Flying Colours:

THE JETHRO TULL REFERENCE MANUAL

GREG RUSSO

CROSSFIRE PUBLICATIONS
P.O. BOX 20406
FLORAL PARK, NY 11002-0406

$22.95

CREDITS:

"Flying Colours: The Jethro Tull Reference Manual" by Greg Russo was completed on December 3, 1999. Updates to the first edition were completed on June 24, 2000.

First edition - January 2000. Updated first edition - July 2000.

Special thanks: Dag Sandbu, Lon R. Horwitz (text editor), Joe Konas, Jim O'Neill, Doug Hinman, Mark Colman, Len Fico, Joe McMichael, Glenn Cornick, Clive Bunker, John Arkle, Jean Pegg, Carmen Garcia, Steve Gugerty, Elizabeth Watson (Scottish Theatre Archive), Janet Snowman (Royal Academy of Music), Hans-Arne Nakrem, Dennis Landau, Martha Klassanos, Andy Taylor, Ann Leighton, Brian Cooper, Michael P. Dawson and my parents (Rita and Rudy Russo).

Also available from Crossfire Publications are Greg Russo's other books (postage is $3.20 per book in the US):
COSMIK DEBRIS: THE COLLECTED HISTORY & IMPROVISATIONS OF FRANK ZAPPA (REVISED) ($23.95)
TIME OF THE SEASON: THE ZOMBIES COLLECTOR'S GUIDE ($13.95)
YARDBIRDS: THE ULTIMATE RAVE-UP ($19.95)
MANNERISMS: THE FIVE PHASES OF MANFRED MANN ($22.95)

For further information, please address all correspondence to: Crossfire Publications, P.O. Box 20406, Floral Park, New York 11002-0406 USA. Phone/Fax: (516) 352-3037.

Outside North America, the above books can be purchased from: John Arkle, 2 Buryfield, Bury, Huntingdon, Cambs. PE17 1LE, England. Please call or fax (01487) 814752 for prices in UK currency.

The following is a list of the most useful Jethro Tull resources on the Internet:

The Official Jethro Tull website: http://j-tull.com

Jethro Tull newsgroup on the Internet: alt.music.jethro-tull

A New Day magazine - 75 Wren Way, Farnborough, Hants. GU14 8TA, England. e-mail: DAVIDREES1@compuserve.com

Living In The Past magazine - Dennis Landau, P.O. Box 1127, New Hyde Park, NY 11040. e-mail: wingedisle@aol.com

Collecting Jethro Tull website - http://collecting-tull.com

Fuel 2000 Records website - http://www.fuel2000.com

Roadrunner Records website - http://www.roadrunnerrecords.de

Laufi's Jethro Tull World website - http://www.laufi.de

The St. Cleve Chronicle website - http://remus.rutgers.edu/JethroTull

Beggar's Farm - German fan club - c/o Harald Eikermann, Sonnenallee 118, 12045 Berlin, Germany

Itullians - Italian fan club - www.megi.it/phoenix/itullians. Contact Aldo Tagliaferro's e-mail: ataglia@hitmail.com

eGroups discussion list for Jethro Tull: http://www.egroups.com/community/JETHRO_TULL

"Somewhere In The Universe" - A Jethro Tull-inspired album by RAY: http://www.universerecords.com/index1.html. Universe Records, P.O. Box 73, Kenmore, NY 14217.

The Tullring Home Page - http://homepages.tig.com.au/~boddo/tullring.htm

"Flying Colours" website: http://www.flying-colours.net

"Cup Of Wonder: The Annotated Jethro Tull Lyrics Page": http://www.angelfire.com/wy/voorbij/tulltext.html. e-mail: jvoorbij@kabelfoon.nl

To purchase Joe Konas' book "Hey Joe," which describes his career and time in The Gods with John Glascock, please send $20 plus $5 Canadian to: Joe Konas, 674 Vimy, Windsor, Ontario, Canada M8W 1M7. A CD-R of Gods BBC perfomances is also available.

ISBN: 0-9648157-6-1

TABLE OF CONTENTS

INTRODUCTION

Well, here it is - my fifth book. The books I have previously written and published on Manfred Mann, The Yardbirds, Frank Zappa and The Zombies were nothing like the one you now have in your hands. "Flying Colours: The Jethro Tull Reference Manual" is quite different from all of those - not only in the way in it was written, but in the way it was created. The text is more like a conversation I'm having with you, the reader, and I think it is the best way to convey Jethro Tull's history and output without losing your interest! Never I have come across such a helpful and giving group of people as the Jethro Tull fans who have contributed to making this book a unique experience for Tull followers. I must also thank all those who have given permission to reprint their interviews. A great deal of thanks goes to Dag Sandbu, Dennis Landau, Jim O'Neill and Lon Horwitz - four people who opened up their vast collections of memorabilia, information, interviews and photos to me with a unified interest in sharing their collective knowledge and enthusiasm of Jethro Tull with fans worldwide. Lon Horwitz also gets the added distinction of being the book's editor! Thanks also to Glenn Cornick and Clive Bunker, who were both instrumental in providing massive amounts of new and updated early Tull information. The large quantity of photos on display in this book are of varying quality, but even the most unprofessional concert photos included here give you the exhilarating feeling of being at that particular show. No professionally posed Jethro Tull photo can approach that unique experience. By including all aspects of the band's history, I have attempted to give the most well-rounded band portrait of Jethro Tull. All of the group's members have unique personalities, and you will find them all here in more detail than you have ever seen.

You will notice that the early years of each band member have been incorporated into the main history of the band, and that their post-Tull years are covered in the solo sections later on in the book. I have come across more information on David Palmer and John Glascock than has ever been revealed in print, and related to this, I must make a few very important points. Both of these mid-period Jethro Tull members have never been properly covered in the past, and this book redresses the balance. Having complete knowledge of their extensive backgrounds is essential to understanding their contributions to Jethro Tull. The fact that more space is given to their introductory sections is irrelevant, and one should not come to the mistaken conclusion that they were more important than the others. Simply, they had more professional involvement with the creation of music than any new Jethro Tull members up until that point. Concerning the amount of space I have devoted to the late John Glascock, this should not be construed as favoritism or as a homage. Rather, you will discover that Glascock's diverse recording and playing experiences at such a young age were nothing but astounding and prepared him well for the rigors of Jethro Tull. With these points in mind, the reader can put the contributions of *every* Jethro Tull musician in the proper light.

So, what am I trying to accomplish with this book? Simply, a comprehensive band history with a lot of inside record company information and photos that I take great pleasure in sharing with fans. One more point that I must stress: I have no conflict of interest with the band and I have no CDs with slight Tull-related involvement to sell. The only thing I have to offer is this book, and it's _all_ about Jethro Tull!

I have devoted a great deal of time (and money!) in making this the book the one that all Jethro Tull fans will return to again and again. At last, I can finally let go of this project, knowing that it is commensurate with the high quality of music that Jethro Tull has created over the past three decades. It is indeed my pleasure to share the labors of my work with all of you, and I look forward to your feedback. Enjoy!

Subj: Re: Jethro Tull Book
Date: 99-04-15 03:04:38 EDT
From: Real tull
To: GRusso2787

Send me a copy when you have it finished. I look forward to reading it. Best wishes and good luck. Sorry I am in a rush.
IA

THE WISDOM OF JETHRO TULL

The gifts of wisdom and foresight can be very useful if possessed by the right person. For the British band Jethro Tull, these traits are personified by its leader Ian Anderson and long-standing guitarist, Martin Barre. Their dedicated professional relationship has enabled Jethro Tull to weather numerous musical storms since the band's inception in 1967.

Jethro Tull's unique and consistent blend of musical and lyrical brilliance has set the band apart from their "progressively" labelled contemporaries. With Ian Anderson's humorous and insightful manner of creatively expressing himself in song, the band has carved a legendary niche for itself in music history. Even though the band is not as popular in the musical mainstream, hundreds of thousands of devoted fans anxiously welcome Jethro Tull's recordings and concert appearances, year after year.

While not squarely in the public eye, Jethro Tull's existence has almost depended solely on the activities of Ian Anderson. In fact, since Ian Anderson has practically written the band's entire recorded output, Ian has been incorrectly referred to as "Jethro Tull" himself. In terms of ability, calling Ian Anderson a multi-instrumentalist is an understatement. Throughout Jethro Tull's career, Ian Anderson has sung and played the following instruments: flute, whistles, acoustic and electric guitars, violin, piano, claghorn, mouth organ (harmonica), Hammond organ, mandolin, balalaika, saxophone, trumpet, drums and assorted percussion. Of these, Ian is most remembered for his flute playing, while perched on one leg! This unique image has led to numerous ill-informed characterizations of Ian Anderson as "a mad-dog Fagin," "a stork with St. Vitus' Dance," "a demented flamingo" and "Toscanini on speed"! With this silliness out of the way, let's get on to the history of Jethro Tull.

THE STAGING AREA – IAN ANDERSON, JEFFREY HAMMOND AND JOHN EVANS

To get away from the watered-down American rhythm and blues that The Beatles and many other "beat" groups were producing in the early to mid-1960s, a different musical approach came into being. British groups such as The Rolling Stones and The Yardbirds explored a more authentic, back-to-basics attack on American blues and they were significantly influenced by records that sailors brought into English seaside towns. Rather than playing straightforward 2 1/2 minute versions of these songs, these two bands (as well as some of their contemporaries) injected new life into these tunes by squeezing out every emotion that was in them. While The Rolling Stones took a hard-edged approach, The Yardbirds fleshed out songs by improvising and making their material more exciting and dramatic. The latter part of the 1960s revealed artists like John Mayall and Fleetwood Mac taking similar exploratory paths with rhythm and blues in an effort to raise that music form to a higher level. As these musical changes started to evolve, three young lads from Blackpool, England took it all in and decided to do something about it for themselves: Ian Anderson, John Evans and Jeffrey Hammond.

Ian Scott Anderson was born August 10, 1947 in Dunfermline, Fifeshire, Scotland. Dunfermine is a small town located in the Scottish lowlands, and the Anderson family moved across the Firth of Forth to Edinburgh, Scotland when Ian was four years old. In 1953, Ian entered Roseburn Primary School in Edinburgh. At the age of eight, Ian felt threatened when his parents forced him to attend Sunday School in full Scottish dress, namely a kilt. In Ian's view, he felt that a kilt would unnecessarily expose his thin legs and bony knees. He went to church once or twice, before deciding to circumvent this "torture." When Ian would walk toward his church, he would hide in the bushes on the church grounds until the conclusion of the service. He would then follow the congregants when they exited the building as if he attended!

Ian's first musical exposure was through the big band music that his parents enjoyed. With the British breakthrough of Elvis Presley in 1956, a Presley "knockoff" ukelele became Ian's first instrument as a nine year old. This toy proved to be near useless, so at the age of 11, Ian persuaded his father to purchase a Spanish guitar for £5 at an Edinburgh music shop. His father encouraged him to play that guitar, but Ian never reached the playing level that his father was expecting him to attain. In 1958, the Andersons moved to Blackpool, England, a seaside town in northern England. Mr. and Mrs. Anderson ran a boarding house and corner grocery store. Ian's father would also work as a night watchman. With his family's move, Ian attended Blackpool Grammar School for Boys and enjoyed math and the sciences to the extent that he aspired to a career that used both disciplines. Musically, at 15 years old he started to go beyond the typical three guitar chords.

The move to Blackpool would prove to be fruitful in 1963. While in the opening days of the 6th form at Blackpool Grammar that

September, Ian Anderson approached fellow student Jeffrey Hammond and told him that he looked like a musician. Obviously, this was a cue from Ian that he wanted to start a band, and Hammond (born July 30, 1947 in Blackpool) readily expressed his interest in such an enterprise. Ian still had his Spanish guitar, and Jeffrey chose the bass guitar because it seemed to be the easiest band instrument to play. They needed a drummer and Ian Anderson soon found another schoolmate, John Evans, that filled the bill.

John Spencer Evans was born in Blackpool on March 28, 1948, but drums was not his original instrument. At the young age of four, John learned piano from his mother, a piano instructor. Even though Evans was picking up valuable technical knowledge about playing piano, he found he was learning more on his own through current pop music - especially The Beatles. The excitement of the "beat boom" in England drove Evans to channel his enthusiasm to a few lessons on the drums. While at Blackpool Grammar, Evans turned Ian Anderson on to pop music by playing his copy of The Beatles' first album "Please Please Me."

The three also acquired rare American R&B records by pooling their resources and got in on the action by practicing the blues with harmonica player Harry Hartley, an older friend of Anderson's. Ian, Jeffrey and John surveyed Blackpool's club scene and found that the members of the hottest band in the Blackpool area, The Atlantics, were rewarded with _female attention_. Seeing the possible female benefits of their work, Ian Anderson & Co.'s amorous intentions motivated them to form a similar band. The Atlantics were playing six or seven nights a week at this time. Ian, Jeffrey and John frequently saw them at the Catholic church-run youth club, The Holy Family. Conveniently, the club was just around the corner from John Evans' house. Evans offered Ian and Jeffrey a rehearsal location in his mother's front room (the garage), but there was a stipulation: they had to acquire another drummer to accommodate John's move back to keyboards. John's hands were traumatized from his primal percussion banging, and he believed that he would be more productive behind a keyboard.

Ian Anderson would later comment on this early period: "When I first learned to play, the main reason was to earn money and meet girls. It was only by going back and re-examining the origins of the music around and developing them in a slightly different direction, that music became satisfying."

The Atlantics were in the process of making the transition from playing pop to R&B. This latter style was the direction that Anderson, Hammond and Evans had expressed as their preference to The Atlantics when they met them offstage. At that point, The Atlantics consisted of Michael Stephens (bass, vocals), Frank Blackburn (guitar), Chris Riley (guitar, vocals) and drummer Ronnie "Lee" Brambles.

John Evans continued to play drums, as a new drummer had yet to materialize. In the fall of 1963, Ian Anderson, Jeffrey Hammond and John Evans formed The Blades. The band name was taken from the London club where "007" (James Bond) played a bridge game in Ian Fleming's 1955 novel "Moonraker." Since no one in the band thought of themselves as a singer, Ian Anderson promptly took on this role. As a three-piece band, plus Harry Hartley on occasional harmonica, The Blades played their first gig at The Holy Family youth club. The Holy Family was also used as a practice area on occasion. On a weekly basis, The Blades played front rooms and church-based youth clubs - their audience was mainly female, but not "old enough" for the band's attention! Their early presentation was as a Johnny Kidd And The Pirates-type of pop group.

Ian Anderson felt his guitar capabilities were inadequate for this band. It was indeed fortuitous that Michael Stephens of The Atlantics quickly decided to defect to The Blades by switching from bass to six-string guitar. The Atlantics replaced him with Brian Hood. The Blades went up a notch when they scored a gig at a Blackpool coffee bar. At the end of 1963, Hartley dropped out and the search continued for a new drummer. The band thought they had acquired a drummer in the shape of art student and fellow R&B fan Paul Jackman, but his playing ability was deemed unsatisfactory in a live setting following a short trial run. Jackman simply couldn't bridge the gap between the Liverpool pop and the blues numbers required of bands at the time by masters like Muddy Waters ("Rock Me Baby"), Howlin' Wolf, T-Bone Walker, Robert Johnson ("Dust My Broom"), John Lee Hooker, Willie Dixon, Sonny Terry & Brownie McGhee ("So Much Trouble"), Little Walter and many others. Ian went through a couple of guitars during this period - the most recent of which was a Harmony Stratotone. This guitar was used to play the blues numbers they learned together as a formal band.

In early 1964, The Blades advertised in the local newspaper, the Blackpool Evening Gazzette, for a drummer that would take them to the next level. Two people answered, and one was more interested in how much money he was going to make rather than the actual joy of playing. The other person was Barrie Barlow, born September 10, 1949 in Birmingham, England. Barlow, who had just completed his final schooling at age 14, had moved to Blackpool to live with his estranged father. Barlow's father was now employed in Blackpool. Barrie already had experience playing as a school band drummer and he played football (soccer) with an Aston Villa boys team. Like John Evans, Barrie was inspired to play drums because of The Beatles. With Barlow in tow, Evans was able to preserve his aching hands by playing a less harmful instrument - the organ. The Blades steadily built up their reputation throughout 1964 by expanding their song selection and diversifying their sound. One of their showpieces at the time was "Bright Lights, Big City" by American bluesman Mathis James "Jimmy" Reed.

After releasing one single ("Bombora"/ "Greensleeves") on November 27, 1964, The Atlantics became Johnny Breeze And The Atlantics when they took on vocalist Breeze. With this direct competition and the massive impact that The Beatles and The Rolling Stones made on the British music scene, The Blades felt the need to progress in a hurry.

Ian Anderson had graduated from Blackpool Grammar with eight "O" (ordinary) levels and worked as a Lewis' Department Store retail sales assistant trainee that summer. His straight-laced life was getting on his nerves, and Ian decided to rebel by wearing an earring. As Ian tells it, "I *really* didn't have an earring, though. It was actually just a curtain ring, broken, and clipped on. I pretended that I had my ear pierced. I didn't really have the guts to do it then." His parents made sure this behavior came to a quick end!

Ian's next plan as a 16 year old graduate was to join the police force as a foot patrolman. He thought that he could become a detective sergeant or inspector by the time he was 25 years old. Reflecting back on his early years, Ian described how his plans were dashed: "I wanted to get into practicing a discipline and into a position of influence within a body of gentlemen that I had, basically, respect for. I had a pen poised over the recruitment form. . .when the officer in charge questioned me about my examination qualifications. He snatched the paper from me and gave me sensible adult advice. He told me to finish college and come back when they could give me a proper job with the police. If I had signed up on the dotted line, who knows? I thought I could change the police force by the time I was forty-five. Maybe Ian Anderson as policeman would have been far better in terms of the good of the society. I might have been much better as a policeman than I am at what I'm doing! Really, I sincerely wanted to do that."

Having no opportunities with the police in 1964, Ian Anderson decided to study painting at Blackpool College of Art. As a typical art student, his musical development outpaced his artistic exploits. Ian had been experimenting with an Irish tin whistle and harmonica while working out the early Blades blues numbers, but his interest in guitar was renewed in school when he purchased a Burns Black Bison guitar and an accompanying Burns 30-watt amplifier. Catching another hot Blackpool band, The Rocking Vicars (formerly known as Reverend Black And The Rocking Vickers), Ian met up with their new bassist Ian "Lemmy" Kilmister (later of Hawkwind and Motorhead) in 1965. Kilmister wanted to unload his white Fender Stratocaster and Anderson quickly traded in his Burns guitar to get the £30 required to complete the desired sale. However, Ian couldn't afford to buy strings for this Fender, so he traded it in during 1967. *Ian only wishes he still had the Fender guitar because it's worth a fortune!*

WE'RE NOT THE BLADES - WE'RE THE JOHN EVAN BAND!

The year 1965 ushered in a series of organ-dominated artists that combined heavy jazz leanings with pop, such as Georgie Fame, Brian Auger & The Trinity, and The Graham Bond Organisation (with Jack Bruce and Ginger Baker). The Graham Bond Organisation LP "The Sound Of '65" had a great deal of influence on the band, and they made sure to learn the whole album because three-quarters of the LP was immediately added to their set. To bolster their sound and to match the lineups of those jazz-influenced bands, they added Jim Doolin (trumpet/ baritone sax) and tenor sax player Martin "Marvo" Skyrme to the core of Ian Anderson, Jeffrey Hammond, John Evans and Barrie Barlow. Michael Stephens was unable to make this musical transition, so he bowed out at this point. With the addition of Doolin and Skyrme, The Blades became The John Evan Band. The suggestion to drop the "s" at the end of Evans' name came from Jeffrey Hammond because he felt it had a better sound. Their earliest confirmed live date was a December 20, 1965 appearance at the Blackpool Grammar School for Boys. They were billed as The John Evan Blues Band. To replace Stephens in early 1966, the band made the move of tapping another Atlantics alumni: Chris Riley. Riley had left The Atlantics because he did not want to play what the band's managers wanted - that is, the pop and R&B hits of the day from the likes of The Beatles and The Rolling Stones. In the meantime, Riley had joined The Hobos in 1965 with Chris "Kriss Manton" Wootton

Early glimpses into the world of The John Evan Blues Band in 1965. At top left, Ian Anderson and Jeffrey Hammond take five. The middle photo has John Evans pretending to show Ian his latest creation while Barrie Barlow and Jeffrey Hammond are oblivious to the action. At right, Ian, Barrie, John and Jeffrey create promotional magic.

Below, Ian Anderson and John Evans take a smoking break, along with Ian posing on his own and with Jeffrey Hammond.

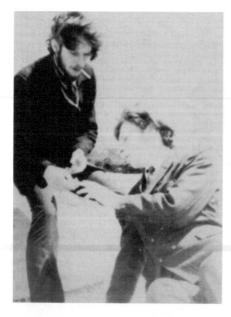

(organ), drummer Ronnie "Lee" Brambles and a bass player that replaced Glenn Cornick. Riley was very impressed with the strides that The Blades had made in becoming The John Evan Band. Before Riley joined in fact, the group linked up with a manager, local electrician Johnny Taylor. This group had to become their livelihood, as only Riley and Barlow had jobs. Barlow, in particular, was an apprentice toolmaker. Another guitar player, Ernie Robinson, was asked to join the band as well, but he made the mistake of telling Ian Anderson that he saw no earning potential for himself with the band! The only problem with Riley's arrival was that they had just taken a group photo for promotion and Chris Riley had to be cut into the photo because no one was interested in shooting another at the time!

Local jobs started to come in as a result of manager Johnny Taylor and the band's own persistence. The first gig they landed was a two-day talent competition at the Elizabethan Club in Kirkam (near Blackpool) on March 5-6, 1966. They won the competition, and it was an auspicious beginning for the new John Evan Band. They didn't play for another ten days after this gig, but they landed another two-night stay at the Elizabethan within two weeks. After this, some weeks had almost completely filled performance calendars. Besides hits like "Knock On Wood," The John Evan Band tried to work in the more esoteric Sonny Terry & Brownie McGhee, John Lee Hooker, Mose Allison ("Parchman Farm"), Graham Bond, Georgie Fame ("In The Meantime" and "Pink Champagne") and James Brown numbers that they enjoyed playing. Unfortunately, their audiences did not share the band's enthusiasm for these songs. It was clear that their set and the venues they played had to undergo a metamorphosis. They did make a solid impact at clubs like The Twisted Wheel in Blackpool, where their early success resulted in four engagements covering six dates throughout the year. Some of these Twisted Wheel dates involved bills with Georgie Fame and John Mayall's Bluesbreakers.

Their first university gig was at Blackpool Tech College on March 23, 1966, and they consistently landed hotel and higher class club dates over the next few months. Music was changing very quickly in 1966 and so was The John Evan Band lineup. Just as they graduated to the university and boat club circuit, personnel changes would haunt the band. The first one took place when baritone sax player Tony Wilkinson came in to replace Jim Doolin in April 1966. Wilkinson was originally a drummer, but he made the move to sax once he learned of the opening. This turned out to be the only band Tony Wilkinson ever played with.

One of the most unusual early dates this new lineup played was at the Bolton Palais on April 24, 1966. They backed up odd looking Bald Brian Rossi, former front man for the Belfast, Ireland group The Wheels. A ten-minute band introduction of the Booker T. & The MG's hit "Green Onions" led to a disastrous stage entrance by Rossi, who leaped onto the stage from above. After he regained his composure and perhaps his brains, The John Evan Band again played "Green Onions" to kick off the concert. Peter Yates, a band booker, got this Bolton show for the band, and the entertaining nature of the show led Yates to suggest that the Evan Band have Don Read, of the Ian Hamilton Organisation in Manchester, England, represent them on a full-time basis. The band felt that this was a necessary step to land higher profile gigs. Little did they know that each member would only be receiving £2 every week! One can only imagine how much revenue management absconded, as the lack of adequate tour proceeds was a typical complaint by music groups of the time. For sure, the band needed to invest in a new Transit van because Evans' van could not accommodate the increasing demands of such a large group. John Evans continued in his responsibility of doing all the driving, especially since he was the only one with a driver's license!

The band's first taste of the "big time" took place at two June club gigs in Barrow at the British Cellophane and "99" clubs when they opened for Herman's Hermits. The June 13 show at the "99" Club in Barrow was not notable in the playing sense (in fact, the audience was unresponsive), but it led to an unusual occurrence for Ian Anderson. At this gig, one of the Hermits approached Ian after The John Evan Band set and said, "You were great, just like Elvo!" Since Ian didn't know what this guy was going on about, Tony Wilkinson informed Anderson that one member of Herman's Hermits thought he sounded just like Elvis Presley - hence the nickname. Even today, Ian Anderson still thinks that Wilkinson gave him this nickname, but Tony was just translating the Hermit's rantings into something comprehensible!

Along with more upmarket club gigs, The John Evan Band made the rounds of boat clubs in Nottingham throughout the summer and fall of 1966. Gigs at Nottingham boat clubs like The Brittania, Trent and Union gained them more exposure to first-name acts. At the Union, they played with The Graham Bond Organisation - one of their main influences, although Jack Bruce and Ginger Baker had already left to form Cream. These boat clubs proved to be their most enjoyable concert environments with more receptive audiences. John Mayall's Bluesbreakers with the returning Eric Clapton shared another bill with The John Evan Band at the Britannia Rowing Club in Nottingham. Another shared bill would have taken place at the Aztec Club in Sunderland if Mayall

Right: The photo of The John Evan Band in front of the Granada television studio on May 23, 1967 used as the cover for the archival release "The John Evan Band - Live '66." From left to right, we have Neil (Chick Murray) Smith, Ian Anderson, Neil "Ranger" Valentine (with sax), John Evans (sitting), Barrie Barlow, Tony Wilkinson and Glenn Cornick.

Below: The early 1966 lineup with a cutout of Chris Riley's top half inserted into the photo! From left to right: Ian Anderson, Chris Riley, Barrie Barlow, Jeffrey Hammond, Jim Doolin, Martin Skyrme, John Evans.

hadn't cancelled his appearance because of a poor audience turnout. A military base gig at Gretna Hall in Carlisle would also provide The John Evan Band with another type of venue and valuable audience experience.

More personnel changes were in store for the John Evans conglomerate. Not only were they also being billed under different names (The John Evan[s] Band, The John Evans Blues Band or even The John Evans Big Soul Band), their member names were rapidly changing. Jeffrey Hammond decided to go to art school and Chris Riley was interested in leaving, but he pledged to stay on until they found a suitable replacement. Jeffrey Hammond enrolled in a preparatory course at Blackpool College of Art before he started three years of paint study at the Central School of Art in London. He was also of assistance to Ian Anderson, whom he had helped locate a Blackpool flat. An ad was placed in the Manchester Evening News for a guitarist, and Neil Smith, a Scotsman like Ian, discovered it and called up Tony Wilkinson for information. To make sure he knew what he was getting into, Smith caught The John Evan Band at the Beachcomber in Bolton on July 20. At that point, Neil Smith expressed his interest to the band, and at this gig, Ian Anderson showed Neil the chords of the Jimmy Smith song "The Cat" that the band was working on. Ian was impressed that Smith picked up the song quickly and improvised guitar parts for it. With this conversation, Neil got the nickname Chick Murray because his speech patterns were very similar to the Scottish comedian of the same name. Smith was born in Aberdeen, Scotland and moved to Bolton at the age of 13. Despite not fully appreciating the commercial potential of The John Evan Band, Neil Smith decided to join after giving a termination notice to his current band. Smith was working with Inland Revenue (tax collection) in Manchester, England, and he decided to keep this position while working with the Evans band at night. There was no need to place an ad to find a replacement for Jeffrey Hammond - Derek "Bo" Ward (from outside the Bolton area) was located at a South Bank Jazz Club show in Grimsby. "Bo" Ward got his name because he was a Bo Diddley fanatic. Fortunately for Ward and Smith, there was a transition period lasting about two months to learn the material. There was no such transition for Barrie Barlow, who wanted to leave after mistakenly thinking that Tony Wilkinson was taking control of the band. Barrie was more than happy when Ian Anderson coordinated things, and he decided to continue his participation until September. Chris Riley also took it upon himself to locate and interview drummers before his own departure.

In the late summer of 1966, The John Evan Band would start their sets with "Sock It To 'Em J.B.," an instrumental taken from a two-part single by Rex Garvin & The Mighty Cravers that was issued in the UK in mid-August. It was a rousing show opener based on an insistent sax and solid organ parts. Also part of their sets at the time were Marvin Gaye's "Pride And Joy," Carole King's "Point Of No Return," The Temptations' "My Girl" and a couple of Big Joe Turner numbers, "Get On The Right Track, Baby" and "Every Day I Have The Blues."

After nearly two years at art school, Ian dropped out in 1966. Anderson's parents were not happy with his decision to pursue music full-time, and Ian found himself selling issues of New Musical Express and Melody Maker at the local newsstand to make some pocket money. Despite dropping out of school, he felt that his training prepared him well for the art of songwriting: "Most of my learning period was spent in solitary confinement up in my room to listen to what went together. I listened to folk and classical and all of it. I never studied music, but I studied painting for two years, and the discipline and analysis of that work wore off and I started writing songs."

The band's workload began to increase substantially. On occasion they would play a club, break their gear down and drive to play an all-nighter at another venue. One example of this took place on August 27, 1966 when the group played at Talk Of The Town in Manchester, England before driving to the Cavern in Liverpool to complete that night's performance.

DHARMA FOR ONE?

The John Evan Band placed a want ad in Melody Maker for a drummer and a tenor sax player and received a number of enquiries. One of the applicants that Chris Riley interviewed was Ritchie Dharma, an Indian drummer from Leicester. The Evan band played at the Top Of The Town in Manchester, where they met up with Dharma. Ritchie got up on stage and got into the proceedings by playing on one song with the band. Afterward, they took Ritchie Dharma to the Manchester pub The Rising Sun and offered him the job. According to Chris Riley's diary, the last date Chris played with the band was on September 18, 1966. The night before, they played at the famed Club A-Go-Go in Newcastle. Just before Jeffrey Hammond, Barrie Barlow and Chris Riley went out and Bo Ward, Ritchie Dharma and Neil Smith came in, the band did some demo recordings in the Evans garage. Two of the numbers they laid down were a cover of Thelonius Monk's "Straight No Chaser" and the first Ian Anderson composition that he presented to the band: "How Can You Work With Mama?". The lineup on these recordings was John Evans, Barrie Barlow, Ian Anderson, Jeffrey Hammond, Martin Skyrme, Tony Wilkinson and Chris Riley. Once Dharma joined the band, Barlow left to form the All Jump Kangaroo Band in early 1967 with Chris Riley, who departed the Evans organization a couple of days after Barrie. They gigged in northern England, specializing in Tamla/Motown soul hits when not backing cabaret comedians. Barrie Barlow's band was named by Jeffrey Hammond, and Barlow and Riley were joined by bassist Paul Hargreaves and Andy Truman on organ. (Truman would later become a road manager for Jethro Tull.) Neil "Ranger" Valentine, a Jehovah Witness member, responded to the sax portion of the Melody Maker ad to replace Martin Skyrme and would join a couple of weeks before Neil Smith came on board. Valentine's nickname came from the Forest Ranger character in "Yogi Bear" cartoons that had a similarly heavy beard. When not in the band, Valentine built coaches for British Rail. With The John Evan Band's inner turmoil, concert dates were few and far between. In addition, the massive van repair expense of repairing its blown piston provided the band with a very cloudy financial picture.

One of the dates that they did play took place within the week after Jeffrey Hammond, and then Chris Riley, left the band. Interestingly, Neil Smith hadn't met either one of them! Smith was still learning the guitar portions for the Evans band set and he decided to make an informal back-of-the-room tape of a gig to practice along with at home. Neil Smith recorded this gig right after joining the band, and for the first time, I am happy to reveal that the show was recorded at a dance hall in Casterton, northeast of Barrow-In-Furness, between September 18 (Riley's last gig) and the end of that month. (Twenty three years later in 1989, Neil Smith saw Jethro Tull at a charity gig at Inverness and met up with Ian Anderson for the first time in 22 years. This pleasant experience triggered Smith to locate the tape of this gig. Smith immediately notified Dave Rees, of A New Day magazine, and the album was released with Ian Anderson's permission as "The John Evan Band - Live '66" in October 1990.) The lineup for the Casterton show was Ian Anderson and John Evans and all their recent hirees: Tony Wilkinson, Bo Ward, Ritchie Dharma, Neil Valentine and Neil Smith.

It is important to note Ian Anderson's development as a front man at this time. Anderson clearly directed the band as they played one song right after another, linked by his rehearsed dialogue, which depended on the audience reaction received after each song performed. Audience disinterest was most noticeable at the Casterton show, and Ian says on-mike to the band before introducing their take of Otis Redding's "Mr. Pitiful": "These people laugh at me - they think there's something wrong with me. Do you know what I mean?"

For his small Blackpool flat, Ian Anderson had just purchased a mono record player. To hear the only record he had, which was fellow Blackpool folkie Roy Harper's debut LP "Sophisticated Beggar," Ian connected his record player to a Vox AC-30 amplifier and listened to it until it was time for bed. It didn't matter that there was only one speaker - that album was only released in mono! Ian noted that Harper's unique, direct songwriting style was not formulaic and this to be was reflected in future Anderson songs.

More interesting gigs carried them on to the end of the year. They did the Stax Club in Manchester a couple of times and the Tower Ballroom in Blackpool. The Tower's banquet rooms provided the venue for Evans, Anderson and the rest, and the ballroom's own band joined in for the occasion as well. Don Read decided to change the band's name to The John Evan Smash to usher the group into that musical era, but its members were annoyed that this change was made without consulting them.

GLENN CORNICK AND THE "FIRSTIMERS" EXPERIENCE

Barrie Barlow's group The All Jump Kangaroo Band dissolved quickly in early 1967. Another Barlow group, The Chicago Line, followed with Chris Riley, Johnny Breeze and Brian Hood (both formerly with The Atlantics), Andy Truman, guitarist Ernie Robinson (the one crazy enough to turn down the John Evan Band gig) and sax player Pete Yoxhall. This group was also short-lived, and Barrie Barlow wanted to take his drumming talents elsewhere. Having heard of a successful Luton group called McGregor's Engine with Mick Abrahams (guitar), Clive Bunker (drums), Andy Pyle on bass and vocalist Pete Fensome, Barlow created his own McGregor's Engine group without any interest of taking the time to come up with another name! For his enterprise, Barlow used three Atlantics members (Frank Blackburn, Johnny Breeze, Brian Hood) and one from The Hobos (Chris Wootton). This group was even less successful than his Kangaroo band. Barlow decided to observe the potential of The John Evan Band (or Smash, as Barlow discovered) at a Blackpool gig in early 1967. With a completely different lineup (other than Ian Anderson, John Evans and Barrie's supposed nemesis Tony Wilkinson), The John Evan Smash had a sound that floored Barrie. Right away, Barlow was asked to replace drummer Ritchie Dharma. Just after Barlow joined, bass player Bo Ward didn't turn up for a gig, so he needed to be replaced. Ward and Dharma had in fact asked guitarist Neil Smith if he wanted to leave Evans because they thought the group had no chance of making decent money. Smith was not interested. Barlow recommended former Hobos/Executives bassist Glenn Cornick and all the pieces of the puzzle were in place. Cornick was living in a flat in Blackpool and was ready for the challenge. Q: What lineup do we have now? A: It's Ian Anderson, John Evans, Neil Smith, Tony Wilkinson, Neil Valentine, Barrie Barlow and Glenn Cornick, of course! On first sight, Cornick thought that Wilkinson was the band leader because his father lent them more money for van upkeep and equipment than anyone else! With Cornick's perception, it is easy to see why Barrie Barlow left in the first place.

Glenn Cornick was born Glenn Douglas Barnard on April 23, 1947 in Barrow-In-Furness, Cumbria, England. Glenn was frequently called "Barnyard," so he changed his identity to Glenn Douglas and later Glenn Cornick - the last name of his stepfather. He started playing guitar at 15 but switched to bass as a 16 year old. Three Barrow-In-Furness groups, Joey And The Jailbreakers, The Vikings and Formula One, engaged Cornick's services for about two years in total. He then left home and moved to Blackpool on March 7, 1965 to form the aforementioned Hobos with fellow Barrow-In-Furness native Chris Wootton. Cornick and Wootton with The Hobos played with a number of extremely popular acts during the two-year life of their group: The Yardbirds (with Eric Clapton), The Hollies and The Walker Brothers. This led to Glenn's short stint in The Executives. After Chris Riley left The John Evan Band and The All Jump Kangaroo Band, he auditioned for Tony Williams' guitar slot in The Executives months after Glenn Cornick's final Executives gig on March 20, 1967. Besides Glenn Cornick, The Executives' lineup was completed by vocalist Roy Carr, Steve Unwin (drums) and keyboardist Robin Dalton. Chris Riley later became a Blackpool school teacher of flute and guitar while playing saxophone and guitar several nights a week in a band. He was also in a 1978 band with guitarist Tony Williams.

The advantages of having the vastly experienced Glenn Cornick in The John Evan Smash were immediate. Tony Wilkinson, much to the chagrin of his mother, offered his kitchen as a practice space and the revised band gelled quickly. The John Evan Smash firmly established themselves in northern England clubs and stretched their performance boundaries in all directions. Their first show with Cornick was at the Lower Chamber in Rochdale on March 25, 1967. With a full and more settled lineup, The John Evan Smash moved from crossover jazz and blues to the soul music that northern English music fans craved. It is interesting to note at this point that even though they started out in Blackpool, not all of The John Evan Smash members were spread out within six or seven miles of Blackpool: Ian Anderson (Devonshire Road, St. Anne's - just outside Blackpool), Tony Wilkinson (also in St. Anne's), John Evans (Warleyroad, North Shore), Glenn Cornick (Carleton), Neil Valentine (Manchester), and Neil Smith and Barrie Barlow respectively remained in Bolton and Blackpool. What a change a few years made - only one member lived in Blackpool now! Barlow would soon move in with his uncle in distant Birmingham.

The band continued to be plagued with management problems. When Don Read heard them doing The Impressions' "It's Alright," Read was outraged and forbid them to play it again because he disliked the song intensely. Another problem was caused on April 7, 1967 when their original Blackpool agent, Johnny Taylor, notified them the day before a Dagenham Irish Social Club gig on the east side of London that was to pay £100. The problem was that the club owner was looking for an Irish show band, and The John Evan Band would have to put on their best Irish presentation. After an exhausting 28-hour drive, the band was in no mood to impersonate any nationality and the owner of the club would not let them perform. The only positive thing they got out of the experience was a meal; the next day, they had to drive all the way back for a gig at the Bolton Beachcomber.

Ian Anderson's writing talents were really starting to blossom and the band's focus turned to incorporating more original material into their sets. In late March 1967, Ian presented to the band another new song he had written called "Take The Easy Way." On April 5, The John Evan Smash entered Regent Sound Studio in London to lay down three Ian Anderson songs that they now had at their disposal: "How Can You Work With Mama?," "Take The Easy Way" and "You Got Me." These recordings only exist on battered tape reels and acetates (test records). As a break from their usual routine of having Ian do all the vocals, guitarist Neil Smith provided the backing vocals on "How Can You Work With Mama?". Don Read (the band's current manager) notified the group that they would be appearing in a talent competition on TV called "Firstimers," so the arrival of this new song was perfectly timed. They passed their audition, and they were greenlighted to appear on the program. If "Take The Easy Way" didn't come along, the band would have performed Ian's "How Can You Work With Mama?". "Firstimers" was a three-month nationwide talent competition produced by the Granada television production company and judges would decide the winner from the artists appearing in a three-minute segment that took place ten minutes before the conclusion of the tea time magazine program "On Air." The John Evan Smash was the second band that auditioned on the "Firstimers" segment during its first week. The filming date was May 3, 1967. On May 24 at 4:50PM, The John Evan Smash's performance of "Take The Easy Way" was aired on TV with John Hamp producing the

Above: The Hobos with Glenn Cornick, Chris Wootton, Chris Riley and Ronnie Brambles.

At left, Ian Anderson tries to emerge from obscurity.

At right, the Roland Kirk LP that gave Ian the motivation to play the flute.

Below, three of the releases in the Derek Lawrence production series that feature John Evan Smash or Jethro Tull material.

14

broadcast. They caught its transmission in a store! They followed the group Foggy Dew-O, who played the previous day. Unfortunately, the Smash would find out in late August that they did not win. Amen Corner, who had already released the single "Gin House," had everything going for them and this record became their first hit. Unfortunately, Granada brilliantly decided to erase the film of The John Evan Smash's performance along with many others. Don Read was able to drum up some interest in the band from their "Firstimers" appearance, and gigs on the south coast of England quickly came in. Then the ultimate gig appeared: the Marquee Club on Wardour Street in London. At the Marquee, The John Evan Smash opened for The Herd (with Peter Frampton) on June 19, 1967 and played "Take The Easy Way" just as they did on television. This success was followed up by a Swanage show supporting Simon Dupree And The Big Sound on July 20. In between, they played again at the Club A-Go-Go in Newcastle. The John Evan Band got their first taste of psychedelia through two shows in mid-1967. A May 3 Moulin Rouge show in Southport paired them with Pink Floyd and a mind-blowing light show. This was the same night as their Granada TV taping. At the other gig on August 19, the inimitable The Crazy World Of Arthur Brown took over a show at the Matlock Bath Pavilion.

The management that the Smash had was not able to cover London with any regularity, and so a change was in order. They needed better advice and they came across Chris Wright, a Manchester-based concert booker and social secretary of Manchester University Union. Wright was on the prowl for talent and met up with the band at Didsbury College in Manchester on June 13, 1967. Here's Ian Anderson's perspective on this occurrence: "My first meeting was with Chris (Wright). It was at a little college somewhere in Manchester (Didsbury College) and we - as The John Evan Band (Smash) at the time - were supporting Ten Years After. Chris was friendly, actually, and encouraged us to make the big move south." Wright recommended that they get a hot guitarist to put them over the top in the hot blues environment prevalent in the London clubs. After all, Chris Wright and fellow social secretary Terry Ellis were doing well managing Ten Years After with their newly formed Ellis/Wright booking agency on London's Regent Street. Terry Ellis was born in Hertfordshire in 1944 and left school at 18 to become a computer programmer for a year. He went to university to study math and metallurgy and obtained a degree. Ellis went back to work for a year, but got bored. He then went into business with Wright. The band signed up with Ellis and Wright's agency, and on August 4, the Smash planned to make another tentative southern move - their second Marquee date in London. However, their van broke down and they never made it there. Glenn Cornick caught The Creation's set at the club instead!

The word about "Firstimers" got to the Feldman publishing empire, and they referred the band to one of Britain's independent record producers, Derek Lawrence. Even though Lawrence was most closely linked with EMI Records in London, England, he had a proven track record of licensing his recordings to a number of labels on both sides of the Atlantic. With this in mind, The John Evan Smash wanted to have a single released on any label that was interested in them.

THE FIRST OFFICIAL RECORDING SESSIONS

Despite all of this activity, money was starting to dry up for the band. Ian Anderson had just turned 20 and was owed some money by a person he knew in St. Anne's. It was time for Ian and Glenn Cornick to call in the debt, but the problem was that the person didn't have the money - he just had a flute. Ian accepted this Selmer Gold Seal concert flute in C as payment, and the deal was done. That same night, Ian Anderson took the flute with him to a gig they were playing that night in northern England. Ian had already traded in the Fender Stratocaster he got from Ian Kilminster in 1965 and obtained a Shure Unidyne Three microphone. Despite Ian's comments that he got the flute as a part trade for his Fender because he could put the flute in his pocket, Glenn Cornick stated in A New Day magazine that debt collection is how Ian got the flute. (*After all, Glenn should know because he accompanied Ian when he took possession of the flute!*)

For the next few weeks, Ian was not able to produce more than a few peeps from the flute, and in embarrassment, he stored it away. At this point in our story, Jeffrey Hammond makes a very important intrusion. Jeffrey started to get into jazz while at the Central College of Art in London. He made some album purchases, including "I Talk With The Spirits" by Roland Kirk and the Ornette Coleman Trio's live recordings from the Golden Circle Club in Stockholm (released separately on two LPs in March and May 1966 in England on the Blue Note label). Jeffrey played both LPs for Ian Anderson when Ian went to Jeffrey's flat near Archway in north London. Of these albums, Ian liked the Kirk LP better because it was simpler, melodic yet improvised, and the songs were shorter and therefore more direct. Unknown to both of them, "I Talk With The Spirits" was the only album Roland Kirk recorded that exclusively involved flute. Ornette Coleman's free alto saxophone playing broke all rules of jazz improvisation, but this playing style did not lend itself to Ian's aspired performance identity. While walking home, Ian couldn't get Roland Kirk's "Serenade To A

Cuckoo" out of his head. This song was the inspiration for Ian Anderson to develop his flute skills.

After just a few minutes effort the next day, Ian worked out the initial bars from the verse of "Senerade To A Cuckoo." Ian was already familiar with the combined singing/playing technique that Roland Kirk used on the album, since he did it with guitar, tin whistle and harmonica. This technique existed long before Kirk came on the scene, but Roland's most notable example of "singing and playing" at the same time was the track "You Did It, You Did It." This song was recorded August 16 and 17, 1961 and appeared on his "We Free Kings" album. Even though the British release of "Serenade To A Cuckoo" took place in September 1965, it was recorded a year earlier - September 16, 1964 at Nola Studios in New York, NY. (The album was released April 19, 1965 in the US.) Ian Anderson knew that Kirk was on the right track, but Ian wanted to incorporate Roland's flute tonality into his own initial playing style. The flute became Ian's primary instrument at this point, since his rudimentary guitar playing ran into a dead end.

Producer Derek Lawrence arranged a recording session for the band, which he wanted to call "Candy Coloured Rain." The Candy Coloured Rain sessions were EMI demos recorded by The John Evan Smash at CBS Studios on London's New Bond Street and EMI's Abbey Road Studios between September and October 1967. Their aim was to produce a single and some album tracks. On September 14 at CBS, the band covered a Barry Mann/ Cynthia Weil song selected by Derek Lawrence entitled "The Man." An October 5 trip to CBS resulted in a recording of the Anderson original "Invasion Of Privacy." Studio 2 at EMI's hallowed Abbey Road facility was freed on October 19 for Candy Coloured Rain to tape two cryptically titled Anderson compositions, "7th Stroke Of 9" and "From 21 Subtract." These tracks were completed on October 24. Two days before, the band laid down "How Can You Work With Mama?," "Letting You Go" and "Aeroplane." While the first song was a remake of Ian's song from earlier in the year, the other two were jointly composed by Glenn Barnard (Cornick) and Ian Anderson. Derek Lawrence kept recommending the use of a hot session guitarist named Ritchie Blackmore to toughen up these somewhat whimsical recordings, but the Smash would have none of it. With the exception of "Letting You Go" and "Aeroplane," these tracks were never released, and they never will because Derek Lawrence never saw fit to keep a copy. (*I have confirmed that EMI destroyed them, thinking that they were taking up space.*)

Derek Lawrence kept acetates of "Aeroplane" and "Letting You Go," and "Aeroplane" would form the B-side of a single in 1968. "Aeroplane" would also feature backing vocals by Tony Wilson, one of Lawrence's favorite singers who became popular a few years later with the pop group Hot Chocolate. Interestingly, "Letting You Go" offered the first released Ian Anderson flute playing on record. He had been playing flute for a little over a month at the time of this recording. That song was written to Ian's girlfriend, Yvonne Nicholson. Despite his flute breakthrough, Ian Anderson still did not have the confidence to play the instrument live and continued to sing and play harmonica. After years of waiting, "Letting You Go" first turned up in 1991 on the German CD single "The Derek Lawrence Story - The Sampler." By the time "Letting You Go" was laid down, its title had changed to "Blues For The 18th" and it appeared on an acetate with this revised title. The 1991 single with "Blues For The 18th" was taken from five volumes of material that Lawrence produced throughout his career. When released, Derek Lawrence created a bit of confusion by vaguely mentioning in the liner notes of this disc that Mick Abrahams and Clive Bunker from the band McGregor's Engine played on "Blues For The 18th." When Mick Abrahams was questioned about "Blues For The 18th," he responded: "What was that - 'Blues for the what?' I don't remember that at all. It seems like Derek Lawrence is making up another one of his stories. He likes to make himself out to be more important than he really is!" *Exactly Mick, but we know better!*

THE BEACHCOMBER MEETING

In addition to being in town for recording, The John Evan Smash had a gig in Luton, Bedfordshire (near London) at the Beachcomber Discotheque on October 21, 1967. This pivotal concert marked the end of one Smash chapter and the beginning of an uncertain future. The Beachcomber was the upstairs location of a discotheque housed within a bowling alley. A casino was downstairs in the same building, and the band playing there was the "real" McGregor's Engine. Having lost their vocalist some months ago, McGregor's Engine was now a three-piece band: Mick Abrahams (guitar and vocals), Andy Pyle (bass) and drummer Clive Bunker. That night, the Smash met McGregor's Engine linchpin Mick Abrahams and everything was turned upside down. Was the meeting a coincidence? Not really. Mick had already heard The John Evan Smash at Caesar's Palace in Luton (his hometown) when McGregor's Engine and the Smash were playing in adjacent rooms on June 17. Mick was very impressed with Ian Anderson's antics and the band's performance in general. It was only a matter of time before Ian and Mick would officially cross paths.

Mick tells how he finally met The John Evan Smash: "One night in October (the 21st), I walked into the Beachcomber, as I often

At left, the ad for the Beachcomber gig on October 21, 1967 at which Ian Anderson met Mick Abrahams.

Above is a February 1967 ad for a McGregor's Engine show.

Above: A promo of the infamous Jethro Toe 45.
Below: A counterfeit of the same record.

Below: A genuine, commercial Jethro Toe single.

A rare youthful photo of the original Jethro Tull lineup: Glenn Cornick, Ian Anderson, Clive Bunker, Mick Abrahams. We're used to seeing them as old men!

did, and had a look at the band, who happened to be The John Evan Smash. They were pretty good, and had this intriguing singer who peppered the set with bursts of flute playing. . .and afterwards, we got into a long conversation which culminated in Ian asking me if I wanted to join the band. They'd heard about me, apparently, and reckoned I was the bloke they needed to help them break out of the circuit they'd become rutted into." How right Mick was: between the Smash's last Luton gig and the Beachcomber, Chris Wright had tipped them off about Mick Abrahams of McGregor's Engine.

Michael Timothy Abrahams was born on April 7, 1943 in Luton. As a 9 year old, Mick mimicked playing guitar in front of a mirror when he saw Elvis Presley on television. He started playing guitar at 10 and was first influenced by folk-based skiffle music, the pop instrumentals of The Shadows (featuring guitarist Hank Marvin) and the gutteral UK blues of Alexis Korner. Soon, Mick took in the guitar playing and/or singing of Chuck Berry, Bo Diddley, Jerry Reed, Chet Atkins, Scotty Moore and Mel Travis. His uncle was a member of the Royal Ancient Buffalo Club and he got Mick his first performance there, where he played the skiffle numbers "Rock Island Line," "Oh Mary Don't You Weep" and "Don't You Rock Me Daddy-O." Of these, he was asked to perform the last song a few times. His payment? Two shillings and a pint of orange juice, naturally!

When presented with the choice of a guitar or a big 21st birthday party, Mick chose a Gibson SG guitar and to turn professional. (He continued to use the same guitar into the '70s.) Abrahams was first in the local band The Jesters, and then in The Hustlers, which played Little Richard, Chuck Berry and their versions of Beatles songs at US air bases for ten pounds a gig and all the hamburgers they could eat. Mick's first big break came in 1964 when he replaced Jimmy Page in the well-known combo Neil Christian (nee Tidmarsh) And The Crusaders. During his three month stay with Christian's band, Mick netted seven pounds a night. Mick's tenure would have lasted longer, but as Mick relates, "We had to dress up in orange shirts, tight black trousers and white boots and wiggle our asses. If you saw how fat I was then you'd know why I didn't fancy it!" Abrahams hit the youth club circuit and met drummer Clive Bunker at a talent competition while with Christian. Over the next five months, Abrahams suffered through five gigs with The Goodtimers with Graham Waller, Dave Cakebread and Bernie Etherington and a revolving cast of others. He rejoined Christian's Crusaders for a short spell, and thanks to Crusaders drummer Carlo Little, Mick got a few gigs with Screaming Lord Sutch And The Savages. This led to Mick's first unfortunate opportunity. One of his idols, Johnny Kidd, offered Abrahams a job with his backup group The Pirates, but the day that he wanted to tell Kidd that he would take the job, Johnny Kidd died in a car crash. He then joined Jenson's Moods with Jimmy Ledgerwood (organ), Andy Pyle (bass) and drummer Clive Bunker. This group survived until early 1966 when Abrahams and Bunker went to Manchester to join The Toggery Five. They were formerly based in Luton and recorded two singles before Mick and Clive joined. Also in this lineup of the band was Paul Young (of later Sad Café and Mike And The Mechanics fame).

The Toggery Five broke up around Christmas 1966 when they came back to Luton, Bedfordshire from Germany. Mick then formed McGregor's Engine in January 1967 with Clive, Pyle and Pete Fensome on vocals. For the majority of 1967, McGregor's Engine developed a strong Luton reputation at the Beachcomber at Chaul End and the Purple Door on Upper George Street. They also received frequent coverage in the Tuesday Pictorial newspaper for these gigs.

THE MOVE SOUTH

The John Evan Smash had reached the point where they were not rehearsing as needed and morale within the band was at an all-time low. The debts to family and friends for equipment were enormous. When Mick Abrahams expressed his interest to Ian Anderson and Glenn Cornick in joining the band, he had no intention of moving. Instead, he suggested that the Smash move down to Luton to make things easier in terms of traveling and getting London-area gigs. Mick tells us why: "I said I'd be happy to join, because McGregor's Engine was beginning to run out of steam at that point, but I told him there was no way that I was going to move to Blackpool, or even to London - because I had a good job in Luton, and was not about to chuck it up to become a pop star . . .I'd been all through that before." Andy Pyle of McGregor's Engine wanted to quit, although they had three months of concert commitments. Mick Abrahams told Pyle and Bunker that instead of playing those gigs, they would take three months off. Clive Bunker's mother wanted him to return to work at Commercial Cars of Luton, where motorized vehicles were produced under the Commer name.

Neil Smith found the traveling from southern gigs to his Bolton home and Inland Revenue tax inspector position too burdonsome, so he decided to return to Bolton. This freed up the guitarist slot for Abrahams. After returning home from the Beachcomber gig, the rest of the band agreed to move to Luton, although it was not a unanimous decision. What was agreed upon was a more blues-based direction, and the southbound move to Luton brought them within striking distance of the center of the entire electrified blues movement - London. After finishing a November 10, 1967 gig at Manchester University, they loaded up the van with their gear and belongings and moved to Luton.

Mick Abrahams and Clive Bunker were still living with their parents in Luton, but the band's move to Luton was easiest for Glenn Cornick because he was now living there. He soon moved in with his recently relocated parents above a Thornton Heath, London pub. As Glenn tells it, "We got back to Blackpool after that gig, Chick Murray (Neil Smith) left the band, and Ian got on the phone to Chris Wright. . .(and) told him we'd got this great new blues guitarist who leaps around, pulls faces and does all the other things - so Chris told us to move down and he said he'd try to get us some work." In Ian's opinion, the move to Luton was another failed promise: "We took his (Chris Wright's) advice and made a loose arrangement with him to do some dates with Mick Abrahams. The carrot that was dangled in front of us was that Chris would get us some work, but within a week of being in London (*actually Luton*), we were flat broke. There was no money and nothing to eat." Rehearsals with Abrahams took place in a Luton classroom and consisted mainly of 12-bar blues workouts.

Glenn Cornick reflects on the same period, "We did a few gigs (with Mick Abrahams) as a seven-piece, but the money ran out almost immediately. . .we simply couldn't make ends meet on our pitiful income - so we had a meeting, during which everything came to a head: Ranger (Neil Valentine) decided to pack it in - partly because he was finding it such a drag to get back to his Jehovah's Witness meetings, and the other sax player (Tony Wilkinson) left too. John Evans decided he didn't want to stick around, and he opted to continue his studies - he'd always wanted to study physics, so he went off and did that. . .he couldn't envisage the band ever making it. Neither could Barrie Barlow - he had a girlfriend back home (in Blackpool) and he left the band too."

After their first week in the London area, The John Evan Smash was without money, food or consistent work. Ian Anderson rarely talks about this period in great detail, but he did make things clear in one interview: "I think we had about four or five dates set *(actually it was a lot more)*, about one a week for the next four weeks or something, but I mean clearly we couldn't live, clearly we weren't going to be able to pay for things. So everybody packed up and went back after a few days because we couldn't even eat. We found some potatoes in a cellar of this rented basement that we managed to get and roasted them over a coke fire. . .nearly all died of carbon monoxide poisoning. We actually had gone down to work with this guitarist, Mick Abrahams, because he was going to join the group. And when the others went back, Mick and I decided that if I could manage to stay down there and exist on nothing as it were, he knew a drummer and I knew a bass player, and we could put together a little group that would be cheaper to run. So I took a job vacuum cleaning a cinema for which I got paid $15 a week which was just enough to pay the rent, and managed to exist for a couple of months while we got some work. That's how it began. It wasn't really that anybody started the group; it was just the remnants of other groups."

Two of the seven-piece gigs they did were in Birmingham, and they averaged only £15 between them. In all likelihood, the last of the four gigs performed by this expanded lineup took place on November 25, 1967 at St. Peter's College in Birmingham. Neil Valentine bailed out immediately afterward. As for Tony Wilkinson, he hung around longer than nearly everyone else - about two weeks. Wilkinson was staying with Mick's mother's friend while Tony's mother paid for his stay. Tony Wilkinson got Barrie Barlow a place to stay, but Barrie found the house that Ian Anderson was sharing with John Evans more to his satisfaction. Besides concerns for his girlfriend, Barlow felt that the blues was not a proper fit to his playing abilities and expressed to the band that he would stay on until a replacement was found. It was now time for Mick Abrahams to submit Clive Bunker's name for approval. As Clive Bunker remembers, Barrie Barlow did not teach him the set or split gigs with him in order to learn the material.

John Evans was extremely disappointed with the band's inability to succeed within the rapidly changing music scene, and decided to return home to college. The touring that took the band further and further away from home led to Evans failing all of his "O" (ordinary) level exams. It was too late for John to enroll for the 1967-1968 school year, so he ended up entering the Chelsea College of Science in London in September 1968. With Clive Bunker firmly established on drums, Evans and Barlow decided to leave together. Tony Wilkinson decided that he didn't have the playing ability or the business acumen to make it in the band and finally went home after Evans and Barlow departed. (Wilkinson died in a 1990 motorcycle accident.) In 1971, Barrie had this to say about where the band was: "The music had changed from jazz blues into a lot of 12-bar rubbish and I couldn't stand it. It had been only the music that kept me going. There was no money, and when there was both no money and no music I went back." Of the entire group, Ian Anderson and Glenn Cornick were the most determined to persevere in this new musical arrangement.

Born December 30, 1946 in the area of Luton, Bedfordshire, Clive William Bunker started out playing guitar at 15 and failed miserably. His desire to have his own group directed him toward the drums, inspired by his drum heroes Buddy Rich, Bobby Elliott of The Hollies and Louie Bellson. This inspiration helped Clive to create a four-piece band that performed in Bedfordshire clubs for free in Dunstable and Luton.

The first gig with the Anderson/Abrahams/Cornick/Bunker lineup occurred on Loughborough University on December 1, 1967. The next day, they played Barking Tech. with Graham Bond. This was just three weeks after Ian and Glenn moved to Luton. Ian Anderson describes this arrangement for us in more detail: "That was the beginning of the group. We played a few gigs that The John Evan Band left in the date sheet but Chris (Wright) never came to see us again. It was a very wise thing to do because the group Chris thought he was booking out wasn't the same group at all. We were being booked out as a seven-piece group and we used to tell the promoters that the other three guys were on their way, travelling in a separate car! Of course, when it came time to go on they hadn't shown up, (so) we said how worried we were about them and we would feign a telephone call. We'd tell the promoter that they'd had a car accident in order to gain his sympathy. When we found ourselves weeks later going back to the same club still without these guys, we'd explain that they were still in the hospital!" According to Glenn Cornick, the Ellis/Wright agency kept hearing from club owners that "the band was very good - it's a shame their brass section didn't show up!".

Chris Wright involved himself completely with the upsurging Ten Years After, so partner Terry Ellis devoted himself to the remains of The John Evan Smash. Ian Anderson consistently invaded the Ellis/Wright office several times a week and he would be adamant about not leaving until he received some gig work from the agency. Ian was a bit of a bad boy - he didn't tell Ellis and Wright that they were a four-piece instead of seven for several weeks! By the middle of December 1967, the band had to admit to being a four-piece. Their northern manager Don Read thought he still had control over the group, but Ellis and Wright had to persuade Read to relinquish his claim to this group as it was an entirely new entity.

The band still had some outstanding John Evan Smash gig commitments to satisfy in soul clubs for a few weeks to carry them through the rest of December. The band then played under variable names like Ian Anderson's Blues Band, Bag O'Blues, Navy Blue and even The John Evan Smash - although Don Read strongly discouraged them from using the latter name. The revised band's first two appearances at the Marquee Club in London used two of these names in fact: Bag O'Blues on December 14, 1967, and Navy Blue on January 16, 1968. Feedback from club owners was generally positive, but not positive enough for the band to retain one name from gig to gig. By using different names, an owner would not know ahead of time that he was getting the same band. This would allow multiple exposures for the same band! Usually, the band checked the poster outside the venue and the name they didn't recognize would be their name for that night! They also made sure to wear different clothes if they played more than once at the same place to avoid recognition.

Ian Anderson spent the Christmas holiday with the Abrahams family and shared a turkey dinner. This would be the last good meal he would have for about three months. Ian had sought out a job to supplement his meager gig income and pay the rent - he cleaned toilets at the Savoy ABC Cinema in the center of Luton for £1 a day. Ian frequently wore a scruffy overcoat that his father gave him as a leaving home present, carrying a paper bag of belongings. (*Envision the Aqualung character!*) He shared a bottom flat in a large house on Studley Road with Glenn Cornick, and occasionally, newly freed inmates from a local prison would find their way into the flat and lay down on Glenn's bed. Ian reflected on his feelings at the time: "I'd never been away from home before. It was just like a yokel hitting the city with all his belongings in a knotted hankie at the end of a stick. I started out as a singer and when the others were playing, I found I was just gazing round the lofty halls. I thought I'd like to be playing something and moving 'round too, so I got hold of a flute and a harmonica and bluffed my way through."

When the four of them got those gigs out of the way, they still had some unfinished business - namely the record that they were in the middle of making with Derek Lawrence before The John Evan Smash splintered. Ian Anderson and Glenn Cornick were intent on completing the recording, even though it would be mixed and matched from two lineups. In early January 1968, Anderson, Cornick, Abrahams and Bunker entered Abbey Road Studios to record a new song that Mick Abrahams just put together - "Sunshine Day." Lawrence thought the song was great, although the band never thought it representative enough of their style to perform it live. As with the previous "Aeroplane," Tony Wilson was the backing vocalist. In this case, Wilson joined Ian Anderson's harmony on this Abrahams-sung tune. In a much later interview, Ian Anderson joked that Candy Coloured Rain recorded The Lemon Pipers' "Green Tambourine" at this session. It turns out that he was not joking - they recorded "Green Tambourine" at the "Sunshine Day" session to create a UK version of the Lemon Pipers US hit!

The songs that the band played live included blues tunes like Sonny Terry & Brownie McGhee's "So Much Trouble," "Rock Me Baby" (by Muddy Waters, born McKinley Morganfield) and the Abrahams-vocalized "I Wonder Who" by Iverson "Louisiana Red" Minter. While rehearsing in late 1967, Ian Anderson felt comfortable enough with his development in flute playing that he suggested doing Roland Kirk's "Serenade To A Cuckoo" as a group showpiece reflecting his newfound ability. Abrahams, Cornick and Bunker were game, and Anderson arranged a version of this Kirk piece that clearly brought out the group's dynamics and stage presence.

By the end of January 1968, agent Dave Robson of the Ellis/Wright agency suggested that the band name themselves after the 18th Century agriculturist Jethro Tull. As Glenn Cornick put it, "'Jethro Tull' has a nice grubby farmer sound to it!" When they did their third Marquee gig on February 2, 1968, Jethro Tull was the name they used. Marquee Club manager John C. Gee was a jazz fan interested in transforming his club from a jazz venue to a more commercially viable forum with cutting edge acts. Gee was highly impressed with the band's presentation and he was especially taken by Ian Anderson's performance on flute, harmonica and vocals. Their enormously successful performance at the Marquee earned them the Friday night residency at the club, in which they headlined usually every other week.

WHO WAS JETHRO TULL, ANYWAY?

After all, no proper discussion of Jethro Tull would be complete without a history of the man who loaned the band his name! In fact, there are many parallels between Jethro Tull (the man) and the band - namely confusion about their careers. Jethro Tull was born in March 1674, but no one knows exactly when because his birth records are lost (*just like those Candy Coloured Rain tapes*). What we do know is that Jethro was born to Jethro and Dorothy Tull and baptized at Basildon Church in England on March 30, 1674. He lived in a country house and was very interested in all things country - farming, sports and recreation. He enrolled at St. John's College in Oxford, England in July 1691 but left to pursue law at Gray's Inn in London on December 11, 1693. (*Please note that Gray's Inn was not a pub - it was a law school!*) Before being called to the Bar on May 19, 1699, our first jolly Jethro did a grand tour in which he visited fields in France and Italy to observe soil, culture and the growing of vegetables. He also studied the methods of plowing, sowing, planting and reaping that were employed in those countries. After studying for over five years and becoming a member of the Bar, Jethro Tull decided not to practice law after all and sought to pursue farming.

Jethro was also a musician in his spare time, playing organ and mastering its entire mechanism. On October 26, 1699, Jethro married the former Sussanah Smith of Burton-Dassett, Warwickshire and moved to a farm in Howberry, Oxfordshire, England. They would bear one son and four daughters. This Jethro was unfortunately a hypochondriac that felt he was always suffering from tuberculosis and calculus - not math, but gall stones! Having calculus and being on a farm was not a good combination, but Tull became a farmer out of necessity. By luck, the composition of the soil on Jethro's land was rich in lime and thus prime for growing heavy crops like wheat and barley. Other crops that flourished in his soil included peas, beans and potatoes. Tull did best with St. Foin (sanfoin), a legume. With such hearty soil, Jethro found it to be excellent for experimentation. The only problem was that plow servants took advantage of their masters by stealing crop proceeds, thereby reducing or eliminating their master's profits. Jethro's view was that these workers were by nature dishonest and bent on stealing and destroying the land they worked on. Since his own workers did not want to follow his orders, Tull had to come up with a way to "eliminate the middleman"!

Tull was interested in producing the largest crop while conserving seed. In an attempt to achieve this goal, Jethro Tull made the decision to invent a machine that would plant the seed in rows with the spacing he desired. He felt that there was no need to cast seed all over the land in the hopes of growing crops anyplace - he mathematically calculated (*not that word again*) the ideal distance between seed rows to maximize crop production. *Remember when I mentioned that Jethro Tull knew all about the organ? Well, the groove, tongue and spring of an organ's sounding-board provided Jethro with the idea of a contraption that delivered the seed through notched barrels.* The year he had conceived and created such a seed laying machine, known as the seed drill, was 1701.

The horse-drawn seed drill had four wheels and three colters (blades) which cut spaced rows for seeds into the soil. Behind the colters, funnels directed seeds from an opening in the seed box mounted on the drill to seed droppers located underneath that seed

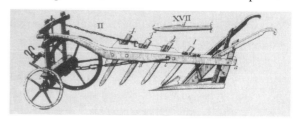

A diagram of Jethro Tull's four-coltered plow.

Above: The REAL Jethro Tull.
Below: Jethro Tull's memorial tombstone.

Published in 1972, this is the most recent book on the first Jethro Tull!

G. E. FUSSELL

Jethro Tull:
his influence on mechanized agriculture

THE GREAT INNOVATORS SERIES

box. An axle attached to the seed droppers turned with the wheels and the passage of seed from box to dropper was controlled by a brass cover and an adjustable spring. By flapping open and dropping seed when engaged, this spring acted like the tongue in an organ mechanism that creates sound when an organ key is pressed.

Farming became his obsession and his wide vocabulary expressed an overall nasty disposition when confronted by fellow farmers that found his seeding theories hilarious. It was no wonder that he complained more of chest pains! His sanfoin seed was growing extremely well using his seed spacing method, and he created a horse-driven hoe and a four-coltered plow. After obtaining a lease to Prosperous Farm in Shalbourne, Berkshire, Tull moved his family there in 1709. Jethro was actually feeling very ill, yet he still chose to visit Italy and southern France in April 1711. To finance his travels, he sold part of his estate. Even though Jethro Tull was not feeling well, he wasn't sick enough to prevent his observation of cultivation methods in Lombardy, Italy and other locations in France in his three years away from home!

Upon his return to England, Jethro Tull became a farming madman. His vastly increased crop growing knowledge and experience enabled him to turn wet or weed-infested soil without purpose into dry, productive soil through soil treatments. By pulverizing the soil without manure, the flow of water to plant roots was markedly increased and so was their crop production. Tull's new cultivation method involved creating two or three furrows (trenches) in the ground with wide intervals between seed rows. The row intervals were hoed by hand to maintain the soil effectiveness and to prevent weeds. Jethro Tull's success quickly spread to farmers across England, who demanded him to document in detail his experimental soil and crop growing successes in book form.

Jethro was not very jolly about writing a book, and he spent a few years writing it on and off. The off years were when that calculus and tuberculosis aggravated him. However, in 1731 he printed a book in London called "The New Horse-Hoeing Husbandry, or an Essay on the Principles of Tillage and Vegetation." He was so self-effacing that he didn't even put his name on it! Tull was outraged to find out that his book notes and chapters were printed out of order by the publisher. Maybe it was a good idea that he didn't sign it after all! Jethro also didn't sign its expanded 1733 edition, "The Horse-Hoeing Husbandry or an Essay on the Principles of Tillage and Vegetation…Vineyard Culture into the Cornfields." This book was properly arranged and included six plates with illustrations of the machinery that Jethro Tull invented in 1701. The 1733 edition was also printed in Dublin by a bootlegger - *another thing that both Jethros have in common!* A supplement to "The New Horse-Hoeing Husbandry…" was included in the third edition, which was printed in 1743. It was first translated into French and then other translations followed.

Tull was the 81st UK agriculturist on record that published a book. When not discussing his machinery or crops in his book, Jethro made the analogy that the life of plants was very much like that of humans. He considered plant roots to be like intestines that take in earth particles and grow further into the earth until hoeing is required to open up spaces for them to grow. In Tull's opinion, the function of leaves was to cleanse those earth particles as human lungs cleanse the blood. By varying the four elements of our world (earth, air, fire and water), Jethro Tull felt that crop growth could be maximized in any soil environment.

Regardless of the edition (and there have been a number of reprints over the past two centuries), Jethro Tull's book was a hot topic. Being the work of a pioneer in agriculture, "The New Horse-Hoeing Husbandry…" was either tremendously praised or slashed. One person that highly regarded Tull's book was renaissance man and US president Thomas Jefferson. Jefferson mentioned it in an August 3, 1771 letter to Robert Skip, who was interested in creating a book library for £50.

Controversy surrounded Jethro Tull's book well into the 20th Century. While he was still alive, Jethro found himself constantly defending his book. His health was also put under a great deal of strain by his useless son John, who never bothered to get work and continued to receive financial support from his father. John Tull was jailed in Fleet Prison for his debts and died in jail. The controversial and financial pressures proved too much for Jethro Tull, who died on February 21, 1741. He was buried at Basildon Church in Berkshire, England on March 9. In the 1960s, a memorial gravestone was erected for Jethro Tull at that church, but they mistakenly listed his year of death as 1740. *Perhaps he needed a better publicist!*

Jethro's book on agriculture has been cited to contain some errors, but the limited agricultural knowledge of the time could not have produced a better work. Other agriculturists came up with their own machines and occasional books, but nearly all of it was counterproductive or just plain useless. Tull's principles of economic conservation and financial maximization proved to be just as important as his seed drill, which evolved into the tractor-driven seed drill that came into use in the 20th Century.

WHAT WAS THAT - JETHRO TOE?

Unlike most singles of the time, their Derek Lawrence-produced recordings were not pressed and released within two to three weeks of their recording. The MGM Records arm of the Metro-Goldwyn-Mayer film studio empire finally set a February 16, 1968 release date on the single - exactly two weeks after their triumphant Marquee debut as Jethro Tull. The only problem was that Derek Lawrence was unable to properly convey the name of the group to an MGM staffer over the telephone. When telling MGM staff about the name of the group, it came out as "Jethro Toe." In recent CD liner notes, Lawrence has blamed MGM staff, but he has also admitted to making the mistake himself in the past. Lawrence has also admitted that it was possible to correct this mistake as mislabelled promo copies were available prior to its release while regular distribution copies had not been pressed. However, no effort was made to make this amendment. Among band members, Mick Abrahams thought Derek Lawrence misheard the name as Jethro Toe before telling MGM, but Glenn Cornick thought Derek didn't think Jethro Tull was "cool enough" and modified it on his own so that it rhymed. Clive Bunker felt that Derek had the right name but suggested Jethro Toe as an improvement. Clive has also stated that the band debated the name for hours and any name would do! (*Since Derek Lawrence has admitted his mistake, let's blame it all on Derek!*)

The other MGM label mistake was on the "Aeroplane" side, with a Len Barnard/ Ian Anderson writing credit instead of reflecting Glenn Cornick's original name, Glenn (not Len!) Barnard. Glenn started using Cornick as his legal last name in May 1969. Two out of three songs recorded over the past few months were chosen for the record: the recently taped "Sunshine Day" as the A-side, and The John Evan Smash's "Aeroplane" on the flip. In order to maintain some continuity over the two sides, Neil Valentine and Tony Wilkinson's saxophone tracks on "Aeroplane" were not included in the final mix.

Contrary to popular belief, the MGM single label was not corrected to reflect Jethro Tull within a few days after its release. The MGM release date for regular copies was February 23, 1968 - a week after the incorrect promos. Even with this extra week of preparation, the record was still credited to Jethro Toe. With the confusion surrounding this MGM release, its failure was ensured. When I asked Mick Abrahams about it, he replied: "I was confused then and all these years on, I'm still confused!" Thanks to MGM's bungling, the first promotional blunder in Jethro Tull's career, "Sunshine Day"/ "Aeroplane" was to be the only Tull product this label would issue. In 1976, insult was added to injury when it was discovered that the single masters were lost when preparing the "Rare Tracks" sampler on the Polydor label in England. In the meantime, MGM went out of business and Polydor gained ownership of the recordings. Both sides of the single were transferred from a record that was in less than mint condition. As a result, "Aeroplane" faded about ten seconds before its complete ending. Both tracks were also released this way on the 20th anniversary box set, and the box remains their only official release in the US. The series "The Derek Lawrence Sessions" and the sampler "25 Very Rare Masters From The Sixties" involved transferring all three John Evan Smash/ Jethro Tull recordings from Lawrence's own acetates, which come very close to distorting on a few occasions. The main saving grace of these transfers is that "Aeroplane" is the complete version. Sadly, it was Derek Lawrence's practice during the '60s to keep only an acetate of a mixed recording and leave the multi-track tape with the record company. As has been proven time and time again with CD reissues, searches for Lawrence's multi-tracks or mixdown masters have come up empty. In September 1979, the single was counterfeited in New York on regular black and colored vinyl using the corrected label and a large spindle hole common to North American singles. These counterfeits have larger labels and list Jethro Tull instead of Jethro Toe. The only problem was that the typeface on the Jethro Tull line was never used by MGM for their 1960s singles. An authentic MGM single now sells for as much as $500 in mint condition. All in all, these Jethro Tull tracks have been poorly presented on a consistent basis. Most telling is Mick Abrahams' royalties for "Sunshine Day" after three decades - a whopping £18!

Chris Wright and Terry Ellis had enough of Derek Lawrence and the whole MGM mess and terminated the relationship between Lawrence and Jethro Tull. Lawrence's parting words to the band were: "Stop trying to be Sounds Incorporated and become a proper rock band!" For those not familiar with the UK pop kitchsters Sounds Incorporated, this was supposed to be an insult. At this point, MGM was the only company interested in the band, and as Chris Wright has pointed out, they couldn't even spell their name right! Wright and Ellis renamed their company Chrysalis Productions and set out to associate with a more responsible recording company for Jethro Tull's future musical creations.

Some thought that Mick Abrahams should have been the front man, and that Ian Anderson and his flute had no place in a blues band. Ian would have none of that, and well aware that Mick was a far superior guitarist, he felt that he had to elevate his performance level in some way to avoid extinction. Since Jethro Tull's performance on record to date gave no indication of Anderson's talent, live audiences had to be the deciding factor. As Ian revealed later: "Ten Years After told their manager (Chris Wright) that it was not right to have a flute in a blues group, so they tried to get me thrown out; they wanted me to play rhythm piano at the back of the stage and let Mick Abrahams do all the singing. That was something I fought strongly against. . .I wasn't a very good singer but he wasn't either. We used to do about half of it each. I mean that was almost like getting thrown out of the group. What it actually was was a polite invitation to leave. But I wasn't completely aware of that. I sort of hung in there and at a certain point in time, some of the songs I had written and some of things I was doing obviously became the feature of the group."

Audiences at the Marquee, and the other clubs where Jethro Tull had played in the late winter and spring 1968, saw a colorful and more confident Ian Anderson direct Jethro Tull's unique blend of jazz and blues interactions within the band. Ian's songs were becoming more individualistic and so was his clothing. The long overcoat that Ian's father bought him helped to combat the winter of 1967/1968, which turned out to be extremely cold. Ian wore it everywhere, on stage and off, and the warmth of the coat was beneficial when he slept in it within his freezing flat. Early Jethro Tull performances included the use of Ian's flute on only two or three songs, and one of them was "Serenade To A Cuckoo." Anderson's stage movements approached the gymnastic, and he took to playing the harmonica on one leg. When concert reviewers mentioned Ian's one-legged playing, they mistakenly attributed it to his flauting, which he did with both legs firmly on the ground! At first, Ian was a bit upset with this rendering of his performance style. Since he and the band were finally getting the attention of the public, Ian decided to make the most of the exposure by occasionally playing his flute on one leg as well. In this way, Ian would give concert goers what they were expecting to see and hear from what they read in the print media. With this attribute working heavily in their favor, Jethro Tull built up a strong British following in the first half of 1968. Here's how Ian viewed his appearance: "I started reading that I was a flute player that stood on one leg. I hadn't been aware that I was doing it, and I was embarrassed: I wanted to be taken as a serious musician. So I stopped doing it for about three weeks. But then, I felt people were expecting me to do it because they'd read about it, so I included it in a sort of dutiful way."

As Ian Anderson tells it, his flute playing initiative came from a famous guitar player: "My biggest influence as a flute player was Eric Clapton. Clapton demonstrated to me, when I listened to his early guitar playing with John Mayall's Bluesbreakers, that I was never going to be a great guitar player. I didn't want to be second, third or tenth best behind Eric. When I took up flute, the logical thing was to refer, musically speaking, to somebody whom I revered for his rhythmic and melodic approach to music. So my flute playing was based on my interpretation of guitar lines, both in terms of riffs and improvisation around the blues scale. And I guess that's what made me a little different from other flute players who had been formally taught and played music based on scales."

In fact, Jethro Tull's initial rehearsals as a four-piece band evolved into flute and guitar improvisation and interplay based around the blues numbers that Mick Abrahams introduced to the band, like "I Wonder Who" and "Rock Me Baby." Abrahams encouraged flute/ guitar/drums interplay and he and Ian worked out the improvisatory bits within the rhythmic structure that Cornick and Bunker laid down. Ian's singing or humming a note while playing it on flute beefed up the sound and gave him confidence, even though he had to struggle to be heard above the guitar-driven racket. Ian did not have anything to do with his Harmony guitar at this point: his Hohner blues harmonica and Selmer flute paved the way. His esoteric instrument arsenal now included an alarm clock, a hot water bottle and a claghorn (a self-constructed and unruly instrument made from a bamboo flute, a taped sax mouthpiece and a sawed off bicycle horn). From this battery of unique instruments and personalities, Jethro Tull forged their own identity. Their reputation as a uniquely creative and exciting band grew in leaps and bounds.

Jethro Tull was asked to open for Pink Floyd at a free concert in London's Hyde Park on June 29, 1968. In preparation for this highly publicized event, the band took their Vox AC-30 amps from their John Evan Smash days and powered them through an Edwards five-channel mixer. Going from one sound extreme to another, the band was invited to record their first mono BBC radio session in early August 1968 for John Peel's "Top Gear" program. The BBC engineers had no idea of how to properly record bands, especially one with the dynamics that Tull offered. The tracks that the band played were "A Song For Jeffrey," "My Sunday Feeling" and "So Much Trouble." The last track was the previously mentioned Sonny Terry & Brownie McGhee number, while the first two were new tunes by the now prolific Ian Anderson. The Jeffrey that inspired "A Song For Jeffrey" was none other than past Blades and John Evan Band bassist Jeffrey Hammond. All three songs were aired on "Top Gear" on September 22, 1968. "A Song For Jeffrey" was the only one to see official release - the "20 Years Of Jethro Tull" box set in 1988.

The second official Jethro Tull promotional photo, and wouldn't you know it, they're already showing no interest for the camera! At least they don't look like old men! The photo was released in May 1968, and left to right, we have Mick Abrahams (in the water), Clive Bunker (fishing with his back to the camera), Ian Anderson (with his liquor supply) and Glenn Cornick (balancing his hat).

THE SUNBURY FESTIVAL AND "THIS WAS"

Prior to their BBC invitation, John Gee of the Marquee Club recommended that Jethro Tull play the 8th Sunbury National Jazz & Blues Festival in Kempton, England on August 10, 1968. Chrysalis Productions was already familiar with this three-day festival because Ten Years After, their most popular client, was the hit of the 7th festival at Balloon Meadow in Windsor on August 12, 1967. Ellis and Wright's proven track record with Ten Years After at Sunbury led to a natural progression for Jethro Tull's participation in the festival. The sold-out crowd numbered 20,000 and Tull gave the most outstanding performance of the entire August 10 lineup, which included Deep Purple, Eclection and Fairport Convention, The Incredible String Band, John Mayall, The Spencer Davis Group and Traffic. Similar to Tull, Deep Purple was making its first large-scale UK appearance. On Saturday, August 9, The Herd, Tyrannosaurus Rex (later T-Rex), Marmalade, Al Stewart, Joe Cocker, The Nice and Taste with Rory Gallagher prepared the scene for Ten Years After, making its second Sunbury festival gig. The stage was then set for another fine day of music on the 10th by new and developing acts. Following The Incredible String Band, Jethro Tull played "Cat's Squirrel" and "Serenade To A Cuckoo." Kirk's "Cuckoo" proved to be the smash hit of the entire festival through Jethro Tull's tight, explosive treatment.

Part of Ian Anderson's routine at gigs of that time was to carry onstage a battered paper bag containing a flute, claghorn and harmonicas, so that he could rummage through it between songs looking for the next instrument to play. At Sunbury, John Gee took the bag onstage before introducing the band, and loud audience recognition of that bag came before Gee even uttered a word! The band thought that the audience would be oblivious as to who they were, but their Marquee devotees were out in force to cheer them on. Mick Abrahams, for one, was floored by the reception: "That was the real turning point for the band. I was playing the whole time with my mouth wide open because I couldn't believe the reception we were getting." A Reprise Records executive from the US went out of his way to see the band at Sunbury and then at the Marquee two weeks later. All of a sudden, everyone took notice of the amazing stage presence of Jethro Tull, including the media and two people that would unknowingly have great influence on the band's future success and accomplishments: Sunbury audience member Martin Barre and David Palmer.

Island Records band Spooky Tooth had asked their label, fronted by Chris Blackwell, to check out Jethro Tull at Sunbury. What Spooky Tooth didn't know was that Island was already in contact with Jethro Tull, and they had already started recording their debut album on June 13, 1968 - sixteen days prior to their appearance with Pink Floyd! Chris Wright and Terry Ellis of Chrysalis signed an Island Records deal for the band, with Chrysalis Productions functioning as the production outlet for Jethro Tull's recordings. At last, Tull had an organized label structure with a genuine interest in their artistic integrity. Tull's Sunbury triumph only confirmed for Island that they had a blazing hot property. Jethro Tull played about 300 gigs throughout England in 1968, and only a handful of them appear in the concert listing in this book. These shows were mainly at clubs holding 40-50 patrons, and Tull had proven at Sunbury that a band could make it solely from a grass roots level. The maximum they received for any of these concerts was £20. The music industry was aghast at such a development! Despite little prior publicity from the music papers and complete ignorance from record companies, Jethro Tull was solidly on the map.

In preparation for their first LP "This Was," Jethro Tull along with Chrysalis looked for a suitable producer. Notable producer and blues purist Mike Vernon passed on the band's offer to produce "This Was." With this turndown, Terry Ellis stepped in by borrowing £1,000 from his father and decided to produce the LP at Sound Techniques Studio in Chelsea, London with the band. Victor Gamm served as the recording engineer, a capacity that he would occasionally fill in Tull's early career. The band's collective inexperience and full gig itinerary stretched out album sessions for over two months (until August 23, 1968), but the results were exemplary. The combination of Ian Anderson's writing and playing talents and the entire band's live excitement formed the blueprint for success on "This Was." The album was called "This Was" because Ian Anderson felt that the band was in a one-off bluesy mood at the time the album was recorded - a mood that they would never fully return to. The album offered powerful musical material and creativity. Whether it was the flute-driven attack of "My Sunday Feeling" or the Roland Kirk jazz instrumental "Serenade To A Cuckoo," it was clear that Ian Anderson was mainly (but not fully) in charge. The band required outside help, and they hired David Palmer to arrange the horns on the Abrahams-written "Move On Alone."

DAVID PALMER

Palmer came to the band's attention through his work at Sound Techniques, including the orchestrations he did for Bert Jansch's album "Nicola" in the spring of 1967. This resulted in the single "Life Depends On Love" / "A Little Sweet Sunshine" (released June

1967) and the album on Transatlantic released the next month. Palmer has always avoided discussing his past, but more background on his early years is in order here.

David Palmer was born July 2, 1937 and his musical activities revolved around London. His boyhood wish was to join the Army and he decided to prepare for this training. As a nine year old, David attended grammar school, but he was expelled at 14 for running a horse bookmaking business in school! Just before being dismissed, a student that recently transferred into school intrigued Palmer with his clarinet. This is when Palmer first became aware of London's prestigious Royal Academy of Music (RAM). Palmer was still too young to enroll in the school, but he did the next best thing: he committed the school's curriculum to memory. As a way to prepare himself for RAM, he answered an Army newspaper ad in which the Royal Military School of Music would prepare soldiers through military and musical training. David then joined the Army while still a teenager and studied at Knellar Hall. The musical instruction he received prepared him well for his eventual enrollment into RAM in 1961. Within the Royal Academy of Music's halls, David Palmer was instructed by Richard Rodney Bennett. David was most interested in piano, brass and composition. Palmer ended up playing London nightclubs and strip joints with the Royal Academy of Music Symphony Orchestra, although one can find the placement of an orchestra in a strip club hard to believe!

David Palmer was also the musical director of the "Cambridge Footlights" review. The cast of the show included John Cleese and Graham Chapman, both of whom would go on to form the enormously popular Monty Python's Flying Circus troupe. This review toured New Zealand for six weeks during the summer of 1964. A US tour began on Broadway on October 6, 1964 for a 23-episode run before an off-Broadway US cast took over the show in early 1965.

Palmer majored in composition at RAM and won the Eric Coates Prize in his graduation year - 1965. Film composer Michael Nyman was one of the many internationally established graduates of that class. The year before graduation, David Palmer had started working as a ghost music music writer for films with Richard Rodney Bennett and others at Sound Techniques Studio in Chelsea, London. On and off, this work would carry him through 1968. At that studio, Bennett scored music for Hammer Films, the largest independent UK film company at the time. Bennett's film credits for Hammer included "The Man Who Could Cheat Death," "The Nanny" and "The Witches." In all likelihood, Palmer worked on at least one of these films. John Barry, known for his musical charts for James Bond movies, also did Hammer work at this time that could have featured contributions from David Palmer. David also kept busy through television music work and as Roy Orbison's musical director, orchestrator and keyboard player for his 1967 UK tour. On this tour, Orbison headlined over The Walker Brothers and Lulu.

In the process of recording "This Was," Terry Ellis asked Sound Techniques engineers Victor Gamm and John Wood if they had any recommendations for a musician that had a background in joining rock music with orchestration. Since John Wood had been working with David Palmer at the studio for the past month, Wood recommended David Palmer for the job. Ellis brought along Ian Anderson to check Palmer out at the studio. Terry and Ian agreed that Palmer would be a perfect fit. (*If only they knew how poorly his work on Bert Jansch's "Nicola" was received, Palmer's participation may not have evolved!*)

David Palmer orchestrated five of the twelve tracks on Jansch's record, and the results were mixed. By Palmer's own admission, he threw in everything but the kitchen sink for those songs. "Life Depends On Love" (with string and horn accompaniment), "Wish My Baby Was Here" (with woodwinds) and "A Little Sweet Sunshine" (featuring a horn section) were pop-based and more successful, but Palmer's overdressed contributions on "Woe Is Love My Dear" and his out of sync playing with Jansch detracted from Bert's songs. The off-kilter effect on "Woe Is Love My Dear" was especially surprising, since the orchestra was recorded at the same time as Jansch. As Melody Maker said of David G. Palmer's orchestral arrangements, "Over-busy and elaborate, they seem to smother the delicate lyrics of Bert's songs until they nearly suffocate under the weight."

David Palmer was brought in to give some fullness to Mick Abrahams' song "Move On Alone." This recording was done when Mick was out of the studio, as he attests: "What Ian Anderson said in the (album) notes was true! I had no idea of what they had done until I listened to the rushes for the album, and along with hearing the guitars of 'Move On Alone,' I heard these horns and I thought that it complemented the song really well." On that track, Abrahams played a guitar with nine strings for an unusual sound.

Unusual was the word for the album, a mélange of well-played music incorporating jazz and rock within a loose blues framework. What removed "This Was" from many of the blues-based albums of 1968 was Anderson's now masterful flute playing. Instead of ornamentation, the flute was the lead instrument when Mick Abrahams' guitar wasn't in charge. It was certainly in charge during "Cat's Squirrel," Mick's stunning guitar showpiece. There has been a lot of confusion as to where the song came from, so to end all confusion, here is its development!

"CAT'S SQUIRREL" - THE REAL STORY

An early Jethro Tull live favorite, "Cat's Squirrel" was a song with a long and previously untold history. If you think Mick Abrahams wrote the song, you're way off! The song was actually created and developed as a vocal number by blues performer Charles Isaiah Ross, aka Dr. Isaiah Ross. Ross was born in Tunica, Mississippi on October 21, 1925 and his grandparents were American Indians. His father, Jake, was a farmer that played harmonica for amusement, and Isaiah was one of eleven Ross children born and raised on the family farm (Isaiah had four brothers and six sisters). At the age of nine, Isaiah would sneak away while his father was in the field harvesting crops to play his father's harmonica. He got his own harmonica that year when one of his sisters got married. Even as a nine year old, Ross aspired to become a musician and started to develop skills on harmonica, drums, guitar and kazoo throughout his childhood. He was left-handed and played the harmonica and guitar upside down, using open G guitar tuning (DGDGBD instead of EADGBE) without restringing the instrument. Isaiah's idol was blues man John Lee "Sonny Boy" Williamson. Isaiah played with Willie Love and toured with Barber Parker's Silver Kings and The King Biscuit Boys between 1936 and 1939. Ross did a lot of live radio in Arkansas, Mississippi and Tennessee. He left Mississippi and went west to Helena, Arkansas in August 1943. Ross went into the Army that December 16 and came home March 1944 on vacation before going overseas. During his Army spare time, he liked to read medical books. His constant medical reading led to fellow US Army buddies calling him Dr. Ross. Ross made the most of his Army hitch by entertaining the troops with a song about his Mississippi childhood called "Mississippi Blues" at the Pacific Theater of Operations in the Philippines. "Mississippi Blues" was an immediate morale booster for the troops.

Isaiah was released from the Army in 1948 and returned to Tunica, Mississippi before being recalled to the Army in 1950. In between, Ross attended a show by Sharon, Mississippi guitarist K.C. Douglas and his group The Lumberjacks. One song Douglas played was called "Catfish Blues" and it had a great guitar riff. Ross learned it and incorporated it into his own "Mississippi Blues." In 1951, he completed his military service and moved to Champaign, Illinois to work for General Motors. He married and quickly divorced the next year. Ross then formed two short-term groups: Doc Ross And His Jump & Jive Boys and Dr. Ross And The Interns. He then decided to be a one-man band, playing all of the instruments that he learned while growing up. When a recording opportunity in Memphis, Tennessee presented itself, a move to Memphis was in order. K.C. Douglas had still not recorded his "Catfish Blues" yet (he wouldn't until 1956), so Ross appropriated that guitar riff and recorded "Mississippi Blues" with washboard player Reuben Martin in Memphis on October 3, 1953. (Although not released at the time, it is currently available on the CD "Boogie Disease" on the Arhoolie label.) He married again, honeymooned in Flint, Michigan in October 1954 and continued to hone his one-man band act there. Over the next few years, the popularity of "Mississippi Blues" and its catchy riff and vocals dictated another recording of it using a distinctive title - this time it was called "Cat Squirrel."

Recorded again in Detroit as Dr. Ross & His Orbits in 1959 for the A-side of Fortune 857 (the flip was called "The Sunnyland"), "Cat Squirrel" became a local R&B favorite. Ross made recordings in the '50s for the legendary Sun label, but none of them had the impact of "Cat Squirrel." When not performing, Ross worked at General Motors in Detroit. His automotive work took precedence until 1964, when blues historian and producer Pete Welding and Don Kent went to Flint, Michigan to meet Ross with an offer to record his first LP for Welding's Testament label. After recording it, Ross toured Europe with the annual American Folk Blues Festival. Ross' 1965 LP, entitled "Call The Doctor," was a highly influential album for blues fans - especially in England. Eric Clapton, of the newly formed group Cream (with Jack Bruce and Ginger Baker), latched onto a copy of the LP, which was issued in England on the Bounty label in August 1966. Clapton loved the LP's first track, a re-recording of "Cat Squirrel," and decided to rework the song as an guitar instrumental showcase while giving himself arranging credit for a song he considered traditional - not to mention that he mistitled it "Cat's Squirrel"! This song became the main Clapton guitar workout on their album "Fresh Cream."

Now that we have the history of the song now known as "Cat's Squirrel," how did Jethro Tull find out about it? Well, Mick can fill us in on that: "The first time I heard it was when Cream did it for their first album. I didn't know where it came from, but we did it differently than their version. I later located where Cream got it from (the aforementioned Dr. Ross LP) and found out that it was far removed from what we did with it!" Ross would record the song a few more times, including an unreleased version for the Blue Horizon label. Ross continued touring until his death in Flint, Michigan on May 28, 1993. Over the years, "Cat Squirrel" has been Ross' most enduring contribution to the blues.

Above: The UK and German releases of "A Song For Jeffrey" along with the ridiculous ad for the single "Love Story."

Above: "Love Story" as written by Ian Henderson (who?) and Ian Anderson, plus the first (and incorrect) Spanish translation of "It's Breaking Me Up" for the Argentine market. The above title means "It's Confusing Me."

Below: The second Argentine issue of "It's Breaking Me Up" - this time, it translates as "It's Destroying Me"! Also shown are the French and US releases of "Love Story."

MAY 1968

PROGRAMME — MAY 1968

Thur. 2nd
THE NICE
Mabel Greer's Toyshop
Members 6/- Non Members 8/6

Fri. 3rd
Blues Night
JETHRO TULL
The New Nadir

Sat. 4th
THE TIME BOX
The Spirit of John Morgan

Mon. 6th
THE NITE PEOPLE
Breakthru

Tue. 7th
MANFRED MANN
The Glass Menagerie
Members' Tickets available in advance.
Non-Members 12/6 on evening)

Thur. 9th
THE GODS
Granny's Intentions

Fri. 10th
Blues Night
AYNSLEY DUNBAR RETALIATION
Tramline

Sat. 11th
DICK MORRISSEY UNIT
Clouds

Mon. 13th
THE NEAT CHANGE
The Exception

Tue. 14th
TRAFFIC
with Stevie Winwood
By Popular Demand: Ireland's Top Blues Group
The Taste
Member's Tickets 10/- available in advance.
Non-Members 12/6 on evening)

Thur. 16th
JOE COCKER (is coming)
Granny's Intentions

Fri. 17th
Blues Night
JETHRO TULL
THE TASTE

Sat. 18th
THE TIME BOX
Circus

Mon. 20th
THE NITE PEOPLE
Rivers Invitation

Tue. 21st
TO BE ANNOUNCED
Dick Morrissey Unit
(Members' Tickets available in advance.
Non-members on evening)

Thur. 23rd
MARMALADE
Granny's Intentions
(Members 6/- Non-members 8/6)

Fri. 24th
Blues Night
TEN YEARS AFTER
Duster Bennett

Sat. 25th
THE TIME BOX
and Support Group

Mon. 27th
SPOOKY TOOTH
Rivers Invitation

Tue. 28th
JOHN MAYALL'S BLUES BREAKERS
Tramline
(Members' Tickets 7/6 available in advance.
Non-Members 10/- on evening.)

Thur. 30th
THE GODS
Juniors Eyes

Fri. 31st
Blues Night
JETHRO TULL
The Spirit of John Morgan

EVERY WEDNESDAY
STUDENTS' NIGHT
Union Cards MUST be presented
Admission : 4/6

EVERY SUNDAY
"WHOLE LOTTA SOUL"
featuring
RADIO ONE DJ STUART HENRY
and the best in recorded "Soul music"
also live groups
Members : 5/-   Guests : 7/6

All Programmes are subject to alteration and the Management cannot be held responsible for non appearance of artistes.

JETHRO TULL — ON RECORD

RS 6336

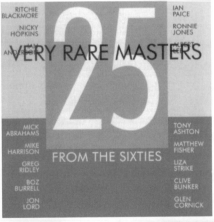

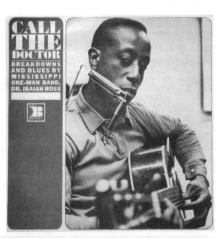

At right is the Italian release of "This Was." Guess who's missing? Yes, none other than Mick Abrahams, who had left the group before its release in that country.

31

The question of who was in charge throughout "This Was" proved to be a sensitive and controversial one on the album, since it went in many directions. Most telling is the fact that only three cuts were collaboratively written. Of these, the concluding "Round" (with Ian on piano) credited all four band members plus Terry Ellis for no purpose other than to provide publishing royalties to everyone in the band. Only two other tracks on the LP featured songwriting combinations: "Beggar's Farm" (the only song written by Ian and Mick together) and Ian and Clive's "Dharma For One." Although Ian's "A Song For Jeffrey" was about former bandmate Jeffrey Hammond, "Dharma For One" had nothing to do with one-time John Evan Band drummer Ritchie Dharma - the song was inspired by a Jack Kerouac rumination. Clive Bunker gave the drums a good thrashing in this forum - perfect for his talents. Clive's drumming with the band was an excellent fit - not flashy or technically precise, with occasional drumstick hits during drum rolls, but his playing added the extra element of tension and unpredictability that worked in their favor far more often than not.

Besides the two Ian Anderson originals previewed on the BBC ("My Sunday Feeling" and "A Song For Jeffrey"), Ian contributed "It's Breaking Me Up." Also breaking fans up, or even confusing them, was the album cover featuring all four of them dressed up as old men along with a mixed litter of dogs. The question remains, did Jethro Tull ever play in make up as old men? Yes, they did, but only once! Glenn Cornick has recently revealed that after the October 16, 1968 front cover photo session at Brian Ward Studios, the band ran from the session right to their gig at The Toby Jug in Tolworth and performed with their make up on! A female BBC makeup artist did the honors. More confusion was caused when Ian insisted that the group's name not appear on the album cover. Anderson hinted in the sleeve notes of this gatefold album that its music revealed where they were musically during its recording phase and that they would not be continuing down the same path: "This was how we were playing then - but things change. Don't they." In many respects, Ian felt that "This Was" formed the band's introductory document to the public. Previewing the album was their first Island single: "A Song For Jeffrey" b/w "One For John Gee" on September 27, 1968. The band thanked Marquee manager John Gee for showing faith in the band above and beyond the call of duty through Mick Abrahams' jazzy instrumental B-side, recorded in July 1968 during the album sessions. While receiving a small measure of airplay, sales were not forthcoming.

However, "This Was" was coming, and it arrived at the end of October 1968. Here is Mick Abrahams' view on the album: "I thought it went really well. It presented a good cross-section of what we played at the time, but I was not comfortable with the musical styles on some of the songs. With the first album, there weren't many opportunities for collaborating with Ian Anderson and that led to a lot of friction with the band. Terry Ellis, our manager, had an idea of what was right for the band, and it proved to be true, but I couldn't play what I felt wasn't me. With songs like 'Serenade To A Cuckoo' and the B-side 'One For John Gee,' I like jazz, but it's not totally me." *It's strange that Mick said that about "One For John Gee" because he wrote it!*

"This Was" sold well immediately upon release, eventually hitting #10 on the UK album chart. The album was released simultaneously in mono and stereo, but the slightly different mono version was withdrawn within a week of release. It has now become a major collector's item along with the original stereo mix, which lasted only for the initial pressing. A slightly revised stereo edition has appeared on all subsequent pressings. One song that worked better in mono was "A Song For Jeffrey," on which Ian Anderson's eclectic vocals came more to the forefront. The stereo mix buried Ian Anderson's studio-treated vocals on the right channel, making the deciphering of the lyrics almost impossible. The vocal effect was produced by plugging a Shure microphone into a Vox AC-30 Top Boost guitar amp. Regardless of the mix, "A Song For Jeffrey" had the authentic feel of a blues recording from the American heartland.

With this UK success in the books, Terry Ellis and Chris Wright were hard at work to get Jethro Tull signed worldwide. A myriad of direct and licensed recording deals were made in many countries: Island (Holland), Fontana (Germany, France, South Africa, Singapore, Portugal, South Africa), Dischi Ricordi International (Italy), and Philips (Argentina and Spain). The most important link was with Reprise Records, the company that handled the US, Canada, Japan and Australia. All of these deals were of varying lengths, depending on how long it took to formally set up Island, Reprise or Chrysalis Records labels in those countries. In the case of Germany, the single "A Song For Jeffrey" was issued on Fontana, but "This Was" appeared on Island. Germany took an unusual step in promoting "This Was": they issued a promotional sampler of the album that helped generate interest. In a similar vein, the Philips label in Argentina released their own single: "It's Breaking Me Up"/ "A Song For Jeffrey." Note that they considered "It's Breaking Me Up" to be a stronger A-side with "Jeffrey" relegated to the flipside and "One For John Gee" nowhere to be found. It was soon reissued on Music Hall/Reprise when Tull's popularity there increased markedly. One more note about "One For John

Gee": the British master tape has disappeared. Despite being released on a German single, "One For John Gee" was transferred from a record when presented on the 20th anniversary box set. Again, the song made its only US appearance on that box.

With their worldwide contracts still in negotiation, Jethro Tull was recording a radio session - this time for "Saturday Club." This program featured new versions of the "This Was" tracks "Beggar's Farm" and "Dharma For One" along with the Billy Eckstine number "Stormy Monday Blues" and the new Ian Anderson song "Love Story." These tracks were first aired on November 5, 1968. The 20th anniversary box released "Stormy Monday Blues" and "Love Story," but the other two new versions remain unreleased. Enjoying their increased exposure, Tull didn't want to be confined to England. They wanted to repeat the success that Alvin Lee and his band Ten Years After were experiencing in the US. Once their UK commitments were out of the way, they could finally mount their attack on America.

The band made their first appearance outside England when they went to Scandinavia between September 28 and October 6. They did two dates with The Jeff Beck Group - the Brondby Pop Club on October 5 and the Star Club the next night. At the Star Club, they had the show all to themselves because Jeff Beck had one of his tantrums and cancelled his band's performance. While in Copenhagen, Ian shared a cabin with Glenn Cornick. Ian had purchased an inexpensive mandolin from a Copenhagen pawn shop, and kept playing the instrument in their room. On their return, they planned to record Ian's BBC number "Love Story." On the overnight ferry home from Copenhagen, Ian wrote "Fat Man" on the mandolin and played it constantly. Shortly after arriving, Ian wrote "Christmas Song" as a single B-side. "Fat Man" entered the Tull set after Ian discovered the right tuning to play the song.

The appearance of Ian Anderson in a tattered coat and disheveled hair while flailing away on his flute provided the media with a field day when it came to his lifestyle. Record Mirror asked Ian about drugs, expecting him to come clean with some admission of drug usage. *Au contrare!* The October 12, 1968 issue of the publication had Ian Anderson laying out for the first time in print his anti-drug stance, a position to which he has steadfastly adhered all these years. Another quote featured Ian saying, "I've never smoked marijuana or taken any of those drugs. The main reason I don't do it is because everybody else does it - it strikes me as boring." To Ian's credit, making his anti-drug stand known right up front provided Ian, and the rest of Jethro Tull, a higher integrity level that raised them above the scores of drug-addled bands requiring such substances to perform their "psychedelic" style of music.

An acetate from Sky Studios in Luton dated October 18, 1968 that McGregor's Engine bassist Andy Pyle gave Clive Bunker has recently come to light. The same unfinished recording appears on both sides and features Ian's flute and vocals along with Abrahams, Cornick and Bunker. None of its participants remember its recording, but it's clearly Jethro Tull! As Glenn Cornick describes it, "The recording quality is abysmal and the playing not much better!". Cornick and Bunker feel that the date on the disc is incorrect as the band had access to much better studios and their performance would have been a lot tighter. It is also important to note that Sky was a very basic demo studio. In all likelihood, the acetate was from one of their first four-piece rehearsals in late 1967.

Booking November time at Morgan Studios in London, the band recorded "Love Story" and "Christmas Song" with Ian Anderson and Terry Ellis handling producing chores. Both sides used Ian's new mandolin. "Love Story" was a calculated attempt by Ian Anderson to get away from the blues format that Abrahams still wanted to pursue. Once again, the Jethro Tull trademark flute was incorporated into the adventurous and continuously evolving band sound. You would think that Mick Abrahams wouldn't have liked "Love Story," but Mick felt differently: "I rather liked it because it reflected all that we stood for musically. It still had a strong blues feel and I'm proud of it. A friend of mine played the solo of 'Love Story' for me the other day and said, 'Do you know who this is?,' and I said that I didn't know. He said, 'It's you - don't you recognize it? You were incredible!' I said, 'We were planning to play it tonight as a cover version!' Seriously, sometimes you forget how good you were and how you played certain things."

The fact that Mick *didn't* play on "Christmas Song" was interesting. This was a slight on Anderson's part, as Cornick and Bunker also played on the recording engineered by Andy Johns. As his first in-charge studio venture, Ian found his timing to be somewhat inaccurate. After laying down his mandolin, tin whistle and vocals with Glenn Cornick and Clive Bunker's parts on "Christmas Song," Ian invited David Palmer to once again arrange and conduct the strings. Palmer recorded his wholly British, classically-tinged orchestration and when Ian played back the result, the orchestration was just as out of sync as it had been with Palmer's session with Bert Jansch! In this case, the timing differences were caused by Ian due to the disjointed recording of the song and not knowing how Palmer's full orchestration would accompany the tracks he already laid down. *Perhaps if drum machines or click tracks were readily available at the time, this would have been avoided!* Ian went back in and re-recorded his parts in sync with

Palmer's orchestration and Terry Ellis added the sleigh bells that completed "Christmas Song." More than anything, this incident convinced Ian Anderson that he could rely on the professionalism and attention to detail that David Palmer's craft afforded.

This recording session naturally drew into question who actually constituted Jethro Tull. Was it Ian Anderson and sidemen, or was it a real band? Jethro Tull was preparing for a US tour to coincide with the February 1969 release of "This Was" on the Reprise label. The run up to this tour escalated the growing friction between Ian Anderson and Mick Abrahams, especially since Anderson and Abrahams did their writing separately. Anderson's compositions showed definite leanings toward a more progressive, evolutionary sound, but Abrahams' playing style was still locked into blues. Ian Anderson had the foresight to know that playing blues was not going to elevate the band. The members of the band also wanted to expand their horizons, and accomplishing this with "bluesy" Abrahams on board was nearly impossible. Since Mick Abrahams only wanted to work four nights a week and only within the UK, his days were numbered. Mick had already skipped out on a gig in the two-week period between their Sunbury appearance and the conclusion of the recording of "This Was." As Ian Anderson puts it: "I quickly became dissatisfied with what we were doing. I found it hard to go onstage and convincingly be a polite shade of black. What really got me was that I was singing something that was essentially stolen. And it wasn't just stealing music, it was stealing somebody's emotions and point of view, almost pretending to have an awareness of what it means to be black."

"Love Story" was released on November 25, 1968 and airplay was slow going at first. The record became their first charted singles entry, hitting the Record Retailer chart on January 1, 1969 and reaching #29 in eight chart weeks. As for New Musical Express (NME), this recording hit the very bottom of their Top 30 on January 11 in a tie with The Move's "Blackberry Way." It fell off the chart the next week, but rebounded for the January 25 issue and made it up to #22 in five charted weeks. Another annoying thing happened with the single that smacked of MGM's ineptitude: initial copies had writer credits by "Ian Henderson." This error was corrected immediately, and copies with the Ian Henderson label mistake are now highly collectable. *For the nitpickers (or trainspotters, for UK readers) out there, the corrected label version of the single comes with and without a centerpiece, the latter being similar to a US pressing. Doesn't that make you feel better?* Some copies even have "Christmas Song" labels on both sides!

Mick Abrahams' days as a Jethro Tull member were coming to an end. Audiences were clearly gravitating to Ian Anderson as the leader of the band, and Terry Ellis and Chris Wright were proved wrong in their initial belief that Ian should have been replaced. A further problem existed as Mick was also not getting along with Glenn Cornick. The last documented concert with Abrahams took place at the School of Economics in London on November 30. At this show, the band Earth also made an appearance. Earth's guitarist was Tony Iommi and he was approached by Ian Anderson to audition for Jethro Tull.

How Mick Abrahams left Jethro Tull is the stuff of legend. Let's hear Mick's side of things: "It was a management thing. Terry Ellis thought that he could dictate what the band should do and I wanted no part of it. I had nothing against Ian or the band, but I felt left out as a result. I told Ian that I couldn't go on and go to America, and then I did things like playing badly on purpose and not showing up for gigs, which I regret. I then went to Terry Ellis' office, turned his desk over on him, called him a motherfucker and then gave him notice that I was leaving the band. A week later, I was called into Terry's office and he 'fired' me. I told him that he couldn't fire me since I had already quit!" More recently, Mick has said that he <u>did</u> want to go the US, but his decision to quit was already made. According to Ian Anderson, Mick told the band one day that he was sick, only to be caught in town with a girl that night! Clearly, Mick and Ian were unable to trust each other, but Mick wanted to explore a more developed blues direction on his own. Ian weighs in with his opinion of Mick's departure: "When Mick Abrahams left, which wasn't a compatible leaving, he and I had just grown apart, he was a blues man and I. . .I didn't know what I was but I wanted to find out. . ." Just after leaving Jethro Tull in late November 1968, Abrahams formed Blodwyn Pig in Luton. Mick put it very succinctly: "That's why I formed Blodwyn Pig - I could play music that I play the best, on my own terms." That music was freer blues than even Tull had attempted. A lengthy overview of Blodwyn Pig and his non-Jethro Tull related activities can be found in his solo section.

A sloppily arranged audition was put together to replace Abrahams. Besides the need to replace Mick, the band was slated to perform during "The Rolling Stones Rock & Roll Circus" TV special. Tony Iommi, Davy O'List from The Nice, Jimmy McCulloch of Thunderclap Newman and another guitarist Ian and the band met at a Vandike Club in Plymouth, England gig the night before Abrahams' last gig - Martin Barre - were in the running. At that November 29 show, Barre's group Gethsemane opened for Jethro Tull. According to Glenn Cornick's diary, O'List was invited to join. After a good first day, Davy O'List's playing disintegrated and he was out within a week. Mick Taylor was invited to join, but he elected to stay with John Mayall. It was at this point that the

At Jethro Tull's appearance during "The Rolling Stones Rock And Roll Circus," Ian wore a button that said "Coffee turns me on." Betcha didn't know that!

Jethro Tull at "The Rolling Stones Rock & Roll Circus" on December 11, 1968: (l. to r.) Glenn Cornick, Clive Bunker,

Ian Anderson and Tony Iommi (hiding underneath a hat with his head down). It was Iommi's only Tull appearance.

auditioning process began. Of the auditionees, three received personal invitations from the band - Tony Iommi, Martin Barre and Tony Williams. Nearly 100 guitarists were auditioned over two days, and the results were disastrous. As Cornick describes it, "I had never realized there were so many incompetent musicians with delusions of grandeur in London!". In fact, Iommi got tired of waiting for the band to get to him at the audition and decided to leave. Tony was called back in with the promise that his turn was coming right up, and he landed the guitar slot after giving a successful tryout. With the exception of Tonny Iommi, all the other guitarists did not perform to the band's satisfaction. Another misunderstanding took place, but this time it was internal and unspoken. Iommi was under the impression that he was a full-time replacement for Mick Abrahams. However, Ian Anderson has recently stated that he brought Iommi in only to do the TV show. Tony Iommi brought his Earth bandmate, Terry "Geezer" Butler, to Jethro Tull rehearsals and expressed his uneasiness within the Tull environment to Butler and Ian Anderson. One of the songs that Tony had difficulty in getting the proper feel of was the as-yet unrecorded Anderson original "Nothing Is Easy." According to Iommi, Ian suggested that Tony give himself some time to get acclimated. Tony still felt out of place within Tull and told Ian that he was not able to play effectively with the band. Ian requested that Iommi do the television show before he went on his way. On December 11, the only performance of the Tony Iommi lineup of Tull took place at Intertel Studios, Wembley, London with the band miming to an instrumental backing track of "A Song For Jeffrey." That is, everyone was miming except for Ian, who provided a new pre-filming studio vocal for the proceedings. Filming rehearsals took place the prior day with the band doing run-throughs of "A Song For Jeffrey" and "Fat Man." However, only the former song was filmed because Who drummer Keith Moon wrecked Clive's gear for "Fat Man"! Iommi used his Tull experience to formalize his band, now named Black Sabbath. To this day, Tony is appreciative of the more attentive work ethic he experienced in Jethro Tull, which he brought to his own band of reknown. It can be debated whether Tony Iommi would have been a success in Tull, but the long-term existence of Black Sabbath and Iommi's guidance of the band through its many incarnations would not have been possible without his influential, albeit brief, Tull detour.

Also appearing during "The Rolling Stones Rock & Roll Circus" were The Who, John Lennon and *vocalist extraordinaire* (!) Yoko Ono, Eric Clapton and of course, The Rolling Stones. After all of these artists went through a lot of effort to perform on the program, The Rolling Stones decided not to air the show. Two main reasons have been given for its cancellation: 1) The Rolling Stones were jealous that The Who outperformed them, and 2) Brian Jones' death. A cursory examination of the program in its eventual video release in 1996 will reveal that while The Who gave a blazing performance, The Rolling Stones held their own quite nicely. Brian Jones died on July 3, 1969 - nearly seven months after the show's taping. Even though Jones had left the band a month before his death, British TV programs of the time were taped for broadcast as soon as post-production was completed. This program was ready for airing the same month as its taping. In all likelihood, The Rolling Stones felt that the program's backward-looking presentation conflicted with where they were headed musically.

Jethro Tull was again without a guitarist and things were not looking good. In fact, the band cancelled a December 20, 1968 appearance at the Marquee Club in London because they still didn't have a guitarist - not to mention their impending US tour. Ian Anderson remembered that one of the unchosen auditionees had a charm about him even though he gave a less than memorable performance. Enter Martin Barre.

MARTIN BARRE

Martin Lancelot Barre was born in Kings Heath, Birmingham, England on November 17, 1946. While in Birmingham, Martin attended Yarwood Primary and then Kings Norton Grammar School. His family moved to Solihull and Barre entered Tudor Grange Grammar, earning 7 "O" levels. Barre had a French grandfather that played violin, but there was no other musical talent in his family. One of Martin Barre's first groups was The Dwellers, who recorded a demo in 1963. That group featured vocalist John Carter, who was also in Martin's next group, The Moonrakers. These bands started off playing the instrumentals of The Shadows and The Ventures before getting into The Beatles. Here's Martin on his formative years: "I started playing guitar when I was 15. In those days it was just a hobby and I used to play with various groups in the local youth club. At 17, I learned flute and had a good teacher. It was good for me because on another instrument, I really got to know about things. On guitar, I tended to learn a load of clichés without really knowing what the instrument was really about."

Martin studied architecture and surveying at Hall Green College in Birmingham and Lanchester University in Coventry. While in college, he employed those skills at the Public Works Department at West Bromwich County Council and then through drawing and general surveying at Bryants. After leaving college and turning professional, Barre got involved with soul music as a sax and flute player because he couldn't get a job otherwise. He joined a touring soul band that travelled for three years throughout

Above left and right: Martin Barre's group The Moonrakers. Barre is on the left in both photos, and vocalist John Carter is located in the lower middle of the left photo. You can't beat those bowling alley gigs!

Below: The first UK pressing of "Living In The Past."

Hello Ian! Below is the second pressing of the same single. Shown is the B-side label - "Driving Song."

A review of Jethro Tull's first US gig.

Tull in a Strong U. S. Set; Tears 'Teariffic'

NEW YORK — Jethro Tull made an auspicious U. S. debut at Fillmore East in the first show on Jan. 24, the first of four weekend performances. Blood, Sweat and Tears, the closing act, gave another magnificent performance. They clearly are in the forefront of blues bands today.

Jethro Tull is a British quartet headed by Ian Anderson, a pixie on stage, but a pixie possessing a firm blues voice. Anderson's fluting also contributed to the group's distinctive sound. The other three members of the unit also displayed good musicianship, but even when drummer Clive Bunker had his extended solo, Anderson remained onstage clowning. Although their equipment had been mis-routed to Boston, the roup came across well.

Also, during Bunker's solo in "Dharma for One, which is on the group's first Reprise album, guitarist Martin Lancelot Barre and Anderson joined in on flute. Barre, a new member of the quartet, and bass guitarist Glenn Cornick also were strong on their own. Other good numbers from the Reprise album were "My Sunday Feeling" and "A Song for Jeffrey."

This group's strong initial impression indicates a successful U. S. tour is ahead of them. Another British group, Parrot's Savoy Brown, also was to have made its U. S. debut on the program, but were delayed in England by immigration authorities, a common occurrence for foreign groups trying to perform in America. As a last-minute replacement, Fillmore East offered the Gay Desparados, a steel band from Trinidad, whose version of the overture to Rossini's "William Tell" was remarkable.

Blood, Sweat and Tears were largely responsible for the packed house and the Columbia artists didn't disappoint. The gutsy blues singing of David Clayton-Thomas, outstanding instrumental solos by trumpeter Louis Soloff, saxophonist Fred Lipsius, lead guitarist Steve Katz, bass guitarist Jim Fields, drummer Bobby Colomby and organist Dick Halligan and fine support by trombonist Jerry (Continued on page 82)

Germany and the UK, backing Lee Dorsey, The Coasters, The Drifters, Ben E. King and Alvin Robertson. When the British soul movement ran its course, blues replaced it. Barre then picked up his guitar again and joined the blues band Gethsemane around the same time as Jethro Tull's formation. The lineup of Gethsemane was Barre on guitar and flute, Mike Ketley (keyboards, vocals), Malcolm Tomlinson (drums, vocals) and bassist Bryan Stevens. Gethsemane supported Jethro Tull on November 29, 1968 at the Vandike Club in Plymouth, England, and we're back to square one!

Looking back on why he started playing guitar, Martin told Guitar Player magazine: "I just liked the guitar, like somebody will like a sports car. And to me having a red Stratocaster was like having a Mercedes or something. It was just a nice thing to have at home and be able to say you played guitar - definitely for the wrong reasons, definitely not for musical reasons. I used to shine it up all the time and everything. . . Where I am today stems out of what started as a joke about five years ago (actually more!). I played as a hobby. I tried to play music, tried to learn to read." As Martin reflected later, Jethro Tull gave him the motivation he needed: "When I joined Jethro, I had to concentrate on the guitar playing and had to learn to push myself, because before that I was a lazy bum musician, getting pissed and doing about two gigs a week! I was dissatisfied with my guitar playing ability for the first year with Jethro, but now I have the confidence to play what I feel."

Ian Anderson granted Martin Barre a second audition and Martin, the hapless soul he was, showed up with an electric guitar but no amplifier. Ian had to place his ear next to the guitar so that he could hear him! Ian felt that Martin's perseverence and effort in trying to audition despite all these drawbacks would make him the ideal replacement for Mick Abrahams. And all this happened just in time to close out 1968: Martin Barre's first Jethro Tull concert was at The Winter Gardens in Penzance, England on January 2, 1969.

In 1969, Ian described how Martin got the job: "Barre was an architectural student at the time and he came to an audition that was advertised in the papers with about fifty others (*actually 100*). And like the fifty others we thought he was awful and sent him on home. But he kept phoning around and saying we ought to give him a second chance, so we despaired and said yes, because we'd found none better. Our first practice was last Christmas Day (1968), with everybody in London in bed or stuffing their stockings or doing whatever they were doing on Christmas. Quiet, no cars running in the streets, and we were playing aloud in a rehearsal room. Frightening, really."

With Mick Abrahams gone, Martin Barre in and the experience of "Christmas Song" as his inspiration, Ian Anderson sought to write a full album of songs that were far removed from blues. Anderson was getting into folk-based albums like Bob Dylan's initial LPs and those of Roy Harper and Bert Jansch. Ian wanted to incorporate some Asian and classical influences into his music, as well as some acoustic pieces that captured the flavor of those folkies. To do this, Ian obtained some new ethnic instruments like a bouzouki and a balalaika along with an inexpensive Yamaha acoustic guitar. These, along with his mandolin, would be ideal instruments for Ian's newly crafted material. The lineup change and Barre's still developing guitar talents freed up some slack for Ian to explore wider ranges for acoustic and electric guitars.

On the classical side, Ian Anderson got a classical introduction from an unlikely source: an English student practicing guitar. Ian was now living in a small Kentish Town flat in London, and this guitar student in an adjacent flat was desperately trying to master Johann Sebastian Bach's "Bourée." After hearing it so many times, Ian learned it on his own and planned a suitable Jethro Tull treatment for later use. Meanwhile, more UK dates took the band through the early part of 1969 along with shows in Sweden and Denmark. Their two shows supporting Jimi Hendrix at Stockholm's Koncerthaus on January 9 were recorded for airing on television and radio. The fact that Hendrix and Jethro Tull were both signed to Reprise in the US was little more than a coincidence, since Jimi had requested their participation at these shows. Other than festivals, they were the only concerts at which both acts appeared together. Tull's set featured "My Sunday Feeling," "Dharma For One," "A Song For Jeffrey," "Nothing Is Easy" and "Back To The Family" (both of which they had not yet recorded), "Martin's Tune" (a still unreleased Martin Barre piece) and Ian's "To Be Sad Is A Mad Way To Be." The latter song remained unissued until the 25th anniversary box set.

The time came for Jethro Tull to invade America. Unbelievably, the Reprise label in the US did not release "This Was" until February 1969. Here was Jethro Tull - touring a strange country with an album featuring a guitarist that had already departed and their tour started before the album was released! Reprise had prepared American audiences for the album by creating print ads that said "Jethro Tull - we're your record company" - as if the band didn't know who they signed with! Promotional radio spots were just as embarrassing. On local radio stations, an announcer would mention the band's show in the area with a song from "This Was" played in the background. Unlike the UK edition, "This Was" in America listed the band's name on the cover with a conspicuous "stereo" credit across its top - as if Reprise had the slightest intention of issuing it in mono in the US! The banning of the UK mono edition put an end to that.

Jethro Tull's first shows in the US took place at the Fillmore East in New York City on January 24-25, 1969. They opened for Blood, Sweat & Tears with The Gay Desperadoes Steel Band as the odd (and long-forgotten) third act on the bill. The Gay Desperadoes replaced Savoy Brown, who were unable to obtain visas in time for their performance. Tull's gear was mistakenly shipped to Boston, so they had to use borrowed equipment that sounded horrible. Despite this, Billboard magazine trumpeted Tull's fine performance and spearheaded the swelling interest in this ragged looking band sporting an odd flute player. "This Was" was finally released and reached #62 on Billboard's album chart. I asked Mick Abrahams about the delay in the American release of "This Was," and he said: "Is that right? I had no idea that so much time went by before it was released in the States! It's really unfortunate how things like that turn out." *Right again, Mick!* Reprise tried to play catch up by releasing the "Love Story" single (backed with the previous A-side "A Song For Jeffrey") in February, but there was no interest. As usual, the strange American practice of coupling two previously released British A-sides worked like a charm - it failed miserably.

The early 1969 tour had the band opening up for Led Zeppelin, Vanilla Fudge and Fleetwood Mac. Again, in a short time, Jethro Tull had won over the US just as they had done in England. Now they were ready for their big breakthrough. The clubs and the ballrooms they supported those bands in led to some headlining gigs at small clubs, including multiple night runs at places like the Boston Tea Party. Despite their intimate setting, these small clubs provided an important training ground for Jethro Tull to discover what worked best with more boisterous American crowds. On this tour, Ian's Selmer flute quit on him and he immediately replaced it with an American made Artley model before moving over to Japanese flutes marketed under the Pearl brand name. Playing with the biggest bands of the era led to some natural rivalries on the road, but Jethro Tull rose to the challenge by giving the best show they could. In the case of Led Zeppelin and the rapidly disintegrating Vanilla Fudge, catching a Jethro Tull performance that was better than their headliner was not an uncommon occurrence. The band's plan was to spend half of 1969 in the US cultivating their audience, but they had to keep the home fires burning as well.

The enthusiastic response Jethro Tull received in the US brought along inevitable comparisons between the flute playing of Ian Anderson and American flute master, Roland Kirk. When asked about this comparison in March 1969, Ian retorted: "Anyone who compares me with Roland Kirk obviously does not understand what Kirk is doing. I don't know how old Roland Kirk is, but I'm 21. I've been playing for 18 months. I mean, technically, there's no comparison whatsoever. Soundwise, there is a similarity. Roland Kirk is a jazz musician who leans heavily towards blues - loose, free blues. Kirk does it because he's a person who understands the instrument, the flute, to a fantastic degree. Now I don't have a style; but I do have a *sound*. I do it because it's the one sound I can make which will blend with a guitar; a strident noisy sound. I have to do it; it's a matter of coming across. The fact that I use my voice with the flute doesn't mean I'm imitating Kirk. Really, the comparison is irksome. He's been playing flute for years - many, many years. I've been playing flute only since 1967. I don't even know the mechanics of my instrument." When the Kirk issue was finally settled, whether Ian was a jazz musician was called into question. To this, Ian responded: "I can't play jazz. I'm not a musician in that sense. I'm a musician in that I understand. . .I have a pretty broad understanding of music and the different sorts of music. But as a player, I can't play jazz; I can't play classical music; I can't play folk music; and I can't play blues. But I know what I can play. It's just music. To categorize might help the listener or the critic. . ."

"LIVING IN THE PAST"

To make the most out of their first US trip, they decided to record some material for the British singles market to hold them over until they returned to England. Terry Ellis was accompanying the band on the road and encouraged Ian Anderson to write another hit single, so Ian worked on putting one together. He wrote it in Boston during the band's three-night stay at the Boston Tea Party (February 13-15). The name of the song was "Living In The Past," a non-formulaic song in a 5/4 time signature. With some time off on March 3, Tull went to tiny Vantone Studio in West Orange, New Jersey of all places to lay down the backing track and vocals in two sessions. Although Ian Anderson thinks that the vocals were done the next month at Western Recorders in L.A., Glenn Cornick remembers everything being done at Vantone Studios. Vantone was the hideaway rehearsal studio that Frankie Valli of The Four Seasons ran. "Living In The Past" was produced by Terry Ellis and Ian Anderson with Lou Toby arranging and conducting members of The New York Symphony Orchestra.

Above left and right: the Japanese and Israeli picture sleeves for "Living In The Past."

Two very rare US promos: "Living In The Past" (stereo mix) and radio commercials for the "This Was" LP.

The British and American 45s of "Sweet Dream."

A flip side was needed, and Ian provided one with "Driving Song." Based on the rigors of the road, it was laid down at a March 18, 1969 Western Recorders session in L.A. and was produced by Ellis and Anderson. Released as a UK single in May of that year, "Living In The Past" provided the major hit that the band was looking for in England, reaching #3 on both the Record Retailer and New Musical Express (NME) listings. Capitalizing on this hit, Jethro Tull appeared on BBC TV's "Top Of The Pops" in June and they achieved full acclaim across the board. Suddenly, Tull had graduated from the underground rock scene. This irritated the underground, but the band wanted a song that crossed over these musical boundaries into new territories and they got one. In the US, "Living In The Past" was not a big seller, but it helped to solidify the band's growing American audience. A little-known fact about this 45 is that the single version of "Living In The Past" has two flute tracks running through it and is mixed differently than the well-known version on the "Living In The Past" album, and "Driving Song" is also a different mix. Glenn Cornick has confirmed that Martin Barre played a wrong chord during the instrumental passage before the final chorus, so that's why the other flute does not appear - Ian's in-tune second flute track clashed with Barre's mistake! In all countries in which it was released, the "Living In The Past" single was only issued in mono. However, US stereo promotional copies of "Living In The Past" b/w "Driving Song" provide unique stereo mixes of these tracks that have not been repeated anywhere else. Not all US promotional copies are stereo, but they are clearly marked "stereo" on their white labels.

Their trip to L.A. was not without incident, as Martin Barre relates: "We had one nasty moment. We were driving a hire car in Los Angeles and got a bit confused on a motorway. In the back was a sealed bottle of whiskey, which was mine. But there was an unsealed one - and it's an offense to have an open bottle in a car - and it was left by the previous person who had the car. Anyway, our long hair and so on - we were suspect. And they found some seeds. They assumed it was marijuana. In fact, they came from a hamburger bun. But we were guilty until we could prove our innocence, which is the opposite way 'round to Britain."

The UK success of "Living In The Past" sparked all kinds of releases in other countries. In Portugal, a unique EP took the hit and its flipside along with the "This Was" tracks "My Sunday Feeling" and "Some Day The Sun Won't Shine For You." An EP in Thailand, most likely illegal, joined "Living In The Past" with tracks by three other artists. For a special French release, "Living In The Past" was coupled with the Aphrodite's Child cut "I Want To Live." The jukebox market was satisfied in Italy by pairing this Tull song with a Box Tops track, and Mexico received Anibal Velasquez's "Linda Carlita" B-side for a Gamma label release.

During their eleven-week initial 1969 tour of the US, the band was frequently ill and tour proceeds did not cover expenses. Another highlight of the tour was their four-night stand at the Fillmore West in San Francisco, where they opened for Creedence Clearwater Revival. Returning home in mid-April, it was now time to plan their sophomore album. As second albums go, it was pivotal in making it big or reverting back to clubs and/or breaking up. The eight-track Morgan Studios location in Willesden, London was booked for the band to record in April, and Ian Anderson had written all of the band's new material on the record - that is, except for "Bourée." That song was recorded at Olympic Studios in Barnes, London. They also had time to film in Paris on April 15 for Johnny Hallyday's show. Ten days later, Morgan Studios footage of the band recording the LP was shot for French TV. A one-hour German documentary, "Swing In," was also being prepared at the same time with the band's cooperation.

"STAND UP"

The album project "Stand Up" was named by Terry Ellis and was another Ellis/Anderson joint production. Terry was also responsible for the album cover. With "Stand Up," Jethro Tull was finally able to present a full album's worth of material coinciding with Ian Anderson's musical visions. Gone were the straight blues songs, and in was a heady brew of rock, folk and classically-influenced songs. Ian whipped out his exotic instruments for the album and contributed the Hammond organ when necessary. As it turned out, the guitar riff-laden "Stand Up" formed an early blueprint for future Tull albums. Martin Barre's presence on the album was immediately felt on guitar-powered numbers like "A New Day Yesterday" and "Back To The Family." Without a Leslie speaker cabinet in Morgan Studios to provide a rotating guitar sound, engineer Andy Johns (not Ian, according to Glenn Cornick) swung the microphone around in a circle in front of the guitar amplifier speaker cabinet while Martin Barre was recording his guitar track. Producing an effect like that by hand could not be duplicated, so it had to be done in a minimal number of takes to avoid wear and tear to Andy! The folk portion of the album included another dedication to friend Jeffrey Hammond ("Jeffrey Goes To Leicester Square"), and the live favorite "Fat Man." The most striking element of "Fat Man" was Ian's balalaika playing. "Bourée," a version of a Bach composition, indicated yet another facet of the Jethro Tull persona, as well as the beautifully orchestrated "Reasons For Waiting." As expected, David Palmer was behind the arrangement and orchestration of the song. Martin Barre and Ian

Anderson shared flute lines on the song as well. In addition, another unusual occurrence within this song and "Jeffrey Goes To Leicester Square" was Barre's switching of instruments with Ian - Martin played flute and Ian played guitar. Although Ian Anderson has frequently stated that the songs were naïve, simplistic and even too personal, many of the tracks on "Stand Up" have formed the backbone of Tull's concerts to this day. One song even formed the backbone of Eagles concerts starting in 1976 - their "Hotel California" was stolen directly from the guitar solo of Tull's "We Used To Know." "Look Into The Sun" used a tremelo-effected vocal, and Martin Barre's ending wah-wah guitar on the song and "We Used To Know" is priceless. To this day, fans hearing the trick ending of "For A Thousand Mothers" still don't know when the song actually ends!

The album's songs may have been too self-centered, but they had to be since the songs on "Stand Up" reflect Ian's relationship with his parents. The songs were written on his now battered Harmony guitar which was missing one pickup, and the remaining pickup was attached to the three-string balalaika that he used on "Fat Man" and "Jeffrey Goes To Leicester Square." In these ways, this LP was a throwback to his youth and the possessions he still retained. As a result of channeling his childhood emotions into "Stand Up," Anderson's songwriting matured tremendously. So did Martin Barre's guitar playing ability. Here's how Ian describes what went into his songs on "Stand Up": "Simplicity - like that of the blues or R&B era. Simplicity of the forthright approach with variations of intensity from the simple songs to the heaviest and rawest." Jethro Tull was now charting its own musical path, with "This Was" a distant memory.

As for Bach's "Bourée," an explanation of the piece is in order here. Bach (1685-1750) wrote "Bourée" (correctly spelled "Bourrée") between 1708 and 1717 as part of his "Suite No. 1 for Lute in E minor" (catalog number: BMV 996). It is Bach's earliest surviving lute composition. The core movements of this suite were all stylized dances: "Allemande," "Courante," "Sarabande" and "Gigue." Bach allowed for additional movements to be improvised between the "Sarabande" and "Gigue" dances, including "Bourrée." The piece was kicked off by a "Prelude," which requires a high degree of virtuosity for a lutentist (*that's a lute player*) to pull off. Lutenists at the time had a great deal of difficulty in fingering the entire piece, so the classical guitar became the favorite instrument for playing this suite - especially Allemande and "Bourrée." In addition, the guitar's E tuning is better suited for this piece because it is in E minor. As for the Jethro Tull version of "Bourée" (note the amended spelling), the band took improvisation to a well-executed extreme by working in jazz and blues influences into the mix. The only unfortunate part about "Bourée" on "Stand Up" was its mistaken credit to Ian Anderson. *Yet another embarrassing mistake for Ian to suffer at the hands of the record company!*

Ian's chance to return some embarrassment came when he told Melody Maker about his bandmates: "Glenn hasn't changed at all in the last two years. He's generally happy and enthusiastic about things. . .Clive is a bit of a mystery man. He comes from a large family and has about seven brothers or something. And they're all identical. . .Martin is a born loser. He trips over things, gets tea over his shirts and gets electrical shocks from door handles." *Now, now Ian!*

Tull went back to touring without time to breathe - first in England and Ireland, then to America. Breaks in their schedule could not take place with the impending release of "Stand Up." Of their British dates, their first gig at the esteemed Royal Albert Hall in London took place on May 8 on a twin bill with Ten Years After. This was one of six dates Tull played with that band early in their career. Their premiere in Dublin took place twenty days later at Dublin National Stadium.

Promotion of their new and past hit product also took place in England during June 1969. "Living In The Past" was performed June 5 and 12 on British TV's "Top Of The Pops." Compared to the squeaky clean Cliff Richard, Jethro Tull looked downright scruffy to viewers that had no idea what the band looked like. Amazingly, Cliff got on well with Ian Anderson during the taping and came away impressed. Ian Anderson's parents were never in agreement with his decision to leave art school to become a musician. However, Ian changed their minds in 1969 when he bought his parents a new home with the royalties he earned from "Living In The Past." Another "Top Gear" radio broadcast was taped June 16 for airing on the 22nd and included "Living In The Past," "A New Day Yesterday" and "Fat Man." The latter song, as usual, featured only Ian and Clive Bunker. Of these, "Fat Man" was first issued on the "21 Years Of Alternative Radio" compilation before its overprocessed, fake stereo inclusion on the 20th anniversary box. "A New Day Yesterday" also appeared on the same box set. The BBC version of the hit single has still not been released.

Their second 1969 US jaunt started out with a festival-driven ten-day period before settling down to regular gigs, mainly with Led Zeppelin. An interesting bill at the Fillmore East in New York featured Jeff Beck and Soft White Underbelly, three years before their album debut as Blue Öyster Cult. The Newport Pop Festival (with Eric Burdon & The Animals and many others) and the

Miami Jazz Festival were perfect setups for the Newport shows that came in early July. The Newport Jazz Festival in Rhode Island allowed rock bands to play for the first time, and Jethro Tull was among the many groups that appeared. One of Ian Anderson's new musical heroes, Frank Zappa, was also on hand for the festivities but Ian and Frank did not meet (among others, Zappa and Led Zeppelin performed on July 5). On Independence Day (July 4), Tull played along with Roland Kirk, Ten Years After, Jeff Beck and Blood, Sweat & Tears. Meeting Roland Kirk was certainly a thrill for Ian Anderson, and Kirk was very happy to meet the band and to express his thanks to Ian for doing "Serenade To A Cuckoo" because it made *him* famous! The Newport Jazz Festival also hit Laurel Springs, MD and Philadelphia, PA and included such luminaries as Ray Charles and Woody Herman. Regardless of the location, Jethro Tull's festival performances were consistently successful. Thanks to the smart thinking of Terry Ellis, Tull would volunteer to play early in each festival in order to maximize the full stage lighting and to catch the audience before they got loaded!

When finally released in the UK on August 1, 1969, Jethro Tull was rewarded with an immediate #1 British album chart entry and its first gold album in the US (a #20 success). It was the first #1 album in Island Records' history. To celebrate, Terry Ellis took the band to Las Vegas to see Elvis Presley on August 11! This album was the band's first lavishly packaged LP, with a "stand up" cut-out caricature of the band appearing when the album's gatefold cover was opened. For promotion of "Stand Up," Reprise Records issued yet another lovely EP containing radio spots for the album. A 24-karat gold CD (with a perfectly duplicated "stand up" cut-out photo in its booklet) was made available in 1989.

"Bourée" was considered to be a strong A-side in many countries, with Norway and Sweden coupling it with "Back To The Family." In Holland and Spain, "Look Into The Sun" was its B-side. Belgium, France, Germany and Japan decided to pair it with "Fat Man," while Italy joined it with "Reasons For Waiting." A further Italian single for jukeboxes had "Bourée" on one side and a Buddy Miles track ("Them Changes") on the flip. All of these releases proved to be intriguing, but uncommercial all the way around.

Jethro Tull was scheduled to play the Fillmore West between August 12-14, but the show on the 13th was cancelled because someone spiked Ian's Coke during the sound check! Glenn Cornick has since discovered that this was a favorite prank that Fillmore personnel played on acts performing there. When the band finished their last-ever gig with Led Zeppelin in San Antonio, TX on August 15, 1969, their days supporting others were virtually over. It was headlining all the way, but there was uneasiness within Tull because the comfort factor of supporting was gone and the potential for failing as a headliner could be enormous! Still, the US gameplan was to establish themselves firmly on both coasts and then move towards the center of the country. Their second trip to the States had financially broken even.

While in New York for their July 28 date at Central Park, the group received an invitation to appear at the Woodstock festival (August 15-17, 1969). Alvin Lee of Ten Years After and co-manager Chris Wright told the band of the rain, the uncontrolled overflow crowd and the lack of payment. Tull passed on the opportunity despite cancelling a Dallas gig on the 17th just in case.

When Island Records made their deal with Terry Ellis and Chris Wright of Chrysalis, the label afforded the two Chrysalis honchos the opportunity to form their own record company if they attained three top ten records with their roster of talent. Since "Living In The Past" was the third Top 10 success by one of their acts, Ellis and Wright immediately formed the Chrysalis Records label with Island distribution. Chrysalis was formed specifically for Jethro Tull at first, then other worthy bands followed later.

A break in the Jethro Tull tour schedule freed up some recording time for a single (their first for Chrysalis) in early September 1969 at Morgan Studios in London. This single would build on their success on both the album and singles fronts. Three Anderson/Ellis produced tracks (notice the change in name order) were recorded, but only two comprised their next single: "Sweet Dream" and "17." The leftover track, "Singing All Day," would be included on the later "Living In The Past" double album in 1972. "Singing All Day" was another multi-instrumental tune for Ian, who contributed balalaika, Hammond organ and flute besides his voice. Glenn Cornick contributed an unusual second Hammond organ to the track along with his usual bass. "Sweet Dream" sported Ian's flute and 12-string guitar accompaniment to Barre's electric riffing and David Palmer's punchy arranging and conducting work. The single reached #7 (#8 NME) in late 1969, but US single success was still in the wings. The British B-side "17" was a meandering, repetitive 6-minute track that Ian Anderson has stated, in no uncertain terms, that he detests! Reprise in the US opted for the "Stand Up" track "Reasons For Waiting," although yet another label error had the record featuring "Back To The Family." To appease fans who wanted to hear the rare "17" on an album, Anderson placed a 3-minute edit of it on the 1988 box set. Therefore, the full version of "17" has yet to make it to an album. Thankfully, no UK label errors occurred this time, and the single came with or without a centerpiece. The most unusual release of "Sweet Dream" was its inclusion on a four-track EP in Portugal.

Above: The Swedish and German issues of "Sweet Dream."

Above are the Italian release of "Sweet Dream" and the extremely rare German Club-Sonderauflage compilation LP.

At left is the first album release of Jethro Tull's BBC take of "Fat Man."

"Stand Up" was the first album with Martin Barre.

Jethro Tull in action with new guitarist Martin Barre.

Ian Anderson in 1969.

Above: Terry Ellis and Chris Wright in the good old days.
Below: Barre, Anderson, Cornick and Bunker.

More radio recordings followed to fill the gap between appearances. For "Top Gear," Tull recorded "Sweet Dream," "Nothing Is Easy," "Bourée," and the as-yet unrecorded "The Witch's Promise." Only "Bourée" has officially seen the light of day, and it's on the 20th anniversary box. Thanks to an argument that John Peel show producer John Walters had with Ian Anderson, Jethro Tull had recorded their last BBC session until 1975. More television programming was on Tull's books during the fall. On September 4, the group filmed a TV stint in Stuttgart. Paris filming for the program "La Jaconde" was done on September 30 and October 31, while "Top Of The Pops" was lensed on October 30 and November 13. The September 20, 1969 issue of Melody Maker had a nice surprise for the band when their poll of most popular British groups revealed Tull as the runner up behind The Beatles. To their amazement, The Rolling Stones came in third. This popularity was borne out by the sold-out ticket sales of their month-long UK tour, where they headlined over Savoy Brown and Terry Reid. This month also included stops in Ireland, Northern Ireland, Belgium, Holland and France, and marked the first time they played in the latter two countries. This tour included Dutch, Belgian and French dates sponsored by Island Records at which they played just a few songs. Just three days into the tour in Dublin, a crazed fan ripped off one pocket of Ian's orange and black checkered coat. That pocket had his flute and harmonicas. Although the flute was mailed back shortly after, Ian was so upset that the band would not return to Ireland until 1993 - 24 years later!

Mid-November marked the third and final US wave of Jethro Tull tours for 1969. Four sold-out nights at the Fillmore West in San Francisco were followed by theaters, large auditorium shows and a tour accompanying Fleetwood Mac and Joe Cocker that lasted until the middle of December. This was their first tour to turn a profit. The band's unusual appearance brought along with it nagging questions about their playing ability and lifestyle. To that, Martin Barre answered those questions head on in Beat Instrumental magazine: "Jethro Tull does have discipline. Ian Anderson especially. When I joined, I was very sloppy. I was an okay musician but I couldn't prove it. There's discipline in getting down to writing, and I don't seem to have that yet. But in terms of playing, we are together, and we do have discipline. People assume that the rest of us are like hermits, because Ian doesn't drink and doesn't get about much. In fact, we are just. . .well, normal." *That settles it!* Martin also expounded upon the nature of recording, as recording studios were preparing to gear up for recording equipment with a greater number of tracks: "Normally, we're on eight-track recordings. I think you need all that. The concept of getting a live sound in the studio isn't really relevant. But on the next album, we'll probably try a few in 16-track. It may not work, but it's worth trying. Basically, I'd say eight-track is enough. When people talk of 32-track. . .well, I just don't see how you'd use it all." *If only Martin knew…then what would he be using today!*

During their Fillmore stay, Ian Anderson proved that he was a master at wordplay and self-effacing humor by directing the following words to the crowd: "Well, thank you for coming tonight, and I hope some of you do come. Or maybe you've come already. For shame on you. Imagine what your parents would say if they were here. (Then fingering his kinky shoulder-length hair. . .) It's frightful, really, this hippy thing with your long hair and nonsense. . .really getting out of hand." The band's final sold-out US show of 1969 was supposed to take place at Chicago's Kinetic Playground. Chicago, being a town known for its - shall we say - organized crime activities, suffered another injustice when those forces burned down this venue within days of Tull's performance. It was moved to the Aragon Ballroom, and the show went on without a hitch.

Returning home to London, Morgan Studios found the band locked in its confines again in mid-December. "Teacher" and "The Witch's Promise" were produced by Ellis and Anderson during the session. John Evans, on a break from college, played Hammond organ on "Teacher" and both piano and mellotron on "The Witch's Promise." Evans brought Jeffrey Hammond with him to observe the session. Since both sides were considered equally strong, the single was marketed as a double-sided disc. As their first record release of the '70s, "The Witch's Promise"/ "Teacher" became a #4 British hit (#3 NME). While "The Witch's Promise" was another elegantly styled Anderson original, "Teacher" was a heavier, Martin Barre-fueled rocker. Martin Barre turned in dual guitar duty on "The Witch's Promise" through the use of acoustic and electric guitars on the track. The single version of "Teacher" made its first appearance on the 1988 box set, but it unfortunately was presented in rechanneled stereo instead of duplicating the original single's true stereo mix. England was the only country to receive the original single in stereo. The belated American single also had "Teacher" on its B-side, but in a shorter, more controlled newly recorded version. Reprise asked the band to produce a commercial single and album track featuring Ian's flute, and Terry Ellis selected "Teacher" despite the band's feeling that it was a throwaway track! You want more label goofs? The UK single appeared with the following title variations: "The Witch's Promise"/ "Teacher," "Witch's Promise"/ "The Teacher" and "Witch's Promise"/ "Teacher." I can happily say that no copies were pressed as "The Witch's Promise"/ "The Teacher"! What is the correct title? The sleeve has it correct! As a special release for the German Sonderauflage record club, Island issued an unusual self-titled compilation LP that featured singles and album tracks. It is the first LP to include "Sweet Dream" and "The Witch's Promise." Since both songs had not yet been mixed in stereo, they

The UK sheet music for "The Witch's Promise."

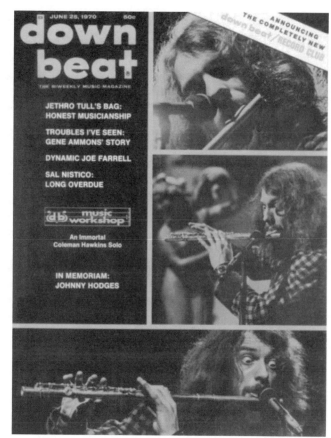

The June 25, 1970 front cover of Down Beat.

Jethro Tull in flight on their tour with Led Zeppelin. Note Zep drummer John Bonham at the left of the photo.

appear in rechanneled stereo. This LP is very difficult to find. Also difficult is the Swedish single release that came on blue vinyl and also on standard black vinyl. On top of this, a unique Mexican release coupled "Sweet Dream" with a Tommy Roe recording.

After "The Witch's Promise," Jethro Tull made an executive decision to stop going after the singles market. The two singles after "Living In The Past" were selling less than their predecessors. The band was not properly reaching the album market (of whom singles buyers formed a subset) by catering to the demands of the singles clientele.

A Jethro Tull stage show became an Ian Anderson showcase for all sorts of flute abuse - waving the flute around like a wand or sword and placing it upward between his legs like a phallus (among other things) when not playing the instrument. The flute was also used as a cheerleading device when Ian twirled it around like a baton. Ian's occasionally bulging eyes gave frenzied audiences reason to stay right there and keep their attentions on his every move. Once offstage, Ian became a more introspective yet eloquent person of integrity. This introspection brought Anderson closer to his songwriting and himself, but further away from the band.

When asked about the dichotomy of his stage personality and off-stage personality, Ian replied somewhat tongue-in-cheek: "Well, if there's a difference in personalities, it's because I have a tremendous range of emotions - as a person and as a performer. I'm glad to see people enjoy one of my concerts, but at the same time, if something goes wrong, I'll get extremely depressed - right on stage. Sure, the people aren't aware that we might have goofed, but it doesn't help me. I know, and if it's particularly bad, I'll disappear behind an amp and cry."

"BENEFIT"

Tull started off 1970 with yet another trek to Morgan Studios to lay down tracks for their next LP. Robin Black was their engineer this time. It was the first encounter in a long-running relationship with the engineer. While the band was recording, NME was tallying the votes that readers sent in for Best New Group nominees. The winner with a plurality of 3,000 votes was none other than Jethro Tull, and the results were printed in the January 24 issue.

The Morgan recordings formed the basis of their "Benefit" album, also named and covered by Terry Ellis. It must be noted that Ian did not like the album titles for this LP and its predecessor! The dead serious "Benefit" contained an eclectic mix of styles again, with no musical overlapping from previous releases. Guitar riffs were in abundance, underpinned by acoustic guitar and/or the piano and organ supplied by guest John Evans. Personally, Ian Anderson was not very happy at the time, feeling out of place with his peers. Optimism was rarely presented in these songs - if it was, the optimism was guarded. What fans did not know was that Ian was very close to calling it quits. Anderson's dissatisfaction with touring and loneliness on the road were the main factors in his introspection, but the songwriting process was therapeutic in getting these feelings out of his system. Songs like "With You There To Help Me" were about Jennie Franks, a secretary in Chrysalis' publishing department. They would marry later that year at Watford Registry Office in England.

The non-stop touring was not doing wonders for the band, and Martin Barre had a problem with spending half of every year in America. He was feeling very low emotionally and most of the others had no time to appreciate anything in life other than touring. The Britishness of Tull was at risk of being swept away and something had to change. Touring was just as involved as it was the previous year, as three passes through the US were made in both 1969 and 1970.

As for the album, John Evans (again shown as Evan to reflect the old days) was invited to play piano and organ. Evans recorded his parts at night after completing his studies, just as he did on "The Witch's Promise." Barre loaned Ian his Gibson SG electric guitar for use as a rhythm instrument on the LP. The US version contained the alternate version of "Teacher," which became a massively popular album track that still receives airplay today. Releases outside North America had "Alive And Well And Living In" instead. Astrononaut Michael Collins, the only one of the Apollo 11 crew that did not walk on the moon, got a name check along with Jeffrey Hammond on "For Michael Collins, Jeffrey And Me." "To Cry You A Song" was an "airplane experience" song that most people misconstrue as being about drugs. It is also unusual for its fade-in introduction. Two other "Benefit" songs were differently constructed: "Son" and "Play In Time." "Son" cut away to an acoustic section in its middle before the band returned to finish the song, while "Play In Time" relied on backward piano and other tape effects to work its magic. Ian Anderson played on the word "society" in his "Sossity; You're A Woman." Martin Barre thought "Sossity" was the name of a girl and purchased a boat (always

The UK and German issues of "The Witch's Promise" are above with the US 45 and Argentine "Teacher" EP below.

Belgium was one of the countries that received "Bourée" as a single. Tull's June 1970 Aragon Ballroom concert in Chicago was released as a free cassette/CD with the Italian publication "Il Dizionario del Rock." You may ask, how did they get away with it? Well, Italian copyright laws are very loose!

Ian Anderson and conductor Zubin Mehta during the rehearsals and filming for "Pop Goes The Symphony."

Yes, it's Zubin Mehta and Ian Anderson trying to enjoy themselves again before "Pop Goes The Symphony"!

For some reason, the obscure Zygote magazine thought it was clever to illustrate the entire band's pregnancy!

Here are radio spot singles for "Stand Up" and "Benefit."

Below are British and French releases of "Inside."

referred to as if a girl) that he named "Sossity." When Ian told Martin that he was just playing on the word "society"'s personification as a woman, Martin promptly sold the boat!

"Benefit" was a May 1970 release, and furthered the band's success throughout the world. British (#3) and American (#11) sales were strong, and the band maintained their US headlining status. Accompanying the album was the single "Inside." For England, the single's B-side was "Alive And Well And Living In," and for the US, Australia and New Zealand, it was "A Time For Everything?". The introspective nature of this single and complete lack of promotion did not translate into sales. In Argentina, Reprise issued the "Teacher" EP with the title number, "Move On Alone," "The Witch's Promise" and "Driving Song." The German issue of "Benefit" was different in that it came with a gatefold cover containing otherwise unused Ian Anderson live photos inside.

On the playing side, Tull started off in Denmark, Finland, Sweden and Germany before tackling the US again. Between February 13-17, the band filmed a Hollywood TV special for the NBC television network with noted UK pop program producer Jack Good, entitled "The Switched-On Symphony." The title was a play on Walter (now Wendy!) Carlos' landmark Moog album "Switched-On Bach." Besides Tull, the other rock acts on the program included The Nice and Santana. The symphony was the L.A. Philharmonic Orchestra conducted by Zubin Mehta. During the program, Jethro Tull did "Nothing Is Easy." The show was well documented in the May 8, 1970 issue of Life magazine and Hit Parader covered it as well. Perhaps due to its misinterpretation as a drug-influenced program, the show was broadcast on March 14 under the title "Pop Goes The Symphony." An uproar occurred during the taping when Tull refused to participate in a show-ending jam with the orchestra. In Ian's view, "I don't know if there was a moral to be put over by bringing rock and the classics together in the program, but if there was, it certainly was not to be served best by each of the units compromising their own standards to find a very low musical common denominator purely for the sake of playing together. I feel we can best serve the cause of entertainment by doing what we know best, to the best of our ability, and allow the audience to be the judge of what conclusions to draw, if any." While the show still exists, it has been long forgotten. A few months later, Zubin Mehta and the L.A. Philharmonic would give an equally disastrous performance at the debut of Frank Zappa's "200 Motels" with The Mothers Of Invention on May 15, 1970. Mehta has since elevated himself with his conducting for The Three Tenors!

Another issue that still dogged the band was if Ian Anderson dominated the group. Glenn Cornick flatly replied, "Yes, he does. Why not? He writes good songs, but what's more, he's able to finish them, which is more than the others can say. Martin and I have both been working on songs for over a year, but we'll never get them done. Ian has the right direction of mind to sit down and write the beginning and end to a song." An attempt to form a Jethro Tull fan club ("Jeffrey's Journal") was accompanied by a letter supposedly by Jeffrey Hammond. It turned out to be bogus (Hammond had no apparent knowledge of it), and the fan club was terminated in September.

THE RETURN OF JOHN EVANS

Jethro Tull's first show in Germany was literally a smashing success on February 21, as fans destroyed the glass walls of the Jahrhunderhalle venue in Frankfurt. It was their last gig until early April, when they came back to Germany. Two days before while in Germany, Tull appeared on the "Beat Club" program. While in German rehearsals to prepare for their April 5 show in Nuremberg, Ian realized that the band was unable to reproduce the fuller recorded sound of "Benefit" on stage. Keyboards were required. Jeffrey Hammond's outside view of the band was helpful to Ian Anderson: "It was Jeffrey Hammond who'd seen us a couple of times and who said the band sounded incomplete. It tended to be all guitar and flute - a formula and limiting to what I could write, because we didn't have enough instruments or tone colors at our disposal."

Ian immediately called John Evans, who gave up his studies at Chelsea College of Science after completing his Easter exams in late March and early April. At the time, John was living in the same house as Ian and Jeffrey Hammond. Despite his mother's classical piano training, John Evans was still considered a musical virgin by Ian's standards! Evans' first work was for the German "Beat Club" TV taping of "The Witch's Promise," which the band mimed. Evans' first two shows with Tull took place in Nuremberg and Hamburg on April 5 and 6, respectively. He was also on the June 23 German "Beat Club" tapings of "Nothing Is Easy," "With You There To Help Me" and "By Kind Permission Of." That performance ended when Ian Anderson, suffering from a bad stomach, left the stage for the bathroom after two aborted attempts to complete the first song during the sound check. These shows were meant to be a trial for Evans, who was then offered a full-time position in Tull. Evans figured that he would give it a go for a year or two, but his full-time relationship with the group lasted for much longer than that - nine years! Similar to his guest appearances, Evans' last name became Evan upon joining. What Evans brought to the table was the ability to color the electric sound that the rest of the band created. This coloring brought to light all sorts of arrangement possibilities and the potential for playing music that required a higher degree of proficiency. As Ian said, "John (Evans) has added a new dimension musically and I can write more freely now. In fact, anything is possible with him at the keyboard." Another facet of Evans' persona was the influence of the harp-playing Marx brother, Harpo, on his stage presentation: a white-suited clown prince with goofy faces to match his virtuosic playing (similar to Harpo's piano-tinkling brother Chico).

After cancelling gigs at the Fillmore West on April 2-4, 1970 with Manfred Mann Chapter Three to do two German shows, Jethro Tull's first US dates with Evans in April 1970 took place at Mammoth Gardens in Denver, Colorado with the nearly 20,000 strong crowd of the Long Beach Coliseum right afterward. Similar to many Jethro Tull members that would join after him, John Evans would go from total obscurity to playing for massive crowds. The Long Beach, CA show was important in a few respects: Evans was given a forum for a piano solo in which he quoted from Beethoven's "Moonlight Sonata," and Tull previewed a recent song Ian had written called "My God." "My God" was in fact written before "Benefit." Part of this show formed the basis of the early bootleg "My God" released later that year. Martin Barre now had his own forum to play a guitar solo lasting as long as ten minutes! Accompanying the group's instrument arsenal was new electronic equipment that further colored their sound. Ian started using an echo unit for his flute that sustained tones just played, forming a musical bed to lay more flute sounds on top of the sustain. Other gimmicky products did not work as well, but the band was coming to terms with the developing sound synthesis technology. A May 10 show at Washington University Field House in St. Louis, MO featured many acts besides Tull, including the Scottish trio Clouds - a Chrysalis act whose album was produced by Terry Ellis. The drummer for Clouds was Harry Hughes, who is sometimes listed (erroneously) as a Tull drummer in some publications! Thanks to Jethro Tull, Chrysalis' client base was growing.

Roland Kirk ran into the band again in Hartford, CT before Tull did their first show in Canada at the Autostade in Montreal. This would be the last time the band crossed paths with Kirk, who died on December 4, 1977. In mid-June they returned home so that Ian could record his new songs "Just Trying To Be" and "Wond'ring Again" at Morgan Studios with Robin Black engineering. This was the first session Ian produced completely on his own. "Just Trying To Be" had just Ian on acoustic guitar and vocals with Evans on celeste. During these sessions, Morgan Studios was building new 16-track recording facilities. "Wond'ring Again" (originally title: "Wond'ring Aloud") was recorded with that new, unfamiliar equipment and included the entire band with Clive Bunker doubling on drums and glockenspiel. The band tried to record the song "My God" that they played in Long Beach, and that song and two other backing tracks slated for their next album (tentatively titled "My God") were failures and quickly scrapped. "Wond'ring Again" was the only track from those 16-track sessions deemed worthy of release, and it made it to the "Living In The Past" album.

The New York Pop Festival (Randall's Island, New York, NY) was the highlight of their 1970 summer return to the US. Their July 7 show in Tanglewood, MA was shot for TV, but it was not broadcast. An unusual occurrence took place at Curtis Hixon Hall in Miami, FL on July 25 when Ian Anderson noticed that fans were being arrested. Ian stopped the show and asked fans to put together money to bail out the arrested audience members. It was a highly unusual and effective move that showed that the band was really aware of what was going on around them during a performance.

Making their way home from yet another successful US trip, Tull did the full-scale Isle of Wight Festival on August 30 before taking three weeks off. Tracks from the band's Isle Of Wight appearance did not appear on the 3LP US Columbia album extracted from the Wight show and the Atlanta Pop Festival (where Tull cancelled out) because Chrysalis did not license them to that label. Their three-week UK and France tour for "Benefit" had more space between the dates to give the band more rest. Of these shows, Birmingham Town Hall (September 25) was the most notable with Tir Na Nog and Procol Harum opening the show.

Their last visit to the US in 1970 started mid-October in California. Their L.A. Forum show became the notorious "Flute Cake" bootleg LP, and the tour introduced another John Evans piano solo creation as part of a medley with "With You There To Help Me." The piece became known later as "By Kind Permission Of" because significant sections were borrowed from classical composers, all of whom were deceased and not in a position to give Evans permission to perform them!

By far, the most impressive show they did in America was at Carnegie Hall. That hallowed institution did not allow rock bands to play there, with a 1964 Beatles concert as the only exception to their policy. Jethro Tull would become the second rock group to play Carnegie Hall, and this occasion was different: it was a charity concert with proceeds going to the New York drug rehabilitation center Phoenix House. Jethro Tull took the opportunity to record the show and parts of it were later released on the "Living

JETHRO TULL
HAS A NEW ALBUM OUT
"BENEFIT"
RS6400
On Reprise Where He Belongs!

Yet another promotional goof: On Reprise where *he* belongs?

Below: "Benefit" and the "Inside" stereo promo single. The regular copy was in mono.

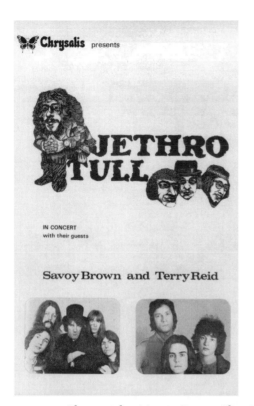

Above right: Martin Barre, Clive Bunker, Jeffrey Hammond-Hammond, Ian Anderson, John Evans.
Below: Ian and Jennie Anderson meet the Duke and Duchess of Bedford after the Carnegie Hall show.

In The Past" album and the 25th anniversary box set. These two albums comprise the entire show without duplication. Politically, Ian felt it was the right thing to do, especially since he was completely against drugs. Here's Ian view on the issue of drug taking in his band: "I don't give a damn what others do as long as they don't louse themselves up physically. I couldn't abide sidemen who are constantly stoned. If I don't take any drugs, it's not due to a moral thing. It's simply that I don't want my personality changed or even influenced by external things." *Notice Ian's use of the word "sidemen"!*

That veiled comment was related to Glenn Cornick, who drank socially but avoided drugs. Even though he married Judy Wong from San Francisco in March and moved to a London suburban house, he frequently chased (and caught!) other women. At the end of the tour in Plattsburgh, NY on November 15, 1970, Ian fired Cornick because he felt Glenn's enjoyment of constant touring was not what he wanted. Cornick was also gravitating towards a heavier riff-based direction that Tull had already moved away from. Terry Ellis had the nasty job of telling Glenn his fate at JFK Airport in New York. Glenn went on to form the group Wild Turkey that recorded two albums and toured America twice. (Cornick's subsequent activities are noted later in his solo section.)

"AQUALUNG" AND JEFFREY HAMMOND-HAMMOND'S BASS CRASH COURSE

With a tour pending, a bass player was needed immediately. Martin Barre knew a bassist but he couldn't contact him. Ian immediately gravitated toward Jeffrey Hammond. Jeffrey had just left art school and had no interest in doing a post-grad course at the Royal Academy Schools because he couldn't see earning a living from artwork. During his redecoration of Ian's house, Jeffrey was asked by Anderson if he wished to replace Glenn Cornick in Jethro Tull. He agreed, and upon joining Tull, Jeffrey was asked by Ian to duplicate his last name to create Jeffrey Hammond-Hammond. As it turned out, his mother's maiden name *was* Hammond - an astonishing coincidence. He had two weeks to revive his bass playing ability.

The month of December 1970 was set aside to record Ian's new batch of songs at Island Studios in London. Ian and Terry Ellis produced the sessions with John Burns engineering. This time, the recording of "My God" was successful. Of course, David Palmer performed his usual orchestral magic throughout the entire collection. Jeffrey Hammond was thrown right into recording, and he had a great deal of difficulty in playing Ian's more intricate music. Hammond was out of his element, but he had to get up to speed very quickly with Ian's instructions for each song. Jeffrey and Martin pitched in by playing recorders (alto and descant, respectively). Finishing off the year was the band's TV appearance on "Top Of The Pops," where they performed "The Witch's Promise."

Ian's depressed feeling on the previous album turned to cynicism on this new collection of songs, which was originally entitled "My God." The appearance of the bootleg of that name forced Ian to change its title. It became "Aqualung," and for once, Ian named the album without any intervention. The title was inspired by one of the many homeless people that Ian's wife Jennie was photographing for a project in London on the embankment next to the Thames River. Accompanying her photos were notes she took on each subject. One of the outcast characters in Jennie's photo collection formed the inspiration for Ian to create the song and album "Aqualung." Parts of Jennie's notes became lyrics to Ian's song and it was the only time Ian wrote lyrics with anyone else. The title character had a rheumatic cough and leering eyes. As Ian explained: "The title character is the outcast from society - in this case, the tramp. In another society, it could have been a starving Britain." The Burton Silverman painting on the album's front cover was supposed to be a vagrant two decades older than Ian, but the final outcome looked more like a slightly older, more disheveled Ian Anderson! As expected, everyone thought the character on the cover was Ian Anderson himself.

It took a long time to put "Aqualung" together. Pre-production involved three days at Ian's Hampstead home, where the band discussed song treatments. These discussions moved into rehearsals, at which numerous arrangements were suggested and attempted. Song difficulties that presented themselves at the first week of rehearsals resulted in Ian scrapping, rewriting or coming up with, new songs. With all of his song crafting, Ian Anderson was now taking his songwriting more seriously with obvious attention to its overall effect on the band and intended listeners. As discussed previously, some of the tracks slated for this album were attempted without success at Morgan Studios in June. With Island's new, more technically advanced studio at their disposal, Tull decided to re-record those tracks. Three other completed Island tracks were recorded again during the winter of 1971 - between their last date in Italy (February 2) and initial UK date of the year (February 26) - because the new live arrangements proved to be more successful than their recently recorded studio renditions. They were working against the clock and final recording was completed using sessions running from midnight to 10AM. All in all, they racked up anywhere between 150 and 200 hours of studio time. With all this time, the production values of the album varied widely from track to track. The time that the album required was in part due to the band's search for perfection, but in main part because the engineers and new equipment at Island Studios were not working to anyone's satisfaction.

The title song "Aqualung," with the album of the same name, became Jethro Tull's most famous work, and "Aqualung"'s signature opening guitar riff is immediately recognizable. Using nearly every root chord in the entire scale, it was a knotted, yet completely engaging and exciting composition. It was ideal for singing along, listening and for musicians interested in learning an intricate musical piece. The music for the song was written in an L.A. hotel room on October 18, 1970 and its recording used an Aria Japanese guitar. What was an "Aqualung"? It was a brand name breathing apparatus produced by the American Aqualung Corporation. When the album was released, their legal department notified Ian Anderson that he used their brand name copyright without their permission. In a highly advantageous settlement for the band, the corporation allowed Tull to keep all of the song and album royalties. Apparently, no one at the corporation was a Jethro Tull fan. A surprise occurred while Martin Barre was recording his solo in "Aqualung": Jimmy Page popped in the control room to say hello during a break from recording the fourth Led Zeppelin LP at Island. Instead of either waving to Jimmy through the studio glass or blowing his solo, Barre got down to business and nailed that take without any hint of distraction. In fact, the take that Page viewed, and listened to, was the one recorded on the album.

"Aqualung" was Jethro Tull's definitive album statement, as the title track, "Locomotive Breath" and "Cross-Eyed Mary" became staples of US AOR (album oriented radio) stations and the band's live set. Besides humor, numerous aspects of life were presented in sharp detail in Ian Anderson's songs. "Wond'ring Aloud" was a love song, "Cross-Eyed Mary" was the town prostitute, "Mother Goose" and "Up To Me" captured everyday London street life, and three songs dealt with dying ("Locomotive Breath," "Cheap Day Return" and the 45-second "Slipstream"). "Cheap Day Return" is the name for a discount British round-trip train ticket requiring a return to origin on the same day. This is the ticket type that Ian used to visit his ailing father in a Blackpool hospital. At the time, Ian was concerned that it would be the last time he would see his father, but Ian's father recovered from his illness. "Locomotive Breath" dealt with dying, in the surreal sense, of being unable to escape an out of control train. This song naturally evolved from an unfinished song Ian had called "The Passenger," in which the title character's train travel was analogous to how he travelled through life. "Locomotive Breath" was the first of Ian's train songs - Ian had never gotten a driver's license, so trains became his preferred method of local travel. Trains have also provided Ian with a good deal of material ever since! Even after all the rehearsals, recording "Locomotive Breath" was very trying because Ian had great difficulty in expressing the feel of the song to the others. Ian took matters into his own hands at Island Studios by first putting down a rudimentary high hat and bass drum track and then overdubbing acoustic and electric guitar tracks before John Evans' distinctive piano introduction was attached to Ian's work. The rest of the band then placed their parts on top of Ian's and the recording was complete. Ian Anderson is the one providing lead guitar on the song because Martin Barre was unable to produce the sound that Ian was searching for. This disjointed recording was unlike anything Tull, or anyone else, had done, but the final result was classic and pure Jethro Tull.

The "My God" suite of songs was the half of the album that received the most media attention. "Hymn 43" was a saving call for, and to, Jesus, but "My God" required more explanation from Ian than anything on the album. Ian explains: "'My God' is a blues for God - not in any way a condemnation for God. It is on His side; a lament that there are so many different ways of worshipping God. He is a social crutch for so many. The thing I'm against is that God is not a God in the spiritual sense but as a figurehead of religion. 'My God' is a slightly humorous lament for God's state of having to be God to everyone, which is my concept of the God He is. But they aren't thinking like that - they say He is my God so He can't be your God. The Catholic God isn't the Jews' God and so on. He can't be the same God for everyone." Ian makes a very valid point, and it's an argument that continues to this day. By extension, Anderson is referring to the wars in our world that are caused by people that claim that their God (or gods) authorize the killing of others that do not adhere to their religious beliefs.

The issue of whether Ian was prosyletizing came to the fore as well. Ian countered: "I'm not a Bible-carrying Billy Graham type. I'm not out to convert people. I'm just having a go at the people who misled me. The religious concept came when, over a period of a year, I found that I'd written four or five songs that had God in the subject matter. But it's not a concept album as such - not in the same way as 'Tommy.' It doesn't tell a story, doesn't have any profound link between the tracks, although there are statements made of a very personal nature. But they are not absolute truths."

This leads us to the next point - the misinterpretation of "Aqualung" as a concept album. Ian has already covered this issue in the prior quote, so we'll move on! As a follow-up to his forced childhood church attendance, "Wind-Up" dealt with Anderson's disagreement that children have to follow the religious beliefs of their parents. Rather, Ian felt through the song that children

The quadrophonic album release of "Aqualung."

The "Sunday Best" LP released only in Australia.

Back: Jeffrey Hammond-Hammond, Martin Barre.
Middle: Ian Anderson, John Evans.
Front: Clive Bunker.

Martin Barre

At left: The French release of "Locomotive Breath." Top right and middle: The three German single issues.

 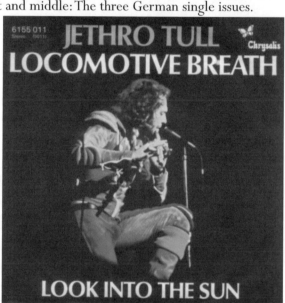

Below: The American releases of "Hymn 43" and "Locomotive Breath" on Reprise.

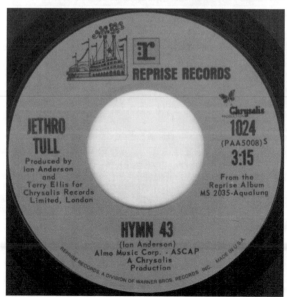 

should use their own minds to come to their own religious conclusions: "To me, religion is something that you grow up to find in your own way. I am sure that a lot people believe in God the same as I do - that faith is a form of goodness 'round which you relate your life. This is where I believe you have to look for God. I don't think you have to look for God in a church or in someone who gives his money for charity."

In January 1971, Chrysalis advertised the single "Lick Your Fingers Clean" b/w "Up To Me." Most likely, it became more and more apparent to the record company that the A-side was not going to be included on the "Aqualung" album, of which it was supposed to precede, so the single was scrapped. "Lick Your Fingers Clean" was later rearranged and re-recorded as the song "Two Fingers" on the "War Child" album in 1974 before the 20th anniversary box set took the original (in an April 1988 mix) under its wing. In one of the most nonsensical reasons for not releasing a single, the record company said that the single was being released too close to the album's release date. Since the single was planned for late January and the album was slated for March, there is no explanation for this statement. A one-sided German acetate of "Lick Your Fingers Clean" was produced to no avail.

The issuance of the "Aqualung" LP in March 1971 (US: May 1971) was the realization of all that the band strove for. Through the strategic placement of the Anderson solo acoustic songs, the Tull fan was able to concentrate more on the full make-up of each song, instead of being blown away by one heavy song after another. This approach has worked very well over the years, as these acoustic numbers have proven to be just as popular as concert favorites like "Aqualung" and "Locomotive Breath." "Aqualung" hit #4 and #7 respectively, on the UK and US album charts. In a unique marketing strategy, the UK market received no singles from the album, but the US received two: "Hymn 43" (a #91 Billboard chart single - their first) and "Locomotive Breath." The Cashbox singles showing for "Hymn 43" was a little better - #77. A few more unusual international releases accompanied the album: Spain released "Aqualung"/ "Up To Me" on Island, while Tull was on an unlawful EP from Vietnam called "Look At Yourself." A US acetate recording was also created for the single coupling "Up To Me" b/w "Wond'ring Aloud," but it went no further when the A-side was then used as a released B-side. A mastering mistake on the US edition of the LP resulted in the omission of the first guitar riff on the title track. The Chrysalis release of "Locomotive Breath" was handled with different flipsides in other countries: "Bourée" in France, Germany and Holland, "Look To The Sun" in Austria, and "Love Story" for the second Dutch release. The German single used "Locomotive Breath" b/w "Hymn 43" as another variation. The Australian EP "This Is Jethro Tull" comprised these tracks: "Living In The Past," "Locomotive Breath," "Hymn 43" and "A Song For Jeffrey."

Further US promotion came in the shape of a jukebox EP and promotional spot single for "Aqualung." On the promotional record, Ian can be heard talking about the LP's religious aspects. A quadrophonic version of the album made the racks in 1974, and this album is a required purchase. In addition to featuring different mixes of the album's tracks, an alternate (almost solo) take of "Wind-Up" was used in place of the correct version. The version of "Aqualung" on the later "M.U. - The Best Of Jethro Tull" and "Original Masters" albums included an alternate mix that was missing the "transistor radio" effect on the song's verses. A collectable half-speed mastered album was also issued in 1981. The 1996 CD comprised the entire album, the quad "Wind-Up," "Lick Your Fingers Clean," an Ian Anderson interview excerpt from a February 22, 1996 interview with Mojo magazine and three previously released BBC tracks. However, the sound was less than ideal. The original US CD of "Aqualung" was missing the last thirty seconds of "Wind-Up," and so was the reissued LP. This error would be a sore spot with American fans until 1997. Ian Anderson's complete two-track master tape was used for the first time since the original LP for the 1997 CD reissue on the DCC label. On another front, Chrysalis Music Publishing's promotional LP "Hardly Beginner's Luck: The Chrysalis Compendium" included a medley of "Living In The Past," "Wond'ring Aloud" and "Locomotive Breath."

Prior to the release of "Aqualung," Ian made a very interesting observation: "It seems a bit silly to say it but if the next album sold only 200 copies and those 200 people were still playing that record in five years time, that would really knock me out. That is what I really want to do. . .to play music that people will remember. Music that will have the same feel in the years to come and not just be the biggest thing of that particular year."

Jeffrey Hammond's first gig was in Odense, Denmark on January 7, 1971. He was sporting new road gear designed to avoid recognition - strange clothing and leather flight goggles. In Odense, his goggles fogged up and he couldn't see what he was playing! The additional humor that Jeffrey provided to the collective Tull persona on stage made him an immediate success with fans. What Ian Anderson calls the "Viking helmet" vocal section of "My God," which involved the use of vocal backing tapes to accompany Ian's flute, had many people scratching their heads inquisitively as to where the voices were coming from!

The tour preceding "Aqualung" marked Jethro Tull's first appearances in Norway, Austria, Switzerland and Italy. Many shows throughout Germany took place for the first time along with numerous shows with Steeleye Span as Tull's opening act. Tull kicked off their US tour a month before the release of the "Aqualung" album, capping it off with two sets of two-night stands at the Fillmore East. Prior to the US tour, Clive Bunker gave Ian Anderson notice that he planned to get off the tour merry-go-round to get married and build a home rehearsal studio. He met his future wife while in England, and he wasn't happy with playing the band's newest material. As Ian said of Bunker at the time, "Sometimes he'd be stuck for ideas on songs I'd written, others he'd be more into playing. Socially, we always got on all right." Clive's last date was the Fillmore East show on May 5, 1971.

"LIFE IS A LONG SONG" WITH BARRIEMORE

With Bunker's departure, Ian was left as the only original member of the band formed as Jethro Tull in 1967. If anything can confirm whose group Jethro Tull was, Clive Bunker's departure proved it and this was still relatively early in the band's career. To replace Bunker, another old John Evan Smash member, Barrie Barlow, became the percussionist. He prepared for his audition by buying the prior three Jethro Tull LPs in a store and John Evans assisted him with the rest. When Barlow saw the band at the Blackpool Opera House on March 14, he came away with the feeling that everyone in the band was not working together. This gave him a sense that something was amiss. Barrie was offered the job on F.A. Cup Final day - a very important day for a football (soccer) aficionado like Barlow. Barrie Barlow, a lathe turner, was in the part-time group Requiem that was formed in 1970 with bassist Tony Williams and Mike Proctor (keyboards). In another mysterious name change, Barlow's first name was lengthened to Barriemore when he joined Tull. This band was the same as the 1965 pre-brass edition of The John Evan Band plus Martin Barre.

Barrie Barlow's first duty as a Tull member was on the five-song Chrysalis EP "Life Is A Long Song," a #11 hit in the fall of 1971. Ian Anderson felt that his new songs were of a higher quality because he didn't have to work with the pressure of a deadline for the first time. Anderson also wanted to give fans more music for their money. Barlow didn't know it at the time, but his inclusion in the band would provide Jethro Tull with five full years of a stable line-up. Barlow, being an expressive drummer, contributed his uniquely boisterous personality to a band that gave equal weight, in each visual and audio presentation, for their devout fans.

The EP was recorded in May 1971 at the home of "This Was," Sound Techniques in London, just days before they started rehearsing for their month-long US tour. Two sessions were required to produce its five tracks, one with Victor Gamm and John Wood engineering, and the other with only Gamm in charge. All of the songs were produced solely by Ian Anderson. The Gamm/Wood session featured the emphasis track "Life Is A Long Song," "Dr. Bogenbroom" and "For Later" (mistitled "From Later"). "Dr. Bogenbroom" featured Evans on piano and harpsichord, while "For Later" had John playing Hammond organ and piano. "Up The 'Pool" and "Nursie" were more personal. "Up The 'Pool" was about Blackpool and Ian described it as "the sort of thing that Ringo might sing." With the other four members, Ian sang and played violin along with his usual flute. The "Edward Bear" referred to in this song was Edward Heath, a Tory party boss that wished to tax more affluent UK residents at an 83% rate. "Nursie" was an Anderson solo recording featuring just acoustic guitar and his vocal. It was another song about his hospital visit to see his father, whom he did not have a good relationship with in his teen years. Like "Cheap Day Return," it was written on a Preston train platform while he was waiting for a southbound train. The EP also hit #10 on the NME chart. Based on sales and airplay, Record Retailer charted the record under the dual titles "Life Is A Long Song" and "Up The 'Pool," while NME charted just the first song. The EP was released in only a handful of countries outside England, such as Italy and Spain, the latter of which presented it with two different covers. It was not released in the US. The Ronco budget label in England released its "20 Star Tracks, Volume 1" hits package that sported a unique edited version of "Life Is A Long Song."

Similar to Hammond and Evans before him, Barlow was thrust into massively populated venues. Barrie's initial show was at the 10,000-seat Salt Palace in Salt Lake City, UT on June 9, 1971. Twelve of the dates on their tour of the US and Canada were supported by Yes. The second date of the tour at Red Rocks Amphitheater in Denver, CO was Tull's first real taste of riot behavior. According to newspaper accounts, 12,000 people showed up at Red Rocks, which held only 10,000. The Denver police department claimed that a riot ensued when 200 to 300 people out of the 2,000 without tickets tried to get in using tear gas. About 1,500 of these people were offered free vantage points from the side of a mountain overlooking the outdoor venue. Another group of these people tried to climb over the wall and threw rocks at the police, knocking one officer off his horse. Another cop, trying to assist his colleague, was hit in the head with a rock. Five stitches were required to close the wound. More rock throwing continued until the police decided to hit the rear of the crowd with tear gas via helicopter. Livingston Taylor opened the show, but

Martin Barre

Ian Anderson

Clive Bunker

Glenn Cornick

John Evans

With new drummer Barriemore Barlow, Jethro Tull appears in whiteface. From left to right: Barriemore Barlow, Martin Barre, Ian Anderson, John Evans and Jeffrey Hammond-Hammond.

The next row has the Italian and UK editions of the "Life Is A Long Song" EP.

At the bottom is the promo radio single for "Aqualung" and the jukebox EP for the album.

Jethro Tull had to play under the influence of tear gas in their eyes. When the disturbance was over, 28 people (including four policemen and three children) had to be taken to a nearby hospital while many more were treated at Red Rocks. Twenty people were arrested for drug and/or weapons possession and public drunkenness. Damage also occurred to many vehicles, including one that was completely destroyed by fire. Denver's Theaters-Arena Division director, Sam Feiner, would disallow future Red Rocks concerts as a result of this incident. This ban remained in effect for about twenty years. In the déjà vu department, tickets for The Casino Ballroom show in Hampton Beach, NH on July 8, 1971 were also oversold, causing a riot there. That venue was closed to concerts for five years.

The record-breaking ticket sales for Jethro Tull were great for the band but bad for promoters, who had to beef up their insurance coverage to protect their venues against possible uprisings at Tull concerts. Shows such as the one at the L.A. Forum revealed more new material from the band, as an expanded "Locomotive Breath" included a Martin Barre solo and the unreleased song "Hard-Headed English General" (also known under the incorrect title "Hot-Headed English General").

After their first 1971 US tour concluded in July, the band moved to Switzerland for tax purposes. Their counsel advised them to pay their regular UK taxes while living as tax exiles in Switzerland in order to lower their overall UK taxable rate. The band established themselves in their new Swiss digs and got ready for their October and November US tour. The November 23, 1971 issue of Rolling Stone mentioned that Chrysalis' planned compilation "The Best Of Jethro Tull" was being cancelled in favor of the band's upcoming album called "Thick As A Brick." Although the album was cancelled, a proof cover exists. At this point, Ian Anderson asked Beatles producer George Martin for production advice. Ian considered using an outside producer instead of handling the chore himself, but George Martin told him that he was doing fine on his own and he should continue self-production.

The success of "Aqualung" and the move to Switzerland took its toll on Ian Anderson's marriage. After being married for about a year, Ian and Jennie Anderson separated and obtained a divorce a few years later. Ian felt that they were too young when they got married, as his successful conquest of taking Jennie, a Jewish woman, away from her traditional parents, proved to be a useless reason for their marriage. After marrying Ian, Jennie could not work at Chrysalis anymore and became a housewife with interests in photography and acting. They parted on good terms, and Jennie became an actress and later, an AIDS activist.

With all of the recent personnel changes, both personally and professionally, Ian Anderson was asked how Jethro Tull managed financially and how he directed his activities at this point in the band's career. To all this, Ian replied: "I have been the front man for three and a half years. I don't like it necessarily all the time, but having assumed the responsibility rather unwillingly at first when Mick left, that is my job now - to write and assume the role of pointing the band in different directions.

"When people join Jethro Tull - this is the way we work it - they come on a wage for the first year. I won't tell you how much, but it's a good wage. Because they don't want to accept the responsibility for the group's expenses, at the same time they want to earn money and we want to find out if we get on all right mutually. So far, everybody has stayed on in the band under those terms. After a year, they come in on an equal split with me. I'm the only one left, so it could be argued that I'm the one the audience comes to see - so I'm told by journalists. I'm the front man, I write the music, it's my group and all the rest of it. Jeffrey Hammond-Hammond comes under a split at Christmas, and Barrie nine or ten months from now.

"I'm the senior member of the group, the senior partner if you like. I dominate things. Maybe I have that much more responsibility when it comes to playing on stage. And I'm the one who's on the stage the least. I know I leap around and might appear to be all action and going potty but I'm not actually making more than one-fifth of a musical contribution. In fact, it is less.

"Let me have the responsibility: if the songs aren't good enough, I'll soon find out. I don't exactly dictate how things should be - I just try to write things hard enough for them to play now. If I write things that are demanding, then they get a kick out of being able to play them."

With all of the tremendous media attention that "Aqualung" generated because of its incorrectly perceived treatment as a concept album, Ian Anderson thought that he could outsmart everyone by actually delivering a genuine Jethro Tull concept album. "Thick As A Brick" became that concept album in the spring of 1972, and a very complex concept it proved to be.

"THICK AS A BRICK"

Just prior to their separation in 1972, the genesis of "Thick As A Brick" came to Ian from eight to ten lines of a letter Jennie wrote to him while Tull was on tour. The lyrics were written on the road in the middle of that tour. The album was created using a different work process, with two weeks of rehearsal at The Rolling Stones' warm-up location in Bermondsey. This was followed by a booked week of studio time taking place two weeks later in December 1971. Even after rehearsals, Ian had still not produced any music - the words were nearly in place, though. Continuing a boyhood theme of his disagreement with the conformity and reliance of British children on society, "Thick As A Brick" employed a satirical, yet humorous, slant on this issue through its musical passages. While this may have produced a tedious album, the serious and fun lyrical and musical elements of the LP were perfectly proportioned. As a strict concept album, "Thick As A Brick," by nature, freed itself from any formulaic blues, jazz or rock structures. Ian Anderson would write a musical segment each morning and audition it for the band. After a few days, these segments would be recorded and linked together in a tentative fashion. Two composite pieces comprising about five or six linked segments formed the sides of the album and the whole output used the singular title "Thick As A Brick." The speed at which such precisely executed material was produced was nothing short of amazing, and all that was left was the cover. It was decided to create the fictional 12-page local newspaper, The St. Cleve Chronicle & Linwell Advertiser, using the front and back pages of the paper as the album's respective covers. The newspaper contained stories that one would find in a typical local British paper, with columns ranging from the embarrassing or uninteresting to absolutely hilarious. Ian, John Evans and Jeffrey Hammond-Hammond were the main contributors to this publication, and former newspaper music journalist (and new Chrysalis employee) Roy Eldridge was responsible for its assembly. The headline of the paper was the award-winning success of a 12 year old prodigy, Gerald Bostock, the writer of the winning title poem who suffered the indignity of having his prize rescinded due to scandal. Ian also became the characters Abraham Gross and Max Quad in two of the paper's stories.

According to Ian Anderson, this is how "Thick As A Brick" developed: "I began with the lyrics actually, and the song was going to be called 'Thick As A Brick.' Somehow I just didn't finish the song until I got to the end. I just forgot to stop, I suppose. It was funny, because in the beginning I just thought it was going to be a longer song. After about ten minutes of music, I knew it was going to be quite a long song. I sort of thought, 'Well Christ, ten minutes. That's half a side of an album, I might as well make it a whole side.' Then having got to the end of side one, I still hadn't finished. I went on and did the rest. It was a satisfying thing to do."

Everyone had their interpretation of "Thick As A Brick," and all of them differed markedly from Ian Anderson's intention. Ian never made the meaning clear because of its personal and complicated nature. The many musical motifs of "Thick As A Brick" came and went in different forms, as the band played the motifs transposed in different keys or in alternate timings. David Palmer provided the linking orchestration that completed the picture.

The album title was a northern England expression assigned to a person without any brains. The same expression could also be attributed to the recording equipment that the album was recorded on. After nearly completing the mix of album's second side, Ian Anderson and engineer Robin Black discovered to their horror that the tape was running almost a semi-tone fast. They had to remix Part 2 again before remastering took place.

Chrysalis told the band that producing the involved packaging for the LP would be too expensive. Ian had the perfect convincing response by asserting that real newspapers could be regularly produced at low cost, so why couldn't their bogus paper be produced in the same way? Taking this one step further, one could also argue that since Tull's paper was only 12 pages and used considerably less paper and ink than that of a real paper, why couldn't Chrysalis handle the cost?

Advance promotion for the album made it easy for music fans to spot the LP. In England, advertising notified the public of the album's impending release. However, the controversial question of whether Gerald Bostock actually wrote "Thick As A Brick," or even if Bostock existed at all, was purposely unanswered. After a period of playfully teasing the public, Roy Eldridge spilled the beans to Circus magazine and revealed that the whole Gerald Bostock story was a hoax.

The album's #1 US and #5 UK placings illustrated that the band's message was definitely getting through. In the US, the album spent two weeks atop the album chart. Radio programmers were included in promoting the album, as Reprise offered radio stations completely banded promo albums for "Thick As A Brick," so that they could easily play the sections of the LP that they

Martin Barre

The German sleeve for the "Thick As A Brick" 45.

When the "Living In The Past" double album was released in 1972, the title song was re-released as a single. This mix is the one that became a US hit that year.

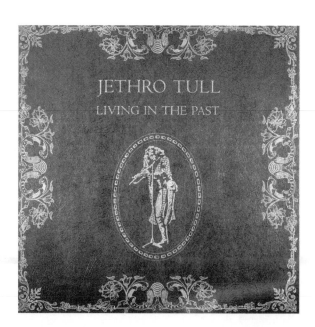

Clockwise: Ian Anderson, Barriemore Barlow, John Evans and Jeffrey Hammond-Hammond.

desired. This was important, because a US or UK single was not going to be released from this single-track album. Chrysalis in England created their own promotional EP with four edits from the album. Other countries, mainly non-English speaking, chose to dissect the album into 45RPM form for easier radio and public consumption. These included Germany, Holland, France, Italy, Brazil, Austria, Denmark and Sweden. Strangely, they chose two edits from the album that did not involve the opening introductory lines and theme. Italy put together a jukebox edition with an edit and the Gentle Giant track "Peel The Paint," while Argentina submitted two edits and a Frank Zappa B-side for the public's approval. An unauthorized 1985 German release of "Thick As A Brick" on the cheapo Platinum/Suisa label clumsily took side one of the LP and abruptly cut it in half over the album's two sides. Chrysalis demanded its immediate withdrawal from the market. (*If you really want this piece of trash, the catalog number is PLP 24020!*)

Tull's January and February 1972 shows in various European countries paired them with progsters Gentle Giant. These shows featured Ian's song "Tomorrow Was Today," which remains unreleased. The following 24-date British tour had Jethro Tull headlining over Tir Na Nog with the predicament of playing a 40-minute piece in its entirety. To lighten things up, humor was called upon to detract from potentially serious audience responses. Their shows were now running an hour in length, and two-thirds of that time had to cover the current album. The "Thick As A Brick" tour was their first concept program, and as such, it was carefully carried out. Just like the newspaper on the album, the concert humor was wide-ranging. In many respects, it was like viewing Monty Python's Flying Circus with a healthy dose of music. To start the show, four old-looking men in overcoats came on stage and disrobed. Who were these men? Why, the guys in Jethro Tull! Ian would dryly say "Thick As A Brick," the band would play the entire "Brick" with an abrupt phone call interruption answered by Ian that immediately thrust the band into concluding that section of the piece. Between its two halves, John Evans read that city's news and weather while threatening to use the urinal connected to his piano! At its conclusion, Ian would refer to what they just played as "a little 12-bar thing." It seemed like a rather cold, serious way to present a satirical piece with humorous elements. When it came time for "Aqualung," an appropriately dressed roadie appeared on stage to assist with the proceedings.

Why would Jethro Tull go through the effort of performing such an elaborate show? In an interview with Audience magazine, Terry Ellis put it in perspective: "The whole thing is based on maintaining an illusion. A kid pays five-fifty for a ticket. He buys it three weeks in advance of the show, and for all those three weeks he's thinking about the show. It's going to be a special night for him; a big band is coming to his little town, to play for him and his friends. He wants to think it's special for us, too. So he blocks out of his mind the obvious - the fact that we play the same set thirty nights in a row. He doesn't want to think that in the morning we'll get on our plane and go to the next town and play the exact same set, the same songs in the same order. He doesn't want to think in terms of the roadies tearing down the equipment and trucking it out to the airport so we can be on the move. He just wants to think about the two hours we're on stage. So we have to go along. We have to make him think that his town is special and unique for us. He has to fight the reality of the rock-and-roll tour, and if we're pros, we help him fight it." *My question is, what happened to those five-fifty tickets?*

As for the band, were they really being themselves? This is an important insight that is rarely revealed by performers. In the same magazine, John Evans reflected: "We imitate what we're supposed to be, that's all. And we're good at it, I hope. We make every performance seem like it's the only one on the tour - at least we try to. But that's not me up there on stage; how could it be, every night? I mean, what kind of guy goes ranting all over the stage, getting down on his knees and waving his arms about? It's just one of the things I do for a living. A lot of people couldn't do it every night, I suppose. Sometimes it's hard for me to (do it)."

The 1972 US tour started with Tull on their own followed by eleven dates in April with another one of Ian's favorites, Captain Beefheart & His Magic Band. US Tull audiences did not appreciate Beefheart at all, and they even had difficulty comprehending the more acoustic passages of "Thick As A Brick." Americans were expecting the rough-and-tumble guitar thrashing they had seen and heard in the past, and Ian Anderson became so exasperated with the ignorance of audiences that he felt like dropping it from the set.

While in New Orleans on May 1, Ian Anderson wrote a piece for orchestra that was recorded there. Along with a 50-piece orchestra and Ian's flute, the composition included Evans on piano, Barre on classical guitar, Hammond-Hammond on double bass and Barlow on timpani. It was the first part of the "War Child" score that Ian was contemplating at the time. This orchestral work remains unissued.

New Zealand, Australia and Japan were new tour territories for the band that summer. In Australia, Reprise issued the unique "Sunday Best" collection in May to alert fans about Tull's Australian appearances in July. Terry Ellis prepared Tokyo, Japan audiences for the humor they were going to be subjected to by translating the jokes into Japanese, printed onto large cards, but the jokes in any language went over their heads. Even though the Japanese audience response was less than enthusiastic, Ian found something to his satisfaction in Tokyo - a Martin 0-16NY parlor guitar that would become important in the future.

The lavishly packaged "Living In The Past" double album (the band's first for US Chrysalis) combined old and new tracks with the 1970 Carnegie Hall live performance taking up one side. John Evans' live piece "By Kind Permission Of" was a classical number that relied heavily on classical music quotes as its basis. In fact, it includes extracts of Beethoven's "Piano Sonata No. 8 in C minor, Opus 13" ("Pathètique" - written 1799), Claude Debussy's "Golliwog's Cakewalk" (the sixth and final section of his 1906-1908 piano piece "Children's Corner" [L113]) and Sergei Rachmaninoff's "Prelude In C# Minor." The other live Carnegie Hall track, "Dharma For One" was completely rearranged with vocal accompaniment by Martin, Glenn and Clive. "Living In The Past" scored another Top 10 hit on both sides of the Atlantic (#8 UK and #3 US), and for good reason. This lavish (*and heavy*) package offered Tull fans many treats to enjoy: old fans took delight in hearing new material, while newer fans were given an opportunity to hear most of what Jethro Tull had accomplished on their prior albums and non-album singles. The US singles market finally caught on to Jethro Tull, as the re-release of "Living In The Past" (backed with "Christmas Song") became their first (and biggest at #11) US hit. Incidentally, the single featured the LP remix, not the original single mix. This edition also hit #15 on the Cashbox singles chart. For CD collectors, original UK and US CDs eliminated tracks, but the current Mobile Fidelity issue collects all of the tracks featured on those two editions on two CDs. The original UK LP had the track "Inside" instead of "Alive And Well And Living In," but the American album, which incorporated the entire "Life Is A Long Song" EP, contained both "Inside" and "Alive And Well And Living In." Later US pressings have "Hymn 43" without "Locomotive Breath"! The album's mix of the previous US-only "Teacher" is ten seconds longer than its appearance on "Benefit." This longer mix of "Teacher" was also included on the recent double CD "The Best Of Jethro Tull." For this album, all mixing was directed by Ian with Robin Black engineering at Morgan Studios, London. "One For John Gee" and the MGM single were not considered to be strong enough for inclusion on the set. To celebrate its creation in the US, Chrysalis issued a promotional five-record set including "Living In The Past."

CHATEAU D'ISASTER AND "A PASSION PLAY"

In August 1972, Jethro Tull went to record a non-concept album at the Chateau D'Herouville studio in Paris, France to build on the success of their recent and archival albums. This studio did not provide the proper atmosphere to record an album, and the studio's equipment was failing the band. Tull finished basic tracks and overdubs for three-quarters of a double album, but they returned to England in disgust after scrapping almost all of their work. The failure of the sessions prompted Ian to name them "The Chateau D'Isaster Tapes." Two tracks ("Only Solitaire" and "Skating Away On The Thin Ice Of The New Day") were rescued from those aborted sessions and would later be included in new mixes on the "War Child" album in 1974.

While writing material for this unnamed album, Ian Anderson noticed a theme of animal life mirroring the cutthroat lives of humans. The songs that reflected this theme best were "Bungle In The Jungle" and "Skating Away On The Thin Ice Of The New Day." The 20th anniversary box provided a first glimpse into these sessions, but Ian could only find one tape reel at that time. Therefore, only three tracks were presented in April 1988 mixes: "Scenario" (featuring Barlow on glockenspiel), "Audition" and "No Rehearsal." When preparing the "Nightcap" double CD in 1993, Ian found the rest of the material but he decided to hold back what he considered the most embarrassing tracks. Still, "Nightcap" comprised, in addition to those three 1988 released tracks, "First Post," "Animalée," "Tiger Toon," "Look At The Animals," "Law Of The Bungle," "Law Of The Bungle Part II" (with a Barre spoken part), "Left Right," "Solitaire," "Critique Oblique" and "Post Last." The tracks that remained in Ian Anderson's possession included "Intro" and "Sailor." "Intro" was an audio collage of humorous vocals and dated, synthesized sounds. "Sailor" was a somewhat repetitive track that segued from "Skating Away," and this was perhaps the reason for its non-inclusion on "Nightcap." For some reason, the "Nightcap" presentation of "No Rehearsal" was 45 seconds shorter than the 1988 box set version.

Here is Ian's view of the proceedings: "When we came to do the album after 'Thick As A Brick,' we went away and started recording separate songs again. But, the excitement of working that way wasn't there anymore, so we scrapped all that stuff. We had done three sides of a double album and threw out the whole thing. We went back and just took one little bit of it and expanded that into 'A Passion Play.' I enjoyed the experience of working in that way. I'm very sad that it's been proved necessary to have to work in conventional song lengths again."

Above: "Thick As A Brick" and the Australian EP "This Is Jethro Tull."

Below: Ian Anderson illustrates the use of a flute as a phallic symbol!

Disappointed Jethro Tull to Drop Touring; Make 1st Film

LOS ANGELES—Jethro Tull will take a leave from concerts after the end of September to rest and then concentrate on their first film. Manager Terry Ellis notes the band has been working continuously for nearly six years. All dates after September have been cancelled.

The band will record an LP featuring songs from the film for release next year. The movie, a musical, is being written by Ian Anderson, lead singer with the British band.

Although they have been selling out huge arenas during their recent American tour, the band has been disappointed by negative critical response to its "A Passion Play" work which has comprised the bulk of their concert presentation.

This has caused a subliminal feeling of frustration among the band. Ellis says the preparation of the music and production of the play began over one year ago. "The abuse heaped on the show by the critics has been bitterly disappointing to the group and as illogical as it may be to identify the opinions of the reviewers with those of the public, it has become increasingly difficult for the group to go on stage without worrying whether the audience is enjoying what they are playing."

Above: The German and French single editions of "A Passion Play (Edit #8)."

In the US, edits 8 and 10 of "A Passion Play" were issued as singles, along with a banded promo version of the LP.

Their return to England coincided with the end of a one-year period in Switzerland, after which they could have become residents. The day their residency papers arrived was the same day on which they made the decision to leave Switzerland. Ian was now living on his own, renting a two-room mews cottage near Baker Street - that's right, a Baker Street mews! The cottage was an ideal setting for Ian to come up with new material upon demand.

The performances between fall 1972 and spring 1973, following their D'Herouville disaster, were filled with numerous musical surprises and confundities - especially since they were playing tracks live that they had previously scrapped. For example, at the Baltimore Civic Center show on November 12, 1972, two aborted Chateau D'Herouville tracks, "The Play (Das Spiel)" and "The Bomb In The Dressing Room" (aka "No Rehearsal") were played in a medley leading into "Thick As A Brick." It would take the band until the end of their European tour in March 1973 to decide on what to do with these songs. The decision was to tackle the dark subject of Ian's rewritten concept piece entitled "A Passion Play," which centered around the possible choices one could make after death. This was another work that required a great deal of analysis, but it was without the humor or ease that endeared fans, and the media, to "Thick As A Brick." "The Play (Das Spiel)" would be renamed "Left Right" when it was eventually released on "Nightcap."

When issued *four months* after the aborted material was first presented, "A Passion Play" still became a #1 album in the US, although Jethro Tull's UK fan base had declined noticeably (it was Jethro Tull's first album to miss the UK Top 10 at #13). With one week at the top, it was one of the most deceiving number one album placements in US chart history. Sales of the album were about half that of their other #1 album "Thick As A Brick." Like "Thick As A Brick," "A Passion Play" had a mock publication included in its packaging - this time, an ersatz theater playbill with the band's members as the play's actors. This playbill was also filled with inside jokes. For one, Ian's character Mark Ridley was making his West End acting debut playing "Elvoe" in Ron Read's play "The Demo." "Elvoe" was the alternate spelling of Ian's old nickname and Ron Read was a slightly amended reference to former John Evan Band manager Don Read.

What to do about singles? Two US 45s were issued: "A Passion Play (Edit #8)" b/w (Edit #9) (a #80 hit in Billboard and #60 in Cashbox), and "A Passion Play (Edit #10)" b/w (Edit #6) (a #105 "Bubbling Under" single). Germany and France also issued the first US single coupling with unique picture sleeves, while Italy's jukebox single took Edit #8 backed with a track by Fausto Leali.

The protagonist of this passion play was the deceased Ronnie Pilgrim, whose inability to get into either heaven or hell had him returning to where he felt his existence was best - earth. This album concept was more difficult than Ian's unrevealed "Thick As A Brick," and the music proved to be just as impenetrable for untrained ears. For Tull fans, it became a very divisive album - it was where your Tull collection stopped or it was the bridge to a higher echelon of the band's future musical development. In retrospect, Ian Anderson admits that it was a bit too serious and highbrow for its own good. In terms of playing, the band was at its most complicated and Ian got the most out of his vocals, sax and flute than ever before. For this LP, Ian used a Martin Nyers guitar. John Evans introduced the synthesizer to the world of Jethro Tull recording, although the organ continued to be the band's main keyboard decoration. The usual top-notch orchestration came from good ol' David Palmer. For the ballet dancer's presentation on the front cover, Ian Anderson received some guidance from his brother Robin, a ballet dancer living in Scotland.

Ian justified creating "A Passion Play" in this way: "I like an album that's difficult to listen to. I like to have to sit down and really work into the music. A listener should make that effort. I don't like music that kind of unconsciously gets your foot tapping. That's Musak. I could write that kind of music, but it's just too easy. That's using music as a tactical weapon to sell records. I think it's important for the listener to feel that an effort has been made, that he has actually contributed in some way to the enjoyment for the music. The only tricks that I use when I play are used to try and help the audience want to make the effort. I admit to doing that. I try to entice the audience into wanting to listen."

Just prior to the conclusion of side one, we are subjected to "The Story Of The Hare Who Lost His Spectacles" - a wholly British, off-the-wall yarn for children that used music written by John Evans and a story told by Jeffrey Hammond-Hammond in his best Monty Python mock interviewer voice. It was credited to John Evans, Hammond-Hammond and Ian Anderson. On the surface, the story seems out of place within "A Passion Play," but a little levity turned out to be what the album needed at that point. When dissecting the album's lyrics, one will find that it refers to Magus Perdé, a medieval passion play writer. However, "Hare"'s presentation on the album was less than ideal. Instead of hearing the hare's story in one piece, the story lost some continuity by ending on side one and starting again on side two. As with the album itself, this section of the album caused either fan hilarity or consternation - those in the latter category would have difficulty finding what parts on the LP to skip. The hare segment was the only part filmed, featuring Tull in costumed animal attire. Amazingly, this short film segment cost an enormous $30,000 to make!

To air "A Passion Play," radio stations again received banded copies for airplay. Reviews of this album were scathing for the most part, and led to many controversies for the band. Chris Welch, a writer for the British magazine Melody Maker, twice took the band to task on "A Passion Play" - once for the album and the other for its UK concert premiere at Empire Pool Wembley. Chris Welch's remarks came as a surprise to the band, since Welch had been an avid supporter up until then. Robert Hilburn of the L.A. Times also produced an unabashedly negative review, and requotes of Welch and Hilburn's slashing reviews spread like wildfire.

A series of enormous press gaffes during 1973 nearly reduced the band to rubble. Jethro Tull had scheduled two dates at London's Wembley Arena in the last week of April but the band's press officer claimed that Ian was suffering from nervous exhaustion. Meanwhile, NME found out that Ian was rehearsing with the band in Canada! The band's press officer did not adequately explain that the shows had to be rescheduled and London-based fans were highly irritated for good reason. More than anything, this lack of communication started the erosion of the goodwill that Jethro Tull had with their fans and the media. As consolation to fans in London, the single April 29 Empire Pool Wembley show that was cancelled along with the Wembley Arena gig was rescheduled for a two-night Pool stay on June 22-23. Ian Anderson felt the delay was necessary for a UK presentation of the US premiere, and doing this required additional time and expense to cart the stage materials and gear to the UK. The sting of the rescheduling was still there because these two shows proved to be the only 1973 Tull dates in their own country. For such an elaborate album, fans thought this treatment was inexcusable and the media preyed on Chris Welch's "slash and burn" concert review.

The next gaffe came when Terry Ellis, without the band's knowledge, made a deal with Melody Maker's editor to lock up a front page story revolving around Jethro Tull's decision to stop performing live as a result of their poor reviews. When the band read the story, they were naturally furious and could not perform damage control without first determining where their internal problems came from. This incident with Ellis was the first sign that his Chrysalis control was counterproductive to the band. His Melody Maker headline deal had created a schism between the band and the media that would never be healed. Ian Anderson tried to disavow any knowledge of the issue, but the damage was irreparable.

Discussing the band's supposed retirement from performing, Ian said, "Well, that meant we were retiring from a situation that had been going on for nearly six years. I had been working very hard and was feeling a bit sorry for myself. After touring America alone 19 times, not counting Europe, England and everywhere else, I thought we had to switch off the motor. It was time to have a sit down and take stock of the situation. I think most groups probably do it more frequently than they let on." Ian still made sure to dig into the printed media: "I have a fairly low opinion of the press because I think it plays way below the average level of intelligence of the audience who reads it."

What about the "Passion Play" show itself - was it really that bad? For a show that lasted almost three hours, it had to have a lot going for it in order to keep fan interest from wavering. In the half-hour period before showtime, a small white dot became an audible, growing, throbbing heartbeat before morphing into a ballerina that crashed through a mirror. The crash got the crowd's attention and the show began. Similar to the previous year's shows, the current album, "A Passion Play," was presented in its entirety. It was a multimedia event, with backing tapes and video accompaniment on "The Story Of The Hare Who Lost His Spectacles." Once again in the middle of "Thick As A Brick," a weather report was read. During the course of the show, one could come across gorillas, bunny rabbits or scuba divers doing their thing. Ian found himself constantly swapping instruments, moving from flute to acoustic guitar to soprano sax to handle the demands of "A Passion Play." The May 17, 1973 Hampton Rhodes Coliseum show in Virginia was one of the first shows featuring unused instrumental segments from "A Passion Play" and the Barriemore Barlow drum showcase "Conundrum" (*get it?*). Even during their L.A. Forum stint in July, the band was using "No Rehearsal" - this time as a lead-in to "Aqualung." That same show included a guitar solo on "Wind-Up" which became the introduction to the album version of "Minstrel In The Gallery" in 1975 - two years later. To sum up, the playing was precise but covered a lot of ground. The band overestimated the audience's comprehension for taking in such a wide range of musical elements in a three-hour period. It was no wonder that critics had no patience for such a concert. After their last show in Boston in September, Jethro Tull took a break - in fact, the longest the group had ever taken. It would be ten months before Tull appeared again on a stage. By this point, the band had earned enough on the road to repay all their British debts and to reinvest additional money in all sorts of lighting, staging, audio and moving equipment.

"WAR CHILD"

To escape from the media onslaught in autumn 1973, Ian started to work on a film tentatively titled "War Child." The plot of "War Child" was the fight of God versus the devil, and the possibility that they could be one and the same entity. Anticipating the "War Child" project to proceed, Jethro Tull recorded most of the film music along with a full orchestral score in 1974. Funding difficulties resulted in numerous delays and eventually grounded the film. As it turned out, film studio funding from the US was the only money available. This studio funding came with stipulations: namely, studio control over which director and American star would be involved with the film. The "War Child" film never materialized because Ian Anderson refused to cede control.

When the "War Child" movie was used as an explanation for their retirement, Ian added: "For us, it was a meaningful thing to stop. In the end, the period was something ridiculous like two days. Which seems like a glib thing to say, but for two days the group did not exist. It was the first time in five years that I could say 'I am not part of the thing called Jethro Tull.' For two days that was an amazing, free feeling. And when it was over, I knew it was time to get working again. Though we had no definite plans about touring again, we started to write a lot of different kinds of music and lay the groundwork for the 'War Child' movie. I don't mind disappointing people from time to time, I just wouldn't like to trade too much on previous success. I don't want to take advantage of people and pour something down their throats that they couldn't possibly enjoy. We've made a lot of music that people could not possibly have enjoyed."

The "War Child" soundtrack would be released on its own, using remixes of two Chateau D'Herouville leftovers ("Skating Away On The Thin Ice Of The New Day" and "Only Solitaire"), the reworked version of "Lick Your Fingers Clean" called "Two Fingers" and some of Ian's intended film songs. For the first time since "Aqualung," Jethro Tull would be creating an album comprised of unrelated songs. Like the previous album, "War Child" was recorded at Morgan Studios. The back cover featured the band illustrating all of the album's song titles, and the sealion trainer was Shona Learoyd (*remember that name, folks!*) - a Chrysalis publicist that was the new woman in Ian Anderson's life. And yes, the queen on the back cover is a man!

Outtakes from the "War Child" sessions included "Rainbow Blues," "Glory Row" and "March, The Mad Scientist." The "Repeat • The Best Of Jethro Tull • Vol. II" album got the first one, "M.U." housed the second and the "Ring Out, Solstice Bells" EP featured the last. In addition, Spanish Chrysalis released a very unusual 1977 version of "Aqualung" with "Glory Row" replacing "Locomotive Breath."

The title "War Child" came from the lyrics of the song "Little Lady" by fellow Blackpool native Roy Harper. That song appeared on Roy's "Lifemask" album from 1973. As for "War Child," the front cover backdrop was Melbourne, Australia. The simpler, more conventional song approach yielded more interest in the US, who appreciated such structure, but the relatively poor #14 UK showing illustrated that audiences continued to look elsewhere in greater numbers. Despite the poorer showing, critical acclaim returned.

For the first time, Jethro Tull was credited for arranging Ian's songs. David Palmer conducted members of the Philomusica of London - an ensemble that joined Palmer for a July 16, 1972 Royal Academy of Music concert with guest guitarist Steve Howe of Yes. Patrick Halling was the Philomusica leader, and Halling selected members from his ensemble that he thought were best suited to the songs on "War Child." These members were violinsts Rita Eddowes, Elizabeth Edwards and a woman named Helen along with cellist Katherine Thulborn. Further sound contouring was provided by John Evans' synthesizer.

While all of this was going on, Ian assisted on outside recording projects for the first time. Ian was a guest musician on the track "Home" on Roy Harper's double LP "Flashes From The Archives Of Oblivion." It was a pleasure for Ian to be on Roy's album since Ian had been a fan of Roy's going back to his first LP. (Remember the story of Ian's mono record player connected to an AC-30 speaker?) Ian was more involved with Steeleye Span's "Now We Are Six" album that was released in March 1974. Steeleye Span had opened for Tull at some UK concerts in 1971 and 1973, and Ian Anderson was happy to help out when the Span lost their way in the middle of recording the album. Ian thought their song "Thomas The Rhymer" was excellent singles material and told Span vocalist Maddy Prior that he would be interested in becoming a production consultant. This is how he was billed on the album, although he mixed it as well. "Now We Are Six" hit #13 on the UK album chart.

Back to "War Child"! Being a more accessible album than either of the two studio albums before it, "War Child" made some strong

Above and middle right: The Yugoslavian and German picture sleeves for "Bungle In The Jungle."

At left, some UK B-sides of "Bungle In The Jungle" left off the "s" on its title.

Below: The promotional US picture sleeve of "Bungle In The Jungle" and the "Skating Away" 45.

The US quad edition of "War Child."

The German sleeve for "Skating Away…"

Jeffrey Hammond-Hammond

Jethro Tull in 1974: Anderson, Hammond-
Hammond, Barre, Evans and Barlow.

statements. "The Third Hoorah" had a dig at music critic Steve Peacock. "Bungle In The Jungle" was an obvious, yet commercial, extension of the animalistic Chateau D'Herouville cut "Law Of The Bungle," and a surprise #12 US Billboard and Cashbox hit single - the band's second and last hit. An added bonus to US promotional copies was a picture sleeve with the "War Child" logo on one side and "Bungle"'s lyrics on its reverse. Those crafty record company people in Thailand even put "Bungle In The Jungle" on two unlawful EPs with other artists!

In Britain, no such sales success was in the cards, although they did manage to "bungle" the B-side title "Back-Door Angels" (they left off the "s" on some copies)! The album spent three weeks at the runner-up position on US listings. Ian made an ecological statement in "Sealion," referring to the effects of sewage dumping in Blackpool. The follow-up US single "Skating Away (On The Thin Ice Of The New Day)" (parentheses added for single release) could not keep up the sales momentum that "Bungle In The Jungle" started. Cashbox was the only publication to list sales action on "Skating Away," and it went up to #75 on their chart. Despite their undeserved commercial fall from grace in the UK, Jethro Tull continued to build upon their stage reputation as an exciting and extremely entertaining theatrical group. Barriemore Barlow almost cancelled out on touring because of some domestic issues, but he did the shows nevertheless. Drummer Gerry Conway was on call in the event Barlow wasn't available.

"War Child" was also issued in quadrophonic, a format that Ian embraced early and had great wishes for. He was also interested in the video market as well: "Our albums will continue to come out as sound albums, in stereo and quadrophonic, but there will also be a visual supplement available. I'm very interested in the possibilities of the videodisc. I'm constantly pushing at the recording company to get behind this, to start getting involved. I wish they'd try and make the consumer aware that there is an incoming market, which is very real." "War Child" was the band's last quad album, as the market's indifference to the numerous incompatible quadrophonic reproduction systems buried the concept. Videodiscs have still not caught on 25 years later!

The "War Child" live show was highly entertaining on numerous visual levels. The four Philomusica players that accompanied the band on tour were dressed identically in black outfits and platinum wigs. Their hilarious costumes nicely balanced the serious sounds they produced on their instruments. As for the band themselves, each member had their own outfit and persona. Ian was colorfully dressed in tights as a minstrel wearing a codpiece - the most memorable stage outfit that Ian would be seen in throughout his career. Assisting on the tour was Shona Learoyd, who wore a skimpy outfit on stage and brought Ian his instruments. As expected, whistles consistently accompanied Shona's stage entrances. The only problem for Shona at the Chrysalis offices was that this chauvinistic practice (among others) forced her to quit her position. Barre was overdone in a floral suit while Hammond-Hammond employed a black and white diagonally-striped motif on his suit and guitars. Continuing the black and white theme, two men in a zebra costume shot out black and white tennis balls from the costume's rear end that Hammond-Hammond would then juggle. Jeffrey was even called upon to sing "How Much Is That Doggie In The Window?" with a tree and a wooden dog on the stage!

This pass involved the first dedicated tour of England since March 1972. The fully-contained all female American group Fanny opened for Tull in England. A special addition to the four shows at London's Rainbow Theatre (November 14-17) was another all-female group - the dance troupe Pan's People. Pan's People danced during the intermission (*the "interval" for our UK readers*) and the dance was accompanied by a specially recorded Jethro Tull track for the occasion: "Pan Dance." This instrumental was laid down by the band and the above string quartet at the Maison Rouge Mobile at Radio Monte Carlo (Monaco) shortly before the tour in 1974. The Maison Rouge Mobile was the name of the band's newest acquisition - a portable recording studio. It was purchased because the band was unhappy with the results they were getting from studios in England. Also recorded at this session was "Quartet" from the aborted "War Child" film. "Quartet" was instead used as the music that fans heard just before Tull took the stage. David Palmer added keyboards on this track, and it was clearly influenced by Bach's "Toccata & Fugue In D Minor" (BMV 565). "Pan Dance" was first issued in 1976 on the "Ring Out, Solstice Bells" EP, but "Quartet" had a much longer wait for its release - the 1993 collection "Nightcap." The UK dates in 1974 would be the band's last in their own country until 1977.

Three other tracks were recorded on the Maison Rouge Mobile prior to the tour: "Saturation," "Paradise Steakhouse" and "Sealion II." The first track was finally issued on the 20th anniversary box, while the other two debuted on "Nightcap." Most unusual about "Sealion II" was that it was also known as "Cecil Was A Sealion" and it featured Jeffrey Hammond-Hammond's vocals.

For the past five years, Tull's emphasis was on developing their US audience. With a solid US following in place, only two American shows took place during 1974. Both of these were at Detroit's Cobo Hall (August 7 and 8). The group made their first inroads into Spain, where they played at the Pabellon Deportivo in Madrid on October 23. Tull more than made up for the US touring oversight in 1974 by putting almost 100 American shows on their calendar in 1975.

The tour for "War Child" would take the band through mid-April 1975. On the US leg of the early 1975 tour for the album, Jethro Tull was joined by the up-and-coming flamenco rock band Carmen. Carmen had just completed a run of shows with Yes, and they were receiving a lot of exposure. The highlight of Carmen's pairing with Tull was the record-breaking five-night run at the L.A. Forum that brought in 93,000 fans. Interestingly, the five shows were broken up into runs of two and three dates with shows in Arizona and Texas in-between. Two shows preceding these were added at the San Diego Sports Arena to make sure fans in southern California got an equal chance of seeing the band.

Sometimes, the fan reaction would get out of hand, as in the case of the February 10 L.A. Forum gig. Fans were so loud during the soft "Wond'ring Aloud" that Ian stopped playing and urged the crowd to get the screaming out of their systems! This show also had an interesting example of Ian's flute tangents on "Pop Goes The Weasel" and the inclusion of "God Rest Ye Merry Gentlemen" during "My God." While in Kiel, Germany on April 1, 1975, Ian twisted his ankle on stage so badly that he required the use of a wheel-chair. The "Ian in a wheelchair" image would be one that Ian would take great pleasure in using as a prop for sympathetic fans before pushing the wheelchair away to perform without it. Ian was able to finish the tour with some wheelchair assistance for a few days. One of these post-accident dates was Jethro Tull's first visit to Yugoslavia on April 15.

At the conclusion of the tour in Switzerland, the band decided to meet the press head on in order to end the war between them. A Montreux press conference was put together, and it was more than a coincidence that the original creation site of "A Passion Play" was chosen as the forum for this discussion. In this televised event, Ian Anderson stated that each music critic's hired role for his publication was that of providing artist feedback, rather than dictating his favorites to that publication's readers. In retrospect, it was a bit of a wishy-washy statement, but the band did meet their critics halfway and scored some political points as a result. They never got back to where they were with critics pre-"A Passion Play," but the press conference provided the best forum for leveling the playing field again.

At this time, Ian Anderson reacquainted himself with Captain Beefheart's Magic Band. Beefheart did that disastrous tour run with Tull in 1972, but it was not the Captain that Ian wanted; it was his band who had recently been cast off by their master. Ian encouraged The Magic Band to reconstitute themselves and lent them money to make an album. The gameplan was that The Magic Band would pay Ian back after making and selling a reasonable quantity of their album. The Magic Band got cold feet and renamed themselves Mallard with the addition of Beefheart replacement vocalist Sam Gilpin. Mallard's album was a disaster (so was their second) and Ian never got his money back.

The two months between the end of April and the end of June 1975 were set aside to record their next album with the Maison Rouge Mobile studio in Monte Carlo, Monaco. The band's accountants had informed them once more that they should record outside England to avoid the country's 98% tax rate on performing artists. The same cast of characters was involved again, with the exception that Bridget Procter replaced Helen on violin.

According to the July 1975 issue of Hit Parader magazine, Ian bought a house in 1974, but he had yet to live in it. Instead, Ian got rid of his London apartment before deciding to live in hotels for about a year. The move to hotels was a more productive one in terms of Ian's writing, as he related: "I want to write some more music. I do that better in hotels than I do in something I'm pretending is my home. I don't worry about selling a million records or selling out tours. I just think about making records that appeal to me. That's enough."

"MINSTREL IN THE GALLERY"

The change in scenery was not therapeutic for the band however, as Ian's songs on the new album project "Minstrel In The Gallery" were more introspective than ever. While isolated in his hotel room, Ian wrote the album's songs between early December 1974 and early January 1975. Not even Christmas could cheer up the extremely personal expressions of sadness and anger Ian Anderson channeled into these songs, as he recorded most of his innermost thoughts on the album separately from Tull. The album received

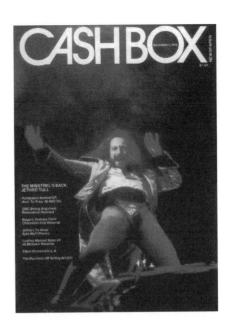

Middle row: (left) The Uruguayan release of the "Minstrel In The Gallery" single. The Spanish translation of the B-side, "Summerday Sands," is shown.
(middle and right) The UK "Minstrel In The Gallery" single and the misspelled B-side of the US issue.

Bottom row: The Yugoslavian release of the same single and the original US LP.

its name as Ian - the minstrel on stage - played as the mobile studio recorded his outpourings in a gallery. Ian's views of street life in London, as a single Baker Street-area man, were combined with the suitcase living he experienced on the road. As previously alluded to, the title of the song "Baker Street Muse" played on the mews cottage Ian rented and wrote the song from. It also alluded to Shona Learoyd, whose relationship with Ian was in its blossoming phase.

If fans were looking for group dynamics within "Minstrel In The Gallery," they had to look elsewhere. Photos of Ian and the band within the album revealed a very haggard looking and unhappy group of musicians that was in great need of some rest. For a group that previously thrived on recording and touring immediately after, they appeared as if the treadmill had thrown them off. Jeffrey was having great difficulty in playing the material, Barlow was very argumentative, and Evans' rock piano playing disintegrated into constant Beethoven performances in a drunken stupor. The fact that Evans' marriage quickly dissoved certainly had a lot to do with his behavior, but his transformation was alarming. David Palmer and his string arrangements were charming as usual.

For some fun, listen for Ian, Martin and David Palmer's voices at the start of the title track. The single edit of "Minstrel" was more like an abortion, sloppily lopping off the first half of the song and catching it in mid-gallop. Another unusual thing about the album is that countoffs for nearly all of the songs were retained on the final album masters, giving them more of a home recording feel. Of these introductions, the US CD of this album has a slightly longer beginning of "Cold Wind To Valhalla."

"Minstrel In The Gallery" still did reasonably well; however, it did not have the staying power of prior Tull albums. The sales figures continued their downward trend, with #20 UK and #7 US album chart peaks. The title track, backed with "Summerday Sands," was a minor hit in the US at #79 in Billboard. "Summerday Sands" was a B-side recorded at the album's sessions which ultimately made its first album appearance on the "20 Years Of Jethro Tull" collection in 1988.

At the beginning of their stay in Monte Carlo, the band did a BBC radio session featuring Ian's solo version of "Cold Wind To Valhalla," Ian and Barlow's duet rearrangement of Minstrel In The Gallery" and "Grace" with Ian, Patrick Halling on violin and David Palmer conducting the Philomusica members. These tracks were included on the 20th anniversary box in 1988.

The July 5 show in Paris, which lasted 70 minutes, was filmed and recorded by Ian Anderson for release on the new videodisc format. Presenting a concert for public consumption via cutting edge technology was one of Ian's wishes, but he was not taken seriously enough by Chrysalis to make it a reality. Ian spent three weeks in Brussels, Belgium to mix the tapes, but it became a wasted effort when the technology and the interest in releasing the show on videodisc or tape was still financially out of reach to the vast fan base that Anderson wanted to target.

Ian Anderson and David Palmer made the unusual move of flying from Texas to Philadelphia to appear on US TV's "The Mike Douglas Show" on August 2. At the time, Ian and David were writing music for a stage musical they hoped '60s pop star Adam Faith would perform. The musical would revolve around the 70-page screenplay outline that Anderson spent quite a bit of time working on. This project would come to fruition in a different form in 1976. In the meantime, Ian on guitar and David on synthesizer were practicing on the Mike Douglas stage before showtime. Cord problems prevented the duo from actually playing on the show, but Terry Ellis of Chrysalis instead offered a Jethro Tull performance clip to accompany Ian's well-received interview with Mike Douglas. After the filming, Anderson and Palmer went back to Texas to do a show that night before doing a gig the next day at Madison Square Garden in New York. *Ah, show business!*

After three tours with the string quartet, Ian finally got tired of their moody personalities and decided to bring in David Palmer and his synthesizer to replace them on a full-time basis in 1976. However, before this took place, Jeffrey Hammond-Hammond quit the band after the November 2, 1975 gig in Athens, GA. Stories of Hammond-Hammond burning his stage clothes afterward have been described by Jeffrey as exaggerated, but let's just say that his clothes met their demise thanks to his desire to paint for a living. Jeffrey moved to Gloucestershire, got married and left the touring and recording routine to create a happier artistic life for himself. Ian had to replace Jeffrey quickly. Anderson recalled Carmen's support of Tull when they did those sold-out L.A. Forum shows earlier in 1975. It was time to call John Glascock. Ian Anderson was unaware of Glascock's extensive musical background.

JOHN GLASCOCK

To say that John Glascock was a seasoned bass player would be to tremendously understate his background. He was the only member that recorded an album before joining Tull. In fact, he did nine - one more than even Tull recorded up to that point! (The "Living In The Past" compilation of older recordings doesn't count.) Glascock's recording history is extensive and his contribution to music essential, yet not properly documented until now. Without this prior training, Glascock would not have been a member of what many fans consider to be Jethro Tull's best performing lineup.

John Glascock was born May 2, 1951 in Islington, London, nearly three years after his brother Brian (born July 17, 1948). When John was two, the Glascock family moved north to Hatfield, Hertfordshire, about twenty-five to thirty miles away, because his father Walter Glascock got a construction job there (Walter was also an Army master sergeant). John and Brian stayed with their family in Hatfield until they decided to move away, and their younger sister Gloria was born in Welwyn Garden City. The Glascock family's musical talent was abundant. Walter played piano, their uncle Albert was a guitar player and maker, and their uncle Bill was a drummer. At weekend family gatherings, John and Brian Glascock would play guitars their cousins made, and all of them would sing around the piano. John and Brian heard their father's 78s before they got into rockers like Elvis Presley and Tommy Steele.

Brian was the more athletic of the two Glascock brothers, and happened to meet fellow Hatfield native Mick Taylor while playing soccer. Taylor (born Michael Kevin Taylor) played guitar, and in 1962 he and Brian decided to put together a group in Hatfield with Brian on drums, John on bass, vocalist Malcolm Collins and Alan Shacklock on lead guitar. Since they were all youngsters, they called themselves The Juniors. John Glascock was only 11 years old, Shacklock was 12 and Brian and Mick Taylor were the old men of the group at 14. Brian Glascock reflected on John's early days: "John wasn't much of a sports guy; he had to in school, but it wasn't his thing. Actually, our musical career preceded that with a band called The Juniors, when John was eleven and I was fourteen. It was a cute thing. We had a recording contract with Decca (*actually Columbia*), and got written up in the fan magazines. We played on summer holidays, and through the school year. We even played at Wembley Stadium once at a pop festival."

A certain Mr. Charles, owner of a local music shop, had the connection to obtain a Columbia Records contract for The Juniors. The band even shared the same publicist as The Beatles, and that publicist contrived a meeting between the two bands at The Fab Four's favorite boutique, Dougie Millan's. The Beatles soon found out that this was a photo op for the fledgling half-pints, and charitably played along with the gag. John and Brian Glascock both met Paul McCartney, as Brian Glascock describes what McCartney meant to his brother: "Paul McCartney was probably the major musical influence in John's life. His bass lines were so melodic, and that impressed John. The other two bass players he really admired (later) were Jack Bruce and Chris Squire."

In the summer of 1964, The Juniors entered Abbey Road Studios, St. John's Wood, London and laid down two tracks for their only single: "There's A Pretty Girl" b/w "Pocket Size" (Columbia DB 7339). It was issued on August 21, 1964, and John Glascock was all of 13! This single pre-dates anything that any other future Jethro Tull member recorded. The single was also issued on MGM in the US. Although the US record was issued using the same titles, the tape box shows the A-side as "Party Girl Next Door." What is most interesting about the record is the most dominant instrument is the bass - it's louder than everything else! Even at such an early age, John Glascock's bass was a standout. The band lasted just a short time after its release, and then its members moved on to other things. Alan Shacklock played with Chris Farlowe, the group Babe Ruth and later went on to produce Roger Daltrey.

John Glascock became a tailor's apprentice in St. Albans as a thirteen year old and he used that skill to design his stage clothes. After the breakup of The Juniors, John concentrated on completing school while Brian and Mick Taylor formed The Strangers. This band was very popular in the area and opened up for The Who and The Kinks during their brief time together. The Strangers evolved into The High Numbers (unrelated to The Who's original band name) and then The Gods. The Gods were formed in Hertfordshire by future Uriah Heep keyboardist/guitarist Ken Hensley in 1965, and Brian and John Glascock were referred to Hensley by Mick Taylor. John had just completed school in time to replace their original bass player, and he also quit his job to devote himself full-time to the band. Unfortunately, John and Brian's father died of a heart ailment in 1965.

When Mick Taylor was sitting in with John Mayall's Bluesbreakers at a Welwyn Garden City gig to fill in for the missing Eric Clapton, Ron Wood of The Birds took his place in The Gods at a US Army base gig in 1965. When Clapton left Mayall for good, Mick Taylor took his place in the summer of 1966. This move put a damper on The Gods, who worked around the moonlighting Taylor. In the spring of 1967, The Gods signed a contract with Polydor Records. With Taylor on board, The Gods recorded the

The Juniors: Malcolm Collins, Allan Shacklock, John Glascock, Mick Taylor, Brian Glascock.

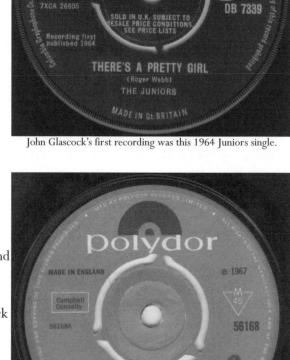

John Glascock's first recording was this 1964 Juniors single.

(This photo and the one above are courtesy of the Glascock family.)

The extremely rare Gods single on Polydor.

Above: The young John Glascock in front of a milk machine!
Below: John Glascock recording with The Gods at Abbey Road Studios and playing live in 1968.
(Bottom row photos courtesy of Joe Konas)

Above are the two Gods albums and the UK edition of the notorious Head Machine LP.
Below: The French edition of the Head Machine album, Toe Fat and Carmen's non-album single.

Toe Fat:
John Glascock, Alan Kendall,
Cliff Bennett and Lee Kerslake

The lineup of Chicken Shack: Paul Hancox, Stan Webb and John Glascock

single "Come On Down To My Boat Baby" b/w "Garage Man" in May 1967. The song had just hit the US charts in a version by the group Every Mother's Son, so The Gods wanted to produce a UK hit version to capitalize on the song's success. The single was billed as The Gods (Thor, Hermes, Olympus and Mars), which were Hensley, Taylor, John Glascock and Brian Glascock. Issued on June 9, 1967, the single was a complete failure and the group broke up by the end of the month. Mick Taylor would move on to The Rolling Stones. (*To give you an idea of how excruciatingly rare the record is, it took me over ten years to find a copy, and when I found one, the price was over $500!*)

After The Gods broke up, Ken Hensley moved to Hampshire, met bass player Paul Newton and put The Gods together again in September 1967 using money from Newton's father. Besides Hensley and Newton, the new Gods lineup included drummer Lee Kerslake and guitarist Joe Konas. They did some club gigs (including two at the Marquee) and did four 1967 demos for the Harvey Block Associates agency. Block's agency signed The Gods as a client and the band moved to London when bass player Greg Lake joined on January 7, 1968. More club gigs with Lake followed, including another 13 Marquee gigs obtained through their residency at the club. One of these Marquee gigs was attended by EMI executive Roy Featherstone, who treated the show as the band's audition for the label. After playing for an hour, Featherstone presented The Gods with a three-year deal to record with Columbia Records at Abbey Road Studios.

Just before they were to go to Abbey Road to record their first album, Greg Lake left to join King Crimson (with Robert Fripp) for the album "In The Court Of The Crimson King - An Observation By King Crimson" before he created Emerson, Lake & Palmer. In July 1968, Ken Hensley called up the band's agency and got John Glascock to replace Greg Lake. Brian Glascock came in as a roadie, and the band lived in the same house in Shepherd's Bush, London. On the occasions when Lee Kerslake was late for a recording session, Brian would fill in. In fact, one of the tracks he played on ended up on their second album "To Samuel A Son."

At Abbey Road's Studio 3, The Gods recorded their first album "Genesis" and their first two singles "Baby's Rich" and "Hey Bulldog," the latter being a cover of The Beatles song from "Yellow Submarine." Their producer was David Paramor, son of noted big band leader and Cliff Richard producer Norrie Paramor. "Genesis" was issued in October 1968 and built up a strong reputation. John and guitarist Joe Konas got their own flat on Fairlane Avenue in Chiswick, and Konas got to spend more time with John Glascock. Even so, Joe Konas told me recently, "I never really knew much about John - he really kept to himself pretty much. He did like to smoke a lot, you know." Konas was impressed by John's steady bass playing and how he played. John Glascock was a leftie that played a right-handed bass guitar with a pick. One of John's other peculiar rituals was the daily changing of his bass strings. This practice was essential to maintain the consistent tone that Glascock strived for and that his band members relied upon. With their album out in the shops, The Gods gigged throughout England, Scotland and Belgium.

Recording at Abbey Road certainly had its advantages, especially when The Beatles were in the building. The Beatles were recording downstairs at Abbey Road's first studio, which was earmarked for the band whenever they had new material to record. The Gods were also in the building to record material for their first album, and one of John Glascock's greatest thrills was taking a leak in the studio's men's room at the same time as Paul McCartney!

Joe Konas and the Glascock brothers were known for rummaging through the Abbey Road stock room to look for any Beatles artifacts (like guitar strings) that they could appropriate. While snooping around, John Glascock found an interesting violin case. He opened it, removed the violin and found some fresh Beatles lyrics that they were about to record for "Abbey Road." On another occasion, John Glascock and Joe Konas felt so guilty about being caught in the stock room that John felt compelled to stuff Paul McCartney's guitar strap down his pants! Joe Konas wanted to make John pay for such an "evil" act, so he told the rest of the band about it. At the Revolution Club in London, Ken Hensley decided to play a joke on John. Ken said to Glascock, "I just saw Paul McCartney come into the club and he's probably looking for his guitar strap!" Glascock turned pale because he was using it! McCartney was not in the club, but Glascock felt he had to play with his bare hands the whole night!

The Bop and Blues Party on New Year's Eve 1968 at London's Alexandra Palace was an extravaganza, with The Gods playing on a bill with Free, The Iveys (pre-Badfinger), Gun, The Small Faces, Spooky Tooth, John Mayall's Bluesbreakers, Amen Corner, Joe Cocker & The Grease Band, The Bonzo Dog Band and other lesser-known groups. They also did some BBC sessions on October 25, 1968 and in early 1969 and released a cover of Leonard Bernstein's "West Side Story" song "Maria" as a single.

Another highlight came on Tuesday, March 11, 1969 at the Speakeasy club in London. The Gods spent their second set playing with Jimi Hendrix, who just happened to be in the club that night. Jimi retrieved his guitar and he played three or four songs with The Gods. Jimi and Joe Konas played fiery leads, and it was the ultimate jam session for the band. On March 31, Hensley decided to leave but agreed to finish off some gigs. Little did he know that this would go on for nearly four months! This four-month period resulted in the completion of a brilliant song suite they created, entitled "To Samuel A Son." On July 26, 1969, The Gods played their last gig. The Columbia label released this suite on one side and some other completed and unfinished tracks as the album "To Samuel A Son" in January 1970. Joe Konas moved to Windsor, Ontario, Canada and now runs a music shop in Windsor.

After Ken Hensley announced his departure, Hensley, Glascock and Kerslake heard that UK '60s pop star Cliff Bennett was interested in creating a more rock-based band. The three moonlighted in Bennett's band, which was unfortunately called Toe Fat. In this group, Hensley concentrated on guitar instead of organ. They were signed to Parlophone in England and the new Rare Earth label in the US. Their first album, produced by disc jockey Jonathan Peel, was self-titled and came out in early 1970. It has one of the worst album covers of all time - a series of people with thumbprints as heads!

Just before the final breakup of The Gods, Ken Hensley, Lee Kerslake and John and Brian Glascock participated in one of the most secretive recording projects done at the time. The name of the album was "Orgasm," produced by David Paramor for the Major Minor label and performed under the group name Head Machine. Recently, Ken Hensley admitted his participation with these Gods members on this album, and that it was done purely for quick money. Each of its partipicants had his last name changed to hide his identity, but I'm removing the curtain now to show you who was involved! Here are their pseudonyms and real names: Ken Leslie (Ken Hensley), John Leadhen (John Glascock) and Brian and Lee Poole (Brian Glascock and Lee Kerslake). As you can see, this is basically the third Gods album. Vocals on the album were provided by Hensley, Glascock and David Paramor. All of the songs were credited to David Paramor, although Hensley wrote the songs "Climax" and "You Tried To Take It All." Since Paramor's last name fit in with the concept of the album, I guess there was no need to change it! "Orgasm" is another Glascock-related record that goes for a fortune because of its Ken Hensley connection, and it has been bootlegged a number of times over the years. It was also notable enough at the time to be released in France with a different cover on the Vogue label. The link between the Head Machine album and the first Toe Fat album is obvious when comparing the track lineups, as "You Tried To Take It All" and "Climax" (retitled "I Can't Believe") were also recorded on the Toe Fat LP.

Ken Hensley and Lee Kerslake were fired from Toe Fat in succession, and they were respectively replaced by Alan Kendall (a friend of John Glascock that was formerly in The Glass Menagerie) and Brian Glascock. Hensley and then Kerslake would respectively join heavy metallers Uriah Heep in 1969 and 1971. The revised Toe Fat lineup recorded the album "Toe Fat Two." Toe Fat rehearsed and recorded this album for three weeks before touring the UK and US, but Cliff Bennett lost his voice in the States and the whole band was forced to return home. While in the US, they supported Derek And The Dominoes for a month. Brian Glascock and Alan Kendall were offered positions with The Bee Gees. Toe Fat broke up when manager Robert Stigwood dropped them in mid-December 1970 after they headlined in the US, and their second album was released after their demise. (Cliff Bennett got another band together to record a one-off Toe Fat single for the Chapter One label.) Toe Fat's best moment was their Fillmore East gig on August 14-15, 1970 with Procol Harum and Country Joe McDonald. Brian met his future wife on this tour and moved to L.A. after Toe Fat's breakup.

After getting married at 21, Brian Glascock was fired from The Bee Gees following his appearance on their hit "How Can You Mend A Broken Heart." Alan Kendall remained with The Bee Gees and had a good run with the brothers Gibb. While Brian and John Glascock were with Kendall and his wife in London, John found out about a bass opening in Stan Webb's group Chicken Shack and joined in late 1970. He stayed with Chicken Shack long enough to record the February 1972 album "Imagination Lady" for the Deram label. "Imagination Lady" was a potent collection of blues-based rock that was popular at the time.

While in L.A., Brian Glascock met David Clark Allen. Allen was of Irish-Andalusian descent and was the son of a flamenco guitarist and a flamenco dancer. As a child, David Allen and his younger sister Angela started their performance lives as performers at their parents' El Cid night club in L.A. David played guitar at this club while Angela danced. Since no one had done it before, David became interested in merging rock and flamenco music in a group format. They soon met Brazilian/Mexican dancer Roberto Amaral, who was raised on the streets of east L.A. Amaral was previously one of Jose Greco's flamenco dance ensemble. The three became known as the group Rose in 1971 before finding Brian Glascock and UK bass player Nigel Griggs the next year.

Local audiences didn't know what to make of Rose, which then called themselves Los Angeles (Spanish for "The Angels"). Nigel Griggs was not happy being in America and left the band, leaving Brian to call John to check them out. Almost as soon as John Glascock joined the band, now named Carmen, Brian left to join Captain Beyond with former Deep Purple vocalist Rod Evans. (Brian Glascock went on to play drums for The Motels, Iggy Pop, Dolly Parton, Joan Armatrading and his California-based band Menthol Hill.) Allen decided to name the band Carmen because of its connotation with the opera of the same name and the images of Spain, gypsies and passions that opera conveyed. They moved to London to find a drummer and came across the volatile Paul Fenton. The search was now on for a record company, but Carmen's highly stylized and fast-moving stage act was difficult for record executives to fathom. They were all brilliantly costumed and their $50,000 sound and stage equipment included the use of 32 microphones to properly present the percussion and dance steps that were integrated into their overall sound. Angela Allen played mellotron and synthesizer when not dancing and fanning herself into a frenzy. Roberto Amaral's vibes, claps, castanets and vocals complemented the rhythm laid down by John Glascock and Paul Fenton. Carmen played dates in England, France and Japan before obtaining a two-album contract with EMI's Regal Zonophone imprint in 1973. The band had already been working on the songs for their initial album for nearly eighteen months.

In 1973, Carmen was assigned David Bowie's producer Tony Visconti and recorded the monumental LP "Fandangos In Space." The album captured the essence and passion of Spain in a medieval setting while seamlessly merging flamenco and rock. Visconti introduced the band to David Bowie at a party, and Bowie was floored. Bowie thought that the band's theatrics would be ideal for the glam rock market and Carmen was David's special guest at a private mid-October gig at the Marquee in London. This show was broadcast for the "Midnight Special" program in the US. This show prepared the music industry for the November 16 British release of "Fandangos In Space." The album immediately silenced any doubts that the music industry had of Carmen being another gimmicky band. Radio Luxembourg immediately embraced the album and its radio airplay topped the station's chart to kick off 1974. "Fandangos In Space" originally appeared on the Paramount label in the US, but that label's demise led to a reissue on ABC. Paramount's difficulties killed any momentum the band had generated to date.

Regal Zonophone released the single "Flamenco Fever" b/w "Lonely House" in 1974, but it was ignored. The label caused a great deal of confusion by incorrectly pressing the record, and replacement copies were not made available quickly enough for radio programmers. The intent of the single was to promote the album, but the A-side was not on it! Its edited follow-up "Bulerias" did not capture the essence of the band because its dance segment was edited out.

Touring continued, but the four hours required to set up their enormous and heavy stage equipment limited the venues they could perform at. They went back into the studio with Tony Visconti to produce the "Dancing On A Cold Wind" album. It was more of a concept piece, with John Glascock taking the role of a lover. Glascock co-wrote the track "Purple Flowers" with Roberto Amaral and he collaborated with the group on the notable cuts "Viva Mi Sevilla" and "Remembrances." Without any singles to promote, the album was immediately ignored upon release.

Carmen returned to the US to do over 40 shows in the fall of 1974. The groups they played with ranged from Sha Na Na, Electric Light Orchestra, Santana, Golden Earring and finally Yes. They got the best supporting gig of their career in late 1974 when they were selected to support Jethro Tull's 13-week US tour starting in January 1975. John Glascock enjoyed watching Jethro Tull's set from the wings of the stage and he hung out with Tull's members after their shows. Without being aware of it at the time, the rapport that Glascock built with Tull would work in his favor. Ian Anderson also took notice from afar. Carmen's association with Tull covered 44 dates, but cracks were developing within David Allen's band.

Carmen found that their tour income was not meeting expenses for their US dates before and with Jethro Tull. The Rolling Stones had planned to use Carmen to open their tour, but the deal did not take place. Paul Fenton fell off a horse during their downtime, and John Glascock was forced to dig potatoes in North Brookfield, MA at Long View Farm to make ends meet. Glascock made an arrangement with the farm's owner to work the land if he could use the farm's recording studio. Glascock stayed at the farm for a few months, writing material for Carmen, who had just obtained a new US recording contract with Mercury. While at the farm, John wrote the song "High Time." This song and another he co-wrote with Carmen, "Margarita," appeared on the band's swansong album "The Gypsies" that was produced by Steve Elson. David Allen tried to incorporate more of the progressive elements that were in vogue at the time, but the album was unable to fuse them properly with their original flamenco direction. "The Gypsies" was dedicated to Ian Anderson and Terry Ellis, among others. "High Time" was the only recording in Glascock's career that he wrote and sang on. Terry Ellis had promised to sign the band to Chrysalis, but it was too late. The group broke up right after the album's recording.

While digging potatoes, Glascock received a call from Ian Anderson to assist with Tull's upcoming album "Too Old To Rock 'N' Roll: Too Young To Die." John auditioned in San Francisco and played some of Ian's new songs slated for the album. Glascock picked up the material immediately and supplied his usual natural, melodic bass lines. A week after his audition, Ian told John that he was in, and John went to L.A. to stay with Brian and his wife. When Angela Allen was also asked to contribute backing vocals on this Tull LP, Carmen's demise was confirmed.

John Glascock was warmly accepted into the Jethro Tull family. Glascock's stage presence as a French aristocrat, resplendent in a fedora and colorful outfit, fed off the energy and live personalities of the other members. Ian Anderson played up John's penchant for extracurricular activities, introducing John as "Old Brittledick" on numerous occasions!

TOO OLD TO ROCK 'N' ROLL?

While Tull fans practically demanded a solo Ian Anderson album featuring acoustic guitar, Ian had no plans for that. Anderson had completed the songs previewed for John Glascock and was ready to record a Jethro Tull album. Once again, the band followed accountant advice and recorded the album "Too Old To Rock 'N' Roll: Too Young To Die" outside England in December 1975 to circumvent a higher taxable rate. The album came about by another set of failed plans.

The stage musical that Ian and David Palmer were writing for Adam Faith was ground to a halt when they discovered that Faith was busy doing another stage production. Jethro Tull took over the project, which became the album "Too Old To Rock 'N' Roll: Too Young To Die." "Too Old To Rock 'N' Roll…" continued the band's string of highly developed albums, with its juxtaposition of moving acoustic numbers and heavy-hitting rock tracks. David Palmer's playing abilities made it onto released Jethro Tull vinyl for the first time, as well as his continued arranging and conducting for the band. With Palmer as a full-time member of Tull, the group had its widest age spread: Palmer was already 38, while Glascock was just 24. It was precisely this lineup's considerable breadth and expertise that worked well both in the studio and on stage.

Upon its spring 1976 release, critics took the title track, another rock classic, as being of an autobiographical nature. The album's protagonist, Ray Lomas, was based on someone that Palmer knew. However, the cover drawing of Lomas looked too close to Ian Anderson to dispel nagging questions. Lomas was positioned as an aging rocker whose career was coming perilously close to an end because of his inability to adapt to current trends. Lomas' motorcyle accident on the M1 motorway was Ray's ticket to discovering that the market would one day come back to appreciate his talents like before. The album title and theme were misconstrued by many as Ian Anderson's current position in the music industry, and critics had a field day personally attributing them to Ian. The LP's gatefold depicted Ray Lomas' life in comic strip form and comedic touches were found all throughout the album.

Still, with all that the album had going for it, "Too Old To Rock 'N' Roll: Too Young To Die" had to fight its way into the US Top 15 (a #14 apex), and British support could only manage a #25 placing. The title track was released as a single, but it failed in nearly all countries despite heavy airplay. While the punk movement has been blamed for the LP's relative failure in England, that movement had not yet taken hold in the US to have any negative impact on album sales. The American B-side was "Bad-Eyed And Loveless" - the unreleased "War Child" outtake "Rainbow Blues" appeared elsewhere. Another difference on US copies was the edited A-side, while most countries issued the record in its album version. Promotional UK copies offered the short and long versions for airplay on all stations.

The album was recorded by the Maison Rouge Mobile Studio at Radio Monte Carlo, and it almost sounded like a field recording. Easily the worst-sounding overall mix on a Tull record, the impact of the LP's songs was reduced somewhat by the muddy sound quality. As evidenced on the remix of the title cut on the 25th anniversary box set, the band got a proper, clean sound on tape but the mix is the culprit. The album still had its share of standout tracks, however. "From A Deadbeat To An Old Greaser," "Salamander" and "Bad-Eyed And Loveless" were just three of the many cuts that stood up to repeated listenings. "Salamander" formed the basis of Ian's new publishing company, "Salamander & Son Ltd.". In the instrument department, Ian Anderson used a Martin

The revised Jethro Tull lineup:
John Glascock, Barriemore
Barlow, Ian Anderson, John
Evans and Martin Barre.

At right is the Italian
release of "Too Old
To Rock 'N' Roll:
Too Young To Die."

Below are the first
and second pressings
of the "Living In The
Past" reissue single
in England.

Above: The UK, US and German singles of "Too Old To Rock 'N' Roll: Too Young To Die."
Below (l. to r.): The Spanish release of the same single, the "Ring Out, Solstice Bells" EP and the "M.U." album.

John Glascock, Ian Anderson and Martin Barre in full flight.
(Photo courtesy of Dennis Landau)

guitar on the title recording, and he rediscovered the harmonica on "Taxi Grab." Maddy Prior was the backing vocalist on "Too Old To Rock 'N' Roll. . ." (the song), and Angela Allen did the same honors on "Crazed Institution" and "Big Dipper." "Quizz Kid" was unusual in that it started with a long quote of the title song. A leftover song from a Ridge Farm Studio session in Surrey, "Strip Cartoon," would be withheld until its use as the B-side of "The Whistler" from the next album "Songs From The Wood."

Also recorded at this session was Anderson's very humorous song "A Small Cigar." The story of a cigar saving the world is preposterous, but great fun, and featured just Ian along with David Palmer on keyboards. It marked its first release on "Nightcap" in 1993.

Album pre-release promotion in England involved the band lip-synching the entire album in a studio setting on a London Weekend Television special simulcast on Capital Radio in London. The TV / radio linkup was the first for two independent stations. Although the singing was canned, the backing tracks were entirely re-recorded for the program. The program's producer was Mike Mansfield. British television got its fill of the band, with the title song's additional performances on the syndicated program "Supersonic" (another Mansfield production) and BBC TV's "Old Grey Whistle Test." Tull took Rod Stewart's place on the latter program when Rod The Mod cancelled with little notice.

The band toured for just over two months during 1976, but they made those shows count despite ignoring England. The first concert with Palmer and Glascock took place in Brussels, Belgium on May 1, 1976. The July 16 gig at Colt Park in Hartford, CT debuted "Tullevision" - the simultaneous video broadcast of the concert in progress. "Tullevision" enabled all concert goers, even those in the cheap seats, to be able to see what Ian and the gang were up to on stage. Although this advanced development in concert enjoyment was not reported in newspaper reviews of the show, a fan stabbing, some drug overdoses and two deaths at the show made the headlines. As with their earlier Red Rocks (Denver, CO) and Hampton Beach Casino (New Hampshire) concerts, Colt Park was closed to future concerts after these incidents.

In between the European and US legs of their 1976 tour, Tull appeared June 19 on the NBC-TV program "Midnight Special." Another highlight was the band's July 23 appearance at Shea Stadium in Flushing, NY in front of 55,000 fans. It was another special event for the band to appear at the home of baseball's New York Mets, especially since concerts are infrequently scheduled there and this was the middle of the baseball season!

Martin Barre enjoyed a special moment of his own on August 8 when he met Julie Weems as he arrived at the Jackson City, MO airport before Jethro Tull's show that night at Arrowhead Stadium in Kansas City. Julie became his wife and they have since produced two daughters and a son, Cameron. Martin was previously living in a cottage in Putney Heath, but this fortuitous meeting changed all this!

Exactly a week later, Ian Anderson received a trophy for the band's highly acclaimed, 100,000 ticket sale extravaganza at the L.A. Memorial Coliseum. Just like the Colt Park show, a video screen behind the stage projected the band's activities for all to see. Tull's live show in 1976 had many new, entertaining bits. Ian employed the use of a baby carriage to hold his guitar and flute, and David Palmer's entrance on stage in a monk's habit caused immediate laughter. Despite his costume, Palmer hovered over his organ like a mortician! The band's performance of "Quizz Kid" had Anderson tossing household appliances from the rear of a trolley. As for John Evans, Harpo Marx mannerisms were still the order of the day. By this point, "Thick As A Brick" was reduced to ten minutes and "A Passion Play," now just a memory, would not be touched upon again until the early 1990s.

After cancelling a similar album five years before, Chrysalis Records decided that the recent change in personnel was the right time to issue a compilation album. Entitled, "M.U. - The Best Of Jethro Tull," the album selected choice cuts from the post-Mick Abrahams era of the band, with the previously issued UK B-side "Rainbow Blues" included as an incentive for US fans to buy the package. Of course, fans from other countries were outraged as they already had the song! British fans for the most part avoided the album, even though "Living In The Past" was reissued as a single there. In the US, response was much more favorable, especially since the album went platinum and the reissued single "Locomotive Breath" gathered some additional sales (#62 Billboard, #74 Cashbox). Most notable about these US singles of "Locomotive Breath" were their different presentations for stores and radio stations. The lyric line "got him by the balls" was bleeped on promo copies. Countries like England and New Zealand received a reissue single of "Living In The Past" b/w "Requiem." On first pressings of the LP and all CDs, "Thick As A Brick Edit #1" segues into "Bungle In The Jungle." Later vinyl pressings separate both tracks.

The promotion budget for "M.U." was the largest in Chrysalis' short history, with numerous print ads, in-store displays and contest prizes. That budget only led to so-so sales, respectively reaching only 44 and 13 in England and the US. Ian recorded half-hour and full-hour versions of a radio program where he introduced and discussed the album's tracks. Chrysalis released both US radio shows on vinyl - one sampler version with the same cuts on both sides and the other with the full track listing. However, they both contained the same Ian Anderson spoken segments. At this point, John Glascock received offers from Ken Hensley (former Gods companion and current Uriah Heep keyboardist) and Ritchie Blackmore of Blackmore's Rainbow to join their respective bands, but John knew what was right for him despite Hensley's repeated requests in the summer of 1976.

The album title "M.U." was from another Terry Ellis brainstorm, in which a "Musician's Union" ("M.U.") of Jethro Tull members was represented in its contents. Current and former members were coerced into appearing at a reunion dinner from which a poster of the dinner table gathering was included in the album. *Why wasn't Mick Abrahams there? He was still on the shit list!*

The moments that would mark a major change in direction for Jethro Tull took place in 1976, when Ian Anderson married Shona Learoyd and finally moved into his 16th Century, 630-acre British redbrick farmhouse in Buckinghamshire. Ian was the last member of the band to move out of the city to pursue country life. Shona had come from an upper-class family that included two duchesses. The feel of the great outdoors literally was a creative breath of fresh air for Ian, since he was now writing at home instead of inhospitable hotel rooms. Through this new atmosphere, Anderson got more in touch with folk music from all throughout Europe, and this folk tradition has continued to influence his writing to this day. Though not always obvious in some of Tull's later work, folk-derived music became the underpinning of Ian Anderson's lyrical and spiritual outlook.

This new, uplifting outlook came with some dividends: Shona soon became pregnant with their son Seamus (James). While expecting, Ian and Shona did only a handful of interviews, but the ones they did were very humorous. Shona revealed this about Ian: "He's one of the most ordinary men I've met in my life." Taking a look at his pregnant wife, Ian added, "She's been having this craving for creamcake. I'm starting to do things I've never done in my life. I pay the rates and electricity bill in our house, which is really a new experience for me. So many people end up living in a make-believe world and go to the extent of having a right-hand man to pay for everything and cushion them from the realities of life. It's necessary for your peace of mind to prove you can handle it. So I usually lock myself in the kitchen when I have to write out all the checks." As for her future stage involvement with Tull, Shona admitted that her onstage time was over: "I try to help out but I stay out of the way for the tuning and such because it has nothing to do with me. Or us. I'd rather be on the road and bored than be alone and busy at home."

Jethro Tull gave their British fans a nice Christmas present in 1976 with an EP, of which its leading track was "Ring Out, Solstice Bells," a song which actually celebrated the change of season to winter (on the 22nd of December) rather than reflecting on Christmas taking place three days later. "Christmas Song" (from the "Living In The Past" collection) was included and "Ring Out, Solstice Bells" eventually made Tull's next LP ("Songs From The Wood"), but the two other tracks from this EP ("Pan Dance" and "March, The Mad Scientist") were unavailable again until 1988. The record was warmly received by fans, providing the band with their first UK Top 30 entry (at #28) since the "Life Is A Long Song" EP. It also reached #29 in NME. The United States did not receive this EP commercially, but it was available as a promotional 12" for radio stations. The band also promoted this single on the UK "Top Of The Pops" program but it did not help one bit - the chart position remained at #28 in Music Week before and after the show! Besides England, at least three other countries received the EP: Germany, Italy and Australia.

"SONGS FROM THE WOOD"

The first fruit of Anderson's new-found relationship with the countryside (and the sexual pleasures that could be derived from it) was "Songs From The Wood," an early 1977 release. "Songs From The Wood" became the first expression of Ian Anderson's new lease on life (so to speak), and was a massive success on many levels. Besides the overflowing reception to the album's tracks, Jethro Tull picked up a whole new legion of fans with this release. The title track, "Cup Of Wonder," "Hunting Girl," the aforementioned "Ring Out, Solstice Bells" and "The Whistler" all created great waves with AOR (album oriented radio) stations. "Songs From The Wood" indicated a sharp upturn in sales, both in the UK and the US (UK: #13, US: #8). With John Glascock and David Palmer firmly established in the line-up, Jethro Tull had all of the elements of a truly complete band. Unlike the previous album, the band really came together to contribute song ideas and their collective humor sparked their renewed energy. Additional musical material was credited to David Palmer and Martin Barre, and the whole band arranged Ian's songs. As a bonus to fans, Ian Anderson proved that he could still go it alone by playing all the instruments on the song "Jack-In-The-Green." On another level, some Top

Ian and Shona Anderson

Top right: Ian Anderson at his swaggering best.

Middle: Martin Barre.

At right is the rare censored US promo single of "Locomotive Breath."

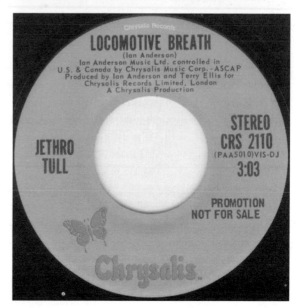

40 stations picked up on the exceptionally catchy jig "The Whistler," bringing the single to a respectable #59 ranking (#52 in Cashbox). The single's bottom side was "Strip Cartoon," a quality track from the "Too Old To Rock 'N' Roll: Too Young To Die" sessions that didn't make an album appearance until 1988. The BBC picked up on the success of "Songs From The Wood" by presenting Tull in an hour-long concert simultaneously broadcast on TV and radio.

Reflecting on his surroundings and the output resulting from them, Ian commented: "All I can be is an illustration of someone who seeks his own way in the world and asks a load of questions. I am an example of an average guy who raised himself intellectually, raised himself musically, raised himself socially, and raised himself in terms of good old entrepreneurial capitalist practice to achieve a state where he is considerably better off than he was when he started. But at the same time, I still react with and around the area of society from which I come."

In the past, the band was in danger of losing their Britishness with all the time they spent in the US. "Songs From The Wood" underscored the pleasures of living in England through its numerous historical, mythological and folkloric references from the English and Celtric traditions. Calling the album "folk" would be completely denigrating its source material and execution. The album's most natural musical settings had the same attributes of the countryside they depicted - sparkling clear instrumentation and Ian's resonant rural tones. In Ian Anderson's musical palette, life's more carnal pleasures were sprinkled with the same free sense of levity. The demand to "pass the word, pass the lady" in the song "Cup Of Wonder" is indicative of Ian's lighthearted treatment of British folklore. At the same time, the disco beat used in one section of that song showed that Ian was aware of the current musical trends in the marketplace. Ian's own more dignified physical appearance with shorter hair, bowler hat and jacket reinforced the images he chose to project.

Creating such a rich musical brew was accomplished through the use of exotic instrumentation within the usual rock band format. David Palmer brought in a portative pipe organ for a denser, more enveloping keyboard sound. (*"Portative" means portable in case you didn't know!*) Unusual string instruments (mandolin, lute) were joined with equally unusual percussion, like marimba, glockenspiel, nakres (small medieval drums) and tabor. The tabor was a small drum usually accompanied by a flute or pipe. This ornamentation was essential on "The Whistler." In a live setting, the song was infrequently played because the multitracking that Ian used on its recording could not be duplicated live. For example, Anderson's switching between tin whistle and acoustic guitar moves too fast - risking missed notes, not to mention his overlapping vocals! When playing the title song live, Ian had to resort to using a tape featuring the backing vocals on the introduction in order to reasonably recreate his vocal treatment. Ian has occasionally joked about this tape's use over the years, and having band members lip-synch the parts has never fooled anyone!

"Fire At Midnight" and "Jack-In-The Green" were the only tracks on the album that Ian wrote while at home. The others were written while he was away from his estate. "Jack-In-The-Green" was most likely the fastest song that Ian did, in terms of its creation to final mix. An hour before leaving home for the London studio on a Sunday morning, Ian wrote "Jack-In-The-Green." He then recorded all the instruments in the studio that afternoon and mixed it the same night before going home! Good old Jack was a short, mythological Celtic figure that revitalized nature after a freezing winter. Taking its meaning one step further, Jack's duty was to restore civilization after our modern world displaced things along the way.

The Renaissance image of dancing to galliard songs was one of the enduring Ian Anderson sketches in the brilliant title track "Songs From The Wood." Its highly involved musical passages captured the band interaction of "A Passion Play" within an uplifting setting. Martin Barre's phased guitar on "Hunting Girl" was another of the album's classics. Martin used a Watkins Copycat tape echo whose sound cannot be duplicated, and it still can't because the unit doesn't work any more! The stalking introduction of "Hunting Girl" was effectively used as the theme music to the local events TV program "Nine On New Jersey" during the late '70s and early '80s. The program originated from WOR-TV's Channel 9 studios in Secaucus, NJ.

"Cup Of Wonder" marked the first use of a Frank Zappa technique that Ian Anderson would use from time to time: conceptual continuity. By referring to his past output, Zappa used it to thematically link his current and past output as one body of work. While not sitting down and purposely crafting his songs like Frank Zappa, Ian Anderson occasionally used conceptual linking to project an overall setting for his similarly themed songs. Even though Ian had previously mentioned the Aqualung character in "Cross-Eyed Mary" and he quoted from "Too Old Too Rock 'N' Roll. . ." in "Quizz Kid," this was the first time that the actual theme of a song was carried over to unrelated projects. On "Cup Of Wonder," the reference to "the green man" was in fact to the dear

"Jack-In-The-Green." "Cup Of Wonder" had a distinctive flute and guitar riff and somewhat bawdy lyrics that endeared itself to US radio programmers who provided it frequent airplay upon release. The song also referred to the beltane, a Gaelic fire festival that replaced all "unholy" house fires with a holy fire. "Beltane" was a song recorded (but not used) for the next album, "Heavy Horses." Equally evocative was "Pibroch (Cap In Hand)," a tune portraying the rugged beauty of the Scottish highlands and inspired by a typical Scottish bagpipe tune known as a *piobaireachd* (Anglicized as "pibroch").

With all of this eating, drinking and merriment going on in Ian Anderson's songs and no mention of any divine intervention, Ian has been accused of promoting a pagan lifestyle. This mistaken criticism continues to this day, with fanatical Christian websites incorrectly reading into what Ian *must have meant* with his songs on this album and its follow-up "Heavy Horses"!

Jethro Tull took their "Songs From The Wood" act on the road in January 1977. Unusually, just seven US dates were planned, their last ever dates in the month of January. This was followed by two February weeks in the UK and a second US pass in March lasting four months. The third American date was a January 16 benefit show organized by Terry Ellis. It took place at the 471-seat Founders' Circle within Dorothy Chandler Pavilion in L.A. The concert raised funds for the Los Angeles Music Center, and Jethro Tull was the first rock group to volunteer on the music center's behalf. It was a private black-tie affair, and being such, the Tull set included Beethoven's Ninth Symphony! (The full title of that Beethoven work from 1824 is "Symphony No. 9 in D minor, op. 125.") The band (minus Ian) had already played that Beehoven piece as a regular part of their 1976 tour.

At the shows open to the public, the band's personality reigned supreme. John Glascock and Martin Barre remained quiet yet flamboyant, while Barlow looked like a tipsy soccer star. The suits that the two keyboardists wore reflected extremes: the seriousness of Palmer's black tailcoat and the "good humor" of Evans' ice cream outfit. Sorry for the bad joke! (For our European residents, Good Humor is a brand of ice cream!) While stirring up action on stage, Ian decided to stir something else: a renewed war with music critics.

Ian's incendiary remarks flowed quite easily during the Hammersmith Odeon show on February 11. While introducing "Thick As A Brick," Anderson called it "Whole Lotta Brick" - a humorous reference to Led Zeppelin's "Whole Lotta Love." It was not a derogatory remark against Led Zep; it was Anderson's annoyance with those in the media that constantly tried to get that band, and their front man Robert Plant, to speak against Tull and Ian Anderson. Circus magazine interviewers even tried to provoke Ian into making negative comments about Plant and Co. as well. Since a "brick" is a euphemism for a penis in some cultures, mostly Spanish-speaking, Ian's retitling of the song was an attack on several levels against media bent on making a sexual escapade of both band's songs and their attempts at creating animosity between Tull and Zep.

After the tour was over, Ian clarified Jethro Tull's position in the music world compared to the other titans: "Stylistically, I've always said that we can't be a heavy riff group because Led Zeppelin are the best in the world. We can't be a blues-influenced R&B rock and roll group because The Stones are the best in the world. We can't be a slightly sort of airy-fairy, mystical sci-fi synthesizing abstract freak-out group because Pink Floyd are the best in the world. And so what's left? And that's what we've always done. We've filled the gap. We've done what's left. That may partly explain our popularity and we've done it for the most part without the aid of gargantuan feats of PR and manipulating the daily press with scandal stories. And we still are one of the most popular groups in the world. There is no explanation. At the same time as being one of these top groups, we are somehow not. We are somehow different."

On the plus side, the Hammersmith Odeon show brought out some other musical treats. A somewhat rehearsed three-minute instrumental passage preceded "To Cry You A Song," and Ian's flute solo included extracts of "Pop Goes The Weasel," "God Rest Ye Merry Gentlemen" and "Bourée." The day before Ian's tirade, Jethro Tull played at the Golders Green Hippodrome in London. This show was recorded for the "Sight 'N' Sound In Concert" program that was broadcast on television a week later. One track from this show, "Velvet Green," was issued on the 20th anniversary box set and featured Martin Barre on marimba.

Anderson's playfulness on stage did not end with critics. Ian's favorite foil on stage was (and continues to be) Martin Barre. Here's a typical Ian Anderson anecdote about Barre: "Our guitarist, Martin Barre, was invited to a high-society party where the hostess was a very attractive and well-off widow. Now Martin, like many small, chubby people, is possessed of a very small *bobo*. Unabashed, Martin secured her amorous attentions for the night and took her upstairs. After very minimal foreplay, they ripped off their clothes. The lady looked down in disgust and said, 'My God, who do you think you can satisfy with that?' And Martin looked her in the eye and said, 'Me, madame.'"

You may ask, with this teasing, why would Martin stay in the band? Barre's response is very serious: "I think that everybody in Jethro Tull is replaceable. . .I'd rather think that I have to work hard to keep my job. I would never take anything for granted. I'm always sweating inside trying to do better, trying to get things right."

Chrysalis really put their heads together in creating promotional materials for the album "Songs From The Wood." Besides standup cardboard displays, mobiles and posters of Ian Anderson and the album cover, three-inch tall tree stumps -with the album title carved into them - were manufactured with an opening for wooden match storage at its top and a striking plate at its bottom! In Australia, a unique single was released: "Songs From The Wood" b/w "Jack-In-The-Green." If you really wanted to get the Guatemalan issue of "The Whistler," you got "Ring Out, Solstice Bells" on the other side. Chrysalis in Canada was very generous to radio stations, providing them with a three-album set entitled "The Jethro Tull Story." It had interview material unique to that country.

The Dorothy Chandler Pavilion show was not the only one with classical elements. At a classical/traditional extravaganza at Anaheim Convention Center on April 6, 1977, Tull played abridged versions of the second and fourth movements of the same Beethoven symphony. The introduction of "Velvet Green" was graced by David Palmer's portative organ quote of the traditional tune "When The Saints Go Marching In." Along with other songs, the encore was Bach's "Double Violin Concerto." The concert concluded with a medley of Eric Coates' "The Dambusters March" and Sir Edward Elgar's "Land Of Hope And Glory." The latter was part of the first march from Elgar's "Pomp And Circumstance." Nowhere else would Jethro Tull perform such a vast quantity of classical material.

Eric Coates' "The Dambusters March" was of great significance to David Palmer, who received a prize in Coates' name when he graduated from the Royal Academy of Music in 1965. The English composer Coates (1886-1957) won a reputation chiefly from light (read: commercial) classical music. His last great success was the march from the film "The Dam Busters," written in 1954 for the 1955 film. Carlene Mair wrote lyrics for it, but the instrumental version has stood the test of time.

If you're wondering why "The Dambusters March" and "Land Of Hope And Glory" were played, they formed a fantastic setup for the concluding element in Jethro Tull concerts: the tossing of two large balloons into the crowd. The balloon ritual was introduced during the band's performance of "Sealion" in 1974, but it had developed into an audience participation magnet. A roadie would hand off each balloon to Ian, who would balance it on his head before pushing it into a different section of the audience. The success of these balloons formed another new Tull tradition that continues today. It was yet another way for the audience to get involved with the band. Invariably, someone with a lit substance of some kind would pop the balloon, but the main goal for fans is to do anything humanly possible to be part of the balloon's journey. (*You know, I have yet to touch a balloon after all these years, and I'll kill to get my hands on one!*)

A European tour followed and Tull would also embark on a twelve-date sellout Australian tour that included four shows in Melbourne. During the band's offtime in the early summer of 1978, Ian Anderson was closing the deal on a second home - the 15,300-acre Strathaird Estate on the Isle of Skye in northern Scotland. The deal was completed in October 1977 and reported immediately afterward. The property had not been taken care of, and $120,000 was spent to restore this eleven-bedroom Victorian mansion. While reading an airline magazine during a European tour flight, Ian came across an article on aquaculture (the cultivation of water-based produce). This intrigued Ian and he developed the idea of farming salmon on his new estate as a way to offset its cost. Additional reading materials helped Ian to set up a salmon farming business with smoking and processing plants in Inverness to develop the salmon that was produced at Strathaird. Anderson's organization started off with three employees and a manager, with salmon grown in cages located in Loch Slapin adjacent to his holdings.

Inverness residents initially expressed their concerns, but the 400 jobs created by Ian Anderson's rapidly thriving business venture had the island's locals proclaiming him a savior - "The Laird Of Strathaird." Ian would later comment on these concerns: "I'm not just trading in salmon, I'm trading in people's lives, in an area of the country where there is very high unemployment and very little in the way of prospects for young people." With the threat of public accusations of monopoly, Anderson forced Marine Harvest, corporate owner of Loch Slapin's lease, to relinquish the loch's lease to him. The maturity of his first salmon coincided with the official founding of Strathaird Salmon Ltd. in 1982. WOR-TV in New Jersey captured the career changes of Ian Anderson and the

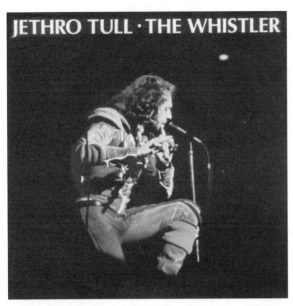

Above are the UK and German editions of "The Whistler," with the US and Dutch copies below.

"Songs From The Wood" and "Repeat • The Best Of Jethro Tull • Vol. II" were the band's releases for 1977.

101

band by compiling the unique Tull documentary entitled "Minstrel In The Gallery." This special captured interviews and live footage recorded on December 3, 1977 in Binghamton, NY. It was aired four days later.

In a hasty decision, Chrysalis Records decided to issue another Jethro Tull compilation in time for Christmas 1977: "Repeat • The Best Of Jethro Tull • Vol. II." Mainly containing favorites that were not included on the first compilation "M.U. - The Best Of Jethro Tull," this album's saving grace was the inclusion of the previously unreleased track "Glory Row" from the "War Child" sessions. Fans thought that the purchase of this album for one new track did not warrant its purchase, and sales really reflected this. It did not hit the sales listings in England, and it only made #94 in the States. To complete the year, Tull toured the US and prepared for the next album.

HEAVY HORSES BREAK DOWN

Ian Anderson's next collection of songs was again written while on tour or aboard trains. The difficulty this time was that quite a bit of Ian's material was not up to standard. Nearly twenty songs were recorded during the album's Maison Rouge Studio sessions in London in January 1978, but most were scrapped as incomplete or inadequate. The Jethro Tull album cycle had evolved into producing a darker album after a more lighthearted affair. With the success of the glorious "Songs From The Wood" in the books, the more downbeat "Heavy Horses" naturally followed.

Unusual for a Jethro Tull album, "Heavy Horses" used the same concept - the outdoors. Its title came from the horse breeds that did heavy labor in England's past times - Shire, Suffolk, Clydesdale and Percheron, to name just four. Tractors and other farm machinery replaced these horses in the 20th Century, leading these breeds to the road of extinction.

Humorous moments were few and far between on "Heavy Horses," but the darkness of the album's songs had its own poignancy. Besides horses, other creatures were covered. Animals have since become a frequent subject of Ian's songs. "One Brown Mouse" was inspired by Robert Burns' poem "Ode To A Mouse." When you have mice, you have to have cats! ". . .And The Mouse Police Never Sleeps" was Ian's tribute to the cats he and Shona had at home, and it mentioned "Weathercock" - another song on the album. Shona also contributed the fine back cover band photo. Author John Le Carré had discussed a game in one of his books that inspired Anderson's love song "Moths." Even though cats ruled, dogs were not forgotten either!

The most unusual track of the album was the nine-minute title track. The song itself seemed to be pieced together from disparate musical sections utilizing different timings. The inclusion of a long, slow guitar-riffed song like "No Lullaby" became a predictable part of the second side of a Jethro Tull album, and its effect was inevitably leaden when placed in its album context. By contrast, "Acres Wild" was the most playful use of the English countryside setting on the album - namely, Ian's new surroundings on the Isle of Skye. Darryl Way of the group Curved Air provided the violin parts heard on that song and the title track. David Palmer's orchestrations on the album were as moving as ever and complemented the songs beautifully. The question on "Heavy Horses" became "What kind of album is it?" Not being folk, rock or orchestral, Jethro Tull had produced an album with a dark, multifaceted identity. John Evans and David Palmer never fully incorporated synthesizers into studio recordings, and the band's guitar/organ sound on record was proving to be past its "sell-by date" in 1978.

In April 1978, the UK single "Moths" accompanied the album "Heavy Horses" into stores. The single did not sell, but Top 20 LP success was nailed down on both sides of the Atlantic (UK: #20; US: #19). The intended B-side was called "Beltane," a track recorded towards the beginning of the album sessions. At the last minute, the song was pulled and "Life Is A Long Song" took its place on the reverse of the record. However, some copies pressed in Ireland show "Beltane" on their labels but play the substituted song. The lack of promotion instantly killed its potential - Chrysalis was apparently too busy creating brass horse shoes that they gave to DJs! "Beltane" would finally be released in the 1988 box, and it is unusual for Ian's sax playing. "Moths" was backed by "Acres Wild" on a French promotional single, while the Polish release chose ". . .And The Mouse Police Never Sleeps" as the other side. An alternate mix of "Moths" was prepared by Ian Anderson in April 1988 for inclusion on the same 1988 box set. Meanwhile, the May 9th edition of BBC2's "Old Grey Whistle Test" broadcast the video of the song "Heavy Horses" that the band shot prior to the album's release.

Three other "Heavy Horses" tracks survived the trashbin: "Living In These Hard Times," "Blues Instrumental (Untitled)" and "Broadford

Bazaar." The first two saw the light of day in 1988, while the last had to wait five years for a "Nightcap" appearance. "Broadford Bazaar" was an acoustic Ian Anderson solo recording. David Palmer conducted the orchestra on "Living In These Hard Times," a track recently mixed for the '88 set. The untitled "Blues Instrumental" had Ian playing flute and an unusual Lyricon wind syntheziser, eliminating the need for Palmer on the cut.

Touring for "Heavy Horses" began in Scotland on May 1, 1978. Eight UK dates, including three at the Hammersmith Odeon and two at the Rainbow, were on tap within this four-week trek. Barriemore Barlow had just played on Richard Digance's "Live At The Queen Elizabeth Hall" LP, so Digance became Tull's last-ever opening act in the UK. All of the tour's gigs were officially recorded and live extracts from the tour were issued on the "Jethro Tull Live - Bursting Out" album later in the year. While this tour was successful from a ticket standpoint, the warning signs of a preventable tragedy were about to show.

During their summer break, Jethro Tull helped out friend Maddy Prior on her solo LP "Woman In The Wings," returning Prior's kindness of singing on Tull's "Too Old To Rock 'N' Roll: Too Young To Die" album. The British release of "Woman In The Wings" came out in 1978, but American copies took two years to surface. Strangely enough, every time this album is mentioned to record collectors, the phrase "Jethro Tull is the backing band" inevitably (and inaccurately) appears. Even though all of Tull's members except for John Evans appear on the album, usually only one or two members play on each track. Still, the Jethro Tull presence and sound is most noticeable on the album. Anderson and Palmer co-produced this LP with Robin Black, who also handled the engineering chores. Even feline-loving Shona Anderson can be heard on backing vocals on the track "Catseyes"! For some reason, Ian's backing vocals on the track "Rollercoaster" escaped the credits.

John Glascock's participation on Maddy Prior's LP was not as extensive as he had hoped. On the "Heavy Horses" tour, John broke a tooth and developed a dental infection. He soon became seriously ill. Glascock's tooth infection spread to his heart and caused damage to a weak valve that he was unaware of. In all likelihood, John inherited his valve weakness from his father Walter, who had died of a heart ailment at a young age in 1965. In an attempt to repair his faulty heart valve, Glascock would have to undergo major surgery in the fall of 1978. Here is Brian Glascock's explanation of John's condition and feelings at that time: "John had, but wasn't aware of, an abcess in his jaw from a broken tooth. It ended up poisoning his blood system, and then an infection settled on a valve in his heart. Later on, they thought he might have had some childhood illness that weakened his heart, but nobody knew about it at the time. When I went to England to see him, he was in the hospital across from Hyde Park. He was on antibiotics because the infection had swollen his heart to twice its size, and he knew that after the infection went away, he'd had to have an operation. He was pretty scared about that. Our father had died from heart trouble, and he knew it ran in the family. He was also worried he wouldn't have his gig with Tull again. I told him, 'There are many other bands out there - besides, you'll be fine. They're not going to cut your hand off - you're having the surgery you need. It's not going to stop you from playing music, but you've got to stop your naughty ways, stop smoking - that stuff." However, John Glascock was not able or willing to change his lifestyle.

Glascock's surgery prevented him from participating in Jethro Tull's US fall tour. Barriemore Barlow, John's good friend in the band, spoke to Chris Riley (remember him from The John Evan Band?) and brought in his Blackpool friend Tony Williams to deputize for John until he recovered. Williams had played in The Executives with Chris Riley and with Barlow in Requiem just before Barriemore joined Jethro Tull. He was a lead guitarist by nature but borrowed a bass from Riley to learn Glascock's parts. His most successful session since then was his bass playing on Stealer's Wheel's first album and hit single "Stuck In The Middle With You."

Early in Jethro Tull's US fall tour, three sets of two-night runs were scheduled at The Spectrum in Philadelphia, Boston Garden and New York's own Madison Square Garden. The Columbus Day performance (October 9) was a landmark show, not only for the band, but for technological advancement. It was broadcast by worldwide satellite and simulcast on BBC2 television and BBC radio, and Tull was the first to broadcast live video and audio from the States to England. They had the last laugh with their nemesis John Peel, since their broadcast pre-empted his program! The show was not without glitches, however, since the broadcast started 40 minutes after the set started. The program's potential audience was exaggerated at 400 million, but the concert captured the band fully at the top of their game - perhaps at their all-time peak. Although numerous requests for the audio release of this show have led to occasional announcements of its future availability, this concert has not been released due to its nearly complete overlap with the "Jethro Tull Live - Bursting Out" album. Parts of the video have been issued on the 20th anniversary videotape. In terms of audio, only "Thick As A Brick" from this show has been released - a bonus track on a reissue CD of the same name. Long Beach

(Photo courtesy of Lon Horwitz)

Above and lower left: the many moves (and moods) of Ian Anderson.

The man that always exudes class - David Palmer.

John Glascock, David Palmer and Martin Barre on the "Heavy Horses" tour.
(Photos courtesy of Giulio Pallone)

John Glascock on the 1978 tour.
(Photos courtesy of Giulio Pallone)

Above: The UK editions of "Moths" and "A Stitch In Time," along with the German single of "Sweet Dream."

Below: The Dutch edition of "Sweet Dream," Maddy Prior's LP and Tull's own "Heavy Horses."

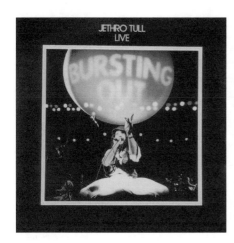  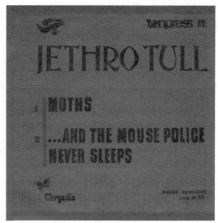

Besides "Jethro Tull Live - Bursting Out," fans trying to catch up on differently packaged foreign releases could purchase "Moths" with its different German and Polish sleeves. Also interesting about the Polish single was its different flipside - "…And The Mouse Police Never Sleeps."

An unusual free publication with Ian on its cover.   (Photo courtesy of Dag Sandbu)

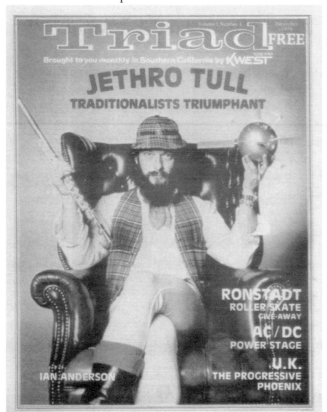 

Auditorium was the concert that capped off a tremendously successful run in the States.

As a stop-gap measure in the fall of 1978, Jethro Tull released their double LP "Jethro Tull Live - Bursting Out" to great acclaim. It was their first complete live release, although some studio overdubs were required from everyone except John Glascock to complete the package. It made #17 in England, and four places lower in the US. "Bursting Out" served well as a live, comprehensive history of the band's accomplishments in their first ten years. As with most live albums, Ian viewed this as the end of one era and the birth of another. In addition to classic tracks, the album offered a few exclusive recordings that they had performing live for a while: Ian's flute medley "Flute Solo Improvisation"/"God Rest Ye Merry Gentlemen"/"Bourée," the instrumentals "Conundrum," "Quatrain" and "The Dambusters March"/"Medley." American CD buyers found their release different from the British CD package. While the British release was a 2CD set, the US version was a single disc which omitted the tracks "Conundrum," "Quatrain" and "Sweet Dream." The US disc wasn't a complete disaster though; it had a longer announcer introduction and ten seconds more of Ian's flute solo. "Quatrain" was a guitar-led instrumental that used the Aaron Copland "Hoedown" segment from his piece "Rodeo" as its source. "Skating Away On The Thin Ice Of The New Day" had the band switching instruments for everyone's amusement: Martin Barre switched to marimba, John Glascock played electric guitar, John Evans manned the accordion, Barlow played glockenspiel and drums, Ian Anderson sang and played his usual acoustic guitar, and David Palmer was away taking a piss! Other fun things to check out: the spine of the original LP says "*Busting Out*" instead of the correct title, and Ian Anderson's introduction of John Glascock before "Hunting Girl" had the word "bastard" bleeped out. Compared to what we hear today on TV and radio, it was not that offensive to censor! It is also interesting to point out that Ian's "Don't strain yourselves" comment before "One Brown Mouse" is very similar to the banter he used in the 1966 recorded show available through A New Day magazine.

To maximize interest in "Jethro Tull Live - Bursting Out," the extremely melodic single "A Stitch In Time" b/w "Sweet Dream (live)" was released in England on white and standard black vinyl. Commercial British singles came with either 3:30 or 4:20 versions on the A-side, while copies from Germany and Holland solely had the complete 4:20 version. The German single had the sides reversed, with "A Stitch In Time" on its B-side. Still, "A Stitch In Time" did not reach an album until 1988, albeit in its 3:30 version. Therefore, the 4:20 version remains a non-album track. As to why it was issued as a single, it was most likely because "Bursting Out" offered no new full-length songs that had not been issued in a studio form. "A Stitch In Time" was recorded in the fall of 1978 at Maison Rouge Studio in London with Anderson, Barre, Barlow and Evans. David Palmer conducted the orchestration. In case you didn't notice on the album cover, Ian Anderson's pants have a strategic hole - you know where! Between the cover balloon and Ian's ripped pants, one can see the dual meaning of the album's title.

Chrysalis managed to confuse the press through an essay by Michael Hooker entitled "The Honest Measure Of Worth." Here's a choice morsel from the essay that describes what Hooker thought of Jethro Tull's current musical stature: "A perhaps simplistic description of Tull's position (in music) might be to portray the manner in which they create as a philosophy of change, a sort of Rock Darwinism that dictates, not follows, the imperative of musical and lyrical evolution." *Huh? And he said that was a simplistic description!* More revealing and to the point was Ian's own songwriting methods: "I'd rather look around me - compose a better song, 'cause that's the honest measure of my worth." *That's more like it!* In Italy, Chrysalis thought of a better way to trumpet "Bursting Out" by coming up with a promotional 12" single containing "Skating Away On The Thin Ice Of The New Day," "Jack-In-The-Green," "Locomotive Breath" and "The Dambusters March"/"Medley."

"THE WATER'S EDGE" AND "STORMWATCH"

Ian Anderson had reason to celebrate again with the birth of his daughter Gael in the last week of December 1978. While recording "Heavy Horses" in the winter of 1977, Ian's brother Robin approached him with a commission to come up with some music for the ballet's tenth anniversary. At the time, Robin was the general administrator for The Scottish Ballet, and he was looking for a piece to coincide with the opening of the ballet's new theater, studio and administrative offices in Glasgow in the fall of 1978. The original gameplan was to present Ian Anderson's work at that Glasgow theater in November, running from the 5th to the 7th and from the 12th to the 14th. With Jethro Tull on the road for this period, and not enough time to put anything together, Ian's writing of the work was put on the back burner until he returned from the US.

The Scottish Ballet put together a show idea called "Underground Rumours" that would consist of three parts with intermissions between each part. The first two parts would be written by rock musicians and then Duke Ellington's "Such Sweet Thunder" would

108

An article on the musical preparations for Ian Anderson and David Palmer's "The Water's Edge." Part of the original ballet program is shown below. Note that Martin Barre is credited for the music as well.

Ian Anderson of "Jethro Tull" with choreographer Robert North working on a number for the new production "Underground Rumours".

Ballet goes Rock!
by George Welsh

"A NEW rock adventure." That's the description for BALLET going rock! And it's going to be one of the most sensational rock happenings in Scotland this year.

For real ballet stars will be able to do more startling stuff than even Travolta can manage! And the company is Scottish Ballet, who have their twirling toes on the ground in knowing what the young want.

Imagine Elvis, Liberace and Marilyn Monroe dancing rock ballet! Well, this is it! A triple bill — with music by Jethro Tull, Jon Anderson of the Yes group and Duke Ellington — will star great names of the Fifties, with dancers in their sensational sequinned gear. They're even attempting Bette Davis in "Baby Jane" 'rig'.

Sensation

"Underground Rumours" is the umbrella name for the three rock events which Scottish Ballet are producing on one bill — as part of their 10th anniversary programme. They're designed to lure (and stun!) young audiences.

The rock sensation will open in Glasgow's Theatre Royal from March 7-24 and hit the King's, Edinburgh between April 3 and 14.

They'll move to Aberdeen (His Majesty's) and Inverness (Eden Court) in May.

Artistry

So congrats to this lively young company for trying to cover a fair swatch of Scotland. They'll also be touring some superb traditional ballets — including "Tales of Hoffman," "Napoli" and "Giselle."

Forget prejudices about ballet being stuck-up and snobbish Scottish Ballet loathe the "sacred" atmosphere which puts young people off.

They have a cheery, very mixed audience and I highly recommend youth organisations to think of booking an evening at the Ballet.

Many seats for a night of LIVE glamour, glitter and artistry cost the same — or less — than that of canned entertainment. And surely such Scottish enterprise deserves support!

For details, write to Scottish Ballet, 261 West Princes Street, Glasgow (041-331 2931) or contact the theatres I've mentioned.

UNDERGROUND RUMOURS

Royal Court Theatre Liverpool

UNSPRUNG (The Source)
Music: Jon Anderson of YES, arranged by Terry Davies
Choreography: Royston Maldoom
Design: Graham Bowers
Lighting: David Hersey

THE SOURCE
PREPARATION
CONSUMMATION
RITUAL

Noriko Ohara (20th)	Robert Ryan
Linda Packer (21st)	Veronica Butcher
Linda Packer (21st mat)	Paulene Laverty
Andrea Durant (21st eve)	Alison O'Neal
Nigel Spencer (20th)	Christopher Long
Vincent Hantam (21st mat)	Anna McCartney
Paul Russell (21st eve)	Ruth Prior
with	Christopher Gillard
Kenneth Burke (20th & 21st mat)	Kenneth Saunders
Vincent Hantam (21st eve)	Linden Currey
Linda Anning	Judy Mohekey
Catherine Evers	Wendy Roe
Eleanor Moore	Garry Trinder
Michael Harper	Paul Tyers
Fiona Dear	Seonaid Macleod
Elizabeth Peden	Ann Sholem
Roy Campbell-Moore	Peter Royston
	Patrick Wood

Stage Manager:
Bill Hammond

Chief Electrician:
Ronnie Anderson

Programme
Subject to Alteration

— INTERVAL —

THE WATER'S EDGE
Music: Ian Anderson, David Palmer & Martin Barre of JETHRO TULL
Choreography: Robert North
Design: Peter Farmer
Lighting: David Hersey

This is a ballet about the sea, its moods, and the Scottish myths and legends that surround it. Three stories appear in the ballet, the Water Horse or Kelpie who rides off with young virgins into the waves; the Selkies, seals that become humans by shedding their skins at night and then dance and weave strange patterns on the shore, and the Mermaids, daughters of the "Fin Folk", half fish, half women, known for their siren songs and their unearthly beauty.

	20th & 21st (eve)	21st (mat)
Young Boy	Kenneth Burke	Leslie Morrison
Narrator	Gordon Aitken	Gordon Aitken
Mary Mackenzie	Elaine McDonald	Sally Collard-Gentle
Water Horse	Paul Russell	Vincent Hantam
Waves, Selkies,	Andrea Durant	Eleanor Moore
Mermaids & Humans	Noriko Ohara	Alison O'Neal
	Wendy Roe	Paulene Laverty
	Anna McCartney	Fiona Dear
	Alison O'Neal	Judy Mohekey
	Elizabeth Peden	Linda Packer
	Linden Currey	Ann Sholem
	Nigel Spencer	Roy Campbell-Moore
	Paul Tyres	Christopher Gillard
	Robert Ryan	Peter Royston
	Christopher Long	Michael Harper
	Patrick Wood	William Bowen

— INTERVAL —

SUCH SWEET THUNDER
Music: Duke Ellington, arranged by Paul Hart
Choreography: Busby Berkeley, assisted by Peter Darrell
Gowns: Adrian, assisted by Bob Ringwood
Lighting: Stanley McCandless, recreated by David Hersey

Featuring in order of appearance: —

		(Understudies)
Othello	Sydney Poitier	Paul Russell
Desdemona	Bette Davis	Gwendoline Edmonds
Caesar	Telly Savalas	Kenneth Saunders
Chorus	James Cagney	Kenneth Burke
		(Peter Royston 21st mat)
	Gene Kelly	Michael Harper
	Donald O'Connor	Jonathan Williams
Hank Cinq	Fred Astaire	Michael Hurren
Lady Macbeth	Fred Perry	Robert Ryan
	Rita Hayworth	Elaine McDonald
		(Judy Mohekey 21st mat)
Iago	Lon Chaney Jnr.	Nigel Spencer
		(Patrick Wood 21st mat)
1st Witch	Norma Shearer	Eleanor Moore
		(Ruth Prior 21st mat)
2nd Witch	Norma Shearer	Linda Anning
3rd Witch	Norma Shearer	Jeanette Newell 21st mat)
		Wendy Roe
		(Catherine Everes 21st mat)
Demetrius	Dan Dailey	Garry Trinder
Helena	Cyd Charisse	Paulene Laverty
Lysander	Danny Kaye	Christopher Long
Hermia	Anne Miller	Seonaid Macleod
Oberon	Liberace	Paul Tyers
Titania	Marilyn Munroe	Sally Collard-Gentle
Puck	Mickey Rooney	Vincent Hantam
Bottom	Norman Wisdom	Gordon Aitken
Kate	Doris Day	Noriko Ohara
Petruchio	John Wayne	Kit Lethby
Romeo	Marlon Brando	Christopher Gillard
		(Roy Campbell-Moore 21st mat)
Juliet	Natalie Wood	Fiona Dear
		(Linda Packer 21st mat)
Hamlet	Elvis Presely	Peter Mallek
Ophelia	Jean Harlow	Andrea Dúrant
Polonius	Edward Arnold	William Bowen
Gertrude	Marlene Dietrich	Linda Currey
Cleopatra	Claudette Colbert	Patricia Merrin
		(Veronica Butcher 21st mat)

Conductor: Bramwell Tovey (Brian Fieldhouse 21st eve)

These ballets under the title UNDERGROUND RUMOURS received their first performance at the Theatre Royal, Glasgow on 7th March, 1979.

UNDERGROUND RUMOURS has been recorded in Benesh Movement Notation by Diana Curry.

David Hersey is a member of the National Theatre Company.

be used to kickoff a tacky Hollywood-style revue with characterizations of Hollywood stars spanning from the 1930s to the present. Purely by coincidence, Ian Anderson, and the unrelated Jon Anderson of Yes, were chosen to provide the music for the first two segments of the show.

Olias Of Sunhillow, aka Jon Anderson, came up with something similar to his contributions to the somewhat overblown Yes 2LP set "Tales From Topographic Oceans." Jon's music was called "Unsprung (The Source)" and it was arranged by Terry Davies. It consisted of four parts, entitled "The Source," "Preparation," "Consummation" and "Ritual." After a well-deserved intermission, it was Ian Anderson's turn.

To create his contribution to the ballet, Ian called in David Palmer to tap his classical experience and orchestration skills. Martin Barre assisted to a much lesser degree. Along with ballet choreographer Robert North, David Palmer developed balletic sequences using Ian's musical sketches. Immediately, problems arose. Anderson and Palmer thought they would be working with a full orchestra, but the theater was too small. This necessitated the use of Palmer's rehearsal score that was originally written for piano. Rehearsal time was minimal (half a day at best), and Ian Anderson was unhappy with the way the musicians fumbled through the timing changes in his music. The work was called "The Water's Edge," and it was finally slated for its Theatre Royal premiere in Glasgow on March 7, 1979. It ran at the theater until the 24th.

The lack of rehearsal time revealed itself at the premiere of "The Water's Edge." It was a complete disaster. Compounding the disaster was a playbill that did not give Palmer credit for the vast amount of time he spent working on it, and Barre's name was barely noticeable. No amount of apologizing from Ian to David and Martin could change things - the ballet was an embarrassment.

If you're still interested in what "The Water's Edge" was about and who else was responsible for its failure, read on! Equally to blame for the ballet's failure was choreographer Robert North, designer Peter Farmer, and light man David Hersey. Ian's intent of "The Water's Edge" was to present three stories concerning Scottish sea myths and legends. The first involved Kelpies (water horses) that run off with young virgins into the waves of the sea. Selkies, seals that become humans at night by shedding their skins to dance on the shore, were dealt with in the second saga. The beauty and song of half women/half fish mermaids were featured in Ian's final tale. On four occasions, the piece known as "The Surface" was played during the performance, and it was surrounded by "Mary's Song," "Kelpie," "Selkies," "Siren Song," "Beneath The Surface" and the concluding segment entitled "The Storm." It is interesting to note that "Siren Song" was later retitled "Elegy" when it was recorded for the "Stormwatch" album, and "Kelpie" would be an outtake from that album session.

Despite the embarrassment "The Water's Edge" brought to its composers (credited or not), more performances of the complete "Underground Rumours" program were presented at the King's Theatre in Edinburgh (April 3-14), His Majesty's in Aberdeen and Eden Court in Inverness in May. If this was not enough, the program then went on to the Royal Court Theatre, Liverpool (May 20-21), Sadlers Wells and its only London performance with piano-only accompaniment. None of the shows were professionally recorded, but at least one audience recording exists. The original Scottish Ballet director later became the musical director of the Winnipeg Symphony Orchestra, and in 1993, he tried to revive "The Water's Edge" by asking David Palmer to provide a full orchestration of "The Water's Edge" in order for that orchestra to record and perform it live. Palmer's full calendar never honored that director's wishes.

In an attempt to put the failure of "The Water's Edge" aside, Ian Anderson wrote more songs for the next album "Stormwatch" prior to the band's one-month US tour between the firsts of April and May 1979. The band convened with the returning John Glascock to rehearse for their upcoming US tour and to do some recording. Glascock had put on some weight during his recovery and was now ready for action. The most popular show from this short tour was at Seattle Coliseum on April 10, bootlegged as "Dark Haiti" because the person taping the show wasn't familiar with the still-unreleased song "Dark Ages" to make out the title properly! "Dark Ages" was the first preview of the next album they had yet to record. The tour ended at the San Antonio Convention Center on May 1, and it turned out to be the final live date John Glascock played with the band - exactly three years after his first Jethro Tull gig. John was starting to experience circulation problems from his surgery that caused numbness in his fingers.

After returning to England, Jethro Tull started work on their "Stormwatch" album at Maison Rouge Studios and their mobile studio. Again, the band was credited for song arrangement. When not recording this album, Barlow, Palmer and Glascock assisted

British DJ Richard Digance on his "Commercial Road" album and all three with John Evans started work on an Evans/Palmer album under the group name Tallis. Digance's LP was finished first, but it was not released until after "Stormwatch." As the sessions progressed, it became very clear that John Glascock's heart condition was becoming progressively worse. After completing three tracks that ended up on "Stormwatch" and two that did not, Glascock had to bow out of the group. Ian persuaded Jeffrey Hammond-Hammond to come to a rehearsal, but Jeffrey had no interest in taking his old job back. Ian Anderson took it upon himself to record all of Glascock's intended bass lines to complete the album. It is interesting to note that Anderson used the same bass model that Glascock used (a Fender Precision) in order to approximate John's intended contributions to the LP.

Spirits were not flying high with the band, and the downright cynical, ecological nature of the songs themselves cast an additional air of doom around the project. "Stormwatch" completed Ian's trilogy of albums based on folk traditions. Ian was reading more and keeping with current events, ecological and otherwise. David Jackson's polar bear on the rear album cover painting was shown co-existing in a nuclear environment with the possibility of outliving it. This theme was borne out in the song "North Sea Oil," in which the then-current oil shortages and reports of world temperature increases potentially threatened the world environment.

Another song based on destruction was the classic "Dun Ringill." What was "Dun Ringill"? Ian reveals: "That's a real place. I can't give you the exact locations for obvious reasons. It's a place on my Scottish estate where I occasionally go; I have a salmon farm and a sheep farm. It's an old hillport about a thousand years old that was built by the primitive inhabitants of the area. It withheld the Nortin invasion - the Vikings - when they invaded the west coast of Scotland. It's like a giant stone dome, really, perched on the edge of a cliff overlooking the sea. Because of its vantage point, it forms a backdrop of snow-covered mountains. It's a very dramatic place in terms of the weather. Whenever I have a chance to go and sit there I do; it's kind of conjured up images that I have tried to put into that song."

A little more background on this Isle of Skye seaside broch (fortress): The chiefs of the MacKinnon clan in Scotland had their seat at Dunringill Castle in the 13th Century. Battles over control of land between clan chiefdoms led to numerous destructions of duns (fortifications). During the Iron Age, Dun Ringill was still offering defensive protection. However, clan chiefs were forced to operate as businessmen in respect of their lands without any ties to their clans. High rents and poor harvests led to the destruction of these duns, leading to mass emigration. By 1808, the Mackinnons were forced to part with their remaining lands. Today, very little of Dun Ringill remains.

Now that we have the setting of "Dun Ringill," what about the song? Quite possibly Ian Anderson's most mesmerizing acoustic song, "Dun Ringill"'s profile has increased tremendously since its release. The reason why the song works in this fashion is the use of cyclical chord changes in 6/8 time before moving to a different chord sequence in 3/4 time during its chorus. This circular effect and backward vocal echo attract the listener immediately. The stone circles that Ian mentions in the song would be revisited on the album "Divinities: Twelve Dances With God" in 1995. Thames TV weatherman Francis Wilson contributed a spoken introduction on the recording to complete the picture.

Sea themes from "The Water's Edge" proved more appropriate for "Stormwatch" than the ballet for which they were originally written. David Palmer's "Elegy" from that ballet was a stunningly beautiful piece with instrumental overtones, and Ian used a solid silver flute to produce the song's lovely melody. "Elegy" was the first complete Tull song since "Bourée" that was not written by Ian Anderson. Along with "Orion" and "Flying Dutchman," "Elegy" was one of the three tracks that John Glascock completed for the LP. The fact that Glascock played on "Elegy," a song for the dead, is purely a coincidence and not open to conjecture. "Flying Dutchman" was inspired by the sea saga in which the title character was doomed to sail the sea for eternity. Another sea-influenced track was "Kelpie," one of the characters in "The Water's Edge." This track featuring John Glascock was first mixed and released in 1988. Palmer was not involved with "Kelpie," but its instrumentation was complete with Ian's flute, whistle and mandolin and John Evans on accordian and keyboards. The other unreleased "Stormwatch" session track with Glascock, but without Palmer, was "Crossword," another 1988 debut release. Glascock was still able to play acoustic guitar and he and Barlow started to work on new songs they collaborated on.

With "Stormwatch," Jethro Tull experienced its last taste of real success for a while, as the album earned the band its last US gold record award for almost a decade. It hit #22 in the US and #27 in England. "Stormwatch" contained many strong and often-played tracks like "Orion" and "Something's On The Move." In England, emphasis was placed on the single "North Sea Oil." As a

A bit of the old and the new: at left is the lineup with David Palmer, Ian Anderson, Barriemore Barlow, Martin Barre, John Glascock and John Evans. At right is David Palmer, Martin Barre, Barriemore Barlow, Ian Anderson, Dave Pegg (Glascock's replacement) and John Evans.

Above: The "Home" EP. The character on the cover looks more like Rod Stewart than Ian Anderson!
Below: The unusual German single for "Warm Sporran."

Dave Pegg

Ian Anderson appeared on the November 11, 1979 edition of comedian Robert Klein's radio program "The Robert Klein Hour." Shown above are Ian Anderson, Robert Klein and Annie Golden of the group The Shirts. (Photo courtesy of Dennis Landau)

Below is the album "Stormwatch" and two of its singles: the US issue of "Home" and the Spanish release of "North Sea Oil."

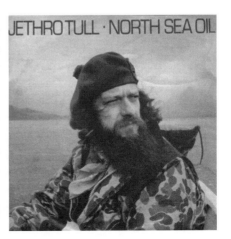

single choice in England, Australia and Spain, "North Sea Oil" b/w "Elegy" was an uncommercial prospect and the record disappeared almost immediately. In France, the flipside was "Something's On The Move." A highly unusual German single from "Stormwatch" featured the album's two instrumentals: "Warm Sporran" b/w "Elegy." Interestingly, the inclusion of two instrumental tracks on "Stormwatch" was its similarity with Tull's first album "This Was." To initially garner attention to the album, Chrysalis in the US issued a promotional 12" single with "Dark Ages" on both sides. "Dark Ages" and "Flying Dutchman," the other long song on the album, were the last vestiges of a song format clearly out of fashion with a record buying public eager for more immediate songs.

Replacing John Glascock was a job that had to be done, as Ian was on the lookout for a suitable replacement for their US tour in October and November 1979. Ian Anderson was considering a Berklee Music School-type from Boston with a funk background, but Barriemore Barlow was not in agreement with Ian's choice at all. Barlow felt a special affinity with Glascock and loved him like a brother. Out of respect for John, Barlow felt that Ian's candidate would not be the kind of player that would properly replace Glascock. After completing the Richard Digance album, Barriemore Barlow and Digance were watching a television broadcast of a July 1979 Fairport Convention farewell concert. Digance recommended that Barlow contact Fairport's bassist Dave Pegg. Afterward, Barlow saw Pegg playing with Richard Thompson in Reading, England. Barlow decided to notify Ian Anderson of Pegg's apparent availability. With Barlow's assistance, Dave Pegg auditioned and got the position in September.

Ian would soon confirm Glascock's departure from the band: "Yes, he has left. After the recurrence of his illness - that's when he left - I had to play the bass on many of the tracks. Later on it became more difficult for John physically to play. After his operation last year, he was really unable to adjust to the kind of life that was necessary for him to lead. We had to say goodbye to John for his own good. It was purely an inherited heart disease which has run in his family. It was a very sad and difficult decision for him and the band. It's better that he got himself out of the rock business, at least until he is able to get himself physically good as possible so that he could slip into music on a different level." Ian Anderson then called Dave Pegg "the new permanent bassist." Pegg provided the backbone and humor that the band needed to make it through this unfortunate period.

DAVE PEGG

Dave Pegg was born November 2, 1947 in Birmingham, England. Pegg's grandfather played banjo and his father was a vocalist. While in school, he started playing guitar in local Birmingham bands. Two of the drummers he ran into were John Bonham (later in Led Zeppelin) and journeyman Cozy Powell. After taking a year off to work in an insurance agency, Dave became the lead guitarist in Roy Everett's Blueshounds. Pegg switched over to bass when he joined The Uglys and then moved over to playing folk with The Ian Campbell Folk Group for a year and a half. In that group, Dave Pegg developed skills on double bass and mandolin. In late 1969, Pegg joined Fairport Convention. The Fairports issued many highly regarded albums until their first breakup in 1979 and Pegg has done numerous sessions over the years. When Ian Anderson called, Dave Pegg did not return Ian's messages because he thought the caller was Folk Roots magazine Ian A. Anderson, who traded on Ian's name after he felt that the Ian Anderson in Jethro Tull caused Island Records to drop his contract! (Fairport Convention and Ian A. Anderson were both recording for Island at the time, but the other Anderson did not have any Island-released product.) Ian Anderson's persistence and final convincing of Pegg that he was the "correct" Ian Anderson took place in July 1979 while Dave was finishing up the final Fairport gigs. Pegg was then chosen for the upcoming US fall tour.

Dave Pegg was indoctrinated in the studio, recording the theme for the new BBC arts program "Mainstream." Ian Anderson was deluged with offers to write film music, but this was the only job he took because he didn't have to write it! The recording was called "King Henry's Madrigal," another outside song with a long history.

The original title of "King Henry's Madrigal" was in fact "Pastime With Good Company" and was one of 34 pieces attributed to King Henry VIII (1491-1547). Henry Tudor's Chapel Royal consisted of 79 musicians, and Henry took along some of them when he traveled. King Henry was a musician himself who appreciated fine playing. Henry's court was constantly filled with music, and many of the published pieces from his court were attributed to him to satisfy his enormous ego! The songs from the king's court date between 1509 and 1520, including the one originally known as "Pastyme With Good Companye." It is listed in the British Library's manuscript Add. MS 5665 under this title and as "The Kynges Balade." While no specific instrumentation for the song was listed in the manuscript, it has been performed in recent times by four or five-piece ensembles. As for the King Henry writing credit, the song was derived from an Italian chord progression used in madrigals. Madrigals were Renaissance melodies usually set to love poems and written for *a cappella* (vocal only) performance. Each line in a madrigal used a different melody instead of a single tune with instrumental accompaniment. The melody of "Pastyme With Good Companye" was already internationally known at the time of King Henry's use of it to form "his" own song. In the hands of Jethro Tull, this madrigal was rearranged by David Palmer as an instrumental, and was produced by Ian Anderson and Robin Black at Maison Rouge Studio. Subsequent live versions were accompanied by David Palmer's spoken introduction and mention of its original title.

"King Henry's Madrigal" was the exclusive track on the UK-only "Home" EP. The record turned out to be one of the band's most obscure records, as it was available for just a couple of weeks. On the cover, Ian Anderson is sitting down with his feet up on a table, looking more like Rod Stewart than himself! Picking up on this EP, "Home" was released as a regular, two-track single (without "King Henry's Madrigal" and the previously released "Ring Out, Solstice Bells") in the US. The other track was "Warm Sporran" from "Stormwatch." Fans were later able to obtain "King Henry's Madrigal" on the much more accessible 1988 box set.

The supporting act on the fall 1979 US tour, Pegg's first with Tull, was U.K. That band originally included former Yes drummer Bill Bruford, bass player John Wetton, guitarist Allan Holdsworth and Eddie Jobson, former keyboardist/violinist for Curved Air, Roxy Music and Frank Zappa. The revised U.K. lineup was without Holdsworth, and former Zappa drummer Terry Bozzio replaced Bruford. In fact, Bozzio and Jobson were in Zappa's band at the same time, although Jobson's stay was much shorter. On stage, Jethro Tull's stage props were ship riggings, and the band unusually started out with five or six songs from their new album before hitting their more familiar material. The problem was that the fan favorites were nonchalantly played, and the newer songs slowed down the pace of the set. With fewer fans interested in their newer material, incorporating fresh songs into their set has been a problem for Tull ever since. John Evans put on a bear costume during "Something's On The Move," emulating the polar bear on "Stormwatch"'s back cover. A large stuffed seagull was brought on stage to demonstrate the ecological effects described in "North Sea Oil." Dave Pegg introduced a jig that Tull never recorded - "Peggy's Pub." "The Dambusters March" marked the balloon phase of the show, which was concluded by Ian shooting confetti into the audience from a cannon. Ian was very appreciative of his fans, although he realized that he had to maintain their interest: "The bottom-line is that people don't sort of like Jethro Tull and nothing else, they might be into Jethro Tull, Frank Zappa or many others. You kind of share your fans with a number of other bands." *Who said Ian Anderson and Frank Zappa don't have anything in common?*

THE DEATH OF JOHN GLASCOCK

Things were a little different when Jethro Tull appeared at Madison Square Garden that October 12. An overzealous fan poked Ian Anderson in the eye with a rose, forcing Ian to cancel two shows and to wear an eye patch at other gigs. Of course, Ian would work his new pirate look into the act! A UNICEF benefit concert at Santa Monica Civic Auditorium sponsored by KMET-FM took place on November 16 with the venue only 75% filled. It was the first inkling that the band was not as popular as they once were. Earlier that day, Barriemore Barlow contacted John Glascock with plans to start another group with David Allen of Carmen and artist Robin Hill once Tull finished their tour on the 18th. Glascock was so interested that he immediately made plane reservations. The plans were not to be, as John Glascock died on November 17, 1979, the day after Barlow called. Glascock had been to a party, and he died in his London bed after he came home. John's body had rejected his new heart valve, and his death was a complete surprise to everyone. He was only 28. As Brian Glascock tells it, "I was in Boston on tour with The Motels (*Brian played drums on their first hit "Only The Lonely"*), when I got a call. It was our second to last gig of that tour. I got a call before the gig, and my wife told me that John had passed on. I was just blown away. But I had to go play a show, so we did the show for John that night. I remember Martha (Davis) crying all the way through it, too." John Glascock had visited Brian with The Motels, and John made such an impression on the band that they dedicated their second album "Careful" to him.

At the time of Glascock's passing, it was also the second to last night of Jethro Tull's US tour. Tull had played very poorly at their San Diego Sports Arena gig that night. However, the band was not told about this tragedy until the next day. Brian Glascock continues about John: "Well, I've met many people over the years who knew him and I don't know anybody who didn't really like him. He was a very spiritual person. It was in his nature. He loved all kinds of people, and he didn't care what class they came from or what they did for a living. John loved to party and have a good time, sing songs, have a drink, fool around, whatever. That was a thing with John; he'd always hang with the roadies, he thought they were more fun (than the musicians)."

John Glascock's death hit Barriemore Barlow very hard, and he had great difficulty in dealing with it for months. With only one more show left on the US tour, Barlow was forced by Chrysalis management to fulfill his playing obligation at Oakland Coliseum. Barlow cried throughout the entire performance. The death of John Glascock created a major chasm between the relationship of Barlow and Ian Anderson - one which has only gotten wider as time passes by. Barlow's immediate reaction was to blame Ian Anderson for his poor treatment of Glascock while he was in the band. To the present day, Barriemore's bitterness remains so strong that he immediately withdrew his biography from the official Jethro Tull website within a week of its online availability.

The sticky issue of how Barlow and Anderson perceived John Glascock is necessary to be discussed at this point. Ian has usually avoided speaking about John in public, but he delivered a response to Martha Klassanos, writer of a series of excellent pieces on Glascock in Living In The Past magazine. Anderson claimed that while in Glascock's presence, he went to the fullest extent to dissuade John from endangering his health by smoking, drinking, etc. after his heart surgery. Sometimes his words to John had to be harsh, and Barlow took exception to this. Jethro Tull was the seventh and last band that Glascock played with, and any of his previous bandmates could have told John about changing his ways. Ian Anderson was simply in the unfortunate position of being the leader of the last band that Glascock interacted with, and Barlow's criticism of Ian is completely unfair when the situation is viewed in this perspective. In fact, Ian's honest concern for John was described in great detail by Brian Glascock: "John never said a bad thing about Ian to me; in fact he was very grateful to Ian for giving him a break. He would tell me how he thought Ian was a wonderful songwriter and a really great showman. As soon as John got sick, Ian paid for me to go to England, and Ian was there at the funeral. He came by himself, and for someone to do that, he's got to care. There was no press there, it was just family and friends. Ian stood off by himself. He seems like a very solitary and lonely person, but that's how he does his work. Still, for him to stand through the whole thing and be sad, I can't say anything bad about that." Adding more fuel to the fire between himself and Barlow, Ian Anderson said in the press that Barriemore was not an instinctive drummer and that he played and acted his best while Ian was playing bass on "Stormwatch."

As for John Glascock's death itself, how could a abscessed tooth cause a heart infection? It can if you are born with a less than perfect heart. During his time in Jethro Tull (1975-1979), the link between dental infections and heart ailments had been correlated. Yet, many dentists still refuse to acknowledge the connection. However, a growing number of cardiologists have studied how these infections cause irreversable and deadly damage upon already imperfect heart tissue. *I should know - I was born with a mitral valve prolapse, in which one of my heart valves occasionally slips (or prolapses) from its usual position and normal blood flow is temporarily interrupted to the heart. The result of this is an irregular heartbeat that comes without warning. My cardiologist instructed me to be pre-medicated with an antibiotic in the penicillin family to prevent a heart infection caused by swallowing bacteria that a dentist would loosen or scrape out of my mouth.* How does this relate to John Glascock's condition? An untreated dental problem, such as an abscess or infection, can cause either pericarditis (inflammation of the membrane enclosing the heart) or endocarditis (inflammation of the lining of the heart and its valves). Since Glascock had a valve weakness, he was in all likelihood suffering from endocarditis. Unfortunately, preparing a patient with *family* heart trouble in advance for dental procedures was not widely practiced during the '70s. Therefore, John Glascock was unable to receive the benefits of antibiotics that was later practiced by dentists. To sum things up, Brian Glascock gives his final thoughts on John: "I still miss him a lot. You never lose the pain, but after time, it gets to be tolerable. But on another level, he's around, absolutely. He definitely believed in life after death. To me, it's not logical otherwise, and I know John felt the same way." John did not ever marry or have children.

Barriemore Barlow's still-unnamed group now included keyboardist Tommy Ayres and Chris Glen on bass, replacing John Glascock. Barlow was required to do another tour with Tull, after which Ian claimed he was taking some time off to devote to his salmon farming. Having made an arrangement with Anderson to rehearse his group in Shepperton for six hours after Jethro Tull's own rehearsal (from 10AM to 6PM), Barriemore found a way to prepare for his future.

On to the '80s! The decade started off nastily with BBC2's January 11 broadcast of a one-hour "Stormwatch" road documentary on the program "Arena." Cracks were clearly showing within the band. John Evans was completely drunk and David Palmer simply stated that Ian Anderson could make any other group of musicians sound like Jethro Tull. Later on, it was revealed that Evans had been experiencing psychological depression since about 1976. The one-month European tour started in mid-March in Drammen, Norway and concluded with five Hammersmith Odeon sellouts in April 1980. The German TV program "Ohne Malkorb" caught the band in Munich on April 1. In London, Jethro Tull performed "North Sea Oil" and "Old Ghosts" on the "Rockpop" television show. The tour festivities were concluded with a live acoustic set on Capital Radio in London. Tull did the program to thank weekly host Richard Digance and to gain exposure from the city's new radio force. Thames weatherman Francis Wilson did the vocal honors again on "Dun Ringill," and "Peggy's Pub" was aired again.

More than ever, the current lineup of Jethro Tull was becoming an anachronism. The band was not making any concessions to current trends and sales were already on a steep decline. This seemed to be the perfect time for the Ian Anderson solo album that everyone was expecting him to record. Chrysalis Records asked Ian if he would be interested in re-recording his acoustic pieces from prior Jethro Tull albums. Ian was able to convince the record company that recording a proper solo album would be the best way to proceed, since fans always wanted to experience Ian's intimate songs in a completely solo setting.

Ian was already hinting at a solo album in an October 1979 Cleveland, OH newspaper interview: "Well, it's something that I suppose has been in the cards for a long time, but I never seem to get the time to do it because my main priority and main *enjoyment*, I suppose, is playing with Jethro Tull. I wouldn't want to make a solo album at the expense of the other people in the group, as a whole. I don't think that it would be fair of me to the other people if I were to shut them out for the sake of doing something that would be rewarding for me artistically and/or financially, and would lessen their chances of paying the rent! If the time presents itself to me one of these years - if I have a couple of months when I'm not touring, recording, farming or whatever - and I have the time to make an album, I *would* like to do it. But it's not a priority in my life. Who knows? It might be next year." It *was* the next year!

Explaining his desire for continually producing music, Ian told the St. Louis Post-Dispatch: "I've grown older and more sophisticated. It gets harder and harder to do something different and yet maintain that special energy. I have the wisdom and experience to tailor my performances to my advancing years."

That wisdom and experience were called into question when Ian Anderson prepared the next project in the spring of 1980. The original intention of the upcoming album was to record Ian and a different set of musicians unrelated to Jethro Tull. Dave Pegg had only recorded two songs as a member of Tull, so Anderson thought his participation here would not be considered as a Tull album project. Eddie Jobson, from Jethro's 1978 support group U.K., accepted Ian's invitation to play keyboards. Anderson approached former Frank Zappa and U.K. drummer Terry Bozzio to act as Barlow's replacement, but Bozzio turned Ian's offer down. American session drummer Mark Craney had worked with Jobson, and Eddie recommended Craney as a potential drum candidate for this recording project. Locating a guitarist proved to be difficult. Anderson started out by asking Martin Barre if he could play on a small number of songs. To everyone's surprise, they gelled as a unit and quickly dashed off seven or eight tracks in a couple of weeks, instead of the two or three songs Ian was planning within that same period. With such a headstart on an album, Anderson came up with additional material to complete the endeavor. After listening to the playbacks, Terry Ellis of Chrysalis started to put pressure on Anderson to call it a Jethro Tull album because of its group dynamics and the overriding fact that Martin Barre participated. Ellis felt that an Ian Anderson solo album would be just Ian and his acoustic guitar. Ian Anderson went along with Chrysalis, although the ramifications of calling this unit Jethro Tull would create tremendous friction between Ian and the group participants from "Stormwatch." This effort became the album "A." In recent years, Ian has openly questioned his agreement to Chrysalis' wishes, as this was additional proof that Jethro Tull *was* Ian Anderson.

EDDIE JOBSON, MARK CRANEY AND THE "A" FALLOUT

Edwin Jobson was born in Billingham, Cleveland, England on April 28, 1955. He started his piano lessons at seven and also studied violin the next year. Immersing himself in classical music, Jobson played with some of the best northern England orchestras until he co-founded his first band in 1971. As a 17 year old, Eddie joined Curved Air and then moved on to Roxy Music. After appearing on five Roxy Music albums in three years, Eddie met (and sat in with) Frank Zappa in Milwaukee, WI during a Roxy US tour in May 1974. Jobson played with one of the earliest versions of Ritchie Blackmore's Rainbow, and he did a couple of Canadian dates with Zappa in December 1975. Roxy Music also opened up for Tull during the mid-'70s. The breakup of Roxy Music led Jobson to move to L.A. and then to join Frank Zappa's band in 1976. In 1978, he formed U.K. with Bill Bruford, John Wetton and Allan Holdsworth. As mentioned earlier, Terry Bozzio came in to replace Bill Bruford for the U.K. lineup that supported Jethro Tull throughout 1979. In addition to bass, John Wetton assumed the guitar duties of the departed Holdsworth. Even in the "A" tour book, Eddie Jobson was listed as a guest of Jethro Tull, in that he had planned to form his own band in April 1981! He was credited for additional musical material on the "A" album along with the band's usual arrangement credit.

Mark Craney came into this world in Sioux Falls, South Dakota on August 15, 1952. He has the distinction of being the first American member of Jethro Tull. He was influenced by Ginger Baker of Cream. Mark's playing breakthrough came when he played on violinist Jean-Luc Ponty's "Imaginary Voyage" LP. He then moved on to Tommy Bolin in 1976, then The Mark-Almond Band, Gino Vannelli and dozens of others. Craney recorded with Eddie Jobson, and developed an excellent working relationship with Jobson that encompassed other recording sessions in L.A.

The album was called "A" because the tape boxes were labelled as such - "A" for Anderson, and not for the symbol of anarchy. Rather, "A" was a warning against such anarchical displays. Like "Stormwatch," "A" revolved around current events with real-life consequences. Anderson would read an interesting topic in his morning paper, write a song based upon it and present it for rehearsal that night with his unknowing Tull prototype lineup. The album was miles beyond anything that the previous lineup had constructed in terms of electronics and forward-thinking arrangements. Why this lineup worked so well in the studio was because they shaped Ian's songs creatively and quickly. Ian Anderson's commented about the making of the album: "I didn't enjoy finishing it, mixing it, because I felt very nervous about calling it a Jethro Tull album. The actual recording of it was great."

The recordings were laid down at Maison Rouge Studio and the mobile unit in the early summer of 1980 with Ian and Robin Black co-producing. With their impending release and Chrysalis' wishes to market them as Jethro Tull, some dirty work had to be done. Barriemore Barlow, John Evans and David Palmer were informed that their services were no longer required. The lineup and the changing musical environment necessitated a change in Jethro Tull, but Chrysalis' strong arm dictated essential personnel changes that were further complicated by their poor communication. Barlow had already notified Ian Anderson and Terry Ellis about his own group, but they had misinterpreted Barriemore's absence as a temporary leave.

The crisis came in June 1980. By making their mark on "A," Jobson and Craney were now official Jethro Tull members even if that was not what they had originally set out to do. Barlow, Evans and Palmer would be treated crudely by management, even though they had all served a decade apiece with various Tull incarnations, replaced by two much younger upstarts - one an American, no less. Chrysalis elected to send the three erstwhile members photocopies of a form letter saying that they were out of the band. The label gave the press a variation of the story that removed them from blame: they said Ian Anderson fired all three! Technically, that's what happened, but Chrysalis wanted to exonerate themselves at all costs - even if Ian Anderson looked like the bad guy.

Almost immediately, Terry Ellis told Melody Maker in a July 1980 issue that all three were gone under the front page headline "SACKED!" Ellis proved to be a loose cannon again, and Ian sent apologetic notes to Barlow, Evans and Palmer before the story was published. This note indicated his intention to work on music with different people that may or may not be marketed as Jethro Tull, but it was something that should have been handled verbally at an earlier date.

Another Melody Maker article, entitled "Did Tull Man Jump Or Was He Pushed?," had more inaccurate statements of Ian's "firing" of the three members. Nothing could have been further from the truth. All three had already been working on other projects, not content to wait around for Ian to call. Evans and Palmer had severed their relationship with Jethro Tull before any correspondence came their way. At the time, Barlow did not attach any blame to Ian Anderson. However, since then, this misunderstanding became Barriemore's second wedge between himself and Ian that compounded the issue of John Glascock's treatment. If Glascock had survived, he would certainly have been terminated as well. Barlow reported that he desired to release an album with his group in September 1980, but he had no recording contract. That group was called Tandoori Cassette and included Zal Cleminson (The Sensational Alex Harvey Band, Nazareth), bassist Charlie Tumahai and Ronnie Leahy on keyboards. They broke up in early 1982 after releasing the single "Angel Talk." You may ask: What happened to David Allen - wasn't he supposed to be in this group? Yes, but he selfishly obtained a record contract on his own and left Barlow behind.

Evans and Palmer were recording under the name Tallis. The group was named after Thomas Tallis, a David Palmer composing favorite. Tallis (c.1505-1585) was a Catholic organist and composer from England that wrote choral works that were mainly intended for the Catholic church along with other orchestral and instrumental works. Thomas Tallis' tour de force "Spem In Alium" ("Hope In Others") used counterpoint heavily and required eight choirs of five voices each to perform it! Palmer, Evans, Barlow, John Glascock and keyboardists David Bristow and Bill Worral were among the musicians that played on the Tallis album. Palmer wrote most of the original works and the other tracks were classical treatments. At the time, there was no market for the music that Tallis created and the LP was not issued.

David Bristow left Tallis, but not until he, Palmer and Evans did a show at Palmer's local Clamden Church. The concert featured a Mozart concerto played by John Evans and the performance of two Palmer songs that would have appeared on the Tallis LP: "The Vicar And The Publican" and "The Cathedral." Dave Rees of A New Day magazine has been hounding Palmer for years to release the album on CD, and one of these days it will come out! When it does appear, proceeds will be donated to the Lupus Foundation. John Evans used the proceeds from mistakenly received Tull royalty checks to build himself up financially after his divorce. He spent half a year working on a friend's farm, wasted money on a boat, and then profitably built up a retired friend's office refurbishment company. A girlfriend got him a British Airways kitchen tiling job at Heathrow Airport, and Evans was on his way. Later, Evans entered the transport business, known as Evans Trucking, in England. David Palmer is one of the world's most distinguished arrangers and conductors today, specializing in classically flavored treatments of rock and pop standards. His work (described in his solo section) continues to be fresh and daring.

Ian Anderson made sure Jethro Tull still functioned with the media circus in full gear. The songs on "A" brought Tull into another time period with no idea of where it would lead. Eddie Jobson's synthesizer playing filled up more of the band's sound than anyone was used to. The sound was perceived as futuristic and cold. Not received well unilaterally, "A" was a 180-degree turn from the band's previous direction. Its chart peaks were #25 (UK) and #30 (US). The single derived from "A," "Working John, Working Joe" b/w "Fylingdale Flyer" was completely ignored. In the US, test pressings exist of this single, but no copies made it to retail shops. In Germany, Spain and Australia, the sides of the record were reversed because those countries correctly thought that "Fylingdale Flyer" was the stronger side. For religious radio stations in the US, Ian recorded an interview for the "What's It All About?" program that hardly deals with religion at all!

"A" contained Ian's wide-ranging perceptions of life and threats to its safety. "Crossfire," the most played track on US radio, was constable Trevor Locke's view of the Iranian embassy hostage freeing in London. A false alarm in England's protectionary Early Warning System inspired Ian's song "Fylingdale Flyer." Related to this topic, "Protect And Survive" criticized the UK for not being prepared for a nuclear attack. The words of "Black Sunday" were written before the final tour of the previous lineup and depicted a relationship breaking up. Despite the poor nature of its recording, "Black Sunday" has survived the longest in the band's set. "Working John, Working Joe" was an even older song (dating from about 1977) that dealt with the plight of the union worker. "Uniform" dealt with the societal roles our clothing dictates. Ian's son James appeared on record for the first time on "Batteries Not Included," a child that becomes the battery-operated toy he receives on Christmas. "4.W.D. (Low Ratio)" is clearly about four wheel drive vehicles, but "The Pine Marten's Jig" is an electric treatment of an outdoorsy piece that would not have been out of place on "Songs From The Wood." Ian's personal, musical goodbye on "A" was "And Further On."

The higher-tech "A" tour brought with it some commensurate equipment upgrades. For the first time, Ian Anderson used a radio-frequency microphone and electrified his flute to enable him to venture into the crowd at will. Prior to this tour, Ian had used nearly 20 Artley flutes, but he switched to the sound of a Pearl model for "A." Tull's flight suits (Ian in white, and the others sporting different colors) were not high-tech and flattering at all - especially for the now rotund Martin Barre! The image of himself in this revealing suit got Martin thinking about how to get himself into shape. Running would become his refuge, but it would take about six years for Martin to realize the benefits of his athletic efforts.

The sales failure of "A" did not let the band down, as live concerts had the same explosive impact as they always had, but with a more modern sense of direction. This new direction worked better on the material of more recent vintage, but the old standbys were sloppily presented. The 1982 home video release of "Slipstream" indicated that this was definitely the case, artfully combining recent live performances and videos of past and present studio tracks. The live cuts on "Slipstream" were recorded on November 12, 1980 from the L.A. Sports Arena. Only two London dates were scheduled out of the many "A" shows played. A 50-second taped electronic introduction called "Slipstream Intro" was played at live shows between 1980 and 1981, and was only released on an LP reserved for radio stations: "1982 Promotion Manual." The October 26 gig at the St. Louis Checkerdome became a "King Biscuit Flower Hour" program and included Martin Barre quoting liberally from the classics during his guitar solo. Other shows from this period included the performance of the traditional instrumental "Jams O'Donnell's Jig" along with Dave Pegg's own "Peggy's Pub." They also managed to work The Champs' "Tequila" into an occasional medley with "Aqualung"!

Eddie Jobson's live deficiencies quickly became apparent during this 1980 tour. While a technical wizard on his instruments, he had no personality to contribute to the band's stage act. He felt it necessary to create his own piano introduction to "Locomotive Breath" instead of playing the John Evans segment that fans desired every time.

Photos of Ian Anderson and Martin Barre from Jethro Tull's first show in 1980 in Drammen, Norway.
(Photos © Hans Arne Nakrem)

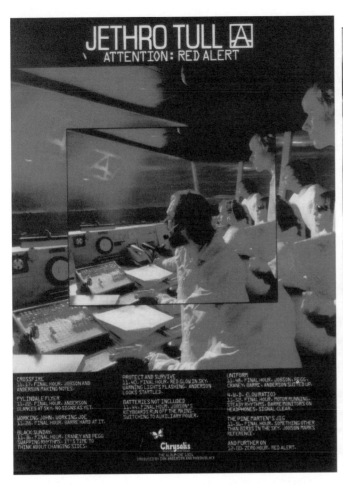

This is the "A" page! At top right is the lineup that recorded the album: Ian Anderson, Eddie Jobson, Mark Craney, Martin Barre and Dave Pegg.

Below is the "A" album in the center, with the "Working John, Working Joe" single and the "What's It All About?" radio interview record for US stations.

As stated earlier, Jobson had his sights on his future plans. During his Tull keyboard solo segment, Jobson took the opportunity to work out material for his upcoming group Zinc's LP "The Green Album" (a 1983 release). Eddie Jobson gave the impression of being in a self-indulgent world of his own, and this did not endear him to fans. As expected, "A" became the only album issued by this line-up, and Eddie Jobson left the band after the tour in February 1981 for a solo career and a brief stop in the group Yes. Mark Craney made a more productive connection with a fellow drummer he met on this tour - the up-and-coming Doane Perry.

Only 22 gigs were on tap in 1981, and they all fell within a 24-day period in February. They did not appear in London, although Tull recorded performances of "Crossfire" and "Fylingdale Flyer" for the "Rockpop" television program. The conclusion of the Palais Des Sports gig in Lyons, France (February 24) would mark the beginning of a fourteen-month group departure from the public eye. The rash personnel changes had not worked as well as their new musical direction. Once again, innovation was looming.

Martin Barre wisely used this time to get seriously involved in running and other outdoor activities like skiing and wind surfing. He would be in better physical shape when the band finally reconvened. In 1980, Barre got into Hamer guitars because he was tired of the same old sounds, as he describes: "I had never played anything but a Gibson. But I could really get the sound I wanted from the Sunburst (by Hamer), and a lot of other sounds too. I've never come to a dead end. It made everything else obsolete." Ian Anderson was also a customer of Paul Hamer's guitar empire and Jethro Tull's sound would make the next evolutionary change.

Record companies in Europe had to do something to keep Tull in the public eye, so they started releasing "best of" collections. Italy put out two volumes, Spain put out a third volume in the series, and countries like France, East Germany, Argentina and Peru had their own single-disc compilations.

Jethro Tull members were not sitting in front of the TV eating chocolates - *perhaps Mick Abrahams was!* Rather, Ian Anderson produced a massive number of songs that were rehearsed and recorded. Twenty seven of the songs recorded in their 14-month "break" period have since been released, and only 12 of these were on the resulting "The Broadsword And The Beast" album! Anderson was familiar with producing albums quickly, but this project would require more effort for a number of reasons.

First of all, Tull replaced drummer Mark Craney with Gerry Conway. Gerry was born in King's Lynn, Norfolk on September 11, 1947. He played drums in various school bands while in London. His parents forbid Gerry from taking a job in The Chico Arnez Orchestra because he was only 13! Conway left school as a 16 year old, worked at EMI and joined a Caribbean band signed to that record label. As everyone did, he played with bluesman Alexis Korner in 1964. Four years later Gerry was in Trevor Lucas' folk/rock band Eclection (where he met Ian Anderson for the first time at Sunbury in 1968) and joined Sandy Denny in Fotheringay. Cat Stevens hired that band's rhythm section for the "Teaser And The Firecat" LP and Conway continued working with Stevens until Cat's retirement in 1978. He had also played with Steeleye Span and other folk-based sessions with Dave Pegg. A miserable late 1980 band stint in L.A. with Gerry Donahue was Conway's saving grace. While in town, Jethro Tull met Conway backstage and he was asked to audition in England after the "A" tour was over in February 1981.

THE BROADSWORD AND THE BEAST"

In 1979, Ian Anderson mentioned to Chrysalis that he wanted an outside producer to work with Jethro Tull. Nothing was done about it at the time, but the extended break in 1981 gave both Anderson and Chrysalis a fresher outlook as to how a producer could maximize the final result of an album project. Ian had already produced nine Jethro Tull tracks on his own, but he was not completely happy with them. These were recorded at Maison Rouge Studio in London, and included "I'm Your Gun," "Down At The End Of Your Road," "Too Many Too," "Mayhem, Maybe," "Overhang," "Commons Brawl," "No Step," "The Curse" and "Lights Out." Of these, "Too Many Too" was the most personal. It was one of the first tracks recorded during this period, and it reflected Ian's dislike of public places and facing people that he did not want to be with. The drum track of "Too Many Too" used a Linn drum machine in combination with Gerry Conway's playing. Anderson's choice of an outside producer for additional recordings proved to be correct when this song was met with audience blahs. Ian played keyboards using four fingers (presumably two from each hand!) on the tracks that required them. None of the tracks from these early sessions were issued at that time. Instead, "Down At The End Of Your Road" was used as the B-side of the 1987 single "Steel Monkey," while that track, "I'm Your Gun" and "Too Many Too" were reserved for the UK 12" release. The 20th anniversary box captured the 1988-mixed "Mayhem, Maybe" (originally known as "3 Day Song") and "Overhang," the former of which included newly recorded vocals, flute and whistles. At the original session, Dave Pegg contributed mandolin, bass mandolin and octavius. "Commons Brawl,""No Step,""The Curse" and "Lights Out" debuted on "Nightcap" in 1993. Two of these songs underwent title changes for their release: "The Curse" was the new name of "Gladys (The Curse)," and the tape of "Commons Brawl" revealed its source as "Folk/Punk/Rock."

After the completion of these tracks, Ian produced another batch of songs. A few producers made the discussion stage, but none went any further. With the new album almost a year behind schedule, Chrysalis brought in an American producer (that no one wants to name!) to assist the band with recording material that was more representative for release on a Jethro Tull album. Two weeks went by and the producer had practically nothing to show for his efforts with the band. Needless to say, the producer was dismissed.

When it became clear that keyboards would continue to play a substantial role in his newest songs, Ian Anderson decided to seek out a modern keyboard contributor with a classical piano background, and more importantly, a _real_ personality! In 1982, Anderson would convey his thoughts for such a player: "I'm particularly interested at the moment in using high-tech instruments to refine the simple acoustic sound that's been consistent in my music. I want to take the sounds of hundreds of years ago and put them into a modern retrieval system where I can use sequencers and every trick in the book to make a keyboard play things nobody but a student of early music could play after spending a lifetime working at it. It's cheating, but if Jethro Tull doesn't do it no one else will." The search for such a classical keyboardist directed Ian Anderson and Martin Barre toward Peter-John Vettese of the Scottish band R.A.F. (Their name stood for Rich And Famous.)

Peter-John Vettese was born on August 15, 1956 in Seafield, Midlothian, Scotland. Vettese started playing piano at four and made his first public appearance five years later with his father's band. Peter-John had his first taste of television when he appeared on "Opportunity Knocks." Vettese joined a dance hall band when he ran away from home as a seventeen year old, but he lost his position when he was caught trying to rehearse his own band during the dance band's own rehearsal time. He went on to a jazz band before joining R.A.F., which played Scottish pubs and clubs and in America. With Ian Anderson using the tried-and-true auditioning method from the John Evan Band days, Jethro Tull placed an ad in Melody Maker for a keyboard player. Peter-John Vettese answered that ad, and Ian and Martin were impressed with his live performance when they caught an R.A.F. gig. Anderson and Barre soon discovered that the playing freedom of Vettese's youth complemented what they did best.

It was now almost Christmas 1981, and Jethro Tull was without a producer and without any acceptable tracks recorded for their next album. The band looked in the Yellow Pages under "record producers" and the first name of note they came across was Paul Samwell-Smith, original Yardbirds bassist and producer of Cat Stevens' most popular recordings, among others. Gerry Conway had already worked with him on most of those Cat Stevens sessions, so his suitability was confirmed. Paul Samwell-Smith met the band and got along well with them. While Paul was producing, Ian Anderson was reading material to prepare himself for purchasing a home recording studio! Even at this time, the idea of having an outside producer would be a one-shot deal. The album Paul Samwell-Smith would work on was called "The Broadsword And The Beast."

After completing the "Broadsword" album, Ian would admit: "We have used a producer for the first time on this album. One of the reasons we wanted a producer was to have someone else take some of the responsibility of putting the public face on the music by giving it that degree of identity that alluded to the traditional idea of what Jethro Tull should be, without letting it become repetitive."

With Peter-John Vettese now in, eighteen more tracks were recorded between the end of December 1981 and the conclusion of February 1982. The tracks that did not make the album were "Jack Frost And The Hooded Crow," "Jack-A-Lynn," "Rhythm In Gold," "Drive On The Young Side Of Life," "Crew Nights" and "Motoreyes." The band's original intention was to have "Jack Frost" on their album, and when it was not included on this LP, Tull failed in convincing Chrysalis to use it as a 1984 Christmas single. It would turn up as the B-side of "Coronach" in 1986 and on the 1988 box set. When they were released, only the tracks selected by Paul Samwell-Smith and Chrysalis carried a Samwell-Smith production credit. Even though Ian ceded control for production and song selection, he would have final approval of the track lineup. "Jack-A-Lynn" and "Rhythm In Gold" made the 1988 box and the others were included later on "Nightcap."

"The Broadsword And The Beast" dealt mainly with the romance and sadness of life while avoiding clichéd statements. It was

Above are the UK's regular and picture disc editions of "Fallen On Hard Times" and the German single "Pussy Willow."

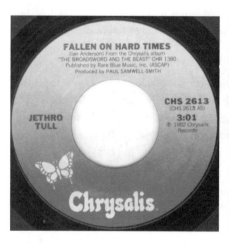

Above: the US edition of "Fallen On Hard Times," the band lineup for the album "The Broadsword And The Beast" (Peter John-Vettese, Gerry Conway, Ian Anderson, Martin Barre and Dave Pegg) and the "1982 Promotion Manual" LP. That album had the exclusive track "Slipstream Intro."

Speaking of "Slipstream," here are its original US videodisc and a reissue of its VHS edition.

124

Gerry Conway

Peter-John Vettese

Below: The 1982 lineup of Gerry Conway, Peter-John Vettese, Ian Anderson, Dave Pegg and Martin Barre.

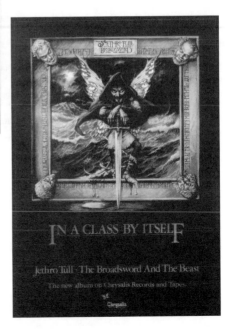

divided into two parts, "Broadsword" and "Beastie." The folkloric concept of protecting the family unit was discussed in the song "Broadsword," and the album's front cover spells out the initial lyrics of this tune. The other half of the album title, "Beastie," was Ian's boyhood euphemism for a feared occurrence. Listen for its reference of "Warm Sporran" - a track from the "Stormwatch" album. The fear of physical contact (namely, a handshake) was covered in "Clasp" and "Fallen On Hard Times" tackled the distrust we have in our politicians. The melody of "Fallen On Hard Times" was derived from Scottish folk tradition and recast in a rock-based setting. Peter-John Vettese's expressive piano and synthesizer runs on "Flying Colours" decorated Ian's lyrics about the arguments he witnessed couples having in public - revealing their disintegrating relationships. The sadness that accompanies a relationship's end was depicted in the side one closer "Slow Marching Band."

The "Broadsword" side of the album was more fantasy-based. The 9-to-5 girl in "Pussy Willow" wishes that her life had more romantic elements, and the fear of constantly being watched in public was covered by "Watching Me Watching You." The dual lyrical meaning of "Seal Driver" applied to either a girl or a boat. *Perhaps Martin Barre should have purchased a boat called "Seal Driver" instead of "Sossity" all those years ago!* With all this gloom, "Cheerio" was an ideal, upbeat side and album closer.

Peter-John Vettese was rewarded with an "additional material" credit - one step short of an actual writing credit. Vettese's credit came as a result of the way the songs developed in the rehearsal stage. Even during recording, Ian was intent on making this a full band recording and recorded most of his parts (including vocals) while the band was playing the backing track. The live approach to recording "The Broadsword And The Beast" made it a more immediate and accessible album for Jethro Tull's fans. It was released in April 1982, and did extremely well in Germany - sales were twice as much as previous releases.

"Broadsword" was the band's most overwhelming album in years, providing the ammunition for the band to compete in 1980s rock culture. Peter-John Vettese's strong, effective keyboard lines had successfully avoided the mechanical feel of keyboard-oriented bands of the '80s, guiding Tull most noticeably on the fan favorites "Clasp," "Pussy Willow" and "Watching Me Watching You."

Despite hitting #27, "The Broadsword And The Beast" had the longest UK album chart stay since "Aqualung," a very encouraging sign. In the US, radio welcomed the band back to the Top 20 (#19) by featuring many tracks from the album, namely "Fallen On Hard Times," "Beastie" and "Flying Colours." On Billboard's new Album Rock Tracks chart, "Fallen On Hard Times" was the 20th most played track on album oriented radio (AOR) stations, and "Beastie" made #50. Just as important, critics also trumpeted the band's performance on the LP. In fact, it was difficult to point out the album's highlights because of the uniformly excellent quality of all of the tracks recorded throughout the album's sessions. In England, "Broadsword" b/w "Beastie" was treated as a double A-sided single and was released as a standard single and a collectible picture disc. The US chose "Fallen On Hard Times" b/w "Pussy Willow" as its single tracks. Shortly after its release, "The Broadsword And The Beast" was also available as a half-speed mastered album. As for the CD format, original UK CDs were obviously mastered by a disgruntled Chrysalis employee that substituted a transfer from noisy vinyl instead of the proper master tape! The US CD became the release of choice in the UK until the British release was corrected. A very rare promotional picture disc was issued by Chrysalis - it was called "Broadsword Townhouse."

The band went through an ordeal to make "Broadsword," and it was finally time to present it live. This tour was just as successful as the album. A European leg was followed by a few special appearances, then the US had the chance to see Tull after a short break. The 1982 Jethro Tull employed more humor than had been exhibited on the "A" tour. Instead of ridiculous looking jumpsuits, the members of Tull were dressed as minstrels. The album title was tied in with Ian carrying an inexpensive-looking broadsword with the glowing eyes of the "Beastie" on his back. The usual white-coated roadie image was used in the strobelighted "Watching Me Watching You," and the old rabbit suit gag was dragged out once again. You may be wondering - was Chris Welch (their nemesis on "A Passion Play") impressed? You bet, and he was just as vocal in his current enthusiasm as he was of his disgust with their 1973 tour.

Oslo, Norway was the site of Gerry Conway and Peter-John Vettese's live debut on April 1, 1982. The Hamburg show a week later formed the basis of another "King Biscuit Flower Hour" show. The 20th anniversary box set was the commercial debut of that show's live tracks "Clasp," "Pibroch"/"Black Satin Dancer (Instrumental)," "Aqualung," "Locomotive Breath," "Sweet Dream" and "Fallen On Hard Times." Tull's "Roma 7 Up" Italian TV broadcast spread "Broadsword"'s impact, and the London Daily Telegraph enthusiastically promoted their Wembley Arena date on May 13 as their best show in a decade. Jethro Tull's renewed energy and completely integrated, complementary lineup were making waves.

The German "Rockpop '82" TV broadcast was drawn from their vital May 29 Westfalenhalle performance at the Dortmund Pop Festival. This concluded Jethro Tull's European tour. On June 7, Tull performed on "The David Letterman Show" on the NBC television network in the US, and a spot on the "Cleveland Afternoon Exchange" program eight days later. Jethro Tull had originally planned to start touring again in September, but a few special European shows came their way.

David Bowie cancelled his July 21 appearance at "The Prince's Trust Rock Gala" with short notice. With little time to prepare and Gerry Conway unavailable, Jethro Tull could only rehearse at the Dominion Theatre in London during the afternoon of that show. Genesis drummer Phil Collins was appearing as a solo act at the concert, so he willingly rehearsed with Tull. If you cannot believe Phil Collins as a drummer for Jethro Tull, the proof (two of the three songs they played) is available in the video that was released shortly after the concert. The verdict? Phil Collins is no Jethro Tull drummer! This was the first in a series of Prince's Trust concerts and included Madness, Kate Bush, Pete Townshend and others.

In an unusual move, a drummer change in Jethro Tull was necessary because of Gerry Conway's continued unavailability. Former 10cc drummer Paul Burgess filled in, and his first gig was at the Theakston Music Festival at Nostell Priory. Dave Pegg was responsible for obtaining Tull's placement on the bill through his business with the Theakston brewery and consumption of their alcoholic products! The support acts at Theakston festival were selected by Jethro Tull. One of these bands was Marillion, a Genesis-influenced band that sent Ian Anderson a demo tape. The up and coming Marillion would pay back Jethro Tull at a Milton Keynes Bowl show in 1986. The day before the Theakston festival, Ian was looking very Scottish as he was dressed in a kilt for a taped Yorkshire television interview in England.

In preparation for the US tour, the American arm of Chrysalis Records released an album sampler called "1982 Promotion Manual." Besides tracks from the band's back catalog, the aforementioned exclusive track "Slipstream Intro" was included. The opening act for the American shows was the Canadian band Saga.

Oustide America, promotion of "The Broadsword And The Beast" came in many different forms. A deluxe cassette edition of the album came out only in England. On the singles front, an unusual array of singles complemented the LP. "Broadsword" b/w "Watching You Watching Me" was a German and Dutch singles coupling, and a Spanish promo paired "Watching You Watching Me" and "Beastie." Germany and Holland were the only countries to receive a follow-up single: the intriguing "Pussy Willow" b/w "Beastie."

The year 1982 also marked the official founding of Strathaird Salmon Ltd., which became Ian Anderson's prime sideline when not on the road. While performing, Ian switched to guitars made by Andrew Manson of Devon, England. The completion of the US tour marked another break for Jethro Tull, but not for Ian Anderson - he was busy producing a genuine solo album. Jethro Tull would not be heard from again until November 1983. To follow up on the American tour, the small Pair Records label produced a rather low-budget 2LP set containing the "Stormwatch" and "Heavy Horses" albums. This release lost much of the original album packaging. During the band's quiet period, Ian and Tull were covered in a five-minute segment on the BBC2 documentary "Food And Drink" that aired on June 2, 1983. The Marquee Club was planning 20th anniversary concerts during the summer of 1983 that involved original group lineups. The club had asked the original Tull to perform, but Ian Anderson's still-distant relationship with Mick Abrahams did not make this a reality.

THE TECHNOLOGY OF "WALK INTO LIGHT" AND "UNDER WRAPS"

The November 1983 release of "Walk Into Light" certainly surprised many Tull fans who were expecting a more acoustic album. Instead, Ian Anderson (who played and/or programmed all of the instruments save for keyboards) collaborated with Peter-John Vettese to create a synthesizer-heavy set of songs with a scarcity of flute or guitar. As a result, Tull fans found this work far removed from the band's sound and shied away from "Walk Into Light." The failure of this album was certainly a surprise to all involved. Still, the album contained one obvious classic single - "Fly By Night," which formed the perfect dynamic backdrop when used as a theme by CBS Sports in the mid-'80s. Initial copies of the "Fly By Night" single reveal yet another record company blunder: quick piano chords preceding the B-side "End Game" were inadvertently included on the 45. This initial segment did not appear on the album version of "End Game." When this error was spotted, the album version was substituted. Interesting promos from Canada (a 12" sampler) and Argentina (a promo 7" with "Fly By Night" backing labelmate Pat Benatar's "Love Is A Battlefield") did their

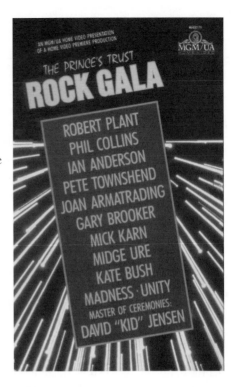

Jethro Tull's last-minute appearance at this Prince's Trust event was captured on this video, which was released in two different package designs.

The only Ian Anderson solo single released commercially to date. Early copies had a slightly longer version of the B-side "End Game."

At left is a Spanish promotional single for Ian Anderson's "Fly By Night." It was the B-side of Pat Benatar's "Love Is A Battlefield."

At right is Ian's first solo LP - "Walk Into Light."

Shots of Ian Anderson, Martin Barre and Dave Pegg at their Hammersmith Odeon show in 1984. On tour to promote the album "Under Wraps," the band released "Lap Of Luxury" as a single and then avoided the song in concert!

Bottom right: Only 1,000 copies were made of the "Under Wraps" picture disc LP. The album features an interesting band photo that does not appear on the standard LP configuration.

best to sustain interest in the album.

The mechanical nature of "Walk Into Light" gave most fans the impression that the technology was controlling Anderson and Vettese instead of the other way around. In a departure from the vast majority of his compositions, Ian Anderson co-wrote half of the tracks with Peter-John Vettese. As time has passed, the cold nature of the album has proven ultimately disappointing. As with most '80s recordings utilizing drum machines, the album sounds like something done in 1983. Looking at it with a wider view, "Walk Into Light" caught Ian Anderson in transition, bridging the gap between standard rock structures and more technical, experimental song stylings.

Two television appearances substituted for a "Walk Into Light" tour. David Palmer manned the control room for a live German appearance of Jethro Tull at the Atlas Circus in Munich - their only appearance that year. Tull did two tracks from Ian's album (including "Fly By Night") with a sloppy orchestra in an event put together by Eberhard Schoener. A formless jam with Ian Anderson, Jack Bruce and African percussionist Fela Kuti was equally embarrassing. More successful was Ian's lip-synch BBC performance of "Fly By Night" on "The Leo Sayer Show" in December. Despite this exposure, "Walk Into Light" only made #78 on the UK chart, and it did not sell enough to appear on the US Top 200 album chart. Chrysalis had also decided to license Tull recordings to an outside company, namely EMI's Fame budget label. "Stand Up" was released in February 1984, but the LP was quickly withdrawn.

Despite the lack of response to "Walk Into Light," Ian Anderson carried this keyboard-driven concept one step further with the next Jethro Tull album "Under Wraps" in 1984. For a Tull LP, the most surprising thing about "Under Wraps" was its lack of a drummer, since Ian Anderson was again responsible for the drum programming here. Even though Ian Anderson could not predict the future direction that rock would take in the '80s, he knew that dealing with its new technology was a necessity for the band to progress and survive. The only concession that Anderson made to the old Tull approach was "Under Wraps #2," a perfectly formed acoustic number. British fans showed that they had short memories about "Walk Into Light," since they brought the band back into the Top 20 (#18) with "Under Wraps." American audiences could only take the album to a #76 peak position despite strong radio play. In addition to its availability as a British picture disc, "Under Wraps" became the first Tull album to appear on compact disc and bonus-tracked cassette, with four bonus tracks included, three of which also appeared as tracks on the UK #70 "Lap Of Luxury" 12" and double 7" singles: "Astronomy," "Tundra" and "Automotive Engineering." (The standard British and Australian 7" single had "Astronomy" on its other side.) The exclusive track on the British cassette and CD was "General Crossing." In a strange chart occurrence, "Lap Of Luxury" actually reached #39 on the NME chart! In the US, this CD did not appear simultaneously with the British version, but appeared the next year instead. The US cassette would only feature "Astronomy" and "Automotive Engineering" as its extra tracks. "Lap Of Luxury" just barely made the Top 30 on US airplay listings in 1984. Certainly, this modern approach to Tull music polarized the band's fan base, but 1984 concerts showed that the band still had the audience in their hands, even though the attendance was noticeably less.

At a separate session, Ian, Martin and Dave Pegg were reunited with David Palmer and Gerry Conway to work on the haunting Scottish funeral song "Coronach" - a song Palmer had written for the British historical series "The Blood Of The British" for Channel 4 television in England. Franz Schubert had also written a piece called "Coronach Op. 52 no.4" (D836) based on Sir Walter Scott's poem "The Lady Of The Lake: Canto 3 (Excerpt)," but Palmer's "Coronach" was completely unlike the Schubert piece in that Palmer composed both music and lyrics. However, Palmer captured the same downcast feel in "Coronach" that Schubert attained in his piece. Palmer also wrote the rest of the music for this series, but "Coronach" was the only complete song featured. David Palmer was also the keyboardist and producer of this recording at Manor Studio, Oxfordshire, and the group was joined by an uncredited oboe player. The intent of the recording was to release it in time for the September 13, 1984 premiere of the series. With "Under Wraps" just in release, Chrysalis shelved the recording. Little did anyone know that they would dust it off two years later when the program was broadcast, and even then, it was released after the repeated television series had started!

"Under Wraps" was the first Jethro Tull album recorded at Ian's home studio ("Walk Into Light" was also recorded there), and its production took nine months. There was no doubting that this time period resulted in the best-sounding Tull LP to date, but fans were either delirious or exasperated by its contents. Learning from "Walk Into Light," Ian Anderson redirected the same technology to create a forward-looking album packed with energetic performances from Martin Barre and Peter-John Vettese. The demanding nature of the songs drove Ian to his most powerful vocal performances on record. As with "Walk Into Light," the songs on "Under Wraps" were almost all collaborations - even the mixing was a collaborative experience. Ian wrote the album's first three tracks on his own, ten were written with Vettese and the other two were composed with Barre and Vettese. Barre stepped up his writing by coming up with most of the music of "Paparazzi" and an equal share on "Nobody's Car."

Jethro Tull enjoyed making the album for the most part, but the long recording time was frustrating, as Martin Barre revealed: "I liked it for a few months, but once was enough. There wasn't a live feel to it. At first it was effortless working with a Linn (electronic) drum because we've always had a problem with drummers. Linn drums are always right, so you're either on or off. But later there is this thing called feel, and they don't have feel. They have volts." Folkster Dave Pegg was not happy with it at all. Neither was Terry Ellis, who originally threatened to block its release. He soon relented and was proved wrong by its UK chart performance. The band did not appreciate Chrysalis' lack of interest in promoting it, however.

"Under Wraps" contained the whimsical and humorous elements that were essential to a well-crafted Tull album. In one of his most priceless lines, Ian Anderson warns the astronaut in "Apogee": "Don't forget to urinate"! Four of the songs make references to cars ("Lap Of Luxury," "Nobody's Car," "Astronomy" and "Automotive Engineering") - amazing since Ian can't drive! Besides these vehicle references, conceptual continuity pops up again with the "science and engineering" lyric linkage between "Automotive Engineering" and "Radio Free Moscow" (listen for it in the background of the latter song!). Just as a point of interest: the Datsun that Ian is referring to in "Lap Of Luxury" is now known as Nissan. For some reason, England and the US were among the last countries to switch over from Datsun to Nissan. Ian went back to his childhood French book to extract the line "Trop tard sera le cri" - the first half of its English translation "Too late will be the cry, when the ice-cream salesman has gone by." The most unusual promotional item for the album was the US 12" featuring both takes of the title track.

While "Under Wraps" was in production, Ian Anderson sought a drummer for the album's tour. In the fall of 1983, Ian placed an ad in the New York publication The Village Voice. The winning auditionee was another American drummer - Doane Perry.

DOANE PERRY

Born June 16, 1954 in Mt. Kisco, NY, Doane Ethredge Perry started playing classical piano at seven for four years. He attended Browning and St. Bernard's, the latter a New York school rooted in British culture. Similar to John Evans, he took up drums when he heard The Beatles and taught himself how to play. At 12, Perry drummed on Beatles and Rolling Stones numbers with The Be-Tones. From 14 until he completed high school, Doane performed at weekend gigs while keeping a part-time job selling Baskin-Robbins ice cream.

In December 1968, Doane heard a radio ad for Jethro Tull's Fillmore East gigs (January 14-15, 1969). The ad also featured "Cat's Squirrel" (*you know that story!*). Doane Perry met Clive Bunker backstage and received his first drum lesson right then and there. He received theory and composition training at music schools, including New York's Juilliard school of music, and played with orchestras. As an 18 year old, he started his professional drumming career, playing with so many rock and jazz-influenced bands that they would require a separate book to list them all (a synopsis is in his solo section)! Most relevant to his entry to Jethro Tull was Maxus, who recorded an album in 1980.

A friend saw Ian's Village Voice ad and told Doane, who was now based in California. While in California, he had started a very strong relationship with former Jethro Tull drummer Mark Craney. He called Chrysalis a few days later and was advised to submit a tape before Christmas. Perry had a connection with a Chrysalis executive, and it was time to take advantage of that connection. Doane submitted the Maxus LP and a tape reflecting his various playing styles to Chrysalis' New York office. Somehow, Ian found out that Perry was staying at his great aunt and uncle's house and called Doane just after Christmas. The audition was less than two weeks away, and Ian promised to follow up with another call. Doane didn't think he did well on the audition, but he got the job months later when "Under Wraps" was complete.

On August 30, 1984 at Caird Hall in Dundee, Scotland, Jethro Tull did their first full-length concert in 22 months. The tour included two shows at the Manchester Apollo, three at Hammersmith Odeon in London and two at Hamburg's Congress Centrum Halle. After Ian appeared on the September 9 "Breakfast TV" program on the BBC that morning, the band took the stage at the Odeon for one of their most important shows of the period. Some of the concert was broadcast on Tommy Vance's BBC1 program on December 27, and most of it formed the basis for the Raw Fruit album "Live At Hammersmith '84 - The Friday Rock Show Sessions" released at the end of 1990 ("Clasp," "Thick As A Brick" and "Aqualung" were omitted). This time, the US tour leg started just a few days after the European part ended. The support act in the US was another Canadian group, Honeymoon Suite.

The US tour was problematic. I personally saw Tull for the first time on October 17, 1984 at Rochester War Memorial (Rochester, NY) and Ian Anderson was in fine voice. However, Ian was forced to cancel the second and third nights of their three-night L.A. run (November 22-24) due to laryngitis. The songs from "Under Wraps" had Ian Anderson straining his voice to duplicate his studio performance, and his vocal chords were giving out under the strain. Only five shows in Australia were completed before Ian was forced to cancel the rest of the shows in that country due to muscular spasms. The shame of all this was that Tull's set was at its most energetic and powerful.

The first of the Australian shows was preceded by a scare that had nothing to do with Ian's voice - his son James was rushed to the hospital due to peritonis. Ian immediately flew to England to attend James' operation, and he actually had time to return to Melbourne, Australia for that night's show!

The "Under Wraps" show started with all five Jethro Tull members under sheets and each broke through their coverings once the first song kicked in. During the show, scantily clad women or astronauts played their characteristic parts. During "Apogee," a mock moon landing was staged in which the astronaut planted a UK flag (which would generate booing at non-UK shows) and then a flag of the country they were playing in, which of course would generate the typical nationalistic reponse! Of course in England, there was no need for any of this flag changing reconciliation!

The year 1984 was closed with Jethro Tull's taped appearance on the American TV show "Rock Influences" which dealt with progressive rock's history. As mentioned previously, Tull had recommended the release of "Jack Frost And The Hooded Crow" and "Coronach" as a Christmas present for their fans, but Chrysalis was not interested. The band was growing increasingly unhappy with their record label, as Chrysalis was not attentive to the wishes of any of its artists. This would become clear in 1985 when Terry Ellis sold his share of the company to Chris Wright.

When Ian returned to England, doctors checked the condition of his throat. He was strongly advised to give his voice a rest for the next year. This included all recording and live performances. Anderson's year of silence ended up being twice as long and fans thought Tull would never be heard from again. On February 1, 1985, Ian Anderon was briefly interviewed on BBC television's "The Tube." Like 1983, Jethro Tull would appear once in 1985. Making just this one exception to his doctor's wishes, Ian Anderson used his voice sparingly while the band played a mostly instrumental set.

Ian Anderson made this exception when Jethro Tull was invited to play in Berlin on March 16, 1985 at a concert honoring the 300th birthday of Johann Sebastian Bach. Eddie Jobson rejoined Tull for just this show, and Eddie's violin skills were put to their best effect in the band's performance of Bach's "Double Violin Concerto." This Bach piece from 1717 is formally known as "Concerto for Two Violins in D minor" (BWV 1043). The show was broadcast by German radio and television, and was a fine way for Jethro Tull to present themselves in a more highbrow music forum.

A CLASSIC CASE OF ORIGINAL MASTERS

Prior to this German trip, the band contributed to the album "A Classic Case • The London Symphony Orchestra Plays The Music Of Jethro Tull" at CBS Studios in London. Originally released in Germany in early 1985, in the US at the end of that year, but not in England, the album contains David Palmer's beautifully orchestrated versions of Jethro Tull favorites. This was the first album in Palmer's arrangement with the RCA Red Seal label as part of his series of orchestrally-arranged rock music. Jethro Tull's RCA album was unlike the later Genesis and Pink Floyd LPs that Palmer created, in that the entire band actually played on the album - despite what the album credits printed. The band's lineup was the same as for "Under Wraps," plus uncredited drummer Paul Burgess. This album did about as well as "Under Wraps" in the US sales department (#93), but the single "Bourrée" b/w "Elegy" was poorly distributed and died a quick death. "A Classic Case" was reissued in England during July 1993 under the new title "Classic Jethro Tull." "Bourrée" was also issued in its album version and single edit on a promotional US 12" release to generate interest in "A Classic Case." However, airplay was almost nonexistent.

At right: Ian Anderson fishing after the conclusion of the 1984 "Under Wraps" tour.

Below: The numerous releases of the album "A Classic Case • The London Symphony Orchestra Plays The Music Of Jethro Tull." The middle row has the original German LP, the original US LP and the "Bourrée" single from America. The bottom row illustrates the original US compact disc, the American CD reissue and the "Original Masters" compilation.

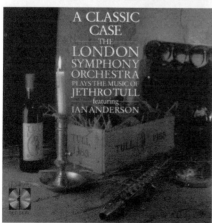

At left, Ian Anderson poses with guitarist Derry Grehan of the band Honeymoon Suite.

The 12" edition of the single "Coronach."

Below: Ian Anderson and Martin Barre at their Denver show in 1987. (Photo courtesy of Lon Horwitz)

Jethro Tull's participation on the album was perceived by some fans as unnecessary rock backing for an album that was released on a classical music label. However, the merging of rock and classical was the intent of Palmer's orchestral exploits in this series. Ian Anderson and Martin Barre were not warm to Palmer's idea for them to participate, but they felt an obligation to deliver because of David Palmer's essential orchestral contributions to Tull over the years. As a result, Ian and Co. have dismissed the album and their participation in it. The only track that did not involve Tull members was "War Child," which utilized Palmer's unused film soundtrack arrangement.

Chrysalis decided to keep Jethro Tull in the minds of fans via a very uninspired and cheaply packaged compilation of old singles and popular album tracks in the album "Original Masters." No new material was offered and none of the band's material after 1977 was included, thereby diluting the necessity of this LP. The expected result was a very poor-selling album. The presentation of the album was similar to the kind of treatment that a cheapo label like Ronco would deliver. If you wanted more in terms of packaging, you had to wait a few years for the additional liner notes included with the Russian release on Melodiya - not that you could read them! In the UK, Chrysalis ran television commercials for "Original Masters" without much effect - only a #63 chart album resulted. American audiences, however, purchased the album over a long period of time. It was certified platinum for sales of 1 million copies in October 1999. The new, younger employees at the label had no idea that the version of "Aqualung" they used was not the one on the original album (it was the mix used on "M.U."). This was all rectified with the 1998 release of "Original Masters" on the DCC Compact Classics label. This CD used the original LP mix of "Aqualung" along with the first 22:42 part of "Thick As A Brick" (with a beginning countoff), replacing the edit on the original "Original Masters" album.

During 1985, Ian Anderson concentrated on Strathaird Salmon Ltd. to ensure that its rapid growth would not necessitate his direct involvement on a regular basis. The previous year, Ian looked at thirty sites in Scotland that would be suitable for salmon farming, and he wanted to select three or four of those locations to create new farms. These locations were soon developed and the worldwide marketing of Strathaird salmon products was in full gear. In 1984, his company harvested 2 1/2 tons of salmon and grossed $500,000. Strathaird salmon found its way into Harrod's and Selfridges shops in London, and the Australian airline Qantas distributed Anderson's product to all airlines operating out of that country. Ian promoted his salmon at Macy's department store in the US, and delis in New York, New Jersey, Florida and Texas were the recipients of twenty tons of Strathaird product. Ian told People magazine in a 1985 interview: "Shoppers are going crazy for Scottish salmon because it's much better than anything they've ever had. I wouldn't like to do this and not ever play music again. But I'm at the point now where there's no way I'd be happy just being a musician the rest of my life." Strangely enough, the only time Ian eats salmon is when he's sampling their quality! When not on tour, Ian would fly from Buckinghamshire to Inverness, Scotland for factory inspections. The inspections would be followed by an 80-mile train or ferry ride to visit his Strathaird property.

The other masterful members of Jethro Tull would also use this long layoff to participate in individual pursuits. Martin Barre wrote and recorded songs when he wasn't involved in his jogging regimen. Barre presented a series of four-track recordings to Chrysalis and Virgin but received turndowns due to the primitive nature of his finished masters. A Dutch radio program announced that Barre's album was called "Top Hat Head" but the negative industry feedback proved that the story was not accurate. Physically, his goal was to get his body down to marathon condition. Barre would look back on his poor physical shape in the December 1996 issue of Runner's World: "It was 10 years ago (1986). I was getting older, and I was getting larger. For the first time, I was feeling uncomfortable on stage. Suddenly, I needed to come to terms with the fact that many people in the audience were half my age. I knew I needed to get fit, so I started running."

Meanwhile, Peter-John Vettese initiated his career as a writer, producer and arranger for films and records. Some of his first sessions were with Go West, Frankie Goes To Hollywood and Simple Minds. Dave Pegg rejoined Fairport Convention for the comeback album "Gladys' Leap." Its surprising success spurred Pegg on to steer the activities of the reconstituted Fairports around his work with Jethro Tull. Ian Anderson offered to play flute on the "Gladys' Leap" track "A Bird From The Mountain," but Fairport Convention did not allow Ian enough time to make this happen. Doane Perry was recording with the Australian group Dragon in February 1986 before he got the call again to rejoin Jethro Tull.

To satisfy fan requirements for up-to-date information, Tull fan Dave Rees created A New Day magazine (AND) in 1985. AND continues today as a magazine and a record company releasing tapes and CDs of artists that are either directly or peripherally related to Jethro Tull.

The Channel 4 television series, "The Blood Of The British," was repeated on June 11, 1986, nearly two years after its premiere. This time, Chrysalis woke up and decided to issue "Coronach" b/w "Jack Frost And The Hooded Crow" to tie in with the repeated series. Even so, Chris Wright of Chrysalis waited too long to assemble its release and distribution was absolutely dreadful. A cassette release was scheduled but never reached the record shops. "Coronach" was billed as "Jethro Tull and David Palmer," and "Jack Frost" as its B-side was odd since the label was issuing a Christmas song right at summer time! Still, "Coronach" was reassuring to fans who fearfully thought Jethro Tull had quietly disappeared for good. The 12" of "Coronach" added "Elegy" and "Living In The Past" - the latter was used to repromote the failing "Original Masters" collection. As a follow-up, David Palmer announced on Radio 2 that the British release of "A Classic Case" would finally surface that October. It would remain unreleased in England for another seven years.

Jethro Tull was now ready to get up to touring speed, even though Ian Anderson's voice was not what it was before. Anderson, Barre, Vettese, Pegg and Perry went the summer festival route in England, Israel, Hungary, Denmark and Germany during the only week they toured in 1986. The first festival came by way of Marillon, who paid back Tull's invitation of the band from the Theakston Music Festival four years earlier. Marillion was now a successful, fully established European act and Tull was now *their* supporting band at Milton Keynes Bowl on June 28, 1986. This did not come cheaply, as Marillon laid out plenty for Jethro Tull's rehearsals and tour preparation.

Out of the five acts at Milton Keynes, Jethro Tull was the third to perform, prior to Gary Moore and Marillion. It was a less than ideal position for the band and their so-so performance reflected this on the Radio 1 broadcast (July 25) and a September 15 television documentary about Ian called "Fish 'n' Sheep 'n' Rock 'n' Roll." Ian Anderson was neither looking nor sounding very well at Milton Keynes. It was very clear that he could not fit into the codpiece that he wore a decade before.

Following Milton Keynes, Tull played its first dates in Israel (Tel Aviv) and Hungary (Budapest). On July 2, 1986, it was a hot night in Budapest, and the lasting images of the city immediately formed the framework of the song "Budapest" that Ian Anderson wrote the next morning. It would become the centerpiece of the band's next album. Originally 20 minutes in length, the song would be broken up into the songs "Budapest" and "Mountain Men." The Danish and German festivals completed Jethro Tull's trial run and got the rust out of their system. A couple of the interesting songs played at these shows included "Fly By Night" and the unreleased instrumental "Unknown Dreams." South American fans were treated to a "Masters Of Rock" collection until Tull delivered their next album.

When this week of shows was completed, the album that became "Crest Of A Knave" started developing. Peter-John Vettese was not available, so Ian decided to play keyboards as he did on the early "Broadsword" sessions. Doane Perry found out that his mother was ill during rehearsals and had to leave temporarily. Perry's mother died a short time later, and Perry returned after a suitable amount of time to complete some drum tracks. The band was working around him through the use of Gerry Conway and electronic drum programs. Perry was dismayed to find out that his efforts appeared on only two tracks: "Farm On The Freeway" and "Mountain Men." As a result, he mistakenly thought he was being treated as a sideman for the band in all their activities. Little did he know how wrong he was! With very few exceptions, based on his own outside activities, Doane Perry has remained a Jethro Tull firmament.

On March 20, 1987, Martin Barre started working with Paul McCartney in Sussex, England. McCartney was not happy with the session, and the first track they completed, "Atlantic Ocean," would not turn up for a decade. The final version of "Atlantic Ocean" was unfortunately typical of the throwaway nature of McCartney's B-sides. "Atlantic Ocean" was included in the second part of Macca's infamous "Oobu Joobu" radio series, and was released on the second CD single for Paul's "Young Boy." Another track that came from this session was "P.S. Love Me Do," on which Martin did some programming. This recording ended up on the Japan-only 2CD edition of McCartney's "Flowers In The Dirt" album in 1990.

"CREST OF A KNAVE"

Ian was now so adept at using keyboards and sampling technology that he had no problem in employing them without creating a mechanized effect. Keyboards took a back seat to the presence of Martin Barre's screaming guitar, as evidenced by "Steel Monkey," "Farm On The Freeway," and "Jump Start," just three of the many wide-exposure tracks on the album. Those tracks respectively made 10, 7 and 12 on US radio frequency playlists. The underpinning of "Steel Monkey" was a sequencer track that formed the foundation for Barre to solo over.

Anderson decided to keep the creation of the album to himself: "I was very, very selfish about making this one. I really just didn't want anybody else to have any creative input on it at all, other than playing the final parts in the studio. The last few albums involved the other guys quite a lot, in the arranging and in writing bits of music, and I felt this time that I wanted to get away from having input from other people - not because I thought I could do it better, but just because I wanted to be very selfish about it and take total charge. A lot of people have gotten the idea that Jethro Tull has always been Ian Anderson being very dictatorial about things. But it's not like that - it has been on occasional songs, but very rarely on whole albums. The music has always been very much the product of the people who were in the group at the time, and everyone's opinion has always gotten a fair hearing." "Crest Of A Knave" was mainly recorded at Ian's home studio with some drum track recording at Black Barn Studio.

The album's family crest artwork was put together first and the title "Crest Of A Knave" played on the phrase "crest of a wave." Fairport Convention violinst Ric Sanders guested on "Budapest" and "The Waking Edge" (uncredited). Gerry Conway was used on "Jump Start," "Said She Was A Dancer," "Budapest" and "The Waking Edge." Between his departure from the band and this session, Conway worked with Richard Thompson, Kate & Anna McGarrigle, John Martyn and Pentangle. Ignored upon release, "Crest Of A Knave" ultimately blew away the competition. The rejuvenated Jethros firmed up their UK audience with a #19 chart rebound. The album drove up to the #35 slot in the US, achieving the first Jethro Tull gold album since 1979's "Stormwatch." It spent more than half a year on US listings. "Crest Of A Knave" was a Top 10 album in Germany, and their last gold US album for an original release. The pre-release signing of their new Chrysalis contract was perfectly timed, considering the success of the album!

The buildup to "Crest Of A Knave" was accompanied by a couple of interesting Tull-related activities. At the Marriott Hotel in Denver, CO, 300 fans won the chance from Boulder, CO radio station KBCO to participate in a focus group/pre-release listening party for "Crest Of A Knave." Ian Anderson wanted to make sure that the tracks that he wanted to include on the album were somewhat in agreement with what fans wanted. This group of people was asked to listen to each track to determine whether it was of high enough quality to include on the album. If not, it would either be considered a bonus track on the CD or the song would remain unissued. The fans were then asked to sequence the tracks that they selected, and the data gathered contributed to the track lineup for the album. Thus, the "Crest Of A Knave" CD contained two bonus tracks: "Dogs In The Midwinter" and "The Waking Edge," while the album's first single, "Steel Monkey," was linked with three 1982 outtakes ("Down At The End Of Your Road," "I'm Your Gun" and "Too Many Too"). It was a #82 UK single, and a special cassette edition included a Tull badge and a competition entry form to win Ian's original tartan frock coat. Everyone should have won because the questions were extremely easy! Check out Ian's "I just woke up" voice on "The Waking Edge" - a brilliant and underrated vocal performance. The press overplayed the fact that Ian Anderson, with Chrysalis, ultimately had the final say on track selection. Yet, stories circulated in Billboard and other publications that fans completely dictated the selection and order of the album's titles. The recommendations by this group of 300 in Denver had at least some impact on how "Crest Of A Knave" was sequenced to the entire world.

In July, Ian Anderson gave the Strange Fruit label permission to release an album extracted from a "Songs From The Wood" live gig. It was meant to be released that October, but Chrysalis withdrew that permission when they expressed their intention on releasing it themselves. It has still not been issued. Despite his misgivings about David Palmer's "A Classic Case" album, Anderson was interested in playing on the track "I Know What I Like" for David's "We Know What We Like - The Music Of Genesis" LP/CD. This album again featured The London Symphony Orchestra. It was released on August 11, 1987.

The completed "Crest Of A Knave" album was aired at Fairport Convention's annual Cropredy Festival in England over the weekend of August 14-15, 1987. This festival celebrated the 20th anniversary of Fairport Convention's founding. Dave Pegg and his wife Chris organized the festival. Because Dave was so proud of his participation in the new Tull album, he felt it was an ideal forum to present the LP along with his invited guests, Ian Anderson and Martin Barre. Near the end of Fairport's set, Ian and Martin came on stage to play a 45-minute set of Jethro Tull fan favorites. The highly enthusiastic response the Tullsters received led Ian to ask Pegg if Fairport Convention would be the US support band for the upcoming "Crest Of A Knave" tour. Pegg jumped at the chance since he was afraid to ask for Ian's participation at Cropredy to begin with! Dave Pegg would play with both bands on the tour, but Ian made one thing clear - the fun-loving Pegg was not to consume alcohol until after the show! The Fairports had just finished recording their new album "In Real Time," and it was one of their few recent albums that received a US release.

Martin Barre and Ian Anderson at a Denver record signing to promote "Crest Of A Knave" in 1987.
(Photos courtesy of Lon Horwitz)

Below: Jethro Tull's main trio in 1987: Dave Pegg, Ian Anderson and Martin Barre.

Before their 1987 tour, the band decided to take a piss! From left to right: Martin Barre, Dave Pegg, Doane Perry, Don Airey and Ian Anderson. Pegg appears to be the most relieved!

Below are the different single releases of "Steel Monkey" from the album "Crest Of A Knave" and the UK "Living In The Past" reissue.

After Cropredy, Jethro Tull was offered a concert at Sun City in Africa, but the tenuous political condition in the country was not suitable for the band to go ahead with such a show. "Crest Of A Knave" would be issued three years after Tull's last proper album "Under Wraps." The album was either ignored or slammed by the press. Billboard magazine usually went out of its way to find an album's high points, but the publication had nothing nice to say about an album they thought had weak lyrics and an overly Dire Straits-derived sound. The reality of the album was that it was completely opposite from what Billboard perceived: it redirected the band's sound with Ian's flute and guitars to the fore. Despite radio ignorance (especially in the UK), "Crest Of A Knave" scored with fans over a long, six-month period and it has become their most durable latter-day album in a live setting. To prevent aggravating his already damaged vocal chords, Ian Anderson cast the songs in lower keys. Ian's lower vocals freed up the high end of the sound spectrum for Martin Barre to weave a tapestry of wide-ranging guitar sounds.

What about the inevitable comparisons to Dire Straits? Ian's vocals on "Budapest" and especially "Said She Was A Dancer" were compared to Mark Knopfler's, but as just discussed, Ian's lower vocal range on the songs came out of necessity. We have also mentioned Martin Barre's choice of Hamer guitars earlier in the decade, and it was Knopfler himself that desired Barre's guitar sound before the album came out! The guitar sound that Martin achieved on "Said She Was A Dancer" was his way of decorating the song. With full knowledge of the negative feedback on the song, Jethro Tull reserved playing it live only during sound checks. In its studio recording, Ian recorded the entire track himself and then Martin and Pegg's double bass was added. At the beginning of 1988, Chrysalis made the mistake of issuing "Said She Was A Dancer" as a single and earned the band a #55 UK chart position in Music Week and more negative press concerning its "supposed" conscious derivation from the Dire Straits songbook.

Peter-John Vettese was unavailable for this tour, so auditions took place to find his replacement. These auditions led them to a keyboardist that would have the poorest fit of anyone they would ever use - Don Airey. Airey was born in Sunderland, England on June 21, 1948 and was classically trained from the age of two. He played organ at working men's clubs in northeast England, before going to Nottingham University and the Royal Manchester College of Music. His band played cruise liners in 1971 and this experience lasted for the next three years. Airey scored some hit singles with Cozy Powell's group Hammer and he toured a year with the noted drummer. He also played with Colosseum II. Powell's group led Airey into the world of heavy metal, with stints in Black Sabbath and Ritchie Blackmore's group Rainbow, the latter also with Cozy Powell. Don Airey joined Ozzy Osbourne's group for three years and had just finished playing with Whitesnake.

Don Airey's live debut was at the Playhouse in Edinburgh, Scotland on October 4, 1987. This tour found the band playing to SRO audiences for the first time in years, and concert openers Fairport Convention (including Dave Pegg, who played with both bands) could not believe the reception. While on the road, Ian Anderson did a guest VJ spot for MTV on the 20th and a short Christmas message for later BBC-TV use. The final show on the UK leg was at the Hammersmith Odeon, and it was broadcast on Capital Radio in London. "Wond'ring Aloud," "Dun Ringill," "Songs From The Wood" and "Thick As A Brick" from that gig were included on the next year's box set.

The American tour was equally productive. The band developed a good relationship with "shock jock" Howard Stern on his November 17 program in New York, playing a medley including "Aqualung" with Howard's golden tones accompanying the band! The same day, Tull was interviewed on MTV and performed two songs live. Four days later, the band's appearance at the "Hungerthon 1987" indicated their dedication toward raising money for world hunger. After flying from Montreal to New York, Ian, Martin and Dave did an acoustic three-song afternoon set at the United Nations before catching a flight to the gig that night in Worcester, MA. The Tower Theater show on the 25th generated two more live tracks on the 20th anniversary box set: "Living In The Past" and "Farm On The Freeway." The tour ended with three nights at Universal Amphitheater in L.A. (the last date at San Diego's Golden Hall was cancelled).

As for the performance quality of these widely viewed shows, it was decidedly mixed. Ian's voice was frequently less than spectacular. Fairport Convention relished their role in the concert, joining Tull's set on the song "Skating Away On The Thin Ice Of The New Day" and joined roadies playing cardboard guitars on the heavy metal frivolity of "Jump Start."

Don Airey's posturing, self-indulgent soloing and pre-programmed keyboard sounds were completely out of whack with what Jethro Tull and their fans wanted to appreciate in concert. The feeling was mutual, and Airey departed after the conclusion of the tour. Don Airey went on to do his noted "K2" album, music for commercials and his creation of a touring band for former Zombies singer Colin Blunstone in 1997 - Colin's first tour in many years. He arranged and conducted the Eurovision Song Contest-winning "Love Shine A Light" for Katrina & The Waves. Don's own band has led him to explore new musical avenues.

With such a hot property on their hands, Chrysalis had no shortage of unusual 12" releases for radio programmers: "Steel Monkey," "Farm On The Freeway" and "Budapest." Canada issued the first two tracks as a promo 7" disc, and "Steel Monkey" was backed by "Dogs In The Midwinter" on the commercial South African release. The German B-side of "Steel Monkey" was "The Waking Edge" and they added "Dogs In The Midwinter" instead of "Too Many Too" on their 12". "Said She Was A Dancer" was also different in those two countries, in that "The Waking Edge" was the flipside. In Australia, the "4 Tracks from 'Crest Of A Knave'" cassette EP was a unique way of presenting the album to radio. The first US appearance of "I'm Your Gun" from the "Broadsword" sessions made it to the Elektra promo only album "Rare Rock Collection - 98KZEW Rock Against AIDS." The proceeds from the LP went to a radiothon at the station on December 3, 1987.

Jethro Tull's final run-in with the music industry took place long after "Crest Of A Knave" was released. The album was released too late to be nominated for the 1988 Grammy awards, but it was submitted for the 1989 awards. To their surprise and confusion, the band found "Crest Of A Knave" nominated for "Best Hard Rock/Metal Performance, Vocal or Instrumental." The Grammy awards ceremony took place on February 22, 1989, but Tull didn't attend because Chrysalis talked them out of appearing! One of the reasons for their avoidance was that Metallica - a band that deserved to be nominated for its "…And Justice For All" album - looked like a cinch for the award. The other nominees, Alice Cooper and AC/DC, were also prime candidates for such a prize. When Metallica played the overwhelming song "One" from that album, the audience was convinced that they had not seen the last of Metallica on the television broadcast. Surprise, surprise - Jethro Tull won the Grammy! The stunned audience greeted the award announcement with boos. As expected, the press mounted a backlash against a band who was appreciative of the award but embarrassed by their categorization. After all, Tull should have been nominated many times earlier and was roundly ignored by the pop-leaning members of the National Association of Recording Arts and Sciences (NARAS)! Chrysalis tried to reassert the band's worthiness of the Grammy by a tongue-in-check Billboard ad stating "The flute is a heavy metal instrument" to no avail. You can check the ad out on the next page and decide for yourself! When Metallica finally won the Grammy in 1992 for their self-titled album, drummer Lars Ulrich said, "Thanks to Jethro Tull for **NOT** putting out an album this year." This comment illustrated the band's ignorance - does anybody remember Tull's 1991 "Catfish Rising" album?

Back to late 1987, Jethro Tull had completed their tour for "Crest Of A Knave" and the ill-suited Don Airey had to be replaced for touring in 1988. Ian Anderson asked Dave Pegg if Fairport Convention lead guitar, mandolin and bouzouki player Martin Allcock was interested in taking on the keyboard role. Allcock was interested and Ian made him the offer on New Year's Day 1988. This offer was made even though he was not a keyboardist by nature!

Born January 5, 1957 in Manchester, Martin Allcock started out on double bass as a 13 year old. Allcock went to Huddersfield School of Music and also studied in Leeds. In 1976, he turned pro and toured with Mike Harding the next year. He played live with Robin Williamson after moving to Brittany and became a chef in the Shetland Islands. The Celtic folk group The Bully Wee Band marked Martin's 1981 music return. Their breakup with followed by Martin's tour with Kieran Halpin in the UK, Ireland and Europe. He joined Fairport Convention in 1985, and since turning pro, Allcock has appeared on dozens of albums. Irish fiddle player Kevin Burke renamed him Maart, and in true Jethro Tull tradition, Allcock brought his amended name into the band. Maart was able to pick up any instrument, and already being a Tull fan, Allcock had no trouble in getting up to speed.

Ian Anderson was looking for a multi-instrumentalist with a personality. Anderson was not looking for a keyboard wizard - he already had that with Don Airey, and look what difficulties that caused! The one thing that Ian had to monitor was Maart's affinity for alcohol, which of course he shared with Dave Pegg!

Jethro Tull's Ian Anderson, Martin Barre and Dave Pegg were inducted into the Hollywood Rock Walk on January 14, 1988 - not an earth-shattering honor by any means, but a well-deserved recognition of their talents. Of their decreased popularity, Ian Anderson said at the time: "It doesn't particularly bother me that we are not as popular a group as we were in the mid-'70s. There's a good chance that maybe I will still be trotting out here and doing this in 10 years time. But if that is the case, I hope the reason I'll be doing it is that it's genuinely a barrel of laughs, and *not* just because I wanted to see if I could get to 50 and still be playing 'Aqualung.'" Ian was further recognized for his salmon exploits on British television in March 1988.

HEAVY

THE FLUTE IS A METAL INSTRUMENT.

CONGRATULATIONS
ON YOUR GRAMMY.
JETHRO TULL
1988 GRAMMY AWARD WINNER
HARD ROCK/HEAVY METAL

DISCOGRAPHY · THICK AS A BRICK PV 41003 · A PASSION PLAY PV 41040 · THIS WAS PV 41041 · STAND UP PV 41042 · BENEFIT PV 41043 · AQUALUNG PV 41044 · WARCHILD PV 41067 · MU – BEST OF... PV 41078 · MINSTREL IN THE GALLERY PV 41082 · TOO OLD TO ROCK 'N' ROLL PV 41111 · SONGS FROM THE WOOD PV 41132 · REPEAT PV 41135 · HEAVY HORSES PV 41175 · STORMWATCH PV 41238 · 'A' PV 41301 · BROADSWORD AND THE BEAST PV 41380 · LIVING IN THE PAST V2X 41035 · BURSTING OUT V2X 41201 · UNDER WRAPS PV 41407 · ORIGINAL MASTERS PV 41515 · CREST OF A KNAVE OV 41590 · 20 YEARS OF JETHRO TULL BOX SET V5X 41653 · 20 YEARS OF JETHRO TULL 21 TRACK COLLECTION VX2 41655

Chrysalis.

Above left: Martin Allcock (left) joins Doane Perry, Ian Anderson, Dave Pegg and Martin Barre.
Above right: Ian Anderson, Dave Pegg and Martin Barre.

Above: The regular and picture disc editions of the British single "Said She Was A Dancer."

Below: The Canadian promo of the same single, along with a promotional CD single of "Part Of The Machine" and the double LP/ single CD compilation "20 Years Of Jethro Tull."

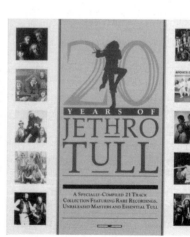

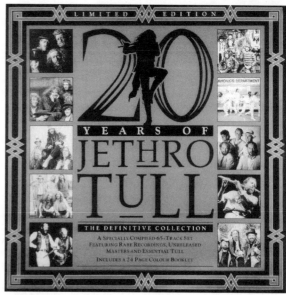

"20 Years Of Jethro Tull" was celebrated by fans through an essential 5LP/3CD set and a video release.

Below: Martin Allcock, Doane Perry, Ian Anderson, Dave Pegg and Martin Barre.

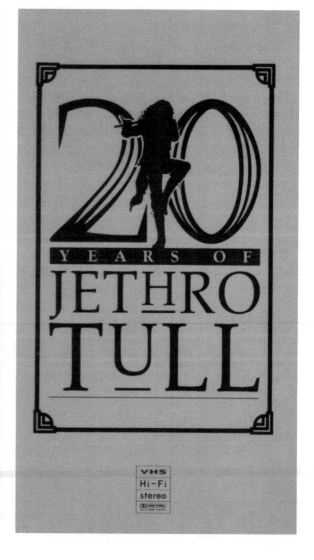

144

RECOGNIZING THE FIRST 20 YEARS

For a couple of years, devoted Tull fans had been writing to Chrysalis Records inquiring about what the label would do to commemorate Jethro Tull's 20th anniversary in 1988. Chrysalis' ambitious anniversary plan called for a five-album box set, a double album, video, television special and radio series. When their ideas were mentioned to Ian Anderson, he originally wanted to minimize his input into the five-album project. As he began working on the anniversary project, Ian became more and more involved and interested in all aspects of the album, from its packaging to its contents. The 5LP/3CD album "20 Years Of Jethro Tull" reached stores in June 1988 (US: July), and was very highly regarded by dedicated fans and casual fans alike. Assembled by A New Day editor Dave Rees and compatriot Martin Webb, "20 Years Of Jethro Tull" was a very ambitious, 65-track limited edition compendium of the aforementioned rare singles tracks, radio show and unreleased live and studio material from all eras of the band, and a new track from 1988 - "Part Of The Machine." The 65 tracks on the final edition were developed from a listing of 90 possible recordings, and only 11 tracks had been issued on previous albums. It remained in print until the spring of 1992. This collection was accompanied by a video of the same name, which included interviews and many exciting live performances of the band, especially a rare Swedish TV appearance from 1969, with Tull playing the previously unavailable Ian Anderson blues tune "To Be Sad Is A Mad Way To Be." This song later appeared on the band's "25th Anniversary Box Set." Former Chrysalis artist Philip Goodhand-Tait was commissioned to create the quickly assembled 80-minute video, which mainly relied on more recent (and easily obtainable) film instead of archive material around the world which would require more research time and expense to license. The UK independent TV program "This Is The First 20 Years" chopped the project down to one-hour in length and would typically be broadcast at the ungodly 3AM time slot.

All of Chrysalis' wishes were realized except for the radio series, as the BBC and Independent Radio Network were not interested. The double album was a sampler taken from the box set. "Part Of The Machine" was one of two tracks recorded at Ian's home studio in March 1988. The other was "Man Of Principle," first issued on "Nightcap" in 1993. Gerry Conway was on both tracks and Martin Allcock was only on "Part Of The Machine," playing electric guitar, keyboards and bouzouki. "Man Of Principle" is interesting for many reasons, including Ian Anderson's quote of Bach's "Toccata & Fugue In D Minor" at its beginning and end. Besides a healthy album chart position for such a large set (UK: #78; US: #97), "20 Years Of Jethro Tull" hit #30 on Billboard's short-lived "Top Compact Disks" (sic) chart. Sales were helped by promotional 12" singles of "Part Of The Machine" and "Thick As A Brick" (in live and edited studio versions). The former was the 10th most played song on US radio that summer.

Maart Allcock first hit the stage with Jethro Tull at the Shoreline Amphitheater in Mountain View, CA. Touring the US took up nearly all of June, and included stops at the reopened Red Rocks Amphitheater (outside Denver, CO) and Pier 84 in New York City. After the Pier 84 show, someone stole the "Crest Of A Knave" tour banner. The next day, Ian Anderson went on the radio and asked for its return as the banner needed Customs clearance for the remainder of the tour and he was planning to give it to his daughter Gael as a present. It was never returned.

With Maart now a Tullie, the band's stage persona was just as varied. Allcock and Pegg hung out with fans, Ian focused on business, Perry concentrated on his playing and the slimmer Barre was more animated than ever on guitar. Jethro Tull was touring on the 1988 box set and the residual effects of "Crest Of A Knave," but only one show at Wembley Arena with Fairport Convention formed their stay in England. Despite the band's diverse personalities, humor remained in the show. Ian used the wheelchair joke again, entering the stage in the contraption with two audience members dressed as his doctor and a lovely nurse. This was Ian's way of showing that he could make fun of his throat condition, as his voice was still showing intermittent effects of trouble. Maart injected more humor into "Aqualung" by performing air guitar on a broom handle. Ian, Martin and Dave mocked being infirmant at the end of each show. This time, it was Dave Pegg's turn to use the wheelchair, while Ian laid upon the stretcher and Martin used crutches!

The Wembley show on July 19, 1988 had a nice surprise: Clive Bunker joined Tull on "Fat Man." Three days before, the first informal Jethro Tull convention took place before the band's concert in Giessen, Germany. The first unofficial Tull convention in the UK was held at a village hall in the northwest London area of Hillingdon, followed by the inaugural sanctioned event on August 5 in Uxbridge, Middlesex.

Jethro Tull's first shows in South America became another media circus. On July 24, Ian was incorrectly quoted as saying he did not like Brazilian music. An uproar resulted. In an effort to put the issue to bed, Jethro Tull performed the Stan Getz/ Astrud Gilberto hit "The Girl From Ipanema" at Belo Horizonte in Brazil on the 26th. The repercussions were still evident, however, when a fan threw a bottle that landed at Martin Barre's feet. Barre demanded that the individual present himself on stage, but the cowardly perpetrator refused.

Ian Anderson was asked to participate in a project designed to raise funds for the Earth Love Fund - Rainforest Appeal. The track "Yes We Can" was written by Manfred Mann's Earth Band vocalist and film/TV composer Harold Faltermeyer. Ian played flute on the track, which was still in a demo form consisting of a drum machine, Chris Thompson's guide vocal, synthesizer and Herbie Hancock's keyboard. Ian Anderson recommended arrangement ideas, but Thompson would have none of it. The final track, which included vocals by Joe Cocker, Stevie Lange, Michael McDonald and Jennifer Rush among others, contains just a few barely audible bars of Ian's flute. *Based on my extensive knowledge of Manfred Mann's Earth Band, Chris Thompson doesn't take orders from anyone, unless his name is Manfred Mann!* It was therefore another disappointing experience for Ian. "Yes We Can" was released as a single in the fall of 1989 in Germany before its UK release three years later. The single was released in four different mixes, all of which include Ian's slight contribution. "Yes We Can" was also included on the benefit album "Earthrise." To sum it up, it's for completists only!

"ROCK ISLAND"

Producing an album to match the success of "Crest Of A Knave" proved to be very difficult for Jethro Tull in 1989. Recording took place this time at the home studios of Dave Pegg (most of the drums) and Ian Anderson. "Rock Island" used the same formula as its predecessor, but it did not generate the same excitement or humor. The musicians for "Rock Island" were Anderson, Barre, Pegg and Doane Perry, with Martin Allcock and Peter-John Vettese guesting on keyboards. For the most part, "Rock Island" was ignored by radio, even though the singles "Another Christmas Song" (UK-only) and "Kissing Willie" (US-only cassette single and promo CD) formed the highlights from the album. "Rock Island" hit #18 in the UK and #56 Stateside, and "Kissing Willie" was the 6th most played song on US AOR stations. The track listing for the UK#95 single "Another Christmas Song" was most complete on the CD, featuring live, direct-to-DAT dressing room medleys of "Intro"/"Christmas Song," "Cheap Day Return"/"Mother Goose" and "Outro"/"Locomotive Breath" recorded in Zurich, Switzerland on October 13, 1989. These performances were supposed to comprise a radio session, but plans fell through. All of these tracks have not yet appeared on a Tull album, and its US release was a promo-only package that duplicated the UK release. Another US CD promo included "The Rattlesnake Trail" and "Another Christmas Song."

Even though "Rock Island" could not meet the high standards set by "Crest Of A Knave," Martin Barre broke through the heavier-hitting material even more. You would have thought that Maart Allcock's arrival would have eliminated the need for other keyboardists, but Ian's intent was to reflect different keyboard playing styles on "Rock Island." John Evans was asked if he wished to participate, but John turned it down because he had lost interest and had already sold his equipment. Ian handled some of this work, and Peter-John Vettese (four tracks) and Maart (two cuts) were called in to do the rest. This blend of musical backgrounds generated more favorable reviews for this album than its predecessor.

"Kissing Willie" was the track that generated the most amusement in the bunch, and it was shot as the album's promotional video. The politically correct crowd developing in society was not in agreement with the lyrics that were considered somewhat sexist. "Big Riff And Mando" also fell into the humorous category, using as its protagonists Martin's riffing guitar and Ian's mandolin - hence the title. The conceptual continuity of "Strange Avenues" involved its mention of the "Aqualung" LP cover!

The somewhat flat emotional nature of "Rock Island" did allow for other direct hits, however. "Ears Of Tin" (originally called "Mainland Blues") was the tale of leaving home to find work, but it evolved into a song dealing with the Scottish landscape. Scotland's Glen Shiel gorge and the gorge's nearby mountain range Five Sisters of Kintail are mentioned in the song. "Heavy Water" was about New York's polluted water (termed "acid rain") and Ian Anderson's experiences with it on Tull's first tours of the city in 1969. The uncredited Maart Allcock played on a third track from this session, "Hard Liner," but it was replaced at the eleventh hour by the final track recorded - "The Rattlesnake Trail." "Hard Liner" was on advance cassettes of the album. "The Rattlesnake Trail" was another strong "Rock Island" track, while "Hard Liner" would turn up later on the B-side of the 1993 "Living In The Past" reissue and the "Nightcap" collection. German Chrysalis would combine "Kissing Willie" and "Heavy Water" for the only official 7" release of the single.

The album "Rock Island" produced two fine singles: "Kissing Willie" and "Another Christmas Song." Although not isued as a single in the UK, a cassette-only US version and the German 7" below were available to fans in those countries.

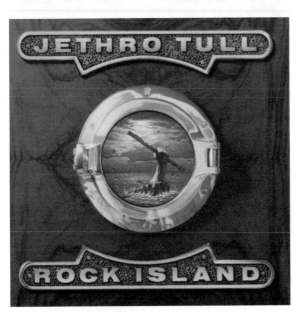

147

David Palmer was preparing for a Royal Philharmonic Orchestra charity concert at the Barbican Theatre in London on October 11, 1989. The program included David's classical rearrangements of the work of Jethro Tull, Genesis and Pink Floyd - his three classical albums on RCA. To promote the concert, Palmer re-recorded his "Elegy," this time without involvement of Jethro Tull. This version was not to be heard, as it still remains unreleased.

A month after Martin Barre appeared at the Cropredy Festival, Jethro Tull (with Allcock back in the fold) went on a three-month tour of England, Germany, Switzerland, Italy and the US. An 800-seater in Inverness, Scotland opened the tour, and Ian found himself selecting a raffle winner midway through the show! Solid laughs were generated by brick-headed props of Margaret Thatcher and George Bush and complaints by "Metallica" concerning how Jethro Tull stole their award. The heavy metal motif was played on again with roadies providing an inexpensive heavy metal-type laser light show with miner helmets. Combined with Maart Allcock's failing steam-powered keyboards, the "Rock Island" tour was a complete crowd pleaser. Instead of Maart, a lucky audience member was selected to play air guitar this time.

Most interesting was the set list inclusions of "Jack-A-Lynn" and occasional medleys of "Requiem" with "Black Satin Dancer" and "The Pine Marten's Jig" with "Drowsy Maggie." "The Third Hoorah" was also aired during this stint. The US opening act was the British band It Bites, led by lead vocalist and guitarist Francis Dunnery. Ian was still having difficulty getting over the top of the band's volume, but nothing could top the notorious "train wreck" on "Songs From The Wood." For some reason, the band completely lost their place for about ten seconds at one 1989 show, creating a wall of noise in front of a stunned crowd. Ric Sanders reprised his violin role on "Budapest" by joining Tull onstage at the Birmingham NEC show on September 25. Eddie Jobson made two guest appearances during the tour, one on each side of the Atlantic: the Hammersmith Odeon (September 29) and the Meadowlands Arena on November 9. Jobson played on "Budapest" and soloed on "The Pine Marten's Jig." Capping off the year, Ian Anderson won the "Highland Business Award" in 1989 for Strathaird Salmon Ltd.

Ian Anderson had no new material to record in early 1990, but there were other projects that required his participation. The first of these fell through. The Rock Aid Armenia charity single "Smoke On The Water" was supposed to feature Ian, but he did not receive a follow-up call with the recording details. A more surprising call came from the New York thrash metal band The Six And Violence. Despite their music genre, the band members loved Jethro Tull and asked Ian Anderson to play flute on their album. The Six And Violence knew that Tull was going to play Nassau Coliseum on November 3, 1989, so they made sure that they played while Ian was in town in order to invite him to one of their gigs. Anderson arrived with the intention to politely show up and leave shortly afterward, but he was quite taken by their overall playing attitude and output. Ian's politeness turned to tremendous enthusiasm over the project, and he played flute on the tracks "Bursting Bladder" and "Theological Guns." The former also included one of Ian's patented barbed comments. It was first issued in May 1990 on Fist Records in the US, before Dave Rees made it available to "A New Day" readers with Jethro Tull cover versions ("Nothing Is Easy" and a "Sunshine Day" medley) included as bonus tracks. The last of these projects was just as unusual and covered the other musical extreme - dance music. Ian Anderson supplied the flute on the 12" mix of Nixon's "Crazy Love" in its "Aqualung Mix." The record was issued in limited quantities in October.

Martin Barre was also busy, but he spent his time pounding the pavement. Martin ran the 1990 London Marathon to raise funds for the Great Ormond Street Children's Hospital and the Great Marlborough Street Wishing Well Appeal. For the latter cause, he enabled a disabled boy to fulfill his desire to visit Disney World.

The 1990 tour kicked off in Scotland in May and loads of UK dates followed. All of the dates on this tour leg were in more intimate venues and received only local advertising. The May 10th concert in Bradford, England was interrupted so that Ian Anderson could wish then-popular WNEW-FM DJ Scott Muni a happy birthday - his 50th. Such was the relaxed nature of the band - they did not have to impress large crowds and there was no push on to promote their latest release. There was none! These shows marked the return of Martin's song "Nellie (The Revenge)," which Tull had dabbled with in live shows around the time of "Crest Of A Knave." The song was so named because its chording bore more than a passing resemblance to the children's song "Nellie The Elephant." Otherwise, the tour was a fine overview of the band's career, drawing upon nearly all of their musical incarnations. Rarely performed numbers like "Love Story" were joined by an interesting interpolation of Bach's "Sleepers Awake" ("Wachet Auf") within "Serenade To A Cuckoo." "Pussy Willow" was also joined with "Pibroch (Cap In Hand)" for another interesting combination. It was no wonder that fans came away very impressed. Jethro Tull was working at its own pace - slower, but more defined. Other musical groups were also working in this fashion, but Tull's adaptation to this more relaxed routine was natural.

Jethro Tull's first and last show in the old East Germany took place at an open air festival in East Berlin (now just Berlin) on August 25. A week later, the group made a joint appearance with Fleetwood Mac at Wembley Stadium in London. The crowd numbered 80,000, but the fans were not able to see Tull's performance on the video screens because they did not work properly until darkness came. By that time, they were already done! The other dates were festivals in Germany and Brazil, the first Brazilian return of Tull since the last blow-up. There were no incidents or misunderstandings this time.

After the conclusion of the 1990 tour, a special event took place at the Jethro Tull convention at Woughton Centre, Milton Keynes on September 22. After years of keeping their distance, Ian Anderson and Mick Abrahams played together with Clive Bunker, Martin Barre and Martin Allcock on bass. They played a 22-minute set at the convention, and they were met backstage by Jeffrey Hammond and John Evans! Also on the bill were Mick's group Blodwyn Pig and Tull cover band Seismic Ring. Ian was very happy with the show and expressed his interest in having Tull perform at these conventions when physically possible. Allcock played on a trio of songs, as most of the set was acoustic.

The December 1990 release of the aforementioned "Live At Hammersmith '84" album was the first non-Chrysalis released album from Jethro Tull outside of the failed "Stand Up" reissue in 1984. The band began recording songs in earnest for the next song cycle, "Catfish Rising." The album's sessions at the home studios of Mssrs. Anderson, Barre and Pegg would lead to a series of changes.

When all was said and done, three keyboardists would appear on the recording sessions. Maart Allcock was not one of them. Ian Anderson was looking for a more natural piano and organ player without the inherent trappings of a synthesist. John "Rabbit" Bundrick, known for his contributions to Free and The Who, was the first keyboardist auditioned in the studio by Ian Anderson. Of the four tracks he played on, only "Sleeping With The Dog" made it to "Catfish Rising." The other three were "Piece Of Cake," "Silver River Turning" and "Rosa On The Factory Floor" - all CD bonus tracks on "Living In The Past" (1993 edition) and on "Nightcap." Bundrick was not the perfect fit Tull was looking for, so Ian again went after Peter-John Vettese. He was busy but recommended another Scottish player, Foss Paterson. Foss was even less successful than Bundrick, but the track he played on, "White Innocence," made it to the album.

"Rosa On The Factory Floor" was a humorous story song that contained the next installment in Ian Anderson's conceptual continuity. At the end of the song, Ian says "Hey! Santa! Pass us that bottle (will you)…oh no, we've done that!" Of course, he was referring to "Christmas Song." It was an unexpected and hilarious ending for such an interesting tale. *It's too bad that we couldn't appreciate it when it was recorded.*

To inject some variety into the proceedings, Ian Anderson placed a local ad for a musician in a low profile group that would play small venues with little notice. Scott Hunter, drummer for The Larry Miller Band and The Blues Project, answered the ad and ended up playing (uncredited) on two Tull tracks - one on the album ("Still Loving You Tonight"). Steve Jackson, the drummer from the Cornish group The Mechanics, also sent Ian an audition tape. Jackson sent a tape of another group he played in, The Chase, because he didn't have anything by The Mechanics that was good enough to submit. Instead of being taken by Jackson's percussion talents, Ian found the keyboard player more interesting! That person was Andy Giddings.

ANDY GIDDINGS SAMPLES SOME "CATFISH RISING"

Andrew Giddings, born July 10, 1963 in Pembury, Kent, was another early piano student. He started at four, and would not form his own band until 15 - they were called X-Static. He earned "O" levels in English, music and art and worked as a sales assistant at Hodges & Johnson Music Store and as a paste-up artist. Giddings joined the group Black Cat and worked the nostalgia circuit before going to London to play with Leo Sayer and Eric Burdon. He just missed out on joining The Cutting Crew, but who remembers them now? Andy's first recording opportunities came with Eric Burdon and other French and German outfits. Giddings also played with Sniff 'N' The Tears and was in the house band for the Granada Television entertainment program "The Funny Side." After linking up with Tull, Andy played on the tracks "This Is Not Love," "Rocks On The Road" and "Doctor To My Disease" - all of which were prime tracks on the "Catfish Rising" album. Of these, "This Is Not Love" was Tull's last heavily played track on US radio, making #14 on Billboard's Top Rock Tracks chart.

The bass situation was starting to become unstable. Dave Pegg's activities were now more involved with Fairport Convention and the operation of his Woodworm studio and record company. There was no time to waste, so Dave did the next best thing - he had his son Matt fill in for him. Matt (born in 1971) played in the band Blinder and did some sessions with It Bites, Tull's support band in 1989. Matt Pegg played on three tracks that turned out to be the singles from "Catfish Rising": "This Is Not Love," "Still Loving You Tonight," and "Rocks On The Road," and another ("Truck Stop Runner") that ended up on "Nightcap." "I Don't Want To Be Me" was another 1993 CD single track that ended up on "Nightcap," and "Night In The Wilderness" was the B-side of "This Is Not Love" along with the Japanese CD edition of "Catfish Rising." Both of these did not involve a keyboardist, but they included Dave Pegg.

"This Is Not Love" preceded "Catfish Rising," and Germany's A-side was "Still Loving You Tonight." This time, the 12" and CD single had the most complete track listings, with the tracks "Night In The Wilderness" and a live version of "Jump Start" from the 1987 Tower Theater show included on both British and German releases. "Catfish Rising" marked Tull's return to a more basic, rustic blues sound - sort of a more refined and experienced "This Was." The response to "Catfish Rising" was adequate, though it barely made the US Top 100 at #88. It made #27 in the UK and hit the Top 10 on both the UK heavy rock and the folk/roots charts - whatever those are! These singles received a muted reaction, but heavy promotion definitely helped the next multi-format single, "Rocks On The Road." Available as a 7" single, cassette, picture disc 12" single or a double CD single, "Rocks On The Road" (a UK #47 Music Week hit in March 1992) provided numerous exclusive tracks for collectors and fans to enjoy. On this occasion, the 12" is a required purchase because its remix of "Rocks On The Road" is full-length and unavailable elsewhere. While the 12" also had a 1981 home demo of the song "Jack-A-Lynn" and a live "Rockline" radio performance of the medley "Aqualung"/"Locomotive Breath," the CD singles included further exclusive live versions of "Rocks On The Road," "Like A Tall Thin Girl," "Fat Man," "Bourée" and "Mother Goose"/"Jack-A-Lynn." "Rocks On The Road," "Mother Goose"/"Jack-A-Lynn" and "Bourée" came from a WMMR radio (Philadelphia, PA) broadcast on August 21, 1991. "Like A Tall Thin Girl" and "Fat Man" were from another 1991 radio broadcast - this time from Electric Ladyland Studios in New York. The six-track US CD single of "Rocks On The Road" was a combination of the "This Is Not Love" and "Rocks On The Road" singles, with the live and album edits of "Rocks On The Road," the live versions of "Bourée" and "Jump Start," the demo of "Jack-A-Lynn" and "Night In The Wilderness." Two other promos worked their magic in Mexico (the double-sided "This Is Not Love") and in Argentina ("This Is Not Love" coupled with another artist). "This Is Not Love" was a single-tracked US CD promo, and another American promo joined "Doctor To My Disease" with "Night In The Wilderness" and the 1987 live version of "Jump Start."

As another move forward, "Catfish Rising" managed to polarize fans. Whether the album was a throwback to the old days, or a fresh outlook, depended on the fan you asked, but its contents reflected all the elements that a Jethro Tull album required to maintain long-term interest. Similar to "Crest Of A Knave," the artwork sparked the album title, and the B-side "Night In The Wilderness" was a song that mentioned catfish. The songs were mainly written on open-tuned mandolins and acoustic guitars. Ian expressed the nature of the album's songs at the time: "This is probably the first time a Jethro Tull album has had so many boy/girl relationship songs. But that's not deliberate, and I'll probably instinctively move away from that on our next record. We tried to make it a balanced album musically. There are a couple of tracks that are fairly straight-ahead rock songs, like 'This Is Not Love' and 'Doctor To My Disease.' There are also a lot of songs with kind of a country-blues feel, like 'Roll Yer Own' and 'Sparrow On The Schoolyard Wall,' which evolved out of me just playing mandolin and filling things in around that. And then there are a couple of songs that are the more typical kind of lengthy, arranged mid-tempo Jethro Tull material, namely 'Rocks On The Road' and 'White Innocence.'" The rustic nature of "Catfish Rising" had Ian commenting more: "What interests me more at this moment is to get back to music that grows on trees - instruments that you actually have to play, as opposed to sitting down and reading some 200-page manual in order to play a part. A lot of the songs on 'Crest Of A Knave' and 'Rock Island' were written on keyboards, but all of the songs on the new album were written on guitar or mandolin, and that gives them a completely different flavor."

That flavor featured Indian cuisine, which Ian and some of the others heartily enjoy. "Like A Tall Thin Girl" was about Doane Perry's longing for an Indian restaurant waitress working on London's Baker Street. Doane saw her at the restaurant while he and Ian were eating there during Doane's 1984 rehearsal period! The other flavor was wordplay, which "Think Round Corners" and the album as a whole artfully crafted.

The album was launched at a bar near Ian's estate in Berkshire, but it was more of a party than a launch - "Catfish Rising" was not played and Tull didn't perform. What did occur was an acoustic Fairport Convention set with guest drummer Chris Welch - yes, *that* Chris Welch! Starting in the third week of June, Jethro Tull played in Europe, including some unusual places like Turkey and Estonia (in the former USSR). Playing countries like Estonia, Ian would remark: "We seem to have become ambassadors for western rock music to Iron Curtain countries." The pre-release set was very much like their 1990 tour. Since they were not to

"Catfish Rising" was preceded by the top-notch single "This Is Not Love."

Two CD volumes of "The Best Of King Biscuit Live" featured tracks from Tull's November 25, 1987 show in Upper Darby, PA.

Lower left photo: Ian is caught in a Denver alley in 1992.
(Photo courtesy of Lon Horwitz)

Lower right: Ian during the "A Little Light Music" tour.
(Photo courtesy of Dag Sandbu)

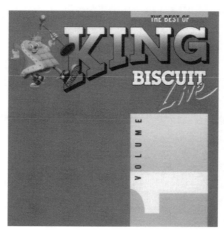

appear in the US until November, the trio of Anderson, Barre and Pegg ventured to the States to appear on radio during a two-week run. They played acoustic sessions at those stations to prepare listeners for the album and to re-energize their back catalog. While this was going on, Doane Perry released his "Creative Listening" drum video for VDO Productions in July.

Prior to the tour, Martin Barre ran the London Marathon on April 21, 1991. This time, Martin raised money for the Royal Schools for the Deaf. Jethro Tull was represented on US television, if you were lucky enough to catch the Miller Beer commercial that featured "Locomotive Breath." As for Ian, he was looking at pricy Sankyo Silversonics and Powell flutes for the future. On stage, he continued to use his Artley models for live playing and other creative manipulation. His Artleys would soon be replaced by tone-rich Powell flutes and the more powerful (and relatively effortless) Sankyos on tour, with Powell models exclusively used for recording.

The last ten weeks of 1991 made up the group's European and US tour with a start in England. At some US shows, heavy metal act Chrissy Steele opened the show. Maart Allcock was retained for the tour, even though his studio involvement with Tull was now nonexistent. However, Maart and Dave Pegg continued to fraternize with fans. Such outgoing social interactions finally rubbed off on Ian. This was the blossoming of Ian Anderson's public outreach to fans and his ongoing interest in their likes and dislikes of Jethro Tull's history and direction.

This sensitivity was reflected in the beautiful pairing of "Reasons For Waiting" and "Look Into The Sun" during the tour. Shows of this period were introduced by a tape of Carl Orff's "O Fortuna" from "Carmina Burana," and Martin Barre blazed through an instrumental version of "Paparazzi" to decorate Jethro Tull's multi-faceted program.

At Portland Civic Center on November 8, 1991, Ian Anderson gave one of his worst performances with Jethro Tull. During this show, Ian vociferously expressed his emotions about the terminal illnesses of Queen's Freddie Mercury as well as that of his highly respected contemporary Frank Zappa. The main problem with these statements was that Ian came onstage in an intoxicated state. What brought this on? A four-night concert event honoring the music of Frank Zappa, entitled "Zappa's Universe: A Celebration," was taking place at The Ritz in New York City from November 7-10. Zappa was scheduled to attend the concerts, but he cancelled at the last minute. On November 8th - the same day as the Tull show in Portland, Maine - Frank Zappa's daughter Moon and son Dweezil announced that Frank had prostate cancer. Word of this announcement reached Ian Anderson right afterward, and Ian was naturally upset. Ian had received a message a few weeks earlier that Zappa wanted to hear from him. Considering that rumors of Zappa's illness had been circulating since 1989, Ian felt awkward about calling him. Ian never completed a call to the Zappa residence even though he dialed and immediately hung up. Ian was so annoyed with himself for not grasping that opportunity of speaking with Frank Zappa that he proceeded to drink three-quarters of a bottle of wine backstage before the show in Portland. That night, Ian Anderson did something that he thought he would never do by appearing onstage under the influence of alcohol. While the potentially terminal illness of a contemporary can be difficult to deal with, cheated fans and critics felt the lack of respect that Anderson showed them that night by performing in that condition. This was the first and (hopefully) last time Ian Anderson appeared in an altered condition on stage. Curiously, Ian misremembered this story during an interview that appeared in Barbara Espinoza's 1999 book "Driving In Diverse: A Collective Profile Of Jethro Tull." In this interview, Ian stated that he started drinking backstage in Portland after hearing of Frank Zappa's death. Zappa died just before 6PM on December 4, 1993. Where was Jethro Tull on December 4, 1993? They had already returned home to England, as their 1993 tour ended on November 22. Therefore, Ian's story is unfortunately incorrect.

With an album called "Catfish Rising," you would expect some kind of fish to be involved. Five thousand pounds of fish were cooked on stage in the week they played in England! Unfortunately, this practice was not continued in the US, but other surprises were in store. Ian Anderson appeared on the Howard Stern morning radio program on November 14 and told Howard that he had lost 30 pounds and quit smoking. Ian was clearly in fine physical condition when he appeared that night at Nassau Coliseum, but the nearly 20,000-seat venue was only half full. Tull was the first band to play Nassau Coliseum on May 13, 1972, but things were now different. It was one of the saddest sights that one could ever witness, but it was clear that the band's days of playing large arenas was in the past. Needless to say, it was the last Jethro Tull gig at Nassau Coliseum. A more upbeat show, at McNichols Arena in Denver on December 7, had an ice cream lady giving out Dove ice cream bars!

Another unusual Ian Anderson appearance came during the fall of 1991 on a Bomb The Bass recording. The "Unknown Territory" album version of "Love So True" covers the flute section from Jethro Tull's "My God," but the 12" mix of the track actually uses the sampled sound of Ian's flute in the recording. It was released in England on the Rhythm King label. Meanwhile, a cassette or CD of Jethro Tull's 1970 appearance at the Aragon Ballroom was a free inclusion with copies of the Italian publication "Il Dizionario del Rock" ("The Dictionary Of Rock"). Subscribers received a CD, while cassettes were packaged with newsstand copies.

Three separate tours were on tap for 1992. Maart Allcock was not verbally notified that he was now out of Jethro Tull - he just got another one of those cold form letters. It came from Ian's secretary. Allcock immersed himself in various recording sessions and Fairport Convention, who he would leave in 1997 to found the band Waz! with Pete Zorn and Dave Whetstone. Andy Giddings would be his full-time replacement, but even that seemed uncertain at first. After playing on "Catfish Rising," drummer Scott Hunter and his lead guitarist Neil Sadler rehearsed acoustic-based material at Ian Anderson's studio during an afternoon and evening with Ian and Martin Barre, but they would not end up with the assignment. Doane Perry had asked Ian Anderson for a leave of absence to fulfill some outside commitments. His stand-in was noted drummer Dave Mattacks.

DAVE MATTACKS AND "A LITTLE LIGHT MUSIC"

David Mattacks was born in Edgeware, Middlesex during March 1948 (he doesn't want his actual birthdate to be revealed!). Mattacks left school to become an apprentice piano tuner before working at Drum City Music Shop in London. He moonlighted three years with a big band. Stage engagements included London, Belfast and Glasgow as well as some jazz groups in the UK. Dave joined Fairport Convention in the fall of 1969, which included recording and touring on seven LPs. He departed in 1974 for session work and returned to the band in late 1985.

The first tour continued with a set very similar to the previous year's jaunt. On March 13, 1992, Giddings and Mattacks made their Jethro Tull debuts at the Plymouth Pavilion. The band performed a month of dates in smaller venues with much more crowd interaction. After this tour segment, the first Jethro Tull convention in the United States was held in Newport, RI over the weekend of April 25-26.

An arrangement change was in order with the popularity of simpler "unplugged" performance styles similar to the MTV acoustic-based program of the same name. To accomplish this, Andy Giddings was not required, but Dave Mattacks was retained. Fans had been clamoring for Jethro Tull to tour acoustically, and the tour named "A Little Light Music" did just that. It walked the line between acoustic and electric by dabbling in both, as the more aggressive guitar numbers like "Aqualung" still used a heavier guitar sound. Defining exactly how Tull would be treating their songs was covered in the catch-all billing "A Little Light Music Featuring The Songs Of Jethro Tull: A More Or Less Acoustic Performance by Ian Anderson, Martin Barre, Dave Pegg and David Mattacks." Whew!

The error-filled May 1, 1992 kickoff gig at Guildford Civic Hall was an unmitigated disaster full of band nervousness. Tull decided to record all the shows of this concert leg for a live album release known as "A Little Light Music," but they were fortunate not to tape their inaugural performance! The other British show at Wembley Conference Centre suffered from poor ticket sales. A week into the tour, Gerry Conway was the surprise drummer at their appearances in Zurich, Switzerland. The week after that, Jethro Tull received another onstage guest while in Athens for a two-night stay - Greek vocal institution George Dalaras. Ian Anderson and George Dalaras worked out an arrangement before the shows in that they would not do their own material onstage. Instead, they would select a pair of outside songs they both enjoyed. The songs performed by Tull with Dalaras were The Rolling Stones' "Ruby Tuesday" and the traditional "John Barleycorn." "John Barleycorn" was an old Celtic ballad which reflected the bread and ale tradition. It was interesting how the song was treated in this mainly acoustic setting. Both Athens live versions draw upon the Traffic version, which is based on both the traditional "Sir John Barleycorn" and Scottish poet Robert Burns' verses of "John Barleycorn." "Ruby Tuesday" would not be released on the "A Little Light Music" album, but two different versions of "John Barleycorn" were issued. In Greece, Italy and Israel, the Anderson/Dalaras duet version of "John Barleycorn" was included, but the standard US and European releases had Ian's studio-overdubbed vocal version of the song. The reason for this overdubbing was that Chrysalis mistakenly thought that George Dalaras was an unknown commodity and no one would be interested in hearing him on the song. Another Chrysalis blunder! To their amazement, George Dalaras was a sell-out artist in England and the US. George's later appearances at Wembley in London and New York's Madison Square Garden were proof of this. The vocal overdub on "John Barleycorn" wasn't the only tampering involved with the live tapes - a guitar track on that song and some other percussion was added to the final masters.

At left is the 1992 lineup of Dave Mattacks, Martin Barre, Andy Giddings, Ian Anderson and Dave Pegg.

At right: Ian Anderson, Dave Mattacks and Martin Barre on that tour. (Photo © 1992 Mark Colman)

Hello again, Ian!

The "Acoustic Aid" CD raised money for AIDS and included Tull's live version of "Bourée" from 1991. The single "Rocks On The Road" was filled with non-album live versions of Jethro Tull favorites. "A Little Light Music" provided an interesting cross-section of the band's music within more intimate settings.

Below: Ian Anderson and Martin Barre at the Hard Rock Café in October 1992. (Photo © 1992 Mark Colman)

Outside England, this tour was improperly promoted as "An Acoustic Jethro Tull Concert" and confused fans with its somewhat electric sound on various songs. Ian Anderson's voice was still presenting a problem, especially since he couldn't soar above a band playing at a lower volume. The set itself tapped a piece of "A Passion Play" for the first time in 17 years and other rarely performed songs, like "From A Deadbeat To An Old Greaser," worked extremely well in this forum.

The week before a trio of Jethro Tull shows in July, Martin Barre played live with a band he put together for occasional summer performances - The Summer Band. Their concerts in Devon, Collumpton, Exeter and the Tull convention in Milton Keynes were recorded and tracks from those shows were included on the CD/cassette "A Summer Band." In late June 1993, it was released on Martin Barre's label named after his studio - Presshouse Records. Copies sold out very quickly and it is a serious collector's piece with Jethro Tull fans. The other acts at the Jethro Tull convention were Elaine Morgan and Dave Dutfield from the group Rose Among Thorns. At the July 24 show, Matt Pegg filled in for his father again and made his live debut with Tull.

Two shows in England and their first in Iceland kicked off the final mini-tour of the year. This trip was different in that it was called the "Light And Dark" tour, and an equal number of dates in Canada were covered as in the US. Mexico was also touched upon for the first time. Ian Anderson felt that North American audiences would not be as receptive to an acoustic Jethro Tull without keyboards, so he brought in Andy Giddings again to fill out the sound. The set remained very much like the previous one without Giddings. On October 17, Ian became ill and was forced to cancel the gig at the Spreckles Theater in San Diego. Another of Ian's prize possessions disappeared on November 9 - the final 1992 tour date - when his harmonica was stolen from Montreal's St. Denis Theatre.

Fans got used to the idea that Jethro Tull was moving at a slower pace, but they were surprised with the release of "A Little Light Music" in September. Its tracks were drawn from 13 of the 17 recorded gigs during the second tour leg. The album reached #34 in the UK and only #150 in the US - a shocking dropoff. Promo CDs of "Some Day The Sun Won't Shine For You" (in the UK) and "Christmas Song" (US-only) were released for radio play, which did not readily take place.

After returning home, Jethro Tull made a series of recordings done at Beacons Bottom and the home studios of Ian Anderson, Martin Barre and Dave Pegg. Doane Perry was back in the fold. These were recorded for the upcoming 25th anniversary box set that Ian Anderson was starting to assemble. Their anniversary year, 1993, would prove to be a bonanza for fans craving unreleased material.

THE 25TH ANNIVERSARY FESTIVITIES AND A "NIGHTCAP"

Also in the works were a 90-minute video and one-hour TV broadcast - "25 Years Of Jethro Tull." During an interview, Ian Anderson gave a wish list of artists he would like to record with, and Ian came up with James Galway, The Stranglers and The Ramones!

US fans were treated to two live Jethro Tull tracks from their 1987 Tower Theater concert ("Aqualung" and "Locomotive Breath"), available on Volumes 1 and 4 of Sandstone Records' "The Best Of King Biscuit Live" series. The benefit album "Acoustic Aid" used the same WMMR version of "Bourée" that appeared on the "Rocks On The Road" single earlier in the year. CD sales proceeds went toward AIDS research, and the collection was made available in England in mid-February 1993.

In the summer of 1992, Ian Anderson found himself caving in to the demands of Chrysalis and the fans, who wanted a multitude of products to honor Jethro Tull's 25th anniversary in 1993. The downside of these archival releases would be the complete impossibility of a new album. Ian Anderson, the forward-looking musician that he is, would have rather spent the same time organizing a new Tull album for release in 1993. Instead, Tull made the Beacons Bottom tapes available from the previous November for potential box set use. Since no one knew if the band would make its next major anniversary (its 30th) in 1998, it was now or never to deliver any prized goodies that were still lurking in Ian's tape library.

Chrysalis wanted Ian Anderson to come up with two 4CD sets, a "best of" and a new video released a few months apart. Dave Rees and Martin Webb, co-compilers of the 20th anniversary box, requested a four-disc set and a double disc "best of" collection. The results stunned everyone: a 4CD box, a 2CD "best of," a video and another double disc set - a total of eight CDs and one video!

The "25th Anniversary Box Set" was the initial 4CD present that Ian Anderson presented to Jethro Tull fans in April 1993. The first disc was entirely made up of remixed Tull favorites, while the other three discs consisted of live recordings from various locations: disc two included the remaining sections of the 1970 Carnegie Hall concert, disc three featured new live takes on old material, and the final disc was a compilation of performances from around the world.

The first disc, entitled "Remixed Classic Songs," presented all of its songs in different frames. There was no mistaking that the reverb and other audio effects liberally used on the vocals, guitars and drums was not in existence when these songs were recorded, so there is a somewhat anachronistic feel on some of the earlier tracks. Having said that, the "most improved mix" awards go to "A Song For Jeffrey," "Too Old To Rock 'N' Roll: Too Young To Die" and "Black Sunday," all of which were not properly balanced upon original release. In fact, the difference in "Too Old Too Rock 'N' Roll..." is quite revelatory. So are "Songs From The Wood" and "Heavy Horses," which contain instrumentation either edited or mixed out on the fine, original mixes. "Life Is A Long Song" had an exclusive announcement at its start from Ian that it was Take 5. The entire Carnegie Hall show, except for the two cuts issued on "Living In The Past," formed the interesting second disc. It was a wasted opportunity to present the entire show on one disc, especially since it would have been no problem timewise.

"The Beacons Bottom Tapes" comprised the third disc. The title is a misnomer because five of the 14 tracks weren't recorded there! Three were recorded at Ian's home studio, one at Dave Pegg's Woodworm Studio and the other at Martin Barre's own Presshouse. The Pegg and Barre tracks were the respective instrumental solo recordings "Cheerio" and "Protect And Survive." Ian's three home pieces were the solo "So Much Trouble" and "Some Day The Sun Won't Shine For You" along with an Anderson/Giddings pairing on "Living In The Past." "A New Day Yesterday" featured an instrumental version of "Kelpie," and it would also be played this way during the tours in 1993 and 1994. Most interesting of all is the performance of Ian's "The Whistler" by the band at his studio - Ian's not on it!

The final "Pot Pourri: Live Across The World & Through The Years" disc leaned heavily on more recent live performances, although some surprises like the aforementioned "To Be Sad Is A Mad Way To Be" and the segments from "A Passion Play" are evident. In an unusual move, EMI in the US decided to import UK copies instead of pressing their own for American fans.

While preparations were being made for the first box set, a February 1993 reunion at the West Morland Arms in London featured Ian Anderson, Martin Barre, John Evans, Jeffrey Hammond-Hammond, Mick Abrahams, Glenn Cornick, Clive Bunker, Barriemore Barlow, Dave Pegg, Mark Craney, Doane Perry, Maart Allcock, Andy Giddings, Tony Williams and Ric Sanders and Simon Nicol of Fairport Convention. We can safely assume that everyone else that was in Tull was not able to make it!

With all of these albums in the pipeline, Chrysalis went into overdrive. Chrysalis was bought out by EMI before the release of "A Little Light Music," and EMI's reissue division was a high-profile participant in the archival release of '60s and '70s music. On March 3, 1993, Ian and Martin recorded an informal discussion about the band's entire back catalog. This was issued to radio stations on two CDs with the hopes of using their comments to precede a track from the album being discussed. (*I don't know about you, but I never heard those CDs on the radio!*) The "25th Anniversary Interview" promo CDs were very difficult to locate, so Dave Rees made them available with Ian and Chrysalis' blessing as a limited edition double cassette package in October. The cassette edition was lacking the 24-page discography and photo booklet that came with the 1993 double CD.

During one of Jethro Tull's stays in Germany in 1992, Ian Anderson was contacted by German drummer Leslie Mandoki to play on some of his songs featuring other musical luminaries. Mandoki was born in Munich on January 7, 1953 and was a member of the '70s group Djingis Khan. Ian ended up singing and playing flute on three tracks for Leslie: "Hold On To Your Dreams," "I Dance Through My Dreams" and "Mother Europe." Ian did a German television special for Mandoki on the 5th of March 1993 with Jack Bruce, Bobby Kimball of Toto and Blood, Sweat & Tears' David Clayton-Thomas. These tracks were included on Mandoki's "People" CD that year.

The band decided to do two radio appearances to celebrate their 25th anniversary and maintain US interest before they returned in August and September with Procol Harum supporting them. These shows took place at the Lone Star Roadhouse in New York (April 26) and The Spectrum in Philadelphia (April 27). The Philadelphia show also marked the 25th anniversary of the station it was being broadcasted on - WMMR. Both shows were broadcast live and were lighthearted fun. A then-untitled instrumental was played at these shows and at others during their tour. It was soon known as "Andy Giddings' Parrot." In case you're wondering, Andy did indeed have a parrot, and its name was Parker!

It was Ian's intention to make sure Jethro Tull's coverage reached as many countries as possible. Territories like the former East Germany (now part of the unified Germany) and the recently formed Czech Republic were getting their first official taste of Jethro Tull and others of the time, since their only exposure to real music was smuggled or poorly bootlegged product.

Two shows in England kicked off Jethro Tull's world tour, with the widest range of country coverage they would ever manage in one sweep. In late May (late June in the US), another Jethro Tull compilation hit the shops: "The Best Of Jethro Tull." Each Tull studio album was represented by at least one track on this double CD, so at last a career retrospective by the band was available. The multi-level promotion for the album included British-only single releases of "Living In The Past," offering numerous non-album tracks. The 7" B-side of this single was "Rock Island" outtake "Hard Liner." On the CD front, two singles were released: the first featured a live version of "Living In The Past" from Montreal (taken from the "25th Anniversary Box Set"), and the studio outtakes "Silver River Turning," "Rosa On The Factory Floor" and "I Don't Want To Be Me" (all from the "Catfish Rising" sessions). The second had the original version of "Living In The Past" joined with "Truck Stop Runner" and "Piece Of Cake" (both outtakes from "Catfish Rising") and 1988's "Man Of Principle." Most upsetting to Tull fans, however, was the limited 12" single, which put four updated dance mixes of "Living In The Past" on display. Most people were outraged, and the others were highly amused. Chrysalis successfully tricked club DJs by calling 12" promo copies "Living In The Dub" and purposely leaving off the "Jethro" from the band's name on the record label. The "Living In The Past" reissue reached #32 in Music Week (#34 NME) and just missed out on being mentioned on UK television's "Top Of The Pops."

October and November 1993 were equally exciting for the band. On October 16 at the Hammersmith Apollo in London, Tull was joind onstage by Mick Abrahams, Clive Bunker and Gerry Conway. The next day, Ian did three songs by himself at a York, England record store before appearing that night at Wolverhampton Civic Hall. Two weeks later, Jethro Tull found themselves in Chile and Argentina for the first time. Ian Anderson also filmed a brief introductory spot for the Spanish-language music video program "El Planeta" ("The Planet"). In case you're wondering: No, Ian didn't speak in Spanish!

Up next for Tull fans in the UK was yet another 2CD set entitled "Nightcap." This November '93 release replaced the originally planned second 25th anniversary 4CD box set and included a healthy selection of previously unreleased studio tracks, with more of the Chateau D'Herouville (pre-"A Passion Play") sessions recently discovered by Ian Anderson. Similar to the 20th anniversary set, Ian's newly recorded flute was added on some outtakes - namely the Chateau D'Herouville tracks. Completed vocals were missing on these recordings, but Ian wisely decided against adding his wartorn 1993 voice to 1972 tapes. All of the non-album tracks on the British "Living In The Past" singles, except for the notorious dance mixes, have been covered on this album. US EMI passed on releasing "Nightcap," but it had no interest in importing it. This was the first clue of EMI's lack of attention in handling the Jethro Tull catalog. Take heart: EMI in the US finally saw the error of its ways and planned a January 2000 release for the collection.

"Nightcap"'s two CDs were called "My Round" and "Your Round." "My Round" was the Chateau D'Herouville material that Ian found after putting up hundreds of reels on a tape machine to identify exactly what was on them. Anderson held back the tracks he considered embarrassing, and these will apparently remain unissued. The three tracks that originally appeared on the 20th anniversary box were repeated here instead of the pieces Ian chose not to share with us. Therefore, we will never get the feel of what the original album would have been, especially since the original unedited edition/mix of "Skating Away On The Thin Ice Of The New Day" was not included here either. All in all, it was a fascinating experience for Tull fans to have reclaimed an outstanding project that everyone thought was forever lost.

The second disc, "Your Round," was an outtake collection and brought fans up-to-date at the same time. The songs spanned from 1974 to 1988, and all of the "Rock Island" and "Catfish Rising" leftovers that appeared on the "Living In The Past" 7" and CD singles were captured here. This was Ian's gesture of good will to fans unable to locate or afford those singles. The number of people upset with the inclusion of these tracks could probably be counted on one hand! In reality, there were no other leftovers that Ian Anderson considered worthy of release even if the 1989-1991 tracks were not included. These leftovers were not presented in chronological order on the disc, but this was of no consequence as the tracks flowed smoothly in the order presented. Ian battled with Chrysalis/EMI to keep the 2CD set affordable and donated his songwriting royalties to Balnain House, Home Of Highland

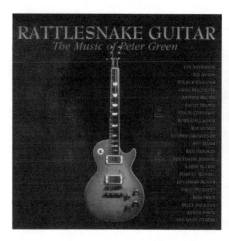 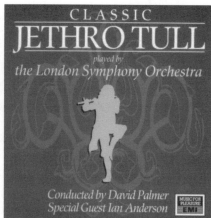 

Some of the many collections and reissues released in the mid-1990s. At left is the CD "Rattlesnake Guitar: The Music Of Peter Green," which includes tracks by Ian Anderson and Mick Abrahams' Blodwyn Pig, among others.

 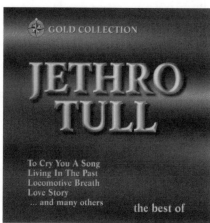 

Two volumes in South Africa's "Platinum" series gathered together what EMI in that country felt was the band's best material. In Poland, four different "best of" CDs were released. All are shown here.

At right is an unusual CD-ROM with Jethro Tull's performance of "With You There To Help Me" on "Beat Club" in Germany.

Above: The French CD "The Very Best Of Jethro Tull."

Ian Anderson on the 1994 tour (Photos © 1994 Mark Colman)

Music, Inverness, Scotland and The Animal Health Trust.

The band's third video was carefully and safely crafted for their anniversary. The February 1993 footage of Jethro Tull alumni in a London pub was edited in such a way that confrontations were left on the cutting room floor. Enlightening interviews, studio videos and live performances (some repeated) were presented in a free-flowing, entertaining package.

Touring for their 25th anniversary would take Jethro Tull well into their 27th year. On January 8, 1994, Ian appeared as an acoustic solo act at the Tull convention in Altenkirchen, Germany. Through his daughter Gael, Ian Anderson made a discovery that would undo all his years of playing flute - he was fingering the instrument incorrectly! On top of this, Ian was told that he was only using the middle of the flute's three-octave range. He found this out just before leaving for Tull's first dates in India (February 16-17). While in India, Ian requested a fax from England containing a fingering diagram. When he returned home, Anderson re-learned the flute over the next few weeks and readjusted his playing style to encompass the flute's complete tonal capabilities.

Martin Barre finally obtained a solo recording contract, but it was with the German dance label ZYX. It was a four-album deal, but it was immediately fraught with problems. In April (UK: May), ZYX released Martin's album "A Trick Of Memory." Saying ZYX "released" the album was similar to saying that a few copies escaped from the warehouse - distribution was practically non-existent and ZYX simply didn't care because it was not a dance release. Musically, the album was a fine representation of Martin's guitar talents and his first released vocals on record. Andy Giddings, Maart Allcock and Ric Sanders from Fairport Convention, Matt Pegg, drummer Marc Parnell and sax player Mel Collins all turned in fine supporting roles. ZYX issued "Suspicion" as a promo CD single, but it was just as hard to locate as the album itself.

The 25th anniversary tour in 1994 mainly hit secondary locations in countries they were already familiar with, and they were back in England for the second time in seven months. The set was essentially the same as in 1993. Some of the most interesting venues they played were the Ko Shan Theater for their Hong Kong debut and TSB Stadium, where they recognized the 20th anniversary of the Magog Motorcycle Club in New Plymouth, New Zealand in two shows. A two-week stay in Australia and a night in Hawaii led to coverage of North America and Europe, concluding with their live debut in Romania at a Bucharest festival.

The shows in June and July would cause scheduling problems for Doane Perry and Dave Pegg. Perry was unable to make the five dates in June, and his poorly rehearsed fill-in Marc Parnell proved inadequate. Parnell came from Martin's group, A Summer Band. More disturbing was the lack of involvement by Dave Pegg. Dave was far too busy with Fairport Convention activities on the recording and live fronts. Once again, his son Matt took his place with Jethro Tull. In this case, Matt's familiarity with Tull's repertoire and the three "Catfish Rising" tracks he recorded with the band prepared him well. Still, the visual and audio images of Jethro Tull with these two temporary replacements were not what they should have been - it was as if the group was playing in a small venue on the nostalgia circuit as Ian Anderson's Jethro Tull.

Three short breaks were broken up by some notable appearances. The Tutbury Summer Music Festival had Jethro Tull and Blodwyn Pig on their bill (among others), and the Friends Of The Earth benefit show by "Jethro Tull & Friends" at Clapham Grand in London, had Tull playing with varying permutations of the following musicians: Mick Abrahams, Clive Bunker, Gary Brooker of Procol Harum and Roy Harper. Ian Anderson joked about the importance of Friends Of The Earth while on stage because he was continually asked about doing the show until he finally agreed. Dave Pegg was preparing the Cropredy Festival, so he remained out of the Tull picture.

A festival in Denmark was followed by a "Euro-Woodstock" festival in Budapest, Hungary on August 19. The next night, Ian Anderson joined Leslie Mandoki's band of has-beens, including Jack Bruce, Bobby Kimball and David Clayton-Thomas. Two more Mandoki tracks with Ian Anderson's involvement were released: "On And On" and "Last Night."

The 1994 tour concluded with seven South African gigs in October. Jethro Tull had not issued an album for three years and there were concerns that Ian Anderson still didn't have material ready to record. It was clearly time to get away from celebratory tours and studio reissues and move on to the future. South Africa released two "best of" packages and France put one out themselves.

"DIVINITIES" AND "ROOTS TO BRANCHES"

In fact, Ian Anderson had been busy putting together two albums: his second solo album, "Divinities: Twelve Dances With God" and the next Jethro Tull CD "Roots To Branches." As Ian described it, doing the "Divinities" album required some convincing: "This record seemed like the least likely thing for me to do. I had thought of making a blues album or a low-key acoustic album. Then EMI came to me with a request from their classical division in London. They persuaded me to do this, thinking it would get into that mysterious area known as 'crossover music.' It was a risk to take and we didn't expect much more than to cover its cost."

Credit Roger Lewis from EMI's classical music division for being persistent with his wishes for Ian to record an instrumental flute album with an overall spiritual or religious theme. Anderson had turned Lewis down a few times, but some late 1993/ early 1994 demos with Andy Giddings turned out much better than expected. Ian and Andy recorded them on DAT and Ian took them on his Indian holiday in early February 1994. Ian Anderson wanted to demo the songs with Giddings first before recording, but they both agreed that these recordings were of releasable quality. The process was that Ian would give Andy song ideas, and Giddings used an orchestral keyboard sound to fill-out the material. Giddings' contributions became a happy accident, since Anderson had not thought of such an accompaniment. Along with Giddings, members of the Royal Philharmonic Orchestra were featured on the album. Being a more serious release, Andy was credited as Andrew Giddings!

Ian Anderson wanted to call the album "Divinities" and EMI desired the title "Twelve Dances With God." They met in the middle by using both titles. "Divinities: Twelve Dances With God" was issued on EMI in England, but on the Angel classical label in the US - the same release mechanism used on Frank Zappa's "The Perfect Stranger" album in 1984.

"Divinities: Twelve Dances With God" was Ian's sophisticated view of the world's religions and God's univeral nature and not his own religious beliefs, as he readily expressed: "What I tried to do initially was to take six world religions that I could present some feeling about, some response in music. Initially, I was going to confine myself totally to the monotheistic religions like Christianity and Judaism where there was a single God. But I decided to include Hinduism because amongst the plethors, the enormous family of Indian gods, there still lies at the back of it, a single creator. So I felt I could stretch the definition a little bit to bring Hinduism in there. One of the reasons we decided to put the various symbols on was because I thought it would be nice to have all the motifs on the cover. Also, I still felt that at the back of all religions you still have a sense of awe, of wonder. At the end of the day, it was just nice to bring all these things in a fun, colorful way. I am not being critical or in any way specific about any religion. I am just trying to give a personal response about the people and the atmosphere that surrounds those religions rather than trying to be too historical."

While in India, Ian made a rediscovery of the bamboo flute - it was originally part of his notorious claghorn. EMI India helped Ian Anderson find a Madras music shop at which he purchased three or four bamboo flutes. The demos of "Divinities" used those bamboo flutes, but most of the final masters used American flutes of that type made by Patrick Olwell as well as other wooden models.

"Divinities: Twelve Dances With God" was an album of modern music with orchestral overtones. Its overall effect was an album that strict classical fans did not like, but novices fully enjoyed. The term "classical" has proven to be an incorrect label for any non-rock music requiring a great deal of technical accomplishment. Ian Anderson addressed this terminology head on: "I can't write classical music. If I could, it wouldn't be deemed classical music until I've been dead 100 years. Classical by virtue seems to suggest not a style or genre but a qualification that comes with history having decided it was up to snuff, on a par with Mozart. That's why John Williams' 'Star Wars' music or Andrew Lloyd Webber's stuff will never be considered classical music. It's show music." Marketing and stocking the album caused problems as a result, and sales figures bore this out. The album received its German release on April 10, 1995, and releases in England (April 24) and the US (May 2) followed shortly after. The fact that it was released around Easter time was a bit of a subliminal religious message.

The album was far different than what fans were expecting, "Divinities: Twelve Dances With God" was more of an instrumental flute showcase for Ian Anderson. In the May 20, 1995 issue of Billboard, the album hit #1 in its first week on the publication's meaningless "Top Classical Crossover" album chart. Ian made sure to make fun of the chart during every live opportunity, with lines like "The album hit #1 on the Top Classical Crossover chart - whatever the fuck that is!" Another Anderson onstage joke related to album's poor overall sales showing: "We had a lot of fun making that. Unfortunately, you didn't have a lot of fun buying it. Never mind, there's still time." EMI in the US put together a promo video for "Divinities" with Ian Anderson interview segments and mimed bits, and the British arm assembled a four-track CD promo entitled "Four Dances With God."

Before Ian went on the road to promote "Divinities" in 1995, he joined the artistic advisory board of a new American non-profit organization - The International Foundation for Performing Arts Medicine (IFPAM). IFPAM raises funds for medical research, injury prevention programs, and the treatment of performance related injuries. The organization is based in North Caldwell, NJ.

By this point, Jethro Tull had sold over 40 million albums with 60+ gold and platinum albums to their credit. Personally, Ian's salmon business was attracting £12 million of business each year. The Windsong label wished to issue the "Sight 'N' Sound In Concert" 1977 show in April 1995, but they had to be content with releasing a "Catfish Rising"-era show instead the next month.

Assembling the lineup for "Divinities" was just as challenging as the album. Ian already had Andy Giddings and Doane Perry, but Dave Pegg was still occupied elsewhere. An orchestra was too cost prohibitive, but an alternative was at hand. Ian Anderson was looking for a violinst with a MIDI (musical instrument digital interface) background, and Dave Pegg came through with his recommendation of Chris Leslie. Leslie had come from the folk group Whippersnapper and he had also played with Fairport Convention. He had an easy going personality that meshed well with the other band members, and he played five-string electric violin on the "Divinities" material. That left the bass slot available in this so-called "pocket orchestra." Jonathan Noyce came to Ian's aid.

JONATHAN NOYCE TO THE RESCUE!

Jonathan Mark Thomas Noyce became the youngest full-time member ever to play with Ian Anderson and then with Jethro Tull. Noyce was born on July 15, 1971 in Sutton, Coldfield, England. His father was Lichfield Cathedral's assistant organist and choir-master, and his mother was a town planner. The Noyce family moved frequently, but Jon continued to attend Hitchin Boys School. Jonathan took a chorister position at Rochester Cathedral until his family moved on to Hertfordshire. Noyce acknowledged being a Jethro Tull fan on a BBC children's program - always a good thing to do! Jon picked up drums, piano, guitar and trumpet before landing a Fender Precision knockoff bass. Noyce earned six "O" (ordinary) levels, two "A" (advanced) levels, a teaching diploma and a professional certificate. In 1987, Jonathan worked for Chiltern Radio before moving on to Machinehead Music Store (Hitchin) and Brian Jordan's Music Store (Cambridge) the next year. He enrolled in London's Royal Academy of Music in 1990, and as a student, became involved in the rock combo section of David Palmer's orchestral touring extravaganza. In between, he worked at the South Cambridgeshire District Council maps division. Noyce's first recording session was with the UK popsters Take That!, and a Sister Sledge session followed. Noyce also played with Diana Ross, Lisa Stansfield, Jimmy Ruffin, Belinda Carlisle, Secret Life and Joey Negro. David Palmer tapped Noyce for his "Orchestral Sgt. Pepper's" project in 1994, and this also included drummer Marc Parnell (remember him?). Martin Barre was looking for a bass player to work on his next album, and Parnell, who had played on Barre's previous "The Meeting," recommended Jonathan Noyce. Jon then worked on Martin's album and the excellent results led Barre to submit Noyce's name to Ian Anderson as a "Divinities" bass candidate. Noyce made the false claim that he played stand-up bass, and he appeared at his audition with a bass that was not his! Noyce got the job, and Ian Anderson was a proud father because his children Gael and James were impressed that he got a Take That! musician to play with him!

The "Divinities" tour consisted of only 18 shows in Europe and North America. It was highly unusual and originally upsetting to see Ian Anderson onstage without Martin Barre by his side. Martin was in fact going to see them in London, but he chickened out! That was unfortunate because he missed out on outstanding and professional displays of musical delight in intimate settings. The tour began in Brussels, Belgium on May 17, 1995 and concluded in L.A. on June 14. The complete "Divinities" album was performed in the show's first half and rearranged Tull favorites comprised the balance. These included nuggets like "Sossity; You're A Woman," "Cheap Day Return," "Nursie" and "Dun Ringill." As expected, Bach's "Bourée" was played, and quite well at that. The fire and brimstone of "Locomotive Breath" and "Aqualung" was replaced by orchestral overtones and sonorities. At some concerts, the otherwise unheard "Dangle The Billies" and the traditional medley "She Moved Through The Fair"/ "Dust Devils" made an appearance. These shows proved that Ian Anderson could develop even further than the album's built-in progression.

The performance issue with Dave Pegg came to a head after Ian Anderson returned to England from the tour. Pegg was completely unable to do anything with Jethro Tull and officially decided to leave. As Pegg said about Jethro Tull, "It's Ian's thing and always has

 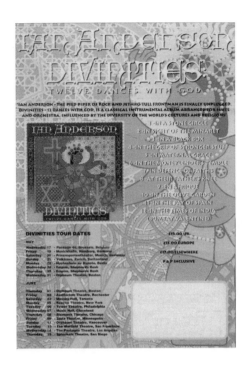

The 1995 lineup that continues to this day. Back row: Jonathan Noyce, Doane Perry, Andy Giddings. Front row: Ian Anderson, Martin Barre.

Ian Anderson played many unusual flutes (like the one shown here) on his album "Divinities: Twelve Dances With God."

Top row: "Divinities: Twelve Dances With God" and two promos for "Roots To Branches" - a US disc (middle) and a UK CD (right).

Middle: "Roots To Branches" and the British promo CD containing four tracks from "Divinities."

At left: Ian Anderson on the "Divinities" tour.
(Photo © 1995 Mark Colman)

been." Giddings would later counter Pegg's comment: "Every band needs someone to make executive decisions, and Ian obviously would be that person. Any Jethro Tull song starts with Ian."

Dave Pegg's last contributions to the band (three tracks) were recorded prior to the "Divinities" tour, and Ian Anderson couldn't wait any longer for Pegg to deliver the goods. Dave was tired of doing the same songs each year and he was not happy with the material on the latest album ("Roots To Branches"). He also had no interest in performing those songs live.

"Roots To Branches" was mainly written and recorded in December 1994 and January 1995. Pegg's unavailability at its start led Ian Anderson to locate noted session bassist Steve Bailey. Bailey is a California-based Bass Institute of Technology instructor and Ampeg technician mainly known for jazz sessions with groups like The Rippingtons. Tull started out with the backing tracks for "Out Of The Noise," "Roots To Branches" and "Wounded, Old And Treacherous." Ian did not return with the lyrics until he returned from a holiday in Goa, India in early February 1995. "Out Of The Noise" started out with bass and drums before the guitar track was worked out in a hotel bedroom in an hour. Barre's guitar portion was then recorded and engineered at Ian's studio by Andy Giddings. The title track was about the world's religious wars and offered hope for more unified beliefs. As for "Wounded, Old And Treacherous," its riff entered Ian's mind while on his way to a June 1994 gig in Austria. Anderson and Giddings got the riff down on DAT during the soundcheck. The demo of the song recorded before his India trip required more of a spoken feel instead of singing. Upon Ian's return, he recorded something resembling a spoken rap over the track. The song was previewed in an instrumental form on the "Divinities" tour as a soloing piece for the band. I will leave it up to you if you think that the lyric "big mother is calling from the underground" refers to Frank Zappa! Completely opposite to these, "Valley" and "Dangerous Veils" were rehearsed and worked out purely in the studio.

"At Last, Forever" was about dying before your domestic partner. The Middle Eastern-influenced "Rare And Precious Chain" was written and recorded during the two day layover between the European and North American "Divinities" tours (May 30-31). The album's final song, "This Free Will," was assembled from three failed backing tracks done at different times. What Doane played on bore no resemblance to the final version, as the final master had different lyrics and an entirely different melody and arrangement. When Perry heard the playback, he didn't even know what it was! Frustrating to most fans is that there are about five unreleased tracks from this album's sessions that we haven't heard yet! I wonder if Doane Perry would recognize those.

Jethro Tull was thrust into the '90s with an album that showed how their own roots could cultivate vital music. The humor on the September 1995 release "Roots To Branches" involved a good deal of cynicism, and fused Eastern, classical and blues influences with guitar riffing and flute passages. Ian now feels that it had more of a live '70s sound instead of a studio work and that it did not have enough variety. Fans did not agree, although the somewhat cerebral nature of the album took a while to sink in. "Roots To Branches" made #20 in the UK and #114 in the States.

How would Chrysalis/EMI promote "Roots To Branches"? A UK two-track CD took "Rare And Precious Chain" and "This Free Will," while the US selected three cuts: "Beside Myself," "Roots To Branches," "Rare And Precious Chain." The US then capitalized on the holidays by issuing a promo "Christmas Sampler" CD with "Ring Out, Solstice Bells," "Christmas Song" and "Another Christmas Song" - none of which were on the current album!

The "Roots To Branches" tour started in England in September and worked its way across Europe and the US over the next two months. The BBC recorded one UK show for an hour broadcast in October on Radio 2 - the new UK radio home for older rock fans. This tour was not without controversy, however. At the November 14 show at the Beacon Theater in New York City, Jethro Tull made the grave mistake of not playing "Aqualung." Of course, there were a few small teases throughout the set, but not even one verse was played. It did not score points with outraged fans - many swore not to see the band again.

During the break in this tour, Ian Anderson also recorded a cover version of Fleetwood Mac's "Man Of The World" with Andy Giddings for inclusion on the Peter Green tribute album "Rattlesnake Guitar" (also known as "The Peter Green Songbook" outside North America). The month after the "Roots To Branches" tour ended, Ian Anderson joined Mick Abrahams in a Buckingham recording studio to record four songs for Mick's solo acoustic CD "One." It was their first joint recording since 1968's "Love Story." "One" was released in February 1996, with Martin Barre's album "The Meeting" soon to follow. Barre celebrated the termination of his disastrous ZYX contract by releasing "The Meeting" as a 1,000 copy limited edition on his own Presshouse Records label. It would be picked up by the Imago label in the US after Martin listened to feedback from fans and changed the vocalist on the track "Running Free" for the American release. In 1995, Jethro Tull was represented through another kind gesture - their donation of the tracks "Warm Sporran," "Broadsword" and "Cheerio" to the charity CD "Heart Of The Lion" to raise funds for the Scottish Highland Hospice. David Pullman of The Pullman Group approached Jethro Tull in an effort to get the band to sell their royalty rights via bonds, but Ian Anderson did not take the proposal seriously. Pullman has worked his magic with David Bowie, James Brown and countless others since 1996, but he had to look elsewhere. By this time, Ian's fish farming and processing holdings were valued between £10 million and £20 million.

WHEELCHAIR BOUND FOR REAL

The year 1996 was loaded with touring difficulties, nearly all of which were caused by their surroundings. "Roots To Branches" was promoted in South America before a short US auditorium run. Aside from Brazil, the Jethro Tull name was carried into Chile, Argentina and Uruguay. Ian Anderson felt that hitting new places like Lima, Peru and other obscure US towns would replace the old intimate days of playing places like the Boston Tea Party. The problem with Lima, Peru was that bombing was taking place there a week before they arrived. After they arrived, good old South American food poisoning hit nearly the entire Jethro Tull crew, and one roadie's serious illness caused his hospitalization. Toward the end of the March 19 show in Lima, Peru, Ian seriously injured his left knee on a rickety stage. The show was interrupted and Ian finished the show seated in a chair. Anderson completed the tour's shows in Bolivia, Venezuela and the US in a wheelchair. For once, Ian's use of a wheelchair was not a joke - it was serious! Ian's knee was finally operated on when the band returned to the UK in April.

Jethro Tull had already scheduled May dates in Australia and New Zealand, but the tour promoter wanted to cancel it based on Ian Anderson's condition. Foolishly, Anderson wanted to go ahead with the tour, even if a wheelchair was required for its entire duration. Sure enough, the pain was enormous and on the fourth night of performances, Ian could not finish the show. He was admitted to the hospital and found that he was suffering from thrombosis (blood clotting) which could be deadly. The rest of the Australian and New Zealand shows were cancelled along with the other European dates scheduled for the next six weeks.

Yet another media circus developed with Ian Anderson's hospitalization. A number of publications had him near death and these stories would persist for weeks. It was time for Ian to take stock of the importance of his life and the future performance limits that he would have to place on himself. Luckily, one of the daily knee rehabilitation exercises that Ian was required to do involved jumping up and down on one leg without falling over - it was a snap for him!

An extensive US tour was arranged with a UK leg arranged after a break of about six weeks. The American shows paired Tull with the reunited Emerson, Lake & Palmer. Ampthitheaters and other midsize venues were lined up for this successful tour of two somewhat broken down monolithic acts. Martin Barre was also having arm and shoulder problems that prevented his playing for a short time. As for ELP, Keith Emerson had his own arm injury, but that didn't stop him from overturning his organ nightly!

Jethro Tull was recognized in a number of other ways in 1996. "Cross-Eyed Mary" was part of the soundtrack of the film "Breaking The Waves." Ian Anderson recorded two more songs with Leslie Mandoki - "Let The Music Show You The Way" and the live Anderson/Mandoki jam "Back To Budapest" recorded in that city during the year. Both tracks appeared on Leslie Mandoki's album "People In Room No. 8," and "Back To Budapest" also made it to Mandoki's "The Jazz Cuts" collection the next year.

A Jethro Tull tribute album called "To Cry You A Song • A Collection Of Tull Tales" gathered together progressive artists and ex-Tull members to mixed effect. Five of the tracks feature Mick Abrahams, Glenn Cornick and Clive Bunker as backing band. Dave and Matt Pegg contributed "Life Is A Long Song" and Dave bravely attempted the vocal! Ian Anderson was not impressed by this collection, although Roy Harper's lyrically changed version of "Up The 'Pool" had such an impact on Ian that Jethro Tull would perform it for the first time *and* with Harper's changes. Also available was a deluxe box set called "The Ultimate Set," which contained a 12" picture disc and CD of "Aqualung" along with the "25th Anniversary Video" and the "Jethro Tull - Complete Lyrics" book.

In between and during all this activity, some Jethro Tull-related albums were recorded and released. "Somewhere In The Universe" by Ray Roehner, performing under the group name RAY, recorded the Jethro Tull songs "Broadford Bazaar" and "Jack-A-Lynn" with other originals that respectfully captured the essence of Tull. Martin Barre recorded an album with his childhood friend John

Ian Anderson in one of the "wheelchair" shows - March 25, 1996 at the Electric Factory in Philadelphia. (Photo courtesy of Dennis Landau)

Ian and Martin live in September 1996.
(Both photos © 1996 Mark Colman)

Above is the tribute CD "To Cry You A Song • A Collection Of Tull Tales," along with the original and reissue of the "BBC Live In Concert" disc on the Windsong label in the UK.

Below are two mid-1990s videos that feature one Jethro Tull track each. They both reveal the power of the band in their pre-"Aqualung" period.

Carter, vocalist of the bands The Dwellers and The Moonrakers. The two had lost touch after Barre joined Jethro Tull and Carter got married, but they have been in regular contact since the mid-'70s. John Carter was not playing or recording professionally, but he was always interested in recording with Barre. They started working together in 1989 on an informal basis. Carter sent a tape of his songs to Martin, who decided then and there that they had to do an album at his Presshouse Studio. The original intention of the album, called "Spirit Flying Free," was for a John Carter solo flight, but Martin Barre's joint credit was due to his vast involvement in all aspects of the sessions. Among the Tull-related luminaries on the album were Jonathan Noyce, "Divinities" tour violinist Chris Leslie and Dave Pegg, who had time to record this one! It was released that November 30 by A New Day Records.

On that same November day in 1996, the next UK Tull convention took place in Gravesend. The proceeds from the show went to the Lupus UK fund on behalf of David Palmer's wife, who had suffered and recently died from the debilitating long-term disease. David wanted to play at the convention and Tull alumni John Evans, Clive Bunker and Mick Abrahams joined the current participants (Ian Anderson, Jonathan Noyce and Andy Giddings). Abrahams appeared with his group Blodwyn Pig and Bunker came with his band Solstice. Glenn Cornick was also scheduled to appear with his reformed Wild Turkey, but he was recovering from the open-heart surgery he underwent just a few weeks before. Wild Turkey would play without Glenn. The convention had Ian Anderson playing with Solstice and Andy Giddings, Jonathan Noyce and Mick Abrahams would play together. The strangest sight was definitely David Palmer with Blodwyn Pig! Where was Martin Barre? He refused to come to the less than spectacular area of Gravesend!

What Martin Barre wanted to do was run. As he told Runner's World at the time: "Running gives me energy. We tour a lot, and the schedule can be ridiculous. Airports, taxis, hotel rooms - travel, travel, travel. Used to be I'd get to the hotel room and just flop on the bed in front of the telly. Now I head out for a run. If it weren't for running, I'd go crazy. While on tour in South America this spring, I decided to run along Lake Titicaca in the Andes, the highest lake in the world (12,500 feet). I hired a van to take me up, and the driver kept trying to talk me out of it. I did it, though, and it was great. I've done three marathons - Paris and two Londons. I ran my 3:40 PR at London. One time, as a challenge, I did the marathon distance 10 times in six weeks. These weren't races, just training runs; I wanted to see if I could do it."

Martin found that there were many motivating factors for running, as he continues: "This morning I read a concert review that referred to me as looking grandfatherly. Ouch! It's true there aren't many rock musicians of my age, but (Camille) Saint-Saëns toured as a concert pianist until he was 86. So why not? There's a lifetime of things I want to do before my fingers seize up. I pick up a guitar every day, wherever I am - on holiday or at work. I never feel fed up. On stage, there's a lot of energy and mental agility needed. Running gives me that energy, that focus."

Even at this point, Martin Barre treats his role in Jethro Tull very seriously. To answer the question of why Barre still does it, he answers: "Every evening on stage is challenging. I know that I can always play better. Eighty percent of what we play live is the same every night. But the rest is open to spontaneity and improvisation. When you try something new, and it clicks, it becomes part of your arsenal. I'm always looking for little oddball, magical things. I would never make too little of what Jethro Tull means to me and its fans. I love the companionship within the band, and we have really good, loyal fans. It's something to be respected."

The German Jethro Tull convention in early 1997 included the now recovered Glenn Cornick and his Wild Turkey, Vikki Clayton, Solstice and Fairport Convention. Clive Bunker, when not playing with Solstice, sat in with the acoustic Clayton and enjoyed it so much that he offered to play in her band. Clive did double duty at a live 100 Club function in London to celebrate the release of albums by Vikki Clayton, Solstice and headliner Blodwyn Pig. At long last, Cornick ended his long-running feud with Mick Abrahams and joined Mick on stage. Glenn did not contribute positively to the proceedings, but another interpersonal difficulty was soon resolved. Vikki Clayton performed with Clive Bunker, Maart Allcock and Martin Barre. In Italy, another Tull acknowledgement was taking place in a recording studio. The Tull cover band Beggar's Farm put together their takes of eleven Jethro Tull classics as their 1997 CD "Jethro Tull Tribute."

Two of Ian Anderson's most unusual outside sessions were done at this time. First up, Ian played on the 15-minute centerpiece "These Fifty Years" on Roy Harper's "The Dream Society." Next, Ian played flute on the track "Play Minstrel Play" on the Blackmore's Night CD "Shadow Of The Moon." This is the oldest piece of music that Ian Anderson had ever played on. Although the song is credited to Pierre Attaignant, Ritchie Blackmore and Candice Night wrote the lyrics. Actually, the song shouldn't even be credited to Attaignant! Pierre Attaignant (c.1494-c.1552) was a French music publisher based in Paris that made popular dance music available to the public via sheet music. The piece that Ritchie Blackmore appropriated to create "Play Minstrel Play" was actually published in 1530 by Attaignant in Paris as "La Basse Dance La Magdalena." The publication that first listed "La Magdalena" was called "Neuf (9) basses dances, deux (2) branles." Basses dances and branles were Renaissance dance pieces that are usually played on lutes, although the original publication did not dictate any specific accompaniment. A basse dance was a graceful Renaissance court dance without the quick steps or jumps prevalent in other dances of the period.

Two budget-priced Tull compilations containing the same titles but different packaging and song order also appeared: "Through The Years" and "A Jethro Tull Collection." England and some other countries got the first one, but Holland got the second. The working title of "Through The Years" was "Journeyman," and it was originally promoted under that name. On May 23, 1997, David Palmer and the Royal Philharmonic Orchestra were on hand to commemorate the release of David's classical CD tribute to Queen. Ian Anderson joined Palmer and the RPO onstage to play flute and sing Tull classics for a decidedly pro-Tull audience uninterested in hearing orchestral Queen.

The 1997 Jethro Tull tour began in Esbjerg, Denmark with three initial UK dates, loads of German shows and other widely scattered gigs. The Slovak Republic was first touched on June 14, and two later British shows were of note: the Derbyshire Rock & Blues Custom Show in Pentrich and the Guildford Festival. The Pentrich gig was a 20,000 strong biker stand featuring Tull, tribute bands and tramps - female tramps, that is! Jethro Tull's strong set was interrupted 20 minutes by generator failure, but bikers can be relied on for keeping themselves busy. The band's biker experience led to an arguable overreaction at Guildford, where a marquee the band requested for protection resulted in a security walkout and an inability for some festival goers to view the band safely and/or properly. Ian Anderson illustrated that he had no problem with Dave Pegg's choice to leave Jethro Tull by promoting the next week's Cropredy Festival at the set's midpoint. The tour ended in Baltimore, MD and some dates in Italy and Germany were cancelled. The elimination of the Italian date at the Naples Blues Festival on September 7 worked out perfectly for Doane Perry.

DOANE PERRY'S HANDS OF KINDNESS

Doane Perry was doing his best to help his good friend, former "A" drummer Mark Craney. After leaving Tull subsequent to the "A" tour, Craney was working on many drum sessions, but his work was halted by kidney failure. Craney tells us what happened: "It was July of '86. I was touring with Tower of Power, and we were using small planes to travel in. I had an ear infection and we dropped altitude really fast into San Francisco. I had the worst pain I'd ever had at the time. And after that, my kidneys shut down. So I went on dialysis for about a year, and then I had some complications with an infection and lost my left big toe. After that, I had more complications with the type of dialysis I was doing, and another infection. I had just complication after complication. I couldn't eat for three weeks: they fed me through my neck, this fluid, and. . .aaahhh. Back then, my mother would wheel me out to one little spot, and we'd just break down for a while. And then dry off and get back at it, and just try to find a way. My mother was here the whole time, she was really my angel. And my father, too. He stayed at home and learned to do things that he had never done in forty-seven years of marriage. After about a three-month stint in the hospital, two months of being in physical rehabilitation, I came out of there in a wheelchair. That was maybe November of '87. In March of '88, just as I was kind of getting myself back together and getting on my feet a little bit, UCLA (Medical Center) called and said, 'We've got a kidney here from a car accident victim. You'd better come down.' I had no time to think about anything, and I went down and that turned into another three-month stay in the hospital. I had a mild stroke when they did the kidney transplant, but it was in a part of the brain that can return completely, and I think a lot of it has. I rejected the kidney at first, so they gave me a drug called OKT3. And I hallucinated my brains out for about three weeks straight. And then just about the time they were going to write me off, the kidney kicked in and it's been perfect ever since. I had a couple more months of physical rehabilitation, first in the hospital and then when I got home, and went from a wheelchair, needing two people to help me out of the wheelchair, to a walker, to two canes, to one cane. Now I use a cane mostly at night. All I have to do is just glance back and I'm real happy with anything I have right now.

"Death looked really, really good to me. It looked like a wonderful, easy way out. I was in one of our better earthquakes when I was in the hospital, and they were talking about all this stuff on the television, and I thought, 'Let it rip. I don't care. Do me a favor.' But at the same time, I realize now that with whatever little bit of energy I had left, I was always thinking of how I could get just a little bit better, like maybe I can dress myself tomorrow, or get out of bed. So it was just a steady climb."

David Palmer's tribute to Queen.

Lon Horwitz and his vest meet John Evans and Glenn Cornick at the Jethro Tull
Convention at Hofstra University on July 27, 1996. Thanks for the photos, Lon!

The Mark Craney tribute CD.

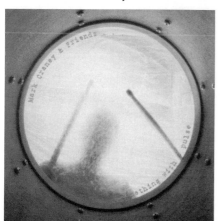  

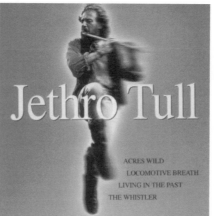

ACRES WILD
LOCOMOTIVE BREATH
LIVING IN THE PAST
THE WHISTLER

3 CD SET

AQUALUNG
LOCOMOTIVE
BREATH
A PASSION PLAY
A MINSTREL IN
THE GALLERY
BUNGLE IN
THE JUNGLE
LIVING IN THE PAST
THICK AS A BRICK
AND MORE!

Extraído de su caja especial:
Aqualung
M.U. The Best of Jethro Tull

Top row: Ian Anderson appeared
on the Blackmore's Night "Shadow
Of The Moon" album in 1997.
Two Jethro Tull compilations
appeared in the first quarter of
1997 - the Dutch "A Jethro Tull
Collection" and the UK CD
"Through The Years."

Middle row: The US mail-order
compilation "36 Greatest Hits"
and the Spanish promo CD for
the track "Aqualung."

Bottom row: Two American videos
that feature Tull appearamces on
the German "Beat Club" program.

174

Mark Craney's stroke affected his right hand, and he also suffered nerve damage in his hands and feet due to the insulin injections he required as a diabetic. Despite his adversity, Mark drummed with artists like Jeff Beck, Tower Of Power and Eric Burdon before he became too sick to play in 1996.

Out of his immense friendship with Mark Craney, Doane Perry assembled the "Something With A Pulse" CD for August 1997 release to cover Craney's medical expenses. The CD included two Jethro Tull-related tracks that are otherwise unavailable: a live 1980 version of "Black Sunday" (from the "Slipstream" video) and a new, March 1997 version of "A Song For Jeffrey." The latter track is credited to Ian Anderson, but Martin Barre and Andy Giddings play on it as well. The CD was originally planned for release on A New Day Records in the UK (AND CD 14), but it was cancelled due to the accessibility of Doane Perry's edition on the Laughing Gull label.

This wasn't enough for Doane Perry. Doane put together a Woodlands Hills Drum Club benefit on September 7, 1997 with drum stars Dennis Elliott (Foreigner), journeyman Gregg Bissonette, Myron Grombacher (Pat Benatar), Steve Smith (Journey), Terry Bozzio (Frank Zappa, U.K., Missing Persons and others), Ricky Lawson, Carmine Appice (Vanilla Fudge), Chad Smith (Red Hot Chili Peppers), Rudy Richmond and Mike Fisher. Eddie Jobson was also on hand. The event was called "Mark Craney & Friends, A Day Of Drums And Music, Pt. II" at the Guitar Center in Hollywood, CA. On September 6, Craney was discharged from UCLA Medical Center, where he received another kidney transplant. Mark was determined to attend and he made it. Not long after the benefit, Gregg Bissonette (a previous roommate at Mark Craney's house) urged Mark to start playing again and he accomplished that as well. Craney has his good days and not so good days, but he is well aware that his fans are out there encouraging him: "The support has been unbelievable. The big thing that I want to try to convey here is my appreciation of the people - to make an official thank you to everybody. I've gotten a lot of letters and support from a lot of stellar drummers, lots of different types of support. I've been so busy on the mend and pushing myself that I haven't really pulled over to think about it myself, but it has been an unbelievable experience. It's one of those things that, now that I'm through it, I wouldn't want to have missed it for what I've gotten out of it. Which takes some figuring out, but that's definitely how I feel now. Life is definitely much different now. I don't sweat the small stuff at all, and to live in the present is the most important thing. It's a little bit easier, as frustrating as it can be playing now, because I can't yet play everything that I'm hearing. I do have this respect from the people that I respect, the players, and that's really important, that really keeps me going." A close personal friend of the tall, lean, unpretentious Craney has shared that other than the use of a cane for his ambulation, he has recovered well. Professionally, Mark continues as a studio session drummer in L.A. and teaches those fortunate enough to have him as a mentor. *We're with you, Mark!*

Ian Anderson's 50th birthday on August 10, 1997 was celebrated at Harbor Lights in Boston. A bagpipe player was on hand to perform for him, and Ian received the wonderful combination of cake and champagne. Just over two months later (October 11), Tull's most recent convention appearance took place in Burlington, VT. This time, the entire band played a special set for conventionees before their normal set that evening at Flynn Theater. More than any other event, the set performed at a cider mill brought the band closer to hundreds of enthusiastic fans and remains a fondly remembered date. The closeness of the situation enabled Tull to play acoustic numbers and solo features before old stand-bys "Locomotive Breath" (with onstage vocal "help"!) and "Aqualung." Another "train wreck" - this time on "Locomotive Breath" - was averted when Tull fan Gary Sexton jumped in on drums to get things back on track. The convention had a question and answer session and a raffle was drawn. How's that for meeting the fans halfway?

The 1997 shows included "Thick As A Brick" in varying lengths, along with an ever-changing Martin Barre solo piece ("Morris Minus," "Misere," "Paparazzi" or "Empty Café"). Some gigs had songs like "Acres Wild," "Up The 'Pool," "Skating Away On The Thin Ice Of The New Day," "We Used To Know" and "Pussy Willow," but these were dropped as the year went by. The encore featured "Aquadiddley" - "Aqualung" played with a Bo Diddley beat. "Aquadiddley" continues to be used today in conjunction with "The Dambusters March" and "Cheerio" during the balloon conclusion of Tull concerts. Another Tull tribute CD made its way to the marketplace in August: "Jethro Tull Classics Played by Jürgen Handke." This was more of an unsuccessful Ian Anderson copy CD compared to the more open "To Cry You A Song" collection. Needless to say, Ian Anderson won't have this one in his collection! By this time, Strathaird Salmon was producing 900 tons of smoked salmon a year and annual revenues were $26 million.

"THE SECRET LANGUAGE OF BIRDS"

The year 1998 was Jethro Tull's 30th anniversary and a rather sedate one at that. The only appearance by the band in the first half of the year was at the April 18 Tull convention in Bedburg-Hau, Germany. Only 700 fans were in attendance, but the intents of the show were to prime the audience for Martin Barre's upcoming solo tour and the inclusion of a new song. Ian Anderson had seen the now-legendary Russian film footage of leader Boris Yeltsin dancing, and "Boris Dancing" became the latest creation in his original song catalog. The song was also meant to be the title of Ian's next solo album, but this was its original performance before the album title was later changed to "The Secret Language Of Birds." The song was proof positive that Ian and the band were in the process of assembling new material for future release. No one in the band knew what songs would end up on which project, but those details were not important at the time.

The previous month, the group recorded three mimed songs for an Austrian television special with James Anderson (Ian's son) on the drum kit. It was not cost effective to bring in Doane Perry for a faked performance. Jeffrey Hammond-Hammond was actually going to mime a bass part for Jonathan Noyce, but the illness of Jeffrey's wife cancelled this plan.

Meanwhile, Ian Anderson kept extremely busy with outside sessions. Along with Martin Barre, Mick Abrahams, Clive Bunker, Big Jim Sullivan, Status Quo's Rick Parfitt and others, Ian played on Jackie Lynton's "Pin-Board Wizards." It was the veteran vocalist's first album in about 15 years. Mick and Martin were on the same recording for the first time. Ian and Martin were also on the Clive Bunker track "Strange Riff" from his first CD "Awakening."

On February 11, Doane Perry replaced Darren Moody in Martin Barre's band in preparation for Martin's solo tour of Germany in May. The set list contained material from Martin's album "The Meeting" and a new version of the popular Jethro Tull riffer "To Cry You A Song." Martin's band also included Jonathan Noyce and Andy Giddings, but very few people came to see this "almost Jethro Tull" band. In the minds of music fans, "almost Jethro Tull" is not Jethro Tull at all. Upon returning home to Britain, Barre prepared for the upcoming 1998 Tull tour and worked on enlarging the capabilities of his Presshouse Studio. In this way, he could increase his production involvement with the acts using his studio.

A New Day editor Dave Rees issued the first Jethro Tull book written in English, "Minstrels In The Gallery - A History Of Jethro Tull," in August. On the first of August, Ian Anderson's original Inverness salmon factory burned down and the building's remains were demolished within the next two weeks. Five per cent of the 300-member staff were out of work.

With "Boris Dancing" just a taster of his next solo album, Ian Anderson completed "The Secret Language Of Birds" for October 1998 release. Without a record company contract, the album was inevitably delayed to spring 1999 and then to February (and then March) 2000 to avoid any promotional conflicts with the next Jethro Tull album. The Tull album was originally planned for April 1999, but it was delayed until August. "The Secret Language Of Birds" was inspired by "The Dawn Chorus" - the natural sound of birds at dawn that is best heard in the world's diminishing rainforests. Radio astronomers and ornithologists have appreciated "The Dawn Chorus" for years, and numerous relaxation CDs have used this chorus for its emotionally restorative properties. By the time "The Secret Language Of Birds" is released, its recordings will be nearly two years old!

With "The Secret Language Of Birds," Ian will finally deliver the acoustic guitar and flute album that he has been expected to produce. Only two of the album's tracks are instrumental - "Boris Dancing" is one of them. The other emphasis tracks on the album are the title track, "Montserrat," "Set Aside" and "Water Carrier." Andy Giddings plays a variety of instruments besides keyboards on the album: accordian, marimba and glockenspiel. Of the CD's other musicians, drummer Gerry Conway is another notable contributor. Ian also plays mandolin, bouzouki and percussion. While in his home studio, Anderson premiered "Set Aside" and "Water Carrier" for an August 10, 1998 birthday radio broadcast in Uruguay of all places. The program on XFM Radio was immediately shared with Tull fans in Uruguay who had their first convention the next day. Ian also played bits of "Bourée," "Thick As A Brick" and "Mother Goose" during the program.

The Jethro Tull machine had generated over $800 million of business as of May 1998. This was to increase with two US mini-tours and one of Spain, with dates in Switzerland and Lichtenstein sandwiched in-between. The record company situation with Chrysalis/EMI was reaching a dead end, and Jethro Tull decided to conveniently let their contract lapse in September 1998 instead of delivering product that would not be properly promoted or distributed. Therefore, two planned EMI projects (the audio documentary "Jethro Tull In Profile" and "30 Years Live") died a quick death on the drawing board. The documentary was slated for May release with the live album set for September. EMI held firm in their ownership of Jethro Tull's back catalog, as they were not interested in selling it.

The secondary venues on the 1998 US tour would provide a rich source of material. At the Atlantic City, NJ show on August 25, Jethro Tull was preceded by a gay, third-rate magician! Ian said the band was "on vacation" in Atlantic City during the show (instead of saying "on holiday"), and Ian's AC casino nightlife experience was reflected in the lyrics of the song "AWOL." By the end of the tour on November 12, the reflections that Ian made on tour were of sufficient quantity to form the basis of the next Jethro Tull album to be demoed just before Christmas.

Before this was to take place, Ian Anderson had to take care of some misleading promotion that accompanied Mick Abrahams' tour for the 30th anniversary of the "This Was" LP. Promoters had mistakenly placed Jethro Tull's name in large name with Mick Abrahams' name in relatively small print. As a result, some deluded UK fans bought tickets to a concert that they had no interest in. In order to put an end to such deceiving practices, Ian Anderson had to direct some threats toward Mick Abrahams and the promoters involved. Mick Abrahams called Ian to tell him that he was unaware of, and upset with, the tour promotion. Mick promised that this would not continue. Mick Abrahams' This Was Band issued a CD of the "This Was" album without the track "Round" in December 1998. While well played, the album came and went very quickly with little interest.

Ian Anderson had always considered computers a necessary evil, but the placement of the Internet as a major conveyor of information would force Ian's hand. With many unofficial Jethro Tull websites on the 'net, it was time to create an official Jethro Tull website. Ian got together with Andy Giddings and created the j-tull.com website for initial uploading in December 1998. The intent of the site was to present the band's history, activities and interests in one informative place. It is the only known "official" website by any band that the group members themselves operate on a day-to-day basis. Besides his musical background, Ian can be found on the site promoting felines, chile peppers and Indian cuisine! The website gave fans consistent updates about the album in progress and extensive world tour plans for 1999. This interaction assured fans that Jethro Tull was still in business and there was a good, clear, solid road ahead.

The band started off 1999 without a record deal but with many companies interested. A Jethro Tull convention at Hofstra University in Hempstead, NY on January 14 and 15 was the first event in a busy year for Tull fans. The first night involved a discussion that was less than successful, but the second day featured the tribute bands A Passion Play and Heresy. The latter played "A Passion Play" in its entirety - a massive undertaking by a group that had little time to prepare for it. Despite the lack of rehearsal time and a few slightly nervous spots, Heresy got through "A Passion Play" in excellent condition.

In March, Ian Anderson met with the German record company Roadrunner to discuss a licensing arrangement. He would record a short interview concerning a Mick Jagger program on the Discovery channel and he demoed Shure Bros.' new in-ear monitoring system at the Frankfurt Music Fair in Germany.

j-tull.com

Three demos were recorded prior to Christmas 1998, and Jethro Tull worked in the studio for three weeks to develop Ian's new songs. Recording continued without a contract, with Ian knowing that contractual matters would be worked out upon their completion. With the enthusiasm and early success of the j-tull.com web site, the band recommended to Ian that the album should be called "j-tull Dot Com." Ian Anderson thought this was clever and instantly wrote a song called "Dot Com" as its final recording. British-born Najma Akhtar provided the female backing vocals on the title track, and her contribution was the last track recorded before the final album mix. Besides her own ethnic recordings, Najma is known to rock audiences as the vocalist on the Jimmy Page & Robert Plant live version of "Battle Of Evermore" on their 1994 "No Quarter: Jimmy Page & Robert Plant Unledded" album.

The "j-tull Dot Com" album was a 24-track recording that encompassed numerous subjects in its 14 tracks. "Hunt By Numbers" dealt with the nature of cats and their impact on nature. Shona Anderson got Ian interested in felines prior to their marriage in 1976. Shona's young cat from her teenage years, Fur, had matured by the time Shona met Ian Anderson. Ian has taken

No, you're not seeing quadruple! Clockwise are the US full album CD promo, the American four-track CD promo, the commerical (and anatomically correct) UK edition of "Dot Com," and the cover-modified US edition.

Below: a serious Jethro Tull for 1999: Andy Giddings, Jonathan Noyce, Martin Barre, Ian Anderson and Doane Perry.

care of two dozen kittens since he met Shona, with a particular interest in Bengal cats. One of these kittens ran into later trouble, as his daughter Gael's cat was run over by a truck. Ian's experiences with cats were captured by a US film crew at the Anderson residence for an in-progress conservation and wildlife program.

Ian's observations of a Caribbean location were expressed in the album's most controversial track, "Hot Mango Flush." Martin Barre came up with the spicy music track and Ian's free word association rap formed its tangy sauce. The song's subject is frequently misinterpreted as either an herbal tea flavored with mango or the reaction of eating food with Hot Mango Pepper sauce! Of the album's tracks, "Hot Mango Flush" and its reprise, "Mango Surprise," have created the strongest negative/positive reactions of any Tull song in years.

"El Niño" dealt with a more serious subject matter - the massive series of rainfall-causing severe destruction across the southern tier of the US and Peru that is accompanied by West Pacific draughts and crippling Australian brushfires. This phenomenon was first detected in Peru in the 16th century, but was named El Niño in the 1890s, as its occurrence peaks in December - the birth of the infant Jesus (el niño is Spanish for baby boy).

"Spiral" dealt with coming out of a dream and the confusion of what is real and what is not, and the fantasy trip of "Far Alaska" realizes the dream. A Frank Zappa technique was used on the middle section of "Spiral" in which the most melodic passage in the song was followed by a "white noise" section of flute and guitar. The juxtaposition of beauty and ugliness within that section was artfully used to reflect the dreamer's emergence into reality.

"Nothing @ All" was a simple Andy Giddings piano introduction that formed a well-executed link to "Wicked Windows." Ian wrote that song after purchasing a new pair of glasses, and those specs generated his comment about what a pair of *"wicked windows"* he had on. The song was inspired by a popular character that we are all familiar with. Who is that, you may ask? If you want my guess, here it is: how about Scrooge from Charles Dickens' "A Christmas Carol"? Hint: the lyric "Christmas was my favorite holiday."

"Black Mamba" is a song about the tree snake variety of the same name and its venomous eating habits! Incidentally, a black mamba is not black, but slate gray. "Bends Like A Willow" uses nautical imagery in a descriptive song that could equally apply to a woman. Only Ian Anderson's self-deprecating humor could poke fun at his 50-something existence in "The Dog-Ear Years": "Vintage and classic, or just plain Jurassic: all words to describe me." Concluding the album is one of the most romantic songs in the Ian Anderson canon: "A Gift Of Roses." Note the reference to "A Passion Play"! "A Gift Of Roses" is a fine, creative closer to an album that can safely be placed in its own time coordinates.

In May 1999, Ian Anderson announced that he and Jethro Tull signed individual and group contracts with Fuel 2000 in North America, and Papillon Records in Europe and the rest of the world. The Ian Anderson Group Of Companies was already formed to license Anderson and Tull recordings to those countries, with Shona Anderson as an active participant in this company as well as the salmon business. Papillon was created by former Chrysalis executive Roy Eldridge (remember the "Thick As A Brick" newspaper?) and Mike Andrews. Eldridge was Chrysalis' executive director when EMI acquired the label in late 1991, and he brought in Andrews as marketing director the next year. Papillon is part of The Hit Label and Chrysalis Group plc. Chris Wright continues to run Chrysalis Group plc, ongoing publisher of Jethro Tull's music. Wright formed Echo Records (a pop/rock label for new acts) and The Hit Label, specializing in compilations and catalog releases. Papillon is French for butterfly, and its logo is very close to the old Chrysalis image without causing any copyright infringements. Jethro Tull's was Papillon's first signing - just as they were for Chrysalis. The European licensee is Roadrunner Records.

What happened to Terry Ellis? He was the chairman of the British Phonographic Institute (BPI) and he launched StarGig.com on the Internet in October 1999 as an alternative to the major record labels. Ellis is the chief executive of StarGig.com.

With Tull's contracts in place, it was decided to leave a six-month sales window between the Jethro Tull album "j-tull Dot Com" and Ian's "The Secret Language Of Birds." Even though Ian Anderson's album was already recorded and "j-tull Dot Com" was still in production at the time of contract negotiations, Ian agreed to delay his own project for proper promotion. (It was delayed again to March 7, 2000.) Ian did not plan concert dates to promote his solo album, however. The cover artwork for "j-tull Dot Com" was also modified for US release, as Fuel 2000 was afraid that the album would not be stocked by some American retailers in its original

Ian Anderson takes off his wicked windows to pose for this photo! From left to right: Andy Giddings, Martin Barre, Ian Anderson, Jonathan Noyce, Doane Perry.

At top right is Jethro Tull's most recent single, "Bends Like A Willow."

Bottom left: Ian Anderson at the House Of Blues in L.A. on October 8, 1999. (Photo © 1999 Mark Colman)

Bottom right: Ian Anderson's third solo album - "The Secret Language Of Birds."

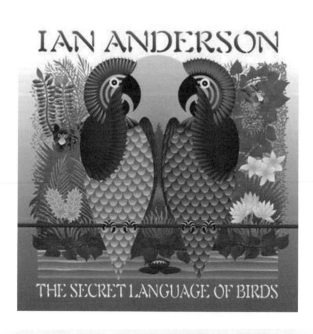

form. Anderson's drawing of the garden statue Amun, a wedding present sculpted for Ian and Shona by their former neighbor Michael Cooper, had to have his genitals painted out for the American CD. His naughty bits were retained for concert memorabilia, however! An unusual, but highly effective, promotional effort by Fuel 2000 and Papillon on initial copies was the unexpected inclusion of an Ian Anderson spoken introduction and his future solo album title track - "The Secret Language Of Birds."

Fuel 2000 went all out to promote "j-tull Dot Com." Unscrupulous characters posing as media reviewers sold some advance "j-tull Dot Com" CDs through the online auction forum eBay prior to the August 24 US release date. Winning bid prices approached the $100 mark. Those copies repeated an edit of the track "Dot Com" as its bonus instead. Another promo CD available by Fuel 2000 included four tracks (two versions of "Spiral," "Dot Com" and "Wicked Windows") with Ian Anderson spoken introductions prior to each title. Most recently, Roadrunner Records has released a one-track promo single of the title track.

Ian Anderson did some unusual guest turns and promoted "j-tull Dot Com" at the same time. Ian appeared with Dr. Joyce Brothers on the comedy/discussion program "Politically Correct With Bill Maher" on May 11 before coming back to New York and L.A. in August for radio and press interviews. After some growing pains with getting audio files to play without crashing other people's computers (!), Giddings and Anderson were finally able to present extracts of four "j-tull Dot Com" songs to illustrate how they developed from Ian Anderson demos to their final forms: "Spiral," "Dot Com," "Hunt By Numbers" and "Black Mamba."

Jethro Tull had a variety of promotional methods at their fingertips to share with fans, such as the ability to download entire songs or segments (such as "Spiral," among others) through websites like Amazon.com or cdnow.com. The current MP3 audio technology enabled many savvy computer nerds to store these downloads on a small digital disc. A live Internet chat took place on September 30 at 8PM on twec.com (The Web's Entertainment Center) - this chat was also shown as it happened in about 900 record stores. Ian Anderson also did a downloadable interview with twec.com for fans to enjoy. Another Internet chat took place at 6PM on October 30 for the Doc Rock Show in Germany. On top of this, an October 8 House Of Blues performance from L.A. became an Internet webcast on the venue's website on December 3, 1999.

The 1999 tour started off with another hot night in Budapest on May 27. Three new "j-tull Dot Com" cuts made their live debuts: "Spiral," "Dot Com" and "AWOL." Some of the early shows also featured a performance of Ian's "Montserrat" from his solo album, and other "j-tull Dot Com" songs like "Hunt By Numbers." Concerts elsewhere, such as the June 15 show in Baden-Baden, Germany, had a different setlist. "Dot Com" (the song) was not part of the gig, but "Nothing @ All" and "Wicked Windows" were included with an Ian Anderson interview. A one-hour segment of the show was broadcast on September 10 on the German TV program "Ohne Filter." Only 250 people were lucky enough to be in the studio to see the band perform live.

Television and radio were still very effective media for the band. While in the Czech Republic, Ian Anderson was filmed for a fall TV program on legendary songwriters. This footage was accompanied by interview footage with Anderson at home. Twenty five minutes of Tull's appearance at the July 18 Pistoia Blues Festival at Duomo Square was filmed for Italian television. Dutch RTL5 radio broadcasted an in-studio Tull appearance at Wisseloord Studios in Hilversum, and Dutch TV aired the same show as "2 Meter Sessies" on December 23, 1999.

Dave Pegg put together a benefit to raise funds for ailing Fairport Convention stalwart Dave Swarbrick at Birmingham Symphony Hall (July 24). Ian Anderson, Martin Barre, Maart Allcock, Fairport Convention, Beverley Craven, Ralph McTell and others gave of themselves to perform at this concert.

The US "j-tull Dot Com" concerts were a little different. As with other Tull shows in the past few years, Frank Zappa music was played before the band took the stage. In case you're a Zappa fan (and you should be!), the songs played were "Jewish Princess," "Dinah-Moe Humm," "Dirty Love" and "The Blimp (troutmaskreplica)" (with Captain Beefheart). Singer/songwriter Vyktoria Pratt Keating opened all but three shows - Ten Years after did the September 1-2 shows. There was no opening act at the Arizona State Fair in Phoenix - the conclusion of the US tour. Keating came to the attention of Ian Anderson through her recordings, and Ian so enjoyed her music that he invited her to open Tull's American shows. Andy Giddings occasionally played during Vyktoria Pratt Keating's set. For the first time, "Serenade To A Cuckoo" was performed at Roland Kirk's original tempo and had Ian switching from bamboo to C flute - similar to the switching Kirk did on the original recording. "Bourée" featured its original classical treatment before the band launched into its own rendition. "The Passion Jig" harkened back to previous humor with a large, costumed hare looking for his spectacles! An acoustic section with "Jeffrey Goes To Leicester Square" was equally enjoyable with hijinks going on during "Fat Man." Even with a new album to promote, Jethro Tull only played three songs from "j-tull Dot Com" at first and they featured six selections from "Stand Up." Initial US gigs were only 90 minutes in length, but shows were extended afterward with the inclusion of "Hunt By Numbers," "Hunting Girl" and an instrumental snatch of "Hot Mango Flush."

After the September 24 show in Detroit, Martin Barre was taken to the hospital. He was suffering from a flare-up of a stomach problem that he thought he left behind a few years ago. After a brief rest, Martin was back in action and had a minor operation in England after the US tour leg was over. In October and November, the entire eight-date concert run in Germany was accompanied by The Mark Gillespie Band.

After "j-tull Dot Com" was released during the last week of August, sales were surprisingly poor, considering the amount of media exposures. "Dot Com" entered the UK album chart at #44 and disappeared the next week. Likewise, the CD made the US chart at #161 and made a quick exit within the following seven days. In Germany, sales were more uplifting - a #15 showing for its initial chart appearance. Additional US promotion came from an even more likely source: the game show "Who Wants To Be A Millionaire?" hosted by Regis Philbin. On August 25, contestant Michael Shutterly, who was going for a $1 million prize on the program, received a question on which band won the Grammy for Best Heavy Metal Album awarded in 1989. Of course, the correct answer was Jethro Tull! However, Jethro Tull was the only band Shutterly had some familiarity with, and he knew the answer couldn't be Tull because they were not considered "heavy metal"! With the option of not answering the question, Michael Shutterly kept his half-million dollars and walked away uncomfortably embarrassed when the unanticipated answer was presented to him. He did end up backstage at their Baltimore show!

Lots of Jethro Tull and related products made their way to fans in 1999. An Emerson, Lake & Palmer tribute album featured Martin Barre and Doane Perry on one track, and EMI in the US reissued many Tull titles that they purposely allowed to go of print. The 25th anniversary 2CD set "Anniversary Collection: The Best Of Jethro Tull" was reissued on October 5. In November, a CD single with edits of "Bends Like A Willow" and "Dot Com" and the unreleased current album session track "It All Trickles Down" was released. At least two other tracks recorded at the "j-tull Dot Com" sessions are still in the can.

Additional Jethro Tull concerts were discussed for 2000, with Scandinavia, Poland, the Czech Republic and Slovenia announced before further US dates in the summer. After the March release of "The Secret Language Of Birds," a live "best of" Jethro Tull album will follow in 2000 and Martin Barre will present his next album. In addition, Ian Anderson plans to start work on remastering Jethro Tull's entire catalog for EMI.

CONCLUSION

With over 2,500 concerts in dozens of countries and album sales (in numerous formats) over the 60 million mark, Jethro Tull is one of the few enduring bands from the '60s. Jethro Tull has been continually guided by one of music's most talented and erudite personalities - Ian Anderson. Similar to Frank Zappa, Ian's education came from following his own unique lifestyle and musical pathway and both found themselves constantly explaining their motives to a completely bewildered and inferior media. *(Another thing that Ian Anderson still has in common with the late Frank Zappa: Ian still doesn't have a driver's license!)* Under Anderson's guidance, Jethro Tull has continued to cultivate its own musical style and unique sound with nary a backward glance.

What of Jethro Tull's music? Equally frustrating to most women and dance types, Jethro Tull's music refuses to bend to the demands of the masses. Rather, it challenges the band's hearty core of fans and newcomers open enough to give it a fair shake. As soon as a Jethro Tull song is played, it is immediately identifiable as Tull. In the instance when another rock musician picks up a flute (Ann Wilson of Heart is one example), his/her flute playing is automatically compared to Ian Anderson's high standards.

Those standards included the deft incorporation of numerous musical forms into Jethro Tull's potent brew of ethnicity and Ian Anderson's lyrical eloquence. The band's humor, stage theatrics and serious playing rolls up to a collective and integrated personality that reflects that they are people just like us. It is this human aspect that fans gravitate and latch on to. With all the money that he would need for several lifetimes, Ian Anderson could just as easily pack it all in and retreat to the relative quiet of his salmon farms. But Ian, lucky for us, simply loves to perform for anyone interested in hearing what he or Jethro Tull has to say musically. Equally important is Ian's interest in spreading Jethro Tull's fanbase into as many free countries as possible. Ian Anderson's natural sharing of music with peoples from all backgrounds is so highly commendable, regardless of how one feels about Ian personally.

Ian Anderson's children, James and Gael, are studying television and media at the university level. With all of the poor press handling that Jethro Tull has received over the years, perhaps Ian's own bloodline can function as Tull's proper PR squad!

Even though venues, ticket sales and CD/cassette sales have dropped off over the years, Jethro Tull has maintained the same honest approach. Ian Anderson originally planned on a 2001 demise of Jethro Tull, but I recently asked Fuel 2000 honcho Len Fico about the contract that Ian and Tull signed with the label: "Suffice to say it is a long term contract. In addition to covering several Jethro Tull albums, it also covers the solo works of Ian Anderson. It is safe to say we will be in the Jethro Tull business well into the next millennium." This is a very encouraging and reassuring thought for thousands of loyal fans.

On the name Jethro Tull, Ian Anderson has recently said, "We borrowed the name, but we'll be happy to return it as soon as we've finished with it!" Now since the band has entered their incredible fourth decade, who knows what Ian Anderson has up his creative sleeve? What's for sure is that Ian is wise enough to carry Jethro Tull on another 30 years, after all of his contemporaries and critics finally realize that his way was legitimate and justified all along.

JETHRO TULL DISCOGRAPHY - SINGLES

(All songs written by Ian Anderson unless otherwise noted)

TITLES	UK & FOREIGN LABEL/NO.	RELEASE DATE	US LABEL/NO.	RELEASE DATE
Sunshine Day/ Aeroplane (promo copy; shown as by JETHRO TOE)	MGM MGM 1384	02/16/68		
Sunshine Day/ Aeroplane (regular copy; shown as JETHRO TOE)	MGM MGM 1384	02/23/68		

A: (Michael Abrahams) Ian Anderson (backing vocals), Mick Abrahams (lead vocal, electric guitar), Glenn Cornick (bass), Clive Bunker (drums), Tony Wilson (backing vocals). Recorded 01/68 at Abbey Road Studios, London. Produced by Derek Lawrence.
B: (Ian Anderson/ Len Barnard [Glenn Cornick]) Ian Anderson (lead vocal), John Evans (keyboards), Glenn Cornick (bass), Barrie Barlow (drums), Neil Smith (Chick Murray) (electric guitar),Tony Wilson (backing vocals). Recorded 10/22/67 at CBS Studios, London. Produced by Derek Lawrence.

(NOTE: This single was counterfeited in New York in September 1979 with Jethro Tull shown on the label. Most of these copies are in colored vinyl, and all are without a centerpiece.)

A Song For Jeffrey/One For John Gee	Island WIP 6043	09/27/68		

A: Ian Anderson (flute, vocal), Mick Abrahams (electric guitar), Glenn Cornick (bass), Clive Bunker (drums). Recorded 07/68 at Sound Techniques, London. Produced by Terry Ellis and Jethro Tull.
B: (Michael Abrahams) Ian Anderson (flute), Mick Abrahams (electric guitar), Glenn Cornick (bass), Clive Bunker (drums). Recorded 07/68 at Sound Techniques, London.

Love Story/Christmas Song	Island WIP 6048	11/29/68		
Love Story/A Song For Jeffrey			Reprise 0815	02/12/69

A: Ian Anderson (mandolin, flute, vocal), Mick Abrahams (electric guitar), Glenn Cornick (bass), Clive Bunker (drums and percussion). Recorded 11/68 at Morgan Studios, London. Produced by Terry Ellis and Jethro Tull. Chart peak: #29 (UK).
B: ("Christmas Song") Ian Anderson (mandolin, tin whistle, vocal), Glenn Cornick (bass), Clive Bunker (drums), David Palmer (string arrangement and conducting). Recorded 11/68 at Morgan Studios, London. Produced by Terry Ellis and Jethro Tull.
B: ("A Song For Jeffrey") Ian Anderson (flute, vocal), Mick Abrahams (electric guitar), Glenn Cornick (bass), Clive Bunker (drums). Recorded 07/68 at Sound Techniques, London. Produced by Terry Ellis and Jethro Tull.

Living In The Past/Driving Song	Island WIP 6056	05/02/69	Reprise 0845	07/28/69
Living In The Past (stereo)/Driving Song (stereo) (promo only)			Reprise 0845	07/28/69

A: Ian Anderson (flute, vocal), Martin Barre (electric guitar), Glenn Cornick (bass), Clive Bunker (drums and percussion), Lou Toby (string arrangement and conducting members of The New York Symphony Orchestra). Backing track and vocals recorded 03/03/69 at Vantone Studio, West Orange, NJ. Produced by Terry Ellis and Ian Anderson. Chart peak: #3 (UK).
B: Ian Anderson (flute, vocal), Martin Barre (electric guitar), Glenn Cornick (bass), Clive Bunker (drums). Recorded 03/18/69 at Western Recorders, L.A., CA. Produced by Terry Ellis and Ian Anderson.

Sweet Dream/17	Chrysalis WIP 6070	10/03/69		
Sweet Dream/Reasons For Waiting (mislabelled B-side; the record plays "Back To The Family")			Reprise 0886	11/26/69

A: Ian Anderson (12-string guitar, flute, vocal), Martin Barre (electric guitar), Glenn Cornick (bass), Clive Bunker (drums), David Palmer (orchestral arrangement and conducting). Recorded 08/31/69 at Morgan Studios, London. Produced by Terry Ellis and Ian Anderson. Chart peak: #7 (UK).
B: ("17") Ian Anderson (flute, vocal), Martin Barre (electric guitar), Glenn Cornick (bass), Clive Bunker (drums). Recorded 09/11/69 at Morgan Studios, London. Produced by Terry Ellis and Ian Anderson.
B: ("Back To The Family") Ian Anderson (flute, vocal), Martin Barre (electric guitar), Glenn Cornick (bass), Clive Bunker (drums). Recorded 04/21/69 at Morgan Studios, London. Produced by Ian Anderson and Terry Ellis.

The Witch's Promise/ Teacher (Version #1) Chrysalis WIP 6077 01/16/70
(NOTE: Some copies labelled as "Witch's Promise" b/w "The Teacher" or "Witch's Promise" b/w "Teacher.")
The Witch's Promise/ Teacher (Version #2) Reprise 0899 03/11/70

A: Ian Anderson (flute, vocal), Martin Barre (electric guitar, acoustic guitar), Glenn Cornick (bass), Clive Bunker (drums), John Evans (piano, mellotron). Recorded 12/19/69 at Morgan Studios, London. Produced by Terry Ellis and Ian Anderson. Chart peak:#4 (UK - double-sided single).
B (both versions): Ian Anderson (vocal, add flute to Version #2), Martin Barre (electric guitar), Glenn Cornick (bass), Clive Bunker (drums), John Evans (Hammond organ). Version #1 recorded 12/19/69 at Morgan Studios, London. Version #2 recorded 01/12/70 - 01/13/70 at Morgan Studios, London. Produced by Terry Ellis and Ian Anderson. Chart peak: #4 (UK - double-sided single).

Inside/Alive And Well And Living In Chrysalis WIP 6081 05/29/70
Inside/A Time For Everything? Reprise 0927 06/10/70

A: Ian Anderson (acoustic guitar, vocal), Martin Barre (electric guitar), Glenn Cornick (bass), Clive Bunker (drums, glockenspiel). Recorded 01/70 at Morgan Studios, London. Produced by Ian Anderson.
B ("Alive And Well And Living In"): Ian Anderson (flute, vocal), Martin Barre (electric guitar), Glenn Cornick (bass), Clive Bunker (drums), John Evans (piano). Recorded 01/70 at Morgan Studios, London. Produced by Ian Anderson.
B ("A Time For Everything?"): Ian Anderson (flute, vocal), Martin Barre (electric guitar), Glenn Cornick (bass), Clive Bunker (drums), John Evans (piano). Recorded 01/70 at Morgan Studios, London. Produced by Ian Anderson.

Lick Your Fingers Clean/Up To Me (cancelled) Chrysalis WIP 6098 01/29/71

A: Ian Anderson (vocal, flute), Martin Barre (electric guitar), Jeffrey Hammond-Hammond (bass), Clive Bunker (drums), John Evans (keyboards). Recorded 12/70 at Island Studios, London. Produced by Ian Anderson and Terry Ellis.
B: Ian Anderson (flute, acoustic guitar, vocal), Martin Barre (electric guitar), Jeffrey Hammond-Hammond (bass), Clive Bunker (drums), John Evans (keyboards), David Palmer (orchestral arrangement and conducting). Recorded 12/70 at Island Studios, London. Produced by Ian Anderson and Terry Ellis.

Hymn 43/Mother Goose Reprise 1024 06/16/71

A: Ian Anderson (flute, vocal), Martin Barre (electric guitar), Jeffrey Hammond-Hammond (bass), Clive Bunker (drums), John Evans (keyboards), David Palmer (orchestral arrangement and conducting). Recorded 12/70 at Island Studios, London. Produced by Ian Anderson and Terry Ellis. Chart peak: #91 (US).
B: Ian Anderson (flute, acoustic guitar, vocal), Martin Barre (electric guitar), Jeffrey Hammond-Hammond (bass), Clive Bunker (drums), John Evans (keyboards), David Palmer (orchestral arrangement and conducting). Recorded 12/70 at Island Studios, London. Produced by Ian Anderson and Terry Ellis.

Life Is A Long Song - Up The 'Pool/
  Dr. Bogenbroom - For Later - Nursie (EP) Chrysalis WIP 6106 09/17/71

A ("Life Is A Long Song"): Ian Anderson (acoustic guitar, flute, vocal), Martin Barre (acoustic guitar), Jeffrey Hammond-Hammond (bass), Barriemore Barlow (drums), John Evans (piano). Recorded 05/71 at Sound Techniques, London. Produced by Ian Anderson. Chart peak: #11 (UK).
A ("Up The 'Pool"): Ian Anderson (acoustic guitar, violin, flute, vocal), Martin Barre (electric guitar), Jeffrey Hammond-Hammond (bass), Barriemore Barlow (drums), John Evans (organ). Recorded 05/71 at Sound Techniques, London. Produced by Ian Anderson.
B ("Dr. Bogenbroom"): Ian Anderson (acoustic guitar, flute, vocal), Martin Barre (electric guitar), Jeffrey Hammond-Hammond (bass), Barriemore Barlow (drums), John Evans (piano, harpsichord). Recorded 05/71 at Sound Techniques, London. Produced by Ian Anderson.
B ("For Later"): Ian Anderson (flute, vocal), Martin Barre (electric guitar), Jeffrey Hammond-Hammond (bass), Barriemore Barlow (drums, percussion), John Evans (Hammond organ, piano). Recorded 05/71 at Sound Techniques, London. Produced by Ian Anderson.
B ("Nursie"): Ian Anderson (acoustic guitar, vocal). Recorded 05/71 at Sound Techniques, London. Produced by Ian Anderson.

Locomotive Breath/Wind-Up Reprise 1054 11/17/71

A: Ian Anderson (flute, electric guitar, acoustic guitar, basic drum track, vocal), Martin Barre (electric guitar), Jeffrey Hammond-Hammond (bass), Clive Bunker (drums), John Evans (keyboards), David Palmer (orchestral arrangement and conducting). Recorded 12/70 at Island Studios, London. Produced by Ian Anderson and Terry Ellis.
B: Ian Anderson (flute, acoustic guitar, vocal), Martin Barre (electric guitar), Jeffrey Hammond-Hammond (bass), Clive Bunker (drums), John Evans (keyboards), David Palmer (orchestral arrangement and conducting). Recorded 12/70 at Island Studios, London. Produced by Ian Anderson and Terry Ellis.

Living In The Past/Christmas Song   Chrysalis CHS 2006   10/30/72

A: Ian Anderson (flute, vocal), Martin Barre (electric guitar), Glenn Cornick (bass), Clive Bunker (drums and percussion), Lou Toby (string arrangement and conducting members of The New York Symphony Orchestra). Backing track and vocals recorded 03/03/69 at Vantone Studio, West Orange, NJ. Produced by Terry Ellis and Ian Anderson. Chart peak: #11 (US).
B: Ian Anderson (mandolin, tin whistle, vocal), Glenn Cornick (bass), Clive Bunker (drums), David Palmer (string arrangement and conducting). Recorded 11/68 at Morgan Studios, London. Produced by Terry Ellis and Jethro Tull.

A Passion Play (Edit #8)/A Passion Play (Edit #9)   Chrysalis CHS 2012   04/30/73

A: Ian Anderson (vocals, acoustic guitars, flute, soprano saxophone, sopranino saxophone), Martin Barre (electric guitar), Barriemore Barlow (drums, timpani, glockenspiel, marimba), Jeffrey Hammond-Hammond (bass, vocals), John Evans (piano, organ, synthesizer). Recorded 03/73 at Morgan Studios, London. Produced by Ian Anderson. Chart peak: #80 (US).
B: Ian Anderson (vocals, acoustic guitars, flute, soprano saxophone, sopranino saxophone), Martin Barre (electric guitar), Barriemore Barlow (drums, timpani, glockenspiel, marimba), Jeffrey Hammond-Hammond (bass, vocals), John Evans (piano, organ, synthesizer). Recorded 03/73 at Morgan Studios, London. Produced by Ian Anderson.

A Passion Play (Edit #10)/A Passion Play (Edit #6)   Chrysalis CHS 2017   09/03/73

A: Ian Anderson (vocals, acoustic guitars, flute, soprano saxophone, sopranino saxophone), Martin Barre (electric guitar), Barriemore Barlow (drums, timpani, glockenspiel, marimba), Jeffrey Hammond-Hammond (bass, vocals), John Evans (piano, organ, synthesizer). Recorded 03/73 at Morgan Studios, London. Produced by Ian Anderson. Chart peak: #105 (US).
B: Ian Anderson (vocals, acoustic guitars, flute, soprano saxophone, sopranino saxophone), Martin Barre (electric guitar), Barriemore Barlow (drums, timpani, glockenspiel, marimba), Jeffrey Hammond-Hammond (bass, vocals), John Evans (piano, organ, synthesizer).Recorded 03/73 at Morgan Studios, London. Produced by Ian Anderson.

Living In The Past/Cross-Eyed Mary   Chrysalis "Back To Back Hits" GCH 0026   01/28/74

A: Ian Anderson (flute, vocal), Martin Barre (electric guitar), Glenn Cornick (bass), Clive Bunker (drums and percussion), Lou Toby (string arrangement and conducting members of The New York Symphony Orchestra). Backing track and vocals recorded 03/03/69 at Vantone Studio, West Orange, NJ. Produced by Terry Ellis and Ian Anderson.
B: Ian Anderson (flute, vocal), Martin Barre (electric guitar), Jeffrey Hammond-Hammond (bass), Clive Bunker (drums), John Evans (keyboards), David Palmer (orchestral arrangement and conducting). Recorded 12/70 at Island Studios, London. Produced by Ian Anderson and Terry Ellis.

Bungle In The Jungle/Back-Door Angels   Chrysalis CHS 2054   11/15/74   Chrysalis CRS 2101   09/23/74
(NOTE: A special picture sleeve was available with US promotional copies only. Some B-sides shown as "Back-Door Angel.")

A: Ian Anderson (vocals, flute, acoustic guitar), Martin Barre (electric guitar), Barriemore Barlow (drums, percussion), Jeffrey Hammond-Hammond (bass), John Evans (keyboards), David Palmer (orchestration and conducting members of the Philomusica of London - leader: Patrick Halling). Recorded spring 1974 at Morgan Studios, London. Produced by Ian Anderson. Chart peak: #12 (US).
B: Ian Anderson (vocals, flute, acoustic guitar), Martin Barre (electric guitar), Barriemore Barlow (drums, percussion), Jeffrey Hammond-Hammond (bass), John Evans (keyboards), David Palmer (orchestration and conducting members of the Philomusica of London - leader: Patrick Halling). Recorded spring 1974 at Morgan Studios, London. Produced by Ian Anderson.

Skating Away (On The Thin Ice Of The New Day)/ Sealion   Chrysalis CRS 2103   02/03/75

A: Ian Anderson (vocals, flute, acoustic guitar), Martin Barre (electric guitar), Barriemore Barlow (drums, glockenspiel, marimba, percussion), Jeffrey Hammond-Hammond (bass), John Evans (keyboards). Recorded 08/72 at Chateau D'Herouville, France. Produced by Ian Anderson.
B: Ian Anderson (vocals, flute, acoustic guitar), Martin Barre (electric guitar), Barriemore Barlow (drums, percussion), Jeffrey Hammond-Hammond (bass), John Evans (keyboards), David Palmer (orchestration and conducting members of the Philomusica of London - leader: Patrick Halling). Recorded spring 1974 at Morgan Studios, London. Produced by Ian Anderson.

Minstrel In The Gallery/Summerday Sands   Chrysalis CHS 2075   08/22/75 Chrysalis CRS 2106   08/11/75

A: Ian Anderson (vocals, flute, electric guitar), Martin Barre (electric guitar), Jeffrey Hammond-Hammond (bass, string bass), John Evans (piano, organ), Barriemore Barlow (drums, percussion), David Palmer [orchestral arrangement and conducting members of the Philomusica of London - leader Patrick Halling, Elizabeth Edwards (violin), Rita Eddowes (violin), Bridget Proctor (violin), Katharine Thulborn (cello)]. Recorded 04/75 using Maison Rouge Mobile somewhere in Europe. Produced by Ian Anderson. Chart peak: #79 (US).
B: Ian Anderson (vocal, acoustic guitar), Martin Barre (electric guitar), Jeffrey Hammond-Hammond (bass), Barriemore Barlow (drums), David Palmer (orchestra conductor). Recorded 1975 using Maison Rouge Mobile at Radio Monte Carlo. Produced by Ian Anderson.

Locomotive Breath/Fat Man   Chrysalis CRS 2110   01/12/76

A: Ian Anderson (flute, electric guitar, acoustic guitar, basic drum track, vocal), Martin Barre (electric guitar), Jeffrey Hammond-Hammond (bass), Clive Bunker (drums), John Evans (keyboards), David Palmer (orchestral arrangement and conducting). Recorded 12/70 at Island Studios, London. Produced by Ian Anderson and Terry Ellis. Chart peak: #62 (US).
B: Ian Anderson (flute, acoustic guitar, balalaika, vocals), Clive Bunker (percussion). Recorded 04/69 at Morgan Studios, London. Produced by Terry Ellis and Ian Anderson for Chrysalis Productions.

Living In The Past/Requiem   Chrysalis CHS 2081   01/16/76

A: Ian Anderson (flute, vocal), Martin Barre (electric guitar), Glenn Cornick (bass), Clive Bunker (drums and percussion), Lou Toby (string arrangement and conducting members of The New York Symphony Orchestra). Backing track and vocals recorded 03/03/69 at Vantone Studio, West Orange, NJ. Produced by Terry Ellis and Ian Anderson.
B: Ian Anderson (vocal, acoustic guitar), Martin Barre (electric guitar), Jeffrey Hammond-Hammond (bass), Barriemore Barlow (drums), David Palmer (orchestra conductor). Recorded 04/75 using Maison Rouge Mobile at Radio Monte Carlo. Produced by Ian Anderson.

Too Old To Rock 'N' Roll: Too Young To Die/ Rainbow Blues   Chrysalis CHS 2086   03/19/76
Too Old To Rock 'N' Roll: Too Young To Die/ Bad-Eyed And Loveless   Chrysalis CRS 2114   06/30/76

A: Ian Anderson (vocals, acoustic guitar, flute), Martin Barre (electric guitar), Barriemore Barlow (drums, percussion), John Glascock (bass, vocals), John Evans (pianos), David Palmer (orchestral arrangement and conducting), Maddy Prior (backing vocals). Recorded 12/75 using the Maison Rouge Mobile at Radio Monte Carlo. Produced by Ian Anderson.
B ("Rainbow Blues"): Ian Anderson (vocal, flute), Martin Barre (electric guitar), John Evans (keyboards), Jeffrey Hammond-Hammond (bass), Barriemore Barlow (drums). Recorded spring 1974 at Morgan Studios, London. Produced by Ian Anderson.
B ("Bad-Eyed And Loveless"): Ian Anderson (vocals, acoustic guitar, flute), Martin Barre (electric guitar), Barriemore Barlow (drums and percussion), John Glascock (bass, vocals), John Evans (pianos), David Palmer (orchestral arrangement and conducting). Recorded 12/75 using Maison Rouge Mobile at Radio Monte Carlo.

Ring Out, Solstice Bells - March, The Mad Scientist/
  Christmas Song - Pan Dance (EP; US issue is a promo-only 12")   Chrysalis CXP 2   12/03/76 Chrysalis CHS-3-PDJ   12/06/76

A ("Ring Out, Solstice Bells"): Ian Anderson (vocals, flute, acoustic guitar), Martin Barre (electric guitar), Barriemore Barlow (drums, percussion), John Glascock (bass, backing vocals), John Evans (piano), David Palmer (synthesizer, backing vocal). Recorded fall 1976 at Maison Rouge Studios, London and Maison Rouge Mobile. Produced by Ian Anderson. Chart peak: #28 (UK).
A ("March, The Mad Scientist"): Ian Anderson (vocal, acoustic guitar), John Evans (keyboards), Jeffrey Hammond-Hammond (acoustic double bass). Recorded 09/74 at Morgan Studio 2, London. Produced by Ian Anderson.
B ("Christmas Song"): Ian Anderson (mandolin, tin whistle, vocal), Glenn Cornick (bass), Clive Bunker (drums), David Palmer (string arrangement and conducting). Recorded 11/68 at Morgan Studios, London. Produced by Terry Ellis and Jethro Tull.
B ("Pan Dance"): Ian Anderson (flute), Martin Barre (electric guitar), John Evans (keyboards), Jeffrey Hammond-Hammond (bass), Barriemore Barlow (drums), Rita Eddowes (violin), Elizabeth Edwards (violin), Helen (violin), Katharine Thulborn (cello). Recorded 09/74 at Morgan Studio 2, London. Produced by Ian Anderson.

The Whistler/Strip Cartoon	Chrysalis CHS 2135	02/04/77	Chrysalis CHS 2135	03/28/77

A: Ian Anderson (vocals, flute, acoustic guitar), Martin Barre (electric guitar), Barriemore Barlow (drums, percussion), John Glascock (bass), John Evans (piano), David Palmer (synthesizer). Recorded fall 1976 at Maison Rouge Studios, London and Maison Rouge Mobile. Produced by Ian Anderson. Chart peak: #59 (US).

B: Ian Anderson (vocal, whistle, acoustic guitar), Martin Barre (electric guitar), John Glascock (bass), Barriemore Barlow (drums), John Evans (keyboards). Recorded 12/75 at Ridge Farm Studio, Surrey. Produced by Ian Anderson.

Moths/Beltane (cancelled)	Chrysalis CHS 2214	03/31/78
Moths/Life Is A Long Song	Chrysalis CHS 2214	04/07/78

A: Ian Anderson (vocals, flute, acoustic guitar, electric guitar, mandolin), Martin Barre (electric guitar), Barriemore Barlow (drums, percussion), John Glascock (bass), John Evans (piano, organ), David Palmer (portative pipe organ, keyboards, orchestral arrangement). Recorded 01/78 at Maison Rouge Studios, London. Produced by Ian Anderson.

B ("Beltane"): Ian Anderson (vocal, flute, saxophones), Martin Barre (electric guitar), John Glascock (bass), John Evans (keyboards), David Palmer (keyboards), Barriemore Barlow (drums). Recorded 12/77 at Maison Rouge Studios, London. Produced by Ian Anderson.

B ("Life Is A Long Song"): Ian Anderson (acoustic guitar, flute, vocal), Martin Barre (acoustic guitar), Jeffrey Hammond-Hammond (bass), Barriemore Barlow (drums), John Evans (piano). Recorded 05/71 at Sound Techniques, London. Produced by Ian Anderson.

A Stitch In Time (4:20)/Sweet Dream (live) (white or black vinyl)	Chrysalis CHS 2260	09/22/78
A Stitch In Time (3:30)/Sweet Dream (live) (white or black vinyl)	Chrysalis CHS 2260	09/22/78
Sweet Dream (live)/A Stitch In Time (4:20)	German Chry. 6155 231	09/22/78

A ("A Stitch In Time"): Ian Anderson (flute, bass, vocals), Martin Barre (electric guitar), Barriemore Barlow (drums), John Evans (keyboards), David Palmer (orchestra conductor). Recorded 1978 at Maison Rouge Studios, London. Produced by Ian Anderson.

B ("Sweet Dream"): Ian Anderson (vocals, flute, acoustic guitar), Martin Barre (electric guitar, mandolin), Barriemore Barlow (drums, glockenspiel), John Glascock (bass, vocals), John Evans (piano, organ, accordion, synthesizers), David Palmer (portative pipe organ, synthesizers). Recorded spring 1978 live somewhere in Europe. Produced by Ian Anderson.

North Sea Oil/Elegy	Chrysalis CHS 2378	10/05/79

A: Ian Anderson (vocals, flute, acoustic guitar, bass), Martin Barre (electric guitar), Barriemore Barlow (drums, percussion), John Evans (piano, organ), David Palmer (synthesizers, portative organ, orchestral arrangement). Recorded spring/summer 1979 at Maison Rouge Mobile and Maison Rouge Studios, London. Produced by Ian Anderson and Robin Black.

B: (David Palmer) Ian Anderson (vocals, flute, acoustic guitar), Martin Barre (electric guitar), Barriemore Barlow (drums, percussion), John Glascock (bass), John Evans (piano, organ), David Palmer (synthesizers, portative organ, orchestral arrangement). Recorded spring/summer 1979 at Maison Rouge Mobile and Maison Rouge Studios, London. Produced by Ian Anderson and Robin Black.

Home/ Warm Sporran		Chrysalis CHS 2387	10/22/79
Home - King Henry's Madrigal (Theme From "Mainstream")/			
Warm Sporran - Ring Out, Solstice Bells (EP)	Chrysalis CHS 2394	11/09/79	

A ("Home"): Ian Anderson (vocals, flute, acoustic guitar, bass), Martin Barre (electric guitar), Barriemore Barlow (drums, percussion), John Evans (piano, organ), David Palmer (synthesizers, portative organ, orchestral arrangement). Recorded spring/summer 1979 at Maison Rouge Mobile and Maison Rouge Studios, London. Produced by Ian Anderson and Robin Black.

A ("King Henry's Madrigal"): (trad., arr. David Palmer) Ian Anderson (flute), Martin Barre (electric guitar), Dave Pegg (bass), Barriemore Barlow (drums), John Evans (keyboards), David Palmer (keyboards). Recorded 09/79 at Maison Rouge Studios, London. Produced by Ian Anderson and Robin Black.

B ("Warm Sporran") - Ian Anderson (flute, acoustic guitar, bass), Martin Barre (electric guitar), Barriemore Barlow (drums, percussion), John Evans (piano, organ), David Palmer (synthesizers, portative organ, orchestral arrangement). Recorded spring/summer 1979 at Maison Rouge Mobile and Maison Rouge Studios, London. Produced by Ian Anderson and Robin Black.

B ("Ring Out, Solstice Bells") - Ian Anderson (vocals, flute, acoustic guitar), Martin Barre (electric guitar), Barriemore Barlow (drums, percussion), John Glascock (bass, backing vocals), John Evans (piano), David Palmer (synthesizer, backing vocal). Recorded fall 1976 at Maison Rouge Studios, London and Maison Rouge Mobile. Produced by Ian Anderson.

Working John, Working Joe/Fylingdale Flyer   Chrysalis CHS 2468   10/17/80

A: Ian Anderson (vocals, flute), Martin Barre (electric guitar), Dave Pegg (bass), Mark Craney (drums), Eddie Jobson (keyboards). Recorded summer 1980 at Maison Rouge Mobile and Maison Rouge Studios, London. Produced by Ian Anderson and Robin Black.
B: Ian Anderson (vocals, flute), Martin Barre (electric guitar), Dave Pegg (bass), Mark Craney (drums), Eddie Jobson (keyboards). Recorded summer 1980 at Maison Rouge Mobile and Maison Rouge Studios, London. Produced by Ian Anderson and Robin Black.

Broadsword/Fallen On Hard Times   Chrysalis CHS 2619   05/28/82
Broadsword/Fallen On Hard Times (7" picture disc)   Chrysalis CHP 2619   05/28/82

A: Ian Anderson (vocals, flute, acoustic guitar), Martin Barre (electric guitar, acoustic guitar), Dave Pegg (bass, backing vocals), Peter-John Vettese (piano, synthesizer), Gerry Conway (drums, percussion). Recorded winter 1982 at Maison Rouge Studio, London. Produced by Paul Samwell-Smith.
B: Ian Anderson (vocals, flute, acoustic guitar), Martin Barre (electric guitar, acoustic guitar), Dave Pegg (bass, mandolin), Peter-John Vettese (piano, synthesizer), Gerry Conway (drums, percussion). Recorded winter 1982 at Maison Rouge Studio, London Produced by Paul Samwell-Smith.

Fallen On Hard Times/Pussy Willow   Chrysalis CHS 2613   06/28/82

A: Ian Anderson (vocals, flute, acoustic guitar), Martin Barre (electric guitar), Dave Pegg (bass, mandolins, vocals), Peter-John Vettese (piano, synthesizer), Gerry Conway (drums, percussion). Recorded winter 1982 at Maison Rouge Studio, London. Produced by Paul Samwell-Smith. Chart peak: #108 (US).
B: Ian Anderson (vocals, flute, acoustic guitar), Martin Barre (electric guitar), Dave Pegg (bass, mandolins, vocals), Peter-John Vettese (piano, synthesizer), Gerry Conway (drums, percussion). Recorded winter 1982 at Maison Rouge Studio, London Produced by Paul Samwell-Smith.

Lap Of Luxury/Astronomy//
   Automotive Engineering/Tundra (double 7")   Chrysalis TULL D1   09/14/84
Lap Of Luxury - Astronomy/Automotive Engineering - Tundra (12")   Chrysalis TULLX 1   09/14/84

A ("Lap Of Luxury"): Ian Anderson (vocals, flute, acoustic guitar), Martin Barre (electric guitar), Dave Pegg (bass), Peter-John Vettese (keyboards). Recorded spring 1984 at Ian Anderson's home studio. Produced by Ian Anderson. Chart peak: #70 (UK).
A ("Astronomy"): Ian Anderson (vocals, flute, acoustic guitar), Martin Barre (electric guitar), Dave Pegg (bass), Peter-John Vettese (keyboards). Recorded spring 1984 at Ian Anderson's home studio. Produced by Ian Anderson.
B ("Automotive Engineering"): Ian Anderson (vocals, flute, acoustic guitar), Martin Barre (electric guitar), Dave Pegg (bass), Peter-John Vettese (keyboards). Recorded spring 1984 at Ian Anderson's home studio. Produced by Ian Anderson.
B ("Tundra"): Ian Anderson (vocals, flute, acoustic guitar), Martin Barre (electric guitar), Dave Pegg (bass), Peter-John Vettese (keyboards). Recorded spring 1984 at Ian Anderson's home studio. Produced by Ian Anderson.

Bourrée/Elegy (shown as by THE LONDON SYMPHONY
   ORCHESTRA featuring Ian Anderson)   RCA Red Seal PB-14262   01/13/86

A: (J.S. Bach) David Palmer (orchestral arrangement, orchestra conductor), London Symphony Orchestra (leader: Ashley Arbuckle), Ian Anderson (flute), Martin Barre (electric guitar), Dave Pegg (bass), Peter-John Vettese (keyboards), Dave Burgess (drums - uncredited). Recorded summer 1984 at CBS Studios, London. Produced by David Palmer.
B: (David Palmer) David Palmer (orchestral arrangement, orchestra conductor), London Symphony Orchestra (leader: Ashley Arbuckle), Ian Anderson (flute), Martin Barre (electric guitar), Dave Pegg (bass), Peter-John Vettese (keyboards), Dave Burgess (drums - uncredited). Recorded summer 1984 at CBS Studios, London. Produced by David Palmer.

Coronach (from the Channel 4 TV Series "The Blood Of The British")/	Chrysalis TULL 2/		
Jack Frost And The Hooded Crow (7" and unreleased cassette)	ZTULL 2	06/20/86	
Coronach (from the Channel 4 TV Series "The Blood Of The British") -			
Jack Frost And The Hooded Crow/Living In The Past - Elegy (12")	Chrysalis TULLX 2	06/20/86	

A: (David Palmer) Ian Anderson (vocal, flute), Martin Barre (electric guitar), Dave Pegg (bass), Gerry Conway (drums), Peter-John Vettese (keyboards), unknown (oboe). Recorded summer 1984 at Manor Studio, Oxfordshire. Produced by David Palmer.
B ("Jack Frost And The Hooded Crow"): Ian Anderson (vocal, flute, keyboards), Martin Barre (electric guitar), Dave Pegg (bass), Gerry Conway (drums), Peter-John Vettese (keyboards). Recorded fall 1981 at Maison Rouge Studios, London. Produced by Ian Anderson.
B ("Living In The Past"): Ian Anderson (flute, vocal), Martin Barre (electric guitar), Glenn Cornick (bass), Clive Bunker (drums and percussion), Lou Toby (string arrangement and conducting members of The New York Symphony Orchestra). Backing track and vocals recorded 03/03/69 at Vantone Studio, West Orange, NJ. Produced by Terry Ellis and Ian Anderson.
B ("Elegy"): (David Palmer) Ian Anderson (vocals, flute, acoustic guitar), Martin Barre (electric guitar), Barriemore Barlow (drums, percussion), John Glascock (bass), John Evans (piano, organ), David Palmer (synthesizers, portative organ, orchestral arrangements). Recorded spring/summer 1979 at Maison Rouge Mobile and Maison Rouge Studios, London. Produced by Ian Anderson and Robin Black.

Living In The Past/ The Witch's Promise	Old Gold OG 9673	02/27/87

A: ("Living In The Past"): Ian Anderson (flute, vocal), Martin Barre (electric guitar), Glenn Cornick (bass), Clive Bunker (drums and percussion), Lou Toby (string arrangement and conducting members of The New York Symphony Orchestra). Backing track and vocals recorded 03/03/69 at Vantone Studio, West Orange, NJ. Produced by Terry Ellis and Ian Anderson.
B: Ian Anderson (flute, vocal), Martin Barre (electric guitar, acoustic guitar), Glenn Cornick (bass), Clive Bunker (drums), John Evans (piano, mellotron). Recorded 12/69 at Morgan Studios, London. Produced by Terry Ellis and Ian Anderson.

Steel Monkey/Down At The End Of Your Road	Chrysalis TULL 3	10/09/87	Chrysalis VS4 43172	10/19/87
Steel Monkey/Down At The End Of Your Road (7" picture disc)	Chrysalis TULLP 3	10/09/87		
Steel Monkey - Down At The End Of Your Road/				
Too Many Too - I'm Your Gun (12")	Chrysalis TULLX 3	10/09/87		

A: Ian Anderson (vocals, guitar, drum programming, percussion), Martin Barre (electric guitar), Dave Pegg (bass). Recorded spring 1987 at Ian Anderson's home studio. Produced by Ian Anderson. Chart peak: #82 (UK).
B ("Down At The End Of Your Road"): Ian Anderson (vocal, keyboards), Martin Barre (electric guitar), Dave Pegg (bass), Gerry Conway (drums). Recorded fall 1981 at Maison Rouge Studios, London. Produced by Ian Anderson.
B ("Too Many Too"): Ian Anderson (vocal, keyboards), Martin Barre (electric guitar), Dave Pegg (bass), Gerry Conway (drums). Recorded fall 1981 at Maison Rouge Studios, London. Produced by Ian Anderson.
B ("I'm Your Gun"): Ian Anderson (vocal, keyboards), Martin Barre (electric guitar), Dave Pegg (bass), Gerry Conway (drums). Recorded fall 1981 at Maison Rouge Studios, London. Produced by Ian Anderson.

Said She Was A Dancer/Dogs In The Midwinter (7")	Chrysalis TULL 4	01/08/88
Said She Was A Dancer/Dogs In The Midwinter (7" picture disc)	Chrysalis TULLP 4	01/08/88
Said She Was A Dancer/ Dogs In The Midwinter -		
The Waking Edge (12")	Chrysalis TULLX 4	01/08/88
Said She Was A Dancer - Dogs In The Midwinter -		
Down At The End Of Your Road - Too Many Too (CD5)	Chrysalis TULLCD 4	01/08/88

A: Ian Anderson (vocals, guitar, keyboards), Martin Barre (electric guitar), Dave Pegg (acoustic bass, acoustic bass), Gerry Conway (drums). Recorded spring 1987 at Ian Anderson's home studio. Produced by Ian Anderson. Chart peak: #55 (UK).
B ("Dogs In The Midwinter"): Ian Anderson (vocal, flute, keyboards, drum programming), Martin Barre (electric guitar), Dave Pegg (bass). Recorded spring 1987 at Ian Anderson's home studio. Produced by Ian Anderson.
B ("The Waking Edge") Ian Anderson (vocal, keyboards, acoustic guitar), Martin Barre (electric guitar), Dave Pegg (bass), Gerry Conway (drums). Recorded spring 1987 at Ian Anderson's home studio. Produced by Ian Anderson.
B ("Down At The End Of Your Road"): Ian Anderson (vocal, keyboards), Martin Barre (electric guitar), Dave Pegg (bass), Gerry Conway (drums). Recorded fall 1981 at Maison Rouge Studios, London. Produced by Ian Anderson.
B ("Too Many Too"): Ian Anderson (vocal, keyboards), Martin Barre (electric guitar), Dave Pegg (bass), Gerry Conway (drums). Recorded fall 1981 at Maison Rouge Studios, London. Produced by Ian Anderson.

Part Of The Machine (edit) - Stormy Monday Blues (live) -
  Lick Your Fingers Clean - Minstrel In The Gallery (live) -
  Farm On The Freeway (live) (CD5)   Chrysalis TULLPCD 1   06/27/88

A: Ian Anderson (vocal, acoustic guitar, flute, whistles), Martin Barre (electric guitar), Dave Pegg (bass), Martin Allcock (bouzouki, electric guitar, keyboards), Gerry Conway (drums). Recorded 03/88 at Ian Anderson's home studio. Produced by Ian Anderson.
B ("Stormy Monday Blues"): (Eckstine/ Crowder/ Hines) Ian Anderson (vocals, flute), Mick Abrahams (electric guitar), Glenn Cornick (bass), Clive Bunker (drums). Recorded and produced by the BBC in 1968.
B ("Lick Your Fingers Clean"): Ian Anderson (vocals, flute), Martin Barre (electric guitar), Jeffrey Hammond-Hammond (bass), Barriemore Barlow (drums), John Evans (keyboards). Recorded 12/70 at Island Studios, London. Mixed 04/88 at Ian Anderson's home studio. Produced by Ian Anderson and Terry Ellis.
B ("Minstrel In The Gallery"): Ian Anderson (vocals, acoustic guitar), Barriemore Barlow (percussion). Recorded 04/75 by the Maison Rouge Mobile at Radio Monte Carlo for the BBC. Produced by Ian Anderson.
B ("Farm On The Freeway"): Ian Anderson (vocals, flute), Martin Barre (electric guitar), Dave Pegg (bass), Doane Perry (drums), Don Airey (keyboards). Recorded live 11/25/87 at The Tower Theater, Upper Darby, PA.

Kissing Willie - Ears Of Tin/ (same tracks; cassette single)   Chrysalis 4JM 23418   10/03/89

A: Ian Anderson (vocals, flute), Martin Barre (electric guitar), Dave Pegg (bass), Doane Perry (drums), Martin Allcock (keyboards). Recorded spring 1989 at Ian Anderson's home studio. Produced by Ian Anderson.
B: Ian Anderson (vocals, flute, keyboards), Martin Barre (electric guitar), Dave Pegg (bass), Doane Perry (drums), Peter-John Vettese (keyboards). Recorded spring 1989 at Ian Anderson's home studio. Produced by Ian Anderson.

Another Christmas Song/ Intro/Christmas Song (live) (7")   Chrysalis TULL 5   12/04/89
Another Christmas Song; Intro/Christmas Song (live);/
  Cheap Day Return (live)/Mother Goose (live);   Chrysalis TULLX 5/
  Outro/Locomotive Breath (live) (12"/CD5)   TULLCD 5   12/04/89

A: Ian Anderson (vocals, flute, keyboards, acoustic guitar), Martin Barre (electric guitar), Dave Pegg (bass), Doane Perry (drums, percussion). Recorded spring 1989 at Ian Anderson's home studio. Produced by Ian Anderson.
B (all tracks): Ian Anderson (vocals, flute, acoustic guitar), Martin Barre (acoustic guitar, electric guitar), Dave Pegg (mandolin, bass). Recorded live 10/13/89 in the dressing room at Zurich Sports Hall, Zurich, Switzerland. Produced by Ian Anderson. Known as "The Dressing Room Tape."

This Is Not Love/ Night In The Wilderness (7")   Chrysalis TULL 6   08/05/91
This Is Not Love/ Night In The Wilderness - Jump Start (live) (12") Chrysalis TULLX 6   08/05/91
This Is Not Love - Night In The Wilderness - Jump Start (live) (CD5) Chrysalis TULLCD 6   08/05/91

A: Ian Anderson (vocals, flute, percussion), Martin Barre (electric guitar), Matt Pegg (bass), Doane Perry (drums and percussion), Andy Giddings (keyboards). Recorded winter/spring 1991 at Ian Anderson's home studio, except Matt Pegg's track (Woodworm Studios). Produced by Ian Anderson.
B ("Night In The Wilderness"): Ian Anderson (vocals, flute), Martin Barre (electric guitar), Dave Pegg (bass), Doane Perry (drums). Recorded winter/spring 1991 at Ian Anderson's home studio. Produced by Ian Anderson.
B: ("Jump Start"): Recorded live 11/25/87 at The Tower Theater, Upper Darby, PA. Produced by Ian Anderson.

Still Loving You Tonight/ Night In The Wilderness (7")   German Chrysalis
                                                               3 23782 7   09/15/91
Still Loving You Tonight - Night In The Wilderness -   German Chrysalis
  Jump Start (live) (CD5)   1c 560-32 3782 2   09/15/91

A: Ian Anderson (vocals, flute, keyboards), Martin Barre (electric guitar), Matt Pegg (bass), Scott Hunter (drums - uncredited). Recorded winter/spring 1991 at Ian Anderson's home studio, except for Matt Pegg and Scott Hunter's contributions (Woodworm Studios). Produced by Ian Anderson.
B ("Night In The Wilderness"): Ian Anderson (vocals, flute), Martin Barre (electric guitar), Dave Pegg (bass), Doane Perry (drums). Recorded winter/spring 1991 at Ian Anderson's home studio. Produced by Ian Anderson.
B: ("Jump Start"): Recorded live 11/25/87 at The Tower Theater, Upper Darby, PA. Produced by Ian Anderson.

Rocks On The Road (remix-edit)/Jack-A-Lynn (demo) (7")	Chrysalis TULL 7	03/09/92
Rocks On The Road (extended remix)/Jack-A-Lynn (demo) -	Chrysalis TULLX 7/	
Aqualung (live) - Locomotive Breath (live) (12" picture disc/ cassette)	TULLMC 7	03/09/92
Rocks On The Road (remix-edit) - Jack-A-Lynn (demo) -		
Like A Tall Thin Girl (live) - Fat Man (live) (first CD5)	Chrysalis TULLCD 7	03/09/92
Rocks On The Road (live) - Bourée (live) - Mother Goose (live) -		
Jack-A-Lynn (live) - Aqualung/Locomotive Breath (live) (second CD5)	Chrysalis BSTULLCD 7	03/09/92

(NOTE: the above CD single was only available in a double CD package.)

Rocks On The Road (remix-edit) - Rocks On The Road (live) -		
Bourée (live) - Jack-A-Lynn (demo) - Night In The Wilderness -		
Jump Start (live) (CD5)	Chrysalis F2 23818	04/14/92

A: Ian Anderson (vocals, acoustic guitar, flute), Martin Barre (electric guitar), Matt Pegg (bass), Doane Perry (drums and percussion), Andy Giddings (keyboards). Recorded winter/spring 1991 at Ian Anderson's home studio, except for Matt Pegg's track, which was recorded at Woodworm Studios. Produced by Ian Anderson. Chart peak: #47 (UK). NOTE: The full-length remix is exclusive to the 12" and cassette.

B ("Jack-A-Lynn [demo]"): Ian Anderson (vocal, acoustic guitar). Recorded fall 1981 at Ian Anderson's home studio. Produced by Ian Anderson.

B ("Like A Tall Thin Girl"): Ian Anderson (vocal, acoustic guitar), Martin Barre (electric guitar), Dave Pegg (bass), Doane Perry (drums), Martin Allcock (keyboards) Recorded 08/21/91 live at WMMR, Philadelphia, PA. Produced by Joe Bonadonna.

B ("Fat Man"): Ian Anderson (vocal, acoustic guitar), Martin Barre (electric guitar), Dave Pegg (bass), Doane Perry (drums, percussion), Martin Allcock (keyboards). Recorded 08/26/91 live on the radio program "Rockline" (KLOS-FM, L.A. with Bob Coburn). Produced by Mark Felsot.

B ("Rocks On The Road"): Ian Anderson (vocal, acoustic guitar), Martin Barre (electric guitar), Dave Pegg (bass), Doane Perry (drums), Martin Allcock (keyboards). Recorded 08/21/91 live at WMMR, Philadelphia, PA. Produced by Joe Bonadonna.

B ("Bourée"): Ian Anderson (vocal, flute), Martin Barre (electric guitar), Dave Pegg (bass), Doane Perry (drums), Martin Allcock (keyboards). Recorded 08/21/91 live at WMMR, Philadelphia, PA. Produced by Joe Bonadonna.

B ("Mother Goose"/"Jack-A-Lynn"): Ian Anderson (vocal, acoustic guitar), Martin Barre (electric guitar), Dave Pegg (bass), Doane Perry (drums), Martin Allcock (keyboards). Recorded live 08/20/91 at Electric Ladyland Studios, New York, NY. Produced by Ian Anderson.

B ("Aqualung"/"Locomotive Breath"): (Ian Anderson/ Jennie Anderson; Ian Anderson) Ian Anderson (vocal, acoustic guitar, flute), Martin Barre (electric guitar), Dave Pegg (bass), Doane Perry (drums), Martin Allcock (keyboards). Recorded live 08/20/91 at Electric Ladyland Studios, New York, NY. Produced by Ian Anderson.

Living In The Past/Hard Liner (7")	Chrysalis CHS 3970	05/10/93
Living In The Past (12" Club Mix) - Living In The Past (7" Mix)/		
Living In The Past (Ravey Master Mix) - Living In The Past		
(N.Y. Tip Mix)(12")	Chrysalis 12CHS 3970	05/10/93
Living In The (Slightly More Recent) Past (Live) - Silver River Turning -		
Rosa On The Factory Floor - I Don't Want To Be Me (first CD5)	Chrysalis 3 23970 2	05/10/93
Living In The Past - Truck Stop Runner - Piece Of Cake -		
Man Of Principle (second CD5)	Chrysalis 3 23971 2	05/10/93

(NOTE: the above singles were available separately, but the first single package could also house both CD5s.)

A (original version): Ian Anderson (flute, vocal), Martin Barre (electric guitar), Glenn Cornick (bass), Clive Bunker (drums and percussion), Lou Toby (string arrangement and conducting members of The New York Symphony Orchestra). Backing track and vocals recorded 03/03/69 at Vantone Studio, West Orange, NJ. Produced by Terry Ellis and Ian Anderson. Chart peak: #32 (UK).

B ("Hard Liner"): Ian Anderson (vocals, drum programming, flute), Martin Barre (electric guitar), Dave Pegg (bass). Recorded spring 1989 at Ian Anderson's home studio. Produced by Ian Anderson.

B ("Living In The [Slightly More Recent] Past") - Ian Anderson (vocals, flute), Martin Barre (electric guitar), Dave Pegg (bass), Dave Mattacks (drums), Andy Giddings (keyboards). Recorded 11/09/92 live in Montreal, QB, Canada. Produced by Ian Anderson.

B ("Silver River Turning"): Ian Anderson (vocals, flute), Martin Barre (electric guitar), Dave Pegg (bass), Doane Perry (drums), John Bundrick (keyboards). Recorded late 1990 at Ian Anderson's home studio. Produced by Ian Anderson.

B ("Rosa On The Factory Floor"): Ian Anderson (vocals, flute), Martin Barre (electric guitar), Dave Pegg (bass), Doane Perry (drums), John Bundrick (keyboards). Recorded late 1990 at Ian Anderson's home studio. Produced by Ian Anderson.

B ("I Don't Want To Be Me"): Ian Anderson (vocals, flute), Martin Barre (electric guitar), Dave Pegg (bass), Doane Perry (drums). Recorded late 1990 at Ian Anderson's home studio. Produced by Ian Anderson.

B ("Truck Stop Runner"): Ian Anderson (vocals, flute), Martin Barre (electric guitar), Dave Pegg (bass), Matt Pegg (bass), Scott Hunter (drums - uncredited). Recorded late 1990 at Ian Anderson's home studio, except Matt Pegg and Scott Hunter's contributions (Woodworm Studios). Produced by Ian Anderson.

B ("Piece Of Cake"): Ian Anderson (vocals, flute), Martin Barre (electric guitar), Dave Pegg (bass), Doane Perry (drums), John Bundrick (keyboards). Recorded late 1990 at Ian Anderson's home studio. Produced by Ian Anderson.

B ("Man Of Principle"): Ian Anderson (vocals, flute), Martin Barre (electric guitar), Dave Pegg (bass), Gerry Conway (drums). Recorded 03/88 at Ian Anderson's home studio. Produced by Ian Anderson.

<table>
<tr><td>Christmas Song/ Skating Away On The Thin Ice Of The New Day
(green vinyl jukebox issue)</td><td>CEMA Special Markets
S7-18211 A/B   11/10/94</td></tr>
</table>

A: Ian Anderson (mandolin, tin whistle, vocal), Glenn Cornick (bass), Clive Bunker (drums), David Palmer (string arrangement and conducting). Recorded 11/68 at Morgan Studios, London. Produced by Terry Ellis and Jethro Tull.
B: Ian Anderson (vocals, flute, acoustic guitar), Martin Barre (electric guitar), Barriemore Barlow (drums, glockenspiel, marimba, percussion), Jeffrey Hammond-Hammond (bass), John Evans (keyboards). Recorded 08/72 at Chateau D'Herouville, France. Produced by Ian Anderson.

Bends Like A Willow (edit) - Dot Com (edit) - It All Trickles Down
   (CD5; limited edition of 5,000 numbered copies)   Papillon BTFLYS0001   11/22/99

A: Ian Anderson (vocals, concert flute, bamboo flute, bouzouki, acoustic guitar), Martin Barre (electric guitar, acoustic guitar), Andy Giddings (Hammond organ, piano, accordion, chromatic and qwerty keyboards), Jonathan Noyce (bass), Doane Perry (drums, percussion). Recorded 01/99-02/99 at Ian Anderson's home studio. Produced by Ian Anderson.
B ("Dot Com"): Ian Anderson (vocals, concert flute, bamboo flute, bouzouki, acoustic guitar), Martin Barre (electric guitar, acoustic guitar), Andy Giddings (Hammond organ, piano, accordion, chromatic and qwerty keyboards), Jonathan Noyce (bass), Doane Perry (drums, percussion), Najma Akhtar (backing vocals). Recorded 01/99-02/99 at Ian Anderson's home studio. Produced by Ian Anderson.
B ("It All Trickles Down"): Ian Anderson (vocals, concert flute, bamboo flute, bouzouki, acoustic guitar), Martin Barre (electric guitar, acoustic guitar), Andy Giddings (Hammond organ, piano, accordion, chromatic and qwerty keyboards), Jonathan Noyce (bass), Doane Perry (drums, percussion). Recorded 01/99-02/99 at Ian Anderson's home studio. Produced by Ian Anderson.

JETHRO TULL DISCOGRAPHY - ALBUMS
(All songs written by Ian Anderson unless otherwise noted)

THIS WAS

MUSICIANS: Ian Anderson (flute, mouth organ, claghorn, piano, vocals), Mick Abrahams (guitar, 9-string guitar, vocals), Clive Bunker (drums, hooter and charm bracelet), Glenn Cornick (bass)
GUEST MUSICIANS: David Palmer (brass arrangement and conducting on "Move On Alone")
PRODUCTION: Terry Ellis and Jethro Tull for Chrysalis Productions
RECORDING LOCATION/ DATE: 06/13/68 to 08/23/68 at Sound Techniques Studio, Chelsea, London
TRACKS: My Sunday Feeling; Some Day The Sun Won't Shine For You; Beggar's Farm (Mick Abrahams/ Ian Anderson); Move On Alone (Mick Abrahams); Serenade To A Cuckoo (Roland Kirk);/ Dharma For One (Ian Anderson/ Clive Bunker); It's Breaking Me Up; Cat's Squirrel (listed as trad. - arranged by Ian Anderson; actually by Dr. Isaiah Ross); A Song For Jeffrey; Round (Ian Anderson/ Mick Abrahams/ Clive Bunker/ Glenn Cornick)
NOTES: Initially released in mono, but recalled in its first week. The original stereo album is a slightly different mix than all future pressings. The first US LP edition came with a poster of the front cover. "This Was" is also part of "The Originals" - see that listing for more details. The cover concept was by Terry Ellis and Ian Anderson.
PEAK CHART POSITION (UK/US): UK#10; US#62
SALES CERTIFICATIONS: Gold (UK)

RELEASES:

	UK & FOREIGN LABEL/NO.	RELEASE DATE	US LABEL/NO.	RELEASE DATE
This Was (mono/stereo LP - first mix)	Island ILP/ILPS 9085	10/25/68		
This Was (LP; second stereo mix)	Island ILPS 9085	01/31/69	Reprise RS 6336	02/03/69
This Was (LP; reissue)	Chrysalis CHR 1041	08/01/73	Chrysalis CHR 1041	07/23/73
This Was (LP; reissue)			Chrysalis FV 41041	07/04/83
This Was (CD)	Chrysalis CCD 1041	04/11/86	Chrysalis VK 41041	11/18/85
This Was (CD; reissue)	Chrys./EMI CCD 1041	03/23/92	Chrys./EMI F2 21041	03/24/92
This Was (LP; reissue)	Chrys./EMI 4 99468 1	03/29/99		
This Was (CD; reissue)			Chrys./EMI F2 21041	09/14/99

STAND UP

MUSICIANS: Ian Anderson (flute, acoustic guitar, Hammond organ, piano, mandolin, balalaika, bouzouki, mouth organ, vocals), Martin Barre (electric guitar, flute on "Jeffrey Goes To Leicester Square" and "Reasons For Waiting"), Clive Bunker (drums, percussion), Glenn Cornick (bass)
GUEST MUSICIANS: David Palmer (string arrangement and conducting on "Reasons For Waiting")
PRODUCTION: Terry Ellis and Ian Anderson for Chrysalis Productions
RECORDING LOCATION/ DATE: 04/17/69 - 05/01/69 at Morgan Studios, London, except "Bourée"(04/24/69 at Olympic Studios, Barnes, London)
TRACKS: A New Day Yesterday; Jeffrey Goes To Leicester Square; Bourée (J.S. Bach, arr. Ian Anderson - incorrect original credit listed Ian Anderson); Back To The Family; Look Into The Sun;/ Nothing Is Easy; Fat Man; We Used To Know; Reasons For Waiting; For A Thousand Mothers
NOTES: Terry Ellis and John Williams thought of the album design, and New York graphic artist Jimmy Grashow did the woodcutting which formed the graphic basis for the entire packaging. The album entered the UK album chart at #1. "Stand Up" is also part of "The Originals" - see that listing for more details.
PEAK CHART POSITION (UK/US): UK#1; US#20
SALES CERTIFICATIONS: Gold (UK and US)

RELEASES:

	UK & FOREIGN LABEL/NO.	RELEASE DATE	US LABEL/NO.	RELEASE DATE
Stand Up (LP)	Island ILPS 9103	08/01/69	Reprise RS 6360	09/29/69
Stand Up (LP; reissue)	Chrysalis CHR 1042	08/01/73	Chrysalis CHR 1042	07/23/73
Stand Up (LP; reissue)			Chrysalis FV 41042	07/04/83
Stand Up (LP; reissue - quickly withdrawn)	Fame/MFP FA 41 3086 1	02/17/84		
Stand Up (CD)	Chrysalis ACCD 1042	04/11/86	Chrysalis VK 41042	11/18/85
Stand Up (CD; reissue)	Chrysalis CCD 1042	01/16/89		
Stand Up (24 karat gold CD)			Mobile Fidelity Sound Lab UDCD 524	09/19/89
Stand Up (CD; reissue)	Chrys./EMI CCD 1042	03/23/92	Chrys./EMI F2 21042	03/24/92
Stand Up (LP; reissue)	Chrys./EMI LPCENT 8	02/17/97		
Stand Up (CD; reissue)			Chrys./EMI F2 21042	09/14/99

BENEFIT

MUSICIANS: Ian Anderson (flute, acoustic guitar, vocals), Martin Barre (electric guitar), Clive Bunker (drums, percussion), Glenn Cornick (bass)
GUEST MUSICIANS: John Evans (piano, organ)
PRODUCTION: Ian Anderson; executive producer: Terry Ellis
RECORDING LOCATION/ DATE: 01/70 at Morgan Studios, London, except "Play In Time" (09/01/69)
TRACKS: With You There To Help Me; Nothing To Say; Alive And Well And Living In*; Son; For Michael Collins, Jeffrey And Me;/ To Cry You A Song; A Time For Everything?; Inside; Play In Time; Sossity;You're A Woman
NOTES: US albums replaced * with "Teacher" (#2). "Benefit" is also part of "The Originals" - see that listing for more details. The cover design was by Terry Ellis and Ruan O'Lochlainn.
PEAK CHART POSITION (UK/US): UK#3; US#11
SALES CERTIFICATIONS: Gold (UK), Platinum (US)

RELEASES:

	UK & FOREIGN LABEL/NO.	RELEASE DATE	US LABEL/NO.	RELEASE DATE
Benefit (LP)	Island ILPS 9123	05/01/70	Reprise RS 6400	04/20/70
Benefit (LP; reissue)	Chrysalis CHR 1043	08/01/73	Chrysalis CHR 1043	07/23/73
Benefit (LP; reissue)			Chrysalis FV 41043	07/04/83
Benefit (CD)	Chrysalis CPCD 1043	06/12/87	Chrysalis VK 41043	11/18/85
Benefit (CD; reissue)	Chrys./EMI CCD 1043	03/23/92	Chrys./EMI F2 21043	03/24/92
Benefit (CD; reissue)			Chrys./EMI F2 21043	09/14/99

AQUALUNG

MUSICIANS: Ian Anderson (flute, acoustic guitar, electric guitar, vocals), Clive Bunker (drums, percussion), Martin Barre (electric guitar, descant recorder), John Evans (piano, organ, mellotron), Jeffrey Hammond-Hammond (bass, alto recorder, backing vocals)
GUEST MUSICIANS: David Palmer (string arrangement and conducting)
PRODUCTION: Ian Anderson and Terry Ellis
RECORDING LOCATION/ DATE: 12/70 and 02/71 at Island Studios, London
TRACKS: Aqualung (Ian Anderson/ Jennie Anderson); Cross-Eyed Mary; Cheap Day Return; Mother Goose; Wond'ring Aloud; Up To Me;/ My God; Hymn 43; Slipstream; Locomotive Breath; Wind-Up; Lick Your Fingers Clean*; Wind-Up (quad version)*; Interview with Ian Anderson*; A Song For Jeffrey

(BBC Version)*; Fat Man (BBC Version)*; Bourée (BBC Version)*

NOTES: The quad LP was a different mix and it contained an alternate take of "Wind-Up." Initial American CDs were missing the initial guitar riff of "Aqualung" and the last 0:30 of "Wind-Up." The UK box set edition uses the same deficient master, but the 25th anniversary collection added the above tracks marked with an asterisk (*). The 24 karat gold edition on DCC Compact Classics is the first CD to use Ian Anderson's original two-track master mixdown tape, but it does not include the bonus tracks. The cover was by Burton Silverman.

PEAK CHART POSITION (UK/US): UK#4; US#7

SALES CERTIFICATIONS: Gold (Austria, France, Germany, Holland, Italy, Spain and South Africa), Platinum (UK, Australia, Canada, New Zealand and Switzerland), Triple Platinum (US)

RELEASES:

	UK & FOREIGN LABEL/NO.	RELEASE DATE	US LABEL/NO.	RELEASE DATE
Aqualung (LP)	Island ILPS 9145	03/19/71	Reprise MS 2035	05/03/71
Aqualung (LP; reissue)	Chrysalis CHR 1044	08/01/73	Chrysalis CHR 1044	07/23/73
Aqualung (quad LP)			Chrysalis CH4 1044	04/02/75
Aqualung (half-speed mastered LP)			Mobile Fidelity Sound Lab MFSL 1-061	11/16/81
Aqualung (LP; reissue)			Chrysalis FV 41044	07/04/83
Aqualung (CD)	Chrysalis CCD 1044	04/11/86	Chrysalis VK 41044	10/08/84
Aqualung (CD; reissue)	Chrys./EMI CCD 1044	03/23/92	Chrys./EMI F2 21044	03/24/92
Aqualung (2LP/CD; reissue - with six bonus tracks)	Chrys./EMI LP25AQUA1/ CD25AQUA 51	06/17/96	Chrys./EMI 8 52213 2	06/18/96
Aqualung (remastered LP/ 24 karat gold CD)			DCC Compact Classics LPZ-2030/GZS-1105	07/04/97

THICK AS A BRICK

MUSICIANS: Ian Anderson (vocals, flute, acoustic guitar, violin, saxophone, trumpet), Martin Barre (electric guitar, lute), Barriemore Barlow (drums, timpani, percussion), Jeffrey Hammond-Hammond (bass, spoken word), John Evans (organ, piano, harpsichord)

GUEST MUSICIANS: David Palmer (string arrangement and conducting)

PRODUCTION: Ian Anderson and Terry Ellis

RECORDING LOCATION/ DATE: 12/71 at Morgan Studios, London

TRACKS: Thick As A Brick - Part 1;/ Thick As A Brick - Part 2; Thick As A Brick (live at Madison Square Garden 1978)*; Interview with Jethro Tull's Ian Anderson, Martin Barre and Jeffrey Hammond*

NOTES: The entire piece was written by Ian Anderson under the pseudonym Gerald Bostock, and Jethro Tull is credited for song arrangements. The 25th anniversary edition added the tracks marked (*) and the entire newspaper from the original LP. The album design and artwork was by CCS.

PEAK CHART POSITION (UK/US): UK#5; US#1

SALES CERTIFICATIONS: Gold (UK), Platinum (US, Australia, Canada, Holland and New Zealand)

RELEASES:

	UK & FOREIGN LABEL/NO.	RELEASE DATE	US LABEL/NO.	RELEASE DATE
Thick As A Brick (LP)	Chrysalis CHR 1003	03/10/72	Reprise MS 2072	05/10/72
Thick As A Brick (banded LP - promo only)			Reprise MS 2072	05/10/72
Thick As A Brick (LP; reissue)			Chrysalis CHR 1003	07/23/73
Thick As A Brick (reissue)			Chrysalis FV 41003	07/04/83
Thick As A Brick (half-speed mastered LP)			Mobile Fidelity Sound Lab MFSL 1-187	07/15/85
Thick As A Brick (CD)	Chrysalis ACCD 1003	12/13/85	Chrysalis VK 41003	11/18/85
Thick As A Brick (24 karat gold CD)			Mobile Fidelity Sound Lab UDCD01-00510	07/18/88
Thick As A Brick (CD; reissue)	Chrys./EMI CCD 1003	03/23/92	Chrys./EMI F2 21003	03/24/92
Thick As A Brick (CD; with live version of title track and interview)	Chrys./EMI 8 57705 2	06/02/97	Chrys./EMI 8 57705 2	10/21/97
Thick As A Brick (LP; reissue)	Chrys./EMI LPCENT 31	11/03/97		

LIVING IN THE PAST

MUSICIANS: various lineups
GUEST MUSICIANS: various, including the Anderson/Barre/Cornick/Evans/Bunker lineup on the two Carnegie Hall tracks. "Singing All Day" lineup: Ian Anderson (vocal, balalaika, Hammond organ, flute), Martin Barre (electric guitar), Glenn Cornick (bass, Hammond organ), Clive Bunker (drums). "Just Trying To Be" lineup: Ian Anderson (acoustic guitar, vocal), John Evans (celeste). "Wond'ring Again" lineup: Ian Anderson (acoustic guitar, vocal), Martin Barre (electric guitar), Glenn Cornick (bass), John Evans (piano), Clive Bunker (drums, glockenspiel).
PRODUCTION: Ian Anderson and Terry Ellis. Executive producer: Terry Ellis.
RECORDING LOCATION/ DATE: see track listing for unreleased recording information.
TRACKS: A Song For Jeffrey (from "This Was"); Love Story (A-side); Christmas Song (B-side); Living In The Past (A-side); Driving Song (B-side); Bourée (J.S. Bach; from "Stand Up");/ Sweet Dream (A-side); Singing All Day (unreleased - recorded 08/31/69 at Morgan Studios, London); Teacher (from US edition of "Benefit"); The Witch's Promise (A-side); Inside (from "Benefit"); Alive And Well And Living In (from UK edition of "Benefit"); Just Trying To Be (unreleased - recorded 06/70 at Morgan Studios, London);// By Kind Permission Of (John Evans; live at Carnegie Hall 11/04/70 - unreleased); Dharma For One (Ian Anderson/Clive Bunker; live at Carnegie Hall 11/04/70 - unreleased);/ Wond'ring Again (unreleased - recorded 06/70 at Morgan Studios, London); Hymn 43 (from "Aqualung"); Locomotive Breath (from "Aqualung"); Life Is A Long Song (EP); Up The 'Pool (EP); Dr. Bogenbroom (EP); For Later (EP); Nursie (EP)
NOTES: A lavishly packaged double LP compilation featuring singles, familiar tracks and unreleased material. The cover design and artwork was by CCS. All non-album tracks have been newly mixed for stereo. On the original 2LP release, "Locomotive Breath" was only on the UK edition, "Hymn 43" was only on the US edition, and "Alive And Well And Living In" was omitted from the US LP re-release. All single CD editions deleted "Bourée" and "Teacher." "Inside" appeared only on the Mobile Fidelity 2CD issue.
PEAK CHART POSITION (UK/US): UK#8; US#3
SALES CERTIFICATIONS: Gold (UK, Australia and Canada), Platinum (US)

RELEASES:

	UK & FOREIGN LABEL/NO.	RELEASE DATE	US LABEL/NO.	RELEASE DATE
Living In The Past (2LP)	Chrysalis CJT 1	06/23/72		
Living In The Past (2LP; different tracks)			Chrysalis 2TS 2106	10/31/72
Living In The Past (2LP; reissue)			Chrysalis CHR 1035	07/23/73
Living In The Past (2LP; reissue)			Chrysalis V2X 41035	10/03/83
Living In The Past (CD; incorrect track listing - 2 tracks missing)	Chrysalis CCD 1035	10/23/87	Chrysalis VK 41035	01/12/88
Living In The Past (CD; incorrect track listing - 2 tracks missing)	Chrys./EMI CCD 1035	03/23/92	Chrys./EMI F2 21035	03/24/92
Living In The Past (CD; reissue - with longbox)	Chrys./EMI CCD 1575	02/28/94		
Living In The Past (2CD; reissue - plus bonus tracks)			Mobile Fidelity Sound Lab UDCD 2-708	09/09/97
Living In The Past (CD; incorrect track listing - 2 tracks missing)			Chrys./EMI F2 21035	09/14/99

A PASSION PLAY

MUSICIANS: Ian Anderson (vocals, acoustic guitars, flute, soprano saxophone, sopranino saxophone), Martin Barre (electric guitar), Barriemore Barlow (drums, timpani, glockenspiel, marimba), Jeffrey Hammond-Hammond (bass, vocals), John Evans (piano, organ, synthesizer, spoken word)
GUEST MUSICIANS: none
PRODUCTION: Jethro Tull (production and arrangement)
RECORDING LOCATION/ DATE: 03/73 at Morgan Studios, London
TRACKS: A PASSION PLAY PT. 1: Lifebeats; Prelude; The Silver Cord; Re-Assuring Tune; Memory Bank; Best Friends; Critique Oblique; Forest Dance #1; The Story Of The Hare Who Lost His Spectacles (Pt. 1) (Hammond-Hammond/ Evans/ Anderson);/ A PASSION PLAY PT. 2: The Story Of The Hare Who Lost His Spectacles (Pt. 2) (Hammond-Hammond/ Evans/ Anderson); Forest Dance #2; The Foot Of Our Stairs; Overseer Overture; Flight From Lucifer; 10.08 To Paddington; Magus Perdé; Epilogue.
NOTES: Mobile Fidelity's gold disc first revealed the subtitles shown above.
PEAK CHART POSITION (UK/US): UK#13; US#1
SALES CERTIFICATIONS: Gold (UK, Canada and US)

RELEASES:

	UK & FOREIGN LABEL/NO.	RELEASE DATE	US LABEL/NO.	RELEASE DATE
A Passion Play (LP)	Chrysalis CHR 1040	07/06/73	Chrysalis CHR 1040	07/23/73
A Passion Play (banded LP - Edited Version for D.J. Use Only)			Chrysalis CHR 1040	07/23/73
A Passion Play (LP; reissue)			Chrysalis PV 41040	08/15/83
A Passion Play (CD)	Chrysalis CCD 1040	01/16/89	Chrysalis VK 41040	04/25/88
A Passion Play (CD; reissue)	Chrys./EMI CCD 1040	03/23/92	Chrys./EMI F2 21040	03/24/92
A Passion Play (24 karat gold CD)			Mobile Fidelity Sound Lab UDCD 720	03/17/98
A Passion Play (CD; reissue)			Chrys./EMI F2 21040	09/14/99

WAR CHILD

MUSICIANS: Ian Anderson (vocals, flute, acoustic guitar, alto saxophone, soprano saxophone, sopranino saxophone), Martin Barre (electric guitar, Spanish guitar), Barriemore Barlow (drums, glockenspiel, marimba, percussion, Jeffrey Hammond-Hammond (bass, string bass), John Evans (organ, piano, synthesizers, piano accordion)
GUEST MUSICIANS: David Palmer (orchestrations and conducting), members of the Philomusica of London (leader: Patrick Halling)
PRODUCTION: Ian Anderson; executive producer: Terry Ellis
RECORDING LOCATION/ DATE: spring 1974 at Morgan Studios, London, except "Skating Away On The Thin Ice Of The New Day" and "Only Solitaire," which are remixes of August 1972 recordings from the Chateau D'Herouville sessions. "Only Solitaire" was originally known as "Solitaire."
TRACKS: Warchild; Queen And Country; Ladies; Back-Door Angels; Sealion;/ Skating Away On The Thin Ice Of The New Day; Bungle In The Jungle; Only Solitaire; The Third Hoorah; Two Fingers
NOTES: none
PEAK CHART POSITION (UK/US): UK#14; US#2
SALES CERTIFICATIONS: Gold (UK, US, Canada and Australia)

RELEASES:

	UK & FOREIGN LABEL/NO.	RELEASE DATE	US LABEL/NO.	RELEASE DATE
War Child (LP)	Chrysalis CHR 1067	10/26/74	Chrysalis CHR 1067	10/14/74
War Child (quad LP)			Chrysalis CH4 1067	04/02/75
War Child (LP; reissue)			Chrysalis PV 41067	10/03/83
War Child (CD)	Chrysalis CCD 1067	04/17/87	Chrysalis VK 41067	01/12/88
War Child (CD; reissue)	Chrys./EMI CCD 1067	03/23/92	Chrys./EMI F2 21067	03/24/92
War Child (24 karat gold CD)			Mobile Fidelity Sound Lab UDCD 745	03/23/99

MINSTREL IN THE GALLERY

MUSICIANS: Ian Anderson (vocals, flute, electric guitar), Martin Barre (electric guitar), Jeffrey Hammond-Hammond (bass, string bass), John Evans (piano, organ), Barriemore Barlow (drums, percussion)
GUEST MUSICIANS: David Palmer (orchestral arrangements and orchestra conductor), members of the London Philomusica: leader Patrick Halling, Elizabeth Edwards (violin), Rita Eddowes (violin), Bridget Proctor (violin), Katharine Thulborn (cello)
PRODUCTION: Ian Anderson
RECORDING LOCATION/ DATE: 04/75 using Maison Rouge Mobile recorded somewhere in Europe
TRACKS: Minstrel In The Gallery; Cold Wind To Valhalla; Black Satin Dancer; Requiem;/ One White Duck/ 0^{10} = Nothing At All; Baker St. Muse, including Pig - Me And The Whore, Nice Little Tune, Crash Barrier Waltzer, Mother England Reverie; Grace
NOTES: The artwork was by R. Kriss and J. Garnett, and it was based on a print by Joseph Nash.
PEAK CHART POSITION (UK/US): UK#20; US#7
SALES CERTIFICATIONS: Gold (UK, US and Canada)

RELEASES:

	UK & FOREIGN LABEL/NO.	RELEASE DATE	US LABEL/NO.	RELEASE DATE
Minstrel In The Gallery (LP)	Chrysalis CHR 1082	09/05/75	Chrysalis CHR 1082	09/08/75
Minstrel In The Gallery (LP; reissue)			Chrysalis FV 41082	08/15/83
Minstrel In The Gallery (CD)	Chrysalis CCD 1082	04/11/86	Chrysalis VK 41082	01/12/88
Minstrel In The Gallery (CD; reissue)	Chrys./EMI CCD 1082	03/23/92	Chrys./EMI F2 21082	03/24/92

M.U. - THE BEST OF JETHRO TULL

MUSICIANS: various; "Rainbow Blues" personnel: Ian Anderson (vocal, flute), Martin Barre (electric guitar), John Evans (keyboards), Jeffrey Hammond-Hammond (bass), Barriemore Barlow (drums)
GUEST MUSICIANS: David Palmer (orchestration, arranging and conducting)
PRODUCTION: Ian Anderson and Terry Ellis
RECORDING LOCATION/ DATE: various; "Rainbow" Blues" recorded spring 1974 at Morgan Studio, London
TRACKS: Teacher (from "Living In The Past" and the US edition of "Benefit"); Aqualung (Ian Anderson/ Jennie Anderson) (different mix; from "Aqualung"); Thick As A Brick Edit #1 (from "Thick As A Brick"); Bungle In The Jungle (from "War Child"); Locomotive Breath (from "Aqualung");/ Fat Man (from "Stand Up"); Living In The Past (from "Living In The Past"); A Passion Play Edit #8 (from "A Passion Play"); Skating Away On The Thin Ice Of The New Day (from "War Child"); Rainbow Blues (unreleased; from the spring 1974 "War Child" sessions); Nothing Is Easy (from "Stand Up")
NOTES: First LP copies and all CDs segued "Thick As A Brick Edit #1" and "Bungle In The Jungle," and reissue LPs had separate tracks. The cover was designed

by Eric Michelson and OZ Studios.
PEAK CHART POSITION (UK/US): UK#44; US#13
SALES CERTIFICATIONS: Gold (UK, Australia and New Zealand), Platinum (US and Canada)

RELEASES:

	UK & FOREIGN LABEL/NO.	RELEASE DATE	US LABEL/NO.	RELEASE DATE
M.U. - The Best Of Jethro Tull (LP)	Chrysalis CHR 1078	01/09/76	Chrysalis CHR 1078	01/12/76
M.U. - The Best Of Jethro Tull/ Repeat • The Best Of Jethro Tull • Vol. II (double cassette)	Chrysalis ZCDP 105	12/03/82		
M.U. - The Best Of Jethro Tull (LP; reissue)			Chrysalis FV 41078	08/15/83
M.U. - The Best Of Jethro Tull (CD)	Chrysalis ACCD 1078	12/13/85	Chrysalis VK 41078	11/18/85
M.U. - The Best Of Jethro Tull (CD; reissue)	Chrys./EMI CCD 1078	03/23/92	Chrys./EMI F2 21078	03/24/92

TOO OLD TO ROCK 'N' ROLL: TOO YOUNG TO DIE

MUSICIANS: Ian Anderson (vocals, acoustic guitar, flute, harmonica, electric guitar, percussion), Martin Barre (electric guitar), Barriemore Barlow (drums and percussion), John Glascock (bass, vocals), John Evans (pianos)
GUEST MUSICIANS: David Palmer (orchestral arrangements, orchestra conductor, Vako Orchestron, late-night saxophone solo on "From A Deadbeat To An Old Greaser"), Maddy Prior (backing vocals on the title track), Angela Allen (backing vocals on "Crazed Institution" and "Big Dipper")
PRODUCTION: Ian Anderson for Five Star Records
RECORDING LOCATION/ DATE: 12/75 at Maison Rouge Mobile Studio, Radio Monte Carlo
TRACKS: Quizz Kid; Crazed Institution; Salamander; Taxi Grab; From A Deadbeat To An Old Greaser;/ Bad-Eyed And Loveless; Big Dipper; Too Old To Rock 'N' Roll: Too Young To Die; Pied Piper; The Chequered Flag (Dead Or Alive)
NOTES: The cover was designed by Michael Farrell and David Gibbons.
PEAK CHART POSITION (UK/US): UK#25; US#14
SALES CERTIFICATIONS: Gold (UK)

RELEASES:

	UK & FOREIGN LABEL/NO.	RELEASE DATE	US LABEL/NO.	RELEASE DATE
Too Old To Rock 'N' Roll: Too Young To Die (LP)	Chrysalis CHR 1111	04/23/76	Chrysalis CHR 1111	05/17/76
Too Old To Rock 'N' Roll: Too Young To Die (LP; reissue)			Chrysalis PV 41111	10/03/83
Too Old To Rock 'N' Roll: Too Young To Die (CD)	Chrysalis CCD 1111	04/11/86	Chrysalis VK 41111	01/12/88
Too Old To Rock 'N' Roll: Too Young To Die (CD; reissue)	Chrys./EMI CCD 1111	03/23/92	Chrys./EMI F2 21111	03/24/92

SONGS FROM THE WOOD

MUSICIANS: Ian Anderson (vocals, flute, acoustic guitar, mandolin, whistles, all instruments on "Jack-In-The-Green"), Martin Barre (electric guitar, lute), Barriemore Barlow (drums, marimba, glockenspiel, bells, nacres, tabor), John Glascock (bass, vocals), John Evans (piano, organ, synthesizers), David Palmer (piano, synthesizer, portative organ)
GUEST MUSICIANS: none
PRODUCTION: Ian Anderson
RECORDING LOCATION/ DATE: fall 1976 at Morgan Studios, London and Maison Rouge Mobile
TRACKS: Songs From The Wood; Jack-In-The-Green; Cup Of Wonder; Hunting Girl; Ring Out, Solstice Bells;/ Velvet Green; The Whistler; Pibroch (Cap In Hand); Fire At Midnight
NOTES: Additional material credited to David Palmer and Martin Barre. The cover was designed by Jay L. Lee.
PEAK CHART POSITION (UK/US): UK#13; US#8
SALES CERTIFICATIONS: Gold (UK, US, Canada and Australia)

RELEASES:

	UK & FOREIGN LABEL/NO.	RELEASE DATE	US LABEL/NO.	RELEASE DATE
Songs From The Wood (LP)	Chrysalis CHR 1132	02/11/77	Chrysalis CHR 1132	02/21/77
Songs From The Wood (LP; reissue)			Chrysalis PV 41132	10/03/83
Songs From The Wood (CD)	Chrysalis CCD 1132	04/11/86	Chrysalis VK 41132	11/18/85
Songs From The Wood (CD; reissue)	Chrys./EMI CCD 1132	03/23/92	Chrys./EMI F2 21132	03/24/92
Songs From The Wood (24 karat gold CD)			Mobile Fidelity Sound Lab UDCD 734	10/20/98
Songs From The Wood (CD; reissue)			Chrys./EMI F2 21132	09/14/99

REPEAT • THE BEST OF JETHRO TULL • VOL. II

MUSICIANS: various; "Glory Row" personnel: Ian Anderson (vocal, acoustic guitar, saxophone, mandolin, flute), Martin Barre (acoustic guitar), John Evans (piano, accordion), Jeffrey Hammond-Hammond (bass), Barriemore Barlow (drums, percussion)
GUEST MUSICIANS: David Palmer (orchestration and arranging); Maddy Prior (backing vocals on "Too Old To Rock 'N' Roll: Too Young To Die")
PRODUCTION: various
RECORDING LOCATION/ DATE: various; "Glory Row" recorded spring 1974 at Morgan Studios, London
TRACKS: Minstrel In The Gallery (from "Minstrel In The Gallery"); Cross-Eyed Mary (from "Aqualung"); A New Day Yesterday (from "Stand Up"); Bourée (J.S. Bach; from "Stand Up"); Thick As A Brick Edit #4 (from "Thick As A Brick");/ War Child (from "War Child"); A Passion Play Edit #9 (from "A Passion Play"); To Cry You A Song (from "Benefit"); Too Old To Rock 'N' Roll: Too Young To Die (from "Too Old To Rock 'N' Roll: Too Young To Die"); Glory Row (unreleased; from the spring 1974 "War Child" sessions)
NOTES: The band's first album to miss the UK chart.
PEAK CHART POSITION (UK/US): US#94
SALES CERTIFICATIONS: none

RELEASES:

	UK & FOREIGN LABEL/NO.	RELEASE DATE	US LABEL/NO.	RELEASE DATE
Repeat • The Best Of Jethro Tull • Vol. II (LP)	Chrysalis CHR 1135	09/09/77	Chrysalis CHR 1135	11/07/77
M.U. - The Best Of Jethro Tull/ Repeat • The Best Of Jethro Tull • Vol. II (double cassette)	Chrysalis ZCDP 105	12/03/82		
Repeat • The Best Of Jethro Tull • Vol. II (LP; reissue)			Chrysalis PV 41135	10/03/83
Repeat • The Best Of Jethro Tull • Vol. II (CD)	Chrysalis CCD 1135	03/14/86	Chrysalis VK 41135	01/12/88
Repeat • The Best Of Jethro Tull • Vol. II (CD; reissue)	Chrys./EMI CCD 1135	03/23/92	Chrys./EMI F2 21135	03/24/92

HEAVY HORSES

MUSICIANS: Ian Anderson (vocals, flute, acoustic guitar, electric guitar, mandolin), Martin Barre (electric guitar), Barriemore Barlow (drums, percussion), John Glascock (bass), John Evans (piano, organ), David Palmer (portative organ, keyboards, orchestral arrangements)
GUEST MUSICIANS: Darryl Way (violin) on "Heavy Horses" and "Acres Wild"
PRODUCTION: Ian Anderson
RECORDING LOCATION/ DATE: 01/78 at Maison Rouge Studio, Fulham, London
TRACKS: . . .And The Mouse Police Never Sleeps; Acres Wild; No Lullaby; Moths; Journeyman;/ Rover; One Brown Mouse; Heavy Horses; Weathercock
NOTES: Additional material was credited to David Palmer and Martin Barre. The front cover photo was taken by James Cotter, and Shona Anderson took the band photo on the back cover.
PEAK CHART POSITION (UK/US): UK#20; UK#19
SALES CERTIFICATIONS: Gold (UK and US)

RELEASES:

	UK & FOREIGN LABEL/NO.	RELEASE DATE	US LABEL/NO.	RELEASE DATE
Heavy Horses (LP)	Chrysalis CHR 1175	04/21/78	Chrysalis CHR 1175	04/10/78
Stormwatch/Heavy Horses (2LP)			Pair CRPDL2-1018	08/15/83
Heavy Horses (LP; reissue)			Chrysalis PV 41175	10/03/83
Heavy Horses (CD)	Chrysalis CCD 1175	04/11/86	Chrysalis VK 41175	04/25/88
Heavy Horses (CD; reissue)	Chrys./EMI CCD 1175	03/23/92	Chrys./EMI F2 21175	03/24/92

JETHRO TULL LIVE - BURSTING OUT

MUSICIANS: Ian Anderson (vocals, flute, acoustic guitar), Martin Barre (electric guitar, mandolin, marimba), Barriemore Barlow (drums, glockenspiel), John Glascock (bass, guitar, vocals), John Evans (piano, organ, accordion, synthesizers), David Palmer (portative organ, synthesizers)
GUEST MUSICIANS: none
PRODUCTION: Ian Anderson
RECORDING LOCATION/ DATE: live in Europe during the "Heavy Horses" tour of 1978. Claude Nobs' band introduction before "No Lullaby" mentions Bern, Switzerland, the location of their 05/28/78 show. Therefore, at least some of the album was recorded at this location.
TRACKS: No Lullaby; Sweet Dream; Skating Away On The Thin Ice Of The New Day; Jack-In-The-Green; One Brown Mouse;/ A New Day Yesterday; Flute Solo Improvisation/ God Rest Ye Merry Gentlemen/ Bourree;/ Songs From The Wood; Thick As A Brick// Hunting Girl; Too Old To Rock 'N' Roll: Too Young To Die; Conundrum (Martin Barre/ Barriemore Barlow); Minstrel In The Gallery;/ Cross-Eyed Mary; Quatrain (Martin Barre); Aqualung (Ian Anderson/ Jennie Anderson); Locomotive Breath; The Dambusters March/ Medley (Eric Coates/ Ian Anderson)
NOTES: The US single CD omits "Sweet Dream," "Conundrum" and "Quatrain," but it has a longer flute improvisation track. The UK 2CD set is incorrectly mastered and has slight edits and fades in the wrong places. On the original 2LP set, Ian Anderson bids the audience farewell after "Cross-Eyed Mary," but on

the double CD, he says goodbye after "Quatrain." "Quatrain" led directly into "Aqualung" on the original double LP. "Aqualung" on the double CD has just the last note of "Quatrain" preceding it. The cover is by Brian Cooke, Ruan O'Lochlainn and Ramey Communications.
PEAK CHART POSITION (UK/US): UK#17; US#21
SALES CERTIFICATIONS: Gold (US)

RELEASES:

	UK & FOREIGN LABEL/NO.	RELEASE DATE	US LABEL/NO.	RELEASE DATE
Jethro Tull Live - Bursting Out (2LP)	Chrysalis CJT 4	09/22/78	Chrysalis CH2 1201	09/29/78
Jethro Tull Live - Bursting Out (2LP; reissue)			Chrysalis V2X 41201	10/03/83
Jethro Tull Live - Bursting Out (single CD; 3 tracks missing)			Chrysalis VK 41201	04/25/88
Jethro Tull Live - Bursting Out (2CD)	Chrysalis CCD 1201	04/25/89		
Jethro Tull Live - Bursting Out (2CD in UK, single CD in US)	Chrys./EMI CCD 1201	03/23/92	Chrys./EMI F2 21201	03/24/92

STORMWATCH

MUSICIANS: Ian Anderson (vocals, flute, acoustic guitar, bass), Martin Barre (electric guitar, mandolin, classical guitar), Barriemore Barlow (drums, percussion), John Glascock (bass on "Orion," "Flying Dutchman" and "Elegy"), John Evans (piano, organ), David Palmer (synthesizers, portative organ, orchestral arrangements)
GUEST MUSICIANS: Francis Wilson (spoken word on "Dun Ringill")
PRODUCTION: Ian Anderson and Robin Black
RECORDING LOCATION/ DATE: spring/summer 1979 using Maison Rouge Mobile and Maison Rouge Studio, Fulham, London
TRACKS: North Sea Oil; Orion; Home; Dark Ages; Warm Sporran;/ Something's On The Move; Old Ghosts; Dun Ringill; Flying Dutchman; Elegy (David Palmer)
NOTES: The band was credited with song arrangements. The cover painting was by David Jackson.
PEAK CHART POSITION (UK/US): UK#27; US#22
SALES CERTIFICATIONS: Gold (US and Canada)

RELEASES:

	UK & FOREIGN LABEL/NO.	RELEASE DATE	US LABEL/NO.	RELEASE DATE
Stormwatch (LP)	Chrysalis CDL 1238	09/14/79	Chrysalis CHR 1238	09/14/79
Stormwatch/Heavy Horses (2LP)			Pair CRPDL2-1018	08/15/83
Stormwatch (LP; reissue)			Chrysalis PV 41238	10/03/83
Stormwatch (CD)	Chrysalis CCD 1238	01/16/89	Chrysalis VK 41238	04/25/88
Stormwatch (CD; reissue)	Chrys./EMI CCD 1238	03/23/92	Chrys./EMI F2 21238	03/24/92

A

MUSICIANS: Ian Anderson (vocals, flute), Martin Barre (electric guitar), Dave Pegg (bass), Mark Craney (drums)
GUEST MUSICIANS: Eddie Jobson (keyboards, electric violin)
PRODUCTION: Ian Anderson and Robin Black
RECORDING LOCATION/ DATE: summer 1980 using Maison Rouge Mobile and Maison Rouge Studios, Fulham, London
TRACKS: Crossfire; Fylingdale Flyer; Working John, Working Joe; Black Sunday; Protect And Survive;/ Batteries Not Included; Uniform; 4.W.D. (Low Ratio); The Pine Marten's Jig; And Further On
NOTES: Additional material was credited to Eddie Jobson, and the entire band was credited with song arrangements. The cover photo was by John Shaw.
PEAK CHART POSITION (UK/US): UK#25; US#30
SALES CERTIFICATIONS: none

RELEASES:

	UK & FOREIGN LABEL/NO.	RELEASE DATE	US LABEL/NO.	RELEASE DATE
A (LP)	Chrysalis CDL 1301	08/29/80	Chrysalis CHE 1301	09/01/80
A (LP; reissue)			Chrysalis PV 41301	10/03/83
A (CD)	Chrysalis CCD 1301	01/16/89	Chrysalis VK 41301	04/25/88
A (CD; reissue)	Chrys./EMI CCD 1301	03/23/92	Chrys./EMI F2 21301	03/24/92

THE BROADSWORD AND THE BEAST

MUSICIANS: Ian Anderson (vocals, flute, acoustic guitar), Martin Barre (electric guitar, acoustic guitar), Dave Pegg (bass, mandolins, vocals), Peter-John Vettese (piano, synthesizer), Gerry Conway (drums, percussion)
GUEST MUSICIANS: none
PRODUCTION: Paul Samwell-Smith
RECORDING LOCATION/ DATE: winter 1982 at Maison Rouge Studios, Fulham, London
TRACKS: Beastie; Clasp; Fallen On Hard Times; Flying Colours; Slow Marching Band;/ Broadsword; Pussy Willow; Watching Me Watching You; Seal Driver; Cheerio
PEAK CHART POSITION (UK/US): UK#27; US#19
NOTES: Additional material credited to Peter-John Vettese. The original UK cassette was issued in a limited edition deluxe outer case resembling a sword sheath. The cover illustration was by Ian McCaig.
SALES CERTIFICATIONS: none

RELEASES:

	UK & FOREIGN LABEL/NO.	RELEASE DATE	US LABEL/NO.	RELEASE DATE
The Broadsword And The Beast (LP)	Chrysalis CDL 1380	04/10/82	Chrysalis CHR 1380	04/19/82
The Broadsword And The Beast (half-speed mastered LP)			Mobile Fidelity Sound Lab MFSL 1-092	10/03/83
The Broadsword And The Beast (LP; reissue)			Chrysalis PV 41380	10/03/83
The Broadsword And The Beast (CD; UK disc mastered from a record!)	Chrysalis CCD 1380	03/14/88	Chrysalis VK 41380	04/25/88
The Broadsword And The Beast (CD; reissue)	Chrys./EMI CCD 1380	03/23/92	Chrys./EMI F2 21380	03/24/92
The Broadsword And The Beast (CD; reissue)			Chrys./EMI F2 21380	09/14/99

UNDER WRAPS

MUSICIANS: Ian Anderson (vocals, flute, acoustic guitar), Martin Barre (electric guitar), Dave Pegg (bass), Peter-John Vettese (keyboards)
GUEST MUSICIANS: none
PRODUCTION: Ian Anderson
RECORDING LOCATION/ DATE: spring 1984 at Ian Anderson's home studio
TRACKS: Lap Of Luxury; Under Wraps #1; European Legacy; Later, That Same Evening (Ian Anderson/ Peter-John Vettese); Saboteur (Ian Anderson/ Peter-John Vettese); Radio Free Moscow (Ian Anderson/Peter-John Vettese); Astronomy (Ian Anderson/Peter-John Vettese); Tundra (Ian Anderson/Peter-John Vettese); Nobody's Car (Ian Anderson/ Martin Barre/ Peter-John Vettese); Heat (Ian Anderson/ Peter-John Vettese); Under Wraps #2; Paparazzi (Ian Anderson/ Martin Barre/ Peter-John Vettese); Apogee (Ian Anderson/ Peter-John Vettese); Automotive Engineering (Ian Anderson/Peter-John Vettese); General Crossing (Ian Anderson/ Peter-John Vettese)
NOTES: "Astronomy," "Tundra," "Automotive Engineering" and "General Crossing" were only on the UK CD, cassette and later US editions, and the US cassette had only two extra tracks: "Astronomy" and "Automotive Engineering." The cover photo was by Trevor Key.
PEAK CHART POSITION (UK/US): UK#18; US#76
SALES CERTIFICATIONS: none

RELEASES:

	UK & FOREIGN LABEL/NO.	RELEASE DATE	US LABEL/NO.	RELEASE DATE
Under Wraps (LP)	Chrysalis CDL 1461	09/07/84	Chrysalis FV 41461	10/08/84
Under Wraps (picture disc LP)	Chrysalis CDP 1461	09/07/84		
Under Wraps (CD; with 4 extra tracks)	Chrysalis CCD 1461	03/15/85	Chrysalis VK 41461	04/25/88
Under Wraps (LP; reissue)			Chrysalis PV 41461	04/25/88
Under Wraps (CD; reissue - with 4 extra tracks)	Chrys./EMI CCD 1461	03/23/92	Chrys./EMI F2 21461	03/24/92

A CLASSIC CASE: THE MUSIC OF JETHRO TULL PLAYED BY THE LONDON SYMPHONY ORCHESTRA (US title - A CLASSIC CASE: THE LONDON SYMPHONY ORCHESTRA PLAYS THE MUSIC OF JETHRO TULL)

MUSICIANS: David Palmer (orchestral arrangement, orchestra conductor), London Symphony Orchestra (leader: Ashley Arbuckle)
GUEST MUSICIANS: Ian Anderson (flute, vocals), Martin Barre (electric guitar), Dave Pegg (bass), Peter-John Vettese (keyboards), Dave Burgess (drums - uncredited)
PRODUCTION: David Palmer
RECORDING LOCATION/ DATE: summer 1984 at CBS Studios, London
TRACKS: Locomotive Breath; Thick As A Brick; Elegy (David Palmer); Bourrée; Fly By Night/ Aqualung (Ian Anderson/ Jennie Anderson); Too Old To

Rock 'N' Roll: Too Young To Die; Medley: Teacher - Bungle In The Jungle - Rainbow Blues - Locomotive Breath; Living In The Past; War Child
NOTES: Even though the album featured all of the members of Jethro Tull, the album was credited to The London Symphony Orchestra featuring Ian Anderson. This album was not released in the UK until 1993, when it was called "Classic Jethro Tull." The original cover photo was by Manfred Vormstein.
PEAK CHART POSITION (UK/US): US#93
SALES CERTIFICATIONS: none

RELEASES:

	UK & FOREIGN LABEL/NO.	RELEASE DATE	US LABEL/NO.	RELEASE DATE
A Classic Case: The Music Of Jethro Tull Played By The London Symphony Orchestra (LP)	German RCA Red Seal RL 71134	02/15/85	RCA Red Seal XRL1-7067	12/31/85
(NOTE: The US edition of the album was quickly changed to RCA Red Seal CRL1-9505.)				
A Classic Case - The London Symphony Orchestra Plays The Music Of Jethro Tull (CD)			RCA Red Seal RCD1-7067	12/31/85
Classic Jethro Tull (CD; repackage of "A Classic Case - The London Symphony Orchestra Plays The Music Of Jethro Tull"	Music For Pleasure 89592 2	06/14/93		
A Classic Case - The London Symphony Orchestra Plays The Music Of Jethro Tull (CD - reissue; shown as by THE LONDON SYMPHONY ORCHESTRA featuring Ian Anderson)			RCA Victor/BMG Classics 09026-62510-2	01/18/94

ORIGINAL MASTERS

MUSICIANS: various
GUEST MUSICIANS: David Palmer (orchestration and conducting), Maddy Prior (backing vocals on "Too Old To Rock 'N' Roll: Too Young To Die"), members of the New York Symphony Orchestra conducted and arranged by Lou Toby ("Living In The Past")
PRODUCTION: various
RECORDING LOCATION/ DATE: various
TRACKS: Living In The Past; Aqualung (Ian Anderson/ Jennie Anderson); Too Old To Rock 'N' Roll: Too Young To Die; Locomotive Breath; Skating Away On The Thin Ice Of The New Day; Bungle In The Jungle;/ Sweet Dream; Songs From The Wood; The Witch's Promise; Thick As A Brick (edit); Minstrel In The Gallery; Life Is A Long Song
NOTES: The DCC gold CD substituted the first half of "Thick As A Brick" plus a countoff instead of Edit #1.
PEAK CHART POSITION (UK/US): UK#63
SALES CERTIFICATIONS: Gold (UK), Platinum (US)

RELEASES:

	UK & FOREIGN LABEL/NO.	RELEASE DATE	US LABEL/NO.	RELEASE DATE
Original Masters (LP)	Chrysalis JTTV 1	10/21/85	Chrysalis FV 41515	11/18/85
Original Masters (LP reissue/CD; UK received only the CD)	Chrysalis CCD 1515	04/11/86	Chrysalis PV/VK 41515	04/25/88
Original Masters (CD)	Chrys./EMI CCD 1515	03/23/92	Chrys./EMI F2 21515	03/24/92
Original Masters (remastered LP/ 24 karat gold CD)			DCC Compact Classics LPZ-2059/ GZS-1126	08/25/98

CREST OF A KNAVE

MUSICIANS: Ian Anderson (vocals, guitars, flute, keyboards, drum programming, percussion), Martin Barre (electric guitar), Dave Pegg (electric bass, acoustic bass)
GUEST MUSICIANS: Doane Perry (drums on "Farm On The Freeway" and "Mountain Men"), Gerry Conway (drums on "Jump Start," "Said She Was A Dancer," "Budapest" and "The Waking Edge"), Ric Sanders (violin on "Budapest" and "The Waking Edge" - the latter uncredited)
PRODUCTION: Ian Anderson
RECORDING LOCATION/ DATE: spring 1987 at Ian Anderson's home studio
TRACKS: Steel Monkey; Farm On The Freeway; Jump Start; Said She Was A Dancer; Dogs In The Midwinter; Budapest; Mountain Men; The Waking Edge; Raising Steam
NOTES: "Dogs In The Midwinter" and "The Waking Edge" only appeared on the cassette and CD. The cover was by Andrew Jamieson.
PEAK CHART POSITION (UK/US): UK#19; US#32
SALES CERTIFICATIONS: Gold (US), Silver (UK)

RELEASES:

	UK & FOREIGN LABEL/NO.	RELEASE DATE	US LABEL/NO.	RELEASE DATE
Crest Of A Knave (LP)	Chrysalis CDL 1590	09/11/87	Chrysalis FV 41590	09/16/87
Crest Of A Knave (CD; with 2 extra tracks)	Chrysalis CCD 1590	09/11/87	Chrysalis VK 41590	01/12/88
Crest Of A Knave (LP; reissue)			Chrysalis OV 41590	04/25/88
Crest Of A Knave (CD; reissue - with 2 extra tracks)	Chrys./EMI CCD 1590	03/23/92	Chrys./EMI F2 21590	03/24/92

20 YEARS OF JETHRO TULL (5LP/ 3CD BOX SET)

MUSICIANS: various; lineups shown next to each track below:

(1) Ian Anderson, Mick Abrahams, Glenn Cornick, Clive Bunker

(2) Ian Anderson, Clive Bunker

(3) Ian Anderson, Martin Barre, Glenn Cornick, Clive Bunker

(4) Ian Anderson

(5) Ian Anderson, Barriemore Barlow

(6) Ian Anderson, Martin Barre, John Glascock, John Evans, David Palmer, Barriemore Barlow

(7) Ian Anderson, David Palmer (conductor of Philomusica of London members with leader Patrick Halling)

(8) Ian Anderson, Martin Barre, Dave Pegg, Peter-John Vettese, Gerry Conway (Ian was taking a pee break during "Pibroch"!)

(9) Ian Anderson, Martin Barre, Dave Pegg, Gerry Conway

(10) Ian Anderson, Martin Barre, Dave Pegg, Gerry Conway, David Palmer, unknown oboe player

(11) Ian Anderson, Martin Barre, Jeffrey Hammond-Hammond, Barriemore Barlow, David Palmer

(12) Ian Anderson, John Evans, Jeffrey Hammond-Hammond

(13) Ian Anderson, Martin Barre, John Evans, Jeffrey Hammond-Hammond, Barriemore Barlow, Rita Eddowes, Elizabeth Edwards, Helen, Katharine Thulborn

(14) Ian Anderson, Martin Barre, John Evans, Barriemore Barlow, John Glascock

(15) Ian Anderson, Martin Barre, Dave Pegg, Barriemore Barlow, John Evans, David Palmer

(16) Ian Anderson, Martin Barre, Barriemore Barlow, John Evans, David Palmer

(17) Ian Anderson, John Evans, Glenn Cornick, Barriemore Barlow, Neil Smith (Chick Murray), Tony Wilson (backing vocals)

(18) Ian Anderson, Mick Abrahams, Glenn Cornick, Clive Bunker, Tony Wilson (backing vocals)

(19) Ian Anderson, Martin Barre, John Evans, Jeffrey Hammond-Hammond, Clive Bunker

(20) Ian Anderson, Martin Barre, John Evans, Jeffrey Hammond-Hammond, Barriemore Barlow

(21) Ian Anderson, Martin Barre, Dave Pegg, Martin Allcock, Gerry Conway

(22) Ian Anderson, Martin Barre, Dave Pegg, Doane Perry, Don Airey

GUEST MUSICIANS: none

PRODUCTION: various

RECORDING LOCATION/ DATE: see track listing for unreleased track information

TRACKS: Album 1 - The Radio Archives: A Song For Jeffrey (1968 BBC) (1); Love Story (1968 BBC) (1); Fat Man (1969 BBC) (2)*; Bourée (J.S. Bach, arr. Ian Anderson; 1969 BBC) (3); Stormy Monday Blues (Eckstine/ Crowder/ Hines; 1968 BBC) (2); A New Day Yesterday (1969 BBC) (3); Cold Wind To Valhalla (1975 BBC) (4); Minstrel In The Gallery (1975 BBC) (5); Velvet Green (1977 BBC "In Concert") (6); Grace (1975 BBC) (7); Clasp (live 04/08/82 in Hamburg) (8); Pibroch/ Black Satin Dancer (instrumental; live 04/08/82 in Hamburg) (8); Fallen On Hard Times (live 04/08/82 in Hamburg) (8);// **Album 2 - The Rare Tracks (Released But Only Just):** Jack Frost And The Hooded Crow (1981 recording issued as a 1986 B-side) (8)*; I'm Your Gun (1981 recording issued as a 1987 B-side) (9)*; Down At The End Of Your Road (1981 recording issued as a 1987 B-side) (9)*; Coronach (David Palmer) (1984 recording issued as a 1986 A-side) (10)*; Summerday Sands (1975 B-side) (11)*; Too Many Too (1981 recording issued as a 1987 B-side) (9)*; March, The Mad Scientist (1974 recording issued as a 1976 B-side) (12)*; Pan Dance (1974 recording issued as a 1976 B-side) (13)*; Strip Cartoon (1976 recording issued as a 1977 B-side) (14)*; King Henry's Madrigal (trad., arr. Palmer) (1979 B-side) (15)*; A Stitch In Time (3:30 edit; 1978 A-side) (16)*; 17 (3:07 edit; edited version of 1969 6:06 B-side) (3)*; One For John Gee (Michael Abrahams; 1968 B-side) (1)*; Aeroplane (Ian Anderson/ Glenn Barnard [Glenn Cornick]; 1968 B-side) (17)*; Sunshine Day (Michael Abrahams; 1968 A-side) (18)*;// **Album 3 - Flawed Gems (Dusted Down):** Lick Your Fingers Clean (1970 recording) (19); The Chateau D'Isaster Tapes (recorded 08/72 at Chateau D'Herouville, France): a) Scenario (5); b) Audition (20); c) No Rehearsal (20); Beltane (recorded 12/77) (6); Crossword (recorded 1979 at Maison Rouge Studios, London) (14); Saturation (recorded 1974 at an unknown studio) (20); Jack-A-Lynn (recorded 1981 at Maison Rouge Studios, London) (8); Motoreyes (recorded 1982 at Maison Rouge Studios, London) (8); Blues Instrumental (Untitled) (recorded 1978 at Maison Rouge Studios, London) (14); Rhythm In Gold (recorded 1981 at Maison Rouge Studios, London) (8);// **Album 4 - The Other Sides Of Tull:** Part Of The Machine (recorded 03/88 at Ian Anderson's home studio) (21); Mayhem, Maybe (recorded 1981 at Maison Rouge Studios, London with vocals, flute and whistles added at Ian Anderson's home studio in 03/88) (9); Overhang (recorded 1981 at Maison Rouge Studios, London) (9); Kelpie (recorded 1979 at Maison Rouge Studios, London) (14); Living In These Hard Times (recorded 1978 at Maison Rouge Studios, London) (6); Under Wraps #2 (4)*; Only Solitaire (4)*; Cheap Day Return (4)*; Wond'ring Aloud (live 10/29/87 in London) (4); Dun Ringill (live 10/29/87 in London) (4); Salamander (6)*; Moths (different mix) (14); Nursie (4)*; Life Is A Long Song (16)*; One White Duck: 0^{10} = Nothing At All (4)*;// **Album 5 - The Essential Tull:** Songs From The Wood (live 10/29/87 in London) (22); Living In The Past (live 11/25/87 at The Tower Theater, Upper Darby, PA) (22); Teacher (single version in rechanneled stereo) (20)*; Aqualung (live 04/08/82 in Hamburg) (8); Locomotive Breath (live 04/08/82 in Hamburg) (8); The Witch's Promise (19)*; Bungle In The Jungle (20)*; Farm On The Freeway (live 11/25/87 at The Tower Theater, Upper Darby, PA) (22); Thick As A Brick (live 10/29/87 in London) (22); Sweet Dream (live 04/08/82 in Hamburg) (8)

NOTES: All of the tracks were previously unreleased except those marked with an asterisk (*). NOTE: Both sides of the "Sunshine Day"/ "Aeroplane" single and "One For John Gee" were transferred from record. "Aeroplane" is about 10 seconds shorter than the original single. "Teacher" is a rechanneled stereo presentation of the original true stereo single version. The booklet introduction was written by Ian Anderson, and the biography was written by Dave Rees and Martin Webb. Art direction and design was by John Pasche and Mainartery.

PEAK CHART POSITION (UK/US): UK#78; US#97

SALES CERTIFICATIONS: none

RELEASES:

	UK & FOREIGN LABEL/NO.	RELEASE DATE	US LABEL/NO.	RELEASE DATE
20 Years Of Jethro Tull (5LP/3CD)	Chry. TBOX/TBOXCD 1	06/27/88	Chry. V5K/V3K 41653	07/26/88

20 YEARS OF JETHRO TULL (2LP/ single CD)

MUSICIANS: see 5CD box for information on tracks below
GUEST MUSICIANS: none
PRODUCTION: various
RECORDING LOCATION/ DATE: various
TRACKS: Stormy Monday Blues (BBC); Love Story (BBC); A New Day Yesterday (BBC); Summerday Sands; Coronach; March, The Mad Scientist; Pibroch/ Black Satin Dancer (live); Lick Your Fingers Clean; Overhang; Crossword; Saturation; Jack-A-Lynn; Motoreyes; Part Of The Machine; Mayhem, Maybe; Kelpie; Under Wraps #2; Wond'ring Aloud; Dun Ringill; Life Is A Long Song; Nursie; Grace; The Witch's Promise; Teacher; Living In The Past; Aqualung; Locomotive Breath
NOTES: All tracks were taken from the 5CD/3LP box set. "Coronach," "Pibroch"/ "Black Satin Dancer" (live), "Saturation," "Motoreyes," "Under Wraps #2" and "Teacher" are not on the CD. The US CD takes the last four tracks and sequences them after "March, The Mad Scientist."
PEAK CHART POSITION (UK/US): none
SALES CERTIFICATIONS: none

RELEASES:

20 Years Of Jethro Tull (2LP/single CD - US only received the CD) Chrys. CJT 7/ CCD 1655 10/10/88 Chrysalis V3K 41655 01/16/89
20 Years Of Jethro Tull (CD; reissue) Chrys./EMI CCD 1655 03/23/92 Chrys./EMI F2 21655 03/24/92

ROCK ISLAND

MUSICIANS: Ian Anderson (vocals, flute, keyboards, mandolin, acoustic guitar, drums on "The Rattlesnake Trail" and "Another Christmas Song"), Martin Barre (electric guitar), Dave Pegg (bass, acoustic bass, mandolin), Doane Perry (drums)
GUEST MUSICIANS: Martin Allcock (keyboards on "Kissing Willie" and "Strange Avenues"), Peter-John Vettese (keyboards on "Ears Of Tin," "Undressed To Kill," "Rock Island" and "Heavy Water")
PRODUCTION: Ian Anderson
RECORDING LOCATION/ DATE: spring 1989 at Ian Anderson's home studio
TRACKS: Kissing Willie; The Rattlesnake Trail; Ears Of Tin; Undressed To Kill; Rock Island;/ Heavy Water; Another Christmas Song; The Whaler's Dues; Big Riff And Mando; Strange Avenues
NOTES: The cover illustration was by Anton Morris.
PEAK CHART POSITION (UK/US): UK#18; US#56
SALES CERTIFICATIONS: Silver (UK)

RELEASES:

	UK & FOREIGN LABEL/NO.	RELEASE DATE	US LABEL/NO.	RELEASE DATE
Rock Island (LP)	Chrysalis CDL 1708	08/21/89	Chrysalis F1 21708	09/12/89
Rock Island (picture disc LP)	Chrysalis CHRP 1708	08/21/89		
Rock Island (CD)	Chrysalis CCD 1708	08/21/89	Chrysalis F2 21708	09/12/89
Rock Island (CD; reissue)			Chrysalis F2 21708	09/14/99

LIVE AT HAMMERSMITH '84 - THE FRIDAY ROCK SHOW SESSIONS

MUSICIANS: Ian Anderson (vocals, flute, acoustic guitar), Martin Barre (electric guitar), Dave Pegg (bass), Peter-John Vettese (keyboards), Doane Perry (drums)
GUEST MUSICIANS: none
PRODUCTION: Tony Wilson and Dale Griffin
RECORDING LOCATION/ DATE: 09/09/84 live at Hammersmith Odeon, London - recorded for the BBC
TRACKS: Locomotive Breath (instrumental); Hunting Girl; Under Wraps; Later, That Same Evening; Pussy Willow; Living In The Past; Locomotive Breath; Too Old To Rock 'N' Roll: Too Young To Die
NOTES: "Clasp," "Thick As A Brick" and "Aqualung" from this concert were omitted from this album.
PEAK CHART POSITION (UK/US): none
SALES CERTIFICATIONS: none

RELEASES:

	UK & FOREIGN LABEL/NO.	RELEASE DATE	US LABEL/NO.	RELEASE DATE
Live At Hammersmith '84 - The Friday Rock Show Sessions (LP/CD)	Raw Fruit FRSLD 004	12/10/90		

CATFISH RISING

MUSICIANS: Ian Anderson (vocals, acoustic guitar, electric guitar, acoustic mandolin, electric mandolin, flute, percussion, occasional drums and keyboards), Martin Barre (electric guitar), Dave Pegg (bass, acoustic bass), Doane Perry (drums and percussion)
GUEST MUSICIANS: Andy Giddings (keyboards on "This Is Not Love," "Rocks On The Road" and "Doctor To My Disease"), Foss Paterson (keyboards on "White Innocence"), John "Rabbit" Bundrick (keyboards on "Sleeping With The Dog"), Matt Pegg (bass on "This Is Not Love," "Rocks On The Road" and "Still Loving You Tonight"), Scott Hunter (uncredited drums on "Still Loving You Tonight")
PRODUCTION: Ian Anderson
RECORDING LOCATION/ DATE: winter/spring 1991 at Ian Anderson's home studio and Woodworm Studios (Matt Pegg and Scott Hunter contributions only)
TRACKS: This Is Not Love; Occasional Demons; Roll Yer Own; Rocks On The Road; Sparrow On The Schoolyard Wall; Thinking Round Corners; Still Loving You Tonight; Doctor To My Disease; Like A Tall Thin Girl; White Innocence; Sleeping With The Dog; Gold Tipped Boots, Black Jacket & Tie; When Jesus Came To Play; Night In The Wilderness
NOTES: "Night In The Wilderness" appears on the Japanese CD only. The cover illustration was by Jim Gibson.
PEAK CHART POSITION (UK/US): UK#27; US#88
SALES CERTIFICATIONS: none

RELEASES:

	UK & FOREIGN LABEL/NO.	RELEASE DATE	US LABEL/NO.	RELEASE DATE
Catfish Rising (CD)	Chrysalis CCD 1863	09/23/91	Chrys./EMI F2 21863	09/10/91
Catfish Rising (LP with limited edition 3-track 12" and lyric inner bag)	Chrysalis CDR 1886	09/23/91		
Catfish Rising (Japanese CD with extra track "Night In The Wilderness")	Jap. Chrysalis TOCP 6872	09/23/91		
Catfish Rising (CD; reissue)			Chrys./EMI F2 21863	09/14/99

A LITTLE LIGHT MUSIC

MUSICIANS: Ian Anderson (vocals, flute, acoustic guitar, mandolin, harmonica, percussion), Martin Barre (electric guitar, acoustic guitar), Dave Pegg (bass, mandolin), Dave Mattacks (snare drum, bass drum, hi-hat, cymbal, glockenspiel, percussion, keyboard)
GUEST MUSICIANS: George Dalaras (vocal on "John Barleycorn")
PRODUCTION: Ian Anderson
RECORDING LOCATION/ DATE: All tracks recorded live on the spring 1992 tour: Athens ("Some Day The Sun Won't Shine For You" and both versions of "John Barleycorn"), London ("Living In Past"), Frankfurt ("Life Is A Long Song"), Zurich ("Under Wraps #2"), Caesarea ("Rocks On The Road," "Look Into The Sun," "Christmas Song" and "This Is Not Love"), Mannheim ("Nursie"), Ankara ("Too Old To Rock 'N' Roll: Too Young To Die"), Prague ("One White Duck"), Graz ("A New Day Yesterday"), Munich ("From A Deadbeat To An Old Greaser"), Berlin ("Bourée"), Dortmund ("Pussy Willow") and Jerusalem ("Locomotive Breath")
TRACKS: Some Day The Sun Won't Shine For You; Living In The Past; Life Is A Long Song; Under Wraps #2; Rocks On The Road; Nursie; Too Old To Rock 'N' Roll: Too Young To Die; One White Duck; A New Day Yesterday; John Barleycorn (trad., arr, Ian Anderson); Look Into The Sun; Christmas Song; From A Deadbeat To An Old Greaser; This Is Not Love; Bourée (J.S. Bach, arr. Ian Anderson); Pussy Willow; Locomotive Breath
NOTES: The version issued in Greece and Italy featured a duet of Ian Anderson and George Dalaras on "John Barleycorn." The more widely released CD has an overdubbed Ian Anderson vocal. The cover was designed and illustrated by Bogdan Zarkowski.
PEAK CHART POSITION (UK/US): US#150
SALES CERTIFICATIONS: none

RELEASES:

	UK & FOREIGN LABEL/NO.	RELEASE DATE	US LABEL/NO.	RELEASE DATE
A Little Light Music (2LP)	Chrys./EMI CDR 1954	09/14/92		
A Little Light Music (CD)	Chrys./EMI CCD 1954	09/14/92	Chrys./EMI F2 21954	09/22/92
A Little Light Music (2LP; with different version of "John Barleycorn")	Greek Chrys. CDL 1957	09/14/92		
A Little Light Music (CD; with different version of "John Barleycorn")	Greek Chrys. 3 21957 2	09/14/92		

25TH ANNIVERSARY BOX SET (4CDs)

MUSICIANS: various; lineups shown next to each track below:
(1) Ian Anderson, Mick Abrahams, Glenn Cornick, Clive Bunker
(2) Ian Anderson, Martin Barre, Glenn Cornick, Clive Bunker, members of The New York Symphony Orchestra with arrangement and conducting by Lou Toby
(3) Ian Anderson, Martin Barre, Glenn Cornick, Clive Bunker, John Evans
(4) Ian Anderson, Martin Barre, Glenn Cornick, Clive Bunker, David Palmer (arranging and conducting)
(5) Ian Anderson, Martin Barre, Jeffrey Hammond-Hammond, Clive Bunker, John Evans
(6) Ian Anderson, Martin Barre, Jeffrey Hammond-Hammond, Barriemore Barlow, John Evans
(7) Ian Anderson, Martin Barre, Jeffrey Hammond-Hammond, Barriemore Barlow, John Evans, David Palmer (arranging and conducting)
(8) Ian Anderson, Martin Barre, John Glascock, Barriemore Barlow, John Evans, David Palmer
(9) Ian Anderson, Martin Barre, Dave Pegg, Mark Craney, Eddie Jobson
(10) Ian Anderson, Martin Barre, Dave Pegg, Peter-John Vettese, Gerry Conway
(11) Ian Anderson
(12) Ian Anderson, Martin Barre, Dave Pegg, Andy Giddings, Doane Perry
(13) Ian Anderson, Andy Giddings
(14) Dave Pegg
(15) Martin Barre
(16) Ian Anderson, Martin Barre, Glenn Cornick, Clive Bunker
(17) Ian Anderson, Martin Barre, Dave Pegg, Peter-John Vettese, Doane Perry
(18) Ian Anderson, Martin Barre, Dave Pegg, Martin Allcock, Doane Perry
(19) Ian Anderson, Martin Barre, Dave Pegg, Andy Giddings, Dave Mattacks

GUEST MUSICIANS: see above
PRODUCTION: Ian Anderson, except "Cheerio" (Dave Pegg) and "Protect And Survive" (Martin Barre)
RECORDING LOCATION/ DATE: The tracks on the disc "The Beacons Bottom Tapes" were recorded November/ December 1992. All other recording locations and dates for unreleased tracks are shown below.
TRACKS: CD1 - Remixed - Classic Songs: My Sunday Feeling (1); A Song For Jeffrey (1); Living In The Past (2); Teacher (3); Sweet Dream (4); Cross-Eyed Mary (5); The Witch's Promise (3); Life Is A Long Song (6); Bungle In The Jungle (7); Minstrel In The Gallery (7); Cold Wind To Valhalla (7); Too Old To Rock 'N' Roll: Too Young To Die (8); Songs From The Wood (8); Heavy Horses (8); Black Sunday (9); Broadsword (10);// **CD2 - At The Carnegie Hall: Live In New York 1970:** Nothing Is Easy (3); My God (3); With You There To Help Me (3); A Song For Jeffrey (3); To Cry You A Song (3); Sossity; You're A Woman (3); Reasons For Waiting (3); We Used To Know (3); Guitar Solo (Martin Barre) (3); For A Thousand Mothers (3);// **CD3 - The Beacons Bottom Tapes:** So Much Trouble (Brownie McGhee) (11); My Sunday Feeling (12); Some Day The Sun Won't Shine For You (11); Living In The Past (11); Bourée (J.S. Bach, arr. Ian Anderson) (13); With You There To Help Me (12); Thick As A Brick (12); Cheerio (14); A New Day Yesterday (12); Protect And Survive (15); Jack-A-Lynn (12); The Whistler (12); My God (12); Aqualung (12);// **CD4 - Pot Pourri - Live Across The World & Through The Years:** To Be Sad Is A Mad Way To Be (Stockholm 01/09/69) (16); Back To The Family (Stockholm 01/09/69) (16); A Passion Play (extract; Paris 07/05/75) (6); Wind-Up/ Locomotive Breath/ Land Of Hope And Glory (last track by Elgar - London 02/10/77) (8); Seal Driver (Hamburg 04/08/82) (10); Nobody's Car (Ian Anderson/ Martin Barre/ Peter-John Vettese) (London 09/07/84 or 09/08/84) (17); Pussy Willow (London 09/07/84 or 09/08/84) (17); Budapest (Leysin, Switzerland 07/10/91) (18); Nothing Is Easy (Leysin, Switzerland 07/10/91) (18); Kissing Willie (Tallin, Estonia 07/20/91) (18); Still Loving You Tonight (London 10/07/91, 10/08/91 or 10/09/91) (18); Beggar's Farm (Washington 10/24/92) (19); Passion Jig (Chicago 10/10/92 or 10/11/92) (19); A Song For Jeffrey (Chicago 10/10/92 or 10/11/92) (19); Living In The Past (Montreal 11/09/92) (19)
NOTES: Remix engineers were Robin Black and Ian Taylor. The concert mixing and recording engineer was Leon Phillips. Bogdan Zarkowski did the artwork, design and layout.
PEAK CHART POSITION (UK/US): none
SALES CERTIFICATIONS: none

RELEASES:

	UK & FOREIGN LABEL/NO.	RELEASE DATE	US LABEL/NO.	RELEASE DATE
25th Anniversary Box Set (4CD; US copies were imported from the UK)	Chrys./EMI 3 26008 2	04/26/93	Chrys./EMI 3 26008 2	04/20/93

THE BEST OF JETHRO TULL - THE ANNIVERSARY COLLECTION (2CD)

MUSICIANS: various
GUEST MUSICIANS: members of The New York Symphony Orchestra with arrangement and conducting by Lou Toby ("Living In The Past"), David Palmer (arranging and conducting), Maddy Prior (backing vocals on "Too Old To Rock 'N' Roll: Too Young To Die"), Francis Wilson (spoken word on "Dun Ringill")
PRODUCTION: various
RECORDING LOCATION/ DATE: various
TRACKS: A Song For Jeffrey; Beggar's Farm; Christmas Song; A New Day Yesterday; Bourée; Nothing Is Easy; Living In The Past; To Cry You A Song; Teacher (#2); Sweet Dream; Cross-Eyed Mary; Mother Goose; Aqualung (Ian Anderson/ Jennie Anderson); Locomotive Breath; Life Is A Long Song; Thick As A Brick (extract); A Passion Play (extract); Skating Away On The Thin Ice Of The New Day; Bungle In The Jungle;// Minstrel In The Gallery (6:10 edit);

Too Old To Rock 'N' Roll: Too Young To Die; Songs From The Wood; Jack-In-The-Green; The Whistler; Heavy Horses; Dun Ringill; Fylingdale Flyer; Jack-A-Lynn; Pussy Willow; Broadsword; Under Wraps #2; Steel Monkey; Farm On The Freeway; Jump Start; Kissing Willie; This Is Not Love

NOTES: none

PEAK CHART POSITION (UK/US): none

SALES CERTIFICATIONS: none

RELEASES:

	UK & FOREIGN LABEL/NO.	RELEASE DATE	US LABEL/NO.	RELEASE DATE
The Best Of Jethro Tull (2CD)	Chrys./EMI 3 21954 2	05/24/93	Chrys./EMI 3 26015 2	06/29/93
The Best Of Jethro Tull (2CD; reissue)			Chrys./EMI 3 26015 2	10/05/99

NIGHTCAP - THE UNRELEASED MASTERS 1973-1991

MUSICIANS:

(1) Ian Anderson, Martin Barre, Jeffrey Hammond-Hammond, John Evans, Barriemore Barlow

(2) Ian Anderson, Barriemore Barlow

(3) Ian Anderson, Martin Barre, Dave Pegg, John Bundrick, Doane Perry

(4) Ian Anderson, Martin Barre, Jeffrey Hammond-Hammond, John Evans, Barriemore Barlow, David Palmer

(5) Ian Anderson, Martin Barre, Dave Pegg, Peter-John Vettese, Gerry Conway

(6) Ian Anderson, Martin Barre, Dave Pegg, Gerry Conway

(7) Ian Anderson, David Palmer

(8) Ian Anderson, Martin Barre, Dave Pegg, Doane Perry

(9) Ian Anderson

(10) Ian Anderson, Martin Barre, Matt Pegg, Scott Hunter (Doane Perry is mistakenly credited on drums)

(11) Ian Anderson, Martin Barre, Dave Pegg

GUEST MUSICIANS: John Bundrick (see tracks marked [2]), Scott Hunter (see track marked [10])

PRODUCTION: Ian Anderson

RECORDING LOCATION/ DATE: The 1972 recordings were taped at Chateau D'Herouville, France that August. The 1974 tracks were recorded at Morgan Studios, Fulham, London, and the 1975 track was taped by the Maison Rouge Mobile. The tracks from 1978 and 1981 were recorded at Maison Rouge Studios, Fulham, London. With the exception of "Truck Stop Runner," all the other tracks were recorded at Ian Anderson's home studio. "Truck Stop Runner" was recorded at Ian Anderson's studio and Woodworm Studio.

TRACKS: CD1 - (My Round): Chateau D'Isaster Tapes 1972 - First Post (1); Animelée (1); Tiger Toon (1); Look At The Animals (1); Law Of The Bungle (1); Law Of The Bungle Part II (1); Left Right (1); Solitaire (original mix; later appeared on "War Child") (1)*; Critique Oblique (1); Post Last (1); Scenario (2)*; Audition (1)*; No Rehearsal (1)*;// **CD2 - (Your Round) - Unreleased & Rare:** Paradise Steakhouse (1974) (1); Sea Lion II (1974) (1); Piece Of Cake* (1990 recording issued as a 1993 CD single bonus track) (3); Quartet (1974) (4); Silver River Turning (1990 recording issued as a 1993 CD single bonus track) (3); Crew Nights (1981) (5); The Curse (1981) (6); Rosa On The Factory Floor (1990 recording issued as a 1993 CD single bonus track) (3); A Small Cigar (1975) (7); Man Of Principle (1988 recording issued as a 1993 CD single bonus track) (6); Commons Brawl (1981) (6); No Step (1981) (6); Drive On The Young Side Of Life (1981) (5); I Don't Want To Be Me (1990 recording issued as a 1993 CD single bonus track) (8); Broadford Bazaar (1978) (9); Lights Out (1981) (6); Truck Stop Runner (1991 recording issued as a 1993 CD single bonus track) (10); Hard Liner (1989 recording issued as a 1993 7" B-side) (11)

NOTES: All tracks previously unreleased except those marked with an asterisk (*).

PEAK CHART POSITION (UK/US): none

SALES CERTIFICATIONS: none

RELEASES:

	UK & FOREIGN LABEL/NO.	RELEASE DATE	US LABEL/NO.	RELEASE DATE
Nightcap (2CD)	Chrys./EMI 8 28157 2	11/22/93	Chrys./EMI 8 28157 2	01/11/00

JETHRO TULL IN CONCERT

MUSICIANS: Ian Anderson (vocals, flute, acoustic guitar), Martin Barre (electric guitar), Dave Pegg (bass), Martin Allcock (keyboards), Doane Perry (drums)

GUEST MUSICIANS: none

PRODUCTION: Pete Ritzema

RECORDING LOCATION/ DATE: 10/08/91 live at Hammersmith Odeon, London for the BBC

TRACKS: Minstrel In The Gallery/ Cross-Eyed Mary; This Is Not Love; Rocks On The Road; Heavy Horses; Like A Tall Thin Girl; Still Loving You Tonight; Thick As A Brick; A New Day Yesterday; Blues Jam; Jump Start

NOTES: none

PEAK CHART POSITION (UK/US): none

SALES CERTIFICATIONS: none

RELEASES:

	UK & FOREIGN LABEL/NO.	RELEASE DATE	US LABEL/NO.	RELEASE DATE
Jethro Tull In Concert (CD)	Windsong WINCD 070	04/24/95	Griffin Mus. GCD-8615-2	02/13/96
Jethro Tull In Concert (CD; reissue)	Windsong SFRSCD051	03/03/98		

ROOTS TO BRANCHES

MUSICIANS: Ian Anderson (vocals, concert flute, bamboo flutes, acoustic guitar), Martin Barre (electric guitar), Andy Giddings (keyboards), Doane Perry (drums, percussion), Dave Pegg (bass on "Out Of The Noise," "Valley" and "Another Harry's Bar")
GUEST MUSICIANS: Steve Bailey (bass on "Roots To Branches," "Dangerous Veils," "Beside Myself," "Wounded, Old And Treacherous" and "At Last, Forever")
PRODUCTION: Ian Anderson
RECORDING LOCATION/ DATE: 12/94 to 06/95 at Ian Anderson's home studio
TRACKS: Roots To Branches; Rare And Precious Chain; Out Of The Noise; This Free Will; Valley; Dangerous Veils; Beside Myself; Wounded, Old And Treacherous; At Last, Forever; Stuck In The August Rain; Another Harry's Bar
NOTES: Zarkowski Designs did the cover art and design.
PEAK CHART POSITION (UK/US): UK#20, US#114
SALES CERTIFICATIONS: none

RELEASES:

	UK & FOREIGN LABEL/NO.	RELEASE DATE	US LABEL/NO.	RELEASE DATE
Roots To Branches (2LP/single CD - US only received the CD)	Chrys/EMI 8 35418 2	09/04/95	Chrys./EMI 8 35418 2	09/12/95
Roots To Branches (CD; reissue)			Chrys./EMI 8 35418 2	09/14/99

THE ULTIMATE SET

MUSICIANS: various
GUEST MUSICIANS: various
PRODUCTION: various
RECORDING LOCATION/ DATE: various
TRACKS: See track listing for "Aqualung"
NOTES: This deluxe box set comes with the 1996 remastered CD of "Aqualung" (Chrysalis/EMI 8 52213 2), an exclusive picture disc of the album (Chrysalis/ EMI SPRO-11634), the "25th Anniversary Video" (Chrysalis/EMI F3 77790), the "Jethro Tull - Complete Lyrics" book (Palmyra Publishing House 3-930378-11-6) and a letter from Ian Anderson.
PEAK CHART POSITION (UK/US): none
SALES CERTIFICATIONS: none

RELEASES:

	UK & FOREIGN LABEL/NO.	RELEASE DATE	US LABEL/NO.	RELEASE DATE
The Ultimate Set			Chrysalis/EMI 7 900510 00516	09/30/96

THROUGH THE YEARS

MUSICIANS: various
GUEST MUSICIANS: David Palmer (arranging and conducting), Darryl Way (violin on "Acres Wild"), Ric Sanders (violin on "Budapest")
PRODUCTION: Ian Anderson
RECORDING LOCATION/ DATE:
TRACKS: Living In The Past (live; from "A Little Light Music"); Wind-Up; War Child; Dharma For One; Acres Wild; Budapest; The Whistler; We Used To Know; Beastie; Locomotive Breath (live; from "Jethro Tull Live - Bursting Out"); Rare And Precious Chain; Quizz Kid; Still Loving You Tonight
NOTES: The original unissued title for this CD was "Journeyman."
PEAK CHART POSITION (UK/US): none
SALES CERTIFICATIONS: none

RELEASES:

	UK & FOREIGN LABEL/NO.	RELEASE DATE	US LABEL/NO.	RELEASE DATE
Through The Years (CD)	EMI Gold CDGOLD 1079	01/23/97		

A JETHRO TULL COLLECTION

MUSICIANS: various
GUEST MUSICIANS: members of the New York Symphony Orchestra arranged and conducted by Lou Toby ("Living In The Past"), David Palmer (arranging and conducting)
PRODUCTION: various
RECORDING LOCATION/ DATE: various
TRACKS: Living In The Past ("Living In The Past" LP Version); Wind-Up; War Child; Dharma For One; Acres Wild; Budapest; The Whistler; We Used To Know; Beastie; Locomotive Breath (live; from "Jethro Tull Live - Bursting Out"); Rare And Precious Chain; Quizz Kid; Still Loving You Tonight

NOTES: The original unissued title of this budget compilation was "Journeyman."
PEAK CHART POSITION (UK/US): none
SALES CERTIFICATIONS: none

RELEASES:

	UK & FOREIGN LABEL/NO.	RELEASE DATE	US LABEL/NO.	RELEASE DATE
A Jethro Tull Collection (CD)	Dutch Disky DC 878612	02/25/97		

THE ORIGINALS

MUSICIANS: Ian Anderson, Mick Abrahams ("This Was" only), Martin Barre ("Stand Up" and "Benefit" only), Glenn Cornick, Clive Bunker
GUEST MUSICIANS: David Palmer (arranging and conducting), John Evans (keyboards)
PRODUCTION: Ian Anderson and Terry Ellis
RECORDING LOCATION/ DATE: various
TRACKS: See the tracks for "This Was," "Stand Up" and "Benefit."
NOTES: A three-CD box set containing the UK editions of the "This Was," "Stand Up" and "Benefit" albums in miniature sleeves.
PEAK CHART POSITION (UK/US): none
SALES CERTIFICATIONS: none

RELEASES:

	UK & FOREIGN LABEL/NO.	RELEASE DATE	US LABEL/NO.	RELEASE DATE
The Originals (3CD set with "This Was," "Stand Up" and "Benefit")	Chrys./EMI CDOMB 021	04/14/97		

36 GREATEST HITS

MUSICIANS: various
GUEST MUSICIANS: various
PRODUCTION: various
RECORDING LOCATION/ DATE: various
TRACKS: Aqualung (Ian Anderson/ Jennie Anderson); Cross-Eyed Mary; Hymn 43; Locomotive Breath; A New Day Yesterday; Glory Row; To Cry You A Song; Teacher (Version #2); Nothing Is Easy; Rock Island; Saboteur; John Barleycorn (trad., arr. Ian Anderson);/ Thick As A Brick (Edit #4); War Child; Skating Away On The Thin Ice Of The New Day; A Passion Play (Edit #8); Fat Man; Rainbow Blues; Minstrel In The Gallery; Requiem; Nursie; Broadsword; Coronach; Roll Yer Own;/ Bungle In The Jungle; Living In The Past; Too Old To Rock 'N' Roll: Too Young To Die; Songs From The Wood; The Whistler; Stormy Monday Blues (BBC); I'm Your Gun; Crossword; Under Wraps #1; Black Sunday; Heavy Horses; Grace
NOTES: A mail-order only 3CD compilation.
PEAK CHART POSITION (UK/US): none
SALES CERTIFICATIONS: none

RELEASES:

	UK & FOREIGN LABEL/NO.	RELEASE DATE	US LABEL/NO.	RELEASE DATE
36 Greatest Hits (3CD)			GSC Music/ EMI-Capitol Special Markets 72434 96580 2 8	09/15/98

j-tull DOT COM

MUSICIANS: Ian Anderson (vocals, concert flute, bamboo flute, bouzouki, acoustic guitar), Martin Barre (electric guitar, acoustic guitar), Andy Giddings (Hammond organ, piano, accordion, chromatic and qwerty keyboards), Jonathan Noyce (bass), Doane Perry (drums)
GUEST MUSICIANS: Najma Akhtar (backing vocals on "Dot Com")
PRODUCTION: Ian Anderson
RECORDING LOCATION/ DATE: 01/99 to 02/99 at Ian Anderson's home studio
TRACKS: Spiral; Dot Com; AWOL; Nothing @ All (Andrew Giddings); Wicked Windows; Hunt By Numbers; Hot Mango Flush (Ian Anderson/ Martin Barre); El Niño; Black Mamba; Mango Surprise; Bends Like A Willow; Far Alaska; The Dog-Ear Years; A Gift Of Roses; (59 seconds of silence); The Secret Language Of Birds (by IAN ANDERSON)
NOTES: The Ian Anderson cover painting was based on a sculpture by Michael Cooper.
PEAK CHART POSITION (UK/US): UK#44; US#161
SALES CERTIFICATIONS: none

RELEASES:

	UK & FOREIGN LABEL/NO.	RELEASE DATE	US LABEL/NO.	RELEASE DATE
j-tull Dot Com (CD)	Papillon BTFLYCD 0001	08/23/99	Fuel 2000 FLD-1043	08/24/99

OTHER ESSENTIAL ALBUMS

RARE TRACKS

MUSICIANS: "Sunshine Day": Ian Anderson (backing vocals), Mick Abrahams (lead vocal, electric guitar), Glenn Cornick (bass), Clive Bunker (drums). "Aeroplane": Ian Anderson (lead vocal), John Evans (keyboards), Glenn Cornick (bass), Barrie Barlow (drums), Neil Smith (Chick Murray) (electric guitar).
GUEST MUSICIANS: Tony Wilson (backing vocals on both tracks)
PRODUCTION: Derek Lawrence (both tracks)
RECORDING LOCATION/ DATE: "Sunshine Day": Recorded 01/68 at Abbey Road Studios, London. "Aeroplane": Recorded 10/22/67 at CBS Studios, London.
TRACKS: Sunshine Day (Michael Abrahams); Aeroplane (Ian Anderson/ Len Barnard [Glenn Cornick]); plus tracks by other artists
NOTES: Both tracks were transferred from records instead of master tapes, and "Aeroplane" is about 10 seconds shorter than the original single.
PEAK CHART POSITION (UK/US): none
SALES CERTIFICATIONS: none

RELEASES:

TITLES	UK & FOREIGN LABEL/NO.	RELEASE DATE	US LABEL/NO.	RELEASE DATE
Rare Tracks (LP)	Polydor 2482 274	05/07/76		

1982 PROMOTION MANUAL

MUSICIANS: various
GUEST MUSICIANS: Eddie Jobson (keyboards on "Slipstream Intro"); Maddy Prior (backing vocals on "Too Old To Rock 'N' Roll: Too Young To Die")
PRODUCTION: various
RECORDING LOCATION/ DATE: various; "Slipstream Intro" recorded summer 1980 at Maison Rouge Studios, London.
TRACKS: Slipstream Intro; Sweet Dream (from "Jethro Tull Live - Bursting Out"); Clasp; Too Old To Rock 'N' Roll: Too Young To Die; Aqualung (Ian Anderson/ Jennie Anderson);/ Fallen On Hard Times; Minstrel In The Gallery; A New Day Yesterday; Locomotive Breath
NOTES: A promotion-only sampler released prior to the band's 1982 tour. "Slipstream Intro," a taped concert opener, is exclusive to this album.
PEAK CHART POSITION (UK/US): none
SALES CERTIFICATIONS: none

RELEASES:

TITLES	UK & FOREIGN LABEL/NO.	RELEASE DATE	US LABEL/NO.	RELEASE DATE
1982 Promotion Manual			Chrysalis CHS-47-PDJ	08/30/82

THE HISTORY OF ROCK VOLUME 18

MUSICIANS: various
GUEST MUSICIANS: various
PRODUCTION: various
RECORDING LOCATION/ DATE: various
TRACKS: Aqualung (Ian Anderson/ Jennie Anderson); Wond'ring Aloud; Sweet Dream; Living In The Past; Life Is A Long Song; Too Old To Rock 'N' Roll: Too Young To Die; plus tracks by other artists
NOTES: One side of this 2LP set is by Jethro Tull.
PEAK CHART POSITION (UK/US): none
SALES CERTIFICATIONS: none

RELEASES:

TITLES	UK & FOREIGN LABEL/NO.	RELEASE DATE	US LABEL/NO.	RELEASE DATE
The History Of Rock Volume 18	Orbis Publishing HRL 018	01/21/83		

RARE ROCK COLLECTION - 98KZEW ROCK AGAINST AIDS

MUSICIANS: Ian Anderson (vocal, keyboards), Martin Barre (electric guitar), Dave Pegg (bass), Gerry Conway (drums)
GUEST MUSICIANS: none
PRODUCTION: Ian Anderson
RECORDING LOCATION/ DATE: fall 1981 at Maison Rouge Studios, London
TRACKS: I'm Your Gun; plus tracks by U2, The Doors, Gregg Allman, Jackson Browne, The Police, Elton John, R.E.M. and Fleetwood Mac.
NOTES: A various artists compilation by radio station 98KZEW to raise funds for a Rock Against AIDS radiothon on December 3, 1987. This is the first US release of "I'm Your Gun."

RELEASES:

TITLES	UK & FOREIGN LABEL/NO.	RELEASE DATE	US LABEL/NO.	RELEASE DATE
Rare Rock Collection - 98KZEW Rock Against AIDS (LP)			Elektra PR-2161	12/03/87

21 YEARS OF ALTERNATIVE RADIO

MUSICIANS: Ian Anderson (vocals, flute, mandolin), Clive Bunker (percussion)
GUEST MUSICIANS: none
PRODUCTION: unknown BBC engineer
RECORDING LOCATION/ DATE: 06/69 for the BBC
TRACKS: Fat Man (BBC version); plus tracks by other artists
NOTES: This is the first release of the BBC version of "Fat Man." This presentation is mono and without the digital echo processing found on the "20 Years Of Jethro Tull" box set.
PEAK CHART POSITION (UK/US): none
SALES CERTIFICATIONS: none

RELEASES:

TITLES	UK & FOREIGN LABEL/NO.	RELEASE DATE	US LABEL/NO.	RELEASE DATE
21 Years Of Alternative Radio (CD)	Strange Fruit SFRCD 200	10/14/88		

THE JOHN EVAN BAND – LIVE '66

MUSICIANS: Ian Anderson (vocals), John Evans (organ), Bo Ward (bass), Ritchie Dharma (drums), Neil Smith (Chick Murray) (guitar), Tony Wilkinson (sax), Neil Valentine (sax), Chris Riley (guitar on "Straight No Chaser")
GUEST MUSICIANS: none
PRODUCTION: Neil Smith and Adrian Wagner
RECORDING LOCATION/ DATE: Casterton, UK, 10/66 and summer 1966 at John Evans' house ("Straight No Chaser" only)
TRACKS: Twine Time (Williams/Wright); Hold On I'm A-Coming (Porter/Haynes); Let The Good Times Roll (Theard/Moore); Don't Fight It (Pickett/Cropper); Respect (Redding); Water (Penn/Hall/Franck); Everything's Gonna Be Alright (Mitchell); Mr. Pitiful (Cropper/Redding); Boot-leg (Axton/Dunn/Hayes/Jackson); Stupidity (Burke); Pink Champagne (Liggins); I Want You (Graham Bond); Wade In The Water (J. Griffin); Work Song (Brown Jr./Adderley); Shake (Cooke); Twine Time (Williams/Wright); Last Night (Mar-Keys); Straight No Chaser (home demo recording) (Monk)
NOTES: This album was the first one released on the A New Day label, and it was exclusively available to its subscribers. Only 500 CDs were pressed, and it was also available on cassette. The sound quality is less than perfect because it's an audience tape made by Neil Smith!
PEAK CHART POSITION (UK/US): none
SALES CERTIFICATIONS: none

RELEASES:

TITLES	UK & FOREIGN LABEL/NO.	RELEASE DATE	US LABEL/NO.	RELEASE DATE
John Evan Band - Live '66 (CD)	A New Day NRS/CD1	11/19/90		

LIVE IN CHICAGO 1970

MUSICIANS: Ian Anderson (vocals, flute, acoustic guitar), Martin Barre (electric guitar), Glenn Cornick (bass), John Evans (piano, organ), Clive Bunker (drums)
GUEST MUSICIANS: none
PRODUCTION: none!
RECORDING LOCATION/ DATE: 06/05/70 live at Aragon Ballroom, Chicago, IL
TRACKS: My Sunday Feeling; My God; To Cry You A Song;/ With You There To Help Me; Sossity: You're A Woman/ Reasons For Waiting; Nothing Is Easy; For A Thousand Mothers
NOTES: A cassette issued free with the Italian publication "Il Dizionario Del Rock" by Armando Curcio Editore. In Italy, such bootlegs are legal!
PEAK CHART POSITION (UK/US): none
SALES CERTIFICATIONS: none

RELEASES:

TITLES	UK & FOREIGN LABEL/NO.	RELEASE DATE	US LABEL/NO.	RELEASE DATE
Live In Chicago 1970 (cassette/CD)	Italy #17A/B / Optimes DIR-17	**/**/91		

THE BEST OF KING BISCUIT LIVE - VOLUME 1

MUSICIANS: Ian Anderson (vocal, flute), Martin Barre (electric guitar), Dave Pegg (bass), Doane Perry (drums), Don Airey (keyboards)
GUEST MUSICIANS: none
PRODUCTION: Bob Meyrowitz and Peter Kauff
RECORDING LOCATION/ DATE: 11/25/87 live from The Tower Theater, Upper Darby, PA
TRACKS: Locomotive Breath (live); plus tracks by other artists
NOTES: none
PEAK CHART POSITION (UK/US): none
SALES CERTIFICATIONS: none

RELEASES:

TITLES	UK & FOREIGN LABEL/NO.	RELEASE DATE	US LABEL/NO.	RELEASE DATE
The Best Of King Biscuit Live - Volume 1 (CD)			Sandstone D233005-2	09/24/91

THE BEST OF KING BISCUIT LIVE - VOLUME 4

MUSICIANS: Ian Anderson (vocal, flute, acoustic guitar), Martin Barre (electric guitar), Dave Pegg (bass), Doane Perry (drums), Don Airey (keyboards)
GUEST MUSICIANS: none
PRODUCTION: Bob Meyerowitz and Peter Kauff
RECORDING LOCATION/ DATE: 11/25/87 live from The Tower Theater, Upper Darby, PA
TRACKS: Aqualung (Ian Anderson/ Jennie Anderson) (live); plus tracks by other artists
NOTES: none
PEAK CHART POSITION (UK/US): none
SALES CERTIFICATIONS: none

RELEASES:

TITLES	UK & FOREIGN LABEL/NO.	RELEASE DATE	US LABEL/NO.	RELEASE DATE
The Best Of King Biscuit Live - Volume 4 (CD)			Sandstone D233008-2	09/24/91

THE DEREK LAWRENCE SESSIONS - TAKE 1

MUSICIANS: Ian Anderson (vocal, flute), John Evans (organ), Glenn Cornick (bass), Barrie Barlow (drums), Neil Smith (Chick Murray) (guitar)
GUEST MUSICIANS: Tony Wilson (backing vocals)
PRODUCTION: Derek Lawrence
RECORDING LOCATION/ DATE: 10/22/67 at CBS Studios, London
TRACKS: Aeroplane (Ian Anderson/ Len Barnard [Glenn Cornick]); plus tracks by other artists
NOTES: This CD contains the complete single version transferred from a cleaned-up acetate.
PEAK CHART POSITION (UK/US): none
SALES CERTIFICATIONS: none

RELEASES:

TITLES	UK & FOREIGN LABEL/NO.	RELEASE DATE	US LABEL/NO.	RELEASE DATE
The Derek Lawrence Sessions - Take 1 (CD)	German Line LICD 9.01118 O	10/28/91		

THE DEREK LAWRENCE STORY - THE SAMPLER

MUSICIANS: Ian Anderson (vocal, flute), John Evans (organ), Glenn Cornick (bass), Barrie Barlow (drums), Neil Smith (Chick Murray) (guitar), Tony Wilkinson (sax), Neil Valentine (sax)
GUEST MUSICIANS: none
PRODUCTION: Derek Lawrence
RECORDING LOCATION/ DATE: 10/22/67 at CBS Studios, London
TRACKS: Blues For The 18th (Ian Anderson/ Glenn Barnard); plus tracks by other artists.
NOTES: This is a CD single containing tracks produced by Derek Lawrence.
PEAK CHART POSITION (UK/US): none
SALES CERTIFICATIONS: none

RELEASES:

TITLES	UK & FOREIGN LABEL/NO.	RELEASE DATE	US LABEL/NO.	RELEASE DATE
The Derek Lawrence Story - The Sampler (CD5)	German Line LICD 9.01138 E	10/28/91		

THE DEREK LAWRENCE SESSIONS - TAKE 3

MUSICIANS: Ian Anderson (backing vocals), Mick Abrahams (lead vocal, electric guitar), Glenn Cornick (bass), Clive Bunker (drums)
GUEST MUSICIANS: Tony Wilson (backing vocals)
PRODUCTION: Derek Lawrence
RECORDING LOCATION/ DATE: 01/68 at Abbey Road Studios, London
TRACKS: Sunshine Day (Mick Abrahams); plus tracks by other artists
NOTES: This track is transferred from a cleaned-up acetate.
PEAK CHART POSITION (UK/US): none
SALES CERTIFICATIONS: none

RELEASES:

TITLES	UK & FOREIGN LABEL/NO.	RELEASE DATE	US LABEL/NO.	RELEASE DATE
The Derek Lawrence Sessions - Take 3 (CD)	German Line LICD 9.01120 O	07/24/92		

1 AND ONLY - 25 YEARS OF RADIO 1

MUSICIANS: Ian Anderson (vocal, flute), Martin Barre (electric guitar), Glenn Cornick (bass), Clive Bunker (drums)
GUEST MUSICIANS: none
PRODUCTION: Tony Wilson and Dale Griffin
RECORDING LOCATION/ DATE: 09/09/84 at Hammersmith Odeon, London for the BBC
TRACKS: Living In The Past (BBC version); plus tracks by other artists
NOTES: none
PEAK CHART POSITION (UK/US): none
SALES CERTIFICATIONS: none

RELEASES:

TITLES	UK & FOREIGN LABEL/NO.	RELEASE DATE	US LABEL/NO.	RELEASE DATE
1 And Only - 25 Years Of Radio 1 (2CD)	Band Of Joy BOJ CD 25	09/07/92		
1 And Only - 25 Years Of Radio 1 (2CD; with different cover)	Band Of Joy BOJ CD 25	06/22/93		

DIAMONDS OF ROCK

MUSICIANS: Ian Anderson (vocal, flute), John Evans (organ), Glenn Cornick (bass), Barrie Barlow (drums), Neil Smith (Chick Murray) (guitar), Tony Wilkinson (sax), Neil Valentine (sax)
GUEST MUSICIANS: none
PRODUCTION: Derek Lawrence
RECORDING LOCATION/ DATE: 10/22/67 at CBS Studios, London
TRACKS: Blues For The 18th; plus tracks by other artists
NOTES: none
PEAK CHART POSITION (UK/US): none
SALES CERTIFICATIONS: none

RELEASES:

TITLES	UK & FOREIGN LABEL/NO.	RELEASE DATE	US LABEL/NO.	RELEASE DATE
Diamonds Of Rock (2CD)	German Castle Communications CBC 8034	09/14/92		

ACOUSTIC AID

MUSICIANS: Ian Anderson (vocal, flute), Martin Barre (electric guitar), Dave Pegg (bass), Doane Perry (drums), Martin Allcock (keyboards)
GUEST MUSICIANS: none
PRODUCTION: Joe Bonadonna
RECORDING LOCATION/ DATE: 08/21/91 live at WMMR, Philadelphia, PA
TRACKS: Bourée (J.S. Bach, arr. Ian Anderson) (live); plus tracks by other artists
NOTES: This is the same live version that previously appeared on the "Rocks On The Road" CD single.
PEAK CHART POSITION (UK/US): none
SALES CERTIFICATIONS: none

RELEASES:

TITLES	UK & FOREIGN LABEL/NO.	RELEASE DATE	US LABEL/NO.	RELEASE DATE
Acoustic Aid (CD)			Oxymoron/KOME 98.5	10/06/92

ROCK LEGENDS II

MUSICIANS: Ian Anderson (vocal, flute, acoustic guitar), Martin Barre (electric guitar), Glenn Cornick (bass), John Evans (keyboards), Clive Bunker (drums)
GUEST MUSICIANS: none
PRODUCTION: none!
RECORDING LOCATION/ DATE: 06/05/70 live at Aragon Ballroom, Chicago, IL
TRACKS: My God
NOTES: Also featured on this disc are tracks by Eric Clapton, Black Sabbath, Led Zeppelin, Bob Dylan, David Bowie, Bruce Springsteen and Bob Marley.
PEAK CHART POSITION (UK/US): none
SALES CERTIFICATIONS: none

RELEASES:

TITLES	UK & FOREIGN LABEL/NO.	RELEASE DATE	US LABEL/NO.	RELEASE DATE
Rock Legends II (CD)	Italy Gruppo Editoriale Fabbri MRL 002	**/**/93		

THE 25TH ANNIVERSARY INTERVIEW

MUSICIANS: Ian Anderson (spoken word), Martin Barre (spoken word)
GUEST MUSICIANS: none
PRODUCTION: Ian Anderson
RECORDING LOCATION/ DATE: 03/09/93 at Ian Anderson's home studio
TRACKS: This Was 1968; Stand Up 1969 ; Benefit 1970; Aqualung 1971; Thick As A Brick 1971/72; A Passion Play 1972/73; War Child 1974; Minstrel In The Gallery & Too Old To Rock 'N' Roll 1975/76; Songs From The Wood 1977; More Songs From The Wood; Stormwatch 1979;/ The 'A' Album 1980; Broadsword 1981/82; Keys, Synths, Flutes & Sax 1983; Under Wraps 1984; A.W.O.L. 1985; Back To The Studio 1986; Crest Of A Knave 1987; 20th Anniversary 1988; Rock Island 1989; A Year Of Touring 1990; Catfish Rising 1991; A Little Light Music Tour 1992; 25th Anniversary & Tull Remastered Packages 1993
NOTES: A commercial two-cassette release of a promotional 2CD item. It was only available to readers of A New Day magazine.
PEAK CHART POSITION (UK/US): none
SALES CERTIFICATIONS: none

RELEASES:

TITLES	UK & FOREIGN LABEL/NO.	RELEASE DATE	US LABEL/NO.	RELEASE DATE
The 25th Anniversary Interview (2 cassettes)	A New Day AND 2	10/11/93		

MESSAGE TO LOVE • THE ISLE OF WIGHT FESTIVAL 1970

MUSICIANS: Ian Anderson (vocal, flute), Martin Barre (electric guitar), Glenn Cornick (bass), Clive Bunker (drums), John Evans (keyboards)
GUEST MUSICIANS: none
PRODUCTION: unknown Pye Records Mobile Studio engineer
RECORDING LOCATION/ DATE: 08/30/70 at Isle Of Wight Festival, Isle Of Wight
TRACKS: My Sunday Feeling (live); plus tracks by other artists
NOTES: The Jethro Tull track is exclusive to this album.
PEAK CHART POSITION (UK/US): none
SALES CERTIFICATIONS: none

RELEASES:

TITLES	UK & FOREIGN LABEL/NO.	RELEASE DATE	US LABEL/NO.	RELEASE DATE
Message To Love • The Isle Of Wight Festival 1970 (2CD)	Essential EDF CD 327	01/08/96	Columbia CK 65068	10/29/96

25 VERY RARE MASTERS FROM THE SIXTIES

MUSICIANS: "Sunshine Day": Ian Anderson (backing vocals), Mick Abrahams (lead vocal, electric guitar), Glenn Cornick (bass), Clive Bunker (drums). "Aeroplane": Ian Anderson (lead vocal), John Evans (keyboards), Glenn Cornick (bass), Barrie Barlow (drums), Neil Smith (Chick Murray) (electric guitar). "Blues For The 18th": Ian Anderson (vocal, flute), John Evans (organ), Glenn Cornick (bass), Barrie Barlow (drums), Neil Smith (Chick Murray) (guitar), Tony Wilkinson (sax), Neil Valentine (sax)
GUEST MUSICIANS: Tony Wilson (backing vocals on "Aeroplane" and "Sunshine Day")
PRODUCTION: Derek Lawrence (all three tracks)
RECORDING LOCATION/ DATE: "Sunshine Day": Recorded 01/68 at Abbey Road Studios, London. "Aeroplane" and "Blues For The 18th": Recorded 10/22/67 at CBS Studios, London.
TRACKS: Sunshine Day (Michael Abrahams); Aeroplane (Ian Anderson/ Len Barnard [Glenn Cornick]; Blues For The 18th (Ian Anderson/ Len Barnard

[Glenn Cornick]); plus tracks by other artists
NOTES: This is the only album to have all three early tracks in one place.
PEAK CHART POSITION (UK/US): none
SALES CERTIFICATIONS: none

RELEASES:

TITLES	UK & FOREIGN LABEL/NO.	RELEASE DATE	US LABEL/NO.	RELEASE DATE
25 Very Rare Masters From The Sixties (CD)	Line Music 9.01333	09/16/96		

THE ROLLING STONES ROCK AND ROLL CIRCUS

MUSICIANS: Ian Anderson (live vocal, flute), Mick Abrahams (electric guitar - backing track only); Tony Iommi (electric guitar - miming to Mick Abrahams' part), Glenn Cornick (bass), Clive Bunker (drums)
GUEST MUSICIANS: none
PRODUCTION: Terry Ellis and Ian Anderson for Chrysalis Productions
RECORDING LOCATION/ DATE: 07/68 at Sound Techniques, Chelsea, London and 12/11/68 at Intertel Studios, Wembley, London (Ian Anderson's live vocal only)
TRACKS: A Song For Jeffrey (live/studio version); plus tracks by other artists
NOTES: This is the only appearance with Tony Iommi in the lineup. The band mimed to the track and Ian mimed a re-recorded studio vocal.
PEAK CHART POSITION (UK/US): none
SALES CERTIFICATIONS: none

RELEASES:

TITLES	UK & FOREIGN LABEL/NO.	RELEASE DATE	US LABEL/NO.	RELEASE DATE
The Rolling Stones Rock And Roll Circus (CD)	Abkco 526-771-2	10/14/96	Abkco 1268-2	10/15/96

SOMETHING WITH A PULSE

MUSICIANS: Ian Anderson (vocals, flute); Martin Barre (electric guitar); Dave Pegg (bass); Mark Craney (drums)
GUEST MUSICIANS: Eddie Jobson (keyboards and violin on "Black Sunday [live]")
PRODUCTION: Ian Anderson
RECORDING LOCATION/ DATE: live 11/12/80 at Los Angeles Sports Arena, L.A., CA
TRACKS: Black Sunday (live); plus tracks by other artists
NOTES: Album credited to Mark Craney & Friends. Please see Ian Anderson's solo section for his track "A Song For Jeffrey" on this album.
PEAK CHART POSITION (UK/US): none
SALES CERTIFICATIONS: none

RELEASES:

TITLES	UK & FOREIGN LABEL/NO.	RELEASE DATE	US LABEL/NO.	RELEASE DATE
Something With A Pulse (by MARK CRANEY & FRIENDS)			Laughing Gull LG002	08/05/97

VIDEOS

TITLES	UK & FOREIGN LABEL/NO.	RELEASE DATE	US LABEL/NO.	RELEASE DATE
Slipstream (VHS/Beta release in the UK, videodisc in the US)	Chrysalis CV1M VH1/ CV1M BE1	08/21/81	RCA Videodiscs 12116	02/07/83
Slipstream (VHS; reissue)			Pacific Arts Video Records PAVR-553	01/30/84
The Prince's Trust Rock Gala (VHS; two tracks: "Pussy Willow" and "Jack-In-The-Green - US edition was issued with two different covers)	MGM/UA Home Video SMV 101792	**/**/87	MGM/UA Home Video MV 400179	**/**/87
Slipstream (VHS; reissue)	Chrysalis Music Video CVHS 5018	01/25/88		
20 Years Of Jethro Tull (VHS)	Virgin Vision VVD 398	10/03/88	Virgin Music Video 3-50136	09/18/89
Slipstream (VHS; reissue)	Chrysalis Music Video CVHS 5018	01/27/94		
Rock In The U.K. (VHS; one track: "With You There To Help Me")			Rhino Home Video R3 2073	02/23/94
Beat Club Vol. 4 (VHS; one track: "The Witch's Promise")	German BMG Video 74321 16019 3	**/**/94		
25th Anniversary Video (VHS)	PMI MVP 4911263	07/04/94	EMI Records/ Chrysalis Video F3-77790	10/21/94
Message To Love • The Isle Of Wight Festival 1970 (VHS/2CD-ROMs; one track - "My Sunday Feeling")	PNE Video PNV 1005/ Castle Commun. UK 143	12/18/95		
Rolling Stones Rock And Roll Circus (VHS/ laserdisc)	Abkco 634-590-3/ 634-590-1	11/11/96 11/11/96	Abkco 1003-3/ Abkco 1003-1	11/12/96 11/12/96
Message To Love • The Isle Of Wight Festival 1970 (VHS/DVD/laserdisc; one track - "My Sunday Feeling")			Sony 49335 (VHS)/ IMG 3424 (laserdisc) Sony 49335 (DVD)	06/03/97 09/17/97 12/10/97
Best Of Musikladen Volume 1 (DVD, with "With You There To Help Me")			Pioneer Artists PA-98-601-D	11/17/98

PROMOTIONAL RELEASES

SINGLES
"This Was" sampler (West Germany Island) (1968)
Radio Spot for Jethro Tull "This Was" - Reprise Album RS 6336 (same two 50-second stereo spots on both sides) (US Reprise PRO 312) (1969)
Radio Spots for Reprise Album RS 6360 - "Stand Up" (same 60- and 50-second stereo spots on both sides) (US Reprise PRO 353) (1969)
Radio Spot for "Benefit" RS 6400: AM Spots (two 60-second mono spots)/ FM Spots (two 60-second stereo spots) (US Reprise PRO 395) (1970)
Radio Spot for Jethro Tull "Aqualung" Reprise Album MS 2035 (same 60-second stereo spot on both sides) (US Reprise PRO 494) (1971)
Aqualung (jukebox-only EP) (US Chrysalis SCH 1044/ Little LP LLP 252) (1971)
Thick As A Brick (promo EP - four edits of the title track) (UK Chrysalis CHRE 1003) (1972)
A Passion Play (promo test pressing EP - four edits of the title track) (Japan Chrysalis 17DY-4810) (1973)
"Jethro Tull Live" EP: Skating Away On The Thin Ice Of The New Day - Jack-In-The-Green/ Locomotive Breath - The Dambusters March (Italy Chrysalis 5001 583) (1978)
Dark Ages (5:24 edit)/ Dark Ages (5:24 edit) (12") (Chrysalis CHS-18-PDJ) (1979)
Watching Me Watching You/ Beastie (Spain Chrysalis ESP 586) (1982)
Walk Into Light (by IAN ANDERSON) (12") (Canada Chrysalis CPR-01) (1983)
El Amor Es Un Campo De Batalla ("Love Is A Battlefield" by Pat Benatar)/ Vuelo De Noche ("Fly By Night" by IAN ANDERSON) (Spanish RCA S-0372) (1984)
Under Wraps #1/ Under Wraps #2 (12") (US Chrysalis AS 1967) (1984)
Lap Of Luxury/ Astronomy (Spain Chrysalis ESP-619) (1984)
Living In The Past/ Cross-Eyed Mary (US Chrysalis GCS 7701) (1985)
Bungle In The Jungle/ Minstrel In The Gallery (US Chrysalis GCS 7702) (1985)
Bourrée (2:48 edit)/ Bourrée (LP Version) (12") (by THE LONDON SYMPHONY ORCHESTRA featuring IAN ANDERSON) (US RCA JB-14262) (1985)
Steel Monkey/ Steel Monkey (12") (US Chrysalis VAS 2796) (1987)
Farm On The Freeway (4:20 edit)/ Farm On The Freeway (4:20 edit) (12") (US Chrysalis VAS 2866) (1987)
Budapest (6:10 edit)/Budapest (6:10 edit) (12") (US Chrysalis VAS 1039) (1988)
Said She Was A Dancer/ Dogs In The Midwinter (12") (Canada Chrysalis CS 8736)
Stormy Monday Blues (BBC Version) - Lick Your Fingers Clean - Minstrel In The Gallery (BBC Version) - Farm On The Freeway (live) - Part Of The Machine (edit) (CD5) (UK Chrysalis TULPCD 1) (1988)
Part Of The Machine (7:01)/ Part Of The Machine (4:34 edit) (12") (US Chrysalis VAS 1170) (1988)
Thick As A Brick (2:58 edit)/Thick As A Brick (5:23 edit) (US Chrysalis VS7 1262) (1988)
Kissing Willie (CD5) (US Chrysalis DPRO 23418) (1989)
The Rattlesnake Trail - Another Christmas Song (CD5) (US Chrysalis DPRO 23457) (1989)
Another Christmas Song - Intro/A Christmas Song (live) - Cheap Day Return/Mother Goose (live) - Outro/Locomotive Breath (live) (CD5) (US Chrysalis DPRO 23471) (1989)
This Is Not Love (CD5) (US Chrysalis DPRO 23760) (1991)
Esto No Es Amor (This Is Not Love) plus tracks by other artists (12") (Argentina EMI Odeon LP 054) (1991)
A Jethro Tull Appeteaser: This Is Not Love (90-second fragment); Doctor To My Disease (90-second fragment); Rocks On The Road (90-second fragment); White Innocence (90-second fragment) (cassette) (US Chrysalis 4PRO 23768) (1991)
Doctor To My Disease - Night In The Wilderness - Jump Start (live) (CD5) (US Chrysalis DPRO 23801) (1991)
Some Day The Sun Won't Shine For You - Living In The Past (CD5) (UK Chrysalis JTPRO 1) (1992)
Christmas Song (live) (CD5) (US Chrysalis DPRO 04657) (1992)
Living In The Dub - Living In N.Y. - Living In The Club (12") (UK Chrysalis 12 CHS DJ3970) (1993)
The Very Best Of Jethro Tull: Locomotive Breath; Bourée; Too Old To Rock 'N' Roll: Too Young To Die; Beggar's Farm (CD5) (France Chrysalis SPCD 1770) (1994)
Rare And Precious Chain - This Free Will (CD5) (UK Chrysalis IAN DJ1) (1995)
Christmas Sampler: Ring Out, Solstice Bells; Christmas Song; Another Christmas Song (CD5) (US Chrysalis DPRO 10421) (1995)
Roots To Branches Sampler: Beside Myself; Roots To Branches; Rare And Precious Chain (CD5) (US Chrysalis DPRO 10425) (1995)
Aqualung (Spain Chrysalis PE 98023) (1998)
j-tull Dot Com Sampler: Spiral (with Ian Anderson spoken intro); Dot Com (with Ian Anderson spoken intro); Wicked Windows (with Ian Anderson spoken intro); Spiral (US Single Version) (CD5) (US Fuel 2000 FLDPRO-1103) (1999)
Dot Com (CD5) (Germany Roadrunner RR promo 456) (1999)

ALBUMS
Thick As a Brick (mono) (US Reprise MS 2072) (1972)
Jethro Tull Radio Show (24 min.): Aqualung; Fat Man; A Passion Play (edit); Thick As A Brick (edit); Bungle In The Jungle; Locomotive Breath; Rainbow Blues; Living In The Past; Nothing Is Easy (all tracks interspersed with Ian Anderson interview segments)/ (same tracks) (US Chrysalis PRO 622) (1976)
Jethro Tull Radio Show (50 min.): Aqualung; Teacher; Fat Man; A Passion Play (edit); Thick As A Brick (edit);/ Locomotive Breath; Skating Away On The Thin Ice Of The New Day; Rainbow Blues; Living In The Past; Nothing Is Easy (all tracks interspersed with Ian Anderson interview segments) (US Chrysalis PRO 623) (1976)
Broadsword Townhouse (picture disc) (UK Chrysalis) (1982)
Rare Rock Collection - 98KZEW Rock Against Aids (US Elektra PR-2161): this promo LP is the first US release of "I'm Your Gun" (1987)
j-tull Dot Com - Advance Promotional Copy: same tracks as original CD except that an edit of "Dot Com" replaces Ian Anderson's "The Secret Language Of Birds" (US Fuel 2000 FLDPRO-1102) (1999)

OTHER PROMOTIONAL ALBUMS
Chrysalis 5LP box set including white label promotion copies of these LPs: Jethro Tull's "Living In The Past," "Turkey" by Wild Turkey, "Below The Salt" by Steeleye Span, and Tir Na Nog's "A Tear And A Smile." No album covers were included in the box set. (Chrysalis no #) (1972)
Hardly Beginner's Luck: The Chrysalis Compendium (UK Chrysalis Music Publishing CHM-1) (with a medley of "Living In The Past," "Wond'ring Aloud" and "Locomotive Breath") (1972)
Live From Central Park (Canada Chrysalis)
Tour Special (Japan Chrysalis)
The Jethro Tull Story (3LP) (Canada Chrysalis): music and interviews

Live In Istanbul (UK Chrysalis PAL VHS) (1992)
Divinities: Twelve Dances With God (by IAN ANDERSON) (US Chrysalis NTSC VHS) (1995)

OTHER PROMOTIONAL ITEMS
"Songs From The Wood": tree stumps with match holder and striking pad
"Heavy Horses": brass horse shoes

UNUSUAL FOREIGN RELEASES

SINGLES
Me Está Destrozando (It's Breaking Me Up)/ Una Canción Para Jeffrey (A Song For Jeffrey) (Argentina Music Hall 31.448) (1969)
Me Confunde (It's Breaking Me Up)/ Una Canción Para Jeffrey (A Song For Jeffrey) (Argentina Philips 83474-PB) (1969)
Bourée/ Back To The Family (Norway Sonet T 9557) (1969) - also issued in Sweden with the same catalog number
Bourée/ Fat Man (West German Island 6014 013) (1969) - also issued by Island in Belgium and France with the catalog number WIP 6068
Bourée/ Fat Man (Japan Reprise JET-1939) (1969)
Bourée/ Living In The Past (Italy Island 6014 029) (1969)
Bourée/ Look Into The Sun (Holland Island 388 859 UF) (1969) - also issued in Spain with the same catalog number
Living In The Past/ (B-side by The Box Tops) (jukebox only) (Italy SIR IL 20105) (1969)
Bourée/ Reasons For Waiting (Italy SIR IL 20107) (1969)
Bourée/ Them Changes (by Buddy Miles) (jukebox only) (Italy Island AS 117) (1969)
Bourée - Living In The Past/ Sweet Dream - Love Story (Japan Reprise SJET-545) (1969)
Living In The Past - Driving Song/ My Sunday Feeling - Some Day The Sun Won't Shine For You (Portugal Fontana 65 027) (1969)
Living In The Past/ I Want To Live (by Aphrodite's Child) (free French single with fold-out cover issued with "Le Metier" magazine) (France Island 17.6.69) (1969)
Viviendo En El Pasado (Living In The Past)/ Linda Catirita (by Anibal Velasquez) (Mexico Gamma No. 238) (1969)
Sweet Dream - Jeffrey Goes To Leicester Square/ Bourée - Fat Man (Portugal Fontana 65 029 TE) (1969)
Maestro (Teacher) - Andare Solo (Walk On Alone)/ La Promesa De La Bruja (The Witch's Promise) - Conducido (Driving Song) (Argentina Reprise/ Music Hall 60.362) (1969)
The Witch's Promise/ Teacher (Sweden Sonet T 7792 - issued on standard black vinyl and blue vinyl) (1970)
The Witch's Promise/ (B-side by Tommy Roe) (jukebox only) (Mexico Gamma No. 261) (1970)
Aqualung/ Hymn 43 (Italy Island 6014 048) (1971)
Hymn 43/ Locomotive Breath (Germany Chrysalis 6014 055) - also issued by Chrysalis in Germany with the same catalog number, and in Holland with the catalog number 10.187 AT (1971)
Locomotive Breath/ Look Into The Sun (Austria Chrysalis 6155 011) (1971) - also issued by Chrysalis in Germany with the same catalog number
Locomotive Breath/ Love Story (Holland Chrysalis 6155 084) (1971)
Himno 43 (Hymn 43)/ Mother Goose (Argentina Reprise/Music Hall 31.719) (1971)
"This Is Jethro Tull" EP: Living In The Past - Locomotive Breath/ Hymn 43 - A Song For Jeffrey (Australia Reprise EPR 252) (1971)
Living In The Past - Life Is A Long Song/ Bourée - Dr. Bogenbroom (Portugal Chrysalis 6285 001) (1971)
Thick As A Brick (Part 1)/ Thick As A Brick (Part 2) (Germany Chrysalis 6155 002) - also issued by Chrysalis in Austria with the same catalog number, and in France with the catalog numbers CHA 103 (jukebox only) and CHA 104, in Italy as 010 1003, in Denmark as 6E00693455, in Holland as 5C 006-93455 and in Sweden as 4E00693455 (1972)
Locomotive Breath/ Bourée (France Chrysalis CHA 111) (1972) - also issued by Chrysalis in Germany and Holland with the catalog number 103 012-100 (1972)
Living In The Past - Christmas Song/ Eat That Question - Cletus Awreetus-Awrightus (both tracks by The Mothers Of Invention) (Argentina Reprise/ Music Hall 40.018) (1972)
Thick As A Brick (Part 1) - Thick As A Brick (Part 2)/ Holiday In Berlin, Full Blown (Part 1) - Holiday In Berlin, Full Blown (Part 2) (both tracks by The Mothers Of Invention) (Argentina Reprise/ Music Hall 183) (1972)
Thick As A Brick/ Peel The Paint (by Gentle Giant) (jukebox only) (Italy Chrysalis AS 156) (1972)
A Passion Play (Edit #8)/ A Passion Play (Edit #9) (Luanda [Angola] Reprise R21 199) (1973)
A Passion Play (Edit #8)/ Samantha (by Fausto Leali) (jukebox only) (Italy Chrysalis AS 223) (1973)
Trovador En La Galeria (Minstrel In The Gallery)/ Arena De Dia Del Verano (Summerday Sands) (Uruguay Chrysalis CRS 2106) (1975)
Living In The Past/ Locomotive Breath (Belgium Chrysalis 6155 058) (1976)
Locomotive Breath ("bleeped" version)/ Wind-Up (New Zealand Reprise RO.584) (1976)
Songs From The Wood (edit)/ Jack-In-The-Green (Australia Chrysalis K 6945) (1977)
The Whistler/ Ring Out, Solstice Bells (Guatemala Chrysalis AC-C-3472) (1977)
Moths/ Beltane (Ireland Chrysalis CHS 2214) - copies play "Life Is A Long Song" on its B-side (1978)
Moths/ . . .And The Mouse Police Never Sleeps (Poland Tonpress S-166) (1978)
Warm Sporran/ Elegy (Germany Chrysalis 6155 278) (1979)
Something's On The Move/ North Sea Oil (France Chrysalis 6837 589) (1979)
Broadsword/ Watching Me Watching You (Germany Chrysalis 104 199-100) (1982) - also issued by Chrysalis in Holland with the catalog number 104 199
Pussy Willow/ Beastie (Germany Chrysalis 104 589-100) (1982) - also issued by Chrysalis in Holland with the catalog number 104 589
Steel Monkey/ The Waking Edge (Germany Chrysalis 109 442) (1987)
Steel Monkey/ The Waking Edge - Dogs In The Midwinter (12") (Germany Chrysalis 609442) (1987)
Steel Monkey/ Dogs In The Midwinter (South Africa Chrysalis [Gallo] PD 2557) (1987)
Crest Of A Knave EP: Steel Monkey/ Jump Start - Budapest (edit) (Bolivia CBS 10523) (1987)
4 Tracks From "Crest Of A Knave" EP: Steel Monkey; Farm On The Freeway; Said She Was A Dancer; Raising Steam (cassette) (Australia Festival/CBS) (1987)
Said She Was A Dancer/ The Waking Edge (South Africa Chrysalis [Gallo] PD 2580) (1988)
Kissing Willie/ Heavy Water (Germany Chrysalis 112 716-000) (1989)

ALBUMS

This Was (Italy Ricordi Dischi SLIR 22031) - different cover design (1969)
Benefit (Germany Chrysalis 6307 516) - with gatefold cover (1969)
Jethro Tull (Club-Sonderauflage mail-order only compilation - Germany Island 92 527) (1970)
Sunday Best (Australia Reprise RS 5259) (1971)
20 Star Tracks, Vol. 1 (UK Ronco RONCOPP 2001) - with a unique edit of "Life Is A Long Song" (1971)
Asi Es Jethro Tull (Spain Philips 63 43 003) (1971)
Beneficio (Benefit) (Spain Chrysalis 6307 516) (1974)
Asi Es Jethro Tull (Spain Chrysalis 6307 517) (1974)
Too Old To Rock 'N' Roll: Too Young To Die (different cover) (Yugoslavia Chrysalis LSCHR 73056) (1976)
Demasiado Viejo Para El Rock: Demasiado Joven Para Morir (different cover) (Argentina Chrysalis 6307 572) (1976)
Lo Mejor De Jethro Tull (same as "M.U. - The Best Of Jethro Tull" with different cover) (Argentina Chrysalis CHR 6307 566) (1976) - also issued by
    Chrysalis in Peru with the same catalog number
Canciones Del Bosque (Songs From The Wood) (Argentina Chrysalis AVI 6307 591) (1977)
Aqualung (Spain Chrysalis AVI 6307 591) - with "Glory Row" instead of "Locomotive Breath" (1977)
The Best (East Germany Amiga 8 55 666) (1978)
A (gatefold album) (Argentina Chrysalis AVSI 4865) (1980)
Story Of Jethro Tull Vol. 1 (France Chrysalis CHM 1363) (1981)
Retrospectivo (Argentina Chrysalis AVI 5011) (1982)
La Espada Y La Bestia (The Broadsword And The Beast) (Argentina Chrysalis AVI 5025) (1982) - also issued by Chrysalis in Spain with catalog number
    CDL 1380
M.U. - The Best Of Jethro Tull/ Repeat: The Best Of Jethro Tull Volume 2 (2LP) (France Music NL 37730) (1983)
Atrapado (Under Wraps) (Argentina Chrysalis TLP 60114) (1984)
Living In The Past (single LP) (Italy EMI 64 3210351) (1985) - with the tracks from the first of the two LPs
Masters Of Rock (South Africa Chrysalis MMTL 1383) (1986)
La Isla Del Rock (Rock Island) (Argentina Chrysalis 10070) (1989)
Giganty Rocka (CD) (Poland Magazyn Silesia ZAIKS 536/98) (1998)
The Best Of Jethro Tull (Gold Collection) (CD) (Poland Club Eve CECD 09-2) (1998)
Gold Collection (CD) (Poland AG-002) (1998)
Giga Collection (CD) (Poland Giga Records GR 015/98) (1998)

RADIO SHOWS

SINGLES

What's It All About?: Jethro Tull (Show #506)/ (B-side by Robert Palmer) (Trav. MA 1785) (01/80)
What's It All About?: Jethro Tull (Show #578)/ (B-side by The Police) (Trav. MA 1921) (05/81)

ALBUMS

Top Gear (LP) (first airdate: 09/22/68): So Much Trouble; A Song For Jeffrey; My Sunday Feeling
Top Gear (LP) (first airdate: 11/05/68): Beggar's Farm; Love Story; Stormy Monday Blues; Dharma For One
Top Gear (LP) (first airdate: 06/22/69): Living In The Past; A New Day Yesterday; Fat Man
Top Of The Pops (LP) (first airdate: 1969): Nothing Is Easy; Bourée; The Witch's Promise; Sweet Dream
BBC Special (open-reel) (first airdate: 03/16/71)
Nightbird & Co., Cosmic Connections, US Army Reserve Programs No. 285-288 (2LP) (airdate: 10/17/76 - 10/24/76): Presented by The Nightbird,
    Alison Steele. Features two music and interview programs with Ian Anderson: #285 (air week of 10/17/76) and #286 (air week of 10/24/76). Other
    shows were with Don Harrison Band and Wishbone Ash.
Inner View, Show #22, Sound Communication, Inc. (LP) (airdate: 1976)
BBC Special - Jethro Tull Story, London Wavelength, National Tape Service 031677 (7" open-reel) (first airdate: 03/16/77): Ian Anderson is interviewed by
    Alexis Korner.
Inner View, Series 13, Program #10 (LP) (airdate: 1978)
The Robert Klein Hour, DIR Broadcasting (2LP) (airdate: 11/11/79): with Ian Anderson, Laraine Newman and The Shirts
Profiles In Rock, Watermark, Program # PRB-802-6 (LP) (air date: 05/10/80 - 05/11/80)
Toyota Presents (2LP) (1980): Ian Anderson profile with music and interviews
King Biscuit Flower Hour, DIR Broadcasting (3-sided LP) (airdate: week of 01/25/81): recorded live at the Checkerdome, St. Louis, MO on 10/26/80
A Night On The Road, RKO (3LP) (ANOTR-581) (airdate: 06/81): recorded live at Los Angeles Sports Arena on 11/12/80 (the "Slipstream" video
    soundtrack)
Best Of The Biscuit, DIR Broadcasting (LP) (airdate: 12/06/81)
Inner View, Series 21, Program #10 (airdate: 1981)
The Source, Program #21 (LP) (airdate: 02/14/82)
BBC Rock Hour, Program #325, London Wavelength (2LP) (airdate: week of 06/20/82): "The Broadsword And The Beast" special
The Source, Program #82-27, NBC Radio (3LP) (airdate: weekend of 07/23/82 - 07/25/82)
Supergroups In Concert, Westwood One, ABC Radio Networks (3LP) (airdate: 07/03/82): recorded live in Freiburg, Ravensburg and Stuttgart - 04/82
Off The Record, Westwood One, Program #82-28 (airdate: 07/82)
The Source (Music Magazine #2), NBC Radio MM-81-1 (LP) (airdate: weekend of 08/13/82 - 08/15/82)
Guest DJ, Rolling Stone (Programs #21/22 - Ian Anderson/ Charlie Daniels) (2LP) (airdates: 08/16/82 and 08/23/82)
Best Of Supergroups In Concert, Westwood One (3LP) (airdate: 09/09/82): live in Germany 1982 plus other artists
King Biscuit Flower Hour, DIR Broadcasting, KB 447 (2LP) (airdate: 11/28/82): recorded live at Hamburg Congress Centrum Halle on 04/08/82
Robert W. Morgan (LP) (airdate: 1982)
Rock Star (with Ian Anderson) (LP) (airdate: 1982)
Captured Live, RKO, Program #CL-583 (3LP) (airdate: 01/83): live from 1980
The Source Music Magazine #2, NBC Radio, MM-82-1 (3LP) (airdate: weekend of 08/13/83 - 08/15/83): Ian Anderson interview
Live Cuts, DIR Broadcasting, LC-11 (LP) (airdate: week of 09/23/83): with Red Rider, The Blasters, John Cougar, Chris DeBurgh and Zebra

Hitline, London Wavelength (LP) (airdate: 10/84): music and interviews

In Concert, BBC Transcription Service CN-4497/S (airdate: 1984): recorded live at Hammersmith Odeon on 09/09/84

BBC Rock Hour, Program #550 (BC 550), London Wavelength (airdate: week of 12/09/84): recorded live at Hammersmith Odeon on 09/09/84

King Biscuit Flower Hour, DIR Broadcasting (LP) (airdate: 12/16/84)

Pioneers In Rock, DIR Broadcasting (2LP) (airdate: 01/86): live tracks from different sources

Off The Record, Westwood One, Program #87-22 (LP) (airdate: 11/02/87)

Rock Stars, Radio Today (2CD) (airdate: 11/16/87 - 11/22/87): music and interviews

Legends Of Rock, Part I, NBC Radio Entertainment (3-sided LP) (airdate: week of 01/04/88 - 01/10/88): Music and interviews with Ian Anderson presented by Ray White.

King Biscuit Flower Hour, DIR Broadcasting (CD) (airdate: 01/10/88): recorded live at The Tower Theater, Upper Darby, PA on 11/25/87

Legends Of Rock, Part II, NBC Radio Entertainment (3-sided LP) (airdate: week of 01/11/88 - 01/17/88): Music and interviews with Ian Anderson presented by Ray White.

King Biscuit Flower Hour, DIR Broadcasting (CD) (airdate: 01/10/88)

King Biscuit Flower Hour, DIR Broadcasting (CD) (airdate: 05/15/88): recorded live at The Tower Theater, Upper Darby, PA on 11/25/87

Ticket To Ride (with Ian Anderson) (CD) (airdate: 06/13/88)

Tune Up #20, Album Network (CD) (airdate: 06/27/88): also contains tracks by The Gregg Allman Band, Ziggy Marley, Gary Wright and Aztec Camera

World Of Rock, DIR Broadcasting (with Ian Anderson and Ron Wood) (2LP) (airdate: 08/20/88)

"Living In The Past" Radio Special (JTSP-88) (airdate: 1988)

"Aqualung" - In The Studio (CD) (airdate: 1988)

King Biscuit Flower Hour Year End Special, DIR Broadcasting (CD) (airdate: 12/25/88): with "Farm On The Freeway" and "Aqualung" recorded live at The Tower Theater in Upper Darby, PA on 11/25/87. The program also features David Bowie, Iggy Pop, Joe Satriani, Grateful Dead, Paul Carrack and Elton John.

King Biscuit Flower Hour, DIR Broadcasting (CD) (airdate: 01/89)

King Biscuit Flower Hour, DIR Broadcasting (CD) (airdate: 03/19/89): recorded live at The Tower Theater, Upper Darby, PA on 11/25/87

Masters Of Rock, Radio Ventures (2CD) (airdate: 06/12/89): music and interviews

Masters Of Rock, Radio Ventures (CD) (airdate: 08/19/89): music and interviews

Legends Of Rock (CD) (airdate: 09/25/89 - 10/02/89)

Pioneers Of Rock (airdate: 1989): with Jethro Tull and Emerson, Lake & Powell

Live Cuts, DIR Broadcasting (CD) (airdate: 10/16/89 - 10/20/89)

In Concert, BBC Classics 89-23, Westwood One (2LP) (airdate: week of 10/30/89): recorded live at Hammersmith Odeon on 09/09/84

King Biscuit Flower Hour, DIR Broadcasting (CD) (airdate: 10/30/89 - 11/05/89)

Rock Stars, Radio Today (2CD) (airdate: 11/20/89 - 12/03/89): music and interviews

World Of Rock, DIR Broadcasting (2LP) (airdate: 12/02/89): Ian Anderson is co-host of the show

Up Close, Media America Radio - Neer Perfect Productions 8926 (2CD) (airdate: 12/11/89 - 12/24/89): music and interviews, including some live tracks

Hitdisc, Century 21 Programming, 819B (airdate: week of 12/15/89): with Crosby, Stills & Nash, D.A.D, Joe Satriani, Bobby Womack, Smokey Robinson and Aaron Neville

"Benefit" - In The Studio, Album Network (CD) (airdate: 12/18/89)

The Live Show, ABC Radio Networks #85 (CD) (airdate: 02/19/90): with "Farm On The Freeway" live from 11/25/87

The Live Show, ABC Radio Networks #111 (CD) (airdate: 08/20/90): with live version of "Aqualung" from 1974-1975

"Aqualung" - In The Studio, The Album Network, Show #126 (airdate: week of 11/19/90): hosted by Redbeard

Classic CDs - "Aqualung", Westwood One (2CD) (airdate: week of 11/26/90)

King Biscuit Flower Hour, DIR Broadcasting (CD) (airdate: 12/31/90 - 01/06/91): with Jethro Tull (from 11/25/87) and King's X

BBC Classic Tracks, Westwood One (CD) (airdate: 03/18/91): with live tracks by Jethro Tull and Procol Harum

Up Close, Media America Radio - Neer Perfect Productions #91-23 (2CD) (airdate: 06/17/91 - 06/21/91)

Classic Cuts, #230 (CD) (airdate: week of 07/01/91): with Ian Anderson, George Martin, Nils Lofgren, Noel Redding and Marty Balin

In Concert, Westwood One, #91-40 (2LP) (airdate: week of 09/30/91): with live tracks by Jethro Tull (from 09/09/84) and Procol Harum (7 tracks)

King Biscuit Flower Hour, DIR Broadcasting (CD) (airdate: 09/30/91 - 10/06/91): live from 11/25/87

The Story Of Jethro Tull, Unistar (3CD) (airdate: 10/91): music and interviews

Rock Over London, 91-38 (LP) (airdate: 10/91)

Schweppes Presents The British Invasion Series Pt. 2 (Rock: From The UK To The USA), Westwood One (6CD) (airdate: 1991)

"Thick As A Brick" - In The Studio, The Album Network, Show #183 (airdate: week of 12/23/91): presented by Redbeard

King Biscuit Flower Hour, DIR Broadcasting (CD) (airdate: 09/27/92)

BBC Classic Tracks, Westwood One, #92-51 (2CD) (airdate: 12/14/92)

In Concert, Westwood One (2CD) (airdate: 02/93)

"Benefit" - In The Studio, The Album Network (CD - reissue of program that aired 12/18/89) (airdate: week of 08/16/93)

BBC Classic Tracks, Westwood One (CD) (airdate: 09/06/93)

In Concert, Westwood One, #94-10 (CD) (airdate: 02/28/94): with live tracks by Jethro Tull (from 09/09/84) and Raging Slab (3 tracks)

King Biscuit Flower Hour, DIR Broadcasting (CD) (airdate: 03/07/94 - 03/13/94): recorded live 11/25/87

BBC Classic Tracks - UK: The Early 70s, Westwood One, #94-18 (CD) (airdate: 04/25/94): with "Beggar's Farm"

King Biscuit Flower Hour, DIR Broadcasting (CD) (airdate: 09/05/94 - 09/11/94): recorded live 11/25/87

King Biscuit Flower Hour, DIR Broadcasting (CD) (airdate: 09/25/95)

King Biscuit Flower Hour, DIR Broadcasting, #95-40 (CD) (airdate: 10/02/95 - 10/08/95): recorded live 11/25/87

Off The Record, Westwood One, #95-42 (CD) (airdate: 10/09/95)

Off The Record, Westwood One, #96-31 (CD) (airdate: 07/29/96)

BBC Classic Tracks, Westwood One, #96-36 (CD) (airdate: 09/02/96)

"Thick As A Brick" - In The Studio, The Album Network, Show #461 (airdate: week of 04/21/97)

Flashback!, Radio Today, Show #28 (3LP) (airdate: week of 07/13/97 - 07/19/97): with other artists

Rick's Café, #97-28 (4CD) (airdate: 07/97)

Superstar Concert Radio Show (2CD) (airdate: 08/18/97)

King Biscuit Flower Hour, DIR Broadcasting, #97-37 (CD) (airdate: 09/08/97 - 09/14/97): recorded live 11/25/87

Blues Deluxe, Music Unlimited, #530 (CD) (airdate: week of 02/15/98 - 02/21/98)

King Biscuit Flower Hour, DIR Broadcasting, #98-19 (CD) (airdate: 05/04/98 - 05/10/98): recorded live from the Spectrum in 1984
BBC Classic Tracks, Westwood One, #98-25 (airdate: 06/15/98)
Flashback!, Radio Today, Show #616 (4CD) (airdate: week of 10/26/98)
The Guitar Show with Kevin Bacon, Show #98-47 (2CD) (airdate: weekend of 11/21/98 - 11/22/98): Kevin Bacon interviews Martin Barre and Rick Nielsen
Rock Legends - "Aqualung", #98-51 (CD) (airdate: week of 12/14/98 - 12/20/98)
BBC Classic Tracks, Westwood One (CD) (airdate: 01/11/99): live from 09/09/84
Superstar Concert Radio Show, #99-08 (2CD) (airdate: 02/20/99 - 02/21/99): live tracks from 09/09/84 and 10/08/91
King Biscuit Flower Hour, DIR Broadcasting (CD) (airdate: 02/22/99 - 02/28/99): live tracks from 09/09/84
Up Close, #99-33 (2CD) (airdate: 08/16/99 - 08/20/99): music and interviews

OTHER UNDATED RADIO SHOWS:
The Live Show (LP): with Crosby, Stills, Nash & Young, Jethro Tull and The Who
King Biscuit Flower Hour Greatest Hits (CD): with two Jethro Tull live tracks
Desert Island Discs (CD): hosted by Ian Anderson
Desert Island Discs (CD): hosted by Martin Barre

TELEVISION APPEARANCES

"Firstimers", Granada TV, UK (filmed 05/03/67; aired 05/24/67): "Take The Easy Way" by The John Evan Smash
"Colour Me Pop", BBC, UK (1968): Four songs played, including "Rock Me Baby"
"Rolling Stones Rock & Roll Circus", UK (filmed 12/11/68; not aired commercially): "A Song For Jeffrey"
Swedish TV (01/09/69): "To Be Sad Is A Mad Way To Be"; "Back To The Family"
"The Johnny Hallyday Show", French TV (filmed 04/15/69): in-studio appearance
French TV (filmed 04/25/69 at Morgan Studios, London): the band in the studio recording "Stand Up"
"Top Of The Pops", BBC, UK (filmed 06/05/69): "Living In The Past"
"Top Of The Pops", BBC, UK (filmed 06/12/69): "Living In The Past"
German TV (filmed 09/04/69): the band performing live in a Stuttgart, Germany TV studio
"La Jaconde", French TV (filmed 09/30/69): in-studio appearance
"La Jaconde", French TV (filmed 10/31/69): in-studio appearance
"Swing In", German TV (Fall 1969): One hour special with Jethro Tull live at the Royal Albert Hall plus footage of Ian Anderson's parents with interviews
"Top Of The Pops", BBC, UK (filmed 10/30/69): "Sweet Dream"
"Top Of The Pops", BBC, UK (filmed 11/13/69): "Sweet Dream"
VPRO, Dutch TV (11/69): film footage from Jethro Tull's 10/10/69 Amsterdam concert
"Top Of The Pops", BBC, UK (02/70): "The Witch's Promise" - a lip-synch performance revealing Ian Anderson's poor teeth prior to dental surgery!
"Beat Club", German TV (filmed in Bremen, Germany 02/19/70): "The Witch's Promise" - another bad miming job by the band!
"Beat Club", German TV (filmed in Bremen, Germany 06/23/70): "With You There To Help Me"/"By Kind Permission Of", "Nothing Is Easy"
"American Bandstand", ABC-TV, US (1970): "Teacher"
"Switched-On Symphony", NBC-TV, US (filmed 02/13/70 - 02/17/70): "Bourée" (with Zubin Mehta and the L.A. Philharmonic, Santana and The Nice.)
"Abendschau Berlin", German TV (01/71): Jethro Tull sightseeing in Berlin and at their hotel
"Beat Club", German TV (1971): "Life Is A Long Song"
"Top Of The Pops", BBC, UK (1971): "Life Is A Long Song"
"The Hare Who Lost His Spectacles" video (1973)
"War Child" video (1974)
"Fritz Rau Special", German TV (1975): contains backstage footage with the band
"All You Need Is Love", US TV (1975): "Minstrel In The Gallery" plus interviews
"Minstrel In The Gallery" (1975): documentary on rock concerts with guest appearance by Jethro Tull
"Supersonic", London Weekend Television, UK (03/27/76): "Too Old To Rock 'N' Roll: Too Young To Die" video directed by Mike Mansfield
"'Too Old To Rock 'N' Roll: Too Young To Die' Special", ITV, UK (1976): "Quizz Kid"; "Crazed Institution"; "Salamander"; "Taxi Grab"; "From A Deadbest To An Old Greaser"; "Bad Eyed And Loveless"; "Big Dipper"; "Too Old To Rock 'N' Roll: Too Young To Die"; "Pied Piper"; "Chequered Flag (Dead Or Alive)". Directed by Mike Mansfield. All backing tracks and vocals were re-recorded especially for the show, but the performance is lip-synched.
"Too Old To Rock 'N' Roll: Too Young To Die", Austrian TV (1976) - Same as above, but German-dubbed interviews replaced "Salamander" and "Bad Eyed And Loveless."
"Midnight Special", NBC-TV (06/19/76): live performance
"The Mike Douglas Show", US TV (filmed 08/02/76): Ian Anderson interview with Jethro Tull film clip
Austrian TV (1977): includes an interview
"The Anne Laurie Show", BBC2, UK (1977): the video for "The Whistler" was shown on this Scottish vocalist's show
"Sight & Sound In Concert", BBC, UK (02/10/77): "Skating Away On The Thin Ice Of The New Day"; "Jack-In-The-Green"; "Thick As A Brick"; "Songs From The Wood"; "Velvet Green"; "Hunting Girl"; "Aqualung"; "Wind-Up"; "Locomotive Breath." The program was recorded live at the Hippodrome in Golders Green and was simultaneously broadcast in stereo on Radio 1.
"Minstrel In The Gallery", WOR-TV (Secaucus, NJ), US (12/07/77): interviews plus live clips of "Too Old To Rock 'N' Roll: Too Young To Die"; "Cross-Eyed Mary"; "Songs From The Wood"; "Thick As A Brick"; "Aqualung"; Beethoven's "Ninth Symphony"
"Old Grey Whistle Test", BBC2, UK (05/09/78): 5-minute edit of "Heavy Horses"
"Live From Madison Square Garden" (10/09/78 worldwide satellite broadcast): "Thick As A Brick"; "No Lullaby"; flute improvisation; "Songs From The Wood"; "Aqualung"; "Locomotive Breath"; "The Dambusters March." This 45-minute program was carried by the UK and some European countries. It was shown by the BBC as part of an "Old Grey Whistle Test" special and broadcast in stereo on Radio 1. It was reshown a few days later on the BBC.
BBC2, UK (1978): a studio panel discussion with Roy Harper, Nick Kent and Rick Wakeman covering the music press, and a 4-minute clip of Ian Anderson's comments on acid was included.
"Arena", BBC2, UK (01/11/80): interviews and film clips from "My God"; "Songs From The Wood"; "Thick As A Brick"; "Dark Ages"; a flute solo; "Heavy Horses"; "The Water's Edge"; "Sweet Dream"; "Dark Ages" (studio version). This was a documentary of the band in and out of action with band interviews and live footage from Seattle, WA (04/10/79) and Portland, OR (04/12/79). The program noted at its end that John Glascock had died in the interim.
Richard Digance program, BBC TV, UK (04/05/80): "Dun Ringill" (live acoustic performance) with Francis Wilson spoken introduction.
"Ohne Maulkorb Spezial", Austrian TV (04/80): interviews plus "Aqualung"; "Dark Ages"; "Home"; "Orion"; "Too Old To Rock 'N' Roll: Too Young To Die"; "Cross-Eyed Mary"; "Minstrel In The Gallery"; "Locomotive Breath"; "The Dambusters March." Live footage from the Munich Olympiahalle was combined with Ian Anderson interview clips.
"Rockpop", German TV (1980): "North Sea Oil"; "Old Ghosts" (both tracks live in the studio)
German TV (1980): "Fylingdale Flyer" (combines "A" promo stills with the audio track)
"Rockpop", German TV (1981): "Crossfire"; "Fylingdale Flyer" (both tracks live in the studio)
"Slipstream" video (1982): "Black Sunday"; "Dun Ringill"; "Flyingdale Flyer"; "Songs From The Wood"; "Heavy Horses"; "Sweet Dream"; "Too Old To Rock 'N' Roll: Too Young To Die"; "Skating Away On The Thin Ice Of The New Day"; "Aqualung"; "Locomotive Breath."
Austrian TV (1982): A 45-minute edit of the above video.

"The David Letterman Show", NBC-TV, US (1982): 13-minutes of music and interviews

"Roma 7 Up", Italian TV (05/02/82): "Clasp"; "Fallen On Hard Times"; "Pussy Willow"; "Broadsword"; "Seal Driver"; "Songs From The Wood"; "Watching Me Watching You"; "Pibroch (instrumental)"; "Beastie"; "Too Old To Rock 'N' Roll: Too Young To Die"; "Cross-Eyed Mary"; "Minstrel In The Gallery"; "Locomotive Breath"; "Cheerio" - all songs live from Rome

"Roma 7 Up", Italian TV (05/02/82): "Beastie"; interview; "Pussy Willow"; "Aqualung" - a pre-concert appearance recorded in a Rome TV studio

"Rockpop", German TV (06/10/82): "Fallen On Hard Times"; "Pussy Willow"; "Heavy Horses"; "Jack-In-The-Green"; instrumental; "Sweet Dream"; "Aqualung"; "Locomotive Breath"; "Black Sunday"; "Cheerio" - all songs live from the 05/29/82 Dortmund Westfalenhalle show

"Drehscheibe", German TV (1982): "Broadsword"

"Munchener Abendschau", German TV (1982): "Broadsword"

"Na Sowas", German TV (1982): "Broadsword" with Bruce Rowlands miming the drums

Swedish TV (1982): "Broadsword"

"Jethro Tull In Concert", London Weekend Television, UK (1982): one hour program including the full-length video of "Heavy Horses"

"The Prince's Trust Gala" (07/21/82): "Jack-In-The-Green"; "Pussy Willow" - live charity gig at London's Dominion Theatre with Phil Collins on drums.

Yorkshire TV, UK (08/27/82): "Aqualung" clip from Slipstream and an interview with Ian Anderson dressed in a kilt

VARA TV, Holland (11/06/82): Ian Anderson interview and Tull performance outtakes. The group R.E.M. was also featured on this program.

"Food And Drink", BBC2, UK (06/02/83): interview and film of Ian Anderson discussing his Scottish salmon farm

"The Leo Sayer Show", BBC, UK (1983): "Fly By Night" mimed by Ian Anderson and Peter-John Vettese

"Rock Classic Nacht", German TV (11/15/83): "Made In England"; "Fly By Night"; "Fat Man"; Jam. Eberhard Schoener put this disastrous show together, and Jethro Tull was accompanied by an orchestra at the Munchen Atlas Circus tent. The jam features Fela Kuti and his band (including Jack Bruce) and Ian Anderson.

"Pebble Mill At One", BBC1, UK (11/30/83): interview; "Fly By Night" (mimed by Ian Anderson and Peter-John Vettese)

"The Blood Of The British", Channel 4, UK (see dates below): This was an eight-episode series that used "Coronach" by Jethro Tull and David Palmer, and that song and other Palmer-written and arranged instrumentals were used on their own and as musical beds for the narrative. The following is the episode information:

   "The Past Is Not Another Place" (first airdate: 09/13/84): Coronach 1 (0:30); Monuments; Ritual Landscape; Coronach 2 (1:30)

   "Ritual Landscape" (first airdate: 09/20/84): Coronach 1; Long Barrows; Tombs; Stone Rings; Monuments; Coronach 2

   "Civil Defence" (first airdate: 09/27/84): Coronach 1; Ritual Landscape; Weapons; Long Barrows; Coronach 2

   "European Community" (first airdate: 10/04/84): Coronach 1; Saxon Museum; Fanfare; Roman Part 2; Hadrian's Wall; Aerials Of Britain; Coronach 2

   "Romans And Countrymen" (first airdate: 10/11/84): Coronach 1; Hadrian's Wall; Treasure; Romans Part 1; South Cadbury; Coronach 2

   "Who Were The English?" (first airdate: 10/18/84): Coronach 1; Saxon Museum (0:51); Saxon Museum (0:52); Saxon Museum (0:20); Saxon Art; Coronach 2

   "Pirates And Pastoralists" (first airdate: 10/25/84): Coronach 1; Viking Raid On Lindisfarne; Birka; Maiden Castle; Viking Village; Coronach 2

   "My Own Ancestor" (first airdate: 11/08/84): Coronach 1; Fanfare; Conquest Of Britain; Roman Part 2; Cadbury Hillfort; Morman Churches; Saxon Art; Opening Title Music; Aerials Of Britain; Coronach 2

"Musik Convoy", German TV (1984): "Lap Of Luxury" (miming in studio)

"Lap Of Luxury" promotional video (1984): its only UK showing was on program below. This video was shown on MTV and other video networks.

"Breakfast TV", BBC 1, UK (09/09/84): clip of "Lap Of Luxury" video and interview with Mike Smith

"Tele Illustrierte", German TV (1984): live clips and an interview

"Rock Influences", MTV, US (12/18/84): interviews; "Aqualung"; "Living In The Past"; "Thick As A Brick"; "Under Wraps"; "Locomotive Breath." This one-hour program covered the history of progressive rock, and half of it was by Jethro Tull! Live tracks were taken from a 10/28/84 performance in Passaic, NJ.

"The Tube", Channel 4, UK (02/01/85): Ian Anderson interview with Jools Holland

"Bach Rock", German TV (03/16/85): "Black Sunday"; "Hunting Girl"; "Elegy"; "Living In The Past"; "Serenade To A Cuckoo"; "Too Old To Rock 'N' Roll: Too Young To Die"; "Wond'ring Aloud"; "Bourée"; Bach's "Double Violin Concerto"; "Aqualung"; "Locomotive Breath" (all tracks live from Berlin)

"Berlin Abendschau", German TV (03/16/85): rehearsal for Berlin gig

"New Lairds Of The Isles", BBC, UK (1985): interviews and film of Ian Anderson working on his salmon farm and on stage plus interview with factory staff

"The Tube", Channel 4, UK (1986): a feature on Blackpool with Jools Holland interviewing Ian Anderson

"The Blood Of The British", Channel 4 (re-broadcast starting on 06/11/86): see above for program details

"Island 25", UK TV (1987): with Jethro Tull, Fairport Convention, John Martyn, Peter Cooke and Dudley Moore

"Fish 'N' Sheep 'N' Rock 'N' Roll", UK TV (09/15/87): Ian Anderson as a businessman, Scottish laird and rock performer. Of the skimpy live footage provided, Hyde Park (1968) and recent Milton Keynes concerts were represented in its 9+ minutes of music.

"Farming Outlook", UK TV (broadcast north of Leeds only) (10/04/87): a shorter version of "Fish 'N' Sheep 'N' Rock 'N' Roll"

"Steel Monkey" promotional video (10/87): shown on MTV and other stations

Guest VJ, MTV (10/20/87): with Ian Anderson

"The Kevin Seal Show", MTV, US (11/18/87): "Serenade To A Cuckoo," "Skating On The Thin Ice Of The New Day"

"Night Network", London Weekend Television, UK (12/87): a repeat of the "Slipstream" video

"20 Years Of Jethro Tull", Sky cable TV (UK), Finland TV and Italian TV (1988): this program was shown a number of times on each station

"Garden Party", BBC, UK (1988): a brief Ian Anderson interview and the "Steel Monkey" video

"Kissing Willie" promotional video (1989): shown on Italian TV and MTV

"Fish 'N' Sheep 'N' Rock 'N' Roll", Discovery, US (08/20/89, 12/22/89 and during one week in 12/90): first US broadcast of this program

Italian TV (1990): Jethro Tull appeared four times early in that year

"The Vet", BBC, UK (1990): this documentary featured Ian and Shona Anderson

"The David Letterman Show", NBC-TV, US (08/19/91): "This Is Not Love"

"Peter's Pop Show", German TV (12/21/92): Jethro Tull lip-synched two songs during this 5-hour program

"The Tonight Show", NBC-TV, US (04/28/93): "Living In The Past"

German TV (06/19/93): "For A Thousand Mothers," "Living In The Past," "Some Day The Sun Won't Shine For You"

"Another Day In Chile", Chilean TV (10/29/93): live footage from Santiago, Chile

"Live with Regis And Kathie Lee", ABC-TV, US (04/05/94): "Rare And Precious Chain" and "Bourée"

Chilean TV (03/06/96): footage from a gig in Santiago, Chile

"1 Day In Caracas, Venezuela", Venezuelan TV (03/23/96): live from that night's gig

"Friday Night", US (12/01/96): A 10-minute appearance with "Life Is A Long Song," "Locomotive Breath" and "Up The 'Pool"

Austrian TV (03/98): three mimed songs with Ian Anderson's son James sitting in on drums

"Mick Jagger - Biography", Discovery Channel (03/99): A short Ian Anderson interview clip discussing Mick Jagger

"Politically Incorrect with Bill Maher", ABC-TV (05/11/99): with Ian Anderson and Dr. Joyce Brothers

"Ohne Filter", German TV (09/10/99): a 06/15/99 televised show in Baden-Baden with an audience of 250

Italian TV (fall 1999): footage from the Pistoia Blues Festival on 07/18/99

Czech TV (fall 1999): Ian Anderson home footage and interview

"House Of Blues" webcast, http://www.houseofblues.com (12/03/99): the 10/08/99 concert from that L.A. venue

"2 Meter Sessies", Dutch TV (RTL5) (12/15/99): 10/19/99 Dutch concert footage from Wisseloord Studios in Hilversum, Holland

JETHRO TULL - TOUR DATE LISTING (1965-2000)
All dates are in the US unless otherwise noted

NOTE: Dates for The Blades (1963 - 1965), The John Evan Band (1965 - February 1966 and September 1966 - March 1967) and Jethro Tull (February - December 1968) are incomplete at this time.

JOHN EVAN BAND
1965
12/20   Blackpool Grammar School for Boys, Blackpool, UK (John Evans Blues Band)

1966
03/05-03/06 Elizabethan Club, Kirkam, UK
03/16   Waterloo Hotel, Waterloo, UK
03/17-03/18 Elizabethan Club, Kirkam, UK
03/19   Golden Torch, Stoke, UK
03/20   Top Twenty, Oldham, UK
03/21   Winsford, Cheshire, UK
03/22   Mecca, Blackpool, UK
03/23   Blackpool Tech College, Blackpool, UK
03/24   Cabus YC, Garstang, UK
03/26   Top Twenty, Oldham, UK
03/28   Marlborough Hotel, Marlborough, UK
03/30   "99" Club, Barrow, UK
04/01   Pilling British Legion, Pilling, UK (John Evans Blues Band with The Dolly Blues)
04/02-04/03 Twisted Wheel, Manchester, UK (John Evan Band)
04/04   Blackpool Grammar School, Blackpool, UK
04/09   Kings Own, Fleetwood, UK
04/11   Oasis, Manchester, UK (John Evans Blues Band)
04/17   Room At The Top, Wigan, UK
04/21   Talbot Conservative Club, Talbot, UK (John Evan Band, plus Jeff Jones and Eddie Martin)
04/22   Garstang, UK
04/23   Warrington Co-Op, Warrington, UK
04/24   Bolton, Palais, UK (with Bald Brian Rossi)
04/30   Peppermint Lounge, Liverpool, UK
05/01   Golden Torch, Stoke, UK
05/03   Mecca, Blackpool, UK
05/06   Wally's Disc Club, Preston, UK
05/07-05/08 "99" Club, Barrow, UK
05/13   Jigsaw, Manchester, UK
05/15   Burnley Miners Home, Burnley, UK
05/19   Savoy Bowl, Blackpool, UK
05/20   Palatine Hotel, Blackpool, UK
05/21   Room At The Top, Wigan, UK
05/22   British Legion, Barrow, UK
05/26   Layton Institute, Layton, UK
05/28   Warrington Co-Op, Warrington, UK
05/29   Top Twenty, Oldham, UK
05/31   Oasis, Manchester, UK
06/04   British Cellophane, Barrow, UK (opened for Herman's Hermits)
06/10   Top Twenty, Oldham, UK
06/11   Room At The Top, Wigan, UK
06/12   Twisted Wheel, Blackpool, UK
06/13   "99" Club, Barrow, UK (opened for Herman's Hermits)
06/24   Oasis, Manchester, UK
06/25   Top Twenty, Oldham, UK
06/27   Palatine Hotel, Blackpool, UK
06/29   Red Robin, Manchester, UK
07/01   Room At The Top, Wigan, UK
07/02   Kings Own, Fleetwood, UK
07/03   Gretna Hall, Carlisle, UK
07/07   Palatine Hotel, Blackpool, UK
07/08   Rialto Rooms, Derby, UK
07/09   Warrington Co-Op, Warrington, UK
07/10   The Dungeon Club, Nottingham, UK (John Evans Band)
07/14   Savoy Bowl, Blackpool, UK
07/15   Assembly Rooms, Garstang, UK
07/16   Top Twenty, Droylsden, UK
07/17   Twisted Wheel, Blackpool, UK
07/20   Beachcomber Club, Bolton, UK (John Evan Band)
07/21   Manor Lounge, Stockport, UK
07/23   Oasis Club, Manchester, UK
07/24   Brittania Rowing Club, Nottingham, UK (with John Mayall's Bluesbreakers)
07/29   Southbank Jazz Club, Grimsby, UK
07/30   Place, Hanley, UK
07/31   Belle Vue, Manchester, UK
08/02   Peppermint Lounge, Liverpool, UK
08/04   BRC Club, Stafford, UK
08/06   Cavern, Liverpool, UK
08/07   Britannia Rowing Club, Nottingham, UK (John Evans Big Soul Band)
08/08   Mr. Smith's, Winsford, UK
08/10-08/12 Twisted Wheel, Blackpool, UK
08/13   Aztec Club, Sunderland, UK (John Mayall cancelled)
08/14   "45" Club, Whitley Bay, UK
08/15   Casino Theatre Club, Blackpool, UK (John Evan Band)
08/22   Beachcomber Club, Preston, UK
08/25   Manor Lounge, Stockport, UK
08/27   Top Of The Town, Manchester, UK (John Evans Band) and Cavern, Liverpool, UK (John Evan Band with Crispian St. Peters, Koobas, Hideaways, Puppets, Times and Mad Monks)
08/28   Victoria Ballroom, Chesterfield, UK

08/29   Royal Lido, Prestatyn, UK
08/30   Peppermint Lounge, Liverpool, UK
09/01   Locarno, Sheffield, UK
09/02   Raven Club, RAF Waddington, UK
09/05   Casino Theatre Club, Blackpool, UK (John Evan Band plus The Outrage)
09/10   Aztec Club, Sunderland, UK
09/12   Quanitways, Chester, UK
09/16   Top Of The Town, Manchester, UK
09/17   Club A-Go-Go, Newcastle, UK
09/18   Nottingham Boat Club, Nottingham, UK (John Evans Big Soul Band; with Bald Brian Rossi)
09/##   Casterton, UK (this was the show recorded by Neil Smith that became the album "The John Evan Band '66")
10/22   Stax, Manchester, UK (John Evans Band) - every Monday gig afterward
11/##   Banqueting Rooms, Tower Ballroom, Blackpool, UK
11/##   Union Rowing Club, Sunderland, UK (with The Graham Bond Organisation)
11/##   Trent Boat Club, Nottingham, UK
11/28   Stax, Manchester, UK (John Evan Band)
12/11   Nottingham Boat Club, Nottingham, UK (John Evans Band)
12/16   Nottingham Boat Club, Nottingham, UK (John Evans Band)

1967
02/04   Union Rowing Club, Sunderland, UK (John Evans Smash)
02/##   Blackpool, UK
03/25   Lower Chamber, Rochdale, UK (John Evans Smash)
03/26   Beachcomber Club, Caesar's, Luton, UK (John Evans Smash)
03/27   Maple Ballroom, Northampton, UK (John Evans Smash)
04/01   Oasis, Manchester, UK (John Evans Smash)
04/02   Jazz Workshop, Scunthorpe, UK (John Evans Smash)
04/07   Nottingham Boat Club, Nottingham, UK (John Evans Smash)
04/08   Dagenham Irish Social Club, Dagenham, UK (John Evans Smash)
04/09   Beachcomber, Bolton, UK (John Evans Smash)
04/14   Co-Op, St. Helens, UK (John Evans Smash)
04/15   Bath, UK (John Evans Smash)
04/21   T.T. Vickers Social Club, Newton-Le-Willows, UK (John Evans Smash)
04/22   Haggerstone Castle, Haggerstone, UK (John Evans Smash)
04/23   Muddersfield Plaza, Muddersfield, UK (John Evans Smash)
04/29   St. Andrew's Hall, Wellingborough, UK (John Evans Smash)
04/30   Grimsby Jazz Club, Grimsby, UK (John Evans Band)
05/01   Carlton, Warrington, UK (John Evans Band)
05/03   Moulin Rouge, Southport (John Evans Smash; opened for Pink Floyd with their psychedelic light show)
05/05   Nottingham Boat Club, Nottingham, UK (John Evans Smash)
05/06   Pendulum Club, Rotherham, UK (John Evans Smash)
05/12   Kendal Town Hall, Kendal, UK (John Evans Smash)
05/13   Iron Curtain Club, Birmingham, UK (John Evans Smash)
05/14   George Hotel, Willby, UK (John Evans Smash)
05/15   Carlton, Warrington (John Evans Smash)
05/18   Beachcomber, Bolton, UK (John Evans Smash)
05/19   Hull Technical College, Hull, UK (John Evans Smash)
05/20   Birmingham Art Centre, Birmingham, UK (John Evans Smash)
05/21   Cosmo Club, Carlisle, UK (John Evans Smash)
05/26   Beachcomber, Nottingham, UK (John Evans Smash)
05/27   Spinning Disc, Leeds, UK (John Evans Smash)
05/28   Cromwellian, Bolton, UK (John Evans Smash)
06/01   Club-A-Go-Go, Newcastle, UK (John Evans Smash)
06/03   The Rink, West Martlepool, UK (John Evans Smash)
06/09   Kenwood Club and Mr. Smith's (both in Manchester, UK) (John Evans Smash)
06/10   Pendulum, Rotherham, UK (John Evans Smash)
06/13   Didsbury College, Manchester, UK (John Evans Smash opened for Ten Years After; Cock A Hoop was also on the bill)
06/16   Nottingham Boat Club, Nottingham, UK (John Evans Band)
06/17   Beachcomber, Caesar's, Luton, UK (John Evans Smash)
06/18   Sportsman's, Wigan, UK (John Evans Smash)
06/19   Marquee Club, London, UK (John Evan Smash; opening for The Herd)
06/23   Nottingham Boat Club, Nottingham, UK (John Evans Band)
06/24   Birmingham University, Birmingham, UK (John Evans Band)
06/30   Nottingham Boat Club, Nottingham, UK (John Evans Band)
07/01   N.E. Cheshire Show, Hazel Grove, Cheshire, UK (John Evans Smash)
07/02   Le Metro, Birmingham, UK (John Evans Smash)
07/03   Quaintways, Chester, UK (John Evans Smash)
07/08   Keighley, UK (John Evans Smash)
07/09   Jazz Workshop, Scunthorpe, UK (John Evans Smash)
07/11   Winter Gardens, Cleethorpes, UK (John Evans Smash)
07/14   Boulevard, Tadcaster, UK (John Evans Smash)
07/15   De Valance Ballroom, Tenby, UK (John Evans Smash)
07/16   Ship & Rainbow, Wolverhampton, UK (John Evans Smash)
07/18   Bournemouth Pavilion, Bournemouth, UK (John Evans Smash)
07/20   Swanage Municipal Hall, Swanage, UK (John Evan Smash; opening for Simon Dupree And The Big Sound)
07/21   Bournemouth Pavilion, Bournemouth, UK (John Evans Smash)
07/22   Lymington, UK (John Evans Smash)
07/23   George Hotel, Willby, UK (John Evans Smash)
07/28   Jazz Club, Grimsby, UK (John Evans Smash)
07/30   The Thing, Oldham, UK (John Evans Smash)
08/04   Marquee Club, London, UK (John Evan Smash was supposed to open for The

	Creation, but their van broke down)
08/07	Eriskay Ballroom, Ammanford, UK (John Evans Smash)
08/09	Glanford Jazz Club, Glanford, UK (John Evans Smash)
08/10	The Ritz, Skewen, UK (John Evans Smash)
08/11	Swansea, Wales, UK (John Evans Smash)
08/12	The Ritz, Skewen, UK (John Evans Smash)
08/19	Matlock Bath Pavilion, Matlock Bath, UK (John Evans Smash; with The Crazy World Of Arthur Brown)
08/26	Club-A-Go-Go, Newcastle, UK (John Evans Smash)
08/27	Peterlee Jazz Club, Peterlee, UK (John Evans Smash)
08/28	Quaintways, Chester, UK (John Evans Smash)
09/09	Cottingham Civic Hall, Cottingham, UK (John Evans Smash)
09/11	The Belfry, Birmingham, UK (John Evans Smash)
09/16	Golden Disc Club, Keighley, UK (John Evans Smash)
09/17	Cromwellian, Bolton, UK (John Evans Smash)
09/22	Hull University, Hull, UK (John Evans Smash)
09/23	Nottingham University, Nottingham, UK (John Evans Smash)
09/24	Tabernacle, Stockport, UK (John Evans Smash)
09/29	Hollins College, Manchester, UK (John Evans Smash)
09/30	The Clouds, Derby, UK (John Evans Smash)
10/01	Nottingham Boat Club, Nottingham, UK (John Evans Smash)
10/07	Bradford University, Bradford, UK (John Evans Smash)
10/08	Morecambe Pier, Morecambe, UK (John Evans Smash)
10/13	Boulevard, Tadcaster, UK (John Evans Smash)
10/14	Manchester University, Manchester, UK (John Evans Smash)
10/20	Chateau Impney, Droitwich, UK (John Evans Smash)
10/21	Beachcomber Club, Caesar's, Luton, UK (John Evans Smash)
10/25	Lancaster University, Lancaster, UK (John Evans Smash)
10/28	York University, York, UK (John Evans Smash)
10/29	Cosmo, Carlisle, UK (John Evans Smash)
10/31	Hunting Hill Lodge, UK (John Evans Smash)
11/04	Sheffield College of Education, Sheffield, UK (John Evans Smash)
11/10	Manchester University, Manchester, UK (John Evans Smash)
11/17	Co-Op, St. Helen's, UK (John Evans Smash)
11/18	Madeley College, Crewe, UK (John Evans Smash)
11/24	Aston University, Birmingham, UK (John Evans Smash)
11/25	St. Peter's College, Birmingham, UK (John Evans Smash)
12/01	Loughborough University, Loughborough, UK (John Evans Smash)
12/02	Barking Tech., Barking, UK (John Evans Smash; with Graham Bond)
12/08	Boulevard, Tadcaster, UK (John Evans Smash)
12/11	Adelphi Ballroom, Slough, UK (John Evans Smash)
12/14	Marquee Club, London, UK (Bag O'Blues; opening act was The Remo Four)
12/15	Salford Technical College, Salford, UK (John Evans Smash)
12/16	Marlow Technical College, Marlow, UK (John Evans Smash)
12/17	Le Metro, Birmingham, UK (John Evans Smash)
12/19	Sixth Form College, Luton, UK (John Evans Smash)
12/22	Club 65, Doncaster, UK (John Evans Smash)

1968

01/16	Marquee Club, London, UK (Navy Blue; opened for Black Cat Bones, who were substituting for Peter Green's Fleetwood Mac and Eddie Boyd)
02/02	Marquee Club, London, UK (with Savoy Brown Blues Band)
02/09	Marquee Club, London, UK (with Eddie Boyd and Black Cat Bones)
02/16	Marquee Club, London, UK (with The Spirit Of John Morgan)
03/15	Marquee Club, London, UK (with Aynsley Dunbar Retaliation)
03/18	Star Hotel, Croydon, UK
03/26	Cromwellian, London, UK
03/29	Marquee Club, London, UK (with Fleetwood Mac)
04/15	Marquee Club, London, UK (with The Bonzo Dog Doo-Dah Band)
04/16	Wood Green Fishmongers Arms, London, UK
04/22	Star Hotel, Croydon, UK
05/03	Marquee Club, London, UK (with The New Nadir)
05/05	The Queens Stag Hounds, Ascot, UK
05/17	Marquee Club, London, UK (with Taste)
05/20	The Nags Head, London, UK
05/25	Bradford, UK
05/26	Coventry, UK (they replaced Jeff Beck for this gig)
05/29	Marlow, UK
05/30	Hull, UK
05/31	Marquee Club, London, UK (with The Spirit Of John Morgan)
06/14	Marquee Club, London, UK (with Duster Bennett)
06/15	Klooks Kleek, West Hampstead, UK
06/18	Klooks Kleek, West Hampstead, UK
06/21	Candle Light Club, Scarborough, UK
06/28	Marquee Club, London, UK (2 shows; with Tramline)
06/29	Hyde Park, London, UK (Jethro Tull opened for Pink Floyd; also appearing: Tyrannosaurus Rex and Roy Harper)
07/05	Marquee Club, London, UK (with Thackery)
07/11	Railway Hotel, Wealdstone, UK
07/19	Marquee Club, London, UK (with Dynaflow Blues Band)
07/20	The Magic Village, Manchester, UK
07/26	Marquee Club, London, UK (with Black Cat Bones)
08/04	Mothers, Birmingham, UK
08/07	The Manor House, London, UK
08/09	Marquee Club, London, UK (with Black Cat Bones)
08/11	8th National Jazz And Blues Festival, Kempton Park, Sunbury, UK (with Deep Purple, Eclection, Fairport Convention, The Incredible String Band, John Mayall, The Spencer Davis Group and Traffic)
08/21	Mothers, Birmingham, UK
08/23	Marquee Club, London, UK (with Duster Bennett)
08/28	The Country Club NW3, London, UK
08/29	Railway Hotel, Wealdstone, UK
09/07	The Magic Village, Manchester, UK
09/09	The Nags Head, London, UK
09/20	Marquee Club, London, UK (with Love Sculpture)
09/21	Mothers, Birmingham, UK
09/23	Edmonton Cooks Ferry Inn, London, UK
10/05	Brondby Pop Club, Copenhagen, Denmark (with The Jeff Beck Group)
10/06	Star Club, Copenhagen, Denmark (another gig with The Jeff Beck Group, but Beck didn't show up. Concert ads for this show and the previous gig definitely list Jethro Tull on the bill.)
10/11	Marquee Club, London, UK (with The Spirit Of John Morgan)
10/15	Royal Albert Hall, London, UK
10/16	The Toby Jug, Tolworth, UK
10/22	Wood Green Fishmongers Arms, London, UK
10/24	Red Lion Hotel, Leytonstone, UK
10/29	Crown Hotel, Birmingham, UK
11/01	California Ballroom, Dunstable, UK
11/02	Chalk Farm Roundhouse, London, UK
11/05	Klooks Kleek, West Hampstead, UK
11/09	Town Hall, Glastonbury, UK
11/15	Hornsey Wood Tavern, London, UK
11/24	Mothers, Birmingham, UK
11/26	Marquee Club, London, UK (with Bakerloo Blues Line)
11/29	Vandike Club, Plymouth, UK (with Gethsemane)
11/30	School of Economics, London, UK (with Earth)
12/11	Intertel Studios, Wembley, London, UK - "Rolling Stones Rock & Roll Circus" TV program
12/20	Marquee Club, London, UK (cancelled)

1969

01/02	Winter Gardens, Penzance, UK
01/03	Ritz, Bournemouth, UK
01/04	Vandike Club, Plymouth, UK
01/05	Nottingham Boat Club, Nottingham, UK
01/07	Bath Pavilion, Bath, UK
01/08	The Toby Jug, Tolworth, UK
01/09	Koncerthaus, Stockholm, Sweden (2 shows; opening for Jimi Hendrix)
01/10	Falconer Theater, Copenhagen, Denmark
01/11	Norwich Gala, Norwich, UK
01/12	Redcar Jazz Club, Redcar, UK
01/14	Speakeasy Club, London, UK
01/15	Keele University, Keele, UK
01/16	Lafayette Club, Wolverhampton, UK
01/18	Manchester University, Manchester, UK
01/24-01/25	Fillmore East, New York, NY (Jethro Tull and Gay Desperados Steel Band opened for Blood, Sweat & Tears)
01/31-02/02	Grande Ballroom, Detroit, MI (with Mitch Ryder on 01/31, Spirit on 02/01, and SRC on 02/02)
02/07-02/08	Kinetic Playground, Chicago, IL (with Led Zeppelin and Jethro Tull opening for The Vanilla Fudge)
02/09	Labor Temple, Minneapolis, MN (with Rotary Connection)
02/13-02/15	Boston Tea Party, Boston, MA (with Silver Apples)
02/16	State University of New York at Stony Brook, Stony Brook, NY (with Mountain - The Jeff Beck Group cancelled)
02/20-02/23	Stone Balloon, New Haven, CT
02/28	Worcester Memorial Auditorium, Worcester, MA (cancelled; this show was to include The Jeff Beck Group and Mountain.)
03/01	Alexandria Roller Rink, Alexandria, VA (2 shows opening for The Jeff Beck Group and Mountain.)
03/02	Symphony Hall, Boston, MA (cancelled; this show was to include The Jeff Beck Group)
03/07-03/09	Eagles Ballroom, Seattle, WA (with Sanpaku, opened for MC5)
03/13-03/16	Fillmore West, San Francisco, CA (opened for Creedence Clearwater Revival)
03/21-03/22	Rose Palace, Pasadena, CA (with The Grateful Dead and Paul Butterfield)
03/23	Sound Factory, Sacramento, CA (with A.B. Skhy and Linn County)
03/28-03/29	Aquarius Theater, Phoenix, AZ (with Zephyr and Goose Creek Symphony)
03/31	Aquarius Theater, Los Angeles, CA (with Chicago Transit Authority)
04/05	Pittsburgh, PA
04/06	Evansville, IL
04/07-04/08	Grande Ballroom, Detroit, MI
04/09	Boston Tea Party, Boston, MA (with Sweetwater)
04/11	Fillmore East, New York, NY (The 8PM show had Jethro Tull opening for Blood, Sweat & Tears. Albert King opened the 11:30PM show for Blood, Sweat & Tears.)
05/03	Leas Cliff Hall, Folkstone, UK
05/06	Free Trade Hall, Manchester, UK (with Ten Years After and Clouds)
05/07	Palais des Sports, Paris, France
05/08	Royal Albert Hall, London, UK (with Ten Years After and Clouds)
05/09	Colston Hall, Bristol, UK (with Ten Years After and Clouds)
05/11	Redcar Jazz Club, Redcar, UK (with Ten Years After and Clouds)
05/13	Guildhall, Portsmouth, UK (with Ten Years After and Clouds)
05/14	City Hall, Newcastle, UK (with Ten Years After and Clouds)
05/15	Town Hall, Birmingham, UK (with Ten Years After and Clouds)
05/17	Gala Ballroom, Norwich, UK
05/23	Abergaveney, UK (with Fleetwood Mac)
05/24	Coventry, UK (with Amen Corner)
05/28	Dublin National Stadium, Dublin, Ireland (with Skid Row and Orphanage)
05/29	Ulster Hall, Belfast, N. Ireland
05/30	Cork, Ireland
05/31	Weston-Super-Mare, UK
06/04	Sherwood Rooms, Nottingham, UK (with Colosseum and Liverpool Scene)
06/05	Assembly Halls, Worthing, UK
06/06	Vandike Club, Plymouth, UK
06/07	Roundhouse, Dagenham, UK
06/09	Cambridge, UK (with Colosseum)
06/12	Locarno, Hull, UK
06/13	Bay Hotel, Sunderland, UK
06/14	Winter Gardens, Malvern, UK
06/15	Lafayette Club, Wolverhampton, UK
06/17	Middlesborough, UK
06/20 - 06/21	Newport Pop Festival, Devonshire Downs, CA (with Eric Burdon & The Animals, Spirit, Cat Mother, Steppenwolf, Creedence Clearwater Revival and The Chambers Brothers. Jimi Hendrix performed on 06/20.)

06/24	Detroit, MI
06/28	Miami Jazz Festival, Miami, FL (with Dave Brubeck, Gerry Mulligan, Miles Davis, Nina Simone, Booker T. & The M.G.'s, George Benson and Roland Kirk)
07/03	Fillmore East, New York, NY (with Jeff Beck Group and Soft White Underbelly, the precursor of Blue Öyster Cult)
07/04	16th Annual Newport Jazz Festival, Festival Field, Newport, RI (also on the bill that night: Blood, Sweat & Tears, Roland Kirk, Steve Marcus, Ten Years After and Jeff Beck - the only time rock bands are invited to play at the event. Frank Zappa and Led Zeppelin played the next night.)
07/05	New York Pop Festival, Downing Stadium, Randall's Island, New York, NY (with The Jeff Beck Group, Grand Funk Railroad, Steppenwolf and John Sebastian - the City Hall, Portland, ME gig was cancelled)
07/11	Newport Jazz Festival, Laurel Springs, MD (with Ray Charles, Woody Herman, Edwin Hawkins, Johnny Winter, Al Kooper, Buddy Guy and Led Zeppelin)
07/12	Newport Jazz Festival, Philadelphia, PA (with Led Zeppelin, Al Kooper, Buddy Guy and Johnny Winter)
07/13	Singer Bowl Music Festival, Flushing Meadows Park, Flushing, NY (not a Jethro Tull show, but Glenn Cornick and Clive Bunker joined members of Vanilla Fudge, The Jeff Beck Group, Ten Years After and Led Zeppelin on the show-ending jam "Jailhouse Rock")
07/15-07/17	The Revolution, Monticello, NY (with Jeff Beck and Ravens)
07/18-07/19	Kinetic Playground, Chicago, IL (with Led Zeppelin and Savoy Brown)
07/22	Stony Brook University, Stony Brook, NY
07/23-07/25	Boston Tea Party, Boston, MA (with Free and Terry Reid 07/24 - 07/25)
07/26	Newport Jazz Festival, New Brunswick, NJ (with B.B. King)
07/27	Grande Ballroom, Detroit, MI (with Jeff Beck, Zephyr, Jim Schwall and MC5 - all groups cancelled out)
07/28	Central Park, New York, NY (with Paul Butterfield)
08/01	Earl Warren Showgrounds (Fairgrounds Arena), Santa Barbara, CA (with Led Zeppelin and Fraternity Of Man)
08/02-08/03	Eagles Ballroom, Seattle, WA
08/08	Swing Auditorium, San Bernardino, CA (with Led Zeppelin)
08/09	Anaheim Convention Center, Anaheim, CA (with Led Zeppelin)
08/10	San Diego Sports Arena, San Diego, CA (with Led Zeppelin)
08/12	Fillmore West, San Francisco, CA (with Chuck Berry)
08/14	Fillmore West, San Francisco, CA (with Chuck Berry; the previous night's show was cancelled)
08/15	San Antonio, TX (with Led Zeppelin)
08/16	Houston, TX
09/25	City Hall, Newcastle, UK (with Savoy Brown and Terry Reid)
09/26	Usher Hall, Edinburgh, Scotland (with Savoy Brown and Terry Reid)
09/27	National Stadium, Dublin, Ireland
09/29	Ulster Hall, Belfast, N. Ireland
10/01	Royal Albert Hall, London, UK (with Savoy Brown and Terry Reid)
10/02	Free Trade Hall, Manchester, UK (with Savoy Brown and Terry Reid)
10/03	Brighton Dome, Brighton, UK (with Savoy Brown and Terry Reid)
10/06	City Hall, Hull, UK (with Savoy Brown and Terry Reid)
10/07	Town Hall, Leeds, UK (with Savoy Brown and Terry Reid)
10/08	Town Hall, Birmingham, UK (with Savoy Brown and Terry Reid)
10/10	Concertgebouw, The Hague, Holland (with Free and Spooky Tooth)
10/11	Town Hall, Antwerp, Belgium (with Free and Spooky Tooth)
10/12	City Hall, Paris, France (with Free and Spooky Tooth)
10/15	City Hall, Sheffield, UK (with Savoy Brown and Terry Reid)
10/19	Rex Cinema, Cambridge, UK (with Savoy Brown and Terry Reid)
10/20	Guildhall, Southampton, UK (with Savoy Brown and Terry Reid)
10/21	Colston Hall, Bristol, UK (with Savoy Brown and Terry Reid)
10/23	De Montfort Hall, Leicester, UK (with Savoy Brown and Terry Reid)
10/25	Guildhall, Plymouth, UK (with Savoy Brown and Terry Reid)
10/26	Town Hall, Oxford, UK (with Savoy Brown and Terry Reid)
10/29	St. Andrews Hall, Norwich, UK (with Savoy Brown and Terry Reid)
11/14	Dane County Coliseum, Madison, WI
11/15	Hartford, CT (with Mountain and Roland Kirk - the Community Concourse, San Diego, CA gig was cancelled)
11/20-11/23	Fillmore West, San Francisco, CA (with MC5 and Sanpaku)
11/26	Civic Auditorium, Santa Monica, CA
11/27	San Diego, CA
11/28-11/29	Riviera Theater, Detroit, MI (with Chicago Transit Authority)
11/30	Spectrum, Philadelphia, PA (with The Sons [Of Champlain])
12/05-12/06	Fillmore East, New York, NY (2 shows both nights; with Grand Funk Railroad and Fat Mattress)
12/07	University of Massachusetts, Amherst, MA (with Spooky Tooth and Johnny Winter)
12/08-12/09	Boston Tea Party, Boston, MA
12/10	Soldiers and Sailors Auditorium, Kansas City, KS (with Joe Cocker and Fleetwood Mac)
12/11	Houston Music Hall, Houston, TX (2 shows; with Joe Cocker and Fleetwood Mac)
12/12	Municipal Auditorium, San Antonio, TX (with Fleetwood Mac)
12/13	Austin, TX (with Fleetwood Mac)
12/14	Aragon Ballroom, Chicago, IL (with Fat Mattress and Fleetwood Mac)
1970	
01/16	Odense, Denmark
01/17	K.B. Hallen, Copenhagen, Denmark
01/19	Helsinki, Finland
01/20	Kongligla Tennis Hallen, Stockholm, Sweden
01/21	Konserthuset, Gothenburg, Sweden
01/22	Lund, Sweden
02/21	Frankfurt Festhalle (Jahrhunderhalle), Frankfurt, Germany
04/05	Nuremberg, Germany
04/07	Musichalle, Hamburg, Germany
04/17-04/18	Mammoth Gardens, Denver, CO (with Zephyr)
04/19	Long Beach Arena, Long Beach, CA (with Eric Burdon & War)
04/20	Civic Auditorium, Honolulu, HI
04/22	Santa Barbara, CA

04/24	Swing Auditorium, San Bernardino, CA
04/25	Convention Hall, San Diego, CA
04/26	Santa Clara, CA (with Elvin Bishop)
04/28	Honolulu, HI
04/30-05/02	Fillmore West, San Francisco, CA (with Fairport Convention, Salt 'N Pepper and Clouds)
05/03	Devonshire Downs, San Fernando, CA
05/07	Tucson, AZ
05/08	Phoenix, AZ
05/09	Las Vegas, NV
05/10	Washington University Field House, St. Louis, MO (with Clouds, Pentangle, David Ackles, Paul Butterfield Band, Mecki Mark Men [from Sweden])
05/13	Dallas, TX
05/14	Houston Music Hall, Houston, TX
05/15	Austin, TX
05/16	University of Miami, Miami, FL (with Pacific Gas & Electric)
05/17	Cape Kennedy, FL
05/20	Hartford, CT (with Roland Kirk and John Sebastian)
05/21-05/23	Fillmore East, New York, NY (with John Sebastian and Clouds)
05/24	The Autostade, Montreal, PQ, Canada (with Johnny Winter, Van Morrison, Mountain and Jefferson Airplane)
05/28	Selby Stadium, Ohio Wesleyan University, Delaware, OH (with Mountain)
05/29-05/30	East Town Theater, Detroit, MI (with Mott The Hoople and Georgie Fame)
05/31	Minneapolis, MN
06/05	Aragon Ballroom, Chicago, IL (with Sha Na Na)
06/06	Cleveland, OH (with Lee Michaels)
07/03	Southampton, NY
07/04	Atlanta Pop Festival, Byron, GA (Jethro Tull cancelled their appearance on the second day of this three-day festival. Also on the bill was Jimi Hendrix, John Sebastian, Mountain, Procol Harum, Poco and Johnny Winter)
07/07	Tanglewood, MA (with The Who and It's A Beautiful Day)
07/08	The Spectrum, Philadelphia, PA (with Cactus and Blodwyn Pig)
07/10-07/11	Boston Tea Party, Boston, MA (with Cactus)
07/13	Shady Grove, MD (with Livingston Taylor)
07/14	Detroit, MI (with Cactus)
07/17	Randall's Island Festival, New York, NY (with Steppenwolf, Jimi Hendrix and Grand Funk Railroad)
07/18	New Orleans Warhouse, New Orleans, LA (with Mott The Hoople)
07/22	West Palm Beach, FL
07/24	Tampa, FL (with Mountain)
07/25	Curtis Hixon Hall, Miami, FL (with Mountain)
07/26	Jacksonville, FL (with Mountain)
07/27	Westbury, NY (with Livingston Taylor)
07/28-07/29	Capitol Theater, Port Chester, NY (with Livingston Taylor)
08/01	Powder Ridge Ski Area, Middlefield, CT (Jethro Tull cancelled their appearance on the second night of the three-day Powder Ridge Festival, which also featured Joe Cocker, Allman Brothers, Cactus, Little Richard, Van Morrison, Rhinocerous and Zephyr)
08/03	Central Park, New York, NY
08/05	Fillmore East, New York, NY (with Cactus)
08/07	Toronto Festival, Toronto, ON, Canada (with Melanie and Mountain)
08/09	Goose Lake Music Festival, Goose Lake Park, Jackson, MI
08/10	Red Rocks Amphitheater, Denver, CO (with Mountain)
08/11	Vancouver Coliseum, Vancouver, BC, Canada (with Fleetwood Mac)
08/15	Lake Geneva, WI
08/16	Aragon Ballroom, Chicago, IL (with Cactus)
08/30	Isle Of Wight Festival, Isle Of Wight, UK (with Jimi Hendrix and many others)
09/23	City Hall, Sheffield, UK
09/24	Albert Hall, Nottingham, UK
09/25	Birmingham Town Hall, Birmingham, UK (2 shows; with Tir Na Nog and Procol Harum)
09/27	City Hall, Newcastle, UK
09/28	De Montfort Hall, Leicester, UK
09/30	Aberdeen Music Hall, Aberdeen, Scotland
10/01	Caird Hall, Dundee, Scotland
10/02	Playhouse Cinema, Glasgow, Scotland
10/03	Free Trade Hall, Manchester, UK
10/04	Colston Hall, Bristol, UK
10/09	Guildhall, Southampton, UK
10/10	Olympia, Paris, France
10/13	Royal Albert Hall, London, UK
10/16	Sacramento, CA (with Charles Lloyd)
10/17	Berkeley Community Theater, Berkeley, CA (with Charles Lloyd)
10/18	Los Angeles Forum, Inglewood, CA (with Charles Lloyd and It's A Beautiful Day)
10/19	Anaheim Convention Center, Anaheim, CA
10/20	The Coliseum, Phoenix, AZ (with Sugarloaf and Leon Russell)
10/22	Swing Auditorium, San Bernardino, CA (with It's A Beautiful Day)
10/23	Oregon State University, Corvallis, OR
10/24	Seattle Arena, Seattle, WA
10/29	Detroit, MI
10/30	Pittsburgh Civic Arena, Pittsburgh, PA (with Mountain)
10/31	War Memorial Auditorium, Syracuse, NY
11/01	The Mosque, Richmond, VA
11/03	Comerford Paramount Theater, Wilkes-Barre, PA (2 shows; with Bob Seger System)
11/04	Carnegie Hall, New York, NY (with McKendree Spring)
11/05	Providence, RI
11/06	St. Anselm's College, Manchester, NH
11/07	Michigan State University, Lansing, MI
11/08	Kiel Opera House, St. Louis, MO (with Mott The Hoople)
11/09	The Ohio Theater, Columbus, OH (with Black Sabbath)
11/10	Derea, OH
11/11	Canton, NY
11/12	Kleinham's University, Buffalo, NY (with Livingston Taylor)
11/13	Union College, Schenectady, NY

11/14	War Memorial Auditorium, Rochester, NY
11/15	State University of New York at Plattsburgh, Plattsburgh, NY

1971

01/07	Odense, Denmark
01/08	Arhus, Denmark
01/09	K.B. Hallen, Copenhagen, Denmark
01/10	Gothenburg, Sweden
01/11	Konserthuset, Oslo, Norway
01/12	Kouserpalast, Bergen, Norway
01/14	Stockholm, Sweden
01/15	Tivoli Konsertsal, Copenhagen, Denmark
01/16	Holsted, Denmark
01/17	Musikhalle, Hamburg, Germany
01/18	Rheinhalle, Dusseldorf, Germany
01/19	Sporthalle Boblingen, Stuttgart, Germany
01/20	Nuremberg, Germany
01/21	Konzerthaus, Vienna, Austria
01/22	Deutsches Museum, Munich, Germany
01/23	Kongresshaus, Frankfurt, Germany
01/24	Deutschlandhalle, Berlin, Germany
01/25	Stadthalle, Wollsburg, Germany
01/26	Munsterlandhalle, Munster, Germany
01/27	Westfalenhalle, Dortmund, Germany
01/28	Stadthalle, Heidelberg, Germany
01/29	Stadthalle, Freiburg, Germany
01/30	Montreux, Switzerland
02/01	Teatro Smeraldo, Milan, Italy
02/02	Rome, Italy
02/26	Gaumont State Theatre, London, UK (2 shows)
02/28	Gaumont State Theatre, London, UK (2 shows)
03/03	Brighton Dome, Brighton, UK (with Steeleye Span)
03/05	Winter Gardens, Bournemouth, UK (with Steeleye Span)
03/07	Guildhall, Plymouth, UK (2 shows; with Steeleye Span)
03/11	Town Hall, Leeds, UK (with Steeleye Span)
03/12	Victoria Guildhall, Stoke-on-Trent, UK (with Steeleye Span)
03/13	Mountford Hall, Liverpool, UK (2 shows; with Steeleye Span)
03/14	Blackpool Opera House, Blackpool, UK (with Steeleye Span)
03/19	Empire Theatre, Edinburgh, Scotland (with Steeleye Span)
03/20	Empire Theatre, Sunderland, UK (2 shows; with Steeleye Span)
04/01	Minneapolis, MN
04/02	Civic Opera House, Chicago, IL
04/03	St. Louis, MO
04/04	Baltimore, MD
04/05-04/06	Fillmore East, New York, NY (with Edgar Winter's White Trash and Tin House. Jethro Tull replaced Cactus and Humble Pie, both of whom cancelled.)
04/13	Atlanta, GA
04/14	Milwaukee Uhlein, Milwaukee, WI (2 shows)
04/16-04/17	Miami, FL
04/18	Roanoke, VA
04/20	Detroit, MI
04/24	W. Long Branch, NJ
04/25	Stony Brook, NY
04/26	Greenville, NY
04/27	Port Chester, NY
04/29	Delhi, NY
05/01	Philadelphia, PA
05/02	Kutztown, PA
05/04-05/05	Fillmore East, New York, NY (with Cowboy)
06/09	Salt Palace, Salt Lake City, UT
06/10	Red Rocks Amphitheater, Denver, CO (with Livingston Taylor)
06/11	Albuquerque, NM
06/12	HIC Arena, Honolulu, HI
06/16-06/17	Golden Hall, San Diego, CA (with Livingston Taylor)
06/18	Los Angeles Forum, Los Angeles, CA
06/19	Anaheim Convention Center, Anaheim, CA
06/20	Berkeley Community Theater, Berkeley, CA
06/24	Edmonton, AB, Canada (with Yes)
06/25	Vancouver, BC, Canada (with Yes)
06/26	Seattle Coliseum, Seattle, WA (with Yes)
06/27	Sacramento, CA (with Yes)
06/29	Kansas City Auditorium, Kansas City, MO (with Yes)
06/30	Oklahoma City State Fairgrounds, Oklahoma City, OK (with Yes)
07/01	San Antonio, TX (with Yes)
07/02	Dallas Memorial Coliseum, Dallas, TX (with Yes)
07/03	Houston, TX (with Yes)
07/04	The Warehouse, New Orleans, LA (with Yes)
07/05	Vancouver Coliseum, Vancouver, BC, Canada
07/09	Wildwood Convention Center, Wildwood, NJ (with Yes)
07/10	Asbury Park Convention Hall, Asbury Park, NJ
07/11	Alexandria Roller Rink, Alexandria, VA (with Yes)
07/29	Port Chester, NY
10/15	Bayfront Center, St. Petersburg, FL
10/16	Civic Center, Springfield, MA
10/17	Columbia, MD
10/18	Madison Square Garden, New York, NY
10/19	Gill Coliseum, Corvallis, OR
10/20	Lowell Technical College, Lowell, MA
10/21	Civic Arena, Pittsburgh, PA
10/22	Detroit, MI
10/23	Veterans Auditorium, Columbus, OH
10/24	Dayton, OH
10/25	Sports Arena, Toledo, OH
10/26	Chicago Amphitheater, Chicago, IL
10/27	New Haven Arena, New Haven, CT
10/30	Rochester War Memorial, Rochester, NY
10/31	Binghamton, NY
11/01	Buffalo, NY
11/06	Durham, NC
11/10	Flint, MI
11/11	Memphis, TN
11/12	Louisville Convention Center, Louisville, KY
11/13	Cleveland Public Hall, Cleveland, OH
11/14	Albany, NY
11/15	Boston Tea Gardens, Boston, MA
11/18	Madison Square Garden, New York, NY

1972

01/06	Holsted, Denmark (with Gentle Giant)
01/07	Odenske, Denmark (with Gentle Giant)
01/08	K.B. Hallen, Copenhagen, Denmark (2 shows; with Gentle Giant)
01/09	Konserthuset, Gothenburg, Sweden (with Gentle Giant)
01/10	Konserthuset, Oslo, Norway (with Gentle Giant)
01/11	Stockholm, Sweden (with Gentle Giant)
01/14	Lund, Sweden (with Gentle Giant)
01/15-01/16	Tivoli Konsertsal, Copenhagen, Denmark (with Gentle Giant)
01/17	Munsterlandhalle, Munster, Germany (with Gentle Giant)
01/18	Deutchlandhalle, Berlin, Germany (with Gentle Giant)
01/19	Congress Centrum Halle, Hamburg, Germany (with Gentle Giant)
01/20	Hansahalle, Lubeck, Germany (with Gentle Giant)
01/21	Grugahalle, Essen, Germany (with Gentle Giant)
01/22	Stadthalle, Offerburg, Germany (with Gentle Giant)
01/23	Nuremberg, Germany (with Gentle Giant)
01/24	Konzerhaus, Vienna, Austria (with Gentle Giant)
01/26	Frederick Eberthalle, Ludwigshafen, Germany (with Gentle Giant)
01/27	Kuppelsaal, Hannover, Germany (with Gentle Giant)
01/28	Oberheimhalle, Offenburg, Germany (with Gentle Giant)
01/29	Hallenstadion, Zurich, Switzerland (with Gentle Giant)
01/30	Festhalle, Berne, Switzerland (with Gentle Giant)
01/31	Milan, Italy (with Gentle Giant)
02/01	Palasport (aka PalaEur), Rome, Italy (with Gentle Giant)
02/02	Naples, Italy (with Gentle Giant)
02/03	Bologna, Italy (with Gentle Giant)
02/04	Palasport, Novara, Italy (with Gentle Giant)
02/05	Palais des Sports, Lyons, France (with Gentle Giant)
02/06	Paris, France (with Gentle Giant)
02/11	De Doelen, Rotterdam, Holland (with Gentle Giant)
02/12	Concertgebouw, Amsterdam, Holland (with Gentle Giant)
03/02	Guildhall, Portsmouth, UK (with Tir Na Nog)
03/03	ABC Cinema, Exeter, UK (with Tir Na Nog)
03/04	Guildhall, Plymouth, UK (with Tir Na Nog)
03/05	Colston Hall, Bristol, UK (with Tir Na Nog)
03/06	Town Hall, Birmingham, UK (with Tir Na Nog)
03/07	City Hall, Newcastle, UK (with Tir Na Nog)
03/08	Central Hall, York, UK (with Tir Na Nog)
03/10	Winter Gardens, Bournemouth, UK (with Tir Na Nog)
03/11	City Hall, Sheffield, UK (with Tir Na Nog)
03/13	St. Andrews Hall, Norwich, UK (with Tir Na Nog)
03/14	De Montfort Hall, Leicester, UK (with Tir Na Nog)
03/15	St. Georges Hall, Bradford, UK (with Tir Na Nog)
03/16	Victoria Hall, Stoke-on-Trent, UK (with Tir Na Nog)
03/17	ABC Cinema, Stockton, UK (with Tir Na Nog)
03/19	Civic Hall, Wolverhampton, UK (with Tir Na Nog)
03/20	Town Hall, Oxford, UK (with Tir Na Nog)
03/21-03/22	Royal Albert Hall, London, UK (with Tir Na Nog)
03/24	Empire Theatre, Edinburgh, Scotland (with Tir Na Nog)
03/25	Caird Hall, Dundee, UK (with Tir Na Nog)
03/26	Playhouse Cinema, Glasgow, Scotland (with Tir Na Nog)
03/27	Liverpool Stadium, Liverpool, UK (with Tir Na Nog)
03/28	Free Trade Hall, Manchester, UK (with Tir Na Nog)
03/29	Royal Albert Hall, London, UK (with Tir Na Nog)
04/14	Montreal, PQ, Canada
04/15	Ithaca, NY
04/16	Syracuse, NY
04/17	Frankfort, OH
04/18	Lorain, OH
04/19	Fayetteville, NC (with Captain Beefheart & His Magic Band)
04/20	Raleigh, NC (with Captain Beefheart & His Magic Band)
04/21	Tuscaloosa, AL (with Captain Beefheart & His Magic Band)
04/22	Norfolk Scope, Hampton, VA (with Captain Beefheart & His Magic Band)
04/23	Salem, NC (with Captain Beefheart & His Magic Band)
04/24	Bowling Green, KY (with Captain Beefheart & His Magic Band)
04/25	Morgantown, WV (with Captain Beefheart & His Magic Band)
04/26	Blacksburg, VA (with Captain Beefheart & His Magic Band)
04/27	Atlanta, GA (with Captain Beefheart & His Magic Band)
04/28	University of Georgia, Athens, GA (with Captain Beefheart & His Magic Band)
04/29	Auditorium, W. Palm Beach, FL (with Captain Beefheart & His Magic Band)
04/30	Miami, FL
05/01	New Orleans, LA
05/02	Indianapolis, IN
05/03	Dane County Coliseum, Madison, WI
05/04	Southern Illinois University, Carbondale, IL
05/05	Kiel Convention Hall, St. Louis, MO
05/06	Knoxville, TN
05/07	Chicago, IL
05/08	Detroit, MI
05/09	The Garden, Cincinnati, OH
05/10	Hershey, PA
05/11	Philadelphia, PA
05/12	Boston Tea Gardens, Boston, MA
05/13-05/14	Nassau Veterans Mem. Coliseum, Uniondale, NY (with Wild Turkey - both shows sold out in 6 hours)
06/02	Quebec Coliseum, Quebec, PQ, Canada

06/03	Ottawa Civic Center, Ottawa, ON, Canada
06/04	Maple Leaf Gardens, Toronto, ON, Canada
06/06	Milwaukee Arena, Milwaukee, WI
06/07	Duluth, MN
06/08	The Gardens, Edmonton, AB, Canada
06/09	Stampede Corral, Calgary, AB, Canada
06/10	Pacific Coliseum, Vancouver, BC, Canada
06/11	Seattle, WA
06/12	Portland, OR
06/14	Oklahoma City State Fairgrounds, Oklahoma City, OK
06/15	Kansas City Municipal Auditorium, Kansas City, MO
06/16	Oakland, CA
06/17	Las Vegas, NV
06/18	Dallas Memorial Coliseum, Dallas, TX
06/19	Fort Worth, TX
06/20	San Antonio, TX
06/21	El Paso, TX
06/22	Albuquerque, NM
06/23-06/24	The Forum, Los Angeles, CA (Heads, Hands & Feet opened)
06/25	San Diego Sports Arena, San Diego, CA (Heads, Hands & Feet opened)
06/26	Tucson, AZ
06/27	Phoenix, AZ
06/28	Salt Palace, Salt Lake City, UT
06/29	HIC Arena, Honolulu, HI
06/30	Denver Coliseum, Denver, CO
07/05	Town Hall, Auckland, New Zealand
07/07	Festival Hall, Melbourne, Australia
07/09	Festival Hall, Melbourne, Australia
07/11	Horden Pavilion, Sydney, Australia
07/14	Festival Hall, Brisbane, Australia
07/15	Koseinenkin-Kaikan, Tokyo, Japan
07/16-07/17	Budokan, Tokyo, Japan
10/13	Buffalo Memorial Auditorium, Buffalo, NY (with Gentle Giant)
10/14	Rochester War Memorial, Rochester, NY (with Gentle Giant)
10/15	Bangor Auditorium, Bangor, ME
10/16	Springfield Civic Center, Springfield, MA
10/17	Pittsburgh, PA
10/18	Charleston, WV
10/19	Columbus, OH
10/21	Cleveland Public Hall, Cleveland, OH
10/22	Memphis, TN
10/23	Barton Coliseum, Little Rock, AR
10/24	Nashville Municipal Auditorium, Nashville, TN
10/25	Louisville Convention Center, Louisville, KY (with Gentle Giant)
10/26	Bowling Green, KY
10/27	Mississippi Coliseum, Jackson, MS (with Gentle Giant)
10/28	Baton Rouge, LA
10/29	Macon, GA
10/30-10/31	Philadelphia, PA
11/01-11/02	Boston Tea Gardens, Boston, MA
11/03	Bayfront Center, St. Petersburg, FL
11/04	Miami Beach Convention Hall, Miami Beach, FL
11/05	Jacksonville, FL
11/06	Wayne, NJ
11/08-11/09	Cobo Hall, Detroit, MI
11/10-11/11	Chicago Stadium, Chicago, IL
11/12	Baltimore Civic Center, Baltimore, MD
11/13	Madison Square Garden, New York, NY (Gentle Giant opened)

1973

02/02	Festhalle, Frankfurt, Germany
02/04	Hallenstadion, Zurich, Switzerland
03/02	Gothenburg, Sweden
03/04	Tivoli Konsertsal, Copenhagen, Denmark
03/06	Congress Centrum Halle, Hamburg, Germany
03/07	Hamburg, Germany
03/08	Munsterlandhalle, Munster, Germany
03/09	Dusseldorf, Germany
03/11	Deutschlandhalle, Berlin, Germany
03/13	Munich, Germany
03/15	Vienna, Austria
03/16	Rome, Italy
03/18-03/19	Palasport, Bologna, Italy
03/20	Milan, Italy
03/26	Phillipshalle, Dusseldorf, Germany
05/04	Tuscaloosa, AL
05/05	Clemson University, Clemson, SC
05/07	Hershey, PA
05/09	Oxford, OH
05/11	Norfolk Scope, Hampton, VA
05/13	Knoxville, TN
05/14	Louisville Convention Center, Louisville, KY
05/15	MSU Jenison Field House, East Lansing, MI
05/16	Memphis, TN
05/17	Hofstra University, Hempstead, NY
05/18	Hampton Rhodes Coliseum, Richmond, VA
05/19	Greensboro, NC
05/20	Atlanta, GA
05/21	Nashville, TN
05/22	Indianapolis, IN
05/23-05/24	Kiel Convention Hall, St. Louis, MO
05/29	Kitchener, ON, Canada
05/30	Maple Leaf Gardens, Toronto, ON, Canada
05/31	Ottawa, ON, Canada
06/02	The Forum, Montreal, PQ, Canada
06/22-06/23	Empire Pool Wembley, London, UK
06/30	Buffalo Memorial Auditorium, Buffalo, NY

07/04	Kansas City Municipal Auditorium, Kansas City, MO
07/07	Berkeley Community Theater, Berkeley, CA
07/08	Albuquerque, NM
07/09	Denver Coliseum, Denver, CO
07/10	State Fair Arena, Oklahoma City, OK
07/12	Dallas Convention Center Auditorium, Dallas, TX
07/14-07/15	Houston, TX
07/16	Fort Worth Convention Center, Fort Worth, TX
07/18	The Forum, Los Angeles, CA
07/19	San Diego Sports Arena, San Diego, CA (with Steeleye Span)
07/20-07/22	The Forum, Los Angeles, CA (with Steeleye Span)
07/23	Oakland Coliseum, Oakland, CA (with Steeleye Span)
07/24	Vancouver Coliseum, Vancouver, BC, Canada
07/25-07/27	Seattle Coliseum, Seattle, WA
07/28	Salt Palace, Salt Lake City, UT
08/26-08/27	Baltimore, MD
08/28-08/29	Madison Square Garden, New York, NY
08/30	Providence Civic Center, Providence, RI
08/31-09/01	Nassau Coliseum, Uniondale, NY
09/03	Madison, WI
09/04-09/05	Chicago Stadium, Chicago, IL
09/06	Cobo Hall, Detroit, MI
09/08-09/09	Cleveland Public Hall, Cleveland, OH
09/10	Rochester, NY
09/11-09/12	Pittsburgh Civic Arena, Pittsburgh, PA
09/13-09/14	Cobo Hall, Detroit, MI
09/15	Milwaukee Arena, Milwaukee, WI
09/18-09/19	New Orleans, LA
09/20	Mobile, AL
09/21	Jacksonville, FL
09/22	Bayfront Center, St. Petersburg, FL
09/23	Miami, FL
09/24	Jai Alai Fronton, Miami, FL
09/26	Roanoke, VA
09/27	Springfield Civic Center, Springfield, MA
09/28-09/29	Boston Tea Gardens, Boston, MA

1974

07/25	Centinal Hall, Adelaide, Australia
07/28	Festival Hall, Melbourne, Australia
07/30-07/31	Sydney Opera House, Sydney, Australia
08/01-08/02	Festival Hall, Brisbane, Australia
08/03-08/05	Horden Pavilion, Sydney, Australia
08/07-08/08	Cobo Hall, Detroit, MI
08/10-08/11	Auckland, New Zealand
08/12-08/13	Town Stage Hall, Christchurch, New Zealand
08/23-08/26	NHK Hall, Tokyo, Japan
08/28	NHK Hall, Tokyo, Japan
10/12	The Ahoy, Rotterdam, Holland
10/13-10/14	Voorst Nationaal, Brussels, Belgium
10/16-10/17	Glenoble, France
10/18	Marseilles, France
10/23-10/24	Madrid, Spain
11/09-11/10	Usher Hall, Edinburgh, Scotland (with Fanny)
11/11-11/12	Apollo Centre, Glasgow, Scotland (with Fanny)
11/13	Newcastle Odeon, Newcastle, UK (with Fanny)
11/14-11/17	Rainbow Theatre, London, UK (with Fanny and Pan's People)
11/18	Colston Hall, Bristol, UK (with Fanny)
11/19-11/20	Birmingham Odeon, Birmingham, UK (with Fanny)
11/21	Empire Theatre, Liverpool, UK (with Fanny)
11/22-11/23	Manchester Opera House, Manchester, UK (with Fanny)
11/24	New Theatre, Oxford, UK (with Fanny)
11/25	Cardiff Capitol, Cardiff, Wales (with Fanny)
11/26	Gaumont Theatre, Southampton, UK (with Fanny)
11/30	Gothenburg, Sweden
12/01	Malmo, Sweden
12/02	Olympen, Lund, Sweden
12/04-12/05	Falkonerteatret, Copenhagen, Denmark

1975

01/17	Asheville Civic Center, Asheville, NC (with Carmen)
01/19	Tuscaloosa, AL (with Carmen)
01/20	The Omni, Atlanta, GA (with Carmen)
01/21	Mid South Coliseum, Memphis, TN (with Carmen)
01/22	Oklahoma City State Fairgrounds, Oklahoma City, OK (with Carmen)
01/23	Convention Center Arena, Fort Worth, TX (with Carmen)
01/24	San Antonio, TX (with Carmen)
01/26	Assembly Center, Tulsa, OK (with Carmen)
01/27	Terrant City Convention Center, Dallas, TX (with Carmen)
01/28	Kemper Arena, Kansas City, MO (with Carmen)
01/29	The Arena, St. Louis, MO (with Carmen)
01/31-02/01	San Diego Sports Arena, San Diego, CA (with Carmen)
02/02	Fresno, CA (with Carmen)
02/03-02/04	Los Angeles Forum, Los Angeles, CA (with Carmen)
02/05	Tucson, AZ (with Carmen)
02/06	El Paso, TX (with Carmen)
02/08-02/10	Los Angeles Forum, Los Angeles, CA (with Carmen)
02/16	Madison, WI (with Carmen)
02/17	Minneapolis, MN (with Carmen)
02/18	Champaign, IL (with Carmen)
02/19-02/20	Chicago Stadium, Chicago, IL (with Carmen)
02/21	Cleveland, OH (with Carmen)
02/23	Niagara Falls Convention Center, Niagara Falls, NY (with Carmen)
02/24	Syracuse, NY (with Carmen)
02/25-02/26	Philadelphia, PA (with Carmen)
02/27	Hershey, PA (with Carmen)
02/28	Hampton Valley, PA (with Carmen)

03/02	New Haven, CT (with Carmen)
03/03-03/04	Nassau Coliseum, Uniondale, NY (with Carmen)
03/05	Pittsburgh, PA (with Carmen)
03/06	Providence Civic Center, Providence, RI (with Carmen)
03/07	Madison Square Garden, New York, NY (with Carmen)
03/08	The Spectrum, Philadelphia, PA (with Carmen)
03/09	Baltimore Civic Center, Baltimore, MD (with Carmen)
03/10	Madison Square Garden, New York, NY (with Carmen)
03/11	Springfield Civic Center, Springfield, MA (with Carmen)
03/12-03/13	Boston Gardens, Boston, MA (with Carmen)
03/30	Deutschlandhalle, Berlin, Germany
04/01	Ostseehalle, Kiel, Germany
04/06	Festhalle, Frankfurt, Germany
04/07	Sporthalle, Cologne, Germany
04/08	Grugahalle, Essen, Germany
04/09	Schartzwaldhalle, Karlsruhe, Germany
04/10	Eberthalle, Ludwigshafen, Germany
04/11	Festhalle, Frankfurt, Germany
04/13-04/14	Festhalle, Frankfurt, Germany
04/15	Pionir Hall, Belgrade, Yugoslavia
04/16	Linz, Austria
04/17	Wienstadthalle, Vienna, Austria
04/18	Olympiahalle, Munich, Germany
04/20	Hallenstadion, Zurich, Switzerland
06/29	Congress Centrum Hall, Hamburg, Germany
06/30-07/01	Munsterlandhalle, Munster, Germany
07/02	Dusseldorf, Germany
07/03	Sportshalle Boblingen, Boblingen, Germany
07/05	Paris, France
07/24	Vancouver, BC, Canada
07/26	Pontiac Stadium, Toledo, OH
07/27	Seattle Coliseum, Seattle, WA
07/28	Oakland Coliseum, Oakland, CA
08/01	Dallas Convention Center, Dallas, TX
08/02	Houston Coliseum, Houston, TX
08/03	Madison Square Garden, New York, NY
08/05	Nashville Municipal Auditorium, Nashville, TN
08/10	Greensboro, NC
08/11	The Gardens, Louisville, KY
08/13	Richmond Coliseum, Richmond, VA
08/15	Roanoke, VA
08/16	Charlotte, NC
08/17	Macon, GA
08/18	Huntsville Civic Center, Huntsville, AL
08/19	Columbus, OH
08/20	Knoxville, TN
08/21	Johnson City, TN
08/23	Jackson, MS
08/24	Little Rock, AR
08/25	Jackson, IN
08/26	Mobile, AL
08/27	Bayfront Center, St. Petersburg, FL
08/28-08/29	Jai Alai Fronton, Miami, FL
08/30	Lakeland, Tampa, FL
09/03	East Lansing, MI
09/26-09/27	War Memorial Auditorium, Buffalo, NY
09/28	Pacific Coliseum, Vancouver, BC, Canada
09/29	Montreal Forum, Montreal, PQ, Canada (with Gary Wright)
10/01	Washington, DC
10/02	Binghamton, NY
10/04	Cincinnati, OH
10/05-10/06	Cobo Hall, Detroit, MI
10/07	Maple Leaf Gardens, Toronto, ON, Canada
10/08	Wings Stadium, Kalamazoo, MI
10/09	Cobo Hall, Detroit, MI
10/12	East Lansing, MI
10/13	Des Moines Veterans Stadium, Des Moines, IA
10/15	Magaw Hall, Evanson, IL
10/16	Evans Field House, DeKalb, IL
10/17	Indiana State University, Terre Haute, IN
10/18	New York, NY
10/19	Morrison, IL
10/21	Horton Field House, Bloomington, IN
10/22	Toledo, OH
10/23	Easton, PA
10/26	Iona, ID
10/27	Milwaukee Arena, Milwaukee, WI
10/28	Madison, WI
10/29	Ornaka, KS
11/02	Athens, GA

1976

05/01	Vorst Nationaal, Brussels, Belgium
05/03	Paris, France
05/05	The Ahoy, Rotterdam, Holland
05/08	Konserthuset, Stockholm, Sweden
05/09	Konserthuset, Stockholm, Sweden
05/10	Tivoli Konsertsal, Copenhagen, Denmark
05/12	Congress Centrum Halle, Hamburg, Germany
05/14	Frankfurt, Germany
05/15	Olympiahalle, Munich, Germany
05/16	Hallenstadion, Zurich, Switzerland
05/18	Barcelona, Spain
05/20	Pabellon Deprtivo, Madrid, Spain
07/15	Providence Civic Center, Providence, RI
07/16	Colt Park, Hartford, CT
07/18	Capital Center, Washington, DC

07/19	Philadelphia, PA
07/21	Boston Tea Gardens, Boston, MA
07/23	Shea Stadium, Flushing, NY (with Robin Trower)
07/25	Pontiac Stadium, Detroit, MI
07/27	Riverfront Stadium, Cincinnati, OH
07/28	Louisville Convention Center, Louisville, KY
07/29	Atlanta, GA
07/31	Tampa Stadium, Tampa, FL
08/03	Cleveland, OH
08/05-08/06	Chicago Stadium, Chicago, IL
08/07	Kiel Auditorium, St. Louis, MO
08/08	Arrowhead Stadium, Kansas City, MO
08/10	Moody Coliseum, Dallas, TX
08/12	Denver, CO
08/13	Salt Palace, Salt Lake City, UT
08/15	Los Angeles Memorial Coliseum, Los Angeles, CA
08/16	Balboa Stadium, San Diego, CA (with Starcastle, Rory Gallagher and Robin Trower)
08/18	Oakland Coliseum, Oakland, CA (with ELO, Rory Gallagher and Camel)
08/20	Portland, OR
08/21	Seattle Coliseum, Seattle, WA
08/23	Edmonton, AB, Canada
08/25	Stampede Corral, Calgary, AB, Canada

1977

01/14-01/15	Pasadena Civic Auditorium, Pasadena, CA
01/16	Dorothy Chandler Pavilion, Los Angeles, CA
01/19-01/20	Masonic Auditorium, Detroit, MI
01/22-01/23	Radio City Music Hall, New York, NY
02/01	Capitol Theatre, Aberdeen, Scotland
02/02	Apollo Theatre, Glasgow, Scotland
02/03	Newcastle City Hall, Newcastle, UK
02/04-02/05	Manchester Apollo, Manchester, UK
02/06	Birmingham Odeon, Birmingham, UK
02/07	Empire Theatre, Liverpool, UK
02/09	Gaumont Theatre, Southampton, UK
02/10	Golders Green Hippodrome (TV), London, UK ("Sight 'N' Sound")
02/11-02/13	Hammersmith Odeon, Hammersmith, UK
02/14	Colston Hall, Bristol, UK
03/01	Oakland Coliseum, Oakland, CA
03/03	Seattle Coliseum, Seattle, WA
03/04	University of Oregon, Eugene, OR
03/05	Washington State University, Pullman, WA
03/06	University of Montana, Missoula, MT
03/08	McNichols Arena, Denver, CO
03/09	Omaha City Auditorium Arena, Omaha, NE
03/10	University of Missouri, Columbia, MO
03/11	Riverfront Coliseum, Cincinnati, OH
03/12	Northwestern Illinois University, Evanston, IL
03/13	Kiel Auditorium, St. Louis, MO
03/14	Municipal Auditorium, Nashville, TN
03/15	Mid-South Coliseum, Memphis, TN
03/16	Louisville Gardens Convention Center, Louisville, KY
03/17	Chicago Stadium, Chicago, IL
03/18	Bradley University, Peoria, IL
03/19	St. John's Arena, Columbus, OH
03/21-03/22	Cobo Hall, Detroit, MI
03/23	Richfield Coliseum, Cleveland, OH
03/24	Maple Leaf Gardens, Toronto, ON, Canada
03/25	Montreal Forum, Montreal, PQ, Canada
03/26	Ottawa Civic Center, Ottawa, ON, Canada
03/28	Boston Gardens, Boston, MA
03/29	Buffalo War Memorial Auditorium, Buffalo, NY
03/30	Syracuse War Memorial, Syracuse, NY
03/31-04/01	New Haven Veterans Memorial Coliseum, New Haven, CT
04/06-04/07	Anaheim Convention Center, Anaheim, CA
04/08	San Diego Sports Arena, San Diego, CA
04/09	Long Beach Arena, Long Beach, CA
04/10	Aladdin Theater, Las Vegas, NV
04/11	Miami Sportatorium, Miami, FL
04/16	Messecentrum, Nuremberg, Germany
04/17	Olympiahalle, Munich, Germany
04/18	Festhalle, Frankfurt, Germany
04/19	Eilenfriedehalle, Hannover, Germany
04/20	Sporthalle, Cologne, Germany
04/21	Grugahalle, Essen, Germany
04/22	Bremen, Germany
04/23-04/24	Deutschlandhalle, Berlin, Germany
05/24	Konserthuset, Stockholm, Sweden
05/25	Gothenburg, Sweden
05/27	Falconerteatret, Copenhagen, Denmark
05/29	Hamburg, Germany
05/30	Saalandhalle, Saarbrucken, Germany
05/31	Palais des Congress, Paris, France
06/02	The Ahoy, Rotterdam, Holland
06/03	Voorst Nationaal, Brussels, Belgium
06/05	St. Jakob Stadium, Basel, Switzerland
06/06	Innsbruck, Austria
06/07	Sporthalle, Linz, Austria
06/08	Stadthalle, Vienna, Austria
09/04-09/05	Perth Entertainment Center, Perth, Australia
09/07	Adelaide, Australia
09/09-09/12	Melbourne, Australia
09/14-09/15	Horden Pavilion, Sydney, Australia
09/17	Festival Hall, Brisbane, Australia
09/19-09/20	Sydney, Australia
11/04-11/05	Jai Alai Fronton, Miami, FL

11/06	Bayfront Center, St. Petersburg, FL
11/07	The Omni, Atlanta, GA
11/08	New Orleans, LA
11/09	Sam Houston Coliseum, Houston, TX
11/10-11/11	Dallas Memorial Coliseum, Dallas, TX
11/12	Oklahoma City, OK
11/13	Kansas City Municipal Auditorium, Kansas City, MO
11/14	Milwaukee Arena, Milwaukee, WI
11/15	St. Paul, MN
11/16	Madison, WI
11/18-11/19	Springfield Civic Center, Springfield, MA
11/20	Nassau Coliseum, Uniondale, NY
11/21	Capital Center, Washington, DC
11/22	Norfolk, VA
11/23	Greensboro Coliseum, Greensboro, NC
11/24	Lexington, KY
11/25	Dayton, OH
11/27	Portland Civic Center, Portland, ME
11/28	Hartford, CT
11/29-11/30	Madison Square Garden, New York, NY
12/01	Rochester, NY
12/02	Wilmington, DE
12/03	Binghamton, NY
12/04	Providence Civic Center, Providence, RI
12/05	The Spectrum, Philadelphia, PA
12/06	Boston Tea Gardens, Boston, MA

1978

05/01	Usher Hall, Edinburgh, Scotland
05/02	Apollo Centre, Glasgow, Scotland
05/03	Manchester Apollo, Manchester, UK (with Richard Digance)
05/07-05/08	Rainbow Theatre, London, UK (with Richard Digance)
05/09-05/11	Hammersmith Odeon, London, UK (with Richard Digance)
05/13	Congresgebouw, The Hague, Holland
05/14	Voorst Nationaal, Brussels, Belgium
05/15	Sporthalle, Cologne, Germany
05/16	Stadthalle, Bremerhaven, Germany
05/17	Munsterlandhalle, Munster, Germany
05/18	Deutschlandhalle, Berlin, Germany
05/20	Grugahalle, Essen, Germany
05/21-05/22	Frederich Eberthalle, Ludwigshafen, Germany
05/23	Sporthalle, Boblingen, Germany
05/25	Strasbourg, Germany
05/26	Saarlandhalle, Saarbrucken, Germany
05/27	Olympiahalle, Munich, Germany
05/28	Festhalle, Berne, Switzerland
05/29-05/30	Walter Kubel Halle, Russelsheim, Germany
05/31	Kuppelsalle, Hannover, Germany
06/02	Ostseehalle, Kiel, Germany
06/04	Birmingham Odeon, Birmingham, UK
06/05	Manchester Apollo, Manchester, UK
10/01	Hampton Valley, PA
10/02	Capital Center, Washington, DC
10/03-10/04	The Spectrum, Philadelphia, PA
10/06-10/07	Boston Tea Gardens, Boston, MA
10/08-10/09	Madison Square Garden, New York, NY
10/11	Madison Square Garden, New York, NY
10/12	Providence Civic Center, Providence, RI
10/13	Montreal Forum, Montreal, PQ, Canada
10/15	Maple Leaf Gardens, Toronto, ON, Canada
10/16	War Memorial Auditorium, Buffalo, NY
10/17-10/18	Cobo Hall, Detroit, MI
10/19	Checkerdome, St. Louis, MO
10/20	Memphis, TN
10/21	Huntsville, AL
10/23	Chicago Stadium, Chicago, IL
10/24	Toledo, OH
10/25	Riverfront Coliseum, Cincinnati, OH
10/26	Pittsburgh Civic Arena, Pittsburgh, PA
10/27	Richfield Coliseum, Cleveland, OH
10/28	Wings Stadium, Kalamazoo, MI
10/30-10/31	Veterans Memorial Coliseum, New Haven, CT
11/01	Syracuse War Memorial, Syracuse, NY
11/02	Rochester, NY
11/07	McNichols Arena, Denver, CO
11/08	Salt Palace Arena, Salt Lake City, UT
11/09	Centennial Coliseum, Reno, NV
11/10	Tempe, AZ
11/12	Oakland Stadium, Oakland, CA
11/13-11/14	Inglewood Forum, Los Angeles, CA (with Uriah Heep)
11/15-11/17	Long Beach Auditorium, Long Beach, CA

1979

04/01	Albuquerque, NM (with U.K.)
04/02	Tampa, FL (with U.K.)
04/03	San Diego Sports Arena, San Diego, CA (with U.K.)
04/04	Selland Arena, Fresno, CA (with U.K.)
04/06	Ogden, UT (with U.K.)
04/07	Pocatello, ID (with U.K.)
04/08	The Metra, Billings, MT (with U.K.)
04/10	Seattle Coliseum, Seattle, WA (with U.K.)
04/11	Pacific Coliseum, Vancouver, BC, Canada (with U.K.)
04/12	Portland, OR (with U.K.)
04/14	Edmonton, AB, Canada (with U.K.)
04/15	Stampede Corral, Calgary, AB, Canada (with U.K.)
04/17	Met Center, St. Paul, MN (with U.K.)
04/18	Cedar Falls Unidome, Cedar Falls, IA (with U.K.)

04/19	Milwaukee Arena, Milwaukee, WI (with U.K.)
04/20	Dane County Coliseum, Madison, WI (with U.K.)
04/21	Lincoln, NE (with U.K.)
04/23	Kemper Arena, Kansas City, MO (with U.K.)
04/24	Wichita, KS (with U.K.)
04/25	The Myriad, Oklahoma City, OK (with U.K.)
04/26	Lubbock Coliseum, Lubbock, TX (with U.K.)
04/28-04/29	Sam Houston Coliseum, Houston, TX (with U.K.)
04/30	Tarrant County Convention Center Arena, Fort Worth, TX (with U.K.)
05/01	San Antonio Convention Center, San Antonio, TX (with U.K.)
10/02	Jacksonville Coliseum, Jacksonville, FL (with U.K.)
10/05	Maple Leaf Gardens, Toronto, ON, Canada (with U.K.)
10/06	Quebec Coliseum, Quebec, PQ, Canada (with U.K.)
10/07	Montreal Forum, Montreal, PQ, Canada (with U.K.)
10/09-10/10	New Haven Coliseum, New Haven, CT (with U.K.)
10/12	Madison Square Garden, New York, NY (with U.K.)
10/15	Providence Civic Center, Providence, RI (with U.K.)
10/16-10/17	The Spectrum, Philadelphia, PA (with U.K.)
10/18	Capital Center, Washington, DC (with U.K.)
10/19	Portland, ME (with U.K.)
10/20	Rochester, NY (with U.K.)
10/21	Boston Gardens, Boston, MA (with U.K.)
10/22	Nassau Coliseum, Uniondale, NY (with U.K.)
10/24	Detroit, MI (with U.K.)
10/25	Pittsburgh, PA (with U.K.)
10/26	Cleveland, OH (with U.K.)
10/27	Cincinnati, OH (with U.K.)
10/29	Chicago, IL (with U.K.)
10/30	Nashville, TN (with U.K.)
10/31	Mid South Coliseum, Memphis, TN (with U.K.)
11/01	The Omni, Atlanta, GA (with U.K.)
11/02	Jacksonville, FL (with U.K.)
11/03	Lakeland Civic Center, Lakeland, FL (with U.K.)
11/04-11/05	Hollywood Sportatorium, Miami, FL (with U.K.)
11/06	Birmingham, AL (with U.K.)
11/07	Carbondale, IL (with U.K.)
11/08	St. Louis, MO (with U.K.)
11/09	Omaha City Auditorium, Omaha, NE (with U.K.)
11/10	McNichols Arena, Denver, CO (with U.K.)
11/12	Las Vegas, NV (with U.K.)
11/13-11/15	Long Beach Arena, Long Beach, CA (with U.K.)
11/16	Santa Monica Civic Auditorium, Santa Monica, CA (with U.K.)
11/17	San Diego Sports Arena, San Diego, CA (with U.K.)
11/18	Oakland Coliseum, Oakland, CA (with U.K.)

1980

03/13	Drammenhallen Mars, Drammen, Norway
03/14	Isstadion, Stockholm, Sweden
03/16	Congresgebouw, The Hague, Holland
03/17	Voorst Nationaal, Brussels, Belgium
03/18	Saarlandhalle, Saarbrucken, Germany
03/19	Frederich Ebert Halle, Ludwigshafen, Germany
03/20	Halle Munsterland, Munster, Germany
03/22	Deutschlandhalle, Berlin, Germany
03/23	Congress Centrum Halle 1, Hamburg, Germany
03/24	Kuppelsaal, Hannover, Germany
03/25	Eissporthalle, Kassel, Germany
03/26	Sporthalle, Cologne, Germany
03/28	Stadthalle, Bremen, Germany
03/29	Philipshalle, Dusseldorf, Germany
03/30	Grugahalle, Essen, Germany
03/31	Sporthalle Boblingen, Stuttgart, Germany
04/01	Olympiahalle, Munich, Germany
04/02	Festhalle, Frankfurt, Germany
04/03	Hallenstadion, Zurich, Switzerland
04/04	Palais des Sports, Dijon, France
04/08	Apollo Centre, Glasgow, Scotland
04/09	ABC Apollo, Manchester, UK
04/10-04/14	Hammersmith Odeon, London, UK
10/04	Salisbury, MD
10/05	Capital Center, Washington, DC
10/06	Hartford Civic Center, Hartford, CT
10/07	Utica Memorial Auditorium, Utica, NY
10/08-10/09	Madison Square Garden, New York, NY
10/10	Providence Civic Center, Providence, RI
10/11	Boston Tea Gardens, Boston, MA
10/12	Nassau Coliseum, Uniondale, NY
10/13	The Spectrum, Philadelphia, PA
10/15	Cleveland, OH
10/16	Riverfront Coliseum, Cincinnati, OH
10/17	Saginaw Civic Center, Saginaw, MI
10/18	Milwaukee Arena, Milwaukee, WI
10/19	Chicago, IL
10/20	St. Paul, MN
10/22	Cobo Hall, Detroit, MI
10/23	Wings Stadium, Kalamazoo, MI
10/24	Champaign, IL
10/25	The Gardens, Louisville, KY
10/26	Checkerdome, St. Louis, MO
10/28	Kansas City Municipal Auditorium, Kansas City, MO
10/29	Tulsa Assembly Center, Tulsa, OK
10/30	Norman, OK
10/31	Reunion Arena, Dallas, TX
11/01	San Antonio, TX
11/02-11/03	Houston, TX
11/04	Tingley Coliseum, Albuquerque, NM
11/05	McNichols Arena, Denver, CO

11/07	Swing Auditorium, San Bernardino, CA
11/08	Selland Arena, Fresno, CA
11/09	Oakland Coliseum, Oakland, CA
11/10	San Diego Sports Arena, San Diego, CA (with Whitesnake)
11/11-11/12	Los Angeles Sports Arena, Los Angeles, CA (with Whitesnake)
11/20-11/21	Royal Albert Hall, London, UK

1981
02/01	Voorst Nationaal, Brussels, Belgium
02/02	Sporthalle, Boblingen, Germany
02/03	Festhalle, Frankfurt, Germany
02/04	The Ahoy, Rotterdam, Holland
02/05	Westfalenhalle, Dortmund, Germany
02/07	Scandinavium, Gothenburg, Sweden
02/08	Copenhagen Forum, Copenhagen, Denmark
02/09-02/10	Congress Centrum Halle, Hamburg, Germany
02/11	Messesportpalast, Hannover, Germany
02/12	Stadthalle, Bremerhaven, Germany
02/13	Munsterlandhalle, Munster, Germany
02/14	Sporthalle, Cologne, Germany
02/16	Deutschlandhalle, Berlin, Germany
02/17	Freiheitshalle, Hof, Germany
02/18	Sporthalle, Augsburg, Germany
02/19	Nibelungenhalle, Passau, Germany
02/20	Rudi Sedlmayerhalle, Munich, Germany
02/21	Fredrich Eberthalle, Ludwigshafen, Germany
02/22	Saarlandhalle, Saarbrucken, Germany
02/23	Hippodrome, Paris, France
02/24	Palais des Sports, Lyons, France

1982
04/01	Konserthut, Oslo, Norway
04/02	Isstadion, Stockholm, Sweden
04/03	Tivoli Konsertsal, Copenhagen, Denmark
04/04	Stadthalle, Bremen, Germany
04/05	Deutschlandhalle, Berlin, Germany
04/06	Olympiahalle, Munich, Germany
04/07	Fredrich Eberthalle, Ludwigshafen, Germany
04/08	Congress Centrum Halle, Hamburg, Germany
04/09	Hannover, Germany
04/10	Congress Centrum Halle, Hamburg, Germany
04/11	Sporthalle, Cologne, Germany
04/12	Grugahalle, Essen, Germany
04/13	Saarlandhalle, Saarbrucken, Germany
04/14	Palais des Sports, Lyons, France
04/15	Maison des Sport, Cermont-Ferrand, France
04/16	Palais des Sports, Dijon, France
04/19	Montpellier, France
04/21	Nantes, France
04/22	Paris, France
04/25	Voorst Nationaal, Brussels, Belgium
04/26	Festhalle, Frankfurt, Germany
04/27	Nibelungenhalle, Passau, Germany
04/28	Oberschwabenhalle, Ravensburg, Austria
04/29	Sporthalle, Boblingen, Germany
04/30	Statdthalle, Freiburg, Germany
05/02	7Up Theatre, Rome, Italy
05/03	Palasport, Bologna, Italy
05/04	Palasport, Genova, Italy
05/05	Palazzo dello Sport, Padova, Italy
05/06	Theatrede Verdur, Nice, France
05/07	Municipal de Deportes, Barcelona, Spain
05/08	Real Madrid Indoor Hall, Madrid, Spain
05/09	Velodromo de Auneta, San Sebastian, Spain
05/11	The Ahoy, Rotterdam, Holland
05/13	Wembley Arena, London, UK
05/14	Edinburgh Playhouse, Edinburgh, Scotland
05/15	Newcastle City Hall, Newcastle, UK
05/16	National Exhibition Centre, Birmingham, UK
05/17	Cornwall Coliseum, St. Austell, UK
05/19	Inverness Ice Rink, Inverness, Scotland
05/29	Westfalenhalle, Dortmund, Germany - "Rockpop" TV
06/10	Dortmund Rockpop Festival, Westfalenhalle, Dortmund, Germany
07/21	Dominion Theatre, London, UK (3 songs at The Prince's Trust Rock Gala)
08/28	Theakston Music Festival, Nostel Priory, Wakefield, UK (other acts at this festival: Marillion, Lindisfarne, The Blues Band, Huang Chang, Huey Lewis And The News)
09/01	Plaza de Toros, Barcelona, Spain
09/04	Reinwiessen, Wiesbaden, Germany (The 5th Golden Summernight Concert, with Neil Young, Michael Schenker Group, April Wine and King Crimson)
09/05	Nurnberg Festival, Nurnberg, Germany
09/09	Merriweather Post Pavilion, Columbia, MD (with Saga)
09/10	War Memorial Hall, Rochester, NY (with Saga)
09/11	Blossom Music Center, Cuyahoga Falls, OH (with Saga)
09/12	Poplar Creek Music Center, Hoffman Estates, IL (with Saga)
09/14-09/15	Pine Knob Music Center, Clarkson, MI (with Saga)
09/16	Hara Arena, Dayton, OH (with Saga)
09/17	Pittsburgh Civic Arena, Pittsburgh, PA (with Saga)
09/18	Nassau Coliseum, Uniondale, NY (with Saga)
09/19	Civic Center, Glens Falls, NY (with Saga)
09/21	The Spectrum, Philadelphia, PA (with Saga)
09/22	War Memorial Auditorium, Buffalo, NY (with Saga)
09/23	Maple Leaf Gardens, Toronto, ON, Canada (with Saga)
09/24	Forum, Montreal, PQ, Canada (with Saga)
09/26	Quebec City Coliseum, Quebec City, PQ, Canada (with Saga)
09/28	New Haven Veterans Memorial Coliseum, New Haven, CT (with Saga)
09/29	Portland Civic Center, Portland, ME (with Saga)

09/30	Meadowlands (aka Brendan Byrne) Arena, East Rutherford, NJ (with Saga)
10/01	Broome County Arena, Binghamton, NY (with Saga)
10/02	Worcester Centrum, Worcester, ME (with Saga)
10/03	Providence Civic Center, Providence, RI (with Saga)
10/05	Hampton Rhodes Coliseum, Hampton Rhodes, VA (with Saga)
10/06	Charlotte Coliseum, Charlotte, NC (with Saga)
10/07	The Omni, Atlanta, GA (with Saga)
10/08	Jai Alai Fronton, Gainesville, FL (with Saga)
10/09	Hollywood Sportatorium, Miami, FL (with Saga)
10/10	Bayfront Center, St. Petersburg, FL (with Saga)
10/12	Leon County Arena, Tallahassee, FL (with Saga)
10/13	Lakefront Arena, New Orleans, LA (with Saga)
10/14	The Summit, Houston, TX (with Saga)
10/15	San Antonio Civic Center, San Antonio, TX (with Saga)
10/16	Reunion Arena, Dallas, TX (with Saga)
10/17	Folsom Field, Boulder, CO (with Saga)
10/19	Alameda Coliseum, Oakland, CA (with Saga)
10/20	Los Angeles Forum, Inglewood, CA (with Saga)
10/21	Swing Auditorium, San Bernardino, CA (with Saga)
10/22	Selland Arena, Fresno, CA (with Saga)
10/23	Lawlor Event Center, Reno, NV (with Saga)
10/24	Stockton, CA (with Saga)

1983
11/15	Atlas Circus, Munich, Germany (3 songs)

1984
08/30	Caird Hall, Dundee, Scotland
09/01	Glasgow Apollo, Glasgow, Scotland
09/02	Newcastle City Hall, Newcastle, UK
09/03-09/04	Manchester Apollo, Manchester, UK
09/06	National Exhibition Centre, Birmingham, UK
09/07-09/09	Hammersmith Odeon, London, UK (09/09/84 show transmitted 12/27/84 on BBC Radio 1)
09/12	Palacio Municipal Deportes, Barcelona, Spain
09/13	Ciudad Portiva del Real Madrid, Madrid, Spain
09/14	Velodromo Anoeta, San Sebastian, Spain
09/15	Palais des Sportes, Toulouse, France
09/16	Les Arenas, Orange, France
09/17	Le Zenith, Paris, France
09/18	Salle Omnisport, Rennes, France
09/21	Isstadion, Stockholm, Sweden
09/22	Falkoner Theatret, Copenhagen, Denmark
09/24	Congresgebouw, The Hague, Holland
09/25	Foret National, Brussels, Belgium
09/26	Sporthalle, Cologne, Germany
09/27	Rheinneckarhalle, Heidelberg, Germany
09/28	Schleyerhalle, Stuttgart, Germany
09/29	Festhalle, Frankfurt, Germany
09/30	Grugahalle, Essen, Germany
10/02-10/03	Congress Centrum Halle, Hamburg, Germany
10/04	International Congress Centrum, Berlin, Germany
10/06	Olympiahalle, Munich, Germany
10/07	Hallenstadion, Zurich, Switzerland
10/12	Veterans Memorial Coliseum, New Haven, CT (with Honeymoon Suite)
10/13	Byrne Arena - Meadowlands, East Rutherford, NJ (with Honeymoon Suite)
10/14	Broome County Arena, Binghamton, NY (with Honeymoon Suite)
10/16	Richfield Coliseum, Cleveland, OH (with Honeymoon Suite)
10/17	Rochester War Memorial Coliseum, Rochester, NY (with Honeymoon Suite)
10/18	Baltimore Civic Center, Baltimore, MD (with Honeymoon Suite)
10/19	The Spectrum, Philadelphia, PA (with Honeymoon Suite)
10/20	Buffalo War Memorial Auditorium, Buffalo, NY (with Honeymoon Suite)
10/21	Ottawa Civic Center, Ottawa, ON, Canada (with Honeymoon Suite)
10/22	Montreal Forum, Montreal, PQ, Canada (with Honeymoon Suite)
10/23	Maple Leaf Gardens, Toronto, ON, Canada (with Honeymoon Suite)
10/24	Quebec Coliseum, Quebec, PQ, Canada (with Honeymoon Suite)
10/26	Nassau Coliseum, Uniondale, NY (with Honeymoon Suite)
10/27	Providence Civic Center, Providence, RI (with Honeymoon Suite)
10/29	Worcester Centrum, Worcester, MA (with Honeymoon Suite)
10/31	Pittsburgh Civic Center, Pittsburgh, PA (with Honeymoon Suite)
11/01	Veterans Auditorium, Columbus, OH (with Honeymoon Suite)
11/02	Dane County Coliseum, Madison, WI (with Honeymoon Suite)
11/03	Joe Louis Arena, Detroit, MI (with Honeymoon Suite)
11/04	Chicago Pavilion, Chicago, IL (with Honeymoon Suite)
11/05	St. Paul Civic Center, St. Paul, MN (with Honeymoon Suite)
11/08	Lakefront Arena, New Orleans, LA (with Honeymoon Suite)
11/09	San Antonio Convention Center, San Antonio, TX (with Honeymoon Suite)
11/10	Sam Houston Coliseum, Houston, TX (with Honeymoon Suite)
11/13	Boulder Events Center, Boulder, CO (with Honeymoon Suite)
11/14	Salt Palace Arena, Salt Lake City, UT (with Honeymoon Suite)
11/17	Pine Coliseum, Vancouver, BC, Canada (with Honeymoon Suite)
11/18	Seattle Arena, Seattle, WA (with Honeymoon Suite)
11/19	Portland Coliseum, Portland, OR (with Honeymoon Suite)
11/21	Cow Palace, San Francisco, CA (with Honeymoon Suite)
11/22	Universal Amphitheater, Los Angeles, CA (with Honeymoon Suite)
12/05	Melbourne Sports Centre, Melbourne, Australia
12/10	Horden Pavilion, Sydney, Australia
12/13	Festival Hall, Brisbane, Australia
12/16	Horden Pavilion, Sydney, Australia
12/18	Melbourne Sports Centre, Melbourne, Australia

1985
03/16	International Congress Centrum, Berlin, Germany (a celebration of Johann Sebastian Bach's 300th birthday with Jan Akkerman, Eberhard Schoener and Ballett der Ungarischen Staatoper)

1986

06/28	Milton Keynes Bowl, Milton Keynes, UK (Jethro Tull was a special guest, plus Mama's Boys, Magnum, Gary Moore and Marillion)
06/30	Yarkon Park, Tel Aviv, Israel
07/02	MKT Stadium (Budapest Old Gymnasium), Budapest, Hungary
07/04	Midtfyns Festival, Ringe, Denmark
07/05	Inselwiese, Dinkelsbuhl, Germany
07/06	Lorelei Freilichtbuhne, St. Goarhausen, Germany (with Status Quo, Nazareth, Lee Aaron, Magnum; special guest: Rory Gallagher)

1987

08/15	Cropredy Festival, Cropredy, UK (with Fairport Convention)
10/04	Edinburgh Playhouse, Edinburgh, Scotland (with Fairport Convention)
10/05	Newcastle City Hall, Newcastle, UK (with Fairport Convention)
10/07-10/08	ABC Apollo, Manchester, UK (with Fairport Convention)
10/09	National Exhibition Centre, Birmingham, UK (with Fairport Convention)
10/11	Congresgebouw, The Hague, Holland (with Fairport Convention)
10/12	Cirque Royale, Brussels, Belgium (with Fairport Convention)
10/14	Carl Diem Halle, Wuertzburg, Germany (with Fairport Convention)
10/15	Schleyer Halle, Stuttgart, Germany (with Fairport Convention)
10/16	Hallenstadion, Zurich, Switzerland (with Fairport Convention)
10/18	Sporthalle, Hamburg, Germany (with Fairport Convention)
10/19	Rhein Neckar Halle, Heidelberg, Germany (with Fairport Convention)
10/20	Olympiahalle, Munich, Germany (with Fairport Convention)
10/22	International Congress Centrum, Berlin, Germany (with Fairport Convention)
10/23	Sporthalle, Cologne, Germany (with Fairport Convention)
10/24	Grugahalle, Essen, Germany (with Fairport Convention)
10/26	Le Zenith, Paris, France (with Fairport Convention)
10/27	Festhalle, Frankfurt, Germany (with Fairport Convention)
10/29	Hammersmith Odeon, London, UK (with Fairport Convention)
11/07	Providence Civic Center, Providence, RI (with Fairport Convention)
11/10	Troy Fieldhouse, Troy, NY (with Fairport Convention)
11/11	Baltimore Civic Center, Baltimore, MD (with Fairport Convention)
11/13	Nassau Coliseum, Uniondale, NY (with Fairport Convention)
11/14	New Haven Coliseum, New Haven, CT (with Fairport Convention)
11/15	Mid Hudson Civic Center, Poughkeepsie, NY (with Fairport Convention)
11/16	Stabler Arena, Allentown, PA (with Fairport Convention - may not have happened)
11/17	Providence Civic Center, Providence, RI (with Fairport Convention)
11/19	Maple Leaf Gardens, Toronto, ON, Canada (with Fairport Convention)
11/20	Forum, Montreal, PQ, Canada (with Fairport Convention)
11/21	United Nations, New York, NY (brief exclusive set for Hungerthon 1987 - a benefit for world hunger; sponsored by WNEW-FM - simultaneous hook-up from L.A.. Ian Anderson, Martin Barre and Dave Pegg flew from Montreal to NY to play at 1PM. After the set ["Skating Away On The Thin Ice Of The New Day;" "Budapest;" "Serenade To A Cuckoo"], they caught a flight for their concert that night.)
11/21	Worcester Centrum, Worcester, MA (with Fairport Convention)
11/22	Meadowlands Arena, East Rutherford, NJ (with Fairport Convention)
11/24-11/25	Tower Theater, Upper Darby, PA (with Fairport Convention)
11/27	Cobo Hall, Detroit, MI (with Fairport Convention)
11/28	Cleveland Public Hall, Cleveland, OH (with Fairport Convention)
11/29	Chicago Pavilion, Chicago, IL (with Fairport Convention)
12/01	St. Paul Forum, St. Paul, MN (with Fairport Convention)
12/02	Milwaukee Arena, Milwaukee, WI (with Fairport Convention)
12/03	Fox Theater, St. Louis, MO (with Fairport Convention)
12/05	McNichols Arena, Denver, CO (with Fairport Convention)
12/07	Salt Palace Arena, Salt Lake City, UT (with Fairport Convention)
12/09	Seattle Arena, Seattle, WA (with Fairport Convention)
12/10	Schnitzer Auditorium, Portland, OR (with Fairport Convention)
12/12	Arco Arena, Sacramento, CA (with Fairport Convention)
12/13	San Francisco Civic Hall, San Francisco, CA (with Fairport Convention)
12/14-12/16	Universal Amphitheater, Los Angeles, CA (with Fairport Convention)
12/17	Golden Hall, San Diego, CA (cancelled; with Fairport Convention)

1988

06/01	Shoreline Amphitheater, Mountain View, CA (with "Fairport Friends")
06/02	Concord Pavilion, Concord, CA (with "Fairport Friends")
06/03	Irvine Meadows Amphitheater, Laguna Hills, CA (with "Fairport Friends")
06/05	San Diego State University Open Air Theater, San Diego, CA (with "Fairport Friends")
06/07	Red Rocks Amphitheater, Denver, CO (with "Fairport Friends")
06/09	Dallas Convention Center Arena, Dallas, TX (with "Fairport Friends")
06/10	Zoo Amphitheater, New Orleans, LA (with "Fairport Friends")
06/12	Poplar Creek Music Theater, Hoffman Estates, IL (with "Fairport Friends")
06/13	Blossom Music Center, Cuyahoga Falls, OH (with "Fairport Friends")
06/14	Pine Knob Music Theater, Clarkson, MI (with "Fairport Friends")
06/16	Chastain Memorial Park Amphitheater, Atlanta, GA (with "Fairport Friends")
06/17	Mud Island, Memphis, TN (with "Fairport Friends")
06/19	Kings Dominion Showplace, Roswell, VA (with "Fairport Friends")
06/20	Riverbend Music Center, Cincinnati, OH (with "Fairport Friends")
06/21	Merriweather Post Pavilion, Columbia, MD (with "Fairport Friends")
06/23	Great Woods Performing Arts Center, Mansfield, MA (with "Fairport Friends")
06/24	Jones Beach Theater, Wantagh, NY (with "Fairport Friends")
06/25	Saratoga Performing Arts Center Amphitheater, Saratoga Springs, NY (with "Fairport Friends")
06/26	Frederick R. Mann Music Center, Philadelphia, PA (with "Fairport Friends")
06/27	Pier 84, New York, NY (with "Fairport Friends")
07/03	Palazzo della Civilta del Lavoro, Rome, Italy
07/04	Palazza de Santa Croce, Florence, Italy
07/05	Palstrussardi, Milan, Italy
07/06	Corregio, Italy
07/08	Tent on Village Green, Imst, Austria
07/09	Volkspark Dutzendteich, Nuremberg, Germany
07/10	Open Air Festival, Frauenfeld, Switzerland
07/12	Open Air Arena, Vienna, Austria

07/13	MTK Stadium, Budapest, Hungary
07/15	Athens, Greece
07/16	VFB Stadion (Waldstadion), Giessen, Germany
07/17	Walsrode, Germany
07/19	Wembley Arena, London, UK
07/26	Belo Horizonte, Belo, Brazil
08/02	Porto Allegre, Brazil
08/06-08/08	Marcanazinho, Sao Paolo, Brazil
08/30	Rio de Janeiro, Brazil

1989

09/18	Eden Court Theatre, Inverness, Scotland
09/20	Newcastle City Hall, Newcastle, UK
09/21	Edinburgh Playhouse, Edinburgh, Scotland
09/23-09/24	ABC Apollo, Manchester, UK
09/25	National Exhibition Centre, Birmingham, UK
09/27-09/29	Hammersmith Odeon, London, UK
10/01	Hamburg Sporthalle, Hamburg, Germany
10/02	Eilenriedenhalle, Hannover, Germany
10/03	Festhalle, Frankfurt, Germany
10/05	Liederhalle, Stuttgart, Germany
10/06	Olympiahalle, Munich, Germany
10/07	Karl Dien Halle, Wuertzburg, Germany
10/09	Grugahalle, Essen, Germany
10/10	Sporthalle, Cologne, Germany
10/11	Frederich Eberthalle, Ludwigshafen, Germany
10/13	Hallenstadion, Zurich, Switzerland
10/14	Halle des Fetes, Lausanne, Switzerland
10/15	Palatrussardi, Milan, Italy
10/16	Palasport, Turin, Italy
10/23	RPI Fieldhouse, Troy, NY (with It Bites)
10/24	Rochester War Memorial, Rochester, NY (with It Bites)
10/26	Copps Arena, Hamilton, ON, Canada (with It Bites - also shown as Maple Leaf Gardens, Toronto, ON, Canada)
10/27	Montreal Forum, Montreal, PQ, Canada (with It Bites)
10/28	Worcester Centrum, Worcester, MA (with It Bites)
10/29	Cumberland Civic Center, Portland, ME (with It Bites)
10/31	New Haven Coliseum, New Haven, CT (with It Bites)
11/01	Providence Civic Center, Providence, RI (with It Bites)
11/02	The Spectrum, Philadelphia, PA (with It Bites)
11/03	Nassau Coliseum, Uniondale, NY (with It Bites)
11/04	Richmond Coliseum, Richmond, VA (with It Bites)
11/06	The Palace, Auburn Hills, MI (with It Bites)
11/07	Cleveland Public Hall, Cleveland, OH (with It Bites)
11/08	Palumbo Center, Pittsburgh, PA (with It Bites)
11/09	Meadowlands Arena, East Rutherford, NJ (with It Bites)
11/11	Hill Auditorium, Ann Arbor, MI (with It Bites)
11/12	Veterans Auditorium, Columbus, OH (with It Bites)
11/14	ARI Crown Theater, Chicago, IL (with It Bites)
11/15	Chicago Theater, Chicago, IL (with It Bites)
11/16	Redbird Arena, Normal, IL (with It Bites - also shown as Riverside Theater, Milwaukee, WI)
11/17	St. Paul Forum, St. Paul, MN (with It Bites)
11/19	Riverfront Coliseum, Cincinnati, OH (with It Bites)
11/20	Fox Theater, St. Louis, MO (with It Bites)
11/21	Von Braun Civic Center, Huntsville, AL (with It Bites - also shown as Birmingham Coliseum, Birmingham, AL)
11/22	The Omni, Atlanta, GA (with It Bites)
11/24	James L. Knight Center, Miami, FL (with It Bites)
11/26	Sun Dome, Tampa, FL (with It Bites)
11/28	Lakefront Arena, New Orleans, LA (with It Bites)
11/29	The Summit, Houston, TX (with It Bites)
11/30	State Fair Coliseum, Dallas, TX (with It Bites)
12/01	Oklahoma City Civic Center, Oklahoma City, OK (with It Bites)
12/03	McNichols Arena, Denver, CO (with It Bites)
12/05-12/06	Universal Amphitheater, Los Angeles, CA (with It Bites)
12/07	Compton Terrace, Phoenix, AZ (with It Bites)
12/08	San Diego Sports Arena, San Diego, CA (with It Bites)
12/10	San Francisco Civic Center, San Francisco, CA (with It Bites)

1990

05/04	Capitol Theatre, Aberdeen, Scotland
05/05	Caird Hall, Dundee, Scotland
05/06	Empire Theatre, Sunderland, UK
05/08	Livingstone Forum, Livingstone, UK
05/09	Harrogate Centre, Harrogate, UK
05/10	St. George's Hall, Bradford, UK
05/11	Sands Theatre, Carlisle, UK
05/13	Guild Hall, Preston, UK
05/14	Victoria Hall, Hanley, UK
05/15	The Dome, Doncaster, UK
05/17	Newport Centre, Newport, UK
05/18	Poole Arts Centre, Poole, UK
05/19	Guild Hall, Portsmouth, UK
05/21	Royal Centre, Nottingham, UK
05/22	Empire Theatre, Liverpool, UK
05/24	Hexagon, Reading, UK
05/25	Dome, Brighton, UK
05/27	Birmingham Town Hall, Birmingham, UK
05/28	Apollo, Oxford, UK
08/25	Weissensee, East Berlin, Germany (festival with Simple Minds, Gary Moore, Tina Turner, Chris De Burgh, Peter Maffay and others - Jethro Tull played with De Burgh, Maffay and others - lineup same for 08/26 and 08/27 below)
08/26	Hockenheim Ring, Hockenheim, Germany
08/27	Blickpunktstudio, Dortmund, Germany
09/01	Wembley Stadium, London, UK (special guests for Fleetwood Mac; Hall & Oates also played)

09/02	Luneburg, Berlin, Germany
09/08	Maracanazinho, Rio de Janeiro, Brazil
09/10	Olympia, Sao Paolo, Brazil
09/11	Gigantinho, Porto Allegro, Brazil
09/13-09/14	Canecao, Rio de Janeiro, Brazil
09/15	Ibirapuera Arena, Sao Paolo, Brazil

1991

06/22	Aalborg Festival, Aalborg, Denmark
06/23	Open Air Theatre, Rostock, Germany
06/25	Open Air Theatre, Dresden, Germany
06/26	Eissporthalle, Halle, Germany
06/28	Freiheitshalle, Hof, Germany
06/29	Cottbus Festival, Cottbus, Germany
06/30	Mayrhofen Festival (Zillertl), Mayrhofen, Germany
07/02	Salzburg Festival, Salzburg, Austria
07/03	Casino Stadion, Vienna, Austria
07/04	Prague City Hall, Prague, Czech Republic
07/06	Palais de Sports, Mulhaus, France
07/07	Patinoire Eissporthalle, Remich, Luxembourg
07/09	Pao Stadium, Athens, Greece
07/10	Leysin Festival, Leysin, Switzerland
07/12-07/13	Istanbul Amphitheater, Istanbul, Turkey
07/15	Ismir Amphitheater, Ismir, Turkey
07/16-07/17	Istanbul Amphitheater, Istanbul, Turkey
07/20	Tallinn Festival, Tallinn, Estonia
10/03-10/04	Manchester Apollo, Manchester, UK
10/05	National Exhibition Centre, Birmingham, UK
10/07-10/09	Hammersmith Odeon, London, UK
10/12	Palasport, Forli, Italy
10/13	Palatrussardi, Milan, Italy
10/14	Palasport, Verona, Italy
10/16	Hallenstadion, Zurich, Switzerland
10/17	Olympiahalle, Munich, Germany
10/18	Karl Diem Halle, Wurzburg, Germany
10/19	Hessenhalle, Alsfeld, Germany
10/21	Grugahalle, Essen, Germany
10/22	Eberthalle, Ludwigshafen, Germany
10/23	Eilenriedenhalle, Hannover, Germany
10/25	Munsterlandhalle, Munster, Germany
10/26	International Congress Centrum, Berlin, Germany
10/27	Sporthalle, Hamburg, Germany
10/29	Sporthalle, Cologne, Germany
10/30	Festhalle, Frankfurt, Germany
10/31	Congresshalle, Stuttgart, Germany
11/01	Stadthalle, Hagen, Germany
11/07	Providence Civic Center, Providence, RI
11/08	Portland Civic Center, Portland, ME
11/10-11/11	Paramount Theater, New York, NY
11/12	Syracuse War Memorial, Syracuse, NY
11/14	Nassau Coliseum, Uniondale, NY
11/15	Knickerbocker Arena, Albany, NY
11/16	Worcester Centrum, Worcester, MA
11/17	Burlington Memorial Coliseum, Burlington, VT
11/19	Richmond Mosque, Richmond, VA
11/20	Palumbo Center, Pittsburgh, PA
11/21	Shoemaker Center, Cincinnati, OH
11/22	Cleveland State University, Cleveland, OH
11/24-11/25	Chicago Theater, Chicago, IL
11/26	Fox Theater, Detroit, MI
11/27	Grand Theater, Grand Rapids, MI
11/29	Fox Theater, St. Louis, MO
11/30	Chattanooga Memorial Auditorium, Chattanooga, TN
12/01	Fox Theater, Atlanta, GA
12/02	USF Sun Dome, Tampa, FL
12/03	James L. Knight Center, Miami, FL
12/06	Delta Center, Salt Lake City, UT
12/07	McNichols Arena, Denver, CO
12/09	Seattle Arena, Seattle, WA
12/10	Orpheum Theater, Vancouver, BC, Canada
12/11	Schnitzer Theater, Portland, OR
12/13	University of California at Davis, Davis, CA
12/14-12/15	Universal Amphitheater, Los Angeles, CA
12/16	Golden Hall, San Diego, CA
12/17	San Francisco Civic Center, San Francisco, CA

1992

03/13	Plymouth Pavilions, Plymouth, UK
03/14	Wolverhampton Civic Hall, Wolverhampton, UK
03/15	City Hall, Hull, UK
03/17	Edinburgh Playhouse, Edinburgh, Scotland
03/18	Royal Concert Hall, Glasgow, Scotland
03/19	City Hall, Newcastle, UK
03/20	City Hall, Sheffield, UK
03/22	Oasis, Swindon, UK
03/23	Hippodrome, Bristol, UK
03/24	Guildhall, Portsmouth, UK
03/27	Saga Rockteatre, Copenhagen, Denmark
03/28	Konserthuset, Gothenburg, Sweden
03/29	The Circus, Stockholm, Sweden
03/30	Konserthus, Oslo, Norway
04/01	Siegenlandhalle, Siegen, Germany
04/02	Musiek Centrum, Utrecht, Holland
04/03	Ancienne Belgique, Brussels, Belgium
04/05	Pabellon la Chimenea, Zaragoza, Spain
04/07	Arena Disco, Valencia, Spain
04/08	Municipal de los Deportes, Barcelona, Spain

04/09	Disco Universal Aqualung, Madrid, Spain
04/10	Disco Xelsa, Salsona, Spain
05/01	Guildford Civic Hall, Guildford, UK
05/02	Wembley Conference Centre, Wembley, UK
05/04	Westfalenhalle, Dortmund, Germany
05/05	Rosengarten Musensaal, Mannheim, Germany
05/06	Kongresshaus, Zurich, Switzerland
05/07	Prinzregentheater, Zurich, Switzerland
05/09	Stefaniensaal, Graz, Austria
05/10	Lucerna Hall, Prague, Czech Republic
05/11	Metropol Theatre, Berlin, Germany
05/12	Alte Oper, Frankfurt, Germany
05/13-05/14	Attikon Theatre, Athens, Greece
05/16-05/17	TRT Ari Studyosu, Ankara, Turkey
05/19	Be'er Sheva University, Be'er Sheva, Israel
05/21	Sultan's Pool, Jerusalem, Israel
05/23	Caesarea Amphitheatre, Caesarea, Israel
07/24	Nyon Festival, Geneva, Switzerland
07/25	Arena Parco Norde, Bologna, Italy
07/26	Burgarenazelt, Finkenstein, Austria
09/22	Regents Theatre, Ipswich, UK
09/23	Derngate, Northampton, UK
09/25	Akranes Sports Hall, Akranes, Iceland
10/01-10/03	Boston Orpheum, Boston, MA
10/05-10/06	Beacon Theater, New York, NY
10/07	Palace Theater, Albany, NY
10/08	Tower Theater, Upper Darby, PA
10/10-10/11	Riviera Theater, Chicago, IL
10/13	Paramount Theater, Denver, CO
10/14	Warfield Theater, San Francisco, CA
10/15-10/16	Wiltern Theater, Los Angeles, CA
10/17	Spreckels Theatre, San Diego, CA
10/20-10/21	Auditorio Nacional, Mexico City, Mexico
10/22	Paramount Theater, Seattle, WA
10/23	Orpheum Theater, Vancouver, BC, Canada
10/24	Beasley Theater Quad, Pullman, WA
10/26	Edmonton Jubilee, Edmonton, AB, Canada
10/27	Saskatoon Centennial Auditorium, Saskatoon, SK, Canada
10/28	Walker Theater, Winnipeg, MB, Canada
10/29	Regina Center of the Arts, Regina, SK, Canada
10/30	Walker Theater, Winnipeg, MB, Canada
11/01	Detroit State Theater, Detroit, MI
11/02	Masonic Auditorium, Toledo, OH
11/03-11/04	Massey Hall, Toronto, ON, Canada
11/06	Congress Centre, Ottawa, ON, Canada
11/07-11/08	Grand Theatre, Quebec, PQ, Canada
11/09	St. Denis Theatre, Montreal, PQ, Canada

1993

04/26	Lone Star Roadhouse, New York, NY
04/27	The Spectrum, Philadelphia, PA
05/25	Cambridge Corn Exchange, Cambridge, UK
05/26	Fairfield Hall, Croydon, UK
05/28	Elysee Montmatre, Paris, France
05/29	Freilichtbuhne, Stuttgart, Germany
05/30	Scherenberghalle, Gemunden, Germany
05/31	Stadthalle, Memmingen, Germany
06/03	Tanzbrunnen, Cologne, Germany
06/04	Congresspark, Wolfsburg, Germany
06/05	Hutbegbuehne, Kamenz, Germany
06/06	Eissporthalle, Halle, Germany
06/10	Westfalen Park, Dortmund, Germany
06/11	Naturbuhne, Elspe, Germany
06/12	Stadion Bremerbruecke, Osnabruck, Germany
06/13	Lubek, Germany
06/15	Cirque Royale, Brussels, Belgium
06/17	Utrecht Music Centre, Utrecht, Holland
06/18	Hamburg Stadtpark, Hamburg, Germany
06/19	Musik-Arena Am Walstadion, Frankfurt, Germany
06/20	Eissporthalle, Grefrath, Germany
06/22	Victovics Sports Hall, Ostrava, Czech Republic
06/23	Petofi Hall, Budapest, Hungary
06/25	St. Gallen, Switzerland
06/26	Bosenbachstadion, St. Wendel, Germany
06/27	Schuetzenanger, Lichtenfels, Germany
06/30	Vienna Arena, Vienna, Austria
07/01	Raiffeisenzelt, Weisen, Austria
07/02	Stadthalle, Wels, Austria
07/03	Sarchinger Weiher, Regensburg, Germany
07/04	Lienz Town Square, Lienz, Austria
07/06	Stadio Briamasco, Trento, Italy
07/07	Rolling Stone, Milan, Italy
07/09	Rostock City Hall, Rostock, Germany
07/11	Ruisrock, Turku, Finland
07/12	Tempodrom, Berlin, Germany
07/13	Gruendelpark, Glauchau, Germany
07/15-07/16	Madrid, Spain
07/17	Liverpool Empire, Liverpool, UK
07/18	Tarlair Music Festival, MacDuff, UK
08/20	Woodlands Pavilion, Houston, TX (with Procol Harum)
08/21	Coca-Cola Starplex, Dallas, TX (with Procol Harum)
08/23	Lakewood Amphitheater, Atlanta, GA (with Procol Harum)
08/24	Walnut Creek Amphitheater, Raleigh, NC (with Procol Harum)
08/26	Garden State Arts Center, Holmdale, NJ (with Procol Harum)
08/27	Jones Beach Theater, Wantagh, NY (with Procol Harum)
08/28	Great Woods Performing Arts Center, Mansfield, MA (with Procol Harum)
08/30	Merriweather Post Pavilion, Columbia, MD (with Procol Harum)

08/31	Mann Music Center, Philadelphia, PA (with Procol Harum)
09/02	Thames River Music Center, Groton, CT (with Procol Harum)
09/03	Darien Center, Darien Lake, CT (with Procol Harum)
09/04	Kingswood Amphitheater, Toronto, ON, Canada (with Procol Harum)
09/05	Star Lake, Pittsburgh, PA (with Procol Harum)
09/08	Marcus Amphitheater, Milwaukee, WI (with Procol Harum)
09/10	Riverbend, Cincinnati, OH (with Procol Harum)
09/11	Deer Creek, Indianapolis, IN (with Procol Harum)
09/12	The World Music Theater, Tinley Park, IL (with Procol Harum)
09/14	Fiddler's Green, Englewood, CO (with Procol Harum)
09/16	Greek Theater, Los Angeles, CA (with Procol Harum)
09/17	Berkeley, CA (with Procol Harum)
09/18	Irvine Meadows, Irvine, CA (with Procol Harum)
09/19	San Diego State University Amphitheater, San Diego, CA (with Procol Harum)
09/22	Shibuya On Air, Tokyo, Japan
10/02	Poole Arts Centre, Poole, UK
10/03	Portsmouth Guildhall, Portsmouth, UK
10/04	Brighton Dome, Brighton, UK
10/06	Birmingham Symphony Hall, Birmingham, UK
10/07	Nottingham Royal Centre, Nottingham, UK
10/08-10/09	Manchester Apollo, Manchester, UK
10/11	Royal Concert Hall, Glasgow, Scotland
10/12	Newcastle City Hall, Newcastle, UK
10/13	Sheffield City Hall, Sheffield, UK
10/15-10/16	Hammersmith Apollo, London, UK (the 10/16 show featured special guests Mick Abrahams and Clive Bunker)
10/17	Wolverhampton Civic Hall, Wolverhampton, UK
10/18	Colston Hall, Bristol, UK
10/20	Dublin Stadium, Dublin, Ireland
10/21	Ulster Hall, Belfast, N. Ireland
10/29	Estadio Chile, Santiago, Chile (TV: "Another Day In Chile")
10/30	Quinta Vergera, Vina del Mar, Chile
11/01	Muelle Uno, Lima, Peru
11/04-11/05	Estadio Obras, Buenos Aires, Argentina
11/09	Mesa Amphitheater, Mesa, AZ
11/10	Kiva Auditorium, Albuquerque, NM
11/12	San Antonio Municipal Auditorium, San Antonio, TX
11/13	Brady Theater, Tulsa, OK
11/14	Oklahoma City Civic Center Music Hall, Oklahoma City, OK
11/16-11/17	Sunrise Musical Theater, Sunrise, FL
11/18	Sundome, Tampa, FL
11/20	Saenger Theater, New Orleans, LA
11/21	Bayfront Auditorium, Pensacola, FL
11/22	Robinson Center, Little Rock, AR

1994

02/16-02/17	Rang Bhawan, Bombay, India
02/19	Bangalore Palace Grounds, Bangalore, India
02/20	Y.M.C.A. Grounds, Madras, India
02/23	Ko Shan Theatre, Hong Kong, Hong Kong
02/26	TSB Stadium, New Plymouth, New Zealand
03/01-03/02	Melbourne Concert Hall, Melbourne, Australia
03/04-03/07	Sydney State Theatre, Sydney, Australia
03/09	Festival Hall, Brisbane, Australia
03/10	Melbourne Sports Centre, Melbourne, Australia
03/12-03/13	Thebarton Theatre, Adelaide, Australia
03/14	Perth Entertainment Centre, Perth, Australia
03/16	Honolulu After Dark, Honolulu, HI
03/18	Warners Theater, Fresno, CA
03/19	San Jose State Events Center, San Jose, CA
03/20	Portland Civic Auditorium, Portland, OR
03/21	Seattle Arena, Seattle, WA
03/22	Vancouver Orpheum, Vancouver, BC, Canada
03/24	Calgary Southern Jubilee, Calgary, AB, Canada
03/26	Walker Theatre, Winnipeg, MB, Canada
03/27	Winnipeg or Thunder Bay, MB, Canada
03/28	Orpheum Theater, Minneapolis, MN
03/30	Massey Hall, Toronto, ON, Canada
03/31	St. Denis, Montreal, PQ, Canada
04/01	Landmark Theater, Syracuse, NY
04/02	Shea's Theater, Buffalo, NY
04/04	Burlington Memorial Auditorium, Burlington, VT
04/05	Mid Hudson Civic Center, Poughkeepsie, NY
04/29	Grieghallen, Bergen, Norway
05/01	Olafshallen, Trondheim, Norway
05/02	Oslo Centrum, Oslo, Norway
05/03	Stockholm Cirkus, Stockholm, Sweden
05/05	House of Culture, Hensinki, Finland
05/06	Typhoon Hall, Turku, Finland
05/08	Lisebergshallen, Gothenburg, Sweden
05/09	Olympen, Lund, Sweden
05/10	Falkoner Theatre, Copenhagen, Denmark
05/12	Evenementenhal, Groningen, Holland
05/13	Queen Elizabeth Hall, Antwerp, Belgium
05/14	Music Centrum, Eindhoven, Holland
05/16	Usher Hall, Edinburgh, Scotland
05/17	Guildhall, Preston, UK
05/18	St. George's Hall, Bradford, UK
05/20	Victoria Halls, Hanley, UK
05/21	Hereford Leisure Centre, Hereford, UK
05/22	Barbican, York, UK
05/24	Oxford Apollo, Oxford, UK
05/25	Ipswich Regent, Ipswich, UK
05/26	Brentwood Leisure Centre, Brentwood, UK
05/28	Kettering Arena, Kettering, UK
05/29	Anvil, Basingstoke, UK

06/07	Graz, Austria
06/08	Klagenfurt, Austria
06/10	Stavanger, Norway
06/11	Nowegian Wood Festival, Frognerbadet, Oslo, Norway
06/12	Festival, Bucharest, Romania
07/10	Festival, Balingen, Germany
07/16	Tutbury Summer Music Festival, Tutbury Castle, Tutbury, UK (with Blodwyn Pig, The Newcranes, The Skeleton Crew, The Cherubims, Harbouring Monsters and The Rye)
07/17	Berne Festival, Berne, Switzerland
08/11	Clapham Grand, London, UK ("Friends Of The Earth" benefit show with Ian Anderson, Martin Barre, Mick Abrahams and Jethro Tull)
08/12	Festival, Aarhus, Denmark
08/19	Budpest Festival, Budapest, Hungary
10/05	Saambou Bank Arena, Pretoria, South Africa
10/06	Standard Bank Arena, Johannesburg, South Africa
10/07	Village Green, Durban, South Africa
10/09-10/11	Three Arts Centre, Cape Town, South Africa
10/13	Standard Bank Arena, Johannesburg, South Africa

1995

Ian Anderson solo shows:

05/17	Passage 44, Brussels, Belgium
05/19	Musikhalle, Hamburg, Germany
05/20	Prinzregententheater, Munich, Germany
05/21	Volkshaus, Zurich, Switzerland
05/22	Hochschule de Kunste, Berlin, Germany
05/24	Shepherds Bush Theatre, London, UK
06/01	Orpheum Theater, Boston, MA
06/02	Auditorium Theater, Rochester, NY
06/03	Massey Hall, Toronto, ON, Canada
06/05	Beacon Theater, New York, NY
06/06	Tower Theater, Upper Darby, PA
06/07	Cleveland Music Hall, Cleveland, OH
06/08	Bismarck Theater, Chicago, IL
06/09	Minneapolis State Theater, Minneapolis, MN
06/11	Orpheum Theater, Vancouver, BC, Canada
06/13	Warfield Theater, San Francisco, CA (a show in Santa Rosa, CA was cancelled in favor of this show)
06/14	The Pantages Theater, Los Angeles, CA

Jethro Tull shows:

09/16	Sands Theatre, Carlisle, UK
09/18	Royal Concert Hall, Glasgow, Scotland
09/19	Newcastle City Hall, Newcastle, UK
09/21	Manchester Apollo, Manchester, UK
09/22	Sheffield City Hall, Sheffield, UK
09/23	Royal Centre, Nottingham, UK
09/25	Guildhall, Portsmouth, UK
09/26	Colston Hall, Bristol, UK
09/27	Birmingham Symphony Hall, Birmingham, UK
09/28	Cambridge Corn Exchange, Cambridge, UK
09/29	Hammersmith Apollo, London, UK
10/02	The Cirkus, Copenhagen, Denmark
10/03	The Cirkus, Stockholm, Sweden
10/04	Centrum, Oslo, Norway
10/06	Lisebergshallen, Gothenburg, Sweden
10/07	Olympen, Lund, Germany
10/09	Tempodrom, Berlin, Germany
10/10	Hannover Musichalle, Hannover, Germany
10/11	Congress Centrum Halle, Hamburg, Germany
10/13	Cirque Royale, Brussels, Belgium
10/14	Sporthalle, Cologne, Germany
10/15	Grugahalle, Essen, Germany
10/17	Stadthalle, Schwerin, Germany
10/18	Aladinhalle, Bremen, Germany
10/19	Muziekcentrum, Utrecht, Holland
10/21	Oberfrankenhalle, Bayreuth, Germany
10/22	Hallenstadion, Zurich, Switzerland
10/23	Mozartsaal, Mannheim, Germany
10/25	Offenbach Stadthalle, Frankfurt, Germany
10/26	Liederhalle, Stuttgart, Germany
10/27	Sedlmeyerhalle, Munich, Germany
11/10	Orpheum, Boston, MA
11/12	Palace, New Haven, CT
11/16	Palumbo, Pittsburgh, PA
11/14	Beacon Theater, New York, NY
11/18	Fox Theater, Detroit, MI
11/19	Veterans Auditorium, Columbus, OH
11/20	E.J. Thomas Theater, Akron, OH
11/21	Chicago Theater, Chicago, IL
11/22	Riverside Theater, Milwaukee, WI
11/24	Universal Amphitheater, Los Angeles, CA

1996

03/06	Estadio Santiago, Santiago, Chile (shown on TV)
03/08-03/09	Gran Rex, Buenos Aires, Argentina
03/10	Montevideo Palacio, Montevideo, Uruguay
03/12	Teatro Ospa, Porto Alegre, Brazil
03/13	Circulo Militar, Curitiba, Brazil
03/14	Metropolitan, Rio de Janeiro, Brazil
03/15-03/17	Olympia, Sao Paolo, Brazil
03/19	Meulle Uno, Lima, Peru
03/21	Estadio Silas, La Paz, Bolivia
03/23	Tereza Careno, Caracas, Venezuela - TV: "1 Day In Caracas, Venezuela")
03/25-03/26	Electric Factory, Philadelphia, PA (wheelchair shows)
03/29	Tupperware Convention Center, Orlando, FL (a wheelchair show)

03/30	Sunrise Musical Theater, Sunrise, FL (a wheelchair show)
03/31	USF Dome, Tampa, FL (a wheelchair show)
04/02	Fox Theater, Atlanta, GA (a wheelchair show)
04/03	Bayfront Auditorium, Pensacola, FL (a wheelchair show)
04/04	Saenger Theater, New Orleans, LA (a wheelchair show)
04/05	Majestic Theater, San Antonio, TX (a wheelchair show)
04/06	The Bronco Bowl, Denver, CO (a wheelchair show)
05/11	Royal Theater, Canberra, Australia
05/12-05/14	Sydney State Theater, Sydney, Australia
08/18	Darien Lakes Center, Darien Lake, CT (with ELP)
08/19	Kingswood Music Theater at Canada's Wonderland, Richmond Hills, ON, Canada (with ELP)
08/21	Montage Mountain, Scranton, PA (with ELP)
08/22	Garden State Arts Center, Holmdel, NJ (with ELP)
08/23	Merriweather Post Pavilion, Columbia, MD (with ELP)
08/25	Meadows Music Theater, Hartford, CT (with ELP)
08/26	Great Woods Performing Arts Center, Mansfield, MA (with ELP)
08/27	New York State Fair Grounds, Syracuse, NY (with ELP)
08/29	Star Pavilion at Hershey Park, Hershey, PA (with ELP)
08/30	Jones Beach Theater, Wantagh, NY (with ELP)
08/31	Blockbuster/Sony Center, Camden, NJ (with ELP)
09/01	Miller Lite Riverplex, West Homestead, PA (with ELP)
09/03	Nautica Stage, Cleveland, OH (with ELP)
09/04	Polaris Amphitheater, Columbus, OH (with ELP)
09/05	Pine Knob Music Theater, Clarkston, MI (with ELP)
09/06	Riverbend Music Theater, Cincinnati, OH (with ELP)
09/07	New World Music Theater, Tinley Park, IL (with ELP)
09/08	The Mark, Moline, IL (with ELP)
09/10	Northrup Auditorium/ Target Center, Minneapolis, MN (with ELP)
09/11	Marcus Amphitheater, Milwaukee, WI (with ELP)
09/13	Riverport Amphitheater, St. Louis, MO (with ELP)
09/14	Sandstone Amphitheater, Bonner Springs, KS (with ELP)
09/15	Riverfest Amphitheater, Little Rock, AR (with ELP)
09/16	Fiddlers Green Amphitheater, Englewood, CO (with ELP)
09/18	Blockbuster Desert Sky Pavilion, Phoenix, AZ (with ELP)
09/19	Aladdin Hotel & Casino Theater, Las Vegas, NV (with ELP)
09/20	Open Air Theater, San Diego, CA (with ELP)
09/21	Irvine Meadows, Laguna Hills, CA (with ELP)
09/22	Universal Amphitheater, Los Angeles, CA (with ELP)
09/24	Concord Pavilion, Concord, CA (with ELP)
09/25	Reno Amphitheater, Reno, NV (with ELP)
09/27	Gorge Amphitheater, George, WA (with ELP)
09/28	L.B. Day Amphitheater, Salem, MA (with ELP)
09/29	BSU Pavilion, Boise State University, Boise, ID (with ELP)
11/11	Plymouth Pavilions, Plymouth, UK
11/13	St. David's Hall, Cardiff, Wales
11/14	Bournemouth CC, Bournemouth, UK
11/16	Hereford Leisure Centre, Hereford, UK
11/17	Reading Hexagon, Reading, UK
11/18	The Dome, Brighton, UK
11/20	Guildford Civic Hall, Guildford, UK (originally scheduled for Brentwood Centre, Brentwood)
11/22	King George's Hall, Blackburn, UK
11/24	Barbican, York, UK
11/25	St. George's Hall, Bradford, UK
11/26	Derngate, Northampton, UK

1997

05/23	Royal Festival Hall, London, UK (David Palmer featuring Ian Anderson)
05/30	Esbjerg Festival, Esbjerg, Denmark
05/31	Beck Theatre, Hayes, UK
06/02	Assembly Hall, Tunbridge Wells, UK
06/03	Dacorum Pavilion, Hemel Hempstead, UK
06/05	Halle Des Sports, Differdange, Luxembourg
06/06	Musiekcentrum, Utrecht, Holland
06/07	Ancienne Belgique, Brussels, Belgium
06/09	Poznan Arena, Poznan, Poland
06/10	Warsaw Coliseum, Warsaw, Poland
06/11	Spodek, Katowice, Poland
06/13	Zimni Stadium, Zlin, Czech Republic
06/14	Presov Amphitheater, Presov, Slovak Republic
06/16	Petofi Csarnok, Budapest, Hungary
06/17	Zimni Stadium, Banska Bystrica, Slovak Republic
06/18	Industrial Palace, Prague, Czech Republic
06/20	Sporthalle, Augsburg, Germany
06/21	Rudi-Sedlmeyer-Halle, Munich, Germany
06/22	Schlossplatz, Bad Mergentheim, Germany
06/23	Rhein-Mosel-Halle, Koblenz, Germany
06/24	Kulturzelt, Tubingen, Germany
06/26	Freilichtbuhne Killesberg, Stuttgart, Germany
06/27	Grosse Jurahalle, Neumarkt, Germany
06/28	Naturtheater, Steinbach-Langenbach, Germany
06/29	Hessentag, Korbach, Germany
06/30	Maximilianpark, Hamm, Germany
07/04	Arena Wuhlheide, Berlin, Germany
07/05	Theaterplatz, Chemnitz, Germany
07/06	Junge Garde, Dresden, Germany
07/07	Messehalle, Cottbus, Germany
07/09	Thuringenhalle, Erfurt, Germany
07/10	Hannover Music Halle, Hannover, Germany
07/11	Westfalenpark, Dortmund, Germany
07/12	Tanzbrunnen, Cologne, Germany
07/13	Freilichtbuhne Schiffenberg, Giessen, Germany
07/17	Ostseehalle, Kiel, Germany
07/18	Stadthalle, Magdeburg, Germany
07/19	Freilichtbuhne Bergen, Rugen, Germany
07/20	Leichtathletikhalle, Neubrandenburg, Germany
07/21	Stadtpark, Hamburg, Germany
07/23	Burgruine, Finkenstein, Austria
07/24	Schlossberg, Graz, Austria (co-headliner was Manfred Mann's Earth Band)
07/25	Festivalzelt, Wiesen, Austria (co-headliner was Manfred Mann's Earth Band)
07/26	Rathausplatz, Telfs, Austria
07/27	Spilimbergo Folkfest Festival, Piazza, Italy
07/29	Velvet, Rimini, Italy
07/30	Cus, Rome, Italy
07/31	Castello, Vigevano, Italy
08/02	Derbyshire Rock & Blues Custom Show, Pentrich, UK (for Outlaws MC England - Derbyshire Chapter; with Limehouse Lizzy, A.B.C.D., Mike Ruthford Band and MacUmbra)
08/03	Stoke Park Festival, Guildford Festival, Guildford, UK
08/07	PNC Bank Arts Center, Holmdel, NJ
08/08	Oakdale Theater, Wallingford, CT
08/09	The Strand Theater, Providence, RI
08/10	Harbor Lights, Boston, MA
08/12	Pine Knob Music Theater, Clarkstown, MI
08/13	Devos Hall, Grand Rapids, MI
08/14	Nat'l Flute Convention, Grant Park, Chicago, IL (not open to the general public)
08/15	Hampton Beach Casino Ballroom, Hampton Beach, NH
08/16	Jones Beach Theater, Wantagh, NY
08/17	Pier 6 Pavilion, Baltimore, MD
09/07	Naples Blues Festival, Naples, Italy
09/12	Stadthalle, Offenbach, Germany (postponed)
09/13	Mobusstadion-Pfingstwiese, Bad Kreuznach, Germany (postponed)
09/14	Schwarzwaldhalle, Appenweiher, Germany (postponed)
09/15	Siegerlandhalle, Siegen, Germany (postponed)
09/16	Mozartsaal, Mannheim, Germany (postponed)
10/09	Mid-Hudson Civic Center, Poughkeepsie, NY
10/10	F.M. Kirby Center, Wilkes-Barre, PA
10/11	Tull Convention (afternoon), Burlington, VT
10/11	Flynn Theater (evening), Burlington, VT
10/12	Merrill Auditorium, Portland, ME
10/14	PQ Grand Theatre, Quebec City, PQ, Canada
10/15	Theatre St. Denis, Montreal, PQ, Canada
10/16	Ottawa Civic Centre, Ottawa, ON, Canada
10/18	Lulu's Roadhouse, Kitchener, ON, Canada
10/19	Centennial Hall, London, ON, Canada
10/20	Massey Hall, Toronto, ON, Canada
10/22	Duluth Entertainment Convention Center, Duluth, MN
10/23	Civic Memorial Auditorium, Fargo, ND
10/24	Walker Theatre, Winnipeg, MB, Canada
10/26	Jack Singer Concert Hall, Calgary, AB, Canada
10/27	Centennial Auditorium, Saskatoon, SK, Canada
10/28	North Alberta Jubilee Auditorium, Edmonton, AB, Canada
10/30	Orpheum Theatre, Vancouver, BC, Canada
11/01	Hult Center for Performing Arts, Eugene, OR
11/02	Paramount Theater, Seattle, WA
11/03	Spokane Opera House, Spokane, WA
11/04	Mount Baker Theater, Bellingham, WA
11/06	E. Center, West Valley, UT
11/07	The Joint, Las Vegas, NV
11/08	Union Hall, Phoenix, AZ
11/09	Centennial Hall, Tucson, AZ
11/10	Popejoy Hall, Albuquerque, NM
11/16	Gera, Germany (cancelled)
11/17	Siegerlandhalle, Siegen, Germany
11/18	Stadthalle, Offenbach, Germany
11/19	Schwarzwaldhalle, Appenweiher, Germany
11/20	Mozartsaal, Mannheim, Germany
11/21	Konrad-Frey-Halle, Bad Kreuznach, Germany

1998

04/18	Tull Convention, Bedburg-Hau, Germany
07/15	Abraham Chavez Theater, El Paso, TX
07/16	Paolo Soleri, Santa Fe, NM
07/18	Starlight Theater, Kansas City, MO
07/19	Coca-Cola Starplex, Dallas, TX
07/21	The Backyard, Austin, TX
07/22	Aerial Theater at Bayou Place, Houston, TX
07/23	Saenger Performing Arts Center, New Orleans, LA
07/24	Mud Island Amphitheater, Memphis, TN
08/22	Open Air, Gampel (VS), Switzerland
08/23	Open Air, Vaduz, Lichtenstein
08/25	Grand Cayman Ballroom - Trump Marina Hotel, Atlantic City, NJ (magician Hobson was the opening act!)
08/27-08/28	Galaxy Concert Theater, Santa Ana, CA
08/30	Humphrey's Concerts by the Bay, San Diego, CA
08/31-09/01	House of Blues, Los Angeles, CA
09/03	Konocti Harbor Resort Amphitheater, Kelseyville, CA
09/04	Washington Park Rose Garden, Portland, OR
09/05	Bumbershoot Festival, Seattle, WA
09/25	Classic Amphitheater, Richmond, VA (changed to Atlantic City - see above)
09/26	Nissan Pavilion, Manassas, VA
09/27	Virginia Beach (GTE) Amphitheater, Virginia Beach, VA
09/29	Palace Theater, Louisville, KY
10/01	Blockbuster Pavilion, Charlotte, NC
10/02	Walnut Creek Amphitheater, Raleigh, NC
10/03	House of Blues, Barefoot Landing, SC
10/04	Florida Theater, Jacksonville, FL
10/06	Ruth Eckerd Hall, Clearwater, FL (with Rhodeside)
10/07	Coral Sky Amphitheater, W. Palm Beach, FL
10/08	House of Blues, Orlando, FL
10/09	Chastain Park Ampthitheater, Atlanta, GA
11/06	Murcia, Spain

11/07	Teatro Villamarta, Jerez de la Frontera, Spain
11/08	Teatro Cervantes, Malaga, Spain
11/10	Barcelona, Spain
11/11	La Riviera, Madrid, Spain
11/12	Santiago de Compostela, Vigo, Spain

1999

05/27	The Round Hall, Budapest, Hungary
05/29	Hala Rondo, Brno, Czech Republic
05/30	Spodek, Katowice, Czech Republic
05/31	Small Sports Hall, Prague, Czech Republic
06/02	Stadtpark, Hamburg, Germany
06/03	Rattenfanger Halle, Hammeln, Germany
06/04	Museumplatz, Bonn, Germany
06/05	Waldbuhne, Schwazenberg, Germany
06/06	Freilichtbuhne, Kamenz, Germany
06/10	Stadthalle, Rostock, Germany
06/11	Columbiahalle, Berlin, Germany
06/12	Open Air Stadthalle, Bamberg, Germany
06/13	Donau-arena, Regensburg, Germany
06/16	Stadthalle, Braunschweig, Germany
06/17	Hessental, Baunatal, Germany
06/18	Naturtheater, Steinbach, Germany
06/19	Rock auf der Burg, Konigstein, Germany
06/20	Greuthalle, Aalen, Germany
06/23	Stadthalle, Magdeburg, Germany
06/24	Messehalle, Erfurt, Germany
06/25	Pelssnitzinsel, Halle/Saale, Germany
06/26	Kanalbuhne, Gelsenkirchen, Germany
07/01	Zeltfestival, Konstanz, Germany
07/02	Feste Marienberg, Wurzburg, Germany
07/03	Landesgartenschau, Mosbach, Germany
07/04	Burg, Esslingen, Germany
07/05	Zeltfestival, Freiberg, Germany
07/14	Neapolis, Bagnoli, Italy
07/16	Folkfest, Udine, Italy
07/17	Musica in Castello, Vigevano, Italy
07/18	Duomo Square, Pistoia, Italy
07/19	Roseto, Italy
08/25	Casino Ballroom, Hampton Beach, NH (with Vyktoria Pratt Keating)
08/26	BankBoston Pavilion, Boston, MA (with Vyktoria Pratt Keating)
08/28	Palace Theater, Albany, NY (with Vyktoria Pratt Keating)
08/29	Oakdale Theater, Wallingford, CT (with Vyktoria Pratt Keating)
08/30	Darien Lake Arts Center, Darien, NY (with Vyktoria Pratt Keating)
09/01	PNC Bank Arts Center, Holmdel, NJ (with Ten Years After)
09/02	Jones Beach Theater, Wantagh, NY (with Ten Years After)
09/03	Montage Mountain Performing Arts Center, Scranton, PA (with Vyktoria Pratt Keating)
09/04	Grand Cayman Ballroom - Trump Marina Hotel, Atlantic City, NJ (with Vyktoria Pratt Keating)
09/05	Pier 6 Pavilion, Baltimore, MD (with Vyktoria Pratt Keating)
09/07	Landmark Theater, Syracuse, NY (with Vyktoria Pratt Keating)
09/09	Blossom Music Center, Cuyahoga Falls, OH (with Vyktoria Pratt Keating)
09/10	Meadowbrook Music Festival at Baldwin Memorial Pavilion, Rochester, MI (with Vyktoria Pratt Keating)
09/11	Auditorium Theater, Chicago, IL (with Vyktoria Pratt Keating)
09/12	Riverport Amphitheater, Maryland Heights (St. Louis), MO (with Vyktoria Pratt Keating)
09/24	Magness Arena (at Daniel L. Ritchie Sports & Wellness Center), University of Denver, Denver, CO (with Vyktoria Pratt Keating)
09/26	Sandy Point Beach (at Lucky Peak Dam in Lucky Peak State Park), Boise, ID (with Vyktoria Pratt Keating)
09/27	Caras Park Pavilion, Missoula, MT (with Vyktoria Pratt Keating)
09/28	Seattle Center Opera House, Seattle, WA (with Vyktoria Pratt Keating)
09/29	Spokane Center Opera House, Spokane, WA (with Vyktoria Pratt Keating)
10/01	Reno Hilton Amphitheater, Reno, NV (with Vyktoria Pratt Keating)
10/02	Centennial Garden & Convention Center, Bakersfield, CA (with Vyktoria Pratt Keating)
10/03	Concord Pavilion, Concord, CA (with Vyktoria Pratt Keating)
10/04	Cal. Poly Performing Arts Center, San Luis Obispo, CA (with Vyktoria Pratt Keating)
10/05	Open Air Theater, San Diego State University, San Diego, CA (with Vyktoria Pratt Keating)
10/07	Greek Theater, Los Angeles, CA (with Vyktoria Pratt Keating)
10/08	House Of Blues, Los Angeles, CA (with Vyktoria Pratt Keating)
10/09	House Of Blues (at Mandalay Bay Resort & Casino), Las Vegas, NV (with Vyktoria Pratt Keating)
10/10	Arizona State Fair, Phoenix, AZ
10/20	Musikcentrum, Utrecht, Holland
10/21	Ancienne Belgique, Brussels, Belgium
10/22	Olympia, Paris, France
10/24	Theatre de Beaulieu, Lausanne, Switzerland
10/26	Stadthalle, Vienna, Austria
10/27	Kongresshaus, Zurich, Switzerland
10/28	Montforthaus, Feldkirch, Austria
10/29	Eberthalle, Ludwigshafen, Germany (with Mark Gillespie Band)
10/30	Phillipshalle, Dusseldorf, Germany (with Mark Gillespie Band)
11/01	Columbiahalle, Berlin, Germany (with Mark Gillespie Band)
11/02	Kulterplast, Dresden, Germany (with Mark Gillespie Band)
11/03	Stadthalle, Erlangen, Germany (with Mark Gillespie Band)
11/05	Musikhalle, Hamburg, Germany (with Mark Gillespie Band)
11/06	Alte Oper, Frankfurt, Germany (with Mark Gillespie Band)
11/07	Rudi Sedlmayer-Halle, Munich, Germany (with Mark Gillespie Band)
11/09	Palacisalfa, Rome, Italy
11/10	Palalido, Milan, Italy
11/15	St. David's Hall, Cardiff, Wales (with Vyktoria Pratt Keating)
11/17	Colston Hall, Bristol, UK (with Vyktoria Pratt Keating)
11/18	Royal Centre, Nottingham, UK (with Vyktoria Pratt Keating)
11/19	Apollo, Manchester, UK (with Vyktoria Pratt Keating)
11/21	Symphony Hall, Birmingham, UK (with Vyktoria Pratt Keating)
11/22	Royal Concert Hall, Glasgow, Scotland (with Vyktoria Pratt Keating)
11/23	City Hall, Newcastle, UK (with Vyktoria Pratt Keating)
11/24	City Hall, Sheffield, UK (with Vyktoria Pratt Keating)
11/26	Corn Exchange, Cambridge, UK (with Vyktoria Pratt Keating)
11/27	Regent, Ipswich, UK (with Vyktoria Pratt Keating)
11/28	Fairfield Hall, Croydon, UK (with Vyktoria Pratt Keating)
11/30-12/01	Shepherds Bush Empire, London, UK (with Vyktoria Pratt Keating)
12/03	Brentwood Centre, Brentwood, UK (with Vyktoria Pratt Keating)
12/04	Anvil, Basingstoke, UK (with Vyktoria Pratt Keating)
12/05	Apollo, Oxford, UK (with Vyktoria Pratt Keating)

2000

04/12	Anfitearo Sambil, Caracas, Venezuela (Ian Anderson with David Palmer conducting the Caracas Symphony Orchestra)
04/13	Universidad de Carabobo Auditorium, Anfiteato de Barbula, Valencia, Venezuela (Ian Anderson with David Palmer conducting the Carabobo Symphonic Orchestra)
04/25	Circus, Stockholm, Sweden
04/27	House of Culture, Helsinki, Finland
04/29	Rockefeller, Oslo, Norway
04/30	Vega, Copenhagen, Denmark
05/02	Lochotin, Pilsen, Germany
05/04	Sala Kongresowa, Warsaw, Poland
05/05	Hala Ludowa, Wroclaw, Poland
05/06	Spodek, Katowice, Poland
05/07	Palac Kultury a Sportu, Ostrava, Czech Republic
05/08	Sports Hall, Zlin, Czech Republic
05/10	Dom Sportiva 2, Zagreb, Croatia, Yugoslavia
05/11	Hala Tivoli 2, Ljubljana, Yugoslavia
05/13	Harbiye Open Air Theatre, Istanbul, Turkey
06/06	The Backyard, Austin, TX
06/08 - 06/09	Bass Performance Hall, Ft. Worth, TX
06/10	Majestic Theatre, San Antonio, TX
06/11	Ariel Theatre, Houston, TX
06/13	Palace Theatre, Louisville, KY
06/14	Riverbend Festival, Chattanooga, TN (headliner of festival)
06/15	Grand Casino Biloxi, Biloxi, MS
06/16	Grand Casino Tunica, Robinsonville, TN
06/17	City Stages Festival, Birmingham, AL (headliner of festival)
06/18	Chastain Park, Atlanta, GA
06/20	Florida Theatre, Jacksonville, FL
06/21	Ruth Eckerd Hall, Clearwater, FL
06/23 - 06/24	Sunrise Musical Theatre, Sunrise, FL
06/25	House of Blues, Orlando, FL
06/27	House of Blues, Myrtle Beach, SC
06/28	Peace Center, Greenville, SC
06/29	Tennessee Theatre, Knoxville, TN
07/01	Walnut Creek, Raleigh, NC (with The Chieftains)
07/02	Blockbuster Pavilion, Charlotte, NC (with The Chieftains)
07/03	GTE Amphitheatre, Virginia Beach, VA (with The Chieftains)
07/17	New Jersey Performing Arts Center, Newark, NJ
07/19	Beacon Theatre, New York, NY
07/20	Star Pavilion, Hershey, PA
07/21	Foxwoods Resort & Casino, Ledyard, CT
07/22	Delaware State Fair, Harrington, DE
07/23	Meadowbrook Farm, Gilford, NH
07/25	L'Agora, Quebec City, PQ, Canada
07/26	Theatre St. Denis, Montreal, PQ, Canada
07/27	Hamilton Place, Hamilton, ON, Canada
07/28	Finger Lakes Performing Arts Center, Canandaigua, NY
07/29	Charles Ives Center, Danbury, CT
07/30	Wolf Trap, Vienna, VA
08/01	Clemens Center, Elmira, NY
08/02	State Theatre, Easton, PA
08/03	Warner Theatre, Erie, PA
08/04	Fraze Pavilion, Kettering, OH
08/05	Palace Theatre, Columbus, OH
08/06	Stambaugh Auditorium, Youngstown, PA
08/08	Ravinia Pavilion, Highland Park, IL
08/09	Interlochen Center, Interlochen, MI
08/10	Oneida Casino, Green Bay, WI
08/11	Embassy Theatre, Ft. Wayne, IN
08/12	N.Y. Erie County Fair, Hamburg, NY
08/13	Stanley Theatre, Utica, NY
08/29	Viejas Casino, Alpine, CA
08/30	Antelope Valley Fairgrounds, Lancaster, CA
09/01	Marin County Civic Center, San Rafael, CA
09/02	Konocti Field Amphitheater, Kelseyville, CA
09/03	Anderson, CA
09/04	Oregon State Fair, Salem, OR
09/06	Deer Valley, Salt Lake City, UT
09/08	Colorado Springs City Auditorium, Colorado Springs, CO
09/09	Kiva Auditorium, Albuquerque, NM
09/10	TCC Music Hall, Tucson, AZ
09/12 - 09/13	Sun Theatre, Anaheim, CA
09/14	House of Blues, Las Vegas, NV
09/15	Tulare County Fair, Tulare, CA
09/16	Civic Arts Plaza, Thousand Oaks, CA
09/17	L.A. County Fair, Pomona, CA
09/19	Carlson Arena, Fairbanks, AK
09/20	Sullivan Arena, Anchorage, AK

(NOTE: Only the original and current members of Jethro Tull and other members that have been in the band at least three years have been included.)

MICK ABRAHAMS

Just after he left Jethro Tull, Mick formed Blodwyn Pig in December 1968 and signed with Island Records. I asked Abrahams about the significance of the band name, and Mick told me: "None whatsoever, really! After I left Jethro Tull, I had asked this guy, Graham Waller, who was mentioned in the music papers from time to time, about what to name my new band. After some thought, Waller said, 'Thy name shall be Blodwyn Pig,' and then he left, and I haven't heard from him since! I have been asked by Welsh people who think that the name offends them, but it's none of my doing!" The band's initial lineup included Abrahams, sax and flute player Jack Lancaster, former McGregor's Engine bassist Andy Pyle and drummer Ron Berg.

Blodwyn Pig's first album "Ahead Rings Out" was Mick's natural progression from Jethro Tull's "This Was." Even though he didn't come up with his band's name, Mick thought of the smoking pig image on the front cover. Blodwyn Pig's stock in trade was a more experimental blues approach with the jazz-leaning contributions of Jack Lancaster. This time, Lancaster's flute playing was more complimentary to Mick's direction. Their interaction helped the album reach #9 in the UK (#149 US). Sales on A&M were strong enough for Blodwyn Pig to tour America, including a stop at the Fillmore East on November 14-15, 1969 with Johnny Winter and Chicago.

"Getting To This" continued Blodwyn Pig's success in the UK, reaching #8. It made #96 in the States and resulted in another US tour. Blodwyn Pig played the Fillmore East with Chicken Shack on August 8, 1970 - three days after Jethro Tull! To promote this album, the band went on "Top Of The Pops." The show wanted the Pig to play the A-side "Same Old Story," but Mick decided to play its B-side, a cover of Larry Williams' "Slow Down." That non-album single was their only output for the Chrysalis label.

Thanks to Andy Pyle, Mick Abrahams was kicked out of his own group in September 1970, replaced by former Yes guitarist Peter Banks. When I asked Mick about it, he answered: "They thought they could continue without me, but after four gigs, they folded. After all, I registered the name Blodwyn Pig - it was my group!" This band was soon renamed Lancaster's Bomber. That December, Banks formed the group Flash and was replaced by guitarist/vocalist Larry Wallis. They quit when Wallis joined UFO. Pyle and Berg went on to Savoy Brown, and Pyle later joined Juicy Lucy and The Kinks.

Undeterred, Mick Abrahams formed Wommet with Pete Fensome (McGregor's Engine vocalist), violinist John Darnborough and ex-John Evan Band drummer Ritchie Dharma. Wommet didn't record, but they did an "In Concert" session for the BBC in November 1970. As Mick says, "Wommet was a name we used before I decided to name the band The Mick Abrahams Band - after all, they can't take my name away from me!" When Wommet evolved into The Mick Abrahams Band, Abrahams and Dharma were joined by Bob Sergeant (keyboards and vocals) and bassist Walt Monaghan. Their first album was called "Mick Abrahams," but it is also known as "A Musical Evening With The Mick Abrahams Band." That LP, although it contained many fine moments, did not chart. Jack Lancaster joined for the album "At Last," but it met the same fate. Mick would withdraw from the recording scene at the end of 1972. Abrahams then went into other lines of work: driving a van, demonstrating Yamaha guitars and as a swim instructor in Luton.

In February 1974, Mick was inspired to reform Blodwyn Pig with Clive Bunker, Jack Lancaster and nemesis Andy Pyle. They did four gigs at the Marquee in London, and one of those was the basis for a BBC Radio 1 "In Concert" session. Blodwyn Pig also did a follow-up session for Radio 1. The last Marquee show they did, on August 15, 1974, was recorded as a demo tape with hopes of obtaining a record contract. However, they broke up soon thereafter when manager June Whyton committed suicide. Clive Bunker and Jack Lancaster would form Aviator with Manfred Mann's Earth Band guitarist/vocalist Mick Rogers two years later. Pyle ended up in Chicken Shack. A 1974 LP session with the gospel group The Mighty Flyers (the "Low Flying Angels" album) featured Mick's playing on all of the tracks except for two.

Out of desperation, Mick recorded the instructional guitar LP "Have Fun Learning To Play The Guitar With Mick Abrahams." After his sales downturn, Mick tells us why he made this album: "Simple - I was broke! The record company, SRT, offered me £1,000 and I did it." Mick then gives us a brief overview of what he did afterward: "After that (the demise of Blodwyn Pig), I got tired of the

The Toggery Five

Blodwyn Pig

The always in-tune Mick Abrahams.

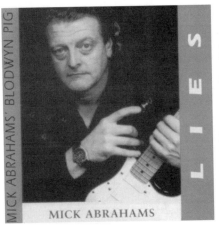

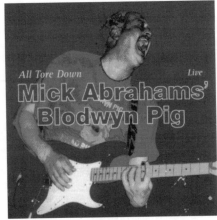

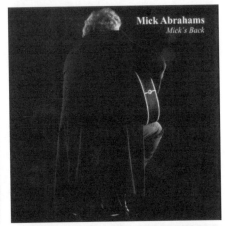

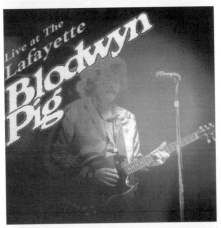

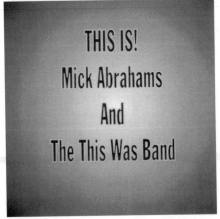

whole business and did lots of jobs. I still play with Ian Anderson and Clive Bunker on occasion, so we still have a good relationship. I have always been a fan of Jethro Tull's work, but not necessarily the folk-oriented material. When Clive is in-between work, he gives me a call and we have a go at each other!"

Mick quit the grind of performing to pursue business interests, including financial consulting at Allied-Dunbar in Milton Keynes, England. He also reacquainted himself with his religious beliefs. I made the mistake of asking Abrahams how he got the itch to play again, and he replied, "Actually, I was going out with this girl. . .really, I reformed Blodwyn Pig in December 1988 to celebrate the opening of a new leisure center in Luton. And, I've been doing it ever since. Most of my income is not from Blodwyn Pig, but from commercials, as I do a lot of voiceover work."

On April 21, 1986, Mick performed at a BAND (Bedfordshire Against Nuclear Dumping) benefit sponsored by the Luton Recreation Services Department. It was held at St. George's Theatre. That November, Abrahams played at the Wheatsheaf in Dunstable. Mick also did the occasional pub date with a band featuring sax player Bernie Hetherington. However, it wasn't until that late 1988 show in Luton that Mick started to get back into playing more regularly. Blodwyn Pig was reformed as Clive Bunker, Andy Pyle, keyboardist Bruce Boardman and Boardman's sax playing friend Dick Heckstall-Smith. Abrahams was already familiar with Heckstall-Smith, since Mick played with him in John Mayall's band before Jethro Tull. Mick had also sat in with Colosseum when Dick Heckstall-Smith was part of their lineup. As for Blodwyn Pig, Mick Abrahams felt this group was only going to do this one gig. However, their performance was a resounding success and Mick decided to continue the band. After some rehearsals, Blodwyn Pig did some warmup gigs in local pubs and clubs. Their gameplan was to hit the Marquee and university touring arena along with some recording. Unfortunately, Heckstall-Smith left due to differences in the band's direction, and Clive Bunker quit shortly after. A new lineup was unveiled in April 1989 with bassist Mike Summerland, drummer Graham Walker and Dave Lennox on keyboards. Here's Mick to tell what the band played: "We played 'My Sunday Feeling' from 'This Was' and the blues number 'So Much Trouble,' tracks from Blodwyn Pig and my solo albums, and 'Slow Down,' which was the B-side of the single 'Same Old Story.'" In late 1989, they did a three-song session on Paul Jones' Rhythm And Blues Show on Radio 2, and it was mentioned that the tracks were from their forthcoming album. A private run of 50 cassettes was prepared for an album called "A Taste Of Things To Come."

Blodwyn Pig recorded a cassette-only release called "Roadroller" which was only sold at gigs in 1990. The intention was to re-release the album as is on CD, but a slight track modification took place when Mick Abrahams signed a recording contract with the Elite label. The revised album was released in 1991 and entitled "All Said And Done." Even though it was by Blodwyn Pig, it was billed as a Mick Abrahams solo release. The Beat Goes On (BGO) label issued three of Mick's previous albums on LP and/or CD with some bonus tracks, with Demon handling "At Last."

The 1991 Jethro Tull convention featured a performance by Blodwyn Pig and guest drummer Clive Bunker. Mick also did a solo set and played with Seismic Ring member Martin Carter. Mick's next Pig album was 1993's "Lies," an impressive release on A New Day Records. It was subsequently licensed to a number of labels, including releases in the US and Germany. These foreign releases contained alternate mixes of two tracks.

Mick surprised everyone when he appeared with Jethro Tull during their 25th anniversary tour, and Ian Anderson returned the favor through an equally surprising appearance at a 1993 Christmas show that Blodwyn Pig played in London.

With the licensing of his officially released masters, Mick Abrahams incorrectly authorized the release of a number of albums of highly variable quality. The poorest sounding collections negatively impacted the integrity of his band. The earliest of these deficient album was "All Tore Down - Live," a 1994 release on Indigo. The album's audience tape quality was further denigrated by the addition of audience responses from some unknown tape! Albums of this nature would not enable Blodwyn Pig to progress beyond the club level. Mick also appeared on the "Quick As A Roof" album by another club veteran, Jackie Lynton. In 1995, Abrahams did the music for the Bury Lawn School production of William Shakespeare's "A Midsummer Night's Dream."

Mick recorded one track for the Peter Green tribute album "Rattlesnake Guitar" (called "The Peter Green Songbook" outside the US), and he recorded with Ian Anderson for the first time since 1968 during the sessions for his "One" album - a 1996 release. "One" was universally praised by fans and critics. Coming right back, Abrahams did a blues covers album called "Mick's Back" before his next Blodwyn Pig album "Pig In The Middle." For the latter album, Mick was joined by bassist Mike Summerland and

Graham Walker on drums. It was produced by Robin Black.

Mick again made the mistake of licensing two more bootleg-like albums to Indigo Records in 1997: "The Modern Alchemist" and "Live At The Lafayette." The former was a 1974 Blodwyn Pig live album that was not billed as such, and the latter was from 1970.

Remember when Mick said he did quite well with voiceovers? Well, his vocal characterizations of Albert Einstein, Joseph Stalin and Mad McGregor were head-on smashes on the House Of Satire album "The Doomsday Clock." Three years in the making, the 1997 release "The Doomsday Clock" contained Mick's finest latter day vocal and guitar performances. Mick's appearance anchored an album that was built for the future and proved that he could more than hold his own in many of today's musical styles.

Mick appeared on Jackie Lynton's "Pin-Board Wizards" album, and released a 1991 Blodwyn Pig concert as the May 1998 album "The Full Porky." Abrahams was asked by a German record company to re-record the most popular Blodwyn Pig track "See My Way," but he turned the offer down. In late 1997, Mick thought of forming a band to play the album "This Was" to mark the 30th anniversary of Jethro Tull and the album. He asked Clive Bunker to join him in an effort to present the album with half of the original Tull lineup, but Clive felt it was a bad idea and passed. Vocalist/flute player Steve Dundon from Tull cover band Seismic Ring teamed up with Mick, bass player Mike Summerland and drummer Graham Walker to rehearse the album for a gig at London's 100 Club. Abrahams quickly nixed the inclusion of "Living In The Past" and tracks from "Stand Up" to concentrate on presenting the tracks he originally played on. The only "This Was" track not played at these shows was the brief "Round." When a family emergency forced Walker to leave, Bunker agreed to fill in temporarily despite his initial feelings. The 100 Club date went over extremely well, and Bunker was so convinced of the viability of the project that he offered his assistance when Mick required it. Six months of gigs were booked, but it became clear why fans flocked to the show - it was misbilled as Jethro Tull with the disclaimer "as performed by original guitarist Mick Abrahams" in very small print! Abrahams was not aware of this major gaffe and called Ian Anderson with his apologies. Ian accepted Mick's apologies and offered to join them on stage if he was able to, but Anderson had to threaten lawsuits if the misleading promotion continued. As a result, Mick Abrahams' reputation took another direct hit. The album "This Is!" was issued in December 1998, but it came and went very quickly. Mick continues to hit the club scene - catch him!

ARTIST CODE:
(1) Blodwyn Pig
(2) The Mick Abrahams Band
(3) Mick Abrahams
(4) Mick Abrahams' Blodwyn Pig
(5) Mick Abrahams' "This Was" Band

SINGLES

TITLES	UK & FOREIGN LABEL/NO.	RELEASE DATE	US LABEL/NO.	RELEASE DATE
(1) Dear Jill/Sweet Caroline	Island WIP 6059	05/16/69	A&M 1158	01/12/70
(1) Summer Day/Walk On The Water	Island WIP 6069	10/03/69		
(1) Same Old Story/Slow Down	Chrysalis WIP 6078	05/29/70		
(4) Going Down (Radio Edit) - Goodbye (Radio Edit) - Hound Dog - Drive Me (CD5)	A New Day AND CD 11	11/25/96		

ALBUMS

TITLES	UK & FOREIGN LABEL/NO.	RELEASE DATE	US LABEL/NO.	RELEASE DATE
(1) Ahead Rings Out (LP)	Island ILPS 9101	07/25/69	A&M SP-4210	10/27/69
(NOTE: US and Australian issues of the above LP substituted "Walk On The Water" for "Sing Me A Song I Know," "See My Way" for "Up And Coming" and "Summer Day" for "Leave It With Me.")				
(1) Getting To This (LP)	Chrysalis ILPS 9122	04/15/70	A&M SP-4243	05/25/70
(NOTE: US issues of the above LP substituted "Meanie Mornay" for "See My Way.")				
(2) The Mick Abrahams Band (LP)	Island ILPS 9147	03/26/71	A&M SP-4312	07/26/71
(2) At Last (LP)	Chrysalis CHR 1005	04/28/72		
(3) Learning To Play Guitar With Mick Abrahams (LP)	SRT SRTM 73313	11/07/75		
(3) Learning To Play Guitar With Mick Abrahams (LP; reissue)	SRT SRTM 73313	01/06/78		
(1) Ahead Rings Out (LP/CD/picture CD)	BGO BGOLP/CD(P) 54	03/13/89		
(4) A Taste Of Things To Come (private cassette demo - 50 copies only)	private release	12/**/89		
(4) Roadroller (private cassette sold at gigs - limited to 500 copies)	private release	10/**/90		
(1) Getting To This (LP/CD; reissue)	BGO BGOLP/CD 81	10/15/90		
(3) All Said And Done (CD; includes 11 of the 12 tracks on the "Roadroller" cassette, plus "Cat's Squirrel" and "Let Me Love You				

"Baby." A studio version of the title track replaces the live version
on the cassette.

Title	UK & Foreign Label/No.	Release Date	US Label/No.	Release Date
(2) At Last (CD)	Elite ELITE 007CD	05/13/91		
(2) The Mick Abrahams Band (CD)	Demon EDCD 335	09/23/91		
(1) Ahead Rings Out (CD; re-promotion)	BGO BGOCD 95	09/14/92		
(4) Lies (CD; fan club version - 1,000 copies only)	BGO BGOCD 54	10/07/93		
(1) Getting To This (CD; re-promotion)	A New Day AND CD3	11/12/93		
(4) Lies (CD; different cover from UK and German issues, plus 2 extra remixed tracks: "I Wonder Who" and "All Said And Done")	BGO BGOCD 81	11/15/93	Viceroy VIC 8013-2	05/23/94
(4) Lies (CD; different cover, plus 2 extra remixed tracks: "I Wonder Who" and "All Said And Done")	German CAS CDVEST 12	06/06/94		
(4) All Tore Down (CD; live in Germany 1993)	Indigo IGOCD 2011	10/24/94		
(2) "Peter Green Songbook 2" (CD; one track: "The Same Way")	Semaphore 32474 422	07/30/95		
(2) "Rattlesnake Guitar: "The Music Of Peter Green" (2CD; one track: "The Same Way," which is actually by Blodwyn Pig)			Viceroy VIC2-8021	08/22/95
(3) "Alexis Korner Memorial Concert Volume 2" (CD)	Indigo IGOCD 2051	11/21/95		
(2) One (CD)	A New Day AND CD 7	02/28/96		
(2) To Cry You A Song • A Collection Of Tull Tales (CD; tribute CD with Mick Abrahams, Clive Bunker and Glenn Cornick)			Magna Carta MA-9009-2	07/02/96
(2) Mick's Back (CD)	Indigo IGOX 501	07/15/96		
(4) Pig In The Middle (CD)	A New Day AND CD 10	11/25/96		
(2) "The Doomsday Clock" by HOUSE OF SATIRE (CD)	Satire CD 1	04/14/97		
(2) Modern Alchemist (CD)	Indigo IGOXCD 507	04/22/97		
(2) "Rattlesnake Guitar: "The Music Of Peter Green" (reissue - 2CD; one track: "The Same Way")			Viceroy/ Lightyear Entertainment 54190-2	06/10/97
(2) Live In Madrid (CD; live in 1974)	Indigo IGOCD 2065	07/29/97		
(3) All Said And Done (CD; re-promotion)	Elite ELITE 007CD	10/08/97		
(4) Live At The Lafayette (CD)	Indigo IGOCD 2067	02/24/98		
(4) The Full Porky: Live In London 1991 (CD; 1,000 copies only)	A New Day AND CD 20	05/08/98		
(5) This Is! (CD)	A New Day AND CD 25	12/10/98		

VIDEOS

TITLES	UK & FOREIGN LABEL/NO.	RELEASE DATE	US LABEL/NO.	RELEASE DATE
A Midsummer Night's Dream (VHS)	A Midsummer Night's Dream Video	03/24/95		
Guitar Tuition For Beginners (VHS)	Masterfield Productions Ltd. MFD	04/17/95		
Guitar Tuition For Intermediate (VHS)	Masterfield Productions Ltd. MFD	04/17/95		
Guitar Tuition For Advanced (VHS)	Masterfield Productions Ltd. MFD	04/17/95		

OUTSIDE SESSIONS - ALBUMS:

Title	UK & Foreign Label/No.	Release Date	US Label/No.	Release Date
"Gary Wright's Extraction" by GARY WRIGHT (LP)	A&M AMLS 2004	02/05/71	A&M SP 4277	01/11/71
"Low Flying Angels" by THE MIGHTY FLYERS (LP; Abrahams plays on all of the tracks except two)	Myrrh MYR 1016	12/06/74		
"Quick As A Roof" by JACKIE LYNTON (CD)	A New Day AND CD 6	02/28/96		
"Pin-Board Wizards" by JACKIE LYNTON (CD; guitar [with Martin Barre] on "If You Wanna Get A Band Together," "Odd Socks Blues," "Hi Lili, Hi Lo," "Getting By Blues," "Shut Up, I'm Playing Me Guitar" [with Martin Barre] and "How Much Do You Cry?")	A New Day AND CD14	06/22/98		

NOTE: Mick Abrahams also recorded with The Hollies. This session has not yet been documented.

RADIO SESSIONS:
Blodwyn Pig (BBC "Top Gear") - The Modern Alchemist; Mr. Green's Blues - 04/13/69 (recorded 03/24/69)
Blodwyn Pig (BBC "Top Gear") - It's Only Love - 07/13/69 (recorded 07/07/69)
Wommet (BBC Radio 1 "In Concert") - Greyhound Bus; How Can You Love Me So?; City Of Gold; Seasons; Slow Down - 11/70 (the transcription disc also includes tracks by Lindisfarne and Marmalade)
The Mick Abrahams Band (BBC Radio 1 "In Concert") - Why Do You Treat Me This Way?; Not To Rearrange; Seasons; Burning Rain Blues - 04/19/71
Blodwyn Pig (BBC Radio 1 "John Peel Show") - See My Way; Blues Of A Dunstable Truck Driving Man; Baby Girl; The Leaving Song - 07/09/74 (recorded 06/17/74; the transcription disc also includes The Spencer Davis Group)
Blodwyn Pig (BBC Radio 1 "In Concert") - See My Way; I Know; Cosmogrification; Blues Of A Dunstable Truck Driving Man; Six Days On The Road; It's Only Love - 09/74 (recorded 08/15/74 live at the Marquee)
Blodwyn Pig (Paul Jones' Rhythm And Blues Show on BBC Radio 2) - Watch Your Step; I Wonder Who Baby; All Tore Down - 12/28/89

NOTE: Mick Abrahams has appeared on radio numerous times. The above list consists of his officially recorded BBC sessions.

TELEVISION SESSIONS:
"Top Of The Pops", BBC, UK: See My Way; Ain't Ya Coming Home, Babe?
"Beat Club", German TV: See My Way; Ain't Ya Coming Home, Babe?
"Top Of The Pops, BBC, UK: "Slow Down"

IAN ANDERSON

TITLES	UK & FOREIGN LABEL/NO.	RELEASE DATE	US LABEL/NO.	RELEASE DATE
Fly By Night/ End Game (early copies have a longer intro on the B-side)	Chrysalis CHS 2746	11/18/83		

ALBUMS

WALK INTO LIGHT

MUSICIANS: Ian Anderson (guitars, flute, bass, drum programming, sequencing, serious vocals)
GUEST MUSICIANS: Peter-John Vettese (synthesizers, piano, blouse vocals)
PRODUCTION: Ian Anderson
RECORDING LOCATION/ DATE: spring/summer 1983 at Ian Anderson's home studio
TRACKS: Fly By Night (Ian Anderson/ Peter-John Vettese); Made In England (Ian Anderson/ Peter-John Vettese); Walk Into Light; Trains (Ian Anderson/ Peter-John Vettese); End Game;/ Black And White Television; Toad In The Hole; Looking For Eden; User-Friendly (Ian Anderson/ Peter-John Vettese); Different Germany (Ian Anderson/ Peter-John Vettese)
NOTES: The cover concept was by Ian Anderson, and the art direction was by John Pasche.
PEAK CHART POSITION (UK/US): #78 (UK)

RELEASES:

TITLES	UK & FOREIGN LABEL/NO.	RELEASE DATE	US LABEL/NO.	RELEASE DATE
Walk Into Light (LP)	Chrysalis CDL 1443	11/18/83	Chrysalis FV 41443	12/05/83
Walk Into Light (CD)	Chrysalis CCD 1443	03/14/88	Chrysalis VK 41443	04/25/88
Walk Into Light (CD; reissue)	Chrys./EMI CCD 1443	03/23/92	Chrys./EMI F2 21443	03/24/92
Walk Into Light (CD; reissue)	BGO BGOCD 350	04/29/97		

DIVINITIES: TWELVE DANCES WITH GOD

MUSICIANS: Ian Anderson (concert flute, alto flute, bamboo flute, wooden flutes, whistles)
GUEST MUSICIANS: Andrew Giddings (keyboards, orchestral tones and colors), Doane Perry (tuned and untuned percussion), Douglas Mitchell (clarinet), Christopher Cowie (oboe), Jonathon Carrey (violin), Nina Gresin (cello), Randy Wigs (harp), Sid Gander (French horn), Dan Redding (trumpet)
PRODUCTION: Ian Anderson
RECORDING LOCATION/ DATE: fall 1994 at Ian Anderson's home studio
TRACKS: In A Stone Circle; In Sight Of The Minaret; In A Black Box; In The Grip Of Stronger Stuff; In Maternal Grace; In The Moneylender's Temple; In Defence Of Faiths; At Their Father's Knee; En Afrique; In The Olive Garden; In The Pay Of Spain; In The Times Of India (Bombay Valentine)
NOTES: Orchestrations were by Ian Anderson and Andrew Giddings, with additional orchestrations and ideas by Gareth Wood and Roger Lewis. The album was designed by Zarkowski Designs.
PEAK CHART POSITION (UK/US): none

RELEASES:

TITLES	UK & FOREIGN LABEL/NO.	RELEASE DATE	US LABEL/NO.	RELEASE DATE
Divinities: Twelve Dances With God (CD)	EMI 5 55262 2	04/24/95	Angel 5 55262 2	05/02/95

"Peter Green Songbook" (CD; one track: "Man Of The World")	Semaphore 32473 422	07/30/95		
"Rattlesnake Guitar: The Music Of Peter Green" (2CD; one track: "Man Of The World")			Viceroy VIC2-8021	08/22/95
"Rattlesnake Guitar: "The Music Of Peter Green" (2CD; reissue - one track: "Man Of The World")			Viceroy/ Lightyear Entertainment 54190-2	06/10/97
Something With A Pulse by MARK CRANEY & FRIENDS (CD; "A Song For Jeffrey" recorded March 1997 with Andy Giddings and Martin Barre - UK issue cancelled)	A New Day AND CD 14	08/04/97	Laughing Gull LG002	08/05/97

TITLES	UK & FOREIGN LABEL/NO.	RELEASE DATE	US LABEL/NO.	RELEASE DATE
Yes We Can / Yes We Can (Native Sounds) by ARTISTS UNITED FOR NATURE (7")	German Virgin 112 764	09/**/89		
Sweet Temptation - Crazy Love - Aqualung Remix by NIXON (12"; flute)	MCA DNXNT 1	10/15/90		
Yes We Can / Yes We Can (Instrumental Mix) by ARTISTS UNITED FOR ANTURE (7")	ELF/PolyGram TV AUN 1	06/22/92		
Yes We Can - Yes We Can (Extended version Featuring Brian May) - Yes We Can (Instrumental Mix) by ARTISTS UNITED FOR NATURE (12"/ CD5)	ELF/PolyGram TV AUND 1/ 863 153-2	06/22/92		

OUTSIDE RECORDING SESSIONS - ALBUMS:

TITLES	UK & FOREIGN LABEL/NO.	RELEASE DATE	US LABEL/NO.	RELEASE DATE
"Now We Are Six" by STEELEYE SPAN (LP; Ian produced and mixed the album)	Chrysalis CHR 1053	02/22/74	Chrysalis CHR 1053	02/25/74
"Flashes From The Archives Of Oblivion" by ROY HARPER (2LP; one track: "Home")	Harvest SHDW 405	11/15/74		
"An Introduction To Roy Harper" by ROY HARPER (promotional LP with spoken comments by Ian Anderson and Paul McCartney)			Chrysalis PRO 620	02/22/76
"I/You" by BRIAN PROTHEROE (LP; flute on "Under The Greenwood Tree")	Chrysalis CHR 1108	04/23/76		
"Flashes From The Archives Of Oblivion" by ROY HARPER (first US release of this 2LP set; one track: "Home")			Chrysalis CHR 1164	02/27/78
"Woman In The Wings" by MADDY PRIOR (LP; produced by Ian Anderson, David Palmer and Robin Black; flute on "Gutter Geese" and uncredited backing vocals on "Rollercoaster")	Chrysalis CHR 1185	05/12/78	Takoma TAK 7078	05/05/80
"The Big Prize" by HONEYMOON SUITE (LP/CD; flute on "All Along You Knew")	Warner Bros. 25293-1/2	02/28/86	Warner Bros. 25293-1/2	02/24/86
"We Know What We Like: The Music Of Genesis" by THE LONDON SYMPHONY ORCHESTRA conducted by DAVID PALMER (CD; flute on "I Know What I Like")	RCA Victor 09026 56242 2	08/10/87	RCA Victor 09026 56242 2	08/11/87
"Pop Goes The World" by MEN WITHOUT HATS (LP/CD; flute on "On Tuesday")	Mercury 832 730-1/2	10/23/87	Mercury 832 730-1/2	10/19/87
"Valentine" (LP/CD; with "Home," which could not fit onto the CD of "Flashes From The Archives Of Oblivion")	Awareness AWL/AWCD 1015	04/17/89		
"The Third Leg" by FAIRPORT CONVENTION (double cassette; "Serenade To A Cuckoo" with Martin Barre and Dave Pegg)	Woodworm (no #)	08/14/89		
"Lettuce Prey" by THE SIX AND VIOLENCE (LP; flute and spoken word on "Bursting Bladder," flute on "Theological Guns")			Fist FR 1069	05/15/90
"Now We Are Six" by STEELEYE SPAN (CD)	Beat Goes On BGOCD 157	06/17/91	Shanachie CD 79060	07/01/91
"Unknown Territory" by BOMB THE BASS (CD; flute on "Love So True" that is only audible on the 12" mix, despite writer credits for both versions on the album. In addition, the flute sampled on "Winter In July [Ubiquity Mix]" could also have been sampled from Ian Anderson)	Rhythm King 4687740	08/19/91		
"Earthrise - The Rainforest Album" (with "Yes We Can" by ARTISTS UNITED FOR NATURE) (LP/CD)	ELF/PolyGram TV 515 419-1/2	06/15/92		
"Lettuce Prey" by THE SIX AND VIOLENCE (CD)			Fist FRCD 1069	05/18/93
"We Know What We Like: The Music Of Genesis" (CD; different cover)			RCA Victor 09026 56242 2	12/14/93
"People" by LESLIE MANDOKI (CD; three tracks: "Hold Onto Your Dreams," "I Dance Through My Dreams" and "Mother Europe")	Germ. Polydor 523 246-2	01/24/94		
"Woman In The Wings" by MADDY PRIOR (CD)	BGO BGOCD 215	03/07/94		
"Earthrise - The Rainforest Album" (belated US CD release)			Rhino/Pyramid R2 71830	10/18/94
"Valentine" (CD; with "Home," which could not fit onto the CD of "Flashes From The Archives Of Oblivion")	Science Friction HUCD 015	11/14/94	Griffin GCD-308-2	11/15/94
"One" by MICK ABRAHAMS (CD; four tracks with Mick: "Driftin' Blues," "How Long Blues," "Billy The Kid" and "Old Mother Nicotine")	A New Day AND CD 7	03/22/96		
"Lettuce Prey" (UKDB "Dog's Bollocks" Edition) by THE SIX AND VIOLENCE (CD; with extra tracks)	A New Day AND CD 9	08/26/96		
"I/You" by BRIAN PROTHEROE (CD)	Basta 30-90452	09/30/96		

"People In Room No. 8" by LESLIE MANDOKI (CD;
   four tracks: "Let The Music Show You The Way," "On And On,"
   "Back To Budapest" [an 08/20/96 Anderson/Mandoki-written live
   recording from Budapest] and "Hold On To Your Dreams")   Polydor 537 213-2   03/15/97
"The Jazz Cuts" by LESLIE MANDOKI (CD; 4 tracks with Ian)   Polydor 537 267-2   03/29/97
"The SAS Band" by THE SAS BAND   Bridge Recordings
   (CD; one track: "Baby, You're A Rich Man")   BRGCD 25   08/18/97
"Shadow Of The Moon" by RITCHIE BLACKMORE (CD; Ian Anderson   Jap. RCA BVCP-6022   09/30/97
   on "Play Minstrel Play" - this edition has a bonus track: "Minstrel Hall")
"Shadow Of The Moon" by RITCHIE BLACKMORE (CD; Ian Anderson
   on "Play Minstrel Play" - this edition has a bonus track: "Possom's Last   Whatever/Edel
   Dance")   0099022WHE   10/20/97
"People" by LESLIE MANDOKI (CD)   Polydor 539 629-2   02/02/98
"Pin-Board Wizards" by JACKIE LYNTON (CD; flute on "Let It
   Rock" and harmonica on "You Gotta Go")   A New Day AND CD 14   02/27/98
"Shadow Of The Moon" by RITCHIE BLACKMORE (CD; Ian Anderson   H.T.D. HTDCD 84   06/19/98
   on "Play Minstrel Play" - this edition has a bonus track: "Possom's Last
   Dance")"
"The Dream Society" by ROY HARPER (CD; flute on "These Fifty Years")   Resurgent 4305   06/22/98
"Awakening" by CLIVE BUNKER (CD; flute on "Strange Riff")   A New Day AND CD 21   08/25/98
"Valentine" by ROY HARPER (CD; reissue)   Resurgent 4066   04/20/99

VIDEOS

TITLES	UK & FOREIGN LABEL/NO.	RELEASE DATE	US LABEL/NO.	RELEASE DATE
Earthrise, The Rainforest Video (PAL VHS, with Ian Anderson on Artists United For Nature's "Yes We Can")	ELF/ PolyGram Video 515 561-3	06/15/92		

BARRIEMORE BARLOW

After the breakup of Tandoori Cassette in 1982, Barrie did separate sessions with Robert Plant and Jimmy Page, and Kerry Livgren of Kansas. Barlow formed the group The Storm in 1988 and he has been quiet ever since.

SINGLES

TITLES	UK & FOREIGN LABEL/NO.	RELEASE DATE	US LABEL/NO.	RELEASE DATE
Angel Talk/ Third World Briefcases (by TANDOORI CASSETTE)	IKA 001	**/**/82		

OUTSIDE SESSIONS - ALBUMS

TITLES	UK & FOREIGN LABEL/NO.	RELEASE DATE	US LABEL/NO.	RELEASE DATE
"I/You" by BRIAN PROTHEROE (LP; drums)	Chrysalis CHR 1108	04/23/76		
"Woman In The Wings" by MADDY PRIOR (LP; drums on "Woman In The Wings," "Cold Flame," "Gutter Geese," "Long Shadows," "I Told You So," Rosettes" and "Catseyes")	Chrysalis CHR 1185	05/12/78	Takoma TAK 7078	05/05/80
"Live At Queen Elizabeth Hall" by RICHARD DIGANCE (LP)	Chrysalis CHR 1187	08/11/78		
"Commercial Road" by RICHARD DIGANCE (LP; producer and drums)	Chrysalis CHR 1262	02/22/80		
"Seeds Of Change" by KERRY LIVGREN (LP)	Kirshner KIR 84453	07/17/80	Kirshner NJZ 36567	07/13/80
"The Principle Of Moments" by ROBERT PLANT (LP)	Swan Song 90101-1	07/15/83	Swan Song 90101-1	07/18/83
"Rising Force" by YNGWIE MALMSTEEN (LP)	Polydor 825 324-1	05/10/85	Polydor 825 324-1	05/13/85
"Transition" by JOHN MILES (LP)	Valentino 7904761	03/21/86		
"Rising Force" by YNGWIE MALMSTEEN (CD)	Polydor 825 324-2	04/08/88	Polydor 825 324-2	04/11/88
"The Principle Of Moments" by ROBERT PLANT (CD)	Swan Song 90101-2	04/29/88	Swan Song 90101-2	05/02/88
"Outrider" by JIMMY PAGE (LP/CD)	Geffen WX155/ 9 24188 1 & 2	06/20/88	Geffen 24188 1 & 2	06/21/88
"Seeds Of Change" by KERRY LIVGREN (CD)	Jap. Sony SRCS 6297	05/21/93		
"Woman In The Wings" by MADDY PRIOR (CD)	BGO BGOCD 215	03/07/94		
"Dark Horse: The Secret Life Of George Harrison" by THE BEATLES (CD; with Barlow interview material)			Laserlight 12595	08/22/95
"In Their Own Words: A Rockumentary" (5CD box set; with Barlow interview material)			Laserlight 15968	09/26/95
"Live At Queen Elizabeth Hall"/ "Commercial Road" by RICHARD DIGANCE (CD)	BGO BGOCD 304	03/08/96		
"I/You" by BRIAN PROTHEROE (CD)	Basta 30-90452	09/30/96		
"Seeds Of Change" by KERRY LIVGREN (CD)			Renaissance RMED00112	11/19/96

MARTIN BARRE

SINGLES

TITLES	UK & FOREIGN LABEL/NO.	RELEASE DATE	US LABEL/NO.	RELEASE DATE
Suspicion (promo CD5)	German ZYX	04/18/94		

ALBUMS

TITLES	UK & FOREIGN LABEL/NO.	RELEASE DATE	US LABEL/NO.	RELEASE DATE
A Summer Band (500 CDs and cassettes sold only through A New Day)	Presshouse MBSBCD 92	06/28/93		
A Trick Of Memory (CD)	ZYX Music 20282-2	05/02/94	ZYX Music 20282-2	04/12/94
The Meeting (CD; 1,000 copies only on Presshouse which were sold through A New Day. Paul Cox's vocal was on the track "Running Free" on the Presshouse edition, but Maggie Reeday's vocal was on the Imago release)	Presshouse 810.135	03/22/96	Imago 72787-23016-2	09/03/96
Spirit Flying Free (JOHN CARTER with MARTIN BARRE) (CD)	A New Day AND CD 16	11/30/96		

OUTSIDE SESSIONS - SINGLES

TITLES	UK & FOREIGN LABEL/NO.	RELEASE DATE	US LABEL/NO.	RELEASE DATE
Young Boy - Broomstick - Oobu Joobu Part 2: Wide Screen Radio; Oobu Joobu We Love You; Oobu Joobu Main Theme; Brilliant, What's Next?; Atlantic Ocean (with Martin Barre); Paul McCartney Reminisces; Bourèe; Oobu Joobu We Love You; Oobu Joobu Main Theme (CD5; second single of a 2CD single set)	Parlophone CDRS 6462	04/28/97		
The Groove by GLOBAL COMMUNICATIONS (12" [three mixes]/CD5 [six mixes]; flute)	Dedicated GLOBA 003 T1/ 003CD	10/27/97		

OUTSIDE SESSIONS - ALBUMS

TITLES	UK & FOREIGN LABEL/NO.	RELEASE DATE	US LABEL/NO.	RELEASE DATE
"You & Me" by CHICK CHURCHILL (LP; four tracks)	Chrysalis CHR 1051	10/13/72	Chrysalis CHR 1051	10/16/72
"Woman In The Wings" by MADDY PRIOR (LP; guitar solo on "Cold Flame")				
"Caught In The Crossfire" by JOHN WETTON (LP)	EG EGLP 107	11/07/80		
"The Third Leg" by FAIRPORT CONVENTION (double cassette; "Serenade To A Cuckoo" with Ian Anderson and Dave Pegg)	Woodworm (no #)	08/14/89		
"Flowers In The Dirt" (2CD; Barre on "P.S. Love Me Do")	Jap. EMI-Toshiba TOCP-6118	10/25/90		
"Woman In The Wings" by MADDY PRIOR (CD)	BGO BGOCD 215	03/07/94		
"Just For The Halibut" by FIVE FURIOUS FISH (cassette; two tracks with Barre: "Cajun Moon" and "People's Limousine")	private release	07/**/95		
"Navigando" by SANTINO DE BARTOLO (CD)	Italian Radio Marconi 270460	**/**/96		
"Movers And Shakers" by VIKKI CLAYTON (CD; Barre on "Beguiled," "Movers And Shakers" and "Sir Hugh Of Lincoln")	A New Day AND CD 15	03/25/97		
"Something With A Pulse" by MARK CRANEY & FRIENDS (CD; "A Song For Jeffrey" recorded March 1997 with Andy Giddings and Martin Barre - UK issue cancelled)	A New Day AND CD 14	08/04/97	Laughing Gull LG002	08/05/97
"Weights And Measures" by SPIRIT OF THE WEST (CD; guitar on "Waking The Lion")			Canadian WEA 19716-2	10/29/97
"Pin-Board Wizards" by JACKIE LYNTON (CD; guitar on "If You Wanna Get A Band Together," "Losing Ground," and "Shut Up, I'm Playing Me Guitar" [first and third tracks with Mick Abrahams])	A New Day AND CD 14	02/27/98		
"Awakening" by CLIVE BUNKER (CD; guitar on "Do We Know Where We're Going?," "Good Times" and "Strange Riff")	A New Day AND CD 21	08/25/98		
"Encores, Legends & Paradox: A Tribute To The Music Of ELP" (CD; one track with Doane Perry: "A Time And A Place")			Magna Carta MA-9026-2	04/06/99
"Clean The Page" by JOHN CARTER (2CD)	A New Day AND CD 31	07/19/99		

NOTE: Martin Barre does not want to reveal his other sessions, on which he plays guitar, flute and sax! On the "25th Anniversary Interview" album, For example, Martin discussed the completion of a sax session he had just finished with a heavy metal band.

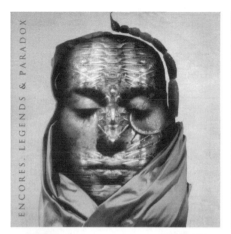

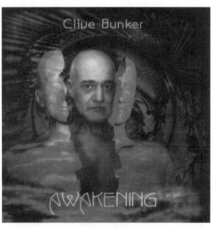

Above middle and left photos: Manfred Mann's Earth Band with Clive Bunker in the lineup. Middle photo lineup: (rear) Clive Bunker, Noel McCalla; (front) Steve Kinch, Manfred Mann, Mick Rogers. (Photo courtesy of Andy Taylor)

At left: Steve Kinch, Clive Bunker, Manfred Mann, Mick Rogers, Noel McCalla.

Middle right: a Clive Bunker self-portrait as a prisoner!

CLIVE BUNKER

After leaving Jethro Tull, Clive Bunker got married and formed the group Jude in July 1971 with ex-Procol Harum guitarist Robin Trower, bassist James Dewar and vocalist Frankie Miller. They were part of the Chrysalis stable, but they broke up in April 1972 after Chris Wright's attempts to make them a guitar hero band caused unnecessary friction. Clive withdrew from the music scene for a while, preparing himself to create an engineering factory and boarding kennels. He re-entered the scene in 1974, joining the short-lived reformation of Mick Abrahams' group Blodwyn Pig. Bunker would not reappear until 1976, when he did Steve Hillage's "L" tour. The tour started with a free concert at Hyde Park that September and lasted until the end of the year. This was followed by album sessions for Gordon Giltrap and former Blodwyn Pig sax/flute player Jack Lancaster in 1978. The latter session led to Clive Bunker's enlistment in Aviator with Mick Rogers (Manfred Mann's Earth Band guitarist/vocalist), Jack Lancaster and bassist John Perry. After two albums ("Aviator" and "Turbulence") that did not express their powerful live act on record, Aviator quit in 1980. While still a member of Aviator, Clive did a notable session for "The Steve Howe Album."

Once again, another break in Clive's activities took place. He worked with Uli Jon Roth's group Electric Sun, and this resulted in the 1985 album "Beyond The Astral Skies." In 1986, Bunker would join the club band Poor Mouth with Jackie McAuley (guitar/vocals), Tommy Lundy (guitar) and Phil Rynhardt on bass. Poor Mouth would soon add members Trader Horne and Cult. They broke up in 1988 in the middle of recording an album, but Clive was back with Blodwyn Pig by the end of that year. Bunker stayed with McAuley and Italian musician Bernardo Lambretti to play the restaurant circuit in Italy. Better things were on the way when Mick Rogers recommended Clive for the drummer slot in the reformed Manfred Mann's Earth Band in early 1991. Bunker got the job and the band did their first gig in Guildford in May 1991. The Earth Band tried out new material while on tour for the next two years, and album recording took place throughout at Manfred's Workhouse Studios in London. During his stint with Manfred, Clive continued to do the odd gig with Blodwyn Pig. Recording for Manfred Mann's Earth Band was slow going. In 1994, Bunker discovered that Manfred wanted to use other drummers on the album, even though he had already been playing and recording the same material for three years. Clive Bunker decided to leave at this point, and the album he was working on, "Soft Vengeance," would not be issued in England until June 1996! Some of the tracks feature Clive's drumming, especially a brilliant version of Bob Dylan's "Shelter From The Storm."

Bunker went through a very down period in which he was forced to make some instructional drum videos to keep things going. Additional work with Mick Abrahams and Vikki Clayton re-energized Clive's playing, and Clive joined the innovative band Solstice. Clive's first solo album, "Awakening," came together in 1998 and was a surprising collection of songs featuring his vocals and percussion talents. In May 1998, he was part of Uli Jon's Roth's band during their segment of Joe Satriani's G3 tour with Roth and Michael Schenker. Bunker then appeared with The Eleanor Rigby Experience between April 30 and May 29, 1999 with Martin Allcock (bass, mandolin and keyboards), Phil Bates (guitar/vocals), Andy Bole (guitar and bouzouki) and vocalist Tina McBain. To promote their concerts, a CD containing their covers of Lennon/McCartney classics was sold during the tour. Unfortunately, Allcock only did the tour and was replaced by Fred T. Baker from Vikki Clayton's band. The album "Raise A Glass To Raymond Jones" has been prepared for their tour in 2000. Clive Bunker remains at the top of his abilities and is ready for action!

ARTIST CODE:
(1) Steve Hillage
(2) Aviator
(3) Uli Jon Roth & Electric Sun
(4) Mick Abrahams' Blodwyn Pig
(5) Manfred Mann's Earth Band
(6) Solstice
(7) Clive Bunker

SINGLES

TITLES	UK & FOREIGN LABEL/NO.	RELEASE DATE	US LABEL/NO.	RELEASE DATE
(2) Lay Down Your Weary Tune/ Greed	Harvest HAR 5171	10/27/78		
(2) Time Traveller/ Rocking Chair	Harvest HAR 5180	02/16/79		
(2) Way Of The World/ Wood Wharf Gumbo	Harvest HAR 5202	02/22/80		
(2) All Your Love Is Gone/ Wood Wharf Gumbo	Harvest HAR 5208	07/11/80		
(5) Nothing Ever Happens (Radio Mix) - Nothing Ever Happens (TV Mix) - Shelter From The Storm (with Clive Bunker) - Adults Only (CD5)	German Virgin 8 93614 2	05/20/96		

ALBUMS

TITLES	UK & FOREIGN LABEL/NO.	RELEASE DATE	US LABEL/NO.	RELEASE DATE
(1) Live Herald (2LP)	Virgin VGD 3502	01/19/79		
(2) Aviator (LP)	Harvest SHSP 4096	04/13/79	EMI America ST-17012	05/21/79
(2) Turbulence (LP)	Harvest SHSP 4107	04/11/80		
(3) Beyond The Astral Skies (LP)	EMI ROTH 1	02/15/85		
(1) Live Herald (2CD)			Blue Plate CAROL 1671 2	07/23/90
(4) All Tore Down (CD)	Indigo IGOCD 2011	10/24/94		
(3) Firewind/Earthquake/Beyond The Astral Skies (3CD; Clive Bunker is on "Beyond The Astral Skies")			Griffin GCD-351-2	06/13/95
(5) Soft Vengeance (CD; Clive Bunker on "Shelter From The Storm" and others)	Grapevine GRACD 213	06/03/96		
(6) Circles (CD)	A New Day AND CD 13	11/04/96		
(3) Beyond The Astral Skies (CD)	Jap. EMI TOCP 3356	10/29/97		
(7) Awakening (CD)	A New Day AND CD 21	08/25/98		
(6) Pathways (2CD)	A New Day AND CD 22	08/10/99		

OUTSIDE SESSIONS - ALBUMS

TITLES	UK & FOREIGN LABEL/NO.	RELEASE DATE	US LABEL/NO.	RELEASE DATE
"Skinningrove Bay" by JACK LANCASTER (LP)	Acrobat ACRO 1	10/20/78		
"Fear Of The Dark" by GORDON GILTRAP (LP)	Electric TRIX 7	11/17/78		
"The Steve Howe Album" by STEVE HOWE (LP; percussion on "Cactus Boogie")	Atlantic K 50621	11/02/79	Atlantic SD 19243	01/21/80
"Skinningrove Bay" by JACK LANCASTER (LP)	Kamera KAM005	02/12/82		
"The Steve Howe Album" by STEVE HOWE (CD)	Jap. Atlantic AMCY-21	**/**/85		
"Wild Connections" by JACK LANCASTER (LP/CD; retitled version of "Skinningrove Bay")	Bold Reprieve BR/ BRMCD 001	06/20/87		
"Skinningrove Bay" by JACK LANCASTER (CD)	C5 C5CD 580	03/16/92		
"The Steve Howe Album" by STEVE HOWE (CD)	Atlantic 765781599-2	09/16/94	Atlantic 81599-2	05/17/94
"Wild Connections" by JACK LANCASTER (CD; billed as Phil Collins, Gary Moore and Rod Argent)	Tring JHD 063	09/23/94		
"To Cry You A Song • A Collection Of Tull Tales" (CD; tribute CD with Mick Abrahams, Clive Bunker and Glenn Cornick)			Magna Carta MA-9009-2	07/02/96
"Pig In The Middle" by MICK ABRAHAMS' BLODWYN PIG (CD)	A New Day AND CD 10	11/25/96		
"Navigando" by SANTINO DE BARTOLO (CD)	Italian Radio Marconi 270460	**/**/96		
"Skinningrove Bay" by JACK LANCASTER (CD)	Zok ZCDJL013	11/26/97		
"Honor-Tokened" by VIKKI CLAYTON (CD; Bunker on 3 live tracks)	A New Day AND CD 18	02/27/98		
"Lost Lady Found" by VIKKI CLAYTON (CD; Bunker on 3 live tracks)	A New Day AND CD 19	03/01/98		
"Pin-Board Wizards" by JACKIE LYNTON (CD; drums on "If You Wanna Get A Band Together," "Getting By Blues" and "Shut Up, I'm Playing Me Guitar")	A New Day AND CD 14	06/22/98		
"Shadowboxing" by JACKIE McAULEY	The Road Goes On Forever RGF/ JMCCD 1041	04/28/99		
"The Eleanor Rigby Experience - The Art Of Lennon And McCartney" by THE ELEANOR RIGBY EXPERIENCE (CD-R)	Notable Music CD/ERE1599	04/30/99		

VIDEOS

TITLES	UK & FOREIGN LABEL/NO.	RELEASE DATE	US LABEL/NO.	RELEASE DATE
Drum Tuition For Beginners	Masterfield Productions Ltd. MFD 0024	04/17/95		
Drum Tuition For Intermediate	Masterfield Productions Ltd. MFD 0025	04/17/95		
Drum Tuition For Advanced	Masterfield Productions Ltd. MFD 0026	04/17/95		
"Live At Cropredy 1998" by SOLSTICE (PAL VHS)	A New Day AND V1	07/19/99		
"Live At Cropredy 1998" by VIKKI CLAYTON (PAL VHS)	A New Day AND V2	07/19/99		

GLENN CORNICK

Glenn formed Wild Turkey after his expulsion from Jethro Tull. Cornick remained in the Chrysalis stable despite being thrown out of Tull, and he was encouraged to form his own band. Wild Turkey consisted of former Eyes Of Blue vocalist Gary Pickford-Hopkins, Tweke Lewis (guitar), guitarist Jon Blackmore and Jeff Jones (drums and percussion). The band's stock in trade was progressive rock, but Blackmore was not happy with it. After their first album "Battle Hymn," Jon Blackmore was replaced by guitarist Mick Dyche and keyboard player Steve Gurl. The album just scraped the US chart, reaching #193. After their second album "Turkey," Wild Turkey disbanded in 1973 and Tweke Lewis joined the group Man. Cornick moved to Berlin in the former West Germany to work on Kathargo's "Rock 'N Roll Testament" album. Cornick was still signed to Chrysalis at the time, but he would not issue any more material for the label. As it turned out, the person Cornick replaced (Gerald Hartwig) returned to the group after the album was recorded. Glenn ran into former Fleetwood Mac guitarist/vocalist Bob Welch and formed the group Paris with Thom Mooney (ex-Nazz). Paris issued two albums in 1976 ("Paris" and "Big Towne, 2061") before they packed it in. Again, both albums had short stays on the US chart, reaching #103 and #152 respectively. Cornick left the music industry in 1977 and became the sales manager of a pet food company in Los Angeles. A decade later, Glenn returned to the music scene by recording an unreleased Irish music album with the group Blended Spirits. The group was made up of Cait Reed (fiddle), Jimmy Keigher (vocals, guitar), Ken O'Malley (vocals, guitar, mandolin), Robbie Rye (drums) and Danny Hannon (drums). Wild Turkey was reformed in 1995 and issued the album "Stealer Of Years." Cornick lives in Downey, CA and regularly attends Tull conventions. Catch him there!

ARTIST CODE:
(1) Wild Turkey
(2) Kathargo
(3) Paris

SINGLES

TITLES	UK & FOREIGN LABEL/NO.	RELEASE DATE	US LABEL/NO.	RELEASE DATE
(1) Good Old Days/ Life Is A Symphony	Chrysalis CHS 2004	09/29/72	Chrysalis CHS 2004	12/04/72
(3) Big Towne, 2061/ Blue Robin			Capitol 4356	11/15/76

ALBUMS

TITLES	UK & FOREIGN LABEL/NO.	RELEASE DATE	US LABEL/NO.	RELEASE DATE
(1) Battle Hymn (LP)	Chrysalis CHR 1002	10/29/71	Reprise MS 2070	03/13/72
(1) Turkey (LP)	Chrysalis CHR 1010	09/29/72	Reprise CHR 1051	12/04/72
(1) Battle Hymn (LP; reissue)			Chrysalis CHR 1045	12/04/72
(2) Rock 'N Roll Testament (LP)	German Bacillus BLPS 19201	02/14/75		
(3) Paris (LP)			Capitol ST-11464	01/26/76
(3) Big Towne, 2061 (LP)			Capitol ST-11560	08/16/76
(1) Battle Hymn (CD)	Edsel EDCD 337	11/15/91		
(1) Turkey (CD)	Edsel EDCD 424	06/20/95		
(1) Stealer Of Years (CD)	H.T.D. HTDCD 58	05/13/96		

OUTSIDE SESSIONS - ALBUMS

TITLES	UK & FOREIGN LABEL/NO.	RELEASE DATE	US LABEL/NO.	RELEASE DATE
"Cast Of Thousands" by LEIGH STEPHENS	Charisma CAS 1040	09/10/71		
"To Cry You A Song • A Collection Of Tull Tales" (CD; tribute CD with Mick Abrahams, Clive Bunker and Glenn Cornick)			Magna Carta MA-9009-2	07/02/96

The original lineup of Wild Turkey: Jeff Jones, Glenn Cornick, Gary Pickford-Hopkins, Tweke Lewis, Jon Blackmore.

In 1973, Glenn Cornick played bass on Karthargo's "Rock 'N Roll Testament" LP. Wild Turkey reconvened to the studio in January and February 1996 to record the album "Stealer Of Years." At right is the revised lineup: Glenn Cornick, Gary Pickford-Hopkins, Tweke Lewis and Brian Thomas.

ANDREW GIDDINGS

ALBUMS

TITLES	UK & FOREIGN LABEL/NO.	RELEASE DATE	US LABEL/NO.	RELEASE DATE
"I Used To Be An Animal" by ERIC BURDON (LP)			Striped Horse SHD 5006	08/15/88
"I'm Your Fan - The Songs Of Leonard Cohen" (various artists tribute to Leonard Cohen) (LP/CD; Andy Giddings played all instruments and produced Eric Burdon's "I'm Your Man")	East West WX 444/ 9031755982	09/30/91	Atlantic 82349-2	11/26/91
"I Used To Be An Animal" by ERIC BURDON (CD)	Success 16153 CD	07/18/94		
"Divinities: Twelve Dances With God" by Ian Anderson (CD)	EMI 5 55262 2	04/24/95	Angel 5 55262 2	05/02/95
"Peter Green Songbook" (CD; one track with Ian Anderson: "Man Of The World")	Semaphore 32473 422	07/30/95		
"Rattlesnake Guitar: The Music Of Peter Green" (2CD; one track: "Man Of The World")			Viceroy VIC2-8021	08/22/95
"I Used To Be An Animal" by ERIC BURDON (CD)			Prime Cuts 2326	06/11/96
"Navigando" by SANTINO DE BARTOLO (CD)	Italian Radio Marconi 270460	**/**/96		
"Rattlesnake Guitar: "The Music Of Peter Green" (2CD; reissue - one track: "Man Of The World")			Viceroy/ Lightyear Entertainment 54190-2	06/10/97
Something With A Pulse by MARK CRANEY & FRIENDS (CD; with "A Song For Jeffrey" [recorded March 1997 with Ian Anderson and Martin Barre] and Eric Burdon's "I'm Your Man" - UK issue cancelled)	A New Day AND CD 14	08/04/97	Laughing Gull LG002	08/05/97

NOTE: Giddings has also recorded with other unidentified German and French acts between his stint with Eric Burdon and his enrollment in Jethro Tull.

JOHN GLASCOCK

ARTIST CODE:
(1) The Juniors
(2) The Gods
(3) Toe Fat
(4) Head Machine
(5) Chicken Shack
(6) Carmen

SINGLES

TITLES	UK & FOREIGN LABEL/NO.	RELEASE DATE	US LABEL/NO.	RELEASE DATE
(1) There's A Pretty Girl/ Pocket Size	Columbia DB 7339	08/21/64	MGM K 13271	09/13/64
(2) Come On Down To My Boat Baby/ Garage Man	Polydor BM 56168	06/09/67		
(2) Baby's Rich/ Somewhere In The Street	Columbia DB 8486	10/11/68		
(2) Hey Bulldog/ Real Love Guaranteed	Columbia DB 8544	02/14/69		
(2) Maria/ Long Time, Sad Time, Bad Time	Columbia DB 8572	05/02/69		
(3) Bad Side Of The Moon/ Working Nights	Parlophone R 5829	02/27/70		
(3) Just Like Me/ Bad Side Of The Moon			Rare Earth 5019	11/02/70
(5) As Time Goes Passing By/ Poor Boy (Glascock on B-side)	Deram DM 381	03/23/73	London 7537	03/26/73
(5) You Know You Could Be Right/ The Loser (Glascock on B-side)	Deram DM 396	07/27/73		
(6) Flamenco Fever/ Lonely House	Regal Zono. RZ 3086	04/05/74		
(6) Bulerias/ Stepping Stone	Regal Zono. RZ 3090	08/09/74		

ALBUMS

TITLES	UK & FOREIGN LABEL/NO.	RELEASE DATE	US LABEL/NO.	RELEASE DATE
(2) The Gods (LP)	Columbia SX/SCX 6286	10/25/68		
(2) To Samuel A Son (LP)	Columbia SCX 6372	01/16/70		
(3) Toe Fat (LP)	Parlophone PCS 7097	05/01/70	Rare Earth RS 511	07/27/70
(4) Orgasm (LP)	Major Minor SMLP 79	05/29/70		
(4) Orgasm (LP; different cover)	French Vogue SLVLX.522	06/26/70		
(3) Toe Fat Two (LP)	Regal Zono. SLRZ 1015	11/13/70	Rare Earth RS 525	09/27/71
(5) Imagination Lady (LP)	Deram SDL 5	02/04/72	Deram DES 18063	02/07/72
(6) Fandangos In Space (LP; US has different cover)	Regal Zono. SRZA 8518	11/16/73	Paramount PAS-1044	01/28/74
(6) Fandangos In Space (LP; reissue with same US cover)			ABC DSDP-50192	10/28/74

TITLES	UK & FOREIGN LABEL/NO.	RELEASE DATE	US LABEL/NO.	RELEASE DATE
(6) Dancing On A Cold Wind (LP)	Regal Zono. SLRZ 1040	01/17/75		
(6) The Gypsies (LP)			Mercury SRM-1-1047	09/22/75
(2) The Gods Featuring Ken Hensley (LP)	Harvest SHSM 2011	11/19/76	Import IMP 102	01/25/77
(6) Fandangos In Space (CD)	German Line LICD 9.00598 O	07/02/88		
(6) Dancing On A Cold Wind (CD)	German Line LICD 9.00601 O	07/02/88		
(6) The Gypsies (CD)	German Line LICD 9.00658 O	07/02/88		
(2) The Gods Featuring Ken Hensley (LP)	C5 C5 537	08/07/89		
(6) Fandangos In Space/ Dancing On A Cold Wind (CD)	German Line LICD 9.21150 O	02/03/92		
(3) Toe Fat (CD)	German Repertoire REP 4416-WY	01/19/94		
(3) Toe Fat Two (CD)	German Repertoire REP 4417-WY	01/19/94		
(2) The Gods (CD)	German Repertoire REP 4418-WY	05/20/94		
(5) Imagination Lady (CD)	Deram 844 169 2	10/07/94		
(3) Toe Fat/ Toe Fat Two (CD)	BGO BGOCD 278	04/26/95		
(2) To Samuel A Son (CD)	German Repertoire REP-4555-WY	05/08/95		
(5) Imagination Lady (CD; reissue)	Indigo IGOXCD 506	04/24/97		
(2) "Psychedelia At Abbey Road 1965-1969" (CD; with first-time stereo mix of The Gods' "Hey Bulldog")	EMI 4 96912 2	08/31/98		

NOTE: The Head Machine album "Orgasm" has been bootlegged three times: German TRC 035 (released 10/29/93), Audio Archives AACD014 (released 02/16/96) and with the album "Weed!" featuring Ken Hensley.

OUTSIDE SESSIONS - ALBUMS

TITLES	UK & FOREIGN LABEL/NO.	RELEASE DATE	US LABEL/NO.	RELEASE DATE
"Woman In The Wings" by MADDY PRIOR (LP; bass on "Woman In The Wings," "Long Shadows," "Rosettes" and "Catseyes")	Chrysalis CHR 1185	05/12/78	Takoma TAK 7078	05/05/80
"Commercial Road" by RICHARD DIGANCE (LP; bass on "East End Ding Dong" and "Beauty Queen")	Chrysalis CHR 1262	02/22/80		
"Woman In The Wings" by MADDY PRIOR (CD)	BGO BGOCD 215	03/07/94		
"Live At Queen Elizabeth Hall"/ "Commercial Road" by RICHARD DIGANCE (CD)	BGO BGOCD 304	03/08/96		

NOTE: John Glascock also recorded material for the Tallis album which remains unreleased.

RADIO SESSIONS:
BBC Radio One, UK (airdate: 10/25/68): Summer In The City; Real Love Guaranteed; You Keep Me Hangin' On; You're My Life; Towards The Sky (As of 01/11/99, these tracks were available on a CD-R [mistitled "Live '67"] from Gods guitarist Joe Konas. Konas' address is shown on page 2.)
Nightbird & Company, Army Reserve Programs #193-#196 (2LP) (airdate: 01/75): #193 Deep Purple; #194 Chick Corea; #195 Kenny Rankin; #196 Carmen

JONATHAN NOYCE

OUTSIDE SESSIONS - SINGLES

TITLES	UK & FOREIGN LABEL/NO.	RELEASE DATE	US LABEL/NO.	RELEASE DATE
Thinking Of You (remixes) by SISTER SLEDGE (CD5)	Warner Bros. A 4515CD	05/17/93		
The Groove (six mixes) by GLOBAL COMMUNICATIONS (12"/CD5)	Dedicated GLOBA 003 T1/ 003CD	10/27/97		

OUTSIDE SESSIONS - ALBUMS

TITLES	UK & FOREIGN LABEL/NO.	RELEASE DATE	US LABEL/NO.	RELEASE DATE
"Everything Changes" by TAKE THAT! (CD; "Relight My Fire")	RCA 16926-2	10/08/93		
"Universe Of Love" by JOEY NEGRO (CD)	Virgin CDV 2714	10/08/93		
"Orchestral Sgt. Pepper's" by THE ROYAL ACADEMY OF MUSIC SYMPHONY ORCHESTRA arranged and conducted by DAVID PALMER (CD)	Premier (MFP) CDDPR 125	10/17/94	EMI (Canada) 5 55321 2	03/14/95
"Love, Love, Love" by SECRET LIFE (CD)	Arcade 3001863	11/24/95		
"The Meeting" by MARTIN BARRE (CD)	Presshouse 810.135	03/22/96	Imago 72787-23016-2	09/03/96
"Spirit Flying Free" by JOHN CARTER with MARTIN BARRE (CD)	A New Day AND CD 16	11/30/96		
"Clean The Page" by JOHN CARTER (2CD)	A New Day AND CD 31	07/19/99		

DAVID PALMER

To say David Palmer is a busy man is a vast understatement. He has consistently moved from one challenging orchestral project to another, all of which have maximized his unique talents. After first working with Bert Jansch and then Jethro Tull on "This Was," Palmer's orchestral contributions were part of nearly every Tull album until he joined the band in 1976. In between, David Palmer worked on a variety of recordings spanning all aspects of pop music. The first of these was a pair of Pye singles for Maxine Nightingale, known later for the hits "Right Back Where We Started From" and "Lead Me On." Palmer also became the youngest conductor of Amsterdam's Royal Concertgebouw Orchestra.

Comedian Max Bygraves was an unlikely source for orchestral assistance, but Palmer helped Max on the first few volumes in his "Singalongamax" series of albums in the early '70s. Of these, "Sing Along With Max" was a #4 UK hit album in 1972, and the 1973 album "Singalongpartysong" generated the #13 British hit "Deck Of Cards." On a more serious note, Palmer conducted the Philomusica of London at the Royal Academy of Music on July 16, 1972. Yes guitarist Steve Howe joined Palmer for this performance. David Palmer then moved on to orchestrations for Gerry Rafferty and Billy Connolly. Palmer co-produced and arranged his orchestrations on Maddy Prior's "Woman In The Wings" LP and he also contributed heavily to Richard Digance's "Commercial Road" album in 1979.

While still in Jethro Tull, David Palmer and John Evans started work on their Tallis album with guest appearances by John Glascock, Barriemore Barlow and others. When this album project fizzled in 1981, Palmer concentrated on the classical treatment of rock classics. Palmer signed with RCA's classical division and set out plans for a series of classical crossover albums. The first of these was a source close to home - Jethro Tull. The album "A Classic Case: The London Symphony Orchestra Plays The Music Of Jethro Tull" was first issued in Germany in 1985 with a US release at year's end. "We Know What We Like" treated the music of Genesis, and Ian Anderson chipped in with a flute solo on one track. Pink Floyd was next, and the album "Objects Of Fantasy" was the result. It was later retitled "Orchestral Maneuvers: The Music Of Pink Floyd." In 1993, "Symphonic Music Of Yes" appeared with considerable involvement by Yes members (similar to the Jethro Tull release). This album hit #1 on Billboard's Classical Crossover chart in December 1993.

In between all of these activities, Palmer worked on a diverse set of orchestral work. He assisted Ian Anderson on his German TV appearance of "Fly By Night" in 1983, and then worked on electronic treatments of Mozart's piano sonatas in Paris. He also did work on advertisements. David Palmer's classical concerts at London's Barbican Theatre and other locations continued, including a June 20, 1991 performance at the Montreal International Festival of Music in Montreal, Canada. In late 1991, a series of video/CD packages on the music of Beethoven, Mozart and Tchaikovsky were released with narrative by David Palmer. These products were produced by Cromwell Productions and were only sold at Boots pharmacies. The programs were also shown on public television in the US.

In 1993, Palmer planned to put together a group called La Salle with guitarist Damian Wilson, Neil Murray (of Whitesnake) and Guy Fletcher (of Dire Straits), but this idea failed to gel. The next year, David Palmer was to be honored in a very special way. Palmer was appointed a Fellow of the Royal Academy of Music in 1994, an honor that is given to at most 250 living holders. He responded in a great way by assisting and advising on the setting up of the Academy's commercial music department.

With the completion of his RCA contract, Palmer created three more crossover albums: "Orchestral Sgt. Pepper's," "Passing Open Windows: A Symphonic Tribute To Queen" and "Norsk Popklassikere." The first of these was a classically-driven treatment of the landmark Beatles album "Sgt. Pepper's Lonely Hearts Club Band." The Queen album was perhaps Palmer's most focused work, and it was honored by a London concert at which Ian Anderson guested. The album was dedicated to Palmer's wife, who had died of Lupus during its production. "Norsk Popklassikere" was a Norway-only release, and hit #13 on the Norwegian album chart. The success of this gold-selling album was not without controversy. The CD was a rearranged collection of Norwegian pop and rock classics, but the general consensus in that country was that Palmer's arrangements were so far removed from the original works that the songs were unrecognizable! Despite his poor showing with the Norwegian press, Palmer was invited to conduct the Bergen Philharmonic Orchestra for a series of Christmas concerts. In the end, David Palmer won the battle.

David Palmer has also discussed another recording album with Bert Jansch. For sure, there's more to come from David Palmer!

TITLES	UK & FOREIGN LABEL/NO.	RELEASE DATE	US LABEL/NO.	RELEASE DATE
Bourrée/Elegy (shown as by THE LONDON SYMPHONY ORCHESTRA featuring Ian Anderson)			RCA Red Seal PB-14262	01/13/86

ALBUMS

TITLES	UK & FOREIGN LABEL/NO.	RELEASE DATE	US LABEL/NO.	RELEASE DATE
A Classic Case: The London Symphony Orchestra Plays The Music Of Jethro Tull (LP; conducting and arranging. Credited to THE LONDON SYMPHONY ORCHESTRA featuring Ian Anderson)	German RCA Red Seal RL 71134	02/15/85	RCA Red Seal XRL1-7067	12/31/85
A Classic Case: The London Symphony Orchestra Plays The Music Of Jethro Tull (CD)			RCA Red Seal RCD1-7067	12/31/85
We Know What We Like: The Music Of Genesis (CD; credited to LONDON SYMPHONY ORCHESTRA conducted by DAVID PALMER (CD)	RCA Victor 09026 56242 2	08/10/87	RCA Victor 09026 56242 2	08/11/87
Objects Of Fantasy: Music Of Pink Floyd (CD; US title: "Orchestral Maneuvers: Music Of Pink Floyd." Credited to DAVID PALMER AND THE ROYAL PHILHARMONIC ORCHESTRA)	RCA Victor 09026-57960-2	08/29/89	RCA Red Seal 07863-57960-2	11/12/91
The Classical Collection - Beethoven (CD/video; with Palmer narration)	Cromwell Productions	12/**/91		
The Classical Collection - Mozart (CD/video; with Palmer narration)	Cromwell Productions	12/**/91		
The Classical Collection - Tchaikovsky (CD/video; with Palmer narration)	Cromwell Productions	12/**/91		
Classic Jethro Tull (reissue of "A Classic Case": The London Symphony Orchestra Plays The Music Of Jethro Tull)	Music For Pleasure 89592 2	06/14/93		
Symphonic Music Of Yes (CD; Palmer arranged and conducted the London Philharmonic Orchestra; produced by Steve Howe and David Palmer)	RCA Victor 09026-61938-2	10/25/93	RCA Victor 09026-61938-2	10/26/93
We Know What We Like: The Music Of Genesis (CD; different cover)			RCA Victor 09026-56242-2	12/14/93
A Classic Case: The London Symphony Orchestra Plays The Music Of Jethro Tull (CD; reissue)			RCA Victor 09026-62510-2	01/18/94
Orchestral Sgt. Pepper's (CD: credited to THE ROYAL ACADEMY OF MUSIC SYMPHONY ORCHESTRA arranged and conducted by DAVID PALMER)	Premier (MFP) CDDPR 125	10/17/94	EMI (Canada) 5 55321 2	03/14/95
Passing Open Windows: A Symphonic Tribute To Queen (CD; credited to THE ROYAL PHILHARMONIC ORCHESTRA)			Columbia CK 62851	11/05/96
Norse Popklassikere (CD; credited to THE LONDON SYMPHONY ORCHESTRA)	Norwegian Columbia 4891462	11/24/97		

OUTSIDE SESSIONS - SINGLES

TITLES	UK & FOREIGN LABEL/NO.	RELEASE DATE	US LABEL/NO.	RELEASE DATE
Life Depends On Love/ A Little Sweet Sunshine by BERT JANSCH (orchestration/conducting)	Big T 102	06/16/67		
Talk To Me/ Spinning Wheel by MAXINE NIGHTINGALE (orchestation/conducting)	Pye 7N 17739	06/06/69		
Don't Push Me Baby/ Thru' Loving You by MAXINE NIGHTINGALE (orchestration/conducting)	Pye 7N 17798	07/25/69		
Love On Borrowed Time/ It's That Hurtin' Thing by MAXINE NIGHTINGALE (orchestration/conducting)	Pye 7N 45046	04/23/71		

OUTSIDE SESSIONS - ALBUMS

TITLES	UK & FOREIGN LABEL/NO.	RELEASE DATE	US LABEL/NO.	RELEASE DATE
"Nicola" by BERT JANSCH (orchestration/conducting)	Transatlantic TRA 157	07/14/67		
"Sing Along With Max" by MAX BYGRAVES (orchestration/conducting)	Pye NSPL 18361	01/29/71		
"Sing Along With Max Vol. 2" by MAX BYGRAVES (orchestration/conducting)	Pye NSPL 18383	11/24/72		
"Singalongamax Vol. 3" by MAX BYGRAVES (orchestration/conducting)	Pye NSPL 18401	04/27/73		
"Singalongamax Vol. 4" by MAX BYGRAVES (orchestration/conducting)	Pye NSPL 18410	09/21/73		
"Singalongpartysong" by MAX BYGRAVES (orchestration/conducting)	Pye NSPL 18419	12/07/73		
"Early Bert Volume 3" by BERT JANSCH (a retitled version of "Nicola")	Xtra XTRA 1165	07/18/76		
"Woman In The Wings" by MADDY PRIOR (LP; produced by Ian Anderson, David Palmer and Robin Black, with arrangements by David Palmer. Palmer played keyboards on "Woman In The Wings" and "Mother And Child.")	Chrysalis CHR 1185	05/12/78	Takoma TAK 7078	05/05/80
"Commercial Road" by RICHARD DIGANCE (LP)	Chrysalis CHR 1262	02/22/80		
"Nicola"/"Birthday Blues" (CD; first album has Palmer involvement)	Transatlantic TDEMD 17	12/06/93		
"Woman In The Wings" by MADDY PRIOR (CD)	BGO BGOCD 215	03/07/94		
"Live At Queen Elizabeth Hall"/"Commercial Road" by RICHARD DIGANCE (CD; second album has Palmer involvement)	BGO BGOCD 304	03/08/96		
"Jack Orion"/"Nicola" (CD; second album has Palmer involvement)	Essential! ESMCD 459	06/24/97		

David Palmer also did orchestrations for Gerry Rafferty, Billy Connolly and others.

DAVE PEGG

<u>ALBUM SESSIONS:</u>
AMORY KANE - Memories Of Time Unwound (1968)
DAVE PEACE - Good Morning (1969)
AMORY KANE - Just To Be There (1970)
JOHN MARTYN - The Road To Ruin (1970)
FAIRPORT CONVENTION - Full House (1970)
NICK DRAKE - Bryter Layter (1970)
FAIRPORT CONVENTION - Angel Delight (1971)
FAIRPORT CONVENTION - Babbacombe Lee (1971)
MARC ELLINGTON - Rains/Reins Of Change (1971)
MICK GREENWOOD - Living Game (1971)
MIKE HERON - Smiling Men With Bad Reputations (1971)
ALLAN TAYLOR - Sometimes (1971)
NICK DRAKE - Nick Drake (1971)
HARVEY ANDREWS - Writer Of Songs (1972)
FAIRPORT CONVENTION - History Of Fairport Convention (1972)
FAIRPORT CONVENTION - Manor (1972; unreleased LP)
FAIRPORT CONVENTION - Rosie (1973)
FAIRPORT CONVENTION - Fairport Nine (1973)
CHRIS DARROW - Chris Darrow (1973)
JOHN MARTYN - Solid Air (1973)
SANDY DENNY - Like An Old Fashioned Waltz (1973)
FAIRPORT CONVENTION - Live Convention (1974)
STEVE ASHLEY - Stroll On (1974)
KRYSIA KOCJAN - Krysia (1974)
FAIRPORT CONVENTION - Rising For The Moon (1975)
FAIRPORT CONVENTION - Fairport Convention (Tour Sampler) (1975)
BRYN HAWORTH - Sunny Side Of The Street (1975)
RALPH McTELL - Streets (1975)
BRIAN MAXINE - Ribbons Of Stainless Steel (1975)
RICHARD THOMPSON - Pour Down Like Silver (1975)
FAIRPORT CONVENTION - Fairport Chronicles (1975)
STEVE ASHLEY - Speedy Return (1976)
RICHARD THOMPSON - Richard Thompson Live! (More Or Less) (1976)
TERRY & GAY WOODS - The Time Is Right (1976)
DAVE SWARBRICK - Swarbrick (1976)
RALPH McTELL - Right Side Up (1976)
FAIRPORT CONVENTION - Gottle O'Geer (1976)
RICHARD THOMPSON - Guitar & Vocal 1967-1976 (1976)
FAIRPORT CONVENTION - Live At The L.A. Troubadour 1970 (1977)
FAIRPORT CONVENTION - Bonny Bunch Of Roses (1977)
DAN AR BRAS - Douar Nevez (1977)
DAVE SWARBRICK - Swarbrick 2 (1977)
JOHN MARTYN - One World (1977)
SANDY DENNY - Rendezvous (1977)
FAIRPORT CONVENTION - Tippler's Tales (1978)
CRAIG NUTTYCOMBE - It's Just A Lifetime (1978)
DAVE SWARBRICK - Lift The Lid & Listen (1978)
FAIRPORT CONVENTION - Farewell Farewell (1979)
RICHARD THOMPSON - Sunny Vista (1979)
RALPH McTELL - Slide Away The Screen (1979)
FAIRPORT CONVENTION - The Airing Cupboard Tapes 71-74 (1981)
RALPH McTELL - Streets Of London (1981)
FAIRPORT CONVENTION - Moat On The Ledge - Live At Broughton (1982)
RICHARD THOMPSON - Shoot Out The Lights (1982)
RICHARD THOMPSON - Hand Of Kindness (1983)
DICK GAUGHAN - Different Kind Of Love Song (1983)
DAVE PEGG - The Cocktail Cowboy Goes It Alone (1984; includes the 1983 single "The Cocktail Cowboy/ The Swirling Pit" [Woodworm WR003])
FAIRPORT CONVENTION - At 2 (The Airing Cupboard Tapes) (1984)

CATHY LE SURF - Surface (1985)
FAIRPORT CONVENTION - Gladys' Leap (1985)
FAIRPORT CONVENTION - The Boot (1985; double cassette)
FAIRPORT CONVENTION - Expletive Delighted! (1986)
SANDY DENNY - Who Knows Where The Time Goes (1986; box set)
NICK DRAKE - Fruit Tree (1986)
JERRY DONAHUE - Telecasting (1986)
FAIRPORT CONVENTION - The Other Boot (1987; double cassette)
FAIRPORT CONVENTION - Heyday (1987)
FAIRPORT CONVENTION - In Real Time: Live '87 (1987)
FAIRPORT CONVENTION - The Third Leg (1989; double cassette)
FAIRPORT CONVENTION - Red And Gold (1989)
SANDY DENNY - Best Of Sandy Denny (1989; best of the box set)
FAIRPORT CONVENTION - The Five Seasons (1990)
SALLY BARKER - This Rhythm Is Mine (1990)
CIRCLE DANCE - Circle Dance (1991)
THE GP's - Saturday Rolling Around (1991; folk-rock supergroup with Dave Pegg, Dave Mattacks, Richard Thompson and Ralph McTell)
FAIRPORT CONVENTION - Bonny Bunch Of Roses/Tippler's Tales (1992)
FAIRPORT CONVENTION - The Woodworm Years (1992)
JERRY DONAHUE - Neck Of The Wood (1992)
RICHARD THOMPSON - Watching The Dark (1993)
FAIRPORT CONVENTION - 25th Anniversary Concert (1994)
NICK DRAKE - Way To Blue: An Introduction To Nick Drake (1994)
SIMON NICOL - Before Your Time (1994)
FAIRPORT CONVENTION - Jewel In The Crown (1995)
A.L. LLOYD - Old Bush Songs (1995)
JOHN MARTYN - Sweet Little Mysteries: The Island Anthology (1995)
RALPH McTELL - Sand In Your Shoes (1996)
RALPH McTELL - From Clare To Here: The Songs Of Ralph McTell (1996)
LINDA THOMPSON - Dreams Fly Away (1996)
VARIOUS ARTISTS - To Cry You A Song • A Collection Of Tull Tales (1996; with Dave and Matt Pegg performing "Life Is A Long Song")
DAVE SWARBRICK - Folk On 2 (1996)
STEVE TILSTON - All Under The Sun (1996)
FAIRPORT CONVENTION - Old.New.Borrowed.Blue (1996)
VARIOUS ARTISTS - Best Of British Rock Folk (1997)
VARIOUS ARTISTS - House On Fire, Vol. 2 (1997)
FAIRPORT CONVENTION - Who Knows Where The Time Goes? (1997)
FAIRPORT CONVENTION - Encore, Encore (1997)
FAIRPORT CONVENTION - The Cropredy Box (1997)
PHILIP PICKETT - Bones Of All Men (1998)
ALLAN TAYLOR - Sometimes/Lady (1998)
DAVE PEGG & FRIENDS - Birthday Party - with Martin Allcock and Fairport Convention (1998)
FAIRPORT CONVENTION - Fiddlestix 1970-1984: The Best Of Fairport Convention (1998)
DAVE PEGG - The Cocktail Cowboy Goes It Alone (1998; reissue on Folkprint)
STEVE ASHLEY - Stroll On Revisited (1999)
STEVE GIBBONS - The Dylan Project (1999)
FAIRPORT CONVENTION - Cropredy 98 (1999)
FAIRPORT CONVENTION - Beyond The Ledge (1999; video)
VARIOUS ARTISTS - All Through The Year

DOANE PERRY

<u>ALBUM SESSIONS (unidentified sessions are covered in the other list below):</u>
BAIRD HERSEY - Have You Heard (1979; the backing band was called The Year Of The Ear)
RIVITS - Rivits (1980)
MAXUS - Maxus (1980)
LOU REED - Blue Mask (1982)
LAURA BRANIGAN - Branigan 2 (1983)
JIM MESSINA - One More Mile (1983)
JAY GRUSKA - Which One Of Us Is Me (1984)
LOU REED - New Sensations (1984)
HUNTER - Dreams Of Ordinary Men (1987)
DOANE PERRY - Creative Listening (1991; video)
TOMMY EMMANUEL - Journey (1994)
IAN ANDERSON - Divinities: Twelve Dances With God (1995)
MAGELLAN - Impending Ascension (1995)
MARTIN BARRE - The Meeting (1996)
STORMING HEAVEN - Life In Paradise (1996; with Vince DiCola)
THREAD - Thread (1997)
PAUL VENTIMIGLIA - Il Bacio (The Kiss) (1997)
VARIOUS ARTISTS - Encores, Legends & Paradox - A Tribute To The Music Of ELP (1999)

<u>OTHER PERFORMERS THAT DOANE PERRY HAS RECORDED AND PERFORMED LIVE WITH:</u>

Pat Alger
Peter Allen
Jon Anderson
Charles Aznavour
Barnes And Barnes
Pat Benatar
Gary "U.S." Bonds
Bridges (with Dave Mason and former Zappa keyboardist Peter Wolf)
Gary Brooker
Peter Cetera
Bill Champlain
Richard Clapton
Marc Cohn
Michael Colombier
Joey Dee And The Starliters
Dragon (aka Hunter)
Fairport Convention
David Foster
Stan Getz
Adrian Gurvitz
Rachel Hart
Debra Holland
Phyllis Hyman (drummer and musical director)
Terry Jones
Kitaro
Stewart Levine
Teo Macero And His Big Band
Barry Mann and Cynthia Weil

Martha And The Vandellas
James McVay
Bette Midler (1978 world tour)
Liza Minnelli
Jenny Morris
Elliott Murphy
Sharon O'Neill
Michael Omartian
Jeffrey Osborne
Tom Pacheco
Freda Payne
Jess Roden
Paul Rothchild
Michael Ruff
Todd Rundgren
Brenda Russell
Katey Sagal
David Schwartz
Patti Scialfa
Scout
Marc Shaiman
Vonda Shepard
Artie Traum
Carlos Vega
Diane Warren
Dionne Warwick
Z (with Dweezil Zappa and Ahmet Zappa) - the unreleased tracks "7/11" and "Svatba" on the "Shampoo Horn" album (the latter track was with former Frank Zappa guitarist Mike Keneally)

<u>TELEVISION AND FILM WORK:</u>
"The Twilight Zone" (film)
"The Texas Chainsaw Massacre" (film)
"Maximum Bob" (TV series; with Beau Bridges)
"The Marriage Fool" (film; with Walter Matthau and Carol Burnett)
various jingles and commercials

COVER VERSIONS

<u>ARTIST</u> - Jethro Tull song covered

ALL ABOUT EVE - "The Witch's Promise"

ANIMAL BAG - "Dun Ringill"

ARCANES - "Locomotive Breath"

BEGGAR'S FARM - "Nothing Is Easy," "A Song For Jeffrey," "A New Day Yesterday," "Cross-Eyed Mary," "Wond'ring Aloud," "Mother Goose," "One White Duck," "Minstrel In The Gallery," "Locomotive Breath" and "Aqualung"

ROBERT BERRY & LIEF SORBYE - "Minstrel In The Gallery" - "To Cry You A Song • A Collection Of Tull Tales" CD

BLACK SABBATH - "A Song For Jeffrey"

BLUE BALL BAND - "Locomotive Breath"

CATGANG - "Locomotive Breath (Special Cat Version and Special Rock Version)"

CCS - "Living In The Past"

CLAW BOYS CLAW - "Locomotive Breath"

THE CONNELLS - "Living In The Past"

CUD - "Living In The Past"

DARKSTAR - "Locomotive Breath"

BILLIE DAVIS - "Living In The Past"

FRANCIS DUNNERY - "Living In The Past"

ECHOLYN - "One Brown Mouse" - "To Cry You A Song • A Collection Of Tull Tales" CD

EKSEPTION - "Dharma For One"

KEITH EMERSON, MICK ABRAHAMS, CLIVE BUNKER & GLENN CORNICK - "Living In The Past" - "To Cry You A Song • A Collection Of Tull Tales" CD

FAIRPORT CONVENTION - "Life Is A Long Song"

MAYNARD FERGUSON - "Living In The Past"

GROUP DU JOUR - "Teacher"

JÜRGEN HANDKE - "A Passion Play," "Aqualung," "At Last, Forever," "Hunting Girl"/ "Heavy Horses," "Locomotive Breath," "Minstrel In The Gallery," "Orion," "Teacher," "Clasp"

ROY HARPER - "Up The 'Pool" - "To Cry You A Song • A Collection Of Tull Tales" CD

HELLOWEEN - "Locomotive Breath"

GLENN HUGHES, MICK ABRAHAMS, CLIVE BUNKER, GLENN CORNICK, DEREK SHERINIAN & ROBERT BERRY - "To Cry You A Song" - "To Cry You A Song • A Collection Of Tull Tales" CD

I TEOREMI - "With You There To Help Me"

IDES OF MARCH - medley of "Dharma For One" and Crosby, Stills & Nash's "Wooden Ships"

IRON MAIDEN - "Cross-Eyed Mary"

JIVE ACES - "Swingin' All Day (Singing All Day)"

JOCO-DEV-SEXTETT - "For A Thousand Mothers" (sung in German)

WAYNE KRANTZ - "Sossity; You're A Woman"

M. WALKING ON THE WATER - "Bungle In The Jungle"

MACK AND THE BOYS - "Living In The Past (From The Hip)"

MAGELLAN - "Aqualung" - "To Cry You A Song • A Collection Of Tull Tales" CD

LENNY McDOWELL - "Locomotive Breath (Mega Dance Mix and LP Version)"

ELAINE MORGAN - "Home"

OVERKILL - "Hymn 43"

DAVE PEGG - "Jack Frost And The Hooded Crow"

DAVE PEGG & MATT PEGG - "Life Is A Long Song" - "To Cry You A Song • A Collection Of Tull Tales" CD

PESKY GEE - "Dharma For One"

PFM - "My God"

RABBITT - "Locomotive Breath"

RAY - "Broadford Bazaar" and "Jack-A-Lynn"

ROYAL PHILHARMONIC ORCHESTRA - "Living In The Past"

SENSATIONAL ALEX HARVEY BAND - "Love Story"

SHEER TERROR - "Hymn 43"

THE SIX AND VIOLENCE - "Sunshine Day Medley" and "Nothing Is Easy"

LIEF SORBYE - "Mother Goose" - "To Cry You A Song • A Collection Of Tull Tales" CD

ROBBIE STEINHARDT, MICK ABRAHAMS, CLIVE BUNKER, GLENN CORNICK, PHIL MANZANERA, IAN McDONALD, ROBERT BERRY & MIKE WIBLE - "A New Day Yesterday" - "To Cry You A Song • A Collection Of Tull Tales" CD

STILETTO - "Locomotive Breath"

TAROT - "Locomotive Breath"

TEMPEST - "Locomotive Breath" - "To Cry You A Song • A Collection Of Tull Tales" CD

MONICA TORNELL - "Nar Jag Var Ung" ("Wind-Up" sung in Swedish)

MIDGE URE - "Living In The Past"

W.A.S.P. - "Locomotive Breath"

JOHN WETTON, MICK ABRAHAMS, CLIVE BUNKER, GLENN CORNICK, IAN McDONALD, PHIL MANZANERA and ROBERT BERRY - "Nothing Is Easy" - "To Cry You A Song • A Collection Of Tull Tales" CD

WOLFSTONE, MICK ABRAHAMS, CLIVE BUNKER & GLENN CORNICK - "Teacher" - "To Cry You A Song • A Collection Of Tull Tales" CD

UNRELEASED TRACKS

"The Beach, Parts 1 & 2" (1974): outtakes from the "War Child" sessions

"Beneath The Surface" (1979): from "The Water's Edge"

"Bug" (1993): a Martin Barre instrumental that later turned up on his album "A Trick Of Memory"

"Carmina Burana" (by Carl Orff) (1989-1991): not by Jethro Tull, this was a taped introduction to their concerts between 1989 and 1991

"Carolan's Concerto" (1988): a song only played live in 1988

"D.J." (1981/1982): an outtake from "The Broadsword And The Beast"

"Dangle The Billies" (1996): a bass and drum solo played throughout 1996

"Dinosaur" (1981/1982): an outtake from "The Broadsword And The Beast"

"Double Violin Concerto" (by J.S. Bach) (03/85): played in Berlin for Bach's 300th birthday concert with Eddie Jobson on violin

"Drowsy Maggy" (1989-1990): played as a live medley at 1989 and 1990 shows

"Dunnmore Lassies" (1980): a traditional jig used at the beginning of Ian Anderson's flute solo during the "A" tour

"Dust Devils" (1996): used as part of a live medley during 1996

"8.40 From Nowhere (Inverness Sleeper)" (1983): another train song from the "Walk Into Light" session

"End Game (instrumental)" (1983): an outtake version from the "Walk Into Light" sessions

"From 21 Subtract" (1967): an Ian Anderson song recorded 10/19/67 at Abbey Road Studios, London under the group name Candy Coloured Rain

"The Girl From Ipanema" (1988): played live in Brazil in 1988

"Green Tambourine" (1968): the Lemon Pipers US hit recorded 01/68 in London under the group name Candy Coloured Rain

"Hard-Headed English General" (aka "Hot-Headed English General") (1972-1975): played during encore medleys of "Aqualung," "Wind-Up" and "Locomotive Breath," among others

"How Can You Work With Mama?" (1966): one of Ian Anderson's first songs played by The John Evan Band

"I Wonder Who" (1993): this blues standard was played at some 1993 shows

"Intro" (08/72): the unused introduction from the Chateau D'Herouville sessions

"Invasion Of Privacy" (1967): an Ian Anderson song recorded 09/67 at CBS Studios, London under the group name Candy Coloured Rain

"Jams O'Donnell's Jig" (1980): an instrumental from the Fairport Convention LP "Bonny Bunch Of Roses"

"Last Night" (1975): a song played live at some shows, including 02/10/75

"Level Pegging" (1984): a song from Dave Pegg's solo LP "The Cocktail Cowboy Goes It Alone"

"The Man" (1967): a track recorded 09/67 at CBS Studios, London under the group name Candy Coloured Rain

"Martin's Tune" (1968/1969): a guitar instrumental played at Stockholm radio on 01/09/69

"Martin's Tune Again" (mid-1969): a guitar workout

"Mary's Song" (1979): from "The Water's Edge"

"Misere" (1995): a live track that was later recorded for Martin Barre's album "The Meeting"

"Nellie (The Revenge)" (1990): an instrumental played live in 1990

"Ninth Symphony" (by Beethoven) (1976-1979): infrequently played during David Palmer's tenure with the band

"Peggy's Pub" (1980): a Dave Pegg instrumental originally recorded on Fairport Convention's "Rosie" album

"Reynard The Fox" (1982): performed only once in Stockholm, Sweden by Ian Anderson and Dave Pegg. It was originally recorded by Fairport Convention for their "Tippler's Tales" album.

"Ring Out, Solstice Bells (Alternate Version) (1976): an unused version of the "Songs From The Wood" track recorded and mixed by Mike Batt

"Ruby Tuesday" (1992): performed twice in Athens, Greece with George Dalaras but not used on the album "A Little Light Music"

"Sailor" (08/72): an unused song that followed after "Skating Away On The Thin Ice Of The New Day" on the original Chateau D'Herouville album

"Selkies" (1979): from "The Water's Edge"

"7th Stroke Of 9" (1967): an Ian Anderson song recorded 10/19/67 at Abbey Road Studios, London under the group name Candy Coloured Rain

"She Moved Through The Fair" (1996): a traditional Irish song used as part of a live medley

"Skating Away On The Thin Ice Of The New Day" (08/72): the unedited version of the song that appeared on the "War Child" album. It is also mixed differently.

"Slipstream Intro" (1980/1981): a taped keyboard intro with song snatches played before the band took the stage. Not officially released on record, it appeared on the "Slipstream" video and the "1982 Promotional Manual" promo LP.

"Soiree" (1972-1994): a piece which is occasionally quoted during "My God," "Bourèe" or Ian Anderson's flute improvisations

"Steal" (1994): a live guitar instrumental that appeared on Martin Barre's album "A Trick Of Memory"

"The Storm" (1979): from "The Water's Edge"

"The Surface" (four themes) (1979): from "The Water's Edge"

"The Swirling Pit" (1982): a Dave Pegg instrumental that was first recorded on Dave Pegg's album "The Cocktail Cowboy Goes It Alone"

"Take The Easy Way" (1967): an Ian Anderson song that The John Evan Smash played on the TV program "Firstimers"

"Tequila" (1987): The Champs' hit used as part of a medley on The Howard Stern radio show on November 17, 1987. It also turns up from time to time in a live setting.

"Tomorrow Was Today" (1972): played at various shows throughout the year

"Trio" (1980): a live instrumental played in 1980

"Unknown Dreams" (1986): a song only played live in 1986

"Untitled Instrumental" (1988): part of this track became "Part Of The Machine"

"Viva L'Espana" (1982): played live in Portugal

"Wachet Auf" (by J.S. Bach) (1990): a piece from Bach's "Cantata No. 140" occasionally quoted during "Serenade To A Cuckoo"

"War Child Waltz" (1974): an unused piece from the "War Child" sessions

"The Water's Edge" (1979): Forty minutes of music written by Ian Anderson, David Palmer and Martin Barre for the Scottish Ballet. Only David Palmer's "Elegy" has been released from this collection of songs. "Elegy was originally known as "Siren Song."

"William Tull Overture" (1987): a Don Airey keyboard introduction to 1987 concerts that quoted from Gershwin and Tull numbers

"You Got Me" (1967): an Ian Anderson song recorded by The John Evan Smash on 04/05/67 at Regent Sound Studios, London

NOTE: At least five unidentified tracks from "Roots To Branches" and at least two more from "j-tull Dot Com" are also unreleased.